Heft J J. Schrage

Dimensions
of Organizational
Behavior

Dimensions
of Organizational
Behavior

Theodore T. Herbert

THE UNIVERSITY OF AKRON

Macmillan Publishing Co., Inc.
NEW YORK

Collier Macmillan Publishers
LONDON

Dedicated with love to my father-in-law, Russell A. Summers

Macmillan Publishing Co., Inc.
866 Third Avenue, New York, New York 10022

Collier Macmillan Canada, Ltd.

Library of Congress Cataloging in Publication Data

Herbert, Theodore T
　Dimensions of organizational behavior.

　Includes index.
　1. Organization. 2. Management. I. Title.
HD31.H473　　　　301.18'32　　　　75-11817
ISBN 0-02-353720-5

Printing: 1 2 3 4 5 6 7 8　　Year: 6 7 8 9 0 1 2

11/26/85

PREFACE

The ways in which organizations function have long fascinated both casual observers and serious students. We all rely on industrial firms, government agencies, health-care institutions, among others, to deliver goods and services; when our needs are *not* met as efficiently or as effectively as we might wish, the nature and operation of the effective organization becomes a subject of real and immediate interest.

Those satisfactions of which organizations are the source accrue to numerous individuals and groups; some of these may be categorized as customers, suppliers, clients, and organizational members themselves. The subject matter of how organizations function—should function—is intrinsically interesting to its students and analysts because of its richness, variety, and challenge; yet an even more important reason for understanding the functioning organization—in all its dimensions—is the critical need for *prescribing* the effective organization. After-the-fact analysis may be quietly satisfying to the researcher/scholar, but the applications of lessons learned to the design or modification of the real firm become critical in our dynamic competitive environment.

One of the last great frontiers of understanding and prescribing the effective organization is the dimension of human behavior; a source of infinite variability—yet consistent and predictable patterns—the sources, mechanisms, and consequences of the behaviors of organizational members constitute an emerging body of knowledge that will one day allow us to design organizations effective according to all criteria, including measures of financial status, production efficiency, product design, customer satisfactions, social responsibility, corporate citizenship, *and* human resources utilization and its maximum development. Such a goal must be striven toward with vigor, because organizational functionings touch us all in many ways;

the potential impact upon both the organization's *internal* as well as *external* environments is considerable.

Given such a perspective, perhaps the rationale for this book may be rather apparent. Ways of looking at the organization in general—frameworks—must be derived from the existing (and rather chaotic) knowledge and effectively transmitted; they can then be tested in application and refined successively as we determine the natures of the important elements, relationships, interactions, and their *effects*. Identification of relevant factors in actual situations, their impacts, and the expected results of changing the individual variables—in what may be considered a complex equation—is a highly desirable skill of significant and eminently pragmatic value.

The modern applications of behavioral science to organizations offer a great deal of excitement and challenge. Executives in business, government, industry, and not-for-profit institutions have seen a dramatic revolution in managerial techniques and methods based upon new insights into the behavioral, the *human*, element.

Yet the pace of new knowledge and of its uses is increasing rather than slackening; one need but thumb through academic journals to appreciate the range and intensity of behavioral research. The student and the executive share the need to develop their perspectives on, and expertise in, this dynamic field. To do so requires some degree of assistance, usually sought in the form of a textbook.

As a human creation, no textbook is perfect and so the student or executive must try to evaluate, as best he can, how well any particular text fits his needs. The professor, too, measures a text against his own criteria. Often the yardsticks of the student and the professor are dissimilar. In cases in which text design is dictated by the wishes of the learner, one finds rather superficial approaches to the subject matter, with insufficient attention paid to new developments, controversial issues, and the complexities resulting from the unique situation. When the text is designed wholly for the academic evaluator, one may find hundreds of pages of rather dry recitation of research and data. With but rare exception in either case, the typical text does not allow the covered materials to be put together into a coherent package, a framework in which the relationships between, and characteristics of, concepts are established.

All of this brings us to the reasons for which *this* text was written. A rather substantial void is perceived to exist between the overly superficial and the too-pedantic alternatives. Neither really provides the means by which complex issues and concepts may be related and understood. Too general a treatment—as well as one that is too detailed—obscures the path a text should illumine: the path to *understanding* and *internalization* by the student.

With this text the intent is to cover the range of behavioral science concepts and their significant applications to human behavior in organized settings. Unlike some texts, this one gives detailed attention to both the individual and the social systems, since they both influence organizational behavior. A primary objective is to provide such coverage in a highly readable form, with materials and logical development that the student can readily follow and identify with; the text is written for the student. At the same time, it is written for the professor, as a major resource to support his classroom activities.

A good balance among conceptual background, theoretical and research findings, and pragmatic applications is sought. Such a goal is instrumental to the overriding purpose of presenting a useful text, one that offers intellectual challenge, deliberative insights, practical guidance, and a stimulating opportunity to discover what is not yet known. In addition, a contribution to the state of the art of organizational behavior is presented through a broad *systems* treatment of the subject matter, including the causal variables found in the *context* of behavior in organizations, such as technology, structure, and authority—not often treated in previous works.

A benefit of such a systems approach is the encouragement to *analyze* and *predict* organizational behavior. The individual professor may choose to emphasize or to play down this aspect of the text, depending upon his objectives and interests; the systems approach is presented and handled in a general (and flexible) fashion so that it can be easily adapted to the specific pedagogical situations in which it is employed. Those who wish to de-emphasize the systems approach will find that the materials and the topical coverage lend themselves to the more usual functional approach, in which conceptual areas are developed rather independently. Those opting for the systems approach will find the model of considerable assistance, since it presents component relationships and major interactions among the elements of organizational behavior. As this is an innovative systems approach, care should be taken to recognize the treatment as a major step *toward* a definitive systems model of organizational behavior; such a model cannot be fully presented here because of the as yet incomplete understanding of relationship and causality in human behavior. I hope the step taken will be seen as a contribution to the ultimate development of such a systems model or of a contingency approach to organizational behavior.

No matter which approach in instruction is taken, benefit will be realized from the use of the companion volume, which incorporates readings and an extensive range of original cases, keyed to the text, by which to challenge and test understanding and ability to translate cognitive knowledge into analytically based and effective behavior.

The text is intended to be used in introductory organizational behavior courses in undergraduate programs, and it may also be used effectively in introductory behavioral sciences in management or organizational behavior courses in graduate business programs, especially when supplemented with the companion volume of cases and readings. No prerequisite courses or preliminary acquaintance with the behavioral or social sciences is assumed or required, which also hints at the text's usefulness in executive development either in self-study, general reading, or formal programs.

The general format followed is based on the recognition that organizational behavior is influenced by three major sets of forces: those of the formal organization itself, factors unique to the individual, and elements that stem from people in groups. Given the understanding of these identifiable and conceptually separable sets of forces, the major techniques and methodologies available to the practicing manager to *intervene in and modify* the nature, direction, and level of behavior are presented. On the whole, a practical synthesis of theory, research, and practice has been sought.

The organization of the volume attempts to reflect its orientation. An introductory section leads the reader to develop an overview of behavioral science applicability to organizational and managerial settings, establish an appreciation of the manager's roles and responsibilities, and initiate a systems view of factors important in the manager's task of attaining results through the resources at his command.

The next three sections investigate the three major dimensions—and their component elements—of organizational behavior: formal organization, individual, and group. In considering the Formal Organizational System attention is paid to the ways in which task technology, organizational structure, authority, and job satisfaction contribute to organizational functioning and purpose. These provide the formal and intended activities of organizational members and are highly related to those elements focused upon in the Classical or Scientific Management schools. They *are* important but cannot explain how and why *actual* behavior deviates from *intended* and *rational* behavior. We must turn to other areas for such explanations.

One such source, factors unique to the individual, is the subject of the third section. Personality, communication, perception, and motivation processes go far to explain how individuals interact as they do with the demands and nature of the formal organization. Another source is that of social forces, the subject of the fourth section. Group dynamics, the informal organization, role theory, status, change, conflict, and leadership are among the topics covered in this section.

Of interest, too, is the use of summary chapters at the *end* of each of these three sections that furnish a unique overview and integration, allowing the reader to put each section's materials into an even more structured and consistent perspective.

Finally, though explanations and predictions of behavior in organization are important, the manager needs more—he needs tools and specific methodologies to build situations sufficient to integrate the individual, the group, and the formal organization into a mutually supportive total entity. The fifth section provides insights into the major modification and adaptation processes of managerial styles, behavior modification, job enrichment, and organizational development. The sixth and final section provides an understanding of the reasons the effective organization is—and becomes even more so—important in our ever-changing world.

A number of people have contributed substantially to the undertaking represented by this text. Thanks are given to James W. Dunlap (Dean, College of Business Administration) and Frank L. Simonetti (Chairman, Department of Management) of The University of Akron for their encouragement and support. For their helpful comments at various stages of the manuscript's completion, grateful recognition is given to Professor Charles Snow of Pennsylvania State University, Professor Christine Habart of Northeastern University, Professor Bernard Hinton of Indiana University, Professor James Conant of California State University at Fullerton, Professor Bruce Meglino of the University of South Carolina, and Professor Kenneth Knight of the University of Texas at Austin. The initial encouragement, and the faith displayed, by Frank Khedouri, my original editor with Macmillan, is acknowledged with gratitude; the efforts and contributions of Sandra Schwede as editor have also been invaluable. Thanks also go to Bea Dagilis, Marg Smicklas, and Karen Crine for their marvelous typing, editing, and assistance in revision. And the essential contributions, assistance, encouragement, and supportiveness of my wife, Jan, are gratefully acknowledged.

T. T. H.

CONTENTS

Section

I

Introduction

Section

II

The Formal Organizational System: Technology and Structure

Section
III
The Individual
as a System

Section
IV
The Social
System

Section
V
Modification
and Integration
Processes

Section
VI
Organizational Behavior:
Perspective for
Tomorrow

SECTION

▌

INTRODUCTION

Chapter

1

Understanding Behavior in Organizations: Contributions from the Past

CHAPTER OBJECTIVES

1. To provide a historical perspective on the major changes in business practice that have occurred over the past seventy-five years.

2. To trace the changing conditions under which the human element in organized settings became increasingly important.

3. To follow the development of new managerial approaches as knowledge of human behavior was incorporated into the practice of management.

4. To develop an appreciation of organizational behavior as an evolving body of knowledge.

5. To set the stage for a forward-looking, analytical approach to behavior in organizations, as developed in succeeding chapters.

CHAPTER OUTLINE

The Industrial Revolution and Changes in Business Practice
Move to Industrialization
Move to Bureaucracy
The Changing Role of Lower Management
Redistribution of Power Between Management and Labor
Changes in Worker Characteristics and Needs
Discovery of Nonrational Man

New Approaches to Management: The Twentieth Century
Impetus from Scientific Management
World War I Developments
The Hawthorne Studies
The Depression Years
The 1940's
Fad of the 1950's
Reevaluation and Reemphasis in the 1960's
Where Are We Now?

We are constantly surrounded by organizations; they employ us, sell to us, provide for us, protect us, and give us—along with others—what we want, need, or are required to do. An organization may be as small as the corner laundry or as large as the federal bureaucracy. It might be devoted to providing a service for a fee or to furnishing relief to disaster victims.

One characteristic that all organizations share is that they are composed of *people*. These people, in turn, have in common the fact that their activities are coordinated and that they therefore cooperate with each other directly or indirectly in order to achieve a goal. Cooperation in a venture that requires the efforts of a number of people means that actions must occur and jobs be done; in short, people must *behave* in certain ways so that the organization fulfills its purpose.

Thanks to psychology, sociology, and anthropology, we have some understanding of why people act as they do. Throughout this book we will examine the reasons behind behavior in organized settings. Only by doing so can we make reasonable predictions of individual actions and reactions.

But first we must understand the history of organizational behavior. How did our understanding of the behavior of people in an organizational setting arise? How does our present knowledge differ from what our fathers (or grandfathers) knew? Can we learn from the ways in which yesterday's managers learned to take the human element into account?

We will take a short tour through the last three quarters of a century, to trace the development of our knowledge about people and their behavior in organizations. In doing so, we will see that this knowledge was not gained evenly or systematically over the years but that it came about in response to changing conditions over which the manager had little or no control.

That human beings make up a vital part of any organization is no secret. No organization could possibly exist without some combination of human beings to set and implement policy and do the work of the company. What is surprising, however, is how new our present understanding is of the importance of the individual and his relationships within the firm.

The Industrial Revolution and Changes in Business Practice

In the early 1800's the United States was caught up in the first waves of change caused by the Industrial Revolution. Major advances in power sources, transportation, and communication[1] had major impacts upon the usual way of doing business. The most apparent and far-reaching of these changes were the dramatic effects they had on the sizes and business practices of enterprises throughout the United States.

With these changes in the basic business processes, came changes in the

---

[1]Daniel A. Wren, *The Evolution of Management Thought* (New York: Ronald Press, 1972), p. 81.

relationships of the employees to the company and to each other. As a result of these major changes new and significant problems arose for which accepted business practices were no longer adequate.

We will look at six broad factors that helped to set the stage for the beginnings of deep interest in the human element in business. These six are (1) the move to industrialization; (2) the accompanying move to bureaucratic organizational forms; (3) the changing role of lower management; (4) the redistribution of power between management and labor; (5) the changing characteristics and needs of the firm's human resource; and (6) the discovery of nonrational man.[2]

Move to Industrialization

The impetus for "big business" was old even at the beginning of the twentieth century. The pioneers were the railroads with their needs for larger systems and more effective management techniques. By 1890 the United States was the world's leading manufacturing nation, and by 1913 it produced one-third of the world's industrial goods. At the turn of the century a period of mergers occurred as it became apparent that large-scale production, distribution, and competitive position created enormous benefits to the industrial firm.[3]

Move to Bureaucracy

This emphasis upon attaining economies of scale hastened changes in the small, personal, and family-owned factory or firm then prevalent. As a result of these mergers and the desire to increase in size, small shops and factories were transformed into relatively large bureaucratic enterprises. These were characterized by a careful attempt to make the operations of the firm more methodical and systematic, particularly by spelling out and limiting the duties, responsibilities, and authority of each job.[4] This approach lessened the total reliance upon the genius of a single "great man's" leadership;[5] logical and rational administration could be attended to through the duties of employee specialists.

The small firms had been typically concerned with only a single product or service; their activities were, with the change to bureaucratization,

[2]Theodore T. Herbert, "The Impact of Historical Forces upon the Integration of Human Relations into Management Theory," in *Management Theory, Research, and Practice—The Search for Unity,* ed. by Thad B. Green and Dennis F. Ray (Mississippi State, Miss.: Southern Management Association, 1972), pp. 269, 270.

[3]Alfred D. Chandler, Jr., "The Rise of Big Business," in *The Changing Economic Order: Readings in American Business and Economic History,* ed. by Alfred D. Chandler, Jr., Stuart Brushey, and Louis Galombos (New York: Harcourt Brace Jovanovich, 1968), pp. 270, 272.

[4]Burleigh B. Gardner and David G. Moore, *Human Relations in Industry: Organizational and Administrative Behavior,* 4th Ed. (Homewood, Ill.: Irwin, 1964), p. 92.

[5]Cf. John M. Pfiffner and Frank P. Sherwood, *Administrative Organization* (Englewood Cliffs, N.J.: Prentice-Hall, 1960), pp. 55, 56.

enlarged to cover multiple products and varieties of services, complicating their operations enormously.[6]

Because the firm had grown from a few employees to many, the relatively close or intimate relationship between workers and owner became impossible to maintain. The owner's nearness to developing problems was decreased by the demands of his new role of administering the entire firm. Relationships between workers or between worker and manager came to be shaped by the formal requirements of the job rather than by the more casual dictates of an informal situation. Workers and managers became specialized as the firm grew larger and more complicated. With this specialization and division of labor, more management levels were required to coordinate the activities of the firm; at the same time, the multiple levels separated the owner and his workers and complicated relationships between people even further.

Larger firms were necessary to reap the benefits of large-scale operations. But they themselves became dependent upon large-scale inputs (and outputs) to continue their level of profitable operations. Large inventories of raw materials, access to large and consistent power sources, and the availability of increased capital were absolutely essential. Also the services of large numbers of workers and managers were required to design, implement, and cope with the new processes, technologies, and complexities of this radically different social organism. As a result, a bewildering variety of specialized jobs came into being, all open to essentially any seeker; he needed only the skills and abilities required by the job he sought. Unprecedented mass mobility resulted; this was coupled with the industrial capabilities brought about by the combination of mass capital, distribution, and consumption. Personal and industrial prosperity resulted.

The Changing Role of Lower Management

The family-owned firms of the early 1900's were many small manufacturing enterprises; management was essentially informal, mainly because of the nature of the market and the production processes and because of the lack of intervening levels of managers between the top manager (the owner) and his workers. Insofar as his subordinates were concerned, the supervisor or foreman was the ultimate authority over the functions for which he had responsibility. His power was absolute. All matters of hiring, firing, compensation, discipline, work standards and quotas, the establishment of relevant policies, and the implementation of company policies stemmed directly from the lower manager. Typically no recourse was available for arbitrary decisions.

In addition, rather simple production processes required little in the way of skilled labor. Laborers were, to a large extent, truly interchangeable

---

[6]Chandler, op. cit., p. 276.

resources. The learning of production jobs was short, simple, and uncomplicated. Labor was then a homogeneous commodity.

As organizations became more complex and technology developed, the several duties of the lower manager became more complicated. Personnel grievances became a source of major concern, rising with the increasing power of labor unions. Labor skills multiplied as the larger firms acquired more specialized functions, thereby complicating the production process. Wages, selection and appraisal, quality, morale, budget, and control were just a few of the additional areas whose scope and technique became complicated.

One by one the separate duties of the lower manager were shorn from him and reassigned to the "staff specialist"; experts were required to handle these more complicated tasks, so that the organization might run more smoothly. Industrial relations experts, personnel managers, industrial psychologists, wage and salary specialists, industrial engineers, quality control engineers, and production engineers—all these narrowed and limited the lower manager's job.[7] Figure 1-1 provides a summary comparison of the changes in the supervisor's duties over the past fifty years.

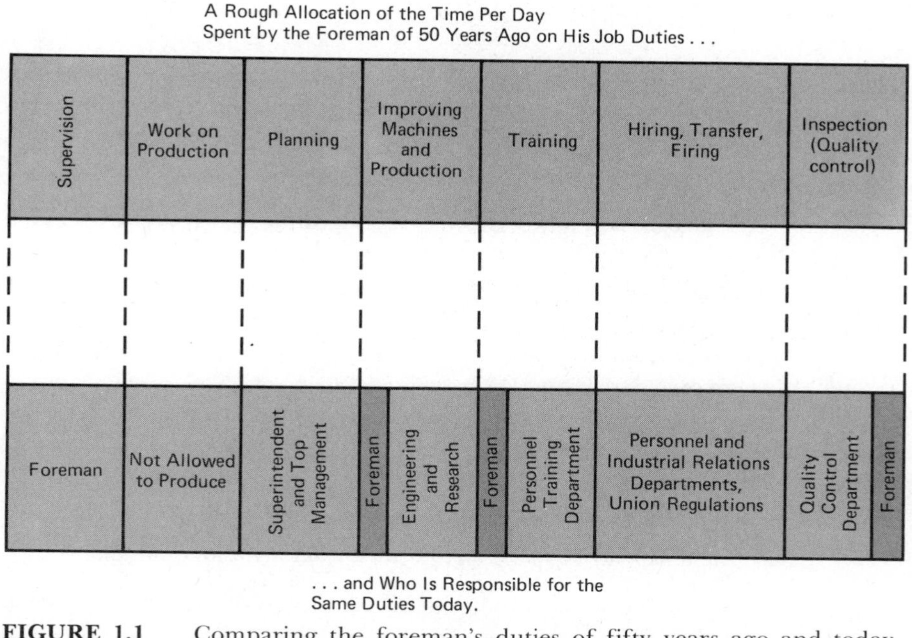

A Rough Allocation of the Time Per Day
Spent by the Foreman of 50 Years Ago on His Job Duties . . .

Supervision	Work on Production	Planning	Improving Machines and Production	Training	Hiring, Transfer, Firing	Inspection (Quality control)
Foreman	Not Allowed to Produce	Superintendent and Top Management / Foreman	Engineering and Research / Foreman	Personnel Training Department	Personnel and Industrial Relations Departments, Union Regulations	Quality Control Department / Foreman

. . . and Who Is Responsible for the
Same Duties Today.

FIGURE 1.1   Comparing the foreman's duties of fifty years ago and today. Source: Adapted from Delbert C. Miller and William H. Form, *Industrial Sociology,* 2nd ed. (New York: Harper & Row, 1964), p. 211.

[7]Cf. William G. Scott, *Organization Theory: A Behavioral Analysis for Management* (Homewood, Ill.: Irwin, 1967), pp. 346–351.

Technological advances continued to have a major impact upon industry; more and more technical knowledge and skills were required by the jobs that the lower manager supervised. As this happened, the supervisor became less competent to be the final authority on the technical details of the jobs he supervised. His became more of an administrative position, with the responsibility for leading and coordinating relatively specialized functions; job knowledge became the almost exclusive domain of his subordinate.

The lower manager's job had changed over time in response to new times and priorities. His authority was narrower and less one-sided. His duties had been redefined, with many having been assigned to staff experts. Subordinates had become more nearly "knowledge" workers. The supervisor had become less of a boss and more of a leader, for effective management of its *human* resources was critical to the bureaucratic organization for the first time.

Redistribution of Power Between Management and Labor

At the turn of the twentieth century, the predominant feeling of capitalists was that labor was a commodity to be purchased in bulk. Power lay with the industries; few of them developed on their own a social conscience about the "proper" utilization of their human commodity. Upton Sinclair was just one social reformer who through his writings[8] appealed to the American sense of morality about work conditions; as a result, the social climate warmed to the point where active concern was felt for workers. What had formerly been "good business practice" was felt by many to be bordering on excess and exploitation.

One result of these excesses was the feeling among workers of a need for some form of power to counteract that of the industrial concern; the form this power took was the union:

Gradually, as the country became more industrial and urban, resistance to unions on the part of the workers themselves began to decrease. By 1904, there were about two million union members in the United States; this figure grew slowly to about five million in 1920. During the next decade, effective anti-union drives by large employers, often with government aid, had the effect of reducing union membership to less than three million by 1933. By then, however, the shock of the great depression with its severe unemployment (about twenty-five percent of the labor force was out of work in 1933, and five years later the jobless rate was still about twenty percent) had helped to make American workers considerably more militant. . . . Union membership rose to a peak of around eighteen million (about one-third of all non-farm workers) by the late 1950's. During this period, unions shifted from the defensive to the aggressive. They underwent an aggressive growth in not only membership but also in financial resources and economic and political power.[9]

[8]Sinclair wrote *The Jungle* in 1906. This exposé of inhuman conditions in the meatpacking industry and in assembly plants created widespread indignation and major legislation to curb industrial abuse.

[9]Saul W. Gellerman, *The Management of Human Relations* (New York: Holt, Rinehart and Winston, 1966), pp. 18, 19.

Changes in Worker Characteristics and Needs

To say that people have changed in the last three quarters of a century is to state the obvious. But for the business manager to recognize that his work force has changed in its characteristics and expectations may be rather difficult. After all, he may have little contact with his workers. He would expect *managers* to have increased their educational attainments; as each manager's aspirations rise, he is given the opportunity to enlarge his sphere of responsibility as he strives for promotion to higher levels.

The job performance of the individual worker, though, may be completely determined by the methods demanded by the job itself or by his supervisor. So his yearning for more "fulfilling" work may never be recognized at all.

It may be helpful to recognize that since 1900 the educational attainments of large numbers of workers have increased dramatically. While the population of the United States was increasing from 76 million (in 1900) to 205 million (in 1970), the percentage of the population seventeen years old who were high school graduates was increasing from 6.4 percent to 78.0 percent! Similarly, the 27,000 college graduates in 1900 increased all the way to 827,000 in 1970.[10] "The number of years of schooling per member of the population over 14 and per member of the labor force both increased by roughly 40 percent between 1900 and the present time. Around 1900, only about 7 percent of all children attended college; by the late 1940's the figure had already risen to approximately 20 percent, and it has more than doubled since."[11] Further advances have been made as recently as the last two decades. In 1952 about 43 percent of workers aged eighteen or over had finished high school; in 1970, about 65 percent had earned the high school diploma. In the same period the portion of the labor force who had completed four or more years of college rose from 8 to about 13 percent.[12] And even now a full one half of *all* high school graduates enter college!

Over time, large numbers of workers were able to rise above mere subsistence living and begin to enjoy the fruits of good living that went with better jobs and higher earnings; industry's control over them tended to wane accordingly. Whereas in the early 1900's substantial numbers of workers were working just to live from day to day, the benefits from large-scale production and distribution resulted in higher standards of living; the worker became correspondingly more concerned about job security and about curtailing the ability of the industrialist to deprive him of what he felt he had earned: his job and all that went with it.

Fears about job security were allayed to a great extent by other factors:

[10]U.S. Bureau of the Census, *Statistical Abstract of the United States: 1972* (93rd ed.) Washington, D.C., 1972, pp. 5, 127.

[11]Richard T. Gill, *Economics: A Text with Included Readings* (Pacific Palisades, Calif.: Goodyear, 1973), p. 397.

[12]Campbell R. McConnell, *Economics: Principles, Problems, and Policies,* 5th ed. (New York: McGraw-Hill, 1972), p. 363.

tight labor markets came about as a direct result of increased production and consumption, which were further reflected in economic growth and a greater demand for labor. These circumstances tended to shift the balance of power to labor and away from the industrialists with their "buyers' market" approach to labor. Through the use of collective bargaining and strike techniques the labor unions likewise decreased the capabilities of businessmen to act without responsibility.

Once these needs for job security had been satisfied, workers and lower managers were more able to aspire to higher or more meaningful—more psychologically challenging, more rewarding, more prestigious—forms of endeavor. Demands for more meaningful employment, concerns about social relationships on the job and more leisure opportunities, and so on became important.

Discovery of Nonrational Man

Along with increasing emphasis on the use of capital goods to mass-produce and mass-distribute myriads of goods came management's natural interest in maximizing efficiency and minimizing costs through scientific management techniques. Management engineers or efficiency experts applied many of the techniques of classical engineering to the workplace. Individual jobs were analyzed and separated into constituent parts, each of which became new jobs. As a result, each worker was doing a smaller number of activities but doing them many more times per day than before, while other workers acquired those activities that had been trimmed from the original job. Shorter periods of learning a job, opportunities to specialize, and increased productivity were direct results of what has been called job rationalization or job atomization. In this way, it was felt, the total production effort would be greatly increased to feed the mass consumption that was the cause and effect of the new industrial society.

Taken out of the old job were such things as judgment (because judgments implies an opportunity to make a mistake), skill (because skilled laborers are relatively expensive and take longer to train), and the creation of handcrafted final products. Each job, then, became highly efficient, largely independent of major human variables, and also divorced from the worker's identification with his end product.

Theoretically the ways in which jobs and products were closely engineered should have lead to greatly increased production with few problems. Management was surprised to find that major problems did occur; they discovered that, amazingly enough, while jobs could be engineered to exceedingly fine tolerances and specifications, people could not be. Moreover, people filling rationalized jobs tended to behave in nonrational ways at times. Many businessmen began to feel uneasily that perhaps all the major factors had not been accounted for when a worker was "engineered" into a job. Unlike machines in impersonal jobs, people were discovered to act in disturbing ways even more when they worked in groups (such as work groups or work teams) than when they worked by themselves.

These unanticipated consequences of a perfectly logical approach to the new demands upon industry began to threaten the very nature of the business process itself. Businessmen became aware that their human resource was not merely another commodity but an important—and unknown—element that exerted a vital influence upon the effectiveness with which business could operate.

New Approaches to Management: The Twentieth Century

As these dramatic changes in business practice occurred, the old tried-and-true management techniques were found to be less and less effective. The increased sizes and complexities of new enterprises created or highlighted problems for which answers did not exist. New solutions were essential.

The ways in which new managerial tools developed with increasing knowledge of the importance of the human element are traced in the remainder of this chapter.

Impetus from Scientific Management

Before Frederick W. Taylor's "scientific management" became popular just prior to World War I, American enterprise had been manufacturing and distributing huge quantities of goods; Taylor, however, was concerned with the gap he saw as existing between *actual* production and costs and *potential* production and costs if his scientific management principles were applied. The crux of his system was the need for proper work methods and standards derived from scientific study of each job and its requirements.

Max Weber, a German sociologist who was a contemporary of Taylor, formulated an ideal organization that would achieve complex goals in the most efficient manner possible.[13] He called it a "bureaucracy," and it was "an apparatus of abstract depersonalization, a system that would rationally dispense solutions without the friction of subjective coloring and human error"[14] through a process guided by rules and procedures and managed by professional bureaucrats who held jobs with precise authority, duties, and limits. A bureaucracy was characterized by

specialization in terms of clearly differentiated functions, divided according to technical criteria, with a corresponding division of authority hierarchically organized, heading up to a central organ, and specialized technical qualifications on the

[13]Max Weber, *The Theory of Social and Economic Organization,* trans. by A. M. Henderson, ed. by Talcott Parsons (New York: Oxford, 1947).

[14]Warren G. Bennis, *Changing Organizations* (New York: McGraw-Hill, 1966), p. 66.

part of the participants. The role of each participant is conceived as an "office" where he acts by virtue of the authority vested in the office and not of his personal influence.[15]

From 1910 to roughly 1935 those schools of thought held sway that tended to view organizations in terms of their functions and activities alone,[16] without people. Their assumption was that man could be "engineered" to fulfill organizational requirements. While man's unpredictability and irrationality would inevitably result in some minor deviations in the planned results, these deviations could be minimized by the use of completely structured job environments, job tools and instructions, and job content. If the worker were not allowed to make judgments and if he were told exactly what to do at every step of the job, the worker would not be able to do otherwise than just what his boss wanted him to, and deviations would not occur. Performance of one's job duties was punished, or rewarded, exclusively through economic sanctions, such as the pay check and threats of being fired. "Rigid hierarchical control, a high degree of specialization"[17] were seen as absolutely essential to this industrial plan, which was a direct reflection of its environment and times.

Taylor did break the ground for studying human behavior in organizations and did a creditable job with the information at his command. He set the direction for business practice for decades.

World War I Developments

The requirements of World War I and a tight labor market greatly increased interest in industrial efficiency—and indirectly in the human element of production. Increased pressure for efficient mass production finally led some to see that thoroughly engineered jobs were simply not functioning the way they were supposed to; all of the obvious outside variables had apparently been carefully accounted for via scientific management analyses, but the predicted maximum human performance never materialized in practice. The underlying assumption of a simple sort of human nature that would be passively fitted into a fragmented, well-engineered, efficient job was found to be questionable at best.

Interestingly enough, World War I brought to the fore the significant problems of human differences in behavior and abilities. The army, as a result of its adopting the military draft, had to find the most effective way to place and use millions of men about whom they had little information. The army had to solve rather quickly such problems as how best to assign people to the various jobs that had to be done so that the jobs would be performed

---

[15]Talcott Parsons, *The Structure of Social Action* (Glencoe, Ill.: Free Press, 1949), p. 506.
[16]Ibid.
[17]George Strauss, "Some Notes on Power Equalization," in *Readings in Organization Theory: A Behavioral Approach,* ed. by Walter A. Hill and Douglas Egan (Boston: Allyn and Bacon, 1967), p. 374.

by people who were best suited to them. For example, who was qualified—or not qualified—to go to officer candidate school? Who was—and who was not—qualified to perform well as an ambulance driver or an infantryman? The American Psychological Association was called in to solve these types of problems, and the activities of psychologists led to major contributions in selection, classification, performance appraisal, and personnel assignment techniques.[18]

Recognition of individual differences and the notion that each worker's characteristics do make a difference in performance, then, received a tremendous boost about this time; the scientific management experience and the army efforts went hand in hand in advancing the cause of consciously taking into account individual differences and needs in the job situation.

At the same time another variable in the worker–job equation changed, complicating the problem for which significant beginnings to solutions were being found. Widespread use of assembly-line techniques led to decreased opportunities for the individualism made possible by the job of the craftsman. Emphasis was upon the quick and accurate performance of standardized operations and therefore qualifications such as speed, dexterity, and accuracy. Pressures, repetition, and monotony advanced even as wage levels rose.[19]

The Hawthorne Studies

The first significant attempts to explore some of the dark regions of human behavior were the famous Chicago Hawthorne Plant studies, conducted jointly by Western Electric and researchers from the Harvard Business School from 1927 to 1932. These studies were a major landmark in the investigation of human behavior at work, but their importance to an understanding of human behavior was discovered almost accidentally. The scientific management school of thought, let us remember, had focused its efforts on the idea of analyzing job conditions and requirements and then redesigning the job to make it as efficient as possible. This approach required the study of almost everything that affected the job. The Hawthorne studies were originally intended to research the effects that job conditions had on job performance; lighting intensity, heat, fatigue, and work layout were examples of the conditions to be investigated.

Using the tried-and-true scientific method, the researchers changed illumination levels (in the most famous test) and for each level observed workers' job performance. In this way they intended to determine the effect that each of the lighting conditions had on job performance. Their confusion can be imagined when the expected results did not occur; in one

[18]Abraham K. Korman, *Industrial and Organizational Psychology* (Englewood Cliffs, New Jersey: Prentice-Hall, 1971), p. 4.
[19]Robert Saltonstall, *Human Relations in Administration: Text and Cases* (New York: McGraw-Hill, 1959), p. 10.

instance, as illumination was increased, production did increase as expected. But when lighting was subsequently decreased, production *still* increased!

The worker himself caused these results: his attitudes and feelings affected his productivity! He formed and participated in informal social groups that satisfied his individual needs and helped him attain his personal goals more nearly than would or could the formal organization or company of which he was a part. The very factors that had made businesses so efficient and able to operate on a large scale gave rise to the personal conflicts and frustrations their members experienced. When the researchers and the company management solicited the workers' opinions and sought their cooperation in the experiments, the workers responded to this unintentional stimulus. Production increased because

First, the workers felt special because they were singled out to participate in the experiment. They believed that this showed management thought them to be important. Second, the workers developed satisfying relationships with each other and their supervisors because they were given considerable freedom to work at their own pace and to divide work in a manner most suitable to them. Third, the social contact and pleasant relations among the workers made the work more agreeable and enjoyable.

Even though the workers could not always describe what was influencing their attitude, informal groups had been formed, teamwork was practiced, and they sensed a feeling of recognition, participation, and increased self-regard. All were beneficial in raising morale and bringing about increased productivity.[20]

A vast productivity resource had been unrecognized and untapped; the Hawthorne studies showed that the economic man concept was insufficient, as were its tools for engineering efficiency. Sentiments and attitudes were important, too. Under the impersonal production system, workers' personal objectives and commitments were divorced from those of the organization by the placing of numerous management levels between the worker and the owner-chief executive. Specialization meant that individual contribution was no longer visible or even apparent and that the ability to identify with the company on either a personal or a product basis was lessened.

The individual worker had found himself faced with only two major alternatives regarding his role in his organization: (1) to accept the role imposed by the "labor-as-a-commodity" concept, doing his job as an "economic man" worker in a rational and dispassionate fashion as the job had been engineered, or (2) to give precedence to his own wants and desires on the job, even if it meant shortchanging the formal organization.

Close identification and social contact with fellow workers made the group more immediate and important, so that the goals of these informal groupings would typically take precedence over the worker's formal or job goals. At best the workers would barely meet the quotas imposed by the

---

[20]Fred J. Carvell, *Human Relations in Business* (New York: Macmillan, 1970), pp. 50, 51.

company, trading off job performance for satisfactions through social identi-fication.

How could this happen? Because of widely available jobs, a livable wage, decent working and living conditions, and lessened uncertainty of what the future might hold, workers had less to fear from the formal authority and methods of punishment the company held.

As a result of these studies, management found out that using tradi-tional stimulus–response techniques was not only inadequate but unrealistic. With this approach, management had automatically assumed that the worker (like any other good and predictable resource) would respond appro-priately when management pushed the right button. If management made changes in the worker's job, it was assumed that greater productivity would automatically occur; to management's dismay, these studies pointed out that the workers' reaction to change was tempered by the *meaning* the change had for the workers:

The meaning a worker assigned to a change depended upon his *social conditioning* (values, hopes, fears), derived from his family and group connections outside the work environment, and upon connections outside the work environment, and upon his *social situation at work,* in which group pressures determined attitudes and sentiments.

It was found that work groups develop a social organization and achieve social stability, in which member roles and status are clearly understood. Any change believed to threaten this stability is thus feared and resisted. This fear of change can offset an increase in output expected from a technical change.

Similar reasoning was shown to apply on a larger scale to the organization as a whole. The formal, official patterns of behavior specified in the rules and policies of the firm are designed to achieve maximum efficiency, e.g., to cut costs, increase output, improve quality, reduce waste, and improve technology. Yet the factors that make for efficiency sometimes oppose factors that make for happiness, collabora-tion, and good morale. The Hawthorne findings suggest that the wise administrator does not exclusively pursue efficiency or morale, but rather seeks an *equilibrium* or balance to provide the best combination of the two.[21]

The Depression Years

After the studies were finished in 1932, industry could afford to take a breather; jobs became relatively scarce, with over one quarter of all workers unemployed. The bases of the boss's ability to extract results from his subordinates reverted once again to the effective use of fear and economic sanctions.

In 1935, however, the Wagner Act required recognition of industrial unions; their powers had been revitalized in the later years of the Depres-

---

[21]Alan C. Filley and Robert J. House, *Managerial Process and Organizational Behavior* (Glenview, Ill.: Scott, Foresman, 1969), p. 22; emphases on the original.

sion. Demanded also was bargaining in good faith, which stripped business and its members of the authoritarian techniques of extracting results. At one fell swoop, power had been more nearly equalized between labor and management; unions had the ability to bargain effectively and strike for their demands. Conditions once again diluted the effectiveness of managerial approaches to workers.

The 1940's

With World War II came more labor shortages, contributing again to the leverage of the labor union; war needs required mass conversion of plants. The war on two fronts, with huge armies committed, called for American industrial know-how to be applied to supplying military needs. The Hawthorne human relations concepts were, unfortunately, misinterpreted and misapplied by industry during the Depression and World War II: the worker's social needs were recognized as existing, but the nature of these needs was not truly understood. Instead of considering *internal,* intensely personal needs, employers improved their workers' social environment with company picnics, assigned status symbols, employee coffee rooms, and so on. The basic idea behind these efforts was the so-called Pet Milk Theory. The Pet Milk Company advertised that they had better milk because their milk came from contented cows; hence the concept that happy workers were productive workers was, with tongue in cheek, labeled the Pet Milk Theory. The findings from the Hawthorne studies were considered helpful; they helped to identify the social buttons to be pushed so that workers' actions would coincide with management's desires.

In the late 1930's Kurt Lewin had conducted some studies in which he examined the effects of not the workers but the supervisors. In one thought-provoking study, he determined that the patterns of behavior by which work-group supervisors related to their workers had a direct effect on worker attitudes and therefore on productivity.[22] Here, then, was evidence of yet another variable that influenced the behavior of humans within the work setting. This time the direct source of the variable (rather than being internal to the worker, like such things as attitude and happiness) was found to be the supervisor himself. The equation became much more complicated.

When peace returned those forces that had united worker and manager disappeared; the autumn of 1945 saw the start of a great wave of strikes. The balance of power had shifted away from business, and now employers had stringent constraints imposed upon their methods of doing business.

Business's model of man had become that of a basically unchanging, constant force (or resource) with known and simple wants; his only variable quantity was some form of output, which could be triggered and maximized

[22]Kurt Lewin, Ronald Lippitt, and Ralph K. White, "Patterns of Progressive Behavior in Experimentally Created 'Social Climates,'" *Journal of Social Psychology* (May 1939), pp. 271–276.

by the external manipulation of his simple economic and social wants. The emphasis was upon employing the *external* stimuli that would elicit the desired response, using only very primitive and exploratory findings about organizational man.

The success of this approach necessarily depended on the correct meshing of the externally applied forces with what man is really like—*inside*. Those things that are uniquely and personally one's own determine his value systems and thence his personality; personality in turn has a bearing on his characteristic patterns of perception and activity. All these interwoven and mutually interdependent links in a causal chain lead to action or reaction. Management did not conceive of them as entering into the equation, held them constant, or ignored them.

During and immediately following World War II, managers began grasping at research straws—too little too late. Human relations training programs presented businessmen with a new perspective on the human element. "Open-door" policies, recognition, and less authoritarian behavior patterns were presented as some ways to increase worker happiness and hence productivity.

As the result of the worker's bargaining through his union, more leisure time and opportunities for interaction on the job had been grudgingly granted by industry. Job security too was a direct result of the countervailing power of the union. Informal organizations had flourished in the industrial environments, which were too sterile for workers' needs to be satisfied by management and the company. By the time industry recognized the importance of these types of needs, the worker had gone a long way toward satisfying them for himself. In what they offered, management was, as usual, one giant step behind critical needs.

Suddenly management's traditional techniques for dealing with employee problems seemed to prove unworkable, for the theory of the nature of man upon which they were based was obsolete. Even as new concepts and techniques were being designed to meet social needs, the worker—although not having his psychological needs entirely met—was discovering that he was experiencing a new set of needs: self-esteem and status through meaningful work, integration into the decision-making process, and recognition of the worker as an important being rather than as a mere cog in a machine. In trying to catch up to where they should have been, researchers began doing significant studies on the embryonic field of group dynamics. This discipline recognizes that groups have properties of their own that are quite different from the properties of the separate individuals that compose the group.

Fad of the 1950's

In the 1950's ideas based on the Hawthorne studies were distilled into simple formulas and techniques that the practicing manager could use on his employees to get them to do what he wanted. Workers had been discovered to value their social relationships sometimes more than their employment commitments, and the ways in which supervisors characteristically dealt with them had been shown to affect worker behavior. The idea of giving employees a social life on the job swept the industrial community. The emphasis seemed right in view of the findings: be considerate of the employee's feelings, make him *feel* important, keep him happy, and he'll produce.

As one writer suggested, the symptom was still being treated instead of the disease:

Research suggests that telling a worker he is an important part of the company, when through *actual experience* he sees he is a very minor part (thanks to task specialization) with little responsibility (thanks to chain of command, directive leadership and management controls) may only *increase* the employee's dissatisfaction with management.

These "fads" assume it is possible to make human relations better, *not* by attacking the causes (formal organization, directive leadership, and management controls) but in effect by making the activities outside the actual work situation more pleasant for the worker (e.g., new toilets, new cafeterias, sports, picnics, newspapers,) or by sugar-coating the work situation.[23]

The "happiness boys" were widely discredited during the later 1950's. The 1957 recession led to a curtailing of human relations training programs. Failure to find indications that these programs (or the application of other "happiness" techniques) made a difference in worker satisfaction and productivity helped, too. Unfortunately it seemed as if many managers used the techniques that were available to them with a short-run Machiavellian purpose, which was not truly to allow workers to satisfy their needs *while* meeting organizational needs. Rather the idea seemed to have been merely to increase production by deluding employees. By 1960 the fad had largely ended.

Reevaluation and Reemphasis in the 1960's

The 1960's ushered in a new era of research and theory concerning human behavior in organized settings. One major area for investigation was the assumption that the goals of the individual and of the organization were not in conflict. Individual "satisfaction" or "happiness" had been felt to indicate how well individual needs were being met; these new indicators were felt to estimate indirectly the degree to which the formal organization was attaining *its* goals. This position seemed to make sense, especially since organizational output and efficiency were the result of individual workers' inputs and efficiency.

Unfortunately, from the viewpoint of the organization, human needs

---

[23]Chris Argyris, *Personality and Organization* (New York: Harper & Row, 1957), pp. 154, 155; emphases in the original.

can be satisfied in many different ways, by diverse paths. And humans possess multiple sets of goals and needs. Need satisfaction and goal attainment that *are* congruent with organizational goals are but a subset of those possible.

The assumption was that no conflict existed between individual and organizational goals. Behavioral researchers and theorists were dealing with what is called a *closed* human system; they had built a simple model to understand the place of the human in the organization, intentionally ignoring other factors that affected organizational behavior. By so doing, they were able to simplify a complicated reality, but oversimplification produces invalid results. Writers like McGregor, Likert, Argyris, and Fiedler opened this closed human system. They took fresh looks at behavior in organizations and saw that explanations would be possible only after the investigation of some of the complicating factors that had been assumed away before. The theory of human behavior in the organization was redefined and refounded. Elements pertinent to describing, understanding, and explaining human behavior in the organization were included. This required the addition of concepts that formerly were on the fringe of accepted theory. Some of the additional items that these writers looked into were such things as leadership characteristics, performance variables, job involvement, and the effects of the organization on the individual. Their new models reflected the organizational setting, as well as direct influences *on* what had been merely relationships *between* workers.

As more research was done, items that were once felt to be completely unrelated were actually found to be intimately intertwined with human performance within the organization. Classical "doctrine," such as organization structure, differentiation of duties, and task specialization, can hardly be realistically separated from their effects on the individuals whose activities are so established and constrained.

Where Are We Now?

We now know that human behavior in the organization cannot be explained totally by human relationships. The organization molds and constrains, modifies and makes demands on human performance. Many different aspects of the organization have an impact on the human subsystem. The nature of the organization's structure, the characteristics of authority attached to different positions, and job and technology requirements, for example, cannot be assumed away and omitted from considerations of behavior. They make crucial demands upon individuals and organizations alike. Even though our present understanding of determinants and effects of behavior in organizations is not complete, we do have a better feel for the ways in which separate factors interact with each other to affect the individual.

In this chapter we have traced the broad outlines of the development of knowledge of organizational behavior. With this as background, the other chapters will elaborate upon the most important determinants of human behavior in organizations, weaving together these contributions from the past with new findings. The ultimate purpose is to allow us to recognize that any managerial activity or decision carries with it possible consequences that the unwary manager might not recognize. At the same time, we will be more able to predict the ultimate effects upon the organizational members affected. We will also recognize that managers are human, too; workers are not the only focus of our predictive efforts, since those charged with the responsibility for supervising exhibit many of the same characteristics of those whom they supervise.

Summary

Our knowledge about how and why people behave the way they do in organizations is continually evolving; the attention given to this vital subject is a relatively recent development. As the area of knowledge has developed, some information has been found to be useless and has been discarded, whereas other areas have been found fruitful for further investigation.

The manager of the early 1900's used a simple "economic man" model of organizational behavior; this model's primary assumption was that people were completely rational and strove only to maximize their own economic well-being. Therefore, to get people to behave in the ways desired by management, the scientific management school taught that people would do what they were paid to do. Since management was at the time primarily interested in economic scales of production, they thought that if people were paid to produce more, they should produce more. Management even felt that by allowing the workers to specialize in repetitive, narrow jobs they were helping the workers to attain their own goals, while helping the company to reach its production goals.

About the same time deeper investigations into the nature and causes of human behavior in business were initiated by a broad-based move to industrialization and an accompanying move to bureaucratic organizational forms, the changing role of lower management, the redistribution of power between management and labor, the changing characteristics and needs of the firm's human resource, and the discovery that humans are not completely rational.

Whatever success that the scientific management approach has had might well be traced to the conditions of the times, in which living standards were not nearly so high (nor were goods as widely distributed) as they are today. The power was on the side of industry, in that economic sanctions really did make a difference at that time. A job—even a low-paying one—was something to hold on to.

With World War I came the tight labor market and an increased interest in fitting the person to the job, which had been analyzed and set up by engineers. Formal recognition of individual differences and the notion that each worker's characteristics do make a difference in performance received a tremendous boost about this time.

The Hawthorne studies in the late 1920's and early 1930's were the first really broad-scale attempts to investigate causes of performance on the job. The researchers discovered that organizations were not merely economic institutions but were composed of many social organizations; people within organizations formed lasting relationships that affected the ways that they behaved on the job. These relationships could even work to the detriment of the company. The landmark Hawthorne studies set the stage for research in the decades to come. Given the new insights into man and his nature, the old "economic man" assumption was dismissed as unrealistic. A new model of the nature of man, that of "social man," took its place.

In striving to reach its own economic goals, industry attempted to use these findings. The techniques they used were primarily those of satisfying the social needs of the worker on the job (by establishing picnics and social outings, coffee rooms, and so on). If happy workers were productive workers, then management would make their workers as happy as possible.

Management's model of the nature of man proved insufficient to influence and predict human behavior. Increased fringe benefits and continuing surveillance by powerful unions eroded the power position of industry.

And the job itself was coming under fire by workers, primarily for not allowing them to realize their potential, or to exercise judgment, or to have an opportunity for meaningful employment. These new and large-scale complaints once again caught management by surprise; they must have thought it terribly unfair that just as they felt they were getting a handle on what workers wanted, these wants changed and changed drastically.

Good research, though, was brought to bear upon the problems faced by business. It was discovered that the things that affect and predict human organizations are very complicated and extremely varied. A number of researchers made significant inroads by focusing not on the social relationships between workers but on factors internal to the firm but external to the social relationships, such as leadership style and organizational effects.

Our understanding of the nature of organizational man has come a long way, and today we can recognize that there are a number of significant factors that affect human behavior in organizations. Understanding these factors and the way that they influence each other gives us a significant opportunity to predict the behavioral consequences of almost any action taken within an organizational setting.

In the next chapter we will investigate the place of the manager in the organizational behavior pattern, considering the nature of his job and the ways in which he typically goes about fulfilling his duties. The manager's role in initiating and maintaining behavioral responses will be discussed.

STUDY AND REVIEW QUESTIONS

1. How did the evolution of large-scale businesses cause changes in traditional business practice?

2. How did labor-management relationships change as a result of bureaucratization?

3. Discuss the changes in educational levels since 1900. How do you think increased education affected the hopes, aspirations, and expectations of workers?

4. What are some direct benefits of making a job more efficient through scientific management techniques such as job rationalization?

5. In what ways were the findings of the Hawthorne studies of major importance to management?

6. The Hawthorne studies showed that the worker's attitudes and feelings affect his productivity. How does this occur?

7. What is the "Pet Milk Theory"?

8. Writers like McGregor, Likert, Arygris, and Fiedler investigated many elements that had not previously been felt to influence behavior. Why were their efforts important?

9. Why do you think that the term *bureaucracy* has such a bad connotation today?

Chapter

2

Role of the Manager

CHAPTER OBJECTIVES

1. To furnish a brief perspective on the function of the organization as an economic and social device.

2. To review the major parts of the process of management, those of planning, organizing, directing, and controlling.

3. To develop an appreciation of the manager's task of balancing and meeting the requirements and needs of the formal organization as well as those of the members of the organization.

4. To show the nature of behavioral cause and effect as an integral part of the manager's overall role.

CHAPTER OUTLINE

The Nature and Function of the Organization
Specialization for Overall Effectiveness
Coordinating the Specialized Efforts of Many

The Managerial Function
Management as a Form of Specialization

Activities of the Manager

Manager and Organization

Managing Organizational Behavior
Stimulus-Response Management
Stimulus-Organism-Response Management
Behavioral Systems Management

We have noted the importance and diversity of organizations in our society. Without them many of the comforts and necessities we take for granted would be either impossible to obtain or far too expensive for many to enjoy.

To satisfy the demands of mass markets, huge quantities of goods and services must be widely available. As was discussed in Chapter 1, the economies of large-scale production and distribution make possible lower costs and, consequently, lower prices.

The Nature and Function of the Organization

In order for the network of goods and services to flow to meet the demands of consumers, a certain amount of specialization of activities must occur. We saw how, up to a point, specialization within an individual's job makes him more efficient and productive. Specialization also occurs at a much more complex level.

Specialization for Overall Effectiveness

We would hardly expect our local telephone company to sell radio equipment, or a supermarket to provide men's clothes. For our economy to provide goods and services efficiently, specialization occurs at the level of the *organization.* An organization exists because something must be done—some objective must be attained—that is too large or complex for one person to accomplish alone. A number of people are gathered together, each of whom is assigned a *part* of the *total* task. When a large task can be broken down into its component parts and individuals can perform these subfunctions, then things that may have been impossible to attain become feasible.

For one example, reflect upon the saying that Thomas Aquinas was the last man to live who knew the total of the knowledge of his time. During his life one who desired a complete education might well have turned to him. Today's total knowledge is well beyond the comprehension of any one person, yet the task of education is carried out nonetheless. Universities and colleges may specialize in the types of education they provide and which branches of knowledge they emphasize.

If you wanted vocational training to prepare you to be, for example, a welder or a mechanic, you would probably not apply for admission to MIT. A vocational program at the community junior college would probably provide the right emphasis and training. But if you wanted advanced knowledge in a highly theoretical or technical field, you might choose to pursue a nationally recognized program of study at one of the top universities. By so specializing at the organizational level, institutions of higher learning may concentrate on doing a particular task and doing it well.

Coordinating the Specialized Efforts of Many

Professors within these organizations similarly specialize. Few professors are capable of thoroughly mastering and remaining competent in fields completely unrelated to each other. Instead, they usually choose to concentrate on a specific branch of knowledge. By having a number of these professors, each specializing in his own discipline and performing a part of the total task, the university can provide educational services to large numbers of students at relatively reasonable prices. Students can even have choices among educational institutions, types of education, quality of instruction, and so on. Without these organizations, of course, higher education as we know it could not exist.

Many other specialized organizations exist. We tend to take them for granted, yet each concentrates its efforts and skills on a particular specialty. Some even specialize on the characteristics or demands of classes of customers. Consider the differences between the fashionable Fifth Avenue designer shop and the dress department of a discount department store! Both are specialists, yet both sell garments. Each employs buyers and sales people who perform the specialized tasks necessary to the organization. These combinations of organizational and task specialization allow each to concentrate on a particular function—and doing it as well as possible.

An organization may then be defined as a social and economic entity in which a number of individuals perform a variety of tasks in order to reach a common objective. This objective is typically too large or too complex for a single person alone.

Implicit in the nature of an organization is the performance of a function that is not directly related to the production of goods or services. This function is the coordination of the activities of the organization to serve the overall goal or function of the entire organization. This coordination results when the organization's many separate activities are *planned, organized, directed,* and *controlled*.

The Managerial Function

The overall function of the manager is to see that desired results are obtained. He must ensure that organizational objectives are reached by planning, organizing, directing, and controlling the activities of organizational members.

Management as a Form of Specialization

Why is management necessary? Management is another form of specialization that helps the organization to perform as efficiently and as smoothly as possible. Were each worker left to perform his duties *and* coordinate his efforts with other workers *and* plan ahead to sidestep possible problems *and* solve disputes or see that someone is responsible for doing each necessary task *and* see that he does the best job possible *and* check to see that work is going according to plan, without disruption or problems, what would happen? Either the job duties would be done *or* these managerial functions would be attended to—most probably not both! These management tasks require the perspective and full-time attention of one who is less immersed in day-to-day production efforts and who can see the overall patterns in the efforts of the workers. To ensure that the work gets done *and* that the management function is performed, these two vital activities are typically split, with workers specializing in directly producing goods and services, and managers specializing in seeing that the overall results are attained.

A manager is not a manager unless he has one or more people reporting to him, for he must perform his function for an identifiable activity done by *people*. If no one reports to him, he cannot be responsible for the results of his subordinates. Without their work, he has no job!

Planning, organizing, directing, and controlling have been presented as activities that the manager performs in his major function of attaining prescribed results through the efforts of his subordinates. These activities are present in every manager's job, sometimes more and sometimes less. Some managers are responsible for much more planning than others, perhaps because they oversee more complicated or more technical activities. Some do more directing, as might the foreman on a production line. Whatever the specifics of any managerial job, though, each of the four management activities is performed.

Activities of the Manager

In order to appreciate the complexity of the managerial function, we should have a somewhat deeper understanding of the manager's activities.

Planning

The manager must carefully and rationally establish specific objectives, so that the organization and its members will have clear ideas of what results are expected. He must also establish the ways in which they will be accomplished. The manager plans for the obvious reason that he needs an objective toward which he may orient his efforts and decisions.

The choice of the objective is critical because what one wishes to accomplish dictates what one must do. A businessman-to-be may wish to obtain a loan from a bank for the purpose of founding a restaurant. The loan officer will want detailed information about the objectives of the applicant and of his restaurant. For example, the plans for a fast-food outlet specializing in hamburgers would be considerably different from those for a four-star establishment featuring French cuisine. The objective of the loan applicant would be critical to the success of his venture; *crepes suzette* and *vichyssoise* made in advance behind a counter and packaged "to go" may encounter some difficulties. Similarly, a forty-five-minute wait for a hamburger and French fries may encounter customer resistance.

After the abstract objectives are established, the necessary tasks, activities, and responsibilities must be concretely defined. Although the organizational objectives or desired end results may have been rationally established, without this stage the individuals within the organization would probably have ill-defined duties and ambiguous responsibilities.

Within this planning function guides must be established to assist organizational members in the performance of their duties. This broad integration of individual performance of assigned duties with the overall organizational objectives is called policy making. Policies set out general expectations that ensure that individual activities will be consistent with organizational objectives. Important issues are preinvestigated and predecided, so that an individual member faced with a decision need not investigate and decide each issue that comes up fairly frequently. Organizational objectives are translated into specific guides for the behavior of the individual in the course of his duties.

"Fixed-price policies," so common here in the United States, are an example of such guides. Most retail outlets, particularly of consumer goods, do not grant discretion to the individual salespersons to haggle or bargain or offer special discounts to selected individuals. The price affixed to the item is the price that will be charged. Should a sales clerk in the appliance section of a department store be requested by a customer to reduce the price of a floor model washing machine by 10 percent, story policy would have predecided the issue for the clerk. This might well be consistent with the store's objective of being a profitable enterprise by encouraging high-volume sales with extremely low profit margins. Should the clerk accept the offer on his own discretion, the objective of the firm may be hindered in its accomplishment.

Planning, to summarize, entails establishing objectives, specifying the activities that must be done to reach the objectives, and setting policies to guide the organization and its members in the pursuit of the objectives.

Organizing

One of the resources necessary to the accomplishment of overall objectives within any organization is the human resource. Duties, activities, functions, and skills reside typically within people. Even machine activities require human operators. No organization can exist without people, but the manager's responsibility of assembling his human resources dictates that these individuals be a great deal more than simply people. Organizational members must be chosen on the basis of their skills and potential; few companies allow a new employee to wander around the company until he finds something that he wants to do. The objective established for the organization dictates the nature of the jobs and skills that are necessary. The manager must then make sure that these jobs are adequately staffed.

In addition, the manager is responsible for organizing the human resources in some way. Similar jobs or skills may be grouped together. Or individual jobs may be grouped because of the benefits of allowing people to specialize on a single product. This organizing of the human resources means facilitating the overall objectives, which have been translated into plans and policies, by grouping people and tasks in such a way that they contribute more effectively to goal accomplishment.

If you were president of a large firm, would you allow each of your vice-presidents to have a private secretary? Would you require that several share one secretary? Or would you have them fill their secretarial needs from a pool of secretaries who are temporarily assigned as needed? This simple organizational problem has far-reaching consequences, as you may have guessed. By creating formal relationships (between vice-president and secretary), one determines the ways in which their work will be done.

Notice that the vice-president who has a full-time private secretary has continuing authority over her. Also, because of the stability of their relationship, he can let her perform some of his routine duties; in this way he can devote himself to exceptional (unusual) matters and to more far-reaching decisions without becoming trapped on a treadmill of routine correspondence, for example. This organizational form then allows the executive's total work load to be divided up for maximum efficiency—but at a considerable payroll cost compared to other organizational alternatives. Other costs would arise from those periods when the secretary is not kept busy because of a light work load.

The pooling of secretaries tends to make more efficient use of the secretaries' time, since they are assigned to an executive only when he has specific duties to be performed. The lack of permanence in the executive–secretary relationship, however, means that the executive probably has to shoulder the routine tasks he would delegate in the private secretary system.

From this brief example we may see that organizing is the creating of relationships among tasks and the people who perform them. The manager must establish authority systems in order to assign responsibility for results *and* to allow the responsible person to influence those who perform the tasks that yield the desired results. This implies creating superior–subordinate relationships as well as grouping tasks that are similar in some ways.

Creating a hierarchy, or a system of superiors and subordinates, allows the successive specialization of individuals in tasks plus the assignment of responsibility for attaining the desired results from the performance of these tasks. Grouping tasks (into departments, for example) makes possible the efficient overseeing of a number of individual efforts. Grouping people who do the same task allows them to identify with, and learn from, each other. The supervisor can also relate to a specific group of individuals and can become familiar with the nature and problems of their work. And since specific duties are assigned to identifiable units, should anything go wrong, errors can be traced to the responsible unit for correction.

A further form of specialization in the organization is found in the separation of *line* and *staff* activities. The simplest organizational form is the line organization, which is composed only of those responsibilities directly related to the firm's output, such as manufacturing and sales. In a line organization, payroll computations, hiring interviews, inventory, and quality control considerations are done by line officers together with their other duties.

As the firm grows, these activities, which *support* (indirectly relate to) line duties, can interfere with the manager's primary responsibilities. When this happens, staff positions are created to relieve line management of the tasks that have grown unwieldy or time-consuming. Thus we see the corporate controller and accountants specializing in information and data services; the personnel department handling payroll changes, interviewing, training, and administering fringe benefit programs; industrial engineers setting up statistical quality control systems and time-study–based work standards; and a corporate planning office analyzing the firm's operations and what changes will be needed in the future.

Staff activities are "carved" out of the line manager's responsibilities and assigned to specialists who devote their full-time attention to their specialty. In this way line management can concentrate on producing the firm's output, while staff specialists can concentrate on the analytical or problem-solving aspects. Through such specialization the overall organization is permitted to function more effectively and more efficiently.

To summarize, organizing entails defining the tasks needed to accomplish organizational goals and subsequently breaking these tasks down into discrete duties and jobs to which individuals can be assigned. The scope of organizing encompasses the creating of superior–subordinate relationships, specialization for efficiency and increased effectiveness, and the grouping of individuals into units. When planning and organizing are combined, the desired end results of the organization are set out and the physical definition of what is to be done and who is to do it is established.

Directing

Planning and organizing are extremely important, as we have seen. The directing activity of the manager relates to the organization's human element. The manager, responsible as he is for results, cannot leave to chance the willingness or capability of his subordinates to contribute their maximum efforts toward desired results. Without direction, organizational members might soon lose their sense of purpose or lose sight of the ways in which their efforts fit into the overall operation. If the manager fails in his directing activity, his subordinates might well find themselves alienated, dissatisfied, unproductive, and at odds with management.

Directing is necessary to provide members with a positive environment within which they may perform activities meaningful both to the organization and to themselves. To direct his subordinates, the manager must be skilled in two important areas: leadership and motivation. He must be capable of bringing forth the best efforts from those for whose results he is responsible. To do this, he must understand the reasons people act as they do and the broad patterns of individual differences. As a manager, he must provide the setting and structure the job requirements so that each individual satisfies his needs while obtaining prescribed results through his own efforts.

How the manager deals with his subordinates also makes a difference. An authoritarian manager might issue commands that must be immediately obeyed to the letter under pain of penalty; he would probably instill little motivation to perform in a creative or a superior fashion. Whatever performance is elicited would probably be from fear rather than commitment.

A manager who actively solicits information and suggestions from his subordinates and who emphasizes how well goals are met rather than how closely procedures are followed might be a good motivator. He might also attain better results than the authoritarian because of greater desire of his subordinates to perform creatively and in a superior fashion.

Similarly, the manager must understand how unofficial groups occur spontaneously and what demands groups place upon individuals. Groups form for many reasons, and they attempt to accomplish something important to their members. If workers form a group because they fear arbitrary actions from managers, they try to satisfy a security need as well as a social need. Because of their new-found strength in numbers, such a group may discover that they can treat with management as equals, or they may emphasize their power and solidarity by restricting output.

However groups behave and for whatever reasons, groups are guided by their leaders. The leader of such an unofficial group is only as good a leader as the group decides he is. If he fails to achieve what the group members believe is important, another leader emerges.

For the manager, the group process is important. If enough subordinates perceive that something important to them is not provided in the context of the job, the natural social nature of man provides a ready vehicle for combined efforts to remedy the deprivation. The remedy might well have negative implications for the formal organization, which implies that the manager's ability to obtain results is diminished.

Thus the directing activity requires the manager to be a leader as well. He must occupy a position as the initiator and the maintainer of activities that are important to the group(s). This can be done only after he is accepted by the members. Without group acceptance, no one can be a leader. And no one can remain a leader for long if the group refuses to go along with him.

Directing is then an important but tenuous portion of the manager's function. He must serve as an agent both of the organization and of his subordinates, attempting to satisfy the requirements of each—at best a difficult task. Unless the directing activity is done well, the planning and organizing activities cannot be implemented completely, and organizational goals will suffer from the efforts of apathetic (or hostile) members. Motivation and leadership are only two of the tools the manager employs.

Controlling

Organizing and directing are both functions that are intended to ensure the effective implementation of the first activity, planning. And planning involves the determination of goals and how they are to be attained. The controlling activity is one in which individual, unit, and organizational performance are *measured*. After all, only by a periodic evaluation of how well something is being done can one determine if the work is going according to plan and to what degree the objective is being attained.

This appraisal is necessary because plans have been made that detail how an objective is to be reached. Without this evaluation, the manager may not recognize problems that may hinder goal accomplishment, slow down the pace of the work, or create bottlenecks. Evaluation of this type occurs within organizations constantly and consistently. Within the college classroom, evaluation—at mid-term and final exams, for example—determines how well course objectives are being achieved and where inadequacies may exist.

Following evaluation the responsibility of the manager is to control the process by comparing units of performance with the established performance standards. If a deviation exists between actual performance and planned performance, the manager must initiate action immediately to remedy the situation. NASA astronauts periodically evaluated their position in space against the planned trajectory from the earth to the moon. If a deviation existed between where they actually were and where they should have been, the astronauts immediately took action to correct the disparity; unless this was done, of course, the astronauts could not hope to attain their goals. Less dramatically, perhaps, the same situation faces the manager. If he has a profit objective of 10 percent of sales for the year and at the end of the first quarter he sees that he has not reached the planned performance level, then he must get performance back on track in order to meet the year's performance objectives.

The activity of controlling makes possible the evaluation of how well objectives are being met, desired results are being obtained, and plans are being carried out. Just as important is the information conveyed about where problems exist. Given that bottlenecks are occurring, information about where the problem areas are, why they are occurring, and how serious they are constitutes vital information that allows quick remedial action.

Manager and Organization

Managing occurs *within* an organization, yet the organization itself is a *result* of the management process. The manager's task is to achieve desired results through the direct efforts of others. His efforts, too, are critical, yet they are only indirectly related to the end products of his subordinates.

The manager is a specialist; his skills are more nearly mental, conceptual, or abstract than the skills of many subordinates. The results of his efforts are not readily visible. Comparisons between a good manager and a poor manager might be possible primarily through inference, by an examination of their subordinates.

In some ways the mark of the good manager is in what *doesn't* happen: dissatisfaction, turnover, unanticipated problems, crises, major "surprises," unnecessary duplication, responsibility disputes, budget overruns, and quality problems. To achieve results, the manager must allow his people to do their jobs. It is his responsibility to foresee and remove roadblocks that might hinder them. He must facilitate their efforts. And he must see that individual, group, and organizational needs are carefully balanced and met.

Because of the nature of the managerial function, we can easily see the importance of understanding human behavior in organized settings. Without this knowledge, the manager's primary vehicle—his subordinates—for fulfilling his responsibility cannot be utilized effectively. And his responsibility to the members of the organization as individuals and as human beings cannot be met.

Managing Organizational Behavior

Our conception of the manager in the organization carries an unspoken assumption: the manager's role is an *action* role. The manager must perform his activities and do his duty so that the organization may be effective in the production and delivery of its goods or service. Such a notion implies that the manager must spark others to action, initiate new programs, and see that plans and orders are carried out. He must be the *stimulus* that brings forth appropriate *responses*.

Stimulus–Response Management

A stimulus is "an external or internal event that brings about an alteration in . . . behavior."[1] A response is the alteration in behavior that occurs. Simplistically speaking, one applies a stimulus and secures a response. Certainly the manager must obtain responses to stimuli—his activities—in order to have work done within the organization.

A danger exists in thinking that a stimulus is directly linked to a response. Were the stimulus–response (S–R) linkage direct, then every time a given stimulus were applied, the same response would be given. This is the

---

[1]G. A. Kimble, *Hillgard and Marquis' Conditioning and Learning*, (New York: Appleton Century Croft, 1961). Cited in Lawrence S. Wrightsman, *Social Psychology in the Seventies*, (Monterey, Cal.: Brooks/Cole, 1972) pp. 10, 11.

FIGURE 2.1 The stimulus–response relationship indicates that a given response may be elicited by the application of a given stimulus.

usual managerial assumption made, that obtaining a desired response is simply a matter of applying a direct, appropriate stimulus.

What's the matter with such an attitude? The shortcoming of the S–R approach was pointed out in Chapter 1. Laws of physics and chemistry encourage direct S–R linkages because of the inanimate and relatively nonvariable characteristics of both stimulus and response. Properties of experimental materials may be measured and held constant while exact voltages are applied to release predetermined volumes of gases. Applying S–R reasoning to situations other than well-defined and predictable physical phenomena is failing to consider the pitfalls of a fallacious analogy. Yet common managerial practice is to define the desired response—and order it to be accomplished! Isn't this a *logical* way of performing the manager's activities?

Using S–R thinking, such an approach is the most *direct* and *efficient* way of getting done what the manager wishes. But why is it that different subordinates respond differently to the same directive? Why do some production workers work at top speed while others loaf—even when they are all under the same incentive (stimulus) system?

Pre-Hawthorne managers noticed these discrepancies between theory and reality in organizations. The Hawthorne studies served to clarify the differences between clear-cut S–R linkages in well-defined and understood situations and the nonlogical process that occurs in the organization, with all its variables and mysteries.

Stimulus–Organism–Response Management

Because something unexplained intervened between stimulus and expected response—yielding a different response—the S–R model was seen as inadequate. The Hawthorne studies pointed out that the *human* factor itself was the missing link. The organism is not a passive element in the stimulus–organism–response (S–O–R) sequence; it directly affects both stimulus and response while *being* affected. A casual remark by one's boss (stimulus) *gains* meaning and added stimulus value if the person has been worried about his job and his performance; an innocuous statement can then be "transformed" by the human organism into a threatening and provocative attack. The organism affects both stimulus and response as he stalks away, raging and anxious.

Managers apply S–O–R concepts when they carefully consider ways of communicating more effectively, so that the meaning sent (stimulus) is the same as the meaning received by another. Response can then be more nearly predicted by a lessening of the variable influence of the individual on the

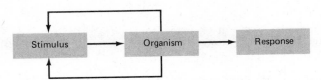

FIGURE 2.2   The stimulus–organism–response
relationship shows how the object of the stimulus (the
organism) intervenes in the S–R process.

S—O—R process. The difference is important because of the recognition that
consideration must be given to the individual as the manager attempts to
elicit the responses required by the functioning organization, for which he is
responsible. Once again the concept underlying S–O–R management is that
of the manager directly influencing and stimulating activity through his role.

Even this more complete behavior sequence seems lacking for the
manager. The organism interacts with stimulus and response, implying that
continuing response patterns may be stimulated either by the manager or by
the motivated individual. Complex patterns of total behavior, such as those
involved in building a dam or assembling an auto, are rather difficult to
handle when we consider *a* stimulus, *one* organism, and a *specific* response
action. Factors that influence the organism and his response are not
accounted for, either, such as desire for achievement or social pressure.

Behavioral Systems Management

The manager cannot physically initiate a stimulus for each person under
his command for each separate activity required until work is done. Instead
he creates a total situation composed for formal expectations and requirements, task technology and work methods, instructions and policies, and
formalized cooperation to integrate specialized work activities.

When the work situation is appropriately defined and established, the
situation itself acts as a continuing stimulus. A moving stream of electronic
parts provides a stimulus for the solderer. An inventory clerk's activities are
initiated by his assigned duty of maintaining records of stock levels. And
what the manager does is a consequence of information that production is
behind schedule or unit costs have risen above tolerance or distributors are
rejecting shipments because of defects.

The *situation* serves to stimulate in lieu of a series of isolated stimuli
stemming directly from the manager. In case it is required, of course, he can
still directly initiate a stimulus designed for a specific activity; such a stimulus
may be needed to supplement situational stimuli (such as questioning someone for excessive tardiness) or to cover a nonroutine or extraordinary need
(such as trying to iron the problems out of a new budget system).

The situation consists of many individual (but related) cues or stimuli, sufficient to bring forth not merely a simple single response but a concerted *pattern* of behavior. Behavior is a much more complex notion than response, because behavior identifies a whole set of related actions (responses).

An additional element in this expansion of behavioral cause and effect is the recognition that a stimulus interacts with individual psychological and emotional forces, as well as group values and pressures, in creating tendencies to behave. How a person *perceives* the stimulus affects how he will react to it. A reference group or a clique may also influence how he behaves because of commonly held values or conceptions of how a group member "ought" to behave.

Managing the complex behavioral systems relationship, then, is substantially more complicated than the simple S–R phenomenon. The manager knows that desired behavior patterns must be initiated and maintained through his activities and the total work situation. Yet both individual and social factors—some beyond his control—also affect the process through which behavior occurs. Understanding the nature of the factors involved and their relationships assists him as he fulfills his role in obtaining results. His is an active part, for he starts, directs, maintains, and terminates organizational activity, and his responsibility lies in bringing forth the behavior necessary to the mission of the firm. The behavior equation is directly influenced by the actions *he* takes. Members of the organization react to their total situation, which includes the manager, *his* behavior, and the manner in which he performs his managerial role.

The activities of the manager are part of an overall system of behavior of which the manager is a part and for which he is responsible. The effective manager is one who knows the limitations of managing by S–R principles and who can analyze and identify the major elements in a more complete conception of behavioral cause and consequence. In the next chapter we will use the behavioral systems process as a fundamental relationship and identify the major components and relationships of human behavior in organized settings.

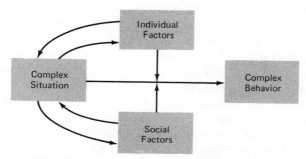

FIGURE 2.3 Behavioral systems management: complex behavior results from the situation, and from individual and social factors.

Summary

The manager operates within the framework provided by the organization. An organization is an economic and social entity in which a number of individuals perform a variety of tasks in order to reach a common objective. This objective is typically too large or too complex for a single person to reach alone.

Organizations are specialized devices, in that each provides a particular or specific service or type of good. Within organizations, too, specialization occurs in the definition and assignment of tasks to individuals. Within limits, this specialization yields benefits of increased efficiency and better ability to perform.

Problems also occur as a result of specialization in organizations; if a number of people are each performing specific tasks associated with a part of the overall objective of the organization, areas of ambiguity and conflict may arise. Some coordination is necessary to meld the efforts of each person into the achievement of the final, desired result.

Specialization of activity allows this coordination to be performed by specific individuals who are charged with the responsibility of ensuring that desired unit results are achieved. These are managers, and their work is an indirect contribution to the firm's product.

The manager performs his function of attaining prescribed results through the process of four activities: planning, organizing, directing, and controlling.

Planning is comprised of establishing objectives to be accomplished, together with the ways in which this will be done. Policies (guides to decision-making and activity) are set up to give predetermined solutions or performance standards to each member. In this way, every member's contribution to overall objectives is broadly directed.

Organizing is the activity in which tasks and individuals are combined. Groups of tasks—or groups of individuals—are set up as units (departments) for efficiency. Formal relationships among tasks and the people who perform them are an integral part of the organizing activity.

Directing is necessary to provide members with a positive environment within which they may perform activities meaningful both to the organization and to themselves. Leadership and motivation are two important skills in this aspect of the managerial role.

Controlling is the final activity in the managerial function. Individual, unit, and organizational performance is measured, in order to see how well plans are being carried out and to what extent objectives are being attained. With this measurement comes information of existing or potential problems which could interfere with attaining objectives; with this information, the manager can take steps to solve or prevent these obstacles.

The manager serves as the agent of the organization, charged with the responsibility of obtaining desired results. As a manager, he must operate *through* the efforts of his subordinates. In other words, he must elicit desired behaviors which contribute to overall objectives. To do this effectively, he must understand those factors which influence or affect the behavior of organizational members and of other managers.

In performing his activities, the manager must obtain required behaviors from organizational members. Using Stimulus–Response approaches fails to recognize the more realistic (but complicated) perspective that behavior is affected by more than a direct stimulus and that behavior is a complex of responses. A given stimulus from the manager may elicit one (or none) or any number of possible responses.

In line with the Hawthorne findings, a stimulus–organism–response conception does build in the need to consider the individual's psychological or emotional response to a stimulus before his overt response is initiated. Such a model of behavior also lacks completeness. The situation–individual/ social factors–behavior (behavioral systems) relationship is presented to identify major factors in behavioral causation. The situation comprises the total range of stimuli operating upon the individual, including the manager, the sociocultural environment, task technology, and so on. The manager stimulates and sustains behavior within the situation. Behavior is the end result of the process and consists of a complex yet interrelated set of responses or activities. Eliciting the *appropriate* behavior patterns is a major part of the manager's role.

Intervening between situation and behavior are additional elements that can distort or influence behavioral tendencies. Psychological and emotional states affect perceptions or identification with the stimulus situation and can change the individual's reaction. Group or social factors can also create a range of behaviors seen as more (or less) desirable than others because they relate to group values or accepted ideas of how a member should act.

The manager finds it important to have a realistic and workable conception of behavioral cause and consequence as he attempts to fulfill his role. The behavioral systems relationship will be used as a fundamental basis for exploring the major factors in organizational behavior in the next chapter.

STUDY AND REVIEW QUESTIONS

1. Why are organizations important?
2. What part does the manager play in the activities of the organization?
3. How are the managerial activities of planning and controlling related?
4. Why should the manager be a leader?
5. Why is an understanding of human behavior vital to the effective manager?
6. What importance has a realistic but workable conception of behavior cause-and-consequence for the manager? Why?
7. How does a response *stimulus* differ from a behavior-affecting *situation*?

8. Why is not a direct S–R relationship adequate for the manager in analyzing and understanding behavior?

9. Identify two separate *situations* with which you are familiar that are consistent with the use of "situation" in the behavioral systems relationship. How is behavior initiated and sustained by the characteristics of each of these situations?

10. What does behavior cause-and-consequence have to do with the manager's activities of planning, organizing, directing, and controlling?

Chapter

3

A Systems View of Organizational Behavior

CHAPTER OBJECTIVES

1. To sketch the overall plan of the text's coverage of organizational behavior.

2. To introduce the concept of interacting behavioral and technological systems.

3. To develop an appreciation of the many variables that affect human behavior.

4. To present the three major organizational behavior systems in brief form.

CHAPTER OUTLINE

As we have seen, the primary job of the manager is to get results; he must initiate and direct those activities that result in the reaching of the goals of the organization. No matter how high or low the manager's position in the company, his position represents a continuing responsibility to give full-time attention to a specific area of the firm's operation. Those who hold management positions—whether they be in a manufacturing firm, the Red Cross, NASA, a bank, or whatever—must get things done in specific areas, so that the overall organization can achieve its purpose. Even the president of a firm or an instituttion has a job that reflects this reality. He is the one who must make sure that the separate activities of the firm are all coordinated and aimed at the success of the entire company.

We've been talking in generalities about the responsibilities of the manager. So far we haven't said much about the things that affect his ability to obtain results. An organization is by no means a mechanical device that whirs into action quickly and efficiently with the pushing of the appropriate button. If the manager could push a button and thereby do his job, managers certainly would not be as well paid as they are. Unfortunately the effective manager must deal with many complexities, all of which seem intent on deterring him from the results he must obtain. Since the manager never directly does the work, he must get things done through the efforts of his subordinates. There is substantial truth in the saying that a big difference exists between theory and practice. Most managers will quickly assure you that their job is critical and difficult because there's an even greater gap between *wanting* to do something and *getting* it done.

After the manager has determined (planned) what he wants to do, what are the resources available by which he can put the plan into appropriate action? What complications and frustrations does he meet in so doing? What types of behavior must he encourage from his subordinates and what are the processes that will affect those behaviors? How can the manager successfully intervene in and influence the course of events in which organizational goals are at stake?

We will be trying to answer these questions through understanding what goes on in the process of attaining results through others, what elements are important, how they affect each other, and how they determine the degree to which the manager does his job. Our focus will be on what causes and makes up human behavior in organizations: organizational behavior. Further, we will be interested in using this information in a *predictive* fashion. We can then make intelligent forecasts of the future and influence or control events, activities, and behavior in fulfilling the manager's role.

Models and Reality

To do this we must first understand that things are not nearly as simple and clear-cut as we might wish them to be. What Seiler calls the "single-cause habit"[1] is rather convenient and widespread. This is the habit of assuming that the result of a cause–effect relationship has a single cause.

If an engineer abruptly quits his job, we might search for the cause. "He wasn't happy," we nod knowingly. The simple cause–effect relationship (unhappiness–quitting) may satisfy our after-the-fact analysis, but can we then apply the same relationship in a *predictive* fashion? If we observe another unhappy job-holder, can we confidently expect his imminent resignation? "Ah," we demur, "we don't know enough about him to predict his actions." Just so. Although we can explicitly assume a single cause for an observed effect in a particular situation, we implicitly recognize that a rather large number of other factors are also important in the relationship.

To explain the engineer's action fully, we might try to determine what personal, professional, social, or organizational (or any combinations thereof) conflicts were bothering him. How did his work stack up against his expectations of it? Had he received another job offer? What kind of job did he take after quitting? We could go on and on, isolating and cataloging single factors that influenced his action. And after that was done, we might look at how certain factors in combination were more influential than they were singly.

In trying to understand any phenomenon, we try to determine the *relationship* between cause(s) and result. Once that is done, we can apply the same general rule (or "law") to different specific instances of the same type. We have built a "model" of a general situation by isolating and extracting major causal factors, examining how they affect each other, and determining how they create or influence the phenomenon in which we are interested. Building a model allows us to simplify reality to the extent that we can grasp its salient characteristics, make an abstract reality rather more concrete, and focus our attention on the most important elements of the situation. Because it is a model, whose function is to simplify reality, it cannot perfectly replicate the situation. Even if it could, would the model be a model or reality?

The law of supply and demand in economic theory is one familiar model. It presents a simplified abstraction of reality by presenting a good's price as being determined by the relationship between aggregate customer demand and the available supply of the good. Is the model realistic? We might complain that the model fails to take into account slight differences in quality or nonprice competition between suppliers or the impact of rapid inflation upon buyers' consumption habits. These are all good criticisms, but the model should be evaluated by how well it represents broad classes of situations for analytical purposes. Recognizing its shortcomings in *individual* or *specific* cases, we can use the model to grasp the *essentials* of the situation, then employ whatever other analyses are appropriate to our particular case.

So it is with human behavior in organized settings. To understand what

[1]John A. Seiler, *Systems Analysis in Organizational Behavior* (Homewood, Ill.: Irwin, 1967), p. 1.

affects behavior, we must represent reality with a model. No matter how complex the model is, some aspects of reality will be omitted.[2] We attempt to describe the relationships among many factors and some resultant behavior. The model must be general enough to provide a good grasp upon the essentials of almost any specific situation, yet concise enough to be usable. It must also represent reality in a significant fashion.

We all employ models by which we operate in the world. Our models are our conceptual understandings of the parts important to us. The model serves as a kind of filter, eliminating or straining out extraneous or confusing data, while highlighting meaningful patterns. We relate to different situations through our understanding of them—through our models. If our models do not effectively represent reality, then our understanding *and* actions can range from being completely inappropriate to being innocuous to being (coincidentally) appropriate.[3] Over time, the odds tilt in favor of "wrong" actions being taken.

Systems and Systems

Intuitively we can accept the existence of models that include *other* models. We may have an overall idea or model of a city, for example; the city may include various transportation networks, health care services, commercial entities, housing complexes, and so on. Each of these components of the city may be modeled in its own right. We may consider the relationships that occur within a business-oriented organization, as well as those by which the firm interacts with other businesses or society as a whole. We can then model specific functions within the organization. The marketing and distribution function might be modeled, as might the inventory control system or performance appraisal techniques.

When component parts of an overall pattern are isolated and modeled, we are actually investigating *systems*. Each of the submodels is discrete in that it is an assembly of related processes or items, each of which contributes to the accomplishment of the overall objective or purpose of the submodel.[4] Each of the elements within a system shares a common purpose for its separate—and interrelated—activities. Those elements can be thought of as working together, even while being made up of elements that we can distinguish readily.

Your automobile may be considered as a transportation system; it is a set

---

[2]"The *primary value of a model is that it does leave things out.* If all models were 'perfect' in the sense that they included *all* aspects of the real system, there would be no models but, rather, simply reproductions of real-world systems. As such, they would be useless for many purposes. . . . *The primary value of a model lies in its simplicity relative to the real world.*" David I. Cleland and William R. King, *Management: A Systems Approach* (New York: McGraw-Hill, 1972), p. 48. Emphases in the original.

[3]Stafford Beer, "The World We Manage," *Behavioral Science*, **18**:199, 200 (1973).

[4]Cf. Fremont E. Kast and James E. Rosenzweig, *Organization and Management: A Systems Approach* (New York: McGraw-Hill, 1970), p. 110.

of interrelated parts and activities that is intended to provide transportation for you. Even when we think of the car as a single system, however, we can recognize that it is composed of an engine, four wheels, a chassis, and a transmission, among other parts. Each of these elements is important to the functioning of the car, but by themselves they can contribute nothing to the end objective of providing transportation. They must work together—in an interrelated fashion—before the end purpose can be achieved.

We can carry the idea of a "system" even further by thinking of the individual elements that make up a transportation system as being themselves systems within a *larger* system. The engine could be thought of as a system composed of pistons, cylinders, a block, and so on. Just as is true of the car, the different elements that make up the engine are worthless unless they function together in an interrelated fashion. When we think of a car as a system, then we can consider the engine to be one of its subsystems. Let us examine the concept of "interrelatedness" among the subsystems that compose the overall system by considering that if we block the auto's exhaust system, the engine (propulsion system) works harder, requiring more fuel from the fuel system, and so on. If a change occurs in one of the systems, changes will occur in the other systems.

We can carry the theme one step farther by considering the extent to which any system is affected by events occurring outside itself. An "open" system

is influenced by, and influences, its environment and reaches a state of dynamic equilibrium in this environment. Such a description of a system adequately fits the typical social organization. For example, the business organization is a man-made system which has a dynamic interplay with its environment—customers, competitors, labor organizations, suppliers, government, and many other agencies. Furthermore, the business organization is a system of interrelated parts working in conjunction with each other in order to accomplish a number of goals, both those of the organization and those of individual participants.[5]

A "closed" system is relatively uninfluenced by or isolated from its environment. Completely closed systems are probably quite rare, if they exist at all; even an alarm clock must be wound by, or receive energy from, an external source. Closed systems are easier to analyze than open systems, because all their constituent elements can be readily identified.[6] Even relatively closed systems are still somewhat open, however.[7]

Using this information about the differences between open and closed systems, and referring back to the definitions of a system, we can portray a simple system as in Figure 3-1.

A simple open system requires that some form of input be provided.

[5]Richard A. Johnson, Fremont E. Kast, and James E. Rosenzweig, *The Theory and Management of Systems,* 3rd Ed. (New York: McGraw-Hill, 1973), p. 12.

[6]Joseph A. Litterer, *The Analysis of Organizations,* 2nd Ed. (New York: Wiley, 1973), pp. 47, 48.

[7]Dalton E. McFarland, *Management: Principles and Practices,* 4th Ed. (New York: Macmillan, 1974), p. 82.

FIGURE 3.1   A simple system.

The input may be money, energy, raw materials, information, or almost anything else that is used to fulfill the system's purpose. These inputs are transformed or used in making an output, such as a manufactured product in a manufacturing system.

The system itself is then the process by which input is transformed into output. In Figure 3-1 the system is represented by the box. This "black box" representation is often used for analytical purposes, to focus attention on input and output rather than on the mechanics of transforming one into the other.

Systems can be "linked" together, with the output of a first system becoming the input of a second. The salesman's order (his output) becomes the input for the order clerk, whose output (a manufacture order) is an input for the manufacturing department, and so on.

The organization can be thought of as an incredibly complex system composed of many subsystems. The organization is obviously an open system, since it interacts with other, external systems in its environment. This idea will be important for our purposes, since we will be examining organizational behavior within the organization. Certainly neither the organization nor the organizational behavior system can be considered as being closed or nonresponsive to their respective external environments.

To understand organizational behavior, we will build a systems model that shows the relationships among its important constituent elements and the ways in which they affect behavior.

The Major Systems in Organizational Behavior

An organization is a collection of people who with consciously coordinated efforts pursue and contribute to the attainment of a common purpose.

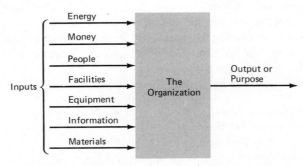

FIGURE 3.2   The organization as a system.

The manager is usually charged with the responsibility of formally directing these activities and of seeing to it that the objective is reached as efficiently and effectively as possible. In order to achieve objectives, he must make sure that proper work and jobs exist and that both the job and the worker are supported by an appropriate technology (suitable knowledge, tools, and design of the work to be done). All these factors we can call the *formal organizational system*. This system is composed of the total work that the organization is to do, the technology by which it attempts to do it, the structure of the organization itself (such as the relationships among groups of specialized jobs), and the distributing of necessary authority and responsibility throughout the organization.

At the same time, the formal organizational system is dependent upon people in some fashion. A job is done only to the extent that the person who *holds* the job wants or allows it to be done; his willingness to fulfill his job role is dramatically affected by job as well as nonjob factors. A splitting headache can hamper a secretary's typing performance just as much as a sticking keyboard letter. Who is to say what or how much effect the boss's sarcastic remarks may have? Or what about the football coach's comment that one of his running-back prospects "has all the equipment—good size and speed, excellent acceleration, great hands, and fine moves. But on any given Saturday he's only as good as he *wants* to be. And I don't know how to make him want to make the starting lineup!"

Each person involved in the organizational process will behave differently, even under the same conditions or in the same situations. Exactly how each individual responds directly affects the extent to which his team or work group can achieve its goal. Have you ever noticed that a "busted" football play can be converted into a touchdown? Often the key block is made by one man who gets up after being blocked out himself, even though he knows the play is going all wrong. Even then he continues while his other teammates may have already conceded lost yardage. Certainly such behavior is of an individual nature and has important consequences for his team. But then, so does the performance of a defensive back who "dogs" it (loafs) on the one play that a pass is thrown into his area—for a touchdown.

Technology—training, skills, knowledge, tools, work design—isn't enough. It takes a person to use the technology. How well he uses it depends on him. How can an individual be encouraged to behave in ways that are consistant with what the organization would like him to do? How can a low producer be encouraged to increase his work rate? Or why is it that the same pay raise will delight one person and make him more productive but discourage or alienate another? We can investigate the factors that affect and influence the individual within the organization by considering the *individual* himself as a system, with particular emphasis on the psychological makeup of the individual and his motivation, or willingness, to behave in ways consistent with the formal organizational system.

Individuals rarely occur alone; the very nature of the organization requires that several individuals be present and active. Within the organization, people tend to band together with others who share their viewpoints or values. For some purposes, groupings of individuals exhibit certain common characteristics. Sometimes we can treat such a grouping as if it were a single entity. What's more, many members of such groups actually think of themselves in this way.

When individuals form into a group, each individual seems to change his behavior somewhat in response to implicit or unstated demands by the group. They all tend to act alike in matters important to the group or clique. Just as the Hawthorne researchers found out, people in groups behave differently from people by themselves. Recognizing this, we can call this important modifier of behavior the *social system*.

These are systems because each is composed of a number of elements, each of which has in common an ultimate specific objective. The purpose of the functioning of the three systems (formal organizational, individual, and social) is the attainment of objectives and getting things done. The formal organizational system, the individual system, and the social system can each be investigated separately for insights into how each system operates and what its major components are. To get a complete understanding of how they contribute to organizational behavior and thence to the objectives, however, we must consider how they affect each other. We know that these separate systems must work together and that they must modify and interact with each other. This approach is necessary in order to be able to understand a very complex process and to *predict* what determines, and what the consequences are, of human behavior in organizations.

The three systems of organizational behavior have important effects upon what happens in a firm. We also know that the manager must somehow intervene in the process to make sure that the behavior that occurs coincides with that necessary to meet organizational objectives. The manager has a number of tools available through which he may influence organizational behavior. They center around the modifying of the determinants of specified behaviors of members and the changing of formal work processes to include recognition of human needs. Further, the manager can and does influence behavior through the ways in which he characteristically relates to, and interacts with, individuals and groups as he fulfills his managerial role. His "style" of management can profoundly influence his subordinates and hence constitutes another of his modification approaches.

A Systems Model of Organizational Behavior

Figure 3-3 shows the general relationships among the three organizational behavior systems. We notice that organizational requirements are directed into this system and that behavior emerges from it. These requirements stem from the purpose of the organization (which in turn derives from the cultural, political, and economic environments). For the organization to survive as an economic entity, these requirements must be met, since

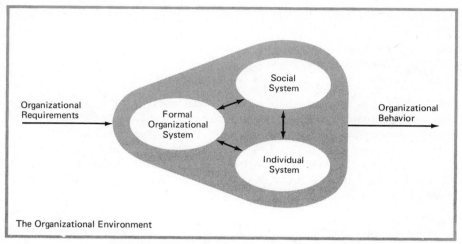

FIGURE 3.3   Organizational systems.

they form its reason for existing. They are translated into the formal definition of the objectives of the organization, which, in turn, establish the activities in which the organization must engage.

The Formal Organizational System

The formal organizational system prescribes such things as specifications of duties and tasks within the broad functions necessary to reach these objectives. Further, the exact ways in which these functions will be performed will be determined through a meshing of available technology and the demands of the firm. Chapters 4 and 5 will detail this phenomenon.

Technology

The formal organizational system can be thought of as the technological and organizational means through which the overall purposes of the firm are intended to be achieved. *Technology* is a rather vague and ambiguous term that encompasses a wide variety of elements and that is extremely broad in its scope. Included in technology are such physical elements as the production process, which includes machinery, raw materials, work flow, and tools—and the relationships among them; the layout or planned placement within a building of desks, people, machines, storage facilities, walls, and so on; and designs of actions and/or activities to be grouped into distinct jobs. More abstractly we can think of technology as any and all knowledge pertaining to the activities of men and/or machines in the pursuit of organizational objectives.[8] Work and technology naturally lend themselves to study, analysis, and emphasis on efficiency. Scientific management techniques have long been

[8]Litterer, p. 283.

employed to determine if the basic technology of an activity is as efficient as possible.

Organization Structure

After the technological and work requirements are set, the organization's *structure* is established. Structure is designed around technology to facilitate the organization's smooth functioning as well as to construct administrative responsibilities and coordination.[9] With this in mind we can recognize that grouping similar tasks—for example, into one distinct department—makes sense. Such a structure might allow a single manager to coordinate and direct the work of many and to become expert at handling recurring problems.

Formal Requirements

The structuring of activities within the organization has other results, too. There are specific results that must be attained, which means that certain specified work must be done. Technology, of course, determines the nature of the work processes. Organization structure breaks down these technologically ordained work processes into jobs and thereby specifies what the holders of the job will do. In other words, the structure (through the design of the job) requires the individual to behave in certain ways.

Going back to the automobile assembly-line example, the basic technology is represented by the mass-production technique of the assembly line. Each worker holds a certain job, does specified actions, and occupies his own work station along the line. The content of each job is determined through the organizing of the firm's structure. But once the job is set, the actions of the holder of the job are set, too. The worker must perform what the job dictates. If he chooses, for example, to leave the door handles off every other car, some customers just might not understand his choice. He is also affected by the technological restrictions on his behavior; the typical assembly-line worker cannot leave his work station for whatever personal or pressing reasons, unless another person takes over his station while he's gone. Technology and structure combine to place requirements and restrictions on behavior.

This might seem harsh and unyielding. We need to bear in mind that the purpose of any organization must be reached or the organization cannot survive. To ensure its existence, work must be done, and the activities of its members cannot be allowed to be haphazard or random. Each job and each

[9]See, for example, Raymond G. Hunt, "Technology and Organization," *Academy of Management Journal*, (September 1970), pp. 240–242; Edward Harvey, "Technology and the Structure of Organizations," *American Sociological Review* (April 1968), pp. 247–259; and F. E. Emery and E. L. Trist, "Socio-Technical Systems," in *Management Sciences: Models and Techniques*, Vol. 2 (Oxford: Pergamon Press, 1960), pp. 86, 87.

person is necessary in some way, and coordination and control are necessary in relating individual specialized jobs to larger segments of the work process.

The specialization of jobs and activities leads to major benefits to the organization in the forms of lower labor costs, higher production, lower training costs, and greater use of mechanization. It also creates the major problems of closely coordinating each work unit's efforts and output with the activities of other units, controlling and monitoring vast work processes, and the human costs of boredom and dissatisfaction.

Authority

The philosophy of specialization and efficiency gives rise to another type of specialization, that of managerial duties. The chief executive of the firm occupies a very broad position, coordinating and controlling many diverse functions. Those reporting to him are allowed to specialize in the various broad areas of the firm, such as manufacturing, marketing, and finance. Given viewpoints narrower than their boss's, they are able to oversee the more detailed functions that their subordinates pursue. This specialization occurs more and more, until one reaches the level of the operative or worker, who usually performs a highly specialized job. With increasing specialization as one goes down the organizational ladder, individual managers act as agents for their superiors and are usually allowed to direct or influence their own subordinates within a specialized area of operations. To do this, they are granted *authority* by their superiors, which is the formal right to influence or direct the behavior of one's subordinates.

Authority is the intermediary by which technology is able to work through the structure of the organization to achieve the benefits of specialization and efficiency in the pursuit of overall organizational goals. Given authority, a manager can control (keep actual performance in line with intended results) and coordinate (mesh activities and output in a timely and proper fashion with other organizational units), so that the firm attains its economic objectives.[10]

Job Satisfaction

Formal task requirements have a result other than economic output; the individual who performs the task experiences some level of satisfaction with his job. His job attitude depends in large measure on the nature of the duties as they have been designed. The extent to which he can identify with the end result of his labors—the meaningfulness of his work—and the impact of technology, organization, and authority all tend to create an overall positive (or negative) attitude. Satisfaction with one's job can mean, in turn, an

[10]Daniel Katz and Robert L. Kahn, *The Social Psychology of Organizations* (New York: Wiley, 1966), p. 203.

increased commitment in the fulfillment of formal requirements. Greater willingness to invest personal energy and time in job performance can also occur with having a satisfying job. Hence we can also show that a tendency to perform or fulfill job expectations stems from the process that culminates in job satisfaction.

Representing the Formal Organizational System

Figure 3-4 sketches the components and relationships of the formal organizational system. Work and technology form the central focus of the system. The organization structure supports or facilitates the technological requirements by job design and task groupings for control and coordination. To attain the benefits of specialization and efficiency, authority is used to ensure adequate role performance and direction of efforts. Job satisfaction is considered as intervening between the requirements of the job and the extent to which these formal expectations are fulfilled by the individual or work group.

We noted in Chapter 1 that technological demands of specialization and efficiency are well suited to analyses. People are usually excluded in these analyses, except for being necessary adjuncts to machines or activities. Exclusive consideration of this formal organizational system can have negative effects on the human beings whose behavior is dictated by the work and technology. Perhaps even more importantly, these humans can have dramatic and drastic effects upon the effectiveness and efficiency with which the formal organizational system operates!

Interface[11]

No organization can exist without people; people compose the organization and perform within it to reach common goals. Exactly what they do is

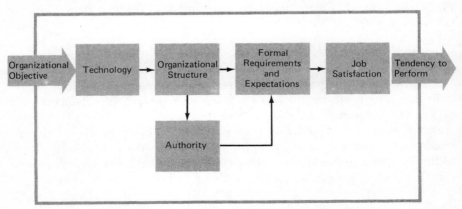

FIGURE 3.4   The formal organizational system.

[11]An *interface* is the area of contact where two systems touch.

largely dictated by technology. Technology allows people to do a job as best they might. It can also hinder them. An assembly-line worker may not finish his task before the product is automatically moved out of his work station and on to the next production step. At the same time, the individual has a considerable effect on how well his job is done. We have probably all seen people who just don't care to work any harder than the bare minimum.

The college classroom provides a good example. Technology supports learning. Technology includes such diverse elements as the textbook, the classroom and its seating arrangement, class notes, the professor and his pedagogical approach (such as lecturing, analyzing cases, question-and-answer sessions), and feedback or control devices like quizzes. The teaching–learning tools within the classroom are not ends in themselves but provide the basic means *through which* the objective (the individual student's learning) may be attained. We have all seen how different aspects of this technology can affect performance. The professor who drones on and on, never looking up from his yellowed notes; an un-air-conditioned classroom in 100-degree heat; the disruption of concentration by construction noise—any or all of these can have serious consequences in how well the student can reach the objective of learning.

Each individual within that classroom is certainly affected by the technology used. At the same time, his own performance is a direct result of the extent to which he chooses to use the available technology and his willingness to put forth his own effort to reach the goal successfully. In the same classroom some students will choose not to take advantage of the technology provided, perhaps by skipping classes excessively; others will use the provided technology but will add little to it in terms of their own efforts, being willing to settle for less than perfect performance. On the other hand, some will use the technology to the fullest, adding to it a dedicated and concentrated amount of personal work, thereby earning accolades for superior performance. It is important to recognize that technology by itself cannot reach organizational goals. The individual must use the technology provided and then must add a considerable amount of human performance to make happen what technology can only make possible.

We must also explicitly recognize that technology does not act in a one-way fashion upon individual behavior: the *individual* affects technology! A new work method would hardly be effective if it required the worker to have four arms. Similarly students directly influence the teaching technologies adopted. If standardized exams show one teaching method to be ineffective in transmitting knowledge, then serious evaluation is in order.

What causes these types of differences in the performance of individuals? To answer this question, we must look at the individual as a representation of many strange and conflicting forces that are continuously in action within him. These are not visible to the naked eye nor directly measureable with yardsticks or other physical standards. These forces are intensely personal and complicated, although they exist in all of us. We will be looking at these forces as they affect the behavior of the individual.

The Individual System

What makes an individual the person that he is? We know that no two individuals in the entire world are exactly the same, just as no two sets of fingerprints are exactly the same. The vast majority of human beings share specific characteristics, such as number of arms and legs, number and placement of internal organs, and so on. How is it, then, that each of us is different?

Despite common physical characteristics, what makes us different is our set of internal characteristics. By *internal* we do not mean the organic or skeletal composition of our bodies, but our psychological makeups. Why are we the way we are? Is it because of our ancestry or heredity? Or have we learned to be what we are through the influence of our environment? We know that environment and heredity are both important in our development—in the development of an individual and unique personality.

Personality

But what is personality? The term is often used very casually. We may speak of a "pleasing personality," or of an "outgoing personality." We might even speak someone as having "a typical football player's personality," when referring to his stage of mental or intellectual development! For our purposes, however, a deeper and more specific meaning will be attached to the term. One way we will use *personality* is to represent "the characteristic traits and patterns of adjustment of the person in his interrelationships with others and his environment."[12] Personality may then be said to be a dynamic psychological process that results in characteristic or predictable patterns of behavior.

Businessmen before the Hawthorne studies, we remember, had thought that their workers exhibited highly predictable behavior. They thought that desired performance could be "turned on" through the application of the correct economic incentive. People are a great deal more complicated than that, as businessmen also found out when workers failed to respond as predicted and limited production instead (and thereby their own wages). What did these businessmen forget? We know now that they failed to take into account what happens *between* the application of the wage incentive (the stimulus) and the elicited job performance (the response). What happens is something not directly observable because it happens within the individual. We can relate what happens in terms of the simple "stimulus–response" thinking of the pre-Hawthorne businessman. A "stimulus" is anything that is applied in an effort to bring forth a given "response" or behavior. If you look into the sun, the brightness (stimulus) will make your eyes water and blink

---

[12]Blair J. Kolasa, *Introduction to Behavioral Science for Business* (New York: Wiley, 1969), p. 242.

(response); this automatic linking of a stimulus to a response requires no effort on your part. Businessmen had likewise felt that this automatic feature would hold when applying economic stimuli and giving greater amounts of work.

Communication

When a stimulus is applied to bring forth such complex and long-lasting activities as are involved in work, the "automatic" response may be lost. The stimulus, whether the boss's order or a promised pay increase, must usually be transmitted in the form of a message of some type. This entails communication, which is the act of transferring meaning or knowledge from one person to another.

Perception

"Meaning" or "knowledge" is no impersonal, automatic stimulus. Rather, it is transmitted in an effort to bring forth behavior that will result in specified outcomes. The meaning communicated goes through a complex (yet sometimes almost instantaneous) process before it results in behavior. Many things can prevent communication, such as simply not understanding what was said. Different people can also "see" the same object or stimulus in different ways; we call this *perception*. This merely means that our vision or understanding is colored or distorted by our own past experiences, what we expect to see, familiarity, feelings or attitudes, or values. The importance of perception may be seen in Figure 3-5.

Perception can literally change the intended stimulus into quite another, and the resultant behavior may well bewilder the one expecting to elicit a different set of actions.

Individual Expectations

The behavior that was desired must undergo a comparison with the individual's own personal needs and personal goals. If there is a conflict between the actions required by the organization and those by which the individual can satisfy his own needs, then serious behavioral difficulties may arise. The individual may be in a quandary because by fulfilling his job role he may be diminishing his ability to satisfy his own personal needs. This commonly happens when a production foreman sets a work quota of so many units per worker. Some workers will accept the quota as a challenge and consistently try to produce more than the quota, thereby increasing their own earnings. Others, on the other hand, see the quota as oppressive and demeaning and assert their own individual needs over organizational requirements by limiting their own production (as well as their own wages).

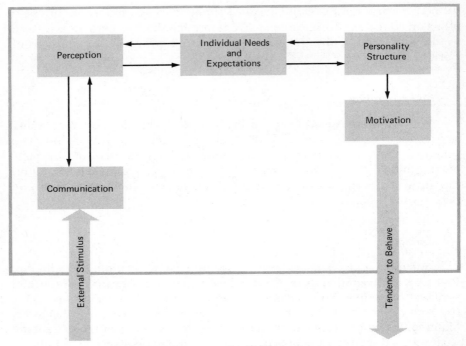

FIGURE 3.5   The individual system.

Motivation

Loosely speaking, when individual needs and organizational requirements are *not* in conflict, we would expect to find that the individual is
enthusiastic in his job. He is then said to be *motivated.* If there is conflict, the
person affected may be put in the position of choosing between organizational requirements and individual needs. He might compromise by doing
his job halfheartedly or by performing at an unsatisfactory level.

Interface

The manager must achieve results through the efforts of individuals.
Job requirements cannot automatically bring forth the desired standard of
performance. His subordinates each have needs of their own, which means
that they will usually respond in slightly different ways to a given stimulus.
Even then, the tendency to act in a certain way may not be directly translated
into actual behavior. Few individuals are able to behave without being
influenced by others.

Effect on the Individual

Technology, and its work-related dictates, have a continuing influence
on the individual. Consider the gregarious machine shop worker who is

effectively isolated from social contact by constant high noise levels. Similarly a middle-level manager may be frustrated in his attempts to influence company policy by requirements for extensive committee deliberations on any major proposal. Technology and organization structure can affect— positively or negatively—the system of the individual.

The Social System's Impact on the Individual

Perhaps just as important is the impact of the social system on individual behavior. No person exists totally independently of his peers. His social relationships and need to belong provide necessary devices to direct behavior into approved channels. Since the group with which the person relates or identifies is, of course, itself composed of people, considerations of the ways group members influence the group as a whole are important. A dominant personality can exert strong pressure on his peer group.

The formal organizational system predetermines some form of relationships among organizational members. These contacts, which occur as a result of stipulated job roles and organizational requirements, can serve to integrate the individual into a web of expectations and demands that may conflict with his own goal-seeking behavior.

The Social System

The Hawthorne studies demonstrated the existence of social organizations within the structure of the formal organization. Such social groupings are neither established nor prescribed by management but form spontaneously from the relationships of individuals at work. The findings of the Hawthorne studies pointed out the fallacy of assuming that each individual consistently behaves in such a way as to maximize his personal well-being. People form groups for many of the same reasons that they form formal organizations: common goals can be more readily reached in a cooperative setting.

Group and Informal Organization

The needs of individuals in informal organizations differ rather drastically from the economic needs of formal organizations. The needs satisfied by social groupings are intangible and are fulfilled through one's social relationships. People can come together, identify with each other, support or reinforce commonly held beliefs or values that are important to them, and *belong*. Figure 3-6 shows how this process ultimately affects individual behavior.

Informal Expectations

Each member willingly gives up a certain amount of "free will," as it were. He gives this up to behave in ways consistent with the expectations of

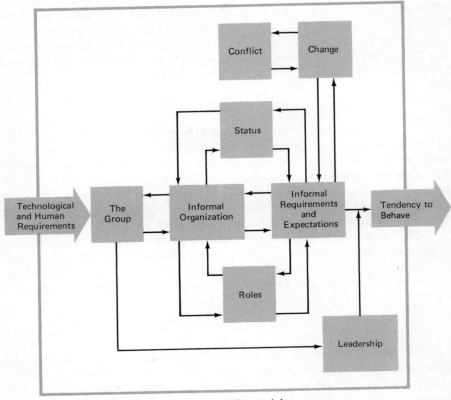

FIGURE 3.6   The social system.

his social-group peers. The more desirable the affiliation is, the more the group can dictate how its members act. You may have seen examples of this, as when fraternity initiates are "required" to undergo rather unusual activities. Dignified pillars of the community may even behave rather strangely, donning outlandish costumes and performing the secret rites of their lodge or civic organization. In both of these cases the individual can choose whether to accede to the expectations of the group. The affiliation is so intensely desired, however, that the members will behave in ways they ordinarily would not.

Role

The Hawthorne researchers observed that, as a result of the informal organization, individuals' behaviors were changed. Because of social or group pressure, workers limited their production and thereby their individual wages. The group is then a powerful device, one that has great influence on the actions of its members. Individual behavior that is not seen as being consistent with the expectations of the group can be quite harshly punished.

Ostracism (the banning of an individual from social contact with group members) is one extreme sanction that can be applied by the group. Others that are more widely used (and less harsh) include ridicule, taking another aside and "cluing him in," and leaving him out of group activities.

Status

Another contributor to the power of the informal or social group is its ability to confer status on members who meet the expectations of the group. These members are looked up to by their peers not for their position in the formal organization but because of their position in the social network. In industrial settings a manager's secretary often occupies a position of high status among those with whom she associates. If her social group is composed of clerk typists, stenographers, and other secretaries, she may be held in high esteem because of her access to information that flows through her formal position to her boss. Information is power, and she may dangle or withhold tidbits of news unavailable to the others.

Change and Conflict

Two subsidiary elements in the social system are change and conflict. The organization's social system is complex, far-reaching—and stable. Management-initiated changes in work procedures may disrupt social relationships and *create* conflict between social and formal organizational systems. Conflict also occurs between subcomponents of the organizational behavior process. For example, departments may contend with each other over budget or access to rewards. The behavior expected of someone may conflict with what he feels he should do, or it may conflict with someone else's expectations. Changes always occur—planned or unanticipated—and create some conflicts before equilibrium is reestablished.

If the informal organization is so widespread yet intangible and can exert such influence, what implications does this complex relationship between the individual and the group have for the manager? This brief introduction to the social system points out that the manager cannot assume that only organizational demands are acting upon his subordinates nor that the desired behavior will be automatically forthcoming. Individual needs and social pressures influence the direction, intensity, and intent of organizational behavior. Many a manager has blundered by selecting for promotion, for example, a low-status member of a tightly knit social group. To his dismay he has found out that the new superior had neither the trust nor the respect necessary to influence his former peers.

Interface

We can readily see how the individual and the group can influence organizational behavior through their interactions. Often we fail to notice that each affects (and is affected by) the formal organizational system. After all, people who work in close proximity to each other would be bound to develop a closer social relationship than people scattered throughout the plant. People working as a team—as members of a football team or as engineers working to solve a complex problem—tend to socialize more. Who has not heard of the frustrations of the individual worker on an assembly line? Certainly technology affects the individual as well.

People, either singly or in groups, can likewise affect technological requirements and effectiveness. One common problem facing managers today stems directly from this: at times auto assembly-line managers have experienced great difficulty in finding people willing to work on the assembly line, even for the relatively high wages paid. Those who did take such jobs had high absenteeism rates and tended to quit after a short period of time. Individual needs and personal characteristics quite literally affect technology and its effectiveness.

Certainly in the analysis and prediction of organizational behavior the manager must be aware of this constant interaction among the three major systems that occur in the organization. If he fails to take into account any one of these three, he may be unpleasantly surprised by the exact nature and direction of the behavior of his subordinates.

Modification and Integration Processes

The manager recognizes that each of these distinct systems influences individual and group behavior as formal requirements are pursued. His major problem is to decrease their negative (counterproductive) effects and to increase their positive effects. A broad strategy by which he can attack this complicated problem is the application of modification and integration processes.

Conflicts between systems are generally disruptive and therefore should be resolved systematically. Each of the systems is then open to modification to ease built-in frictions and sources of ineffectiveness. Through such modifications the entire organization can be made to be more effective and satisfying.

We can expand our basic systems model to show the relationship of modification and integration processes to the organizational behavior systems, as shown in Figure 3-7. Behavior is a continuously emerging phenomenon that can be satisfying or counterproductive. The manager must act to modify behavior in such a way that the separate objectives of each system are simultaneously attained. In this way total organizational effectiveness is maximized.

A feedback loop is shown as emerging from the processes by which organizational behavior is modified and integrated. The loop indicates that these processes have a dual role: emerging organizational behavior can be acted upon and negative consequences prevented before they occur, and the very systems themselves can be acted upon to forestall or eliminate the causes

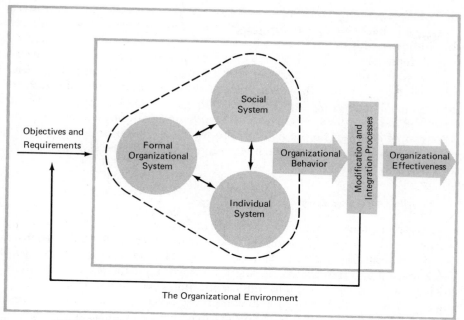

FIGURE 3.7   Systemic components of organizational behavior.

of conflict and to structure the total organization to be humanly satisfying and economically viable.

Four major processes of modifying and integrating organizational behavior are managerial styles, positive behavior reinforcement, job enrichment, and organizational development. All are methods that have humanistic objectives, primarily those of creating work situations at once more economically effective and more intrinsically satisfying to members.

The manager who does not employ appropriate modification and integration tools can find himself in the unenviable position of being unable to change the patterns of organizational behavior. Organizational effectiveness—overall attainment of results by the manager—might be attempted through an increase in the pressure for production, threats, incentive systems, and so on. We will see that these traditional approaches are less effective than the newer applications of behavioral science.

Managerial Styles

The overall pattern of behavior exhibited by the manager as he fulfills his responsibilities may be termed his *style*. The term *managerial style* may also be applied to the manner in which the superior–subordinate relationship is carried out. An authoritarian style, for example, creates dependency on the decisions and favor of the superior; members are expected to follow orders and perform as expected. The democratic style is quite different, however; a democratic manager solicits the suggestions of his subordinates and shares his authority with them.

A manager's overall style reflects his basic philosophy of the nature of man as well as personality considerations. Through a consistent style pattern the manager can cause his subordinates to respond and behave in predictable ways. Acknowledging his style, the manager can consciously identify the effect he has on others, modifying his own behavior in order to modify the behavior of others. The use of an appropriate style (according to criteria to be identified later) enhances the integration of individual, social, and formal organizational systems.

Positive Behavior Reinforcement

Another tool is made available through the application of learning theories and concepts. We know that the manager is responsible for attaining results, typically through the efforts of others. The manager manages *behavior,* attempting to create work situations in which subordinates will contribute (behave in productive ways) to the organization's goal attainment. Learning theory provides suggestions for making those behaviors rewarding to organization and individual. Rewarding constructive behavior and eliminating undesirable activities are major contributions. Rewards are an important part of positive behavior reinforcement because people tend to repeat pleasurable (rewarding) actions. Performance feedback itself can be a reward because it satisfies a human need of knowing how one is doing.

A complete and systematic program of positive behavior reinforcement calls for identifying and rewarding behaviors that contribute to formal goals. As obvious as this statement sounds, such programs are quite rare in business and other organizations. Formal expectations are usually established and subordinates are periodically appraised on how well they meet the expectations or quotas. Failure to perform as required is punished, and success is taken for granted. Positive behavior reinforcement intervenes in the usual process by correcting behaviors that lead to failure and rewarding successful behaviors, thereby modifying organizational behavior and allowing the goals of individuals and organization to become congruent.

Job Enrichment

Another approach entails the investigation of the formal requirements of the individual as expressed by the nature of his job. When people are bored or turned off by their jobs, they cannot be expected to exert maximum energy, apply great initiative or creativity, or express much interest or commitment. Because of the nature of the job, attitudes emerge that color the whole range of behaviors open to the individual.

A "better" job can often mean "better" attitudes and greater willingness to perform task duties. It can also provide greater satisfactions and opportunities for growth, challenge, and meaningful work. Extensive specialization and routinization of tasks can eliminate costly errors—as well as motivation and satisfaction.

Enriching the job means adding individual responsibility, challenge, initiative, meaningful work, and commitment to a job by redesigning its duties and scope. The job holder can produce an identifiable product, for which he is responsible, rather than performing a single specialized operation on the objects on the assembly line.

Behaviors are modified when the definition of formal task requirements is changed to duties that comprise an enjoyable, satisfying, and meaningful job. Individual and organization are more effectively integrated because the job does not come between what the individual seeks and what the organization requires.

Organizational Development

A fourth method for modifying and integrating organizational behavior consists of a group of techniques loosely grouped under the heading of organizational development (OD). In its complete sense OD allows for the humanization of the formal organization by pinning down specific barriers to organizational effectiveness, letting members work on the problems identified, and giving feedback on the development of skills found to be necessary or important—all under the tutelage of a trained behavioral scientist. The emphasis is generally on interpersonal skills, conflict resolution, and the creating of mutual trust and openness.

Because the organization may be considered a form of ritualized cooperation among members in the pursuit of task goals, anything that hinders cooperation takes away from the organization's total effectiveness. OD fosters a cooperative interpersonal climate and the development of a community of purpose.

Behaviors are modified through the teaching of new skills and insights into how teams may best work together—for example, skills that may be assumed to be present but are rarely trained and developed are intellectual or cognitive skills. OD provides the ways by which members may function together with trust and openness and without disruptive competition and conflict. Open communication and a focus on overall goals (rather than narrow or immediate objectives) are two additional OD purposes.

We noted earlier that a fundamental concept in the systems approach is that of interrelatedness or interaction among systems. In this chapter so far we have isolated the major systems of organizational behavior for ease in understanding their differences and functions. If we are to understand the ways in which the systems interact and relate to each other, they must be combined into our overall systems model. Figure 3-8 presents the total model we will be analyzing in depth throughout the rest of this text. In

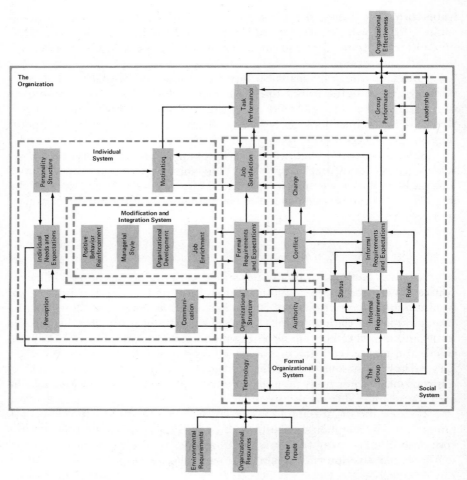

FIGURE 3.8   A systems model of organizational behavior.

carefully comparing the model's individual systems to their earlier sketches (Figures 3-4, 3-5, and 3-6), we note that the three systems are intricately interwoven. Our model, complex as it is, still oversimplifies human behavior, but by using this conceptual framework we can more nearly understand organizational behavior.

Organizational behavior is a complicated but fascinating field for study. It is also a vital area for the results-oriented student and manager because he must actively and effectively use the insights we will develop in this book to fulfill his job. We must understand people to the best of our abilities. Their behavior must be analyzed so that the individual and the organization may be effectively integrated to the mutual benefit of both.

Summary

The organization can be seen as composed of three major systems: the formal organization, the individual, and the social system. The manager of today must be intimately familiar with their characteristics and interactions with each other because they affect and determine organizational behavior.

The formal organizational system is composed of the organization structure and the technology upon which the organization bases the fundamental work that it does. *Technology* is broadly defined to include all of the aspects of knowledge that are applicable to the attainment of the firm's objectives. The organization structure is the relationship between specialized activities and duties into which that work is broken down for efficiency. The organizational structure is characterized by specialization of duties and jobs both horizontally, as in different jobs at the same level of the organization, and vertically, through the successive specialization of managerial activities. Organizational structure and technology affect the behavior and the prescribed roles of individuals within the organization every day because they determine to whom the individual reports, what his job is, and the nature of his activities.

Each person may be considered as possessing a uniquely internal and personal system. It consists of the individual's personality and his motivational systems, connected as he is through the communication and perception process to his external environment.

The social system is composed of the relationships between individuals and is typically illustrated in the concept of the informal organization that coexists with the formal organization. The informal organization (the social group) arises in response to individuals' needs for social activity, affiliation, and influence. The nature of the group is such that individual behavior is prescribed by the group and sanctioned through rewards and punishments different from those provided by the formal organization. In some instances, the informal organization and the formal organization and their requirements are diametrically opposed to each other. The individual may then seem to be in the middle. Certainly the behavior that results from this dilemma may be detrimental to the formal organization.

These three elements determine and affect organizational behavior, but the individual manager can still intervene in the process through which organizational behavior is derived. He can consider the consequences of his characteristic way of behaving, his managerial style, and evaluate the extent to which it is appropriate to the total situation being managed.

The manager also has available to him more formal programs that allow for the integration of individual and organizational needs. Job enrichment calls for individual jobs to be analyzed and enriched with additional opportunities for individual growth. Positive behavior reinforcement uses learning-theory bases in identifying and modifying job-related behaviors. Organizational development is a more far-reaching field that emphasizes the development and reorganization of the firm with particular reference to the needs of the individual.

STUDY AND REVIEW QUESTIONS

1. What is the difference between a *model* and a *system?*

2. Why is a systems approach appropriate to the study of human behavior in organizations?

3. Refer back to the Chapter 1 discussion of the Hawthorne experiments. Show how the formal organizational, individual, and social systems affected human behavior.

4. What are the ways in which the manager can intervene in or exert influence on the organizational behavior system? Why does he need the capability to influence it?

5. How does our use of the term *technology* compare and contrast to common usage?

6. Think of a situation with which you are familiar. Write a description of the situation. Identify the ways in which the three systems affected human behavior.

THE FORMAL ORGANIZATIONAL SYSTEM: TECHNOLOGY AND STRUCTURE

Chapter

Work and Technology

CHAPTER OBJECTIVES

1. To present the organization as an entity in dynamic interaction with its external environment.

2. To outline the vital impact that the enterprise's environment has on internal operations.

3. To discuss technology and patterns of technology as organizational attempts to respond effectively to external requirements.

4. To show how the various technological strategies provide the formal structure of task and expectations for organizational members.

5. To indicate the types of work situations and requisite skills under the classes of work technology.

6. To develop an overall appreciation of the technological structure that surrounds and molds organizational behavior.

**Environmental Impacts on
Technology**

Technological Determinants of Work
Work in Craft Technology

Work in Small Batch Technology
Work in Mass-Production Technology
Work in Continuous Process
  Technology
Work in Advanced Technology

Organizations exist to produce goods or deliver services. They evolve as the total work required exceeds the capacity of one person. The device of the organization, then, provides the structure for dividing this work into units (jobs) that can be assigned to individuals.

The nature of each job—its design and content—is directly related to the characteristics of the total flow of work. This workflow consists of all the operations involved in changing the firm's inputs into the specified output. The patterns of work and characteristics of jobs are important to understanding organizational behavior; work requirements provide continuing sets of expectations of the individual, as well as dictating necessary interpersonal contacts.

As organizations differ in their objectives and operations, what are some of the factors that result in varying work requirements? Major elements are those of the organization's environment, output requirements, technology, and skill. Too often we ignore technology in considering organizational behavior, perhaps under the assumption that technology and behavior are independent of each other. We can make no such simplifying assumption. In this chapter and the next two, we will examine recent important findings that have significant implications for technology as "an important determinant of organizational behavior . . ., affecting such factors as group formation, organization, structure, communication, and needed qualities of managerial leadership."[1]

Approval of or demand for the output of the organization greatly affects the nature of the internal operations of the firm. Without an output of some product valuable to another, no organization can exist for long in our economic system. Without people to buy washing machines, washing machine manufacturers could not long afford to stay in business. Without the explicit or implicit approval of the American taxpayer–voter, NASA could not have provided its high-technology product. And unless some measure of value is perceived by its clients, a university faces the real threat of being forced to close its doors.

Recognition of the direct relationship between the firm and its external environment is critical if we are to understand why organizations differ from

---

[1]Elmer H. Burack, "Technology and Some Aspects of Industrial Supervision: A Model Building Approach," *Academy of Management Journal* (March 1966), p. 43.

each other in important ways. Different demands are *imposed* on a firm by its environment; these demands are translated, through their technological and work implications, into constraints on and requirements of each organizational member and group.

To examine the causes and effects of organizational behavior, we first must appreciate the ways in which forces external to the firm influence the framework within which we work. Each enterprise adapts to the demands of its relevant environments, incorporating technologies and activities that allow effective responses. These technological and structural adaptations, in turn, directly influence the members of the organization by imposing their own demands on effective behavior. Because this process is complex, we will first examine the nature of the organization's external environment.

The Organizational Environment

There are, of course, a number of different viewpoints from which we could examine the environment of the organization. We could consider such things as the social, legal, economic, political, cultural, and competitive environments. Certainly each of these and other elements that go to make up the total environment of the firm are important. For our purposes, however, we will focus upon the ways in which the organization *responds* to its diverse environments, and especially to the demands and requirements of its most immediately important group—its customers and clients. A simplifying assumption we are making here is that social, cultural, legal competitive, economic, and political influences express themselves either *through the requirements* placed on the output by customers (product specifications) or *as restraining factors* that provide boundaries beyond which neither client nor producer may go (this is especially evident in legal, political, and cultural restraints).

Given the purpose of the enterprise, there are three major strategic responses that are important in gearing internal operations to external demands. These are (1) nature and rate of change, (2) standardization of operations, and (3) scale of operations. As we will see, these three are not independent of each other.

Nature and Rate of Change

The nature and rate with which changes are demanded influences the operations of the organization. The importance of the external environment may be seen if we consider that "any change in the kind or quantity of output" is "largely externally induced."[2]

[2]Shirley Terreberry, "The Evolution of Organizational Environments," *Administrative Science Quarterly* (March 1968), pp. 610, 611.

When the firm needs to change its output or operations very little over time, it can become very familiar with its customers, their desires, and the functions that go into producing its product. Procedures and policies can cover almost every situation that might be encountered by a worker or a manager. Decision making tends to become "programmed" because few completely new types of decisions occur. Old techniques can be easily adapted to cover new situations, which are usually merely new versions of old problems.[3]

We might contrast this environment with one that demands rapid technological change or great product improvements over fairly short periods of time. The rapid change in the state of the art in materials and energy technology, for example, means that aerospace organizations must develop their capabilities extremely rapidly in order to stay abreast of the knowledge of their competitors. With new customer needs and government regulation continually being encountered and new demands imposed by these, very few programmed decisions exist at any level of the organization. Rather, as in the research and development laboratory, creative approaches to new problem situations are demanded, for which previously developed rules and methods are probably inappropriate. In addition, the need to adopt to constant changes and new requirements mean that workers themselves must be able to shift from one project to another. Flexibility and adaptability are emphasized, with overspecialization being economically unjustifiable.

Within the context of this environmental change feature, we have presented the conditions of stable demands (no changes) and continual, dynamic change. We must recognize that these are but two ends of a continuum. Relatively few of the organizations with which we are familiar would be considered classic examples of these. More likely, the vast majority of organizations fall somewhere in the middle. We might typify these as being characterized by their need for regulated flexibility.[4] Those firms that operate with regulated flexibility encounter change in their environment, but change at a relatively constant or predictable rate. So planning for change is facilitated and can be incorporated within the operations of the firm. Furthermore the nature of the problems that are encountered remain much the same as previous problems, so existing patterns of coping with problems can be quickly adapted to the specifics of the new problem situation. Examples of organizations that face a *stable change environment* are paper

---

[3]Kast and Rosenzweig point out that "Through repetitive processes . . . a choice becomes more and more automatic, given similar stimuli. Organizations develop habits in the form of standard operating procedures and computer programs for coping with repetitive situations. Programmed decisions reduce the amount of rethinking necessary in repetitive situations" (Fremont E. Kast and James E. Rosenzweig, *Organization and Management: A Systems Approach,* 2nd ed. New York: McGraw-Hill 1974, p. 360).

[4]William H. Newman, Charles E. Summer, and E. Kirby Warren, *The Process of Management: Concepts, Behavior and Practice,* 3rd ed. (Englewood Cliffs, N.J.: Prentice-Hall, 1972), p. 697.

mills, retirement homes, social security offices, and telephone operations. Firms that operate with *regulated flexibility* with regard to their change in environments are job shops, hospitals, unemployment compensation offices, and newspaper offices. Organizations that must respond to *frequent and unprecedented changes* are aerospace plants, medical research laboratories, the training of the hard-core unemployed, and management consulting offices.[5]

Standardization of Operations

The degree to which one produces a limited product line, with few or no differences between individual items within each product line, the more one can take advantage of the advantages of the scientific management approaches discussed in Chapter 1. After all, there are few complications involved in producing a thousand or a million ballpoint pens, after one has discovered how to produce the first one. Consider the problems involved in manufacturing one ballpoint pen, then changing one's operations to make a turret lathe, then to performing surgery. In each case, a product is to be produced, but there are significant differences in what must be done to produce that product. There is opportunity to achieve learning or economies of producing large numbers of the same unit.

Similarly the less one needs to be concerned with even minor differences in each product produced, the more routine can be the task of the individual worker; few surprises would come his way, very little judgment or adaptability would be necessary, and work indeed could be done "by the book."

We can readily see this in research and development laboratories. In that setting, a research team (or a single researcher) is involved in developing an idea or a product on a one-time-only basis. There is little opportunity to modify or adapt the results of previous projects because of significant dissimilarities. In addition, few of the technical problems can be foreseen. Rigid policies and procedures cannot easily be established because of the uncertain direction of the researcher's future efforts. The scope of the work and its progress are entirely a function of the creative skills of those working on the project. New and unique problem situations have to be dealt with as they occur rather than by standard solutions.

Another factor important in standardization of operations must be mentioned. Standardization can be used advantageously, as we pointed out, when few changes in output are required by the external environment. Standardizing tasks and workflow can also be *internally* initiated to ensure that the output does not vary. Telephone company engineers, in designing the circuits for new or expanded service, follow extensive checklists and consult voluminous manuals. Innovations or shortcuts are not encouraged because of the potential effects a mistake could have on the entire communications system.

[5]Ibid.

Other advantages may be reaped from the routinizing of tasks. The simpler the task—the less demanding it is of initiative, intelligence, and judgment—the quicker a worker may be trained to perform effectively. Productivity is thereby increased over a task that requires long and intensive training. Also, the simpler the job, the lower the wage rate typically required to fill the position.[6]

Scale of Operations

The quantity of output demanded is also significant in influencing the operations of the organization. As has been pointed out, producing a large number of the same or similar items allows learning to take place and skill to be increased. With the repetition of a particular task, the planning and problem solving that went into the first try are decreased, resulting in greater overall production efficiency.

In addition, if one knows that he will be producing a large number of exactly the same items over the next few years, he might very well be able to justify the purchase of special-purpose machinery that can take over some of the repetitive and onerous aspects of the job. Without this long production run (great quantity demanded), such an investment might very well not be worth making.

Great quantities demanded also allow for the benefits of specialization and training for specific jobs. Workers can become more and more knowledgeable or skillful in a relatively specialized aspect of the total production of an item, when the time span and quantity demanded justify this investment by the organization.

Should the quantity demanded not allow such specialization and training, the firm would of necessity use workers with higher overall skill levels and great flexibility or adaptability. Each higher-skilled worker—who would be available at higher wage rates than a less skilled worker—would probably not perform a relatively limited number of operations as would the less skilled worker. If his higher adaptability and skill level are to be used to advantage, he would probably do a greater portion of the overall tasks. This would be consistent with the scope of operations, because of the lack of time to break down and specialize a task into component jobs.[7] And the scope of operations would probably not justify the investment in special-purpose machine and specialized training.

As the external environment affects internal operations through the separate or combined demands of standardization, scale, and rate of change, how does the organization adapt? Organizational effectiveness is enhanced

---

[6]Cf. John B. Miner and Mary Green Miner, *Personnel and Industrial Relations: A Managerial Approach*, 2nd ed. (New York: Macmillan, 1973), p. 388.

[7]Joseph E. Litterer, *The Analysis of Organizations*, 2nd ed. (New York: Wiley, 1973), pp. 357–362.

through the application of operations technologies, the characteristics of which fit the nature of environmental demands and constraints.

The Technology Base for Operations

In the broadest sense, we can think of technology as being the broad patterns underlying the methods, procedures, and techniques by which inputs are transformed into outputs. Litterer points out that

Technology is a body of knowledge, but a particular type of knowledge. Furthermore, although it frequently is, it need not be knowledge developed through the scientific method.

Second, at the most basic level, technology is not only knowledge the way the term is typically used and the way we shall use it . . . but it also includes things: tool, machines, devices, and gadgets.

Third, technology is related to solving problems and producing desired outcomes, goods, or services through activities performed by men or machines or a combination of both.

Fourth, more is needed than to have activities performed, they must be performed in a specific order or pattern. To do this there must often be some layout of machines and men who will perform the activities.

It consists of equipment, machines, or tools, sets of activities, methods, or processes, and layouts, arrangements, or patterns. At a more abstract level it is the knowledge of all these things, what activities to perform and how to perform them, how to use machines and how to make or acquire the machines, how to order the machines and activities.[8]

So technology can be thought of as the total of knowledge, skills, and equipment applied within the transformation process of the operations of the organization. Obviously different types of firms require different types of technologies. We may even observe the use of different technologies in producing the same output, such as the housewife making bread who employs techniques and procedures different from those of a large-scale commercial bakery.

Are there ways in which we might classify, for analytical purposes, the major differences and common characteristics of these technologies? Fortunately, we can abstract common elements from the bewildering variety of specific technologies employed in all organizations and group them into a relatively small number of classifications.

One such classification scheme is to present the range of technologies as they are distributed along a coninuum of complexity. Technologies might be grouped, in order of increasing complexity, as craft; small batch; massproduction–assembly-line; continous process; and advanced technology.[9] At

[8]Ibid., p. 283.
[9]Cf. Kast and Rosenzweig, p. 187.

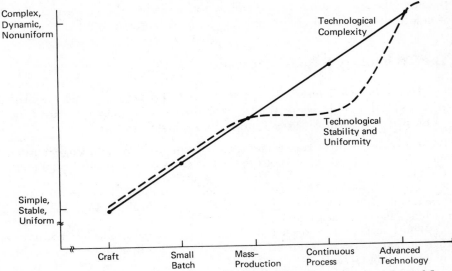

FIGURE 4.1   Technological types and their relationships. Source: Adapted from Fremont E. Kast and James E. Rosenzweig, *Organization and Management: A Systems Approach*, 2nd ed. (New York: McGraw-Hill, 1974), p. 187.

the same time, these types of technology can be rated according to the frequency of change—stability—that accompanies each. Figure 4-1 illustrates the relationships among technologies in their relative complexities and stabilities. Technological complexity increases rather steadily as we move from craft to advanced technology. Stability displays a bit more complicated pattern, as its curve rises steadily to indicate movement from the most stable technology, that of craft. Small batch and mass production allow (or require) more and more variations in the "events, tasks, or decisions which the organization faces."[10]

The stability of mass production and continuous process technologies are approximately equal, for reasons we shall see, reflecting the volume and interrelatedness of the production processes. Uniformity and stability then quickly decrease in the advanced technology of an aerospace firm, for example.

Craft Technology

Craft technology requires relatively high levels of individual skills in the production of custom-made products. The work on each product is typically the responsibility of a single craftsman, who draws on relatively long periods of learning or apprenticeship and who uses judgment and the lessons learned from experience in the pursuit of his craft. We might say that this

---

[10]Kast and Rosenzweig, p. 186.

technology is skill-intensive. Each craftsman has the opportunity of seeing the final product grow or develop under the application of his skilled work. These skills tend to be manually related skills, such as those learned in one's apprenticeship to become a carpenter or a diamond cutter.

Small Batch Technology

Another, more complex technology is that involved in small batch operations. We can see this exemplified in many job shops or small machine shops:

Production is in batches, often for individual orders for specific customers or for finished goods inventory with an extensive product line. The job shop is characterized by a variable routine of the flow. Jobs flow through the system via different routes depending on the tasks required. The facilities and machines are almost always general purpose, meaning that they can be adjusted for a variety of outputs. Examples of job shops are specialty metal fabricating plants, automobile service centers, and hospitals.[11]

We might notice that this requires that the operations of the organization be oriented to producing relatively small numbers of items, typically in direct response to the outside environment. This would require flexibility in the applications of technologies to the specific characteristics of the client's or the customer's demands, and these would differ in some respects from one batch to another.

Mass-Production Technology

Even more complex is the technology involved in mass production or the assembly line. It is more complex because significantly more detailed planning must be done in order that the specified output be produced. Intricate patterns of relationships and coordination are essential for the establishment of the mass-production or assembly-line system. This technology requires that workers specialize in only one or a few specified and narrowly limited tasks. The tasks tend to be very repetitive, being of short cycle, and rather mechanical. In some cases, every single movement that the worker makes is carefully and fully detailed.

Under these technological systems, with individual workers specializing in a minute aspect of the overall operations, work is serially dependent upon completion of the previous work stage. A worker on an automobile assembly line cannot meaningfully complete his task of attaching a door handle to an automobile unless the door has been attached to the chassis.

With all this detail of planning and establishment of routine and procedure, obviously a mass-production operation or an assembly line is not very

---

[11]Richard I. Levin et al., *Production/Operations Management: Contemporary Policy for Managing Operation Systems* (New York: McGraw-Hill, 1972), pp. 75–76.

flexible. A minor design change in the product being assembled has major implications and repercussions for the work and procedures of many individual workers. These technologies might be said to be production-intensive, because they require the scientific management skills and techniques of efficiency and specialization.

Continuous Process Technology

A further technological grouping on this continuum is that of continuous process production. Within this category are such organizations as petroleum refineries and chemical process plants. Because they rely heavily upon technological requirements for continuous production of their products, little is left for the operative worker but to monitor the operations of the organization. Such highly complex, sensitive, and sophisticated production technologies require a closed operations system, independent of the individual. Thus we may see a number of white-smocked workers in a chemical plant taking samples or reading gauges or dials. These activities merely measure the manner in which the self-sustaining operational technology of refining is being conducted. The mixing of the various elements; the establishment of proper pressure, volume, and temperature variables; and any other necessary processes are conducted automatically within the design of the operations system.

Advanced Technology

The most complex technology along this scale is advanced technology. Here we might see such organizations as aerospace firms and research and development laboratories. These might be said to be knowledge-intensive, because manual skills and production orientation are not the inputs critical to the creation of the desired organizational outputs. For example, the individual creativity of large numbers of highly qualified scientists and engineers are necessary to advances in the state of the art in aerospace technology. Each problem or program that they work on is unique unto itself, with few or no rules or solutions that can be directly transferred from another problem or program.

Also complicating this technology is a high degree of uncertainty; engineers may be designing spacecraft while uncomfortably aware that they do not fully understand all of the variables that pertain to a successful mission. In a way, advanced technology almost comes full circle to the craft technology that we discussed earlier—with the major difference being that advanced technology requires the inputs of large numbers of specialists (each specializing in different technical areas and each employing conceptual and analytical skills). The craftsman, we remember, used primarily manual skills and typically worked by himself.

Environmental Impacts on Technology

We recognized previously that the outside environment of each organization has a major impact on what the firm does and the way that it goes about achieving its major objective. And this interaction between technology and environment has an immediate and longlasting effect upon the work and expectations of each organizational member. In considering the critical environmental factors, we pointed out that the degree of standardization of operations, scale of operations, and degree and nature of change were three important factors.

The five basic technologies that we classified can be considered as strategies adopted by the concern to respond effectively to environmental demands. For optimum performance the firm's basic technological characteristics should roughly match the demands of the major factors of the environment. Certainly environmental and technological demands should not conflict in major ways. (See Table 4-1.)

On several occasions we have used the example of the automobile assembly line. If we postulated a new automobile manufacturer entering the industry, we might first look at the demands of his external environment. Should his customers demand an automobile individually customized to taste, conflict with the basic requirements of standardization would immediately be obvious. Further, if the design of these customized autos could not be reused, then the quantity demanded of each product would be only one. And change would be very dynamic—one order might call for a small racing-quality sportscar and the next call for a vanlike vehicle incorporating features of a mobile office and an apartment. Perhaps next year a customer will demand a vehicle that floats on an air cushion, whereas another seeks one with balloon tires and a turbine engine.

We might expect that the organization facing such an environment

TABLE 4-1   Technology as Strategic Response to External Requirements

	Environmental Requirements					
	Change		Standardization		Scale	
Technology	Great or Constant	Stable or None	Identical Products	Unique Product	Large	Small
Craft	x			Similar products		x
Small Batch	x	x	x			x
Mass Production		x	x		x	
Continuous Process		x	x		x	
Advanced	x			x		x

would have two feasible alternatives: to employ a craft technology, perhaps with skilled mechanics (craftsmen) operating as a team on each individual order; or to employ an advanced technology system, in which the design stage is performed by highly qualified scientists and engineers, with the operations phase being performed by craftsmen. In either of these two technologies, we might see the taking advantage of another technology in order to achieve some economical returns. For instance, for specified classes of orders, the chassis might be relatively standardized. Or standard engine sizes in internal combustion engines might be employed. Certainly we might expect standard sizes and designs of tires to be employed on the less far-out automobiles. After this amount of standardization has been used as far as possible, then an assembly-line approach might be used, with workers adapting the standardized parts for compatibility with the unique design characteristics. This is essentially the technological approach used in the mass-producing of automobiles, as the choice of options and colors differs from customer to customer.[12]

Another example points out, perhaps more clearly, the ways in which environment and technology interact. Consider the artist who depends on selling his paintings for his living. The typical technology he might use is that of craft technology. He employs his highly developed skills in order to produce a single canvas of high quality, which he then attempts to sell at the highest possible price. The price that the artist charges would reflect, to a degree, the amount of time and the amount of skill required in the producing of the painting. It might also, of course, reflect his own artistic judgment of the quality of the painting, not to mention his estimate of the potential buyer's ability to pay. In any event, the craft technology means a great deal of personal involvement by the artist and a relatively high price for the unique product. Environmental change in tastes, the uniqueness of the product, and the demand for a quantity of one would dictate the craft technology.

You may have heard of the artists along the Seine River in Paris who also earn a living by selling the fruits of their labors. Some, it is said, are able to enjoy and reap the benefits of economies of scale in their efforts. Recognizing the benefits to be obtained by foregoing the deeply artistic processes involved in creating each painting anew, and attempting to increase productivity as well as revenue, some of these artists paint or sketch several duplicates of the same work of art. Each can then be sold to a customer at a price lower than would be demanded for an original, since the number of paintings produced per unit of time would be greatly increased. This is the use of a small batch approach, of course. This is a time-honored approach, for some of the old masters used much the same approach in maximizing their own productivity. The master would sketch and lay out the design of a

---

[12]Richard J. Hopeman, *Production: Concepts, Analysis, Control*, 2nd ed. (Columbus, Ohio: Charles E. Merrill, 1971), p. 282.

painting, then delegate the relatively routine tasks of actually painting to an apprentice, who was only too happy to serve and learn from the master.

Fairly recently several galleries have been established that employ mass-production techniques, selling oils or prints to large numbers of customers. The products are standardized and duplicated for much the same reasons as the Parisian artists have. Selling popularly priced paintings requires a rather large turnover of inventory, because of the low price category of the paintings. This also means that large segments of the popular art market must be tapped. Each painting to be mass-produced must meet the test of acceptance by relatively large numbers of people. So the paintings must be designed and painted for broad appeal, rather than for the unique tastes of one particular patron.

Technological Determinants of Work

We pointed out earlier that environmental characteristics dictate the broad nature of the appropriate technology. In a similar fashion the technology employed directly affects the nature of the work done by each organizational member and particularly those directly involved in the operations system.

Work in Craft Technology

Under the craft form of technology, the individual craftsman is, in one way, a rather flexible and adaptable input into the operations process. He is an expert in a particular skill area and can apply that skill in a number of slightly different situations equally well. For instance, a first-class woodworker could easily shift from making a table to making a cabinet. Because of the high level of skill and years of experience required to meet the standards of the job, and because of the applications of judgment necessary in the craft, craftsmen command relatively high wages. This is also true because of their qualifications, because there is a restricted supply of craftsmen, and also because of their flexibility.

Additionally the nature of the craftsmen's work is such that he typically works by himself and has control over the choice of tools with which he works. Some craftsmen, as a matter of fact, insist upon providing their own tools. This again reflects the skill of the craftsmen and the importance of recognizing his experience and his expertise in the conduct of his work. This also translates into the tendency for craftsmen to perform more effectively when they are granted greater autonomy.[13]

[13]Y. K. Shetty and Harold M. Carlisle, "A Contingency Model of Organization Design," *California Management Review* (Fall 1972), p. 42.

Since the craftsman employs his skills and experience in a nonstandardized fashion, dependent upon his peculiar habits and personality makeup, procedures typically cannot be routinized. The craftsman, within wide latitudes, must be allowed to pursue his craft as he sees fit. The quality of his work is usually a matter of great pride to him and directly reflects upon his qualifications. Thus his work provides great ego satisfaction and esteem among his fellow craftsmen. A common topic of discussion among craftsmen is the encroaching on their craft by managements that insist on efficiency at the expense of quality. Quality, in this case, is dictated by the high standards of the craftsman.

Craft technology is well suited to the environment in which products are customized to tastes of individual customers and in which standardization of items is not particularly important. Because craftsmen are relatively high-priced, the quantity demanded cannot be very great, so a premium price is charged for the handiwork of the craftsman, who works for a relatively select audience. Despite the constraints and high cost factors built into this technology, one major benefit is its capability of quick responsiveness to changes in environmental demands. As quickly as a craftsman is informed of a new design, he can begin producing it.

Work in Small Batch Technology

Small batch technology is similar to that of the craftsman, with a major exception: the skill of the craftsman is transferred to and routinized in a machine and/or in mechanical processes. Workers then tend to become machine tenders. The machines retain a certain amount of flexibility in that they may be multipurpose machines. Within the job shop, orders for relatively small batches of standardized (customized to each customer's order) output must be filled, and they are routed through the job shop, with multipurpose machines performing the first operation required by the order. After that operation is concluded, the items are sent on to another machine for further work, and so on through the course of the production process.

The work of the job-shop operative is then relegated almost to a secondary position—secondary to the primary work that is done by the machine. The skill of the worker has been decreased to feeding the machine, inspecting its work, and setting its adjustments. The turret-lathe operator and the punch-press operator perform very similar operations on their own jobs, no matter what the individual specifications of the product on which they work. So the skill required of the operative under small batch technology is (compared to that of the craftsman) rather low. This implies that wage rates are lower and also that economies of scale can begin to be realized with the repetition of the process on batches of the same standardized product. One caution is in the relatively large initial investment in the multipurpose machinery.

This technology offers advantages in that some standardization does exist. Quantity can be greater than that met by the craftsman technology, but if demand for the product or service provided does not exist, then the initial investment in the machinery cannot readily be paid off, and the organization suffers. Also, the multipurpose machinery and relatively unskilled labor mean that, within limits, external changes from the environment can be relatively rapidly implemented. Each new product order brings with it changes as a matter of course, so individual operators are conditioned to expect change and to modify current operating techniques to the demands of each order.

Work in Mass-Production Technology

Mass production or the assembly-line technology further dilutes the impact of individual skill or craftsmanship of the individual. Mass production requires an extremely standardized product, to be produced in great numbers. When this is done, and when the external environment is very stable and nondynamic, every single process, every single motion of each worker can be studied and preplanned before the first unit is produced. Each worker is required to specialize in a minute part or aspect of the overall operation associated with producing or providing the firm's good or service. As we pointed out before, the work of each worker is sequentially dependent upon what went before, all the way through to the end of the process. The level of skill is extremely low, with almost anyone being able to fill a place on the assembly line. This means, again, that labor savings can be significant.

We recognize that, for this technology to be consistent with an environment, the environment must call for relatively large quantities of very standardized products. Further, changes in the design or quality of the products cannot vary much over time. Mass production requires an extremely stable environment. This would be reflected in the work of the individual, for he would perform a set and unchanging routine, a narrowly limited and specialized function in which any opportunity for error has been carefully eliminated from each position, along with almost all opportunities for individual judgment and skill. Because of the specialization of task, the individual worker rarely has an opportunity to see his contribution to the overall product or service provided.

Work in Continuous Process Technology

Within continuous process technology organizations, the individual is relegated to a status even more clearly secondary than in small batch technology. The continuous flow process technology comprises a closed-system, continuous flow process in which the major variables and inputs are automatically determined and manipulated through the process itself. The individual worker operates outside this system, typically in a service capacity (driving trucks or providing input services), monitoring the transformation process or providing service for the process's output. This type of work requires more skill than that involved in mass-production or assembly-line technologies, since a certain level of knowledge and skill is requisite for the individual to interpret the operations of the process intelligently. The overall skill level required to support this technology, therefore, remains relatively high, with conceptual and analytical skills predominating, as exemplified by higher education in the sciences. Even the operatives providing input and output services must have basic skills far beyond those required for mass production or the assembly line and typically far beyond those necessary for small batch technology.

Once again the individual worker remains relatively autonomous in the conduct of his job and (more than likely) functions independently of co-workers. Whatever group or team efforts are required consist of problem-solving sessions or input to management decisions.

Work in Advanced Technology

Finally, the advanced technology mode again reinforces the increasing skill level developed within the continuous process technology. Again, the manual skills diminish to almost zero, and the conceptual and analytical skills assume predominance. Under this technology, the intellectual skills of the organizational members are prime determinants of organizational effectiveness. Within a dynamic and nonstable environment and at the leading edge of new knowledge, the product of the advanced technological firm (such as the aerospace firm) is predicated largely on the quality and the creativity of the input from its highly skilled and highly trained members. The environment and the tools of these members are both ambiguous and uncertain, calling for a premium to be placed on individual responsibility, knowledge, experience, and judgment.

Standardization of product is almost nonexistent because almost as soon as one engineering design is approved and implemented, program characteristics and requirements change significantly, so that repetition of the same process is usually not possible. In addition, different programs with different characteristics require that almost completely new problems be met and solved, with little or no transfer of learning from the last program involved.

Organizational members, then, do extremely nonprogrammed and nonrepetitive types of work, operating with inputs that are neither concrete nor stable. Team efforts are extremely important, because of their synergistic effects upon overall effectiveness. That is the concept that two plus two equals five, because of the extenuating and creative effects that a team of highly involved and highly qualified individuals have on the intellectual and innovative outputs of others.

All this also assumes that the quantity demanded does not allow for repetition of the design. We can certainly see this in the space program: very few space capsules have the same purposes or are very similar to previous designs.

Summary

In this chapter, we have examined the complex interrelationships among work, technology, and the organization's external environment. We have seen that they affect each other in important ways.

The characteristics of the environment external to the organization provide the major determinants of the organization's choice of technology. The major characteristics of the external environment are degree of standardization of operations; scale of operations; and rate and nature of change in the external environment.

The basic technologies available to the organization are craft, small batch, mass-production–assembly-line, continuous process, and advanced technology. Craft technology is typified by fairly low standardization, relatively small quantity, and capability of coping effectively with rather substantial changes in the demand characteristics of the external environment. Each worker under craft technology is relatively highly skilled and relatively well paid. A major feature of the work of the craftsman is his close identification with the final product, upon which he exerts his considerable skill and experience.

Small batch technology offers great flexibility in meeting changing external demands, within relatively wide limits. The skills of the craftsman are diluted and transferred to machines, which are operated by machine tenders. Greater flexibility is given the organization to meet external demands because multipurpose machines can provide adaptability to the individual orders and relatively customized modifications of existing product lines. Workers' skills are relatively low because the skills exist primarily within the design of the machines. Relatively little standardization of product need be provided under this technology, because of the flexibility of the operations processes. Quantity demanded overall must be relatively greater than that involved in the craft technology, although individual orders need not be particularly great. A relatively steady stream of orders must be received, so that the entire flexible system of production can be continuously used. Relatively great changes in the external environment and its demands can be rather quickly met because of this technology's flexibility.

Mass production is much more inflexible than the technologies of craft or small batch. Operating in a stable environment with a standardized product and with extremely large quantities demanded, the overall work involved in production can be divided up into extremely small units to which workers are assigned. Judgment and individual skill are largely designed out of these jobs because of the absolute necessity of completely interchangeable parts and components, as they progress toward integration within a final product. All work is sequential and each job depends on the work done at the previous stage. Skill levels of workers are extremely low because the production line or assembly line provides the rationale and technique of operations. Individual workers, operating under scientific management principles, merely provide relatively undifferentiated inputs.

The continuous process technology begins to emphasize different types of skills on the part of the workers. Continuous process technologies are closed systems, with individuals rarely able to intervene in the process. Rather, the individual worker provides a service to the self-contained and self-sustaining process. Conceptual and analytical skills are necessary, as the workers monitor the processes.

Finally, advanced technologies, such as those involved in aerospace firms, continue the upward trend in conceptual and intellectual skills required. These skills are the major input into the operations of the advanced technology firm. These firms operate in a dynamic, nonstable environment, with little standardization or learning from previous programs. The operative engineers and designers in advanced technological firms typically operate as multidisciplinary teams rather than as discrete individuals.

STUDY AND REVIEW QUESTIONS

1. The concept of an "open" and a "closed" system was introduced in Chapter 3. Discuss each of the five technological classes from the perspective of determining which are open and which are closed systems.

2. Rate and nature of change, standardization of operations, and scale of operations: these were the three elements examined in the discussion of how the external environment influences the appropriate technological response of the firm's operations. What are some other elements that might be important?

3. Compare the skills required of the worker in craft and in advanced technologies. How do they differ?

4. Would the role of the effective manager differ according to his organization's basic technology? His functions? Why or why not?

5. "We live in an age of constant change." How does this statement related to each of the technologies discussed in the chapter? Does this mean that some of the technologies are becoming obsolete?

Chapter

5

Authority and the Human Effects of Formal Organization

We have seen previously that the organization is the vehicle by which large-scale efforts are blended together in the pursuit of a major objective. We pointed out that the formal organization is really nothing but a set of relationships among the activities that are part of the total work necessary to attain the end purpose. With the definition of these activities and the grouping of them into specific jobs and with the gathering of similar jobs into departments comes the obvious requirement of coordination. Only by making sure that each subsystem and its output function according to the larger plan of the total organization and that individual subsystems and departments (or even specific jobs) do not work at cross purposes can one implement this overall plan.

Integrating Organizational Activities Through Coordination

The manufacturing function and the marketing function must, for example, be coordinated because of their completely different perspectives on how their own work—and that of the other functions—should be performed. The manufacturing function, emphasizing production as it must, would much prefer to produce identical products, with mass-production techniques, completely standardized parts, and long production runs. Marketing, on the other hand, would much prefer to sell and distribute products that are customized to the specific needs of each customer, which would require a craft technology of production, with extremely short production runs and high unit costs of production and sales, yet with relatively higher revenues.

A superior common to both is necessary to reconcile these different perspectives and to allow the two functions to arrive at a compromise, one that is in the best interests of the overall organization. This coordination can then be easily accomplished through the hierarchy. After initial conflicts are discovered and confronted, this coordination can be achieved through administrative procedures such as policies, job descriptions, production technology, and paperwork.[1]

The end result of using such hierarchical and procedural techniques for coordinating the individual and group activity is greater rationality and predictability.[2] Only by having a logical set of relationships and activities can the overall organization accomplish its purpose efficiently, that is, provide maximum service or value while incurring minimum social or economic costs to its members and itself.

[1]Joseph A. Litterer, *The Analysis of Organizations,* 2nd ed. (New York: Wiley, 1973), pp. 465–470.

[2]"Every organization faces the task of somehow reducing the variability, instability, and spontaneity of individual human acts. . . . The need for reliability of role performance increases with the complexity and sophistication of the organization." (Daniel Katz and Robert L. Kahn, *The Social Psychology of Organizations,* New York: Wiley, 1966, pp. 199, 200.)

Coordination as Requirement for Predictability

Predictability is important because the organization is an ongoing entity that serves particular plans and customers. These have expectations about the product or service to be provided, and the organization must meet these expectations to the best of its ability. This implies that constraints must be set upon the whims and vagaries of the individual. The apple-carton packer who elects to fill every other carton with golden delicious apples instead of winesap apples might be expressing his individuality, but grocery store clients might not see it that way. Predictability of individual activity and subsystem outputs is necessary because of the vast network of relationships and the complex varieties of activities necessary for the organization to function effectively. Without some guidance and coordination of individuals toward some set of expectations of individual contribution to the organization, the firm would indeed be in chaos, with corresponding dropoffs in ability to meet the expectations of client, customer, and society.

In the pursuit of rationality and predictability, coordination is extremely important. When coordination finds its expression in the hierarchy, the coordinator is held responsible for the actions and performance of the units he is coordinating—whether they be turret-lathe operators or federal agencies. Each individual within the organization, as a direct result of division of labor and specialization of duties, then incurs responsibility for the performance of the activity assigned to him—this being an obligation agreed to with the acceptance of an assignment or of employment.

Responsibility and Authority

If one is responsible for job performance or the performance of coordinated units, then an organizationally granted right to influence the factors effecting performance is a necessity. The manager and the subordinate should have control over the aspects of the job that affect performance. Unless this happens, of course, it becomes impossible to measure how well the individual himself performs in that position. The manufacturing manager who runs out of raw materials because of the purchasing department's failure to reorder depleted stocks and has to shut down his assembly line cannot be evaluated completely by the costs his unit incurs—his performance and that of his unit are affected by conditions completely outside his control.

For rationality and predictability, then, each individual within the organization must be able to exert influence over the aspects of his job that affect his performance and his ability to discharge the responsibility. To structure predictable patterns of influence, the process is formalized as authority. This is the organizationally granted *right* to influence the actions and behavior of others. When authority is granted, the responsible person need not resort to arguments, pleading, bribes, or favors to elicit behavior that allows him to discharge his responsibility effectively. He has the right to expect appropriate behavior.

In Weber's conception of bureaucracy, authority is influence institutionalized. It is not a function of personality, charisma, or tradition. Rather, authority resides in the *position* the individual holds and is rationally and directly tied to formal goals.[3]

This authority may typically be backed up with a reward system or appropriate sanctions. The superior may be able to reward superior performance by the people over whom he has authority with salary increases, increases in responsibility, or increased status. On the other hand, he may punish undesirable or unsatisfactory performance with admonitions, demotion, or firing. The sanctions available to the responsible individual are all clearly laid out within his scope of authority.

Classical writers referred to the need for "parity" between authority and responsibility. This simply meant that one should not have more authority than responsibility nor more responsibility than the authority granted him gives control over—responsibility and authority should be equal.

Views of Authority

The Downward Flow of Formal Authority

That the superior has more authority than the subordinate has rarely been questioned. Certainly the chairman of the board of directors is the ultimate source of authority within the organization—he possesses the right to influence every other single member or group of members in the entire organization. This is only fair, since the chairman is ultimately responsible for the performance of the entire organization. The classical theory of authority derives from this logic. The chairman, through the successive specialization of tasks and responsibilities, delegates or transmits pieces of his authority downward in the organization along with the obligation to perform specific duties. The president might be granted authority over the day-to-day operations of the firm. He, in turn, grants further authority (hopefully the sum of which totals the authority granted to him) to his vice-presidents, granting them influence rights over such specialized areas as finance, manufacturing, and marketing. Each of them, in turn, grants pieces of the authority given to them to their subordinates, who are responsible for more detailed segments of the vice-president's responsiblities.

Through this process, coordination through the hierarchy is empha-

---

[3]Max Weber, *The Theory of Social and Economic Organization,* trans. by A. M. Henderson and T. Parsons (New York: Free Press, 1947), p. 45. See also Peter M. Blau and W. Richard Scott, *Formal Organizations: A Comparative Approach* (San Francisco: Chandler, 1962), pp. 27–33.

sized, through the vehicle of the downward flow of authority and the eliciting of responsibility for the wise use of the authority granted. This is the usual perspective taken on authority. This concept of the authority process also has several negative implications and connotations.

This conceptualization of authority clearly implies a directive, authoritarian relationship between the superior and the subordinate. The superior issues orders or commands, and the subordinates carry them out.

Such a process can readily be tied to a system of influence by fear.[4] As we noted in Chapter 1, the downward flow of authority based on fear takes very little account of a subordinate's willingness to perform, his understanding of the order, or his capability of performing under minimal supervision. Rather, it seems to assume that the subordinate is but the hands and legs of the commander and that the superior has all the facts relevant to the situation. The subordinate is then not felt to be able to participate effectively, to render appropriate inputs to the superior, or to be trusted to make judgments regarding his own performance or activities.

Authority as Effective Influence

That the formal theory of authority, the so-called trickle-down theory, does not explain every influence situation is apparent. Some years ago Chester Barnard suggested that the authority process be considered from the perspective of the subordinate. He pointed out that an order (the exercise of authority) that the subordinate receives may or may not be carried out.[5] Should the order be disobeyed, then authority has not been *effectively* exercised. Even though the vast majority of orders are carried out, the subordinate is capable of refusing to obey the order. If the order is obeyed, then the authority of the order over the subordinate is established or confirmed, since it is the basis of action. Disobedience would be a denial of the authority of the superior over the subordinate in a particular matter.[6]

What are the conditions under which a subordinate will accept the authority of an order? Barnard stated that an order will be seen as authoritative:

Only when four conditions simultaneously obtain:

- (a) he can and does understand the communication (order)
- (b) *at the time of his decision* he believes that it is not inconsistent with the purpose of the organization
- (c) *at the time of his decision,* he believes it to be compatible with his personal interest as a whole; and
- (d) he is able mentally and physically to comply with it.[7]

---

[4]David R. Hampton, Charles E. Summer, and Ross A. Webber, *Organizational Behavior and the Practice of Management,* rev. ed. (Glenview, Ill.: Scott, Foresman, 1973), p. 144.

[5]Chester I. Barnard, *The Functions of the Executive,* Thirtieth Anniversary Edition (Cambridge, Mass.: Harvard University Press, 1968), P. 162.

[6]Ibid., p. 163.

[7]Ibid., p. 165.

This implies that every attempt at influence based in authority requires a yes-or-no decision to be made by a subordinate. Without some simplifying mechanism, this would certainly seem to be a monumental task for any subordinate. Barnard proposed that there exists a *zone of indifference* for each individual. Within this zone, orders are acceptable without his consciously questioning the authority behind them. There will be many that are clearly acceptable to the subordinate—that is, clearly within the authority of the superior to expect compliance—and there will be some (probably quite a small number) that are clearly unacceptable and that will not be obeyed. Finally, there will be another group that is neither clearly acceptable nor clearly unacceptable.[8]

One study[9] sought to examine the characteristics of items that fall inside and outside the zone of indifference. Falling within the zone of indifference, that is, perceived as legitimate areas of influence over subordinates, included:

Amount of time spent on personal business on the telephone.
Neatness of the office.
Work hours.
Kind of temperament displayed at work.[10]

Items that were seen as falling *outside* the zone of indifference included:

The church he attends.
Charge accounts he has for shopping purposes.
Choice of vacation location.
School his children attend.
Political party affiliations.[11]

·The superior's right to unquestioned obedience regarding the first set of items is largely unquestioned. Attempting to influence the latter items, however, is likely to meet with resistance or outright disobedience.

The acceptance theory of authority is not one based on fear. Rather, it is a theory that assumes a rational basis of obedience based on the legitimacy of the intended behavior. The acceptance theory focuses on the subordinate and his willingness to obey the orders of his superior—a situation far removed from that of the formal theory of authority, in which orders are given unilaterally and are blindly obeyed because of the superior's control of sanctions.

Sources of Influence

A third way of viewing influence comes from classifying its source or basis. After all, one obeys another for different reasons, and the source of

---

[8]Ibid., pp. 167–169.
[9]Keith Davis, "Attitudes Toward the Legitimacy of Management Efforts to Influence Employees," *Academy of Management Journal* (June 1968).
[10]Ibid., p. 157.
[11]Ibid.

the ability to elicit obedience becomes important. French and Raven identified five types of influence,[12] which enable us to develop an integrated framework consistent with the characteristics of formal authority and the acceptance view.

Reward

Obedience may occur because of the perception that the other has the ability to reward compliance with desirable outcomes. Such rewards may be financial (a pay raise), psychological (praise), or instrumental (a promotion that enables the subordinate to achieve other desired outcomes, such as status). The reward is exchanged for compliance.

Coercion

Just as reward entails a desired outcome, coercion entails fear that punishment will be administered if the influence attempt is not obeyed. Punishment for noncompliance can range from physical abuse to psychological discomfort. Punishments have in common their undesirability as outcomes rather than their forms. Being dismissed or demoted from a job is one punishment. The laying-on of the cat-o'-nine-tails or a forced diet of bread and water is another, more physical form of punishment. Fear of being punished unless one obeys can result in compliance to the extent that the person seeking obedience actually has the ability to punish.

Legitimate Influence

Influence attempts are usually obeyed if they are seen as legitimate, a complex property the roots of which lie in one's internalized values. A command is legitimate, and obedience occurs, when the recipient of the command believes that he "ought to" comply. No reward or punishment is necessarily implicit in the influence relationship; he simply believes that the other "has a legitimate right to influence" him and that he, in turn, "has an obligation to accept this influence.[13]

Legitimacy stems from several possible bases: cultural values, acceptance of the social structure, and designation by a legitimizing agent. The culture may grant the possessor of certain characteristics the right to prescribe another's behavior. At the turn of the century men—because they were men—were seen as legitimately able to prescribe their wives' behavior. The aged, in some cases, are seen as legitimate in offering advice to, or making decisions for, family members.

---

[12]John R. P. French, Jr., and Bertram Raven, "The Bases of Social Power," in *Group Dynamics: Research and Theory*, 3rd ed., ed. by Dorwin Cartwright and Alvin Zander (New York: Harper & Row, 1968), pp. 259–269. French and Raven used the term *power*, yet defined ⁚ in terms of influence. Their concept parallels closely the applications of administrative authority as influence, which is being considered at this point.

[13]Ibid., p. 265.

Accepting the social structure of the group, the organization, or the society implies the acceptance of the legitimacy of one who occupies a superior office in the hierarchy and hence the creation of an obligation to obey him. This basis of legitimacy comes quite close to the acceptance theory of authority previously discussed, and it suggests the basis for acceptance of the judge's right to levy fines, the priest's right to prescribe religious beliefs, or the manager's right to issue a work-related order to a subordinate.[14]

The third basis of legitimacy is the designation by a legitimizing agent. One (whose influence is accepted) may grant the right to prescribe behavior to yet another, *delegating* his original authority. "A department head may accept the authority of his vice-president in a certain area because that authority has been specifically delegated by the president. An election is perhaps the most common example of a group's serving to legitimize the authority of one individual or office for other individuals in the group."[15] The legitimizing process described has strong overtones of the formal theory of authority.

Referent Influence

The ability of one to influence another's behavior can also arise from the degree of personal attraction to, or identification with, the former. Such identification with—the desire to be like or be associated with—another can result in behaving, believing, and perceiving as does the referent person or group. Influence can then be exerted because of the imitation and desire for association. One example of referent influence is that of the "reference group," a group with whom one identifies and who is imitated in the desire to become one of that group.

Expertise

The final influence source lies in the expertise or superior knowledge of the expert. The advice of an attorney in a legal matter will probably be accepted and implemented quite readily by the layman. His expertise is acknowledged—as is the client's *lack* of knowledge—and usually accepted, which is just one form of influence over another. The expert is seen as having unique or special competence, and his "authority of expertise" and his prescription are accepted. Medical doctors (and professors) may possess expert influence, resulting in the acceptance of their pronouncements. Staff or technical experts also display this form of influence. Line managers or the uninitiated may quietly defer to their expert opinion in a matter simply because of ignorance in a complex area, such as data-processing systems.

These influence bases probably seem clear-cut in their pure forms. They

[14]Ibid.
[15]Ibid.

can be rather easily confused in real situations, however. Several different types may operate simultaneously, making analysis of the situation difficult:

We must try to distinguish between referent power and other types of power which might be operative at the same time. If a member is attracted to a group and he conforms to its norms only because he fears ridicule or expulsion from the group for nonconformity, we would call this coercive power. On the other hand if he conforms in order to obtain praise for conformity, it is a case of reward power. The basic criterion for distinguishing referent power from both coercive and reward power is the mediation of the punishment and the reward by [the superior]: to the extent that [the superior] mediates the sanctions (i.e., has means controls over [the subordinate]) we are dealing with coercive and reward power; but to the extent that [the subordinate] avoids discomfort or gains satisfaction by conformity based on identification, regardless of [the superior's] responses, we are dealing with referent power. Conformity with majority opinion is sometimes based on a respect for the collective wisdom of the group, in which case it is expert power.[16]

Authority and the Question of Obedience

A prerequisite for the effective use of authority, as we pointed out in the acceptance theory, is obedience. Mutiny or rebellion against following orders hardly advances the overall cause of the organization—assuming that the orders are legitimate and directly related to the organization's purpose. Authority is the "binding force in organization."[17] And the mechanism that links individual action to organizational purpose is obedience.[18] Although obedience to legitimate authority is something we take for granted, the acceptance theory points out that each individual must decide whether or not to obey any particular order, obeying those that fall within his own individual zone of indifference, and resisting or disobeying those that are clearly outside his zone. One of the important factors in this decision is perception of whether or not the order is directly related to the purpose of the organization.

Although obedience is essential for the carrying out of the beneficial and essential purposes of most organizations, we might consider questions of authority and obedience less in the best interests of society. The Nuremberg Trials following World War II shocked the world with the disavowals of personal responsibility of many individuals who maintained and operated the death camps and gas chambers from 1933 to 1945. The systematic slaughter of millions of innocent persons was ordered—and obeyed. Although a single person might have originated the policy, the purpose

---

[16]Ibid., p. 266.

[17]Harold Koontz and Cyril O'Donnell, *Principles of Management: An Analysis of Managerial Functions,* 5th ed. (New York: McGraw-Hill, 1972), p. 57.

[18]Stanley Milgram, "Behavioral Study of Obedience," *Journal of Abnormal and Social Psychology,* **67**:371 (1963).

could only be carried out on such a massive scale if a great number of persons obeyed the orders they received.[19]

It is inconceivable that basic humanitarian tendencies could be so submerged and ignored in favor of such obedience, yet it happened. Although this example is hardly likely to be encountered in today's organizations, we may ponder our personal reactions to orders or job pressures that encourage us to go against our ethical codes or sense of values. Many persons might well piously exclaim that, under such circumstances, they would rather quit than obey. But how realistic is this in actual practice? What *are* some of the conditions of obedience and disobedience to authority?

Milgram conducted a landmark study in which he investigated exactly this question. He conducted a complex set of experiments in which almost a thousand individuals participated. The major objective was to determine patterns of obedience and disobedience to authority in a situation that went against basic, widely held ethical values. The subjects were male adults, ranging in age from twenty to fifty years and engaged in a wide variety of occupations.[20]

Briefly, each subject was introduced to a situation in which he thought he was administering an electric shock to another human being as part of an experiment in learning. The experimenter arranged the situation so that the subject was called upon to administer increasingly high levels of voltage "punishment" for failure to learn to another person in an electric chair in another room. This other room was wired for sound, so that the subject could hear what he thought were the responses of the person receiving the shock—but what was actually a tape recording. The subject delivered the shock through a simulated shock generator, which had clearly marked voltage levels that ranged from 15 to 450 volts and which had designations that ranged from "slight shock" to "danger: severe shock."

With increasing voltage, the tape recording of the supposed victim became increasingly agitated. Grunting and moaning started at the 75-volt level, and at 150 volts the "victim" demanded to end the experiment. When the subject administered 180 volts, the "victim" cried out that he could no longer stand the pain, and at 300 volts he insisted that he would no longer consent to receive the shocks and must be freed. At each level, should the subject attempt to break off the experiment, the experimenter urged him on, saying, "You have no other choice; you must go on!"[21]

What were the results? We would expect (or hope) that basic humanitarian values would assert themselves at a very low level of shock. Certainly hurting another human being is not something that we would think that most people would continue doing, even if urged on by an authority figure. A group of forty psychiatrists at a leading medical school were asked to

[19]Ibid.

[20]Stanley Milgram, "Some Conditions of Obedience and Disobedience to Authority," *Human Relations* (February 1965), p. 59.

[21]Ibid., p. 60.

estimate the performance of the subjects in the experiment. They predicted that most of the subjects would not continue to obey beyond the tenth shock level (150 volts, at which point the victim made his first explicit demand to be freed). Further, they predicted that by the twentieth shock level (300 volts) only 3.73 percent of the subjects would still obey and that the highest shock on the generator would be administered by only a little over one tenth of 1 percent of the subjects.

Is this consistent with your expectations? What *actually* happened was this: a full 62 percent of the subjects complied fully with the experimenter's commands, administering the successive shocks all the way up to and including the maximum, 450 volts![22]

We should point out that few of the subjects blithely or uncomplainingly carried out these orders. Most, in fact, expressed deep disapproval, and others denounced it as senseless and stupid. Yet they complied even while they protested.[23] The conflict between "the deeply ingrained disposition not to harm others and the equally compelling tendency to obey others who are in authority"[24] seemed to be resolved in favor of obedience.

An important determinant of obedience, we must hasten to add, is proximity to either the victim or the authority figure (experimenter). The subject tended to disobey when the victim was more visible or closer to him. When he actually had to physically administer the shock directly to the subject, obedience dropped off sharply. But when the *experimenter* became physically closer to the subject, obedience became the rule. When the experimenter was physically out of the room, communicating by intercom and physically removed, obedience was again relatively less. Interestingly, some subjects reported obedience to the experimenter over the intercom, yet never administered any shock higher than the very lowest level, even while reporting that they were increasing the shock level according to orders.

The implications of this study are great for our consideration of authority and the obedience to authority that is essential to the conduct of the operations of any organization. The zone of indifference presented in the acceptance theory of authority takes on a somewhat new light; certainly individuals may refuse to obey an order if it conflicts with their values or perceptions of its legitimacy. Another consideration, not taken into account in the acceptance theory, is that of the individual's blindly obeying authority, even while recognizing the results of such obedience. Does the individual then refuse to assume responsibility for his actions? Does he merely take the path of least resistance and place responsibility on the shoulders of the authority figure, thereby seeking to absolve himself of responsibility? Authority is then a powerful instrument, the unwise use of which we cannot assume will be checked by the ethics or conscience of the subordinate. "Just following orders" becomes a substitute for disobeying authority. The individ-

[22]Ibid., p. 72.
[23]Ibid.
[24]Ibid., p. 69.

ual's zone of indifference cannot be completely relied upon to control abuses of authority. Rather, responsible authority must be initiated at the top levels of the organization, or considerable freedom must be given subordinates to conduct autonomous operations and thereby be relatively freed from the demands of proximity to the authority for complete compliance.

Criticisms of the Formal Organization's Effects on the Individual

A number of criticisms have been leveled against the formal organization, primarily for what is seen to be its "inhumanity," its "degradation of the human spirit," or its "subordination of the human will to that of the organization." One of the most outspoken critics of the organization is William H. Whyte, Jr., who wrote *The Organization Man.*[25] He asserts that, with the advent of large organizations or bureaucracies, dominant value systems have swung far from those of imagination and independence to the requirement of conformity, unswerving and unthinking loyalty to the organization, and adaptability at the expense of individual ethics or values.[26] Individualism, then, is dead; conformity and subservient behavior are required for success in the organization, as are cooperativeness and a careful attunement to the expectations of others (particularly one's superior). The result of such value systems and criteria for organizational success is that of "artificiality and a facelessness in ... organization life ... the regularized and deadening uniformity of suburbia, the 9 to 5 beat, of 'the man in the gray flannel suit.'"[27]

Another major critic of the formal organization's effect on the individual is Chris Argyris. He contends that the basic structural elements and demands of the organization are diametrically opposed to the needs of the human personality for full development. The personality tends to develop according to specific trends:

1. From a state of being passive as an infant to a state of increasing activity as an adult.
2. From a state of dependence upon others as an infant to a state of relative independence as an adult.
3. From being capable of behaving in only a few ways as an infant to being capable of behaving in many different ways as an adult.
4. From having erratic, casual, shallow, quickly dropped interest as an infant to possessing a deepening of interest as an adult. The mature state is characterized by an endless series of challenges where the reward comes from doing something for its own sake.

[25]William H. Whyte, Jr., *The Organization Man* (New York: Simon and Schuster, 1956).
[26]Cf. Fremont E. Kast and James E. Rosenzweig, *Organization and Management: A Systems Approach* (New York: McGraw-Hill, 1970), pp. 269, 270.
[27]John M. Pfiffner and Frank P. Sherwood, *Administrative Organization* (Englewood Cliffs, N.J.: Prentice-Hall, 1960), p. 427.

5. From having a short-time perspective . . . as an infant to having a much longer time perspective as an adult.
6. From being in a subordinate position in the family and society as an infant to aspiring to occupy at least an equal and/or superordinate position relative to his peers.
7. From having a lack of awareness of the self as an infant to having an awareness of and control over the self as an adult. The adult who experiences adequate and successful control over his own behavior develops a sense of integrity . . . and feelings of self-worth.[28]

The basic principles of effective organization, Argyris avers, create situations that are detrimental to personality development. These are summarized below.

TASK OR WORK SPECIALIZATION   In concentrating effort on a limited field of endeavor in order to increase the quality and quantity of output, the individual is required to curtail his continuous, ego-involving process of growth and to use only a few of his total abilities. As specialization increases, it also requires use of the less complex abilities rather than the more complex abilities.[29]

CHAIN OF COMMAND   Leadership is created in the organization to control, direct and coordinate each of the separate activities and to make certain that each unit performs satisfactorily. The leader is additionally assigned formal authority to hire, discharge, reward, and penalize individuals in order to elicit appropriate behaviors, requiring that individuals be dependent upon, passive toward, and subordinate to the leader. As a result, subordinates have little control over their working environment. Time perspective is shortened because they do not have complete access to all the information necessary to predict the future.[30]

UNITY OF DIRECTION   Efficiency increases if a unit has only one activity (or one homogeneous set of activities) that is planned and directed by only one person, the leader. Since psychological success is achieved when each individual is allowed to define his own goals in relation to his own inner/needs and in relation to the strength of the barriers to be overcome in order to reach these goals, Argyris states that ideal conditions for psychological *failure* have been created, since no allowance for aspiration for psychological success has been provided.[31]

SPAN OF CONTROL   Efficiency is increased through the limiting of the span of control of the leader to no more than five or six subordinates whose work interlocks. If the number of subordinates is kept to a minimum, great emphasis is placed upon close supervision. This leads the subordinates to become dependent upon, passive toward, and subordinate

[28]Chris Argyris, *Personality and Organization: The Conflict Between System and the Individual* (New York: Harper & Row, 1957), pp.50, 51.
[29]Ibid., pp. 59–60.
[30]Ibid., pp. 60–62.
[31]Ibid., pp. 63–64.

to the leader. Close supervision also tends to place control in the hands of the superior.[32]

As a result of this analysis, Argyris cites what he considers a clear case of incongruence between the demands of the formal organization and the needs of the healthy individual. Work requirements yield situations in which individuals are dependent and passive and in which they use few and unimportant abilities. As a result, frustration, failure, short time perspective, and conflict naturally occur because of the warping of their own personality developmental needs.[33]

Are Whyte's and Argyris's finding inevitable? Must the formal organization, in its pursuit of service to its customers, perform disservices to its members by stunting their psychological growth or by conditioning them into conformist or robotlike roles? Hansell points out that organizations need not do so.[34] In order for organizations to be consistent in proving some service or product, structure is necessary for continuity. Structure can become prey to rigor mortis, in which case the hierarchy becomes inflexible, concerns revolve increasingly around self-administration, and the original purpose may have become lost. When these happen, you may say that the bureaucracy or organization has "frozen."

Individual behaviors must be ordered, because a human under ordinary circumstances tends to wander and create in response to changing environmental forces, unless constrained by some external force. A bureaucracy and an organization are instituted to impose some standardizing, stabilizing structure on variable human behavior. So a person within the organization performs in much the same way from day to day. The freezing organization consists of individuals who lose interest in the end purpose of their endeavors—work becomes the result of the command to work rather than of personal motivation to work. Additionally, increased specialization creates narrow interests and jobs, with responsibilities of narrower scope. Coordination becomes necessary to minimize the dangerous gaps that appear in the coverage of the total amount of work to be done. Another indicator of the freezing process is the movement from effective problem-solving behaviors to the ritual performance of duties. Specialization and routinization of activities similarly do away with involvement and interest in the job, having removed the excitement and challenge of the unexpected.

To summarize, the frozen organization is one in which the bureaucratic process effectively eliminates identification of the individual with the end product of the firm. Jobs are specialized and routinized in order to ensure maximum efficiency and predictability.

Hansell suggests three strategies for fending off this freezing process. One strategy is the constant expectation that a person enlarge his role in the system by direct rotation of jobs, or changes in the location a job is per-

[32]Ibid., pp. 64–66.
[33]Ibid., pp. 233, 234.
[34]Norris Hansell, "Cracking the Bureaucratic Ice," *Innovation* (November 1971).

formed, to keep him from forming arbitrary boundaries around his concerns. The second strategy involves arranging the structure of small groups that work within the overall organization so that they too are constantly involved in working toward the goals of the overall organization. Employee units are regrouped into small, temporary group structures and assigned tasks that are not normally considered within their job scope. This allows a reorientation of the work group to the basic purpose of the firm.

The third and final strategy is to design the culture of the bureaucracy in ways that make freezing less likely. The freezing process will be stymied if the organizational structure is designed so as to involve each individual in constant challenge and contribution to the overall organization and so as to form a tradition or organizationwide policy of redesigning structure and tasks toward this end. And the potential negative effects that the formal structure has upon the individual can be effectively diminished.

We have spent a great deal of time in these last sections reviewing criticisms of the formal organization and pointing out how potentially negative its effects can be on the human being. We want to point out that, at its best, the formal organization can be a most positive and developmental vehicle for society as well as for the individual. At its worst, it can create situations that degrade and humiliate people and that may provide a social disservice to society even while delivering an economic benefit to its customers.

The formal organization, however, is and remains the context in which the individual behaves. Only by thoroughly understanding some of the aspects of the nature of the organization can we better appreciate how complex the subject of organizational behavior is. People do not exist or behave in a vacuum. Their actions and activities are structured or affected by the demands and expectations of the formal organization and the authority by which any individual is directed in the conduct of his job task. Formal organization sets the structure within which he works; it provides his reporting relationships, job content, social contacts, and so on. These are the elements that directly go to make up the individual's attitude toward his work. *Job satisfaction* is a term that is heard quite often in this respect. In the next chapter, we will consider the determinants of job satisfaction, primarily as they reflect the structural organizational elements and content of a job.

Summary

In this chapter, we noted that an organization is composed of interdependent activity systems and that rationality and predictability are essential to the conduct of the firm's operations. The necessity of coordination of diverse activity also creates the need for authority to ensure compliance with organizational requirements. Authority was considered to be the organizationally granted right to influence the behavior or activities of others.

Considered were two of the major theories of authority, the formal authority theory and the acceptance theory of authority. Formal authority is conceived of as a downward trickling of delegated authority, by which successively specialized tasks are coordinated and directed. The sources of influence were identified as reward, coercion, legitimate influence, referent influence, and expertise.

The acceptance theory is traced to Chester Barnard, who recognized that authority is not effective unless it elicits obedience. He postulated the existence of a "zone of indifference" within each organizational member. Each organizational member considers each command as being unquestionably legitimate and thereby worthy of obedience, marginal and subject to further scrutiny, or not a legitimate demand and therefore not worthy of obedience.

Milgram's classic study on conditions of obedience and disobedience to authority was briefly reviewed. The findings of this study cast some doubt on the total validity of the zone of indifference concept, since the majority of subjects were found to continue to comply with orders that were repugnant to the individual and contrary to humanitarian values.

Whyte and Argyris criticized the formal organization for its negative effects on the human being. Whyte stressed the bureaucratic necessity of conformity and lack of independence, and Argyris decried the inability of normal personalities to develop fully in situations in which classical organizational principles are followed.

Hansell pointed out that these are possible but not essential within formal organizations. Given a formal organization that is designed around the needs of the individual, negative effects need not occur.

STUDY AND REVIEW QUESTIONS

1. May authority be exercised only over one's subordinates or employees in the organization? Explain.

2. "With increasing specialization of labor comes the direct requirement for increasing coordination." Discuss.

3. Are the formal and the acceptance theories of authority compatible or reconcilable? Discuss.

4. Relate the relevance of the findings of Milgram's obedience study to the formal theory of authority.

5. Relate the relevance of the findings of Milgram's obedience study to the acceptance theory of authority.

6. Are Whyte's and Argyris's criticisms of the effects of formal organization on the individual valid? Under what conditions are they valid or invalid?

7. Are the organizational requirements of predictability and rationality related to Whyte's and Argyris's arguments?

8. Analyze the findings of Milgram's obedience study as they relate to French and Raven's influence types.

Chapter

6

Technology, Structure and Job Satisfaction

CHAPTER OBJECTIVES

1. To consider the impact of technology on attitudes and job satisfaction.

2. To appreciate how organizational structure directly influences job attitudes.

3. To develop a frame of reference for understanding the technological and structural determinants of organizational behavior.

CHAPTER OUTLINE

The Human Effects of Formal Organization
Attitudes and Behavior
Job Satisfaction and Morale

Technology and Job Satisfaction
Specialization
Job Scope

Organization Structure and Job Satisfaction
Effects of Organization Size
"Tall" and "Flat" Organization Structure

Job Satisfaction and Performance

An Integrating View of Job Satisfaction
Herzberg's Dual-Factor Theory
Factors Determining Satisfaction and
    Dissatisfaction
Satisfaction from Job Content and
    Dissatisfaction from Job Content
Dual-Factor Theory, Technology, and
    Structure
Criticisms of the Dual-Factor Theory

Technology, organization structure, authority, work: these are elements that make up the formal organizational system. Taken together, they provide the vehicles for accomplishing the main purposes of the firm. They establish the framework within which the individual performs his activities. More importantly, they *determine* and directly *affect* the nature and content *of* those activities.

The Human Effects of Formal Organization

What is missing is the consideration of the person who *holds* the position, performs the work, or manages the efforts of others. We must avoid the pitfall of the Frederick W. Taylors of the early twentieth century. They chose to emphasize the "rational," engineering, or technological aspects of job design, without considering the human aspects of the job. In Chapter 1 we discussed how the economic man model, the assumption of homogeneous human inputs, and the disregarding of worker attitudes resulted in a management philosophy that was quite unrealistic. However, as long as the conditions of the times were consistent with this philosophy, the workers did perform largely as predicted. Performance was a direct consequence of technology and structure, with the individual playing a minor and secondary role.

Attitudes and Behavior

In the 1930's the Hawthorne studies clearly pointed out that individual behavior is not the result of a simple and direct stimulus–response relationship. The work situation is *interpreted* by the individual, and attitudes play an important part in the manner in which the situation is interpreted. Only after individual interpretation and comparison with attitudes does the response occur. This means that the response expected from a purely objective and rational consideration of the work situation and its characteristics may or may not be the actual response of the individual. His response depends completely on how he interprets the situation and on his own personal attitudes toward the situation.[1]

Obviously attitudes are an important consideration, because of their central position in the process of transforming work requirements into effort. Attitudes toward one's job are especially important, and *morale* is a term of great importance. An *attitude* "is a predisposition to respond, positively or negatively, to a certain set of facts."[2] Job attitudes would then be

[1]Fritz J. Roethlisberger, *Management and Morale* (Cambridge, Mass.: Harvard University Press, 1941), p. 21.
[2]Blair J. Kolasa, *Introduction to Behavioral Science for Business* (New York: Wiley, 1969), p. 406.

predispositions or tendencies to respond to particular aspects of the job. *Job satisfaction* is one job attitude that is of great interest.

Since attitudes intervene between work requirements and work responses, information about how people feel about their jobs can be quite useful in predictions about work response. In addition, these types of attitudes can portray fertile areas of investigation for making the individual and the organization more compatible.

Job Satisfaction and Morale

Job satisfaction and *morale* are sometimes used interchangeably, but morale is a concept related to the job satisfactions of a group of people, rather than of one individual.[3] We might then say that a particular worker experiences a certain level of *job satisfaction;* his work group, as a result of commonly held job satisfactions, might be said to have a certain level of *morale.*

In a recent report of a national sampling of work attitudes by the University of Michigan,[4] 17 percent of the 709 blue-collar workers interviewed reported negative job attitudes, compared with only 13 percent of 753 white-collar workers. (This finding compares with a median percentage of 13 percent dissatisfied in a study of several hundred job satisfaction studies in the late 1950's.[5])

These national survey figures illustrate broad, overall patterns. However, we cannot forget that within any particular organization, job attitudes and morale may be quite negative and detrimental to the organization's purpose. Perhaps more importantly, they may indicate that technological and structural elements ignore human capabilities and aspirations.

Technology and Job Satisfaction

Specialization

The increasing trend away from craft technologies toward those of batch or mass production has been discussed. We often hear complaints about the content and satisfaction of mass-production jobs, especially in comparison to the "good old days" of craftsmanship. As a matter of fact, less than 10 percent of the medieval labor force consisted of craftsmen; even in

---

[3]Kolasa, p. 407.

[4]Harold L. Sheppard and Neal Q. Herrick, *Where Have All the Robots Gone? Worker Dissatisfaction in the 70's* (New York: Free Press, 1972).

[5]Robert Blauner, "Extent of Satisfaction: A Review of General Research," in *Psychology in Administration: A Research Orientation,* ed. by Timothy W. Costello and Sheldon S. Zalkind, (Englewood Cliffs, N.J.: Prentice-Hall, 1963), pp. 80–81.

the automobile industry in the late 1960's less than 5 percent of all workers were on the assembly line.[6] Further, the approximately 120,000 line assemblers were outnumbered by the approximately 200,000 *skilled* automobile workers.[7]

The question still remains: Does specialization have an effect on job attitudes and job satisfaction? Numerous studies indicate that there is a relationship between job specialization and satisfaction. Most of them, however, focus on *over*specialization. We might well be able to think of a job, the total content of which is too large and complex for any individual to handle competently, with resulting frustration and low job satisfaction. Such an *under*defined job might well lend itself to some form of functional specialization, with certain tasks being removed and reassigned to another individual and with resultant *increases* in job satisfaction.

A concept called *job purification* accounts for this process. We can see this applied in the assignment of the medical doctors' duties of rather routine nature to either nurses or paramedical professionals. The medical doctor can then concentrate his efforts on those aspects of his job that require his qualifications and training.

With increasing specialization will probably come diminishing returns in job satisfaction. At some (undefined) point, increased specialization probably *detracts* from job satisfaction, giving way to relative job dissatisfaction. At what point this occurs cannot be stated for certain, because (as we pointed out earlier) job satisfaction is a result of job attitudes, and attitudes are an intensely personal and subjective factor, not common to all individuals or classes of individuals. Munsterberg pointed out over sixty years ago that there is always someone for whom extremely routine jobs provide significant challenge and satisfaction.[8] In one study, for example, women workers who did light repetitive work in a knitwear mill were surveyed. The boredom they reported stemmed from individual characteristics (youth; restlessness in daily habits and leisure-time activities; and dissatisfaction with plant, home, and personal circumstances) rather than from the task.[9]

In another study, women workers in routine assembly were interviewed over a two-year period. Despite the highly repetitive nature of the jobs, dissatisfaction was not found to stem from monotony or boredom; in fact, less than 20 percent reported that they thought their work was monotonous or boring. Repetitive work, as a matter of fact, was not seen as dissatisfying when distractions were absent; distractions that created dissatisfaction with

[6]Robert Blauner, "Work Satisfaction and Industrial Trends in Modern Society," in *Readings in Organization Theory: A Behavioral Approach*, ed. by Walter A. Hill and Douglas M. Egan (Boston: Allyn & Bacon, 1967), p. 227.

[7]Ibid.

[8]H. Munsterberg, *Psychology and Industrial Efficiency* (Boston: Houghton Mifflin, 1913), pp. 190–205, cited in A. C. MacKinney, P. F. Wernimont, and W. O. Galitz, "Has Specialization Reduced Job Satisfaction?" *Personnel* (January–February 1962), p. 9.

[9]P. C. Smith, "The Prediction of Individual Differences in Susceptibility to Industrial Monotony," *Journal of Applied Psychology* (August 1959), pp. 322–329.

the work were having an excessive pressure for quantity, interruptions from outsiders, or problems from materials or equipment.[10]

Meanwhile, others feel that decreasing job specialization results in increased job satisfaction. This implies that specialization has decreased job satisfaction. Early impetus came when Walker and Guest found (in their early 1950's study of workers on automobile assembly lines) that only 28 percent of the automobile assemblers who had repetitive jobs liked their jobs. In contrast, 90 percent of those holding *non*repetitive jobs liked their jobs. "Of the workers interviewed, 85% said they liked repetitive work, and the remaining 7% said it made no difference."[11] The repetitive jobs generally repeated one or several operations continuously throughout the workday. Walker and Guest thought there might be some connection between the number of operations the worker did and his job interest. They found a strong connection. Of the workers who performed only one operation and repeated it numerous times in the workday, only one third reported their jobs to be interesting. Of the workers who performed two, three, or four operations, 44 percent reported the job to be interesting. Almost 70 percent of those who performed five or more operations reported their jobs to be interesting.[12]

Another such study was done by Kilbridge at the Maytag Company. On a conveyor assembly line, six operators assembled a washing machine water pump with twenty-seven parts. Successive changes were made in the system. After about a year, the work that had been done on a conveyor line was done at four one-man work stations. Specialization had been successfully eliminated, and each assembler put together a complete washing machine water pump. Forty-seven of the sixty-one workers, when asked whether they liked or disliked a number of specific characteristics of the assembly line and the one-man work-station methods, reported that the one-man work stations' variety was liked. At the same time, thirty-two (a bare majority) reported that they liked the task specialization on the assembly line. Social interaction was preferred on the assembly line to that on the one-man work bench, by 45 to 33. Overall, fifteen reported that they had negative attitudes toward the assembly-line technique, whereas only four disliked the one-man work station.[13]

Finally, the concept of specialization is directly linked to the concept of production technologies we considered in Chapter 4. Shepard conducted a study of job attitudes of three groups of workers, each of whom had

[10]A. M. Turner and A. L. Miclette, "Sources of Satisfaction in Repetitive Work," *Occupational Psychology* (July 1962), pp. 215–227.

[11]Charles R. Walker and Robert H. Guest, *The Man on the Assembly Line* (Cambridge, Mass.: Harvard University Press, 1952), p. 53.

[12]Ibid, p. 54.

[13]M. D. Kilbridge, "Reduced Costs Through Job Enlargement: A Case," *The Journal of Business* (October 1960), pp. 357–362. See also E. H. Conant and M. D. Kilbridge, "An Interdisciplinary Analysis of Job Enlargement: Technology, Costs, and Behavioral Implications," *Industrial and Labor Relations Review* (April 1965), pp. 377–395.

different degrees of task specialization.[14] The three groups of workers he studied were chosen to represent the basic production technologies: craft, mechanized (mass production), and automation. Craft workers are skilled artisans; division of labor is not carried very far, because workers fashion the end product from raw materials. Mechanization requires many special-purpose machines, each of which performs limited operations on the end product. Semiskilled operators performing an occupational specialty are needed to operate the machines. Thus under mechanization or mass-production technology, each operator's specialty contributes to the end product, but only in a small way. A high degree of functional specialization character-izes division of labor in mechanized or mass-production technology.

Automated technology workers are monitors of special-purpose machinery or of a completely integrated process production system. As we pointed out in Chapter 4, essentially the worker is responsible for checking gauges that monitor the way in which the production process is functioning. Specialization is decreased by automation, because the number of separate job classifications is reduced, with the result that each worker is responsible for a larger share in the overall production process.[15]

The workers who were studied as representing automated technology workers were oil-refining control-room monitors. The mechanized and craft workers were, respectively, automobile assembly-line workers and journey-men who did maintenance work.[16] Table 6-1 illustrates the relationship between job satisfaction and degree of functional specialization found in this study. We might also observe the strong effect that production technology has on job satisfaction because of the technological requirements that dictate job design and amount of specialization. Notice that job satisfaction is

TABLE 6-1   Job Satisfaction by Degree of Functional Specialization

| | | Degree of Functional Specialization | | | | | |
| | | High (assemblers) | | Moderate (monitors) | | Low (craftsmen) | |
		n	%	n	%	n	%
Job Satisfaction	High	13	14	48	52	102	87
	Low	83	86	44	48	15	13
	Totals	96	100	92	100	117	100

Pattern of responses statistically significant ($p < .001$).

SOURCE: Adapted from Jon M. Shepard, "Functional Specialization and Work Attitudes," *Industrial Relations* (February 1969), p. 191.

[14]Jon M. Shepard, "Specialization, Autonomy, and Job Satisfaction," *Industrial Relations* (October 1973). See also Shepard's "Functional Specialization and Work Attitudes," *Industrial Relations* (February 1969), and his "Functional Specialization, Alienation, and Job Satisfac-tion," *Industrial and Labor Relations Review* (January 1970).
[15]Shepard, "Functional Specialization and Work Attitudes," pp. 186, 187.
[16]Ibid., p. 190.

reportedly much lower among the automobile assembly-line workers (highly specialized positions). Job satisfaction increases quite dramatically at the moderate level of specialization, with over one half of the control-room monitors reporting high job satisfaction. And craftsmen, the least specialized workers of the three groups studied, overwhelmingly reported high job satisfaction. This pattern was found to be statistically significant at the 0.001 level, which means that this pattern would have occurred by chance no more than one time in one thousand.

Job Scope

Closely related to specialization and number of operations of the job is the scope of the job. By *scope* we simply mean the number of separate tasks assigned to an individual. The difference between scope and numbers of operations is essentially this: a task exists whenever an individual exerts effort in order to accomplish a specific purpose, which may require a number of specific movements (operations).[17] When the number of tasks economically justifies a person's being assigned to perform them, a position or job is created.[18] So in its very simplest form, a job must consist of at least one task, and this task must require at least one movement or operation, although a single task may require many separate movements or operations.

The job design, then, is determined by the optimum *scope* of the job. We can see that there are several options open. The job may be narrowly defined in terms of great specialization, which means that the job is defined as the basic task unit only; this just means that the job cannot be subdivided any further. For example, one could not divide any further the task of tightening a nut on a bolt. This single task (composed of several movements or operations) is a basic task unit. A job composed of relatively few operations tends to be repetitive and to have a short cycle time (time from the beginning of the task to its completion). A task that required a rather large number of separate operations tends to be much less repetitive.

Consider the college professor. One of his tasks might be to teach a course in organizational behavior, a task that is composed of many separate operations and that has as cycle time the college term—hardly a repetitive task, even though he might repeat the task every term for years.

Based in large part on the studies of numbers of operations and task specialization, advocates of unspecializing jobs have arisen. One study reports the experience of a large manufacturing company that changed its basic production technology and consequently the jobs associated with the manufacturing process. These jobs were enlarged by requirements of higher technical complexity and the inclusion of new tasks in the content of the

[17]David J. Chesler, Richard H. Lukart, and Jay L. Otis, "Job Evaluation," in *Industrial Engineering Handbook,* 2nd Ed., ed. by H. B. Maynard (New York: McGraw-Hill, 1963), pp. 6–75.

[18]Ibid.

enlarged jobs. These new tasks included some accounting, personnel, and scheduling functions.[19] The employees who held the enlarged jobs reported significantly higher job satisfaction, primarily because of increased use of their abilities and skills.[20]

The Maytag study mentioned before also illustrates a decrease in specialization through an increase in the scope of the job. Washing machine water pumps had been assembled on a conveyor assembly line. The assembly line was discontinued and the assemblers were each given a work station at which they assembled the complete twenty-seven-part water pump. The variety of tasks for each worker was increased. Work technology was changed from continuous to batch operation. Each worker was also given the right to adopt whatever work methods he chose, rather than being required to follow prescribed techniques. Kilbridge reported that overall satisfaction increased.[21]

The concept of increasing the scope of the job will be taken up in considerable detail in Chapter 22, "Job Enrichment."

Organization Structure and Job Satisfaction

Effects of Organization Size

One characteristic of any organization is its size in numbers of members. With the advent of large bureaucratic organizations has come criticism of the production technologies found to be "most appropriate" to the scale of operations required to support or create such an entity. Among the criticisms, as we noted earlier, are the meaninglessness of any particular job, the separation of the worker from the end product, regimentation, boredom and monotony, and so on. These criticisms probably stem from our observation that organizations require rationality and predictability and consequently increasingly structured or specialized tasks.

Accordingly, we might expect that (all other things remaining equal) job satisfaction in larger organizations would tend to be less than in smaller organizations. Indik suggested the following explanatory sequence:

1. As the size of organization increases, there is an increased tendency for more role specialization to occur.
2. With the increase in role specialization, the complexity of the job decreases.
3. The less complex the job, the less satisfying its performance is to the individual.
4. The less satisfied an individual is with his job, the less likely he is to be highly attracted to the organization.

[19]Clayton P. Alderfer, "Job Enlargement and the Organizational Context," *Personnel Psychology* (March 1959), p. 421.
[20]Ibid., p. 423.
[21]M. D. Kilbridge, "Do Workers Prefer Larger Jobs?" *Personnel* (September-October 1960), pp. 45–48.

5. The less highly attracted to the organization the member is, the more likely he is to be absent or to leave the organization.
6. As the size of organizations increases, there will be more members leaving the organization both temporarily and permanently.[22]

Talacchi, for one, found that job satisfaction decreased as organizational size increased.[23]

We must recognize that an additional component of organizational size that must be considered is the size of the subunits that make up the total organization. An organization may be extremely large, yet might be made up of extremely small work units or teams, which could have extremely high morale. Conversely, a relatively small organization might be composed of a single huge assembly line, on which job satisfaction is extremely low. So the size of subunits within organizations and their effects on job satisfaction should be taken into account. Porter and Lawler pointed out in their review of the literature that a large subunit contains built-in obstacles to the maintenance of good communications between subunit members as well as to close personal relationships. Task specialization would probably also be found, and the interaction of these three factors might well lead to the high job dissatisfaction that we might expect and which has been found in several studies.[24]

Following twelve years of surveying over 100,000 employees who worked in several hundred different company units, Worthy reported that "mere size is unquestionably one of the most important factors in determining the quality of employe (sic) relationships: the smaller the unit the higher the morale, and vice versa."[25] He cited the opportunities for closer contact between workers and managers and consequently less impersonality in small organizations. He also agreed that smaller organizations are less specialized in terms of labor, with more meaningful work for the employee and a more ready identification with the purpose and end product of his labors.[26]

"Tall" and "Flat" Organization Structure

Another structural characteristic that might affect job satisfaction and morale is the shape of the organization structure, "tall" or "flat." These simple descriptive terms are actually reflections of several other characteristics, such as numbers of hierarchical levels and spans of control for organizations of a given total size.

[22]Bernard P. Indik, "Some Effects of Organization Size on Member Attitudes and Behavior," *Human Relations* (November 1963), p. 380.
[23]Sergio Talacchi, "Organizational Size, Individual Attitudes and Behavior: An Empirical Study," *Administrative Science Quarterly* (December 1960), pp. 398–420.
[24]Lyman W. Porter and Edward E. Lawler, III, "Properties of Organization Structure in Relation to Job Attitudes and Job Behavior," *Psychological Bulletin,* **64:** 40 July (1965). For an excellent review of the studies that have been done on size of organizational subunits and total organization related to job satisfaction and morale, see especially their pp. 34–43.
[25]James C. Worthy, "Organizational Structure and Employe Morale," *American Sociological Review* (April 1950), p. 173.
[26]Ibid.

In Worthy's study of Sears and Roebuck, he noted from the large numbers of interviews that there were sharp contrasts between what were otherwise comparable units. The major differences in structure between these units were the complexity and amount of decentralization. The results of these differences in organizational complexity and decentralization level were two important ones: development of effective executives and level of employee morale. He found that organizations and units whose functions were highly specialized needed a relatively large number of administrative levels and controls to coordinate the many specialized activities and to push for production. To support these administrative activities, staff units were added to the administrative structure, further complicating the process. To facilitate what was seen as a need for close control and direction of subordinates, and to ensure that approved procedures were followed strictly, the span of control of each successive administrative level was narrowed. This allowed each executive to "exercise the detailed direction and control which is generally considered necessary" over his subordinates.[27]

This approach was compared with units that had relatively large spans of control, with consequently fewer levels of administration. Morale was higher and more effective executives were developed in those with large spans of control. As a matter of fact, Worthy pointed out that in some of these organizations managers quite deliberately were given "so many subordinates that it is impossible to exercise too close supervision over their activities."[28] This emphasizes executive ability and capacity and demands that the supervisor be "able to secure the willing, enthusiastic support of his colleagues and subordinates" by building and maintaining cooperation, teamwork, and a high level of employee morale.[29]

In a national study of managers, some rather complex relationships were found to exist between satisfaction and organizational shape. In companies that employed fewer than 5,000 people, managerial satisfactions were reported to be slightly greater in flat than in tall organizations. Managers in companies of *more* than 5,000 employees reported greater satisfaction in tall structures than in flat structures.[30] The same general types of results were found in an international study of middle and top management executives in thirteen countries. As before, managers in flat companies of less than 5,000 employees reported greater satisfaction than those in tall structures, but managers in companies of 5,000 employees or more were not more satisfied in flat than in tall structures.[31]

---

[27]Ibid., pp. 177, 178.
[28]Ibid., p. 178.
[29]Ibid.
[30]Lyman W. Porter and Edward E. Lawler, III, "The Effects of 'Tall' Versus 'Flat' Organization Structures on Managerial Job Satisfaction," *Personnel Psychology* (Summer 1964) pp. 146, 147.
[31]Lyman W. Porter and Jacob Siegel, "Relationships of Tall and Flat Organization Structures to the Satisfaction of Foreign Managers," *Personnel Psychology* (Winter 1965), pp. 388, 389.

One explanation for the tendency for the advantages of a flat organization structure to decrease with increasing organization size can be found in the characteristics generally attributed to tall and flat organization structures. Advocates of flat organization structures claim that because of the large average span of control, subordinates will have greater freedom and autonomy to make decisions. As a result of this relatively greater freedom and autonomy, individuals are supposed to contribute more to the organization and receive greater satisfaction from their jobs. On the other hand, a tall structure increases supervisory controls and allows superiors to better coordinate the activities of their subordinates. In a small organization problems of coordination and communication do not tend to be severe, simply because the organization is small. Thus, in a small organization there would be little advantage in a tall structure and, in fact, since it tends to amplify the disadvantages associated with tight managerial control, a tall structure probably is a liability in a typical small organization. In large organizations, on the other hand, problems of coordination and communication are complex. Thus, for large organizations a taller type of structure may be needed to overcome these problems and allow managers to supervise their subordinates more effectively.[32]

Job Satisfaction and Performance

The level of job satisfaction of an organizational member is important. Unwise is the thoughtless design of individual jobs, the structuring of positions and organizations, and the imposing of technologies likely to invoke strongly negative feelings in the holders of these positions. Creating a more human and a more humane organizational setting is certainly more in tune with the expectations and requirements of workers and managers alike in our postindustrial society.

But what are the economic returns from job satisfaction? Can an organization that operates on a razor-thin margin of profit *afford* to design a more human organization? How does job satisfaction affect job performance?

In Chapter 1 we pointed out the fallacy of the "Pet Milk Theory," that happy workers are productive workers. Does this mean that increasing job satisfaction will have no effect on performance or on lowering the costs of production? We can draw a clear distinction between the "happiness days" of human relations and the concept of job satisfaction. Employers had tried to make their workers happy by furnishing them with items that were not directly related to the jobs they performed—that did not affect job content. Remember that when we consider job satisfaction we restrict our vision to the feelings, positive and negative, that the position holder has toward his *job*. So the concepts of general happiness and job satisfaction are independent of each other.

Generally speaking, we might assume that job satisfaction is directly related to performance. It makes intuitive sense that a person who enjoys his

[32]Porter and Lawler, "Properties of Organization Structure in Relation to Job Attitudes and Job Behavior," pp. 44, 45.

work works harder at it than would a person who does not like his work. And a person involved in his job should have a stronger commitment to doing a *better* job.

For example, in one Maytag plant the assembly of a water pump was gradually changed from an assembly-line procedure to one-person work stations; the complete pump was assembled at each person's work station. Job satisfaction went up quite a bit, but other results were also observed: the time that it took to assemble each pump dropped from 1.77 minutes per pump to 1.49 minutes. And the company reported saving about $2,000 per year.[33]

On the other hand, a group of laborers and a group of engineers were studied in an attempt to discern their patterns of job satisfaction as they related to productivity. The steel plant laborers did show a positive relationship between job satisfaction and their overall productivity. The engineers and skilled technicians displayed a *negative* relationship between job satisfaction and productivity—as job satisfaction went up, productivity went *down;* the *less* satisfied an engineer was, the greater his productivity tended to be. The researchers attempted to explain this by concluding that the engineers and technicians were performing types of work that were below their aspiration level or desire, while the laborers were strictly limited by the terms of their union contracts and, perhaps, by the more structured nature of the tasks they performed.[34] Since the engineers and technicians valued their relative freedom in the performance of their job more highly than did the production workers, frustration of this desire might well have resulted in this peculiar finding.[35]

Along the same lines, each member of work groups of carpenters and bricklayers was allowed to nominate, in order of preference, three co-workers to be his work partner. Twenty-two of these received as partners the co-worker nominated as first choice; twenty-eight more received their second choice; sixteen were assigned their third choice. The result of this change in work practices was that labor costs and materials costs were greatly reduced. There was also a significant drop in turnover, suggesting greater job satisfaction.[36]

An Integrating View of Job Satisfaction

So far we have considered job satisfaction and morale as they are influenced by the organization's structural characteristics and by the physical characteristics of the job. Organizational shape and size, degree of job

---

[33]Kilbridge, "Reduced Costs Through Job Enlargement: A Case," pp. 359, 360.

[34]John W. Slocum, Jr. and Michael J. Misshauk, "Job Satisfaction and Productivity," *Personnel Administration* (March–April, 1970), p. 57.

[35]Ibid.

[36]Raymond H. Van Zelst, "Sociometrically Selected Work Teams Increase Production," *Personnel Psychology* (Autumn 1952), pp. 181–183.

specialization, and monotony and repetitiveness are each important. But which of the many aspects of a job is the most important in inducing satisfaction or dissatisfaction? If a new college graduate were looking for his first job, what should he look for as indicators of a potentially satisfying position? Is it possible to "balance off" rather dissatisfying job characteristics with more important elements that might make a job satisfying overall? As a future manager, what would *you* consider in evaluating the job satisfactions and morale of your subordinates? What would you change in their jobs to make them more satisfying?

These questions are complex and necessarily frustrating. They are important, however, and cannot be ignored. After all, they stem directly from the basic reasons that the organization exists *and* that people are members of the organization. For our purposes, these questions must be considered because they directly influence organizational behavior. Frustration, discontent, conflict, and alienation are inevitable in dissatisfying jobs and must affect the actions and attitudes of individuals.

Herzberg's Dual-Factor Theory

The notion of factors, associated with the job, that affect satisfaction in different ways is the contribution of Frederick Herzberg. Although highly controversial, his "dual-factor" theory provides an excellent framework for considering job satisfaction and bringing together our previous discussions.

If a job holder is not satisfied with his job, is he *dis*satisfied? We might feel this is obviously so. But is it? One might simply be neutral or ambivalent toward his job. Considering the opposite of job satisfaction to be job *dis*satisfaction assumes that we can measure this complex phenomenon on a single continuum or scale, as in Figure 6-1.

Herzberg and his associates conducted a series of interviews with 200 engineers and accountants.[37] Those interviewed were asked to describe periods of their lives during which they were extremely happy and unhappy with their jobs. Experiences or events were then related to these periods. When these events were analyzed, the concepts of job satisfaction and job dissatisfaction were found to be two *separate* factors and not elements related to each other by degrees along a single scale. Figure 6-2 shows how this might be represented. The opposite of job satisfaction was not found to be job dissatisfaction; rather it was *no* job satisfaction. Similarly, the opposite of job dissatisfaction was *no* job dissatisfaction instead of job satisfaction.

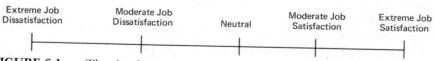

FIGURE 6-1   The simple continuum concept of job satisfaction–dissatisfaction.

[37]For a detailed treatment of the study, see F. Herzberg, B. Mausner, and B. Snyderman, *The Motivation to Work* (New York: Wiley, 1959).

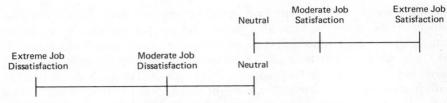

FIGURE 6-2   Job satisfaction as separate dual continua.

Factors Determining Satisfaction and Dissatisfaction

The study by Herzberg et al. suggested that the factors that contribute to job satisfaction are *distinct* and *separate* from those that contribute to job dissatisfaction. The factors associated with job satisfaction were termed *satisfiers;* those associated with job dissatisfaction were called *dissatisfiers* or *hygiene factors.* The latter term was derived from its analogous use in preventive medicine. After all, sound programs of medical hygiene do not of themselves make people healthier—but they do help keep them from becoming ill! In the same way, if those factors classified as hygienic or dissatisfiers are *not* present, job dissatisfaction results. If they *are* present, job dissatisfaction diminishes—but does not become transformed into job satisfaction; it simply becomes a neutral attitude.

If those factors classified as satisfiers are *not* present, job dissatisfaction does not result; rather, no job satisfaction occurs. As satisfiers are added to the job, satisfaction increases correspondingly. The satisfiers and dissatisfiers, as reported in twelve studies, are shown in Figure 6-3. Notice that the factors associated with extreme satisfaction (satisfiers) are quite different from those associated with dissatisfaction.

Satisfaction from Job Content and Dissatisfaction from Job Content

More importantly, hygiene factors are characterized by their being directly related to the *context* of the job; that is, they are factors peripheral to the actual duties of the job. Hygiene factors describe the individual's "relationship to the . . . environment in which he does his job. [They relate] to the situation"[38] in which he does his job. The satisfiers relate to what he actually does: his job duties and the content of the job.

This fundamental difference between satisfiers and dissatisfiers may be clearer after an examination of Table 6-2. Descriptions of the factors are provided to illustrate what the labels mean.

If satisfiers are the primary cause of job satisfaction, and dissatisfiers the primary cause of dissatisfaction, why the preoccupation with hygiene factors? Unfortunately job satisfaction cannot take place until the causes of job dissatisfaction are removed:

[38]Frederick Herzberg, "The Motivation–Hygiene Concept and Problems of Manpower," in *Modern Management: Issues and Ideas,* ed. by David R. Hampton (Belmont, Calif.: Dickenson, 1969), p. 317.

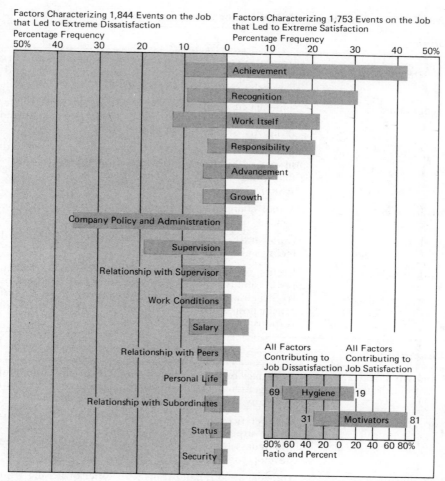

FIGURE 6-3 Factors affecting job attitudes as reported in twelve investigations. Source: Frederick Herzberg, "One More Time: How Do You Motivate Employees?" *Harvard Business Review* (January–February 1968), p. 57.

In brief, the hygiene factors meet man's needs to avoid unpleasantness. "I don't like to be treated this way; I don't want to suffer the deprivation of low salary; bad interpersonal relationships make me uncomfortable." In other words, they want their lives to be hygienically clean. The motivator [satisfier] factors on the other hand make people happy with their jobs because they serve man's basic and human need for psychological growth; a need to become more competent.[39]

Hygiene factors must be provided *before* satisfaction is possible. After all, can a manager be completely happy with his job if he cannot know whether or not he will be laid off next week? Adding more and more hygiene factors

[39]Ibid., p. 318.

TABLE 6-2   Explanation of Dual-Factor Theory Items

Satisfier

Achievement:	Event of success, failure, or absence of achievement. Includes such items as successful completion of a job and seeing the results of one's work.
Recognition:	Some act of recognition of the job holder, the source of which could be superior, subordinate, peer, client, and so on. Act of notice, praise, or blame.
Possibility of Growth:	Likelihood that one will be able to move upward and onward within his organization; situation in which he is able to advance in skill development and in his profession.
Advancement:	Actual change in status or position in the organization.
Work Itself:	Duties (tasks) of a position as a source of good or bad feelings about it.
Responsibility:	Events of satisfaction stemming from being given responsibility for one's own work, the work of others, or from being given new responsibility. Includes loss of satisfaction or dissatisfaction with job because of a lack of responsibility.

Dissatisfier

Company Policy and Administration:	Adequacy or inadequacy of company organization and management. Harmfulness or beneficial effects of company policies, primarily personnel policies.
Supervision–Technical:	Competence or incompetence, fairness or unfairness of the supervisor. Includes items such as supervisor's willingness (unwillingness) to delegate authority or to develop subordinates.
Relationship with Supervisor:	Interpersonal relationships with superior arising from interactions in the performance of their jobs.
Work Conditions:	Physical conditions of work, amount of work, facilities available for doing the work. Includes factors such as adequacy of ventilation, tools, and space.
Salary:	Wage or salary increases, unfulfilled expectation of salary increases.
Relationship with Peers:	Interpersonal relationships with co-workers arising from interactions in the performance of their jobs.
Personal Life:	Job-related factors in personal life. Includes such items as family needs for salary and other family problems stemming from the job situation.
Relationship with Subordinates:	Interpersonal relationships with subordinates arising from interaction in the performance of their jobs.
Status:	Some sign or appurtenance of status directly related to job attitude. Includes such items as having a secretary

TABLE 6-2   *(Continued)*

	in his new position, being allowed to drive a company car, or being unable to use a company eating facility.
Job Security:	Excludes *feelings* of security. Limited to objective signs of the presence (absence) of job security. Includes such items as tenure and company stability or instability.

SOURCE: Adapted from Frederick Herzberg, *Work and the Nature of Man* (Cleveland: World, 1966), pp. 193–198.

rapidly causes the point of diminishing marginal returns to be passed. Just how secure can one be, or how nice one's work station?

Decreases in dissatisfaction (from added hygiene factors) also tend to be short-lived because they become the new status quo. After a while even a sizable salary increase will no longer forestall dissatisfaction—the recipient wants another increase. Satisfiers, however, do have a relatively long-term effect on job satisfaction because of their direct connection with acquiring competence and performing in a meaningful fashion at a meaningful or challenging task. Managers in the "happiness days" of the early human relations era discussed in Chapter 1 discovered, to their chagrin, that company picnics or new lavatories might decrease dissatisfaction for a while but that satisfaction did not increase.

Dual-Factor Theory, Technology, and Structure

The specialization of a task and its negative effects on satisfaction might well be explained through the dual-factor theory. In a highly specialized job, few satisfiers can be present. The work itself might be inherently boring and largely determined by a machine or the assembly line. When a worker's performance is limited to specified acts, what achievement is there? Without the opportunity to excel, recognition cannot be earned and, consequently, opportunities for advancement might be limited. So—at best—such a job would be so designed that *no* job satisfaction is possible. With any hygiene deficiencies, the job would become more and more dissatisfying.

Organization size and job satisfaction might similarly be analyzed. At its worst, a very large organization might cause the individual to become just "another face in the crowd," without identity or opportunity for recognition. Dissatisfiers such as relationships with superiors, peers, and subordinates could well deteriorate because of the anonymity-producing firm size. Company policy and administration—not to mention the technical competence of one's supervisor—assume much more importance and more opportunity to fail to meet the expectations or needs of large segments of the membership.

Specialization and organizational size can be expressed in the "tallness" or the "flatness" of the pyramidal structure. As Worthy pointed out, great specialization creates need for increased coordination (supervision) and therefore more hierarchical levels: a tall organization. Large, tall organizations could well fall prey to few satisfiers and insufficient hygiene factors.

Criticisms of the Dual-Factor Theory

Herzberg's dual-factor theory of job satisfaction seems to provide a good basis for explaining job satisfaction and what causes it. We would be remiss if we did not consider the possible weaknesses in the theory.

A theory should be considered valid if repeated studies consistently support its major findings. Herzberg reported nine studies, with seventeen different occupations represented, which replicated his initial study.[40] The dual-factor theory was supported by the findings.

Common criticisms of the theory are that the results obtained are a direct result of the research methodology alone and that the research technique itself was deficient.[41]

A Method-Bound Theory

Herzberg's research methodology included asking those interviewed to cite job incidents that were either extremely satisfying or extremely dissatisfying. Vroom suggested that "obtained differences between stated sources of satisfaction and dissatisfaction stem from defensive processes within the individual respondent."[42] People might be more inclined to trace satisfaction to their own achievements, while projecting the causes of dissatisfaction to factors other than those directly related to themselves.

Further, when studies were done using Herzberg's incident-telling method, results invariably supported his theory. Studies that used *other* research methods conflicted with the dual-factor theory in their results.[43]

Technical Deficiency

No measure of overall satisfaction or dissatisfaction was used, so it is impossible to state how these satisfier–dissatisfier factors actually contribute to overall job satisfaction. They are just factors that are associated with job satisfaction.[44]

Another criticism of the research technique is the categorization method. The interviewer classified the responses, which required his evaluation of the category in which an incident should be placed—whether satisfier or dissatisfier and so on.[45]

[40]Frederick Herzberg, *Work and the Nature of Man* (Cleveland: World, 1966), pp. 92–129.

[41]Robert J. House and Lawrence A. Wigdor, "Herzberg's Dual-Factor Theory of Job Satisfaction and Motivation: A Review of the Evidence and a Criticism," *Personnel Psychology* (Winter 1967), pp. 371–373.

[42]Victor H. Vroom, *Work and Motivation* (New York: Wiley, 1964), p. 129.

[43]Orlando Behling, George Labovitz, and Richard Kozmo, "The Herzberg Controversy: A Critical Reappraisal," *Academy of Management Journal* (March 1968), p. 105.

[44]Robert B. Ewen, "Some Determinants of Job Satisfaction: A Study of the Generality of Herzberg's Theory," *Journal of Applied Psychology* (1964), **48,** p. 161.

[45]House and Wigdor, p. 372.

Recognition of possible weaknesses in the theory is necessary. On the whole, however, the dual-factor theory does provide a most convenient method of grappling with the complex issue of job satisfaction and its determinants.

Up to this point we have considered the formal context of organizational behavior—those factors that shape or mold human behavior in organized settings but that are technical and impersonal in nature. Our introduction to them is important because no individual behaves completely apart from them; they shape his interactions with co-workers, affect his attitudes, create conflicts, and structure his activities.

In the next chapter—a brief one—we will, look back over the three chapters on the formal organizational system. Our intent will be to integrate and consolidate them, thereby firming our conceptual foundation before considering the other dimensions and processes of organizational behavior as they occur *within* the formal organizational system.

Summary

In this chapter we have been concerned with the human results of formal organization, as they are reflected in the organizational member's satisfaction with his job and in the level of morale that the organizational context creates. We noted that technology is a major determinant of job satisfaction because it directly affects the implicit nature of the workflow itself; it provides the framework within which jobs are designed.

Specialization of jobs was found to be related to job dissatisfaction, with the narrower the scope of the job—the fewer the number of operations—the less the job satisfaction of members.

Organizational structure was also found to be related to job satisfaction, because it creates relationships between individual jobs and operations and reflects the characteristics of the organization as a totality. The size of the company was found to be related to job satisfaction, with smaller companies providing relatively greater opportunities for job satisfaction than larger companies (over 5,000 employees). And the famous Worthy study pointed out that flat organization structures created positive requirements for managers to develop initiative and also to delegate decision-making capabilities to their subordinates, from a sheer lack of time. A large number of employees or subordinates precludes the superior's ability to direct the activities of his unit closely. Along the same lines, the smaller the size of the work group, the greater the job satisfaction.

Finally, job satisfaction and productivity were found to be related, although in a somewhat complex way. To relate these complex factors and findings in a systematic way, Herzberg's dual-factor theory of job satisfaction was presented. His theory considers job satisfaction and job dissatisfaction as being separate and distinct from each other and as being affected by separate sets of factors.

Factors associated with job satisfaction (and called *satisfiers*) are achievement, recognition, possibility of growth, advancement, the work itself, and responsibility. When present, these job content factors increase satisfaction; when absent, they decrease satisfaction until a *neutral* job attitude is attained.

Factors associated with job dissatisfaction (and called *dissatisfiers* or *hygiene factors*) are company policy and administration, technical competence of supervision, interpersonal relationships, work conditions, salary, status, and job security. When deficient, these *job context* factors increase dissatisfaction; when present, they decrease dissatisfaction until a *neutral* job attitude is attained.

STUDY AND REVIEW QUESTIONS

1. How do job attitudes affect job behavior?
2. Discuss the ways in which the production technologies (Chapter 4) require various levels of task specialization. Under which technology would you expect highest morale? Lowest morale? Why?
3. The chapter points out that *over*specialization is a more correct term by which to identify one cause of job dissatisfaction. How can overspecialization create dissatisfaction?
4. Under what conditions would task specialization create job satisfaction?
5. How important are organization size and shape in affecting job satisfaction?
6. Is job satisfaction related to job performance? Discuss.
7. Why, in the dual-factor theory, are satisfiers and dissatisfiers considered separate and distinct from each other?
8. Is salary level a satisfier or a dissatisfier? Why? Is a salary increase a satisfier or a dissatisfier? Why?
9. Use the dual-factor theory to analyze the effect of job scope on job satisfaction.
10. Use the dual-factor theory to predict probable job satisfaction/morale levels in a mass-production technology; in a craftsman production technology.

Chapter
7

Integrating Perspective: The Formal Organizational System

CHAPTER OBJECTIVES

1. To provide a brief overview of the major components of the formal organizational system.

2. To integrate these components in a coherent fashion, reminding the student that analysis is facilitated by the separation of components but that understanding of the overall system demands successive reintegration of its parts.

3. To illustrate how the components of the formal organizational system relate to and affect each other.

CHAPTER OUTLINE

Major Characteristics

The Causal Nature of Technology

A Craftsman's Formal Organizational System

Structure as Adaptation to External Environment

Interface: Formal Organization, the Individual, and Social System

---

In the last three chapters we have examined some major characteristics of the formal organizational system. At this point, reviewing some of our terms might be beneficial. Then we can begin to weave back together the separate strands into which we unraveled the fabric of the formal organizational system.

Major Characteristics

This system is called *formal* because the organization is an artificial mechanism by which prescribed objectives are attained. This term also allows us to distinguish the work-related structure from the purely personal interactions of the individuals of whom the organization is composed.

The device we have considered is an *organization* because its major formally prescribed segments are organized or related to each other in a rational fashion. Each of these components contributes to the efficient meeting of overall goals. In its simplest, classical terms the organization is a *goal*-directed entity employing a characteristic *technology* through a formal *structure* that integrates the specialized portions of the overall task toward the reaching of the firm's purpose. *Authority* relationships are created to ensure the effective performance of prescribed tasks.

We consider the organization to be a *system* because it is made up *internally* of specialized components that mutually affect each other as well as affecting the overall organization. From *external* considerations, the organization also exhibits the characteristics of a system; it interacts with, affects and is affected by its environment as it adapts to demand for the organization's output and to changes in expectations and restrictions. It translates requirements from the environment into activities and work by which the prescribed good or service is produced or delivered. Presented again, as Figure 7-1, is our model of the formal organizational system. We will

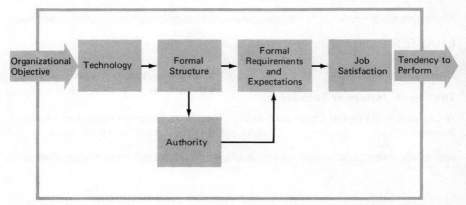

FIGURE 7-1   Systems framework for studying the formal organizational system.

continue to refer to it as we trace effects through the system and integrate the separate components.

When we examine the nature of the formal organizational system, we become aware of the primacy of the organization's goals and work requirements. But this important system is not sufficient to explain how and why people behave in organized settings as they do. The other major systems that also influence behavior—and that, in turn, are affected by behavior—will be the thrust of the ensuing chapters. For now, however, we will attempt to show more concretely how the parts of the formal organizational system may be summarized and integrated.

The Causal Nature of Technology

Probably the most important single factor in this system is the type of technology employed to achieve the purpose of the organization. Because work must be done in some way, the nature of the tools, knowledge, and task scope are critical because they are the primary determinants of what an individual—worker or manager—does within the organized setting. The craftsman employs a high level of skill and consequently is expected to make certain judgments and evaluations (decisions) based on professional experience or training. The formal requirements imposed on him and the expectations of him cannot be nearly as specific or rigorous as they might be for an assembly-line worker. Greater leeway or latitude must be given to the more highly trained and highly skilled craftsman. In essence a large number of decision-making rights and a large amount of authority are delegated to him. Because he can make decisions on day-to-day job factors, his superior must have a great degree of confidence in the craftsman's abilities.

One of the major reasons for this phenomenon is that the craftsman must operate within a unit-production or small batch production technology, in which scales of operations are not large enough to allow automated machinery to be used in place of the craftsman. There may be many different ways to do the job or numbers of variables affecting it ("beauty" or "proportion"), which are subjective and require a person with the appropriate skills.

For a more concrete understanding of technology as a major factor, we may consider an extended example of an organizational member whose everyday activities and relationships are established and constrained by his firm's basic technology. We could choose a representative from any of the five technologies, including an assembly-line worker (mass production), an aerospace engineer (advanced technology), or a college student (small batch?). We could well also consider the impact of technology on holders of managerial positions, but the operative worker is more clearly and directly affected by technology. A furniture designer will be considered as representing craft technology.

A Craftsman's Formal Organizational System

The duties of a furniture designer are dependent on the skill and performance of the craftsman. Subjective factors constitute major portions of his job. Evaluation of his performance is similarly subjective, because quality and quantity of production may be independent of each other.

To a furniture designer the "lines" of a wingback chair are extremely important. Even though there now exist automated drafting machines, the creating of pleasing proportions and designs resides with the highly skilled and knowledgeable designer. Formal requirements and expectations must be largely limited to the end product produced by the designer—the design and specifications for the piece of furniture assigned to him. There may be certain guidelines that the designer follows, but the criterion of the successful and high-performing designer is the quality and salability of his designs. If he chooses to ignore the guidelines, yet still produces outstanding designs, then few criticisms can be leveled at him.

The broad purview of authority to which he is subject must then be largely limited. The ability to be accountable for one's own activities is a large part of the particular craftsmanship we are considering. We might consequently expect considerable emphasis to be placed on the acceptance theory of authority.

Indeed, the formal structure of a unit of designers is a reflection of the unique capabilities, requirements, and technological processes that are part of this process. In other words, the design activities would probably not be divided up and assigned to individual specialists; a designer specializing in chair backs would probably not be assigned one portion of the design responsibility, while an arm specialist works on designing the appropriate type and style of arm for the chair, and a leg man contemplates the positioning, number, and composition of the legs of the chair. Rather, the overall design would probably be assigned to one person. He might well choose to consult spring specialists, of course, for their suggestions regarding whether or not to use a thinner cushion and whether or not a spring were available to give comfort even within a thinner cushion.

From the perspective of the dual-factor theory, we might expect that a person performing this type of highly responsible job would have many opportunities for achieving a high level of job satisfaction. Many of the satisfiers are present, such as the opportunity to achieve professional growth and recognition, enjoyment of the work itself, and the development of responsibility for the design of a complete chair.

Given these satisfactions, due as they are to the work and the technological characteristics of such a job, we expect increased involvement of the craftsman in his job, with a corresponding sense of professional accomplishment in doing a superior job. Because each designer is *not* an undifferentiated or homogeneous labor input, identity is not lost within the work group. Probably the greatest detriment to job satisfaction would be line management's lack of appreciation of the design function. Many engineers, too, suffer from this when cost and quality are traded off in their designs to the detriment of quality because of command decisions made by superiors.

While broad policy-making authority might be recognized by the craftsman as being the prerogative of his superiors, the "zone of indifference" of the craftsman is limited. The commands of his superior regarding job *context* matters, such as assignment of parking spaces, minimum hours of work, pay scale, salary structure, and so on, would rarely be questioned. Factors regarding the *content* of the work for which the craftsman is responsible would, however, fall on the periphery of or even outside the zone of indifference. Few specialists or craftsmen would be willing to modify practices that they have arrived at by trial and error after many years of experience or that are consistent with their training or profession, on the whim of an administrator.

In one engineering firm, administrative stipulations for less than "perfect" engineering designs (on the grounds that "the company cannot afford a perfect job") directly violated the high standards of the engineers involved. Rather than lowering their standards, the engineers simply worked harder to keep up the efficiency rating of the department ("production quota") *and* maintain their standards of performance. The authority of the administrator to influence their performance standards negatively was not accepted. Even though a number of engineers did resign under this pressure, those who remained found an effective way to subvert or disobey the command.

We can then readily see that the formal organizational system imposes continuing demands on the individual for behaviors of specified type, content, and duration. The behaviors so specified are activities that further the goals of the organization. They constitute jobs and departments. This is the rational or bureaucratic side of the organizational face.

Structure as Adaptation to External Environment

Because the technology employed by the organization is dictated by external or environmental factors, it makes sense to consider that the form of the organization, its structure, is also modified to an extent by different sets of demands from external sources. When we entertain the notion that an organization is oppressive or degrading to its members, stultifies creativity and independence, or rewards conformity rather than innovation, almost automatically we think in terms of the *bureaucratic* form of organization. If we consider the forms of authority in such an organization, we typically think of authoritarian superiors, many rules and procedures by which the work must be done, and vast spaces in buildings filled with people performing identical routine tasks.

We must recognize that this bureaucratic form is only one of several possible organizational forms. It requires—even demands—a stable environment, with almost completely know or certain information, stable demands for its product or service, and a fairly large demand for its output. If we have such an external environment, then and only then can we design an effective organization in which we have a "tall" organization structure, small spans of control, great specialization of task, little or no decentralization of authority, and a relative separation of worker and final output. Because of these peculiar conditions, the bureaucratic form of organization exists. Studies have even suggested that, given these specific characteristics of its environment, the bureaucratic form of organization is a most effective form.

But this is not to say that the bureaucratic form is the most effective under *all* conditions. Under conditions in which the external environment is "turbulent" or unstable, or in which the information necessary to the internal operations of the firm is uncertain or dynamic, great specialization of task and knowledge would clearly be ineffective. If the state of knowledge changes greatly with time, then no sooner would a job be completely set up or the machines programmed for a certain set of characteristics of work than they would be obsolete.

Aerospace firms, among others, developed new organizational forms to cope with their highly dynamic environments and rapidly changing technical inputs and high-technology outputs. They did this by creating temporary task forces, "programs" that bore striking resemblances to minicompanies with a single objective, far-ranging committee structures, and so on. The organizational members of necessity were given wider latitudes of authority discretion, even at relatively low levels. A superior manager, perhaps by being out of engineering for only a few years, had probably lost his familiarity with his technical specialization or had been bypassed by recent advances. Authority then was largely decentralized and delegated to relatively low managerial and operative levels. A superior may have formal authority granted by the organization, but his subordinates may exert influence upon *him* by virtue of their greater specialized knowledge. With relatively less specialization of task, and demand for complicated tasks to be accomplished, interdisciplinary teams of experts could be set up to work together, pool their knowledge, and attack an assignment far beyond the range of a single expert.

These types of tasks and assignments, then, mean that authority is far more likely to be based on acceptance rather than fear. Further, with wide-ranging assignments and far-flung co-workers on a temporary basis, the individual organizational member has far greater freedom than his bureaucratic counterpart. He must be held responsible for keeping up with his profession and the application of its new findings to practical problems. This cannot be programmed or established by quota, as the assembling of a stapler might be. Rather, the member of the newer forms of organization is usually allowed to have great latitude in deciding how and when he will perform his function. This requires a certain amount of identification with the problem, ability to see the overall aspects of the assignment and where everything "fits," and a high level of involvement in one's work. In such an organization formal requirements and expectations have to be modified to meet the requirements and expectations of professional members. And the question of job satisfaction assumes even more importance, in part because of the relatively small supply of potential members with the requisite skills.

The newer organizational forms modify or discard parts of the bureaucratic form that are inappropriate for a different technology and set of characteristics. Electronic Data Systems, of Dallas, carefully refrains from establishing job descriptions and authority restraints on managers. As a result, individual initiative creates new market opportunities for the company.

Interface: Formal Organization, the Individual, and Social System

The formal organizational system provides the framework within which people are to behave in prescribed ways. We noted earlier that human behavior is not a simple reflex reaction to a stimulus. The classical organizational "engineering" approach to the problem of individual differences and unpredictability was to design a job that would be done acceptably *regardless* of the characteristics of the individual performing this work. Specialization and routine work were direct results of this approach. But if the environment was not completely stable or predictable, the ability to design such a job was largely lost. With greatly increasing rates of change in knowledge and methods, decreasing reliance on established markets, greater environmental unpredictability and instability, newer approaches are required. These demand that greater knowledge about behavior be accumulated. Individual differences do exist, but how do they affect the organizations? Why do people in groups behave differently from isolated individuals? How can desired behaviors be encouraged and counterproductive behaviors be minimized? How can the organization fulfill a responsibility to be less restrictive and more aware of human (organizational members' and/or society's) needs?

A job can demand strict conformity or compliance to imposed standards simply through its "built-in" technological characteristics. Initiative can be quashed, and dependence be required by authority relationships and by the requirements of the way the organization's overall task is broken down. A job can be designed so that a person can make a difference in performance through initiative—or it can be designed to *exclude* such an unpredictable and uncontrollable contingency as individual contribution.

In Chapter 3 the major components of organizational behavior were identified as the formal organization, individual, and social systems. Having become familiar with the characteristics and processes of the formal organization, we may turn our attention to considerations of the two remaining systems. At the same time, Figure 7-2 reminds us that organizational behav-

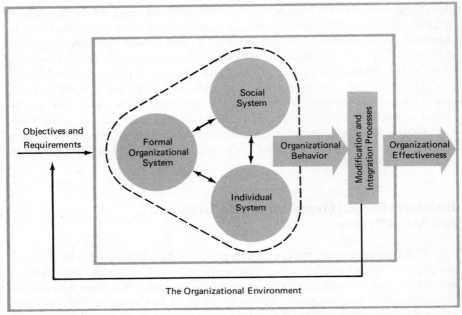

FIGURE 7-2   Systemic components of organizational behavior.

ior is the result of the interactions among all three major systems. We will study the portions of each system, one at a time, only for ease in understanding. Eventually the ways in which component affects component and system influences system must be considered.

In Section III the personal processes of the individual will be considered. We will investigate how and why a person behaves as he does within an organization. Differences in behavior may be traced to personality factors that predispose one to behave in certain identifiable patterns. Communication processes and the distinctly different ways in which people interpret their immediate environments will be considered. Finally, the complicated question of what initiates behavior and what affects rate or quality of behavior—motivation—completes the subject of the individual considered as a system.

Section IV brings us face to face with individuals in social systems, that is, in situations in which they relate and identify with others. The ways in which groups form, grow, and function are important because of the ways in which an individual's behavior is modified by group influence. A common type of group, the informal organization, composed of the unanticipated interactions and the shared sentiments of organizational members, exists within the formal organization and modifies the responses of its members to formal requirements and expectations. Questions of behaviors expected by others will be taken up as roles as well as the informal prestige (status) attached to formally prescribed and informally derived roles. Conflict and its resolution, especially between individual and system, will set the stage for an investigation of leadership as an activity and a goal-related social process.

We can see that the formal organizational system, requiring as it does the integration of work, technology, and performance, creates an environment within which people work and behave. Many of the behaviors they exhibit are directly dictated by the nature of the job they hold. These work characteristics create satisfactions and dissatisfactions, provide opportunities for interactions between people, create conflicts both within and between individuals, and establish informal patterns of behavior.

In the next section we will be considering some of the more important processes that are necessary to the understanding of the individual. The section we are now completing has been important because now we have a better idea of the reasons that the individual may be found in the organized setting. If we are to consider organizational behavior, we must recognize that people do *not* behave within organizations for *no* reason but that they meet expectations created by technology and work, *and also* by themselves, their peers, and other people. The dictates and the impact of the formal organizational system are constantly felt by the individual and the social system within organizations. Without the formal organizational system the individual and the social system could not exist within organizations. The interactions among these three systems, their mutual accommodations to each other, and their possible and potential conflicts will be discussed throughout the remainder of the text.

STUDY AND REVIEW QUESTIONS

1. In this chapter we considered the characteristics of the formal organizational system in which a craftsman might perform his duties. Discuss the characteristics of the formal organizational system of an organization in which a worker would be employed. In doing so, compare and contrast these characteristics which would be associated with the following technologies:
   a. Mass production.
   b. Advanced technology.
   c. Small batch.
   d. Continuous process technology.

2. Why are "formal requirements and expectations" of importance in the formal organizational system? How do they affect job satisfaction and performance?

3. "Probably the most important single factor in the formal organizational system is the type of technology employed." Discuss thoroughly the reasons for its importance and trace other factors in the system.

SECTION

III

THE INDIVIDUAL
AS A SYSTEM

Chapter

8

Insights from Personality Theory and Development

CHAPTER OBJECTIVES

1. To develop an overall framework with which to understand more nearly the extent of behavioral differences between individuals.

2. To gain understanding of the ways in which behavioral differences develop in individuals.

3. To review theories of personality and show how they may be applied to the analysis and prediction of behavior.

4. To show the direct connection between groups of related major personality traits and behavioral tendencies in organized settings.

CHAPTER OUTLINE

Why Personality?

Personality Development
Heredity and Environment
Culture and Personality Development
Personality Development: A
 Psychoanalytic View

Theories of Personality
The Influence of Surface Factors
Personality Influences from Within
Personality Defenses

Relating Surface and Source Traits to
 Behavior

Personality and Behavior
Achievement Motives
Power Needs
Affiliation Needs
Manipulation Needs: The Machiavellians

**Personality and Organizational
Behavior**

In the last several chapters we have seen that the organizational system generates and maintains the required behaviors of its members. These behaviors may often be formalized as jobs and attendant duties. Technological characteristics and demands of particular types of jobs have different work-related effects on people. We might wonder, for instance, why—if assembly-line work is demeaning and boring—*some* people say that they *enjoy* that type of work? And why do some craftsmen claim frustration and dissatisfaction with their jobs, when the majority of their fellow craftsmen report being satisfied?

"That's easy!" we might exclaim. "People are just different." But why? And how? And how do these differences cause people to behave differently from others? How do people *get* to be different from each other? As a matter of fact, how do they get to be who they are?

To answer these types of questions, we need to understand the major determinants of *individual* behavior—the processes that make people behave in unique patterns. This section of chapters will delve into four important areas: personality, communication, perception, and motivation. The areas are related as indicated in Figure 8-1. We can see that central to the individual system is the concept of "individual needs and expectations," a theme that underlies each of this system's components and mutual interactions.

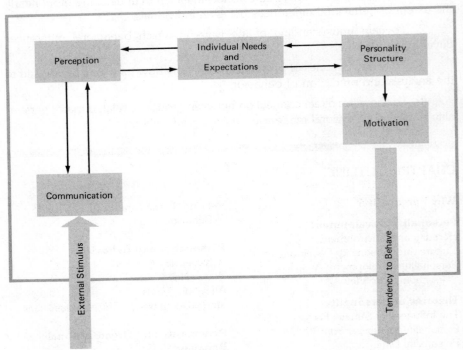

FIGURE 8-1   The individual system.

Why Personality?

Understanding individual behavior requires that we know something about the influences that tend to make a person behave in a particular situation. This calls for the suspension (for the moment) of the rational–economic model of human behavior; we cannot continue to assume away those factors other than the ones by which we might calculate the benefits and costs of various alternative choices in order to decide how to behave. Haven't we all shaken our heads in dismay or consternation at another's behavior and wondered out loud why in the world he acted that way? An executive's decision to leave a highly promising career in order to till the soil of a small farm in a rural community might not make *economic* sense, when the expected incomes for the choices are compared. It might be most sensible when other factors are considered.

These patterns of individual differences are the substance of the study of personality theory and development. Naturally when we hear the term *personality*, we jump to the conclusion that we might be considering only such things as why we like another or that we are contemplating the acquisition or display of social graces. Isn't a pleasing personality a major criterion by which we select or reject potential friends? Personality is much more than these.

Personality is "an individual's characteristics and ways of behaving which are organized in such a way that they reflect the unique adjustments he makes to his environment."[1] Further, these behaviors and adaptations that go to make up one's personality are relatively stable over time. Any one individual's behavior will certainly differ from one situation to another, but there will be some consistent pattern or group of characteristics that will identify the behavior pattern as uniquely his.[2]

We observe and make inferences about how our colleagues and acquaintances behave, thereby gaining some rather practical information. Often behaviors that recur can be grouped together and labeled as specific personality characteristics. Through this process we are apt to become more knowledgeable about the inner workings of another individual. We can then much more confidently predict how he might react in a particular situation. This provides us with a handy method by which we can gather our observations of another, group them in a manner acceptable to us, simplify them, and predict how the other will act. After all, we probably have all experienced this development of expectations. The process is even more noticeable when we are disappointed by what another does, while thinking, "That's just not like him."

A basic understanding of personality and how it develops is of direct importance to organizational behavior. Personality characteristics demonstrate the broad patterns of ways in which we tend to react and behave. If we

[1]Stanley K. Fitch, *Insights into Human Behavior* (Boston: Holbrook Press, 1970), p. 158.
[2]David F. Wrench and Chris Wrench, *Psychology: A Social Approach*, 2nd Ed. (New York: McGraw-Hill, 1973), p. 169.

know that a candidate for a managerial position is shy and unsure of himself, tends to be submissive and conforming, and lacks initiative (all of which are personality characteristics), we might very well draw some direct conclusions about his future performance in a position that demands confidence, initiative, and the capacity to influence others. Certainly an antisocial and reticent person would probably not make a very good outside salesman.

Even while personality is a stable pattern of characteristics and behaviors, we know that personality is constantly developing and changing. Your present personality has changed dramatically since infancy. How does personality originate and develop? What are some of the influences that make personalities develop in certain paths and certain patterns?

Personality Development

Which is the more important in setting the state for determining which behavioral characteristics you will display, your heredity or the environment in which you are reared? Given that your hereditary and environmental background are important, through which distinctive stages will your personality progress?

Heredity and Environment

The relative effects of heredity and environment comprise an extremely old argument in personality theory. Certain characteristics are inherited from one's parents. At conception, each parent normally contributes twenty-three chromosomes. These chromosomes contain thousands of genes, which seem to be the transmitters of traits. Even separate children of the same parents do not have identical genetic makeups. Only identical twins, who develop from a single fertilized ovum, possess the same pattern of genes.[3]

Physical attributes may be inherited. As a matter of fact, we expect this to happen. We are usually prepared to proclaim that a newborn baby "has" his father's ears, his mother's mouth, and so on. A proud grandmother might attribute personality characteristics or behaviors to inheritance, noting that the child is unusually active or aggressive, "just like his father was." A classification of essential characteristics inherited (present at birth) by all humans is as follows:

1. Physical structure (how tall or short one is, whether one has a long or short nose, large or small feet—briefly, how one is put together).
2. Reflexes (direct responses to stimuli, such as withdrawing from a pin prick, blinking when something approaches the eye).

[3]Gerald L. Hershey and James O. Lugo, *Living Psychology: An Experiential Approach* (New York: Macmillan, 1970), pp. 240, 241.

3. Innate drives (impulses to act based on physiological tensions; but these must be linked through learning with activities which will reduce the tensions).
4. Intelligence (the capacity to learn, to modify responses).
5. Temperament (patterned and recurrent responses associated with basic emotional makeup—for example, phlegmatic, excitable, or lethargic).[4]

The effect of environment, we might intuitively feel, is quite strong. "Knowledge, skill, and language are obviously acquired and represent important modifications of behavior. Learned modifications in behavior are not passed on to children, they must be acquired by them through their own personal experience."[5]

Even further, perhaps as a result of training (or could we argue that an inborn tendency steered him to seek this type of training?), we might expect a mathematician or an engineer to be highly analytical and rather objective in his relationships with others. If these personality characteristics were acquired as a result of intellectual and analytical training, obviously environment was extremely important in the development of this trait.

Another type of influence, although less dramatic, is the impact on behavior of one's endocrine glands. Should the thyroid gland be underactive, one becomes tired, sluggish, and unable to concentrate. If it overfunctions, then one becomes restless, irritable, and prone to excessive worry. Further, hunger or tiredness seems to *create* irritability and lack of cooperation, whereas rest and adequate nutrition tend to make people more congenial and generous.[6] Body functions, determined completely neither by heredity nor environment, also affect behavior tendencies.

The argument over which is more important in determining personality—heredity or environment—is probably moot. In comparison with other people, a man who makes a hobby of lifting weights is strong because of environmental factors—but is quite weak, when compared to an elephant, because of *heredity*.[7] The conflict between the two positions may be resolved if we recognize that heredity and environment affect personality development not only separately but jointly; they must interact to produce any meaningful personality characteristic. The complex set of genes with which we are endowed at birth provide for our *potential* development in physical and psychological terms. Heredity may then be considered to set the limits, whereas the full potential of a person is achieved or not achieved according to the demands and requirements of his social *environment*.[8]

---

[4]Kimball Young and Raymond W. Mack, *Systematic Sociology: Text and Readings,* 2nd Ed. (New York: American, 1962), p. 120.
[5]Norman R. F. Maier, *Psychology in Industrial Organizations,* 4th Ed. (Boston: Houghton Mifflin, 1973), p. 25.
[6]Ibid., pp. 250, 251.
[7]Wrench and Wrench, p. 18.
[8]Hershey and Lugo, p. 240.

Culture and Personality Development

One of the important determinants of personality and personality development is the *culture* within which one is brought up, an environmental influence. Culture is the complex of "those beliefs, values, and techniques for dealing with the environment which are *shared* among contemporaries and transmitted by one generation to the next."[9]

Each culture requires *acceptance* and *conformity* from its members, or the culture would eventually cease to exist from lack of being transmitted to successive generations. There are several ways of making sure that members comply with the dictates of the culture. Such socialization can take place through the early training given to the young of a culture, through mores (required ways of behaving, enforced by laws), and through informal pressures to obey folkways (expected or "proper" ways of behaving).[10]

For example, the Zuñi Indian culture of the United States Southwest has a great effect on the personality development of its members. Kluckhohn[11] studied white and Zuñi babies at birth, noting that there were no apparent differences among them; both sets were very active. When he observed them again two years later, the Zuñi babies displayed much less activity than the white babies. This he traced to the culture of the Zuñis. They emphasized living lives that were peaceful, calm, and satisfied. On the other hand, the white mothers generally *encouraged* and *rewarded* activity. The Zuñi babies probably became more passive under the influence of rewards and punishment from their mothers when the babies displayed behavior (activity or passiveness) that was in accord with the dictates of Zuñi culture.

This type of training through reward or punishment eventually results in the transmitting of one's culture from generation to generation. As a result, the culture is perpetuated and behavior patterns are set. That culture actually makes a significant difference in behavior patterns is illustrated by the studies of Benedict.[12] She also studied the Zuñis. She found that they were quiet, dignified, reserved, and restrained. Group considerations took precedence over individualism. Very little conflict existed among individuals. Kindness, consideration, and respect were the hallmarks of the relationships between Zuñis. In addition, there was a lack of competition, aggression, and even leadership. Zuñis believed in moderation in all things. Diet and other factors did not create these behavior patterns. The cultural patterns of the Zuñis were in great contrast to the violence and aggression of the surround-

[9]James D. Thompson and Donald R. Van Houten, *The Behavioral Sciences: An Interpretation* (Reading, Mass.: Addison-Wesley, 1970), p. 22.

[10]Fitch, pp. 164, 165.

[11]Clyde Kluckhohn and H. A. Murray, "Personality Formation: The Determinants," in *Personality in Nature, Society and Culture* ed. by C. Kluckhohn and H. A. Murray (New York: Knopf, 1948), cited in Fitch, pp. 166, 167.

[12]Ruth Benedict, *Patterns of Culture* (New York: Houghton Mifflin, 1934), cited in Kolasa, pp. 308, 309.

ing Indian groups who had dietary resources and other factors common to those of the Zuñis.

The Kwakiutl Indians of the Pacific Northwest were an example of a culture quite different from that of the Zuñis. The Kwakiutl were highly individualistic, and fierce competition was displayed in almost every conceivable way. They were obsessed with the amassing of material wealth and also exhibited an extreme degree of competition in outdistancing rivals in wealth. At the same time, merely increasing one's wealth was not enough. For high status, one had to give away more of his own wealth than did his neighbor or else destroy it.[13]

Another tribe studied by Benedict was the Dobu, who lived on an island off the coast of eastern New Guinea. They were a people characterized by extreme jealousy, resentment, and suspicion. The world to them was an evil place. As a result, they felt that any means were justified in getting ahead.[14] Hostility and aggression, secrecy and treachery, and extreme competition were characteristic of both males and females in their everyday activities. One who schemed and cheated, humiliated others, and exalted himself at the expense of another was held in high esteem.[15]

These primitive societies show quite clearly the effects of culture on behaviors. A few studies have even been done on major complex societies, such as our own. The Russian Research Center at Harvard University, in an attempt to discover Soviet behavioral patterns, studied Russian refugees in Western Europe.[16] Compared to Americans:

The Russians showed a great need for interpersonal face-to-face relationships without, however, undue concern for the opinions of others. They were more emotional and more willing to express their emotions. They had fewer defense mechanisms. Americans may be concerned about being liked, but the Russians expected to receive moral responses from the group (loyalty, sincerity, and respect). Autonomy and achievement are part of American attitudes but are not present in the Russian scheme of things.[17]

Another study that outlined one writer's view of the characteristics of American personality was that of Williams.[18] As we might expect, these characteristics included "trends to personal achievement through activity and work, humanitarianism with a moral orientation, and progress toward material comfort through greater efficiency and practicality."[19]

The attitudes and values that are encouraged within a particular culture are transmitted to the young. In this way the basic qualities of the culture are

[13]Kolasa, p. 308.

[14]Benedict, cited in Fitch, p. 166.

[15]Benedict, cited in Kolasa, pp. 308, 309.

[16]R. Bauer, A. Inkeles, and C. Kluckhohn, *How the Soviet System Works* (Cambridge, Mass.: Harvard University Press, 1957), cited in Kolasa, pp. 310, 311.

[17]Kolasa, p. 310.

[18]R. Williams, *American Society: A Sociological Interpretation* (New York: Knopf, 1951), cited in Kolasa, p. 311.

[19]Kolasa, p. 311.

preserved for generations. Children's stories in public school textbooks are a prime example of perpetuating cultural values by illustrating approved (or disapproved) behavior.

Similar stories can be found in many countries, with varying emphasis. In one country a public school textbook contained a story about children building a boat; the construction of the boat was emphasized, with the details of making it so it wouldn't tip over or sink—emphasizing accomplishment and success through examples. Another country's textbooks took the same story but changed the emphasis: the fun the children had as they worked on the boat and sailed it—emphasizing social skills. Finally, a third country's textbooks showed a boy who persuaded other children to undertake the task and who told them what to do—emphasizing dominance and influence.[20]

Interestingly enough, these analyses were found to be good predictors of rate of economic growth for the countries studied, showing that transmitted cultural values can create behaviors.[21]

Personality Development: A Psychoanalytic View

The first to trace the development of personality from birth to adulthood was Sigmund Freud. Freud's sequence parallels the states of sexual development. The emphasis Freud placed on the influences encountered in early childhood are especially meaningful, because he felt that "the child was father to the man."[22] The final configuration of one's personality is determined or limited by the underlying and basic initial components of the personality, on which are based modifications and additions with age. Eventually the personality ceases changing in major ways and assumes a rather stable configuration. The distinct stages in this sequence are the oral, anal, phallic, and latent stages.

The Oral Stage

The oral stage occurs from birth until the individual is approximately one year old. The oral sensory stage is important, because the types of oral experiences the child encounters can strongly determine the early development of personality as well as the fully developed personality of the adult. The mouth, and especially the sucking reflex, is extremely important here because the infant uses the reflex in feeding.

Trust develops at the oral stage if hunger is quickly satisfied by a mother on whom the infant can rely. The trust so developed can then be ascribed to

[20]David C. McClelland and T. George Harris, "To Know Why Men Do What They Do," *Psychology Today* (January 1971) p. 39.

[21]Ibid., pp. 39, 70, 71.

[22]Ledford J. Bischof, *Interpreting Personality Theories*, 2nd Ed. (New York: Harper &Row, 1970), p. 43.

others. If trust is not developed at this basic level, anxiety results toward the mother and other people in general.[23] (See Table 8-1.)

The Anal Stage

The anal stage is primarily concerned with toilet training, between eighteen months and three years of age. Overly strict toilet training can yield compulsions toward excessive tidiness and orderliness. Other direct results of the anal stage seem to be generosity, masochism, destructiveness, and uncontrolled temper tantrums. Overly strict toilet training creates feelings of being controlled by others and of having no voice in one's own fate. Training that is not too strict, on the other hand, creates feelings of autonomy and some degree of power over one's own future.

The Genital Stage

Occurring between three and six years of age is the genital stage. What the child must learn is the development of satisfactory attitudes toward his own and the opposite sex. The so-called Oedipus complex occurs in this stage. This is a reflection of Freud's belief that a child both loves and hates his parents, with these feelings being strongest toward the parent of the same sex as the child. If the Oedipus complex is not successfully resolved, severe anxiety and guilt feelings may impact normal personality development.

The Latency Period

Finally, the latency period follows the phallic phase, lasting until puberty. In this stage sexual interest and behavior declines, with (for example) boys preferring to be with boys and being very little interested in girls. Sharing and cooperation are learned through what might be called the "gang" aspect of this period.

Erikson extended the basic work of Freud into eight stages. Unlike Freud, Erikson did not believe that personality cannot be changed after childhood. He felt that personality was still flexible throughout the adult years. However, he did feel that if the individual failed to adapt adequately to the *requirements* of each of these stages, then full personality development would be made correspondingly more difficult, stressful, and anxiety-filled.

Table 8-1 details the stages of Erikson's personality development, showing how the first four are compatible with Freud's stages and illustrating how success or failure at any of the eight stages affects the personality. It is easy to see, for example, how failure in the second period (inadequacy, self-doubt)

[23]This analysis and the following analysis of Freud's psychoanalytic theory of personality development are based on Fitch, pp. 180–184.

TABLE 8-1   Erickson's Stages of Personality Development

Erickson's Stage	Compares with Freud's Stage	Age	Success in Meeting Requirements of Stage Brings:	Failure to Meet Requirements of Stage Brings:
1. Early Infancy	Oral	birth to about one year	*Basic Trust* Result of affection and gratification of needs, mutual recognition.	*vs.* *Mistrust* Result of consistent abuse, neglect, deprivation of love; too early or hard weaning, autistic isolation.
2. Later Infancy	Anal	about ages one to three years	*Autonomy* Child views self as person in his own right apart from parents but still dependent.	*vs.* *Shame and Doubt* Feels inadequate, doubts self, curtails learning basic skills like walking, talking, wants to "hide" inadequacies.
3. Early Childhood	Genital	about ages four to five years	*Initiative* Lively imagination, vigorous reality testing, imitates adults, anticipates roles.	*vs.* *Guilt* Lacks spontaneity, infantile jealousy, "castration complex," suspicious, evasive, role inhibition.
4. Middle Childhood	Latency	about ages six to eleven years	*Industry* Has sense of duty and accomplishment, develops scholastic and social competencies, undertakes real tasks, puts fantasy and play in better perspective, learns world of tools, task identification.	*vs.* *Inferiority* Poor work habits, avoids strong competition, feels doomed to mediocrity, lull before the storms of puberty, may conform as slavish behavior, sense of futility.
5. Puberty and Adolescence	—	about ages twelve to twenty years	*Ego Identity* Temporal perspective. Self-certain. Role experimenter	*vs.* *Role Confusion* Time confusion. Self-conscious. Role fixation.

			Work paralysis. Bisexual confusion. Authority confusion. Value confusion.
	Apprenticeship. Sexual polarization. Leader–followership. Ideological commitment.		
6. Early Adulthood	*Intimacy* Capacity to commit self to others, *Lieben und Arbeiten*—"to love and to work."	*vs.*	*Isolation* Avoids intimacy, "character problems," promiscuous behavior; repudiates, isolates, destroys seemingly dangerous forces.
7. Middle Adulthood	*Generativity* Productive and creative for self and others, parental pride and pleasure, mature, enriches life, establishes and guides next generation.	*vs.*	*Stagnation* Egocentric, nonproductive, early invalidism, excessive self-love, personal impoverishment, self-indulgence.
8. Late Adulthood	*Integrity* Appreciates continuity of past, present, and future, acceptance of life cycle and life style, has learned to cooperate with inevitabilities of life, "state or quality of being complete, undivided, or unbroken; entirety" (Webster's Dictionary); "death loses its sting."	*vs.*	*Despair* Time is too short; finds no meaning in human existence, has lost faith in self and others, wants second chance at life cycle with more advantages, no feeling of world order or spiritual sense, "fear of death."

SOURCE: Adapted from Bischof, op. cit., pp. 578–580.

has a direct effect on successive stages. For instance, an unsuccessful second stage hinders the chance of successfully meeting the sixth stage (early adulthood) and achieving ability to attain intimacy.[24]

Finally, we must reconsider Argyris's contention that, in maturing, individuals tend to develop

- From being passive to a state of increasing activity.
- From dependence on others to being independent.
- From having only a few ways to behave to possessing many behavioral alternatives.
- From having shallow or passing interests to having deeper interests.
- From having short time perspective to having a much longer time perspective.
- From being in a subordinate position to aspiring to occupy an equal or superordinate position.
- From lack of awareness of self to an awareness of and control over self.[25]

From the preceding discussions of the development of personality, we can see that personality is a complex concept that reflects many influences both within and outside of the individual. Personality progresses through identifiable stages and never really stops developing. We can, however, examine personality at any point in time within its developmental sequence in order to compare and contrast individual personalities. We can also do this to show more effectively some of the more important components of personality.

Theories of Personality

If you were asked to describe the personality of a close friend, you might well describe him as being athletic, considerate, well-adjusted, realistic, and extroverted and as seeing himself as a modern-day Don Juan. Each of these descriptions reflects a different component of or approach to the study of personality. In the following sections we will take a closer look at how these components are analyzed and described. For the moment, we can recognize that important implications for personality are contained in the consideration of personality traits and types, self-concept, body type, and psychoanalytic personality theories, Lewin's path–goal concept, and psychological defenses.

The structure or composition of personality comes from three areas: the external environment, factors unique or internal to the person himself, and the relationship (adjustment) of inner factors to the external environment.[26]

---

[24]Bischof, pp. 576–580.

[25]Adapted from Chris Argyris, *Personality and Organization: The Conflict Between System and the Individual* (New York: Harper & Row, 1957), p. 50.

[26]Another set of determinants, roughly analogous to this, are constitutional, group membership, role, and situational factors. See Clyde Kluckhohn and Henry A. Murray,

One's internal factors consist of his biological, physiological, and inherent psychological processes. These are considered internal determinants in contrast with external environmental forces.

Personality-shaping influences from the external environment are those that surround the individual, exerting pressures to incorporate attitudes, values, or behaviors of others. Culture is one such external environmental force.

The adjustment processes through which the individual relates to external pressures is the third determinant of personality structure. This provides opportunities for successfully integrating internal and external pressures.

The Influence of Surface Factors

A direct way of investigating personality is to group and classify one's behaviors, rating them by the frequency with which they recur. Careful consideration of these activities allows us to make rather good conclusions or inferences about the personality that is expressed in the behaviors. We pointed out earlier in the chapter that one of the two components of personality is an individual's typical ways of behaving; the other is the individual's characteristics.

Personality traits and types are useful in describing stable behavior patterns. They provide rather concrete insights into one's underlying personality processes by being directly and readily observed and thus are called *surface factors*.

Traits

One of the major ways of attempting to measure or discern personality is through the trait approach. A trait can be simply defined as an action or behavior that is consistently exhibited.[27] Because it occurs in diverse settings, we might consider any trait to be a disposition or a tendency to behave in a particular way.[28] For example, a person is observed in a number of different situations, and he always lets someone else take the initiative in deciding what to do. We might conclude that this tendency is a consistent personality element for that person and so qualifies as a personality trait. We can even name it with a term that describes the behavior, such as *submissiveness*.[29] Appropriately designed personality tests allow the degree of submissiveness (or any other trait) exhibited by an individual to be measured. This can be compared with the "normal" pattern exhibited by large numbers of other individuals.

"Personality Formation: The Determinants," in *Personality in Nature, Society, and Culture*, 2nd Ed., ed. by Clyde Kluckhohn and Henry A. Murray (New York: Knopf, 1967), p. 56.

[27] Hershey and Lugo, p. 252.

[28] Nathan Brody, *Personality: Research and Theory* (New York: Academic Press, 1972), p. 7.

[29] Richard S. Lazarus, *Personality and Adjustment* (Englewood Cliffs, N.J.: Prentice-Hall, 1963), p. 54.

To be most useful, we can think of traits as being divided into small increments along a scale. Then we can consider individuals, one of whom exhibits *more* submissiveness than another. Extending this reasoning, still another person might not display a clear-cut tendency either to be or not to be submissive. If we consider that the opposite of submissiveness is the tendency to be *domineering,* such an individual would probably fall at the neutral point of a scale representing domineering–submissive tendencies.

The trait approach offers a number of advantages in describing personality and its reflection in behavior. We can describe personality fairly effectively through the use of traits such as impulsiveness–seriousness, uninhibited–restrained, dependent–self-reliant, and shrewd–naïve.

Types

Hippocrates, 2,400 years ago, attempted to characterize people and to explain characteristic behaviors by relating personality characteristics to the "humors" or fluids of the body. These humors, when mixed in proper proportions, constituted health; disease resulted from improper proportions. The more enduring, but relatively minor, imbalances were assumed to yield four corresponding types of temperament. Thus a "melancholic" person exhibited his characteristic sad behavior because of an excess of black bile. Sanguineness (cheerfulness, vigor) was attributed to the effect of yellow bile. Choleric (inclined to anger, easily irritated) people received this temperament from the influence of red bile (blood), and phlegmatic (sluggish in temperament, not easily excited) ones were influenced by white bile (phlegm).[30] This attempt at classifying people into "types" by their characteristic behaviors and to attribute these behaviors to underlying personality traits received wide distribution.

When traits are organized into general personality factors, we begin to speak of personality *types.* A person with a certain personality *type* exhibits a common set of *traits.* This identifiable pattern of traits can then be used to classify personalities into common categories or types.

Freud identified three adult personality types, which display tendencies characteristic of one or more of the developmental stages. These types occur from failure to progress normally through the Freudian stages because of the traumatic experiences encountered. The *oral* type exhibits dependent attitudes toward others.

He continues to seek sustenance, or feeding, from others, and, depending on when during the oral stage fixation occurred, is either optimistic, immature, and trusting, or pessimistic, suspicious, and sarcastic about the prospects of continuing support. The *anal* type is also characterized by two substages, the first identified by outbursts of aggression, sloppiness, and petulance, the second associated with obstinacy, orderliness, and parsimoniousness. The *phallic* type is characterized by

[30]Donald W. MacKinnon, "The Structure of Personality," in *Personality and the Behavior Disorders,* Vol. 1, ed. by J. McV. Hunt (New York: Ronald Press, 1944), p. 8.

an adolescent immaturity in which the predominant conflicts are heterosexual, stemming from the Oedipus Complex and the anxieties associated with it. The phallic period is stormy, with sharp emotional swings and preoccupation with love object choices. [31]

Introverted and Extroverted Types

Another, more common type theory is Jung's introversion–extroversion schema. A person who has few friends, avoids social contacts, and rarely speaks to others unless they speak to him first might be characterized as being introverted or withdrawn. On the other hand, a person who is interested in people and expresses his feelings and thoughts openly would probably be characterized as very expressive or extroverted.[32] Other traits associated with the introvert are his being "quiet, retiring, enjoying solitude, and the extrovert being friendly, enjoying interaction with others, craving excitement, and disliking solitude."[33]

Besides these descriptive traits, the dynamics of the extrovert's and the introvert's behavior patterns can be analyzed. The decisions and actions of the extrovert are determined mainly by objective considerations rather than by subjective, personal feelings. His attention and interest are focused on the task at hand and his immediate surroundings; this might indicate his action orientation and realistic attitude.

The introvert, by contrast, is more of an inward-directed, thoughtful person. His actions are guided by his own philosophy or ideas rather than by another's. He tends to be rather rigid or inflexible, preferring subjective evaluations and dominance of his own values.[34]

Body Type

Sheldon's conception of physical characteristics as an indicator of personality must be considered as a personality type theory of importance if only for its analytical research base. Julius Caesar, in Shakespeare's play, notes that Cassius has a "lean and hungry look" and suspects that Cassius thinks too much and might perhaps be overly ambitious or untrustworthy. Later, Cassius also shows a similar tendency to judge personality by body type by expressing his conviction that fat men are inherently good-natured. Following their example, Sheldon[35] developed a theory that relates body form and personality.

The three body types he identified are the endomorph (inclined toward fatness), the mesomorph (tends to be muscular), and the ectomorph (ten-

---

[31]Ibid., p. 57.
[32]Hershey and Lugo, p. 252.
[33]Thompson and Van Houten, p. 49.
[34]Robert M. Fulmer, *The New Management* (New York: Macmillan, 1974), p. 115.
[35]William Sheldon, *The Varieties of Human Physique: An Introduction to Constitutional Psychology* (New York: Harper & Row, 1940), and *The Varieties of Temperament: A Psychology of Constitutional Differences* (New York: Harper & Row, 1942).

dency toward thinness and fragility). As a result of classifying body types into three ideal structures and recognizing that almost all people are *combinations* of these three, Sheldon was able to devise an index by which one's body structure could be classified. He used a numerical rating system by which to indicate the amounts of variation there are in body–behavior types, with the numbers ranging from an absolute minimum (1) to the absolute maximum (7). In this system, the endomorphic figure is always given first, the mesomorphic figure is always given second, and the ectomorphic figure is always given last. So the numbers 1-1-7 would be the rating of a person low in endomorphism, low in mesomorphism, and extremely high in ectomorphism.

Since he called his primary body classifications "somatotypes," this process of numerically rating or classifying body type is called somatotyping. Table 8-2 summarizes the major relationships found in Sheldon's theory of personality.

Sheldon composed his personality theory on the correlation between his somatotypes and personality types. The three basic personality types that he found were each made up of a cluster of twenty specific traits. In arriving at a personality rating, he again used the 1–7 scheme.

Personality Influences from Within

These trait and type theories we have discussed point out the external environmental influences on personality and behavior. They are external in that they comprise characteristics that affect the personality from extramental or extracognitive sources. To now consider the factors that influence personality from within, those that develop and operate in the form of intensely personal and subjective elements, we must turn back to Freud, to the concept of self and to field theory.

Freud's Psychoanalytic Personality Theory

Freud's greatest contribution to personality theory was his concept of the unconscious. He thought that, rather than being fully in rational control of all behavior, all individuals are often influenced by unconscious factors.[36] His primary assumption was that "man came into the world at birth equipped with certain instincts," unlearned, unacquired, and inherent behaviors. These he reduced to two ultimate instincts: the instinct for love or life and the instinct for death or destruction.[37]

His personality theory is based on the mechanisms through which these instincts operate and influence conscious behavior. He thought, first of all, that personality must basically be a hedonistic or pleasure-seeking vehicle.

[36]Kolasa, p. 243.
[37]Bischof, pp. 41, 42.

TABLE 8-2   Summary of Sheldon's Body-Type Personality Theory

Behavioral Characteristic	Sheldon's Somatotypes		
	Endomorph (fat)	*Mesomorph* (muscular)	*Ectomorph* (thin)
Posture and movement	Relaxed	Assertive	Restrained
Physical attitude	Comfort	Adventure	Alert, controlled
Reaction time	Slow	Fast, energetic	Overly fast
Major needs	Eating and socialization	Exercise and domination, risk	Privacy and mental overintensity
Relationships with people	Loves people	Loves competition, even socially	Dislikes people
Temperament	Even-tempered, complacent, tolerant	Ruthless, unrestrained, noisy	Unpredictable because of secrecy
Mental and decision processes	Majority rules	Stereotyped thinking	Highly analytical
Effect of alcohol*	Relaxed and happy	Assertive and aggressive	Resistant
When troubled, needs . . .*	People (no secrets or private sorrows)	Action to remedy the problem	Solitude, withdrawal
Orientation is toward . . .	Childhood and family relationships; sensitive and generous	Goals and activities of youth; competitive and purposeful.	Later periods of life; "old before his time"

*Key Characteristics

SOURCE: Adapted from Ledford J. Bischof, *Interpreting Personality Theories*, 2nd ed. (New York: Harper & Row, Publishers, 1970), pp. 418–429.

At the basic personality level is the *id*. The id serves as the repository for the deep-seated instincts, seeking pleasure insatiably in an undisciplined and selfish manner. At the same time, it serves as the ultimate source of energy for man's existence and "gives man his will to continue."[38] If the id were to be left to its own devices, without control, it would probably destroy itself.

The *ego* is the reality-oriented part of the human personality. It directs and polices the energy of the id toward realistic fulfillment. It is an extension of the id, and it is not independent of it. The ego may be considered to be the psychological part of man's personality, while the id might be considered the organic part of man's personality.[39] The more the ego permits the id its satisfactions, within the bounds of reality, the happier we seem to be.

Last to develop in Freud's concept of the personality is the *superego*. This might loosely be considered the conscience. The superego compares dramatically with the ego; the ego is realistic, whereas the superego is idealistic. It is the ethical and moral arm of the personality and is internalized from the standards of society that it accepts. Its goal is perfection rather than pleasure, so it serves as a "censor."

These three separate personality characteristics are not separate or distinct entities; although each has its own function, it can never exist alone. One of the three might well dominate, yielding some extreme forms of personality function. An overdeveloped superego would probably generate strong feelings of guilt or shame and would result in an underdeveloped ego; the ego would have failed to develop because of the small amount of control the individual has over his relations with the real world. Because of this, the id would probably be effectively sealed up. A danger in this personality pattern is the possibility of a "personality explosion," in which the id erupts. In the eruption, the fundamental forces bottled up in the id (hostility, aggression, or sex) are indulged in a spree.[40]

An underdeveloped superego would characterize the individual who has very few morals or values. The ability of the superego to serve as an effective conscience over the id would be very weak, so that id-based impulses might easily be acted on without much concern for their effects on society.[41]

The Concept of Self

Even while the Freudian personality segments struggle to maintain a balance, the idea of *personality expectations* must be considered. After all, we would hardly anticipate that a self-proclaimed "lady's man" would suddenly swear off dating. We tend to act in ways consistent with our own *image* of who or what we are. This personality theory, which is organized around the

[38]Ibid.
[39]Bischof, p. 40.
[40]Hershey and Lugo, pp. 248, 249.
[41]Ibid.

concept of self, is one in which personality and behavior are largely *determined by* the individual. In other theories, the individual is only the medium through which behavior is elicited after having been acted on by elements over which he has little or no control. According to Rogers, the major proponent of the self-concept, "The best vantage point for understanding behavior is from the internal frame of reference of the individual himself."[42] To Rogers, the individual is the center of experience. To understand his behavior, one must understand how another views his experiences and what sort of image he has of himself. His self-concept "constitutes the person's picture of who he is and who he is in the process of becoming. It is generally regarded as having two components: a private picture or estimate of the self, plus a view of the self which is reflected in the way others behave toward the person."[43]

Experiences are encountered and the self-concept is modified or extended as a result of relationships with others. The ideas of our self are then organized into the self-concept.[44] "Thus, in our discovery of the environment and in our realization that other people exist and have attitudes which affect us, we begin to become persons."[45]

The "personal" self is a result of the experiences we have undergone, including all those characteristics and qualities by which we are distinguished from all other individuals. It also comprises all that we have "learned and accepted as a part of ourself. It also includes all the repressed experiences or unconscious motivations which affect our behavior in ways of which we are unaware. From this internal vantage point we idealize all the various roles we play in life; that is, we assume the characteristics or qualities each one of us would like to think he represents to the world."[46]

In contrast, the "social" self is constituted of the various ways we appear to other individuals plus the way we *think* they see us; obviously each other person sees us in completely different ways. Fortunately, there is a consensus or relatively common image that is perceived by others and that allows for a certain amount of consistency.[47]

The more the personal self and the social self overlap, the more consistent and harmonious are our relationships with others, because "normal" or "expected" behavior and other expectations are thoroughly shared. If we consider our self (the personal self) to be rather awkward socially and more comfortable or skilled in dealing with objects or analytical problems, yet we

[42]Carl Rogers, "A Theory of Therapy, Personality and Interpersonal Relationships as Developed in the Client-Centered Framework," in *Psychology: A Study of a Science*, Vol. 3: *Formulations of the Person in the Social Context*, ed. by S. Koch (New York: McGraw-Hill, 1959), pp. 184–256, quoted in Bischof, p. 337.
[43]Thompson and Van Houten, p. 53.
[44]Henry P. Knowles and Borje O. Saxberg, *Personality and Leadership Behavior* (Reading, Mass.: Addison-Wesley, 1971), pp. 67, 72.
[45]Ibid., p. 73.
[46]Ibid., p. 76.
[47]Ibid., p. 77.

find our self (perhaps through social contacts) in the constant company of socially oriented companions, then incongruence exists between our self-image and the expectations of others (social self). This creates anxiety, because their expectations of us are not consistent with our personal self. Some behavior must result. Either we must reevaluate our self-image, or we must move to reduce the tension either by having less and less to do with these companions or by allowing the conflict to continue as well as its discomfort.

Field Theory

Extending the concept of the social self and the personal self, the field theory of Kurt Lewin suggests that an individual is in constant interaction with his *total* environment. His behavior is modified by his own subjective processes, and he "is thus viewed as active in the behavioral process and not as just a passive recipient of discrete stimuli."[48]

Through the use of diagrams, one can represent the individual and the external forces acting on him. These environmental forces occur in what is called the "life span" of the particular individual and include all the forces that "impinge upon a person and determine his behavior" and affect his personality.[49] Barriers or other frustrating blockages can be diagramed, representing those things or events that make accomplishment of a goal relatively more difficult or impossible.

The major importance of field theory for our concept of personality is the extension it provides in considering the influences on the individual personality and also in recognizing that the individual reacts to outside forces in a goal-oriented fashion.

Personality Defenses

The personality is the very essence of the individual. As such, it is vulnerable to attack and must be protected at all costs. A generally positive self-concept is important to the development and maintenance of a healthy personality.

Techniques of protecting the personality are important behaviors. Not only do they protect the personality, but the defense mechanism used may *reflect* the personality.

In Table 8-3 we can see common types of defense mechanisms. We recognize that they might be classified into three categories: aggression, withdrawal, or compromise.[50] Those that are forms of aggression (displacement, negativism, and fixation) are mechanisms by which we can attack—

---

[48]Cary M. Lichtman and Raymond G. Hunt, "Personality and Organization Theory: A Review of Some Conceptual Literature," *Psychological Bulletin,* **76:** 280 (1971).
[49]Bischof, p. 526.
[50]Fitch, p. 261.

directly or indirectly—what is threatening our ego or self-concept. With-drawal mechanisms (conversion, fantasy, regression, repression, resignation, and flight) attempt to reduce the threat by physically or psychologically withdrawing from the situation in which the threat is perceived. When the threat cannot be reduced by aggression or withdrawal, another common defense—compromise—allows the individual to make a relatively satisfac-tory adjustment. Examples of these are compensation (because it consists of a "partial withdrawal by a person trying to disguise the presence of a weak or undesirable trait while at the same time emphasizing a desirable one"[51]), identification, projection, rationalization (because it is an excuse based on "logic" in an attempt to "save face"), and reaction formation.

Relating Surface and Source Traits to Behavior

The concepts of surface factors and of influences from within, we recognize, are not independent. Certainly many of the directly observable (surface) traits we exhibit may be traced to psychoanalytic roots.

Cattell has developed a dynamic theory of personality that integrates surface and internal ("source") traits through factor-analytic statistical tech-niques. Surface traits tend to be rather unstable and lacking in descriptive power. On the other hand, source traits are the basic, stable, and actual underlying *causes* of surface traits.[52]

The sixteen source traits are listed with brief descriptions in Table 8-4. In comparison with other theories, Cattell's (1) presents source traits that are *universal* and (2) allows *prediction* of behavior of specific individuals in specific situations through a "specification equation" that relates the "characteristics of the given person . . . , each weighted by its relevance in the present situation,"[53] obviously a complex undertaking.

Personality and Behavior

We have seen that the personality is a major influence on tendencies to behave in ways that are consistent with cultural values and self-concept. Individual traits and types, such as aggression or extroversion, are powerful in explaining causes of diverse behaviors. However, by themselves they cannot describe or explain broad ranges of activities, such as those involved in a manager's refusal to delegate authority and his delight in his successful handling of problems that would ordinarily be the responsibility of his subordinates.

Lewin presented the concept of the goal-oriented personality operating

[51]Ibid., p. 271.
[52]Bischof, p. 463.
[53]Calvin S. Hall and Gardner Lindzey, *Theories of Personality,* 2nd Ed. (New York: Wiley, 1970), p. 391.

TABLE 8-3   Common Mechanisms of Personality Defense

Defense Mechanism	Psychological Process	Illustration
	Aggressive	
Fixation	Maintaining a persistent nonadjustive reaction even though all the cues indicate the behavior will not cope with the problems.	Persisting in carrying out an operational procedure long since declared by management to be uneconomical as a protest because the employee's opinion wasn't asked.
Displacement	Redirecting pent-up emotions toward persons, ideas, or objects other than the primary source of the emotion.	Roughly rejecting a simple request from a subordinate after receiving a rebuff from the boss.
Negativism	Active or passive resistance, operating unconsciously.	The manager who, having been unsuccessful in getting out of a committee assignment, picks apart every suggestion that anyone makes in the meetings.
	Compromise	
Compensation	Individual devotes himself to a pursuit with increased vigor to make up for some feeling of real or imagined inadequacy.	Zealous, hard-working president of the twenty-five year club who has never advanced very far in the company hierarchy.
Identification	Individual enhances his self-esteem by patterning his own behavior after another's, frequently also internalizing the values and beliefs of the other; also vicariously sharing the glories or suffering in the reversals of other individuals or groups.	The "assistant-to" who takes on the vocabulary, mannerisms, or even pomposity of his vice-presidential boss.
Projection	Individual protects himself from awareness of his own undesirable traits or unacceptable feelings by attributing them to others.	Unsuccessful person who, deep down, would like to block the rise of others in the organization and who continually feels that others are out to "get him."

154

Rationalization	Justifying inconsistent or undesirable behavior, beliefs, statements, and motivations by providing acceptable explanations for them.	Padding the expense account because "everybody does it."
Reaction formation	Urges not acceptable to consciousness are repressed, and in their stead opposite attitudes or modes of behavior are expressed with considerable force.	Employee who has not been promoted who overdoes the defense of his boss, vigorously upholding the company's policies.
Withdrawal		
Conversion	Emotional conflicts are expressed in muscular, sensory, or bodily symptoms of disability, malfunctioning, or pain.	A disabling headache keeping a staff member off the job the day after a cherished project has been rejected.
Fantasy	Daydreaming or other forms of imaginative activity provides an escape from reality and imagined satisfactions.	An employee's daydream of the day in the staff meeting when he corrects the boss's mistakes and is publicly acknowledged as the real leader of the industry.
Regression	Individual returns to an earlier and less mature level of adjustment in the face of frustration.	A manager having been blocked in some administrative pursuit busies himself with clerical duties or technical details more appropriate for his subordinates.
Repression	Completely excluding from consciousness impulses, experiences, and feelings that are psychologically disturbing because they arouse a sense of guilt or anxiety.	A subordinate "forgetting" to tell his boss the circumstances of an embarrassing situation.
Resignation, apathy, and boredom	Breaking psychological contact with the environment, withholding any sense of emotional or personal involvement.	Employee who, receiving no reward, praise, or encouragement, no longer cares whether or not he does a good job.
Flight or withdrawal	Leaving the field in which frustration, anxiety, or conflict is experienced, either physically or psychologically.	The salesman's big order falls through, and he takes the rest of the day off; constant rebuff or rejection by superiors and colleagues pushes an older worker toward being a loner and ignoring what friendly gestures are made.

SOURCE: Adapted from Timothy W. Costello and Sheldon S. Zalkind, *Psychology in Administration: A Research Orientation* (Englewood Cliffs, N.J.: Prentice-Hall, 1963), pp. 148, 149.

TABLE 8-4   Cattell's Personality Source Traits

Source Trait	Description		
Outgoing–reserved	Warmhearted, easy-going participating	vs.	Detached, critical, cool
More intelligent–less intelligent	Abstract thinking, bright	vs.	Concrete thinking
Emotionally stable–affected by feelings	Faces reality, calm, mature	vs.	Emotionally less stable, easily upset
Dominant–submissive	Independent, aggressive, stubborn		Mild, accommodating, conforming
Happy-go-lucky–serious	Impulsively lively, gay, enthusiastic	vs.	Sober, serious, taciturn
Conscientious–expedient	Persevering, staid, rule-bound	vs.	Evades rules, feels few obligations
Venturesome–timid	Socially bold, uninhibited, spontaneous	vs.	Withdrawn, restrained, diffident
Sensitive–tough-minded	Dependent, overprotected	vs.	Self-reliant, realistic, no-nonsense
Suspicious–trusting	Self-opinionated, hard to fool	vs.	Adaptable, free of jealousy, easy to get on with
Imaginative–practical	Wrapped up in inner urgencies, careless of practical matters, Bohemian	vs.	Careful, conventional, proper
Shrewd–forthright	Calculating, wordly, penetrating	vs.	Natural, artless, sentimental
Apprehensive–self-assured	Worrying, depressive, troubled	vs.	Placid self-confidence, serene
Experimenting–conservative	Critical, liberal, analytical, free thinking	vs.	Respecting established ideas
Self-sufficient–group-dependent	Prefers own decisions, resourceful	vs.	A "joiner" and sound follower
Controlled–uncontrolled	Socially precise, following self-image	vs.	Careless of protocol
Tense–relaxed	Nervous tension, frutrated, driven, overwrought	vs.	Tranquil, torpid, unfrustrated

SOURCE: Adapted from Raymond B. Cattell, "Personality Pinned Down," *Psychology Today* (July 1973), pp. 40, 41: and Bischof, pp. 464–466.

in its life space. Each individual behaves in consistent ways because of basic personality factors that organize his behavior into certain patterns. These patterns of behavior may be traced to needs that are *acquired* by the individual. The behavioral patterns are the expressions of how the personality orders and arranges activities to fulfill the acquired needs.

These are to be distinguished from biological or physiological needs, such as hunger or sex. Biological needs are powerful influences but are usually satisfied rather directly and easily. Acquired needs, on the other hand, result from personality development and from interactions with others. They are *socially* based needs, the four most common of which are achievement (abbreviated *Ach*), power *(Pow)*, affiliation *(Aff)*, and manipulation *(Mach,* for "Machiavellianism").[54]

In discussing these acquired needs and the behavior patterns that characterize them, we will typically be considering a person who displays the motive—and its attendant behaviors—to a great extent. This should not preclude considering the behavior patterns of an individual who displays *little* of the particular motive.

Achievement Motives[55]

The need for achievement ("need Achievement" or *n-Ach*) is a global concept. It does not measure one specific trait of the personality but shows the orientation of the constellation of personality traits.[56] In general terms, it consists of success orientation and is not restricted to any occupation or profession. The individual high in need Achievement must succeed. This being the case, he is unwilling to share the burden with others. Even within an organizational setting, he prefers to work alone and to have fewer meetings than other executives even though many organizational problems would probably be more effectively solved through collaboration.[57] He is strongly concerned with competition and might be described as task-oriented. He needs to have some standard of excellence against which to gauge his performance and will use this standard to measure his competition with himself, with others, or in the accomplishment of something new and unique.

Because the person high in n-Ach is personally involved in task accom-

[54]For detailed descriptions and research on n-Ach, n-Aff, and n-Pow, see John W. Atkinson (ed.), *Motives in Fantasy, Action and Society: A Method of Assessment and Study* (Princeton, N.J.: Van Nostrand, 1958).

[55]The summaries of the behavior characteristics associated with n-Ach, n-Aff, and n-Pow are based on the excellent descriptions in David A. Kolb, Irwin M. Rubin, and James M. McIntyre, *Organizational Psychology: An Experiential Approach* (Englewood Cliffs, N.J.: Prentice-Hall, 1971), pp. 81–83, 110, 176.

[56]Abraham Zaleznik and David Moment, *The Dynamics of Interpersonal Behavior* (New York: Wiley, 1964), p. 389.

[57]Kahlil Noujaim, "Some Motivational Determinants of Effort Allocation and Performance" (Ph.D. thesis, Sloan School of Management, Massachusetts Institute of Technology, 1968), cited in Kolb, Rubin, and McIntyre, p. 82.

plishment to the conscious exclusion of others, he dislikes sharing responsibility for his success or failure—he will go so far as to try to structure or define the situation in such a way that he and he alone is personally responsible for the way in which the situation comes out. This is consistent with the fact that he is not a gambler; he will take calculated—but moderate—risks but is quite realistic about the level of risk he is willing to accept. The moderate risks he accepts are those that are challenging while being attainable. Because of the nature of these risks, and because he requires personal responsibility, he is most comfortable in situations in which he gets immediate and concrete feedback on his performance. This intimates that he will be most effective in tasks that are rather well structured as opposed to those that are exploratory or open-ended. This will also allow him to keep from delegating authority and to perform the task himself.

It would be unfair to say that the individual high in need Achievement is antisocial; he is unconcerned with other people, rather than being negative toward them. His concern about other people occurs only insofar as they might be useful to him in accomplishing his task.

Finally, he has a realistic attitude toward both success and failure. He regards both as learning experiences and as opportunities by which he might improve himself.

Power Needs

While need Achievement is task-oriented, need for Affiliation and Power (n-Aff and n-Pow, respectively) govern interpersonal relationships. People with high n-Pow find satisfactions in controlling or influencing the activities of others. The term *power* might have negative connotations because of its implications of dominance and superiority. Perhaps the negative aspects of the term derive from *abuses* of power; certainly power and need for power are critical in organizations and in leadership situations. Veroff defined the power motive as "that disposition directing behavior toward satisfactions contingent upon the control of the means of influencing another person(s). In the phenomenal sphere of the power-motivated individual, he considers himself the 'gatekeeper' to certain decision-making of others. The means of control can be anything at all that can be used to manipulate another person."[58] In studying n-Pow in a group of college students, Veroff found significant differences between those high in n-Pow and those low in n-Pow. The students who were high in n-Pow expressed greater interest in the satisfactions of being a leader, expressed significantly greater interest in the prestige and status aspects of a job, were rated as highly argumentative by their instructors, and were significantly more active in attempting to sway others to their ways of thinking.[59]

[58]Joseph Veroff, "Development and Validation of a Projective Measure of Power Motivation," in Atkinson, p. 105.
[59]Ibid., p. 113.

People with high n-Pow attempt very strongly to achieve influence over other people; there also seem to be intimations of needs for recognition and acceptance, not to mention aggressive tendencies, among these individuals. As a result, they prefer participation in situations that are competitive and that will tend to provide status. An organizational member high in n-Pow would probably try to control the sources and uses of information in an attempt to improve prestige and self-image. This may result in behavior that is not conducive to improving task performance.

Affiliation Needs

The need for affiliation is a truly social motive; it reflects the desire for social acceptance. The person high in n-Aff is primarily concerned with establishing, maintaining, or restoring positive affective relationships with others. His general orientation is most descriptively expressed by "friendship." Because of his focus on warm and friendly relationships, the person high in n-Aff is probably in a supervisory position or a job in which the maintenance of interpersonal relationships is more important than the quality of decision making.

High n-Aff can create problems for the individual, because he may fear disrupting his relationships by being forthright or by confronting problem situations. Warm and friendly communication with others and collaboration on tasks is, of course, important within an organizational setting, yet creates difficulties when these become ends in themselves.

Manipulation Needs: The Machiavellians

The fourth behavior pattern is that of Machiavellianism. The name for the pattern of behavior stems naturally from traits attributed to Niccolo Machiavelli, who wrote *The Prince* in the 1500's. Cynicism and the manipulation of others for one's own purposes are associated with Machiavelli. Those high in n-Mach are those who have an implicit assumption that man is basically weak and gullible and that a rational man will take advantage of the weaknesses of others.[60] As a result, such an individual has four general characteristics:

1. He is not basically concerned with morality in the conventional sense.
2. He is basically cool and detached with other people. Once a person becomes emotionally involved with another person it is difficult to treat him as an object.
3. He is more concerned with means than ends, thus more interested in conning others than in what he is conning them for.
4. He is not pathologically disturbed nor would he have clinical symptoms of

---

[60]Richard Christie, "The Machiavellis Among Us," *Psychology Today* (November 1970), p. 82.

neurosis or psychosis. The manipulator must be able to function successfully in the real world, and thus must have an undistorted view of reality.
If anything, he would be overrational in dealing with others.[61]

Persons high in n-Mach (called High Machs) are also much more
capable of lying successfully in the course of achieving their goals; this is
consistent with their lack of concern with conventional morality.

High Machs are much more effective when three critical conditions are
met: (1) when they interact face to face with another person; (2) when the
rules are not highly structured, thereby giving the High Mach wide latitude
for improvising in his face-to-face interaction; and (3) when the situation
permits emotions to be aroused, for instance, when the High Mach can
achieve a goal important to him through the situation.[62]

The person who scores high in Machiavellianism is highly resistant to
social influence, although he can be persuaded when rational arguments are
used; he approaches a situation logically and thoughtfully, rather than
emotionally; and when possible, he tends to initiate and control the situation.
His effectiveness at manipulation seems to be largely due to his insensitivity
to the other person, which permits him to ignore social influences in the
pursuit of his own goals.

Personality and Organizational Behavior

In this chapter we have rather extensively reviewed some of the major
theories of personality. At this point we must stop and consider the implications of our deliberations for organizational behavior. We have seen that:

Personality is possessed by every person.
Personality is a pattern of consistent behaviors and characteristics.
Personality is partially inborn and partially acquired.
Personality develops.
Personality is influenced by internal, external, and adjustment processes.
Personality can be described by characteristic behavior traits or constellations
    of "related" traits (types).
Personality is dynamic rather than static.
Personality predisposes an individual to certain behavioral patterns.
Personality provides defenses—and outlets—for the self-concept and
    acquired motives.

Probably the simplest statement we can derive from all this is that "each
individual is different from, yet similar to, each other individual."[63] These
differences and similarities are significant in explaining and predicting
behavior in organized settings.

[61]Ibid.
[62]Ibid., p. 85.
[63]Cf. Clyde Kluckhohn and Henry A. Murray, in Kluckhohn and Murray, p. 53.

At the beginning of the chapter we asked why some workers report that they prefer what might be considered boring or monotonous work. Or why some people steadfastly refuse additional responsibility in the form of a promotion. Or why a supervisor cannot bring himself to reprimand an unruly subordinate. Or why a middle-level manager callously ignores ethical considerations in his climb to the top.

These questions—and other, similar ones—can be answered through thoughtful application of personality concepts. Admittedly subjective, such an approach allows us to begin to understand unique beings and groups with similar personality characteristics.

Unfortunately technological characteristics or required behavior patterns are not examined in the light of personality theory. Consider an assembly job. Satisfactions of people with definite personality patterns could be predicted. Consider an individual low in n-Ach, moderate in n-Aff, high in n-Pow, and high in autonomy, self-acceptance, dominance, responsibility, achievement-through-independence, and flexibility: Would you predict job satisfaction on the assembly line? What about another person who is high in n-Ach, low in n-Aff, low in n-Pow, low in dominance, responsibility, and flexibility, and high in self-control, tolerance, and achievement through conformance?

We can see, too, how a challenging job, requiring judgment and skill, might be most frustrating to an individual high in dependence, low in tolerance of ambiguity, and low in n-Ach, for example. And what about the instructor who (1) is not specific enough, gives ambiguous essay quizzes, and should lecture more or (2) is too rigid and inflexible in his presentations, tests only memory through lengthy true–false and multiple-choice tests, and is fond of "laundry lists" as rules to handle situations? Certainly we can draw inferences about the personalities of these instructors.

Consider the implications of personality theory for organization structure. We reiterated earlier in the chapter Argyris's conclusions about personality development during the maturation process. A major conclusion was that traditional organizational forms are restrictive, failing to allow members to develop psychologically and encouraging immature behavior patterns.[64] In this regard he cited feelings of dependence, subordination, and passiveness as creating frustration and conflict. He thereby falls prey to the same overgeneralizations about personality characteristics as did earlier researchers and practitioners as they applied the rational–economic man model, the human relations model, and so on.[65] When individuals are considered as exhibiting the same behavioral tendencies and the tendencies are evaluated *normatively*, differences in the personalities of individuals are aggregated and hence lost.

We can by now easily imagine individuals who respond most positively to the most protective, security-laden, rules-conscious, conformity-demand-

[64]Argyris, p. 50.
[65]Litchman and Hunt, p. 276.

ing bureaucracy. High dependence needs, low flexibility, and high achieve-ment-through-conformity, for example, represent characteristics that illus-trate a good match between individual and bureaucracy. Talcott Parsons pointed out that the American bureaucracy

is characterized by the relative predominance of patterns of rationality, universal-ism, and functional specificity of roles. Clearly the ability to function in roles requiring such action patterns depends upon the presence of certain appropriate constellations in the personalities of the participants in the occupational structure. It appears that our society develops adequate numbers of individuals whose per-sonality is such as to enable them to operate in such roles, at least to the extent necessary to maintain both their individual personality integration and the effective functioning of the occupational structure.[66]

Organizational form may itself be a personality determinant. This may be observed if we remember the emphasis on rationality and predictability of behavior demanded by the formal organization. In its extreme form, reliabil-ity of response and strict devotion to regulation are demanded. Inflexibility is encouraged, as is a dependent relationship between subordinate and his superior. The bureaucrat's career path is guided and rewarded by salary increments, pensions, and promotion based on seniority, disciplined action, and conformity to official regulations. Induced at the same time is timidness and conservatism.

Mismatches between personality characteristics and organizational requirements are bound to happen. Probably a certain amount of selective screening occurs, however, so that highly independent people are not attracted to, or do not stay with, a large bureaucratic organization.[67]

The "organization man," the individual attracted to and retained by the highly structured large organization, probably brings definite personality characteristics to this affiliation. He is probably highly dependent, uncon-sciously attributing the parental role to the enterprise; he unconsciously expects the firm to meet his dependency needs just as he does his parents. He strongly identifies with the organization, as he wished to identify with his parents. Unconscious conflict may result from his resenting his dependence on the organization and seeking to avoid the dependence, even while fearing detachment from his unconscious parent substitute. The hostility that occurs is often internalized, giving rise to one or a number of psychosomatic symptoms, such as headaches, ulcers, and hypertension.[68]

Note that this "organization man" is presented in the spirit of the preceding paragraph, representing personality "fits" between a preexisting

[66]Paraphrased by Alex Inkeles, "Some Sociological Observations on Culture and Person-ality Studies," in Kluckhohn and Murray, p. 585; Parson's original language is in "The Professions and Social Structure," *Social Forces*, **17**:457–467 (1939).

[67]Robert K. Merton, "Bureaucratic Structure and Personality," *Social Forces*, **18**:564 (1939–1940).

[68]Herbert Holt and Melvin E. Salveson, "Psychoanalytic Processes in Management," in *Management Sciences: Models and Techniques*, Vol. 2, ed. by C. West Churchman and Michel Verhulst (Oxford: Pergamon Press, 1960), p. 63.

disposition and a *very structured* bureaucracy. The bureaucracy did not *make* the individual dependent or conformity-oriented; the individual was already predisposed toward these traits. Further, such an organization may or may not be representative or typical, and certainly we must qualify any rash generalization by considering such factors as task specialization and management level.

Indeed, one empirical study contradicts such conclusions of organizational impact on dependency or conformity. In comparing bureaucrats and nonbureaucrats, Kohn found bureaucratization to be associated with "greater intellectual flexibility, higher valuation of self-direction, greater openness to new experience, and more personally rewarding moral standards."[69] These findings were partially related to a more educated work force but were more strongly related to job conditions such as greater job security, higher income, and much more complex job content.[70]

However, Graham and Calendo studied the relationship of the supervisor's ratings and the personality characteristics of clerks. They found supervisory ratings of personal characteristics positively related to measures such as deference, endurance, and self-control. *High* supervisory ratings on personal characteristics were associated with *high* ratings on the personality measures, and *low* supervisory ratings with *low* personality ratings. Aggression, autonomy, initiative, self-assurance, and self-confidence were negatively related to supervisory ratings. This indicates that *high* supervisory ratings were associated with *low* ratings on these personality measures, and *low* supervisory ratings with *high* personality measure ratings. "The general impression created by this pattern is one of a rather restrictive work environment in which high value is placed upon conformity to organizational rules and standard operating procedures."[71]

The importance and potential of personality theory should be apparent. Its relevance to organizational behavior is great, but widespread applications to real organizations are quite rare. Perhaps the most developed area of application is found in industrial psychology's psychological testing and selection instruments.

The broader problem of the mutual adjustment of organization and individual is still developing. The nature of the organization is rather well known; the characteristics of the individual within the organized setting are still largely unexplored. Many questions remain to be answered, and many have not even been *asked* yet. Is there a *type* of person most suited to monotonous assembly-line work? Are there differences in the basic *characteristics* of line managers and staff experts that create conflicts? Are technology and personality *development* incompatible? Is there a universal leadership style that is independent of socially acquired *motives*?

---

[69]Melvin L. Kohn, "Bureaucratic Man: A Portrait and an Interpretation," *American Sociological Review* (June 1971), p. 472.
[70]Ibid.
[71]William K. Graham and James T. Calendo, "Personality Correlates of Supervisory Ratings," *Personnel Psychology* **22:**485 (1969).

Certainly people are alike, yet different. The extent of the differences and similarities—and their underlying personality *causes*—gives an additional important dimension to explaining human behavior in organizations.

Summary

The basic building block of the organization is the individual. Scientific management advocates largely ignored the human element beyond considerations of skill. Human relations adherents similarly oversimplified the importance and complexity of individual differences.

The study of personality and its development provides an opportunity to consider the individual as a unique entity. We have defined *personality* as "the stable pattern of an individual's characteristics and behaviors which are so organized that they reflect the unique adjustments he makes to his environment." These patterns result from hereditary inputs *and* from environmental (acquired or learned) behaviors. Heredity provides basic capabilities, such as intelligence or physique, and cultural values and opportunities to realize one's capabilities are acquired from the social environment. Culture guides behavioral tendencies and attitudes into paths consistent with its values.

Personality is also influenced during its development by psychoanalytic factors. Stages of personality development, each with opportunities for trauma or crisis, were presented by Freud and by Erickson. Trauma or lack of ability to adapt to the requirements of successive stages results in stunted personality development.

Ways to describe, evaluate, or compare personalities are available through theories of the personality. One set of theories focuses on the directly observable behaviors of the individual as they are consistently exhibited. These can be classified into distinct *traits*. Traits can be grouped into *types*, which describe overall behavior patterns. Freud identified oral, anal, and genital types, who display characteristic behaviors of unsuccessfully resolved developmental stages. Jung developed the concept of the introverted and extroverted types. Sheldon presented a body-type theory that relates physique to behavioral tendencies.

Influences on personality from *internal* sources constitute another perspective. Freud's id–ego–superego construct presents a mechanism through which instincts affect behavior, largely unconsciously. The image that the individual has of himself, his self-concept, gives him a set of expectations or consistent benchmarks by which to order his behavior. Field theory allows the individual, forces acting upon him, and his resultant behavior to be diagramed, allowing an analysis of the dynamic interaction between the individual and his life space. More importantly, field theory explicitly recognizes that the individual is not just a passive recipient of external stimuli but actively modifies his behaviors in goal-directed and subjective ways.

The relationship of the individual and external forces is summarized by the nature of the psychological defenses of the personality. Through aggressive, withdrawal, or compromise activities his self-concept is protected.

Four motives serve as direct personality extensions and as consistent behavior patterns: achievement, power, affiliation, and manipulation. Each is characterized by distinct trait sets and may be effectively used to integrate the separate personality concepts. Prediction of behavior is then facilitated.

Finally, the relevance of personality theory to the broader canvas of organizational behavior is quite direct. Individual responses to various job characteristics cannot be meaningfully explained unless underlying—and unique—behavior tendencies are recognized. Naturally this complicates the task of studying organizational behavior, because simplistic models of organizational man cannot be blindly used. The increase in the validity and usefulness of our explanations and predictions makes the effort well worthwhile.

In the next chapter we will investigate the nature of the ways in which individuals communicate with each other, finding and sharing common grounds.

STUDY AND REVIEW QUESTIONS

1. What are some of the ways in which culture influences personality development? How has your culture influenced you?

2. In what ways do you think culture interacts with the psychoanalytic stages of personality development, improving or restricting one's chances of successfully or unsuccessfully meeting the demands of each stage?

3. Compare and contrast the "surface factors" and the "influences from within" personality theories.

4. How are the concepts of traits and types related? Which is more relevant to personality and behavior predictions? Why?

5. Identify at least three ways each in which the id, the ego, and the superego directly influence the behavior of someone with whom you are familiar.

6. What is self-concept? How does self-concept *restrict* one's personality?

7. Review Lewin's field theory and diagram the interaction of *your* psychological field (life space) and *your* personality. (See, for example, Richard S. Lazarus, *Personality and Adjustment,* pp. 60–62; or C. S. Hall and G. Lindzey, *Theories of Personality,* pp. 211–226) What evaluative comments have you on the theory? What comments have you on your ability, after diagraming, to predict your behavior? To analyze your past behavior?

8. How are personality defenses mechanisms that "may *reflect* the personality"? What traits might characterize individuals consistently displaying each of the mechanisms in Table 8-3?

9. What comments can you make about the personality development of an individual very high in n-Ach? What might be the nature of the self-concept held by one high in n-Ach?

10. What comments can you make about the personality development of an

individual very high in n-Pow? What might be the nature of the self-concept held by one high in n-Pow?

11. Under what technological and structural conditions (include management level as well as organizational structure considerations) would each of the following be *most* effective? *Least* effective?

   a. An individual very high in n-Ach, very low in n-Pow and n-Aff.
   b. An individual very high in n-Pow, very low in n-Ach and n-Aff.
   c. An individual very high in n-Aff, very low in n-Ach and n-Pow.
   d. An individual very high in n-Mach *and* n-Pow, very low in n-Aff.

Chapter

9

Communication:
Bridge Between People

CHAPTER OBJECTIVES

1. To explore the nature of communication as a process.

2. To consider the factors that affect communication effectiveness.

3. To show the importance and pervasiveness of communication within the organized setting.

CHAPTER OUTLINE

The Process of Communicating
The Communication Model

Determinants of Effectiveness in Communication
Efficiency Versus Effectiveness
Communication Efficiency and
   Effectiveness
Noise in the Communication Process
The Role of the Receiver in
   Communication Effectiveness

Barriers to Communication Effectiveness
Evaluating Source Credibility

Communication as a Process of Influence

Organizational Communication
Communication Technology
Communication Engineering for Results

The development of personality takes place during, and as a result of, interaction with other people. These may be people who are part of an overall society or culture or people with whom we come in contact in a random fashion. Whoever they are and whatever they believe, they have a subtle effect on us. In a larger perspective individuals influence us in ways sanctioned by our culture; in early stages of development, they reward or punish us for the patterns of behavior we exhibit as our behaviors compare with the standards of society. For this to happen, some form of communication must take place. Our personalities develop to their full potential as a direct result of this process of socialization. We develop better ideas of what our possibilities are for behavior by observing and analyzing the behaviors of others. All of this requires that we have available some sort of a linkage between two or more people. The communication process is what bridges the gap between diverse and divergent personalities. Communication provides the means whereby meaning and understanding may be passed from one person to another.

Communication is one of the most common processes of human behavior. Because it is so widespread and universal, the importance of communication cannot be underestimated. Without communication no organization could long exist because of the basic coordination so essential. Coordination of individuals, work processes, or departments requires that those being coordinated know what they are to do and when it is to be done. Through the authority of a superior, this vital understanding and direction is passed on, or *communicated*. Looked at from another way, managers vitally need information on which to base decisions; communication is the process by which the manager is apprised of relevant information.

The process of communication, although widely engaged in, is yet not well understood. Perhaps part of its mystery derives from the many and diverse ways in which messages are transmitted: facial expressions, gestures, textbooks, television, newspapers, radio, conversations, phonograph records, lectures, and so on. To study each of these communications media is surely an overwhelming task. However, we can examine the processes *common* to most attempts to communicate and draw generalizations from them. The applications of communication to human behavior in organizations may then be investigated.

The Process of Communicating

For our purposes, we can define communication as a "dynamic process in which man consciously or unconsciously affects the cognitions of another through materials or agencies used in symbolic ways."[1] A person who is

---

[1]Kenneth E. Andersen, *Introduction to Communication Theory and Practice* (Menlo Park, Calif.: Cummings, 1972), p. 5.

attempting to communicate to another uses symbols to influence another in desired ways. The person receiving the communication perceives, interprets, and responds to this communication. Communication is considered a dynamic process because it requires action or energy and involves a series of linked energies or actions for the process to be complete. We include the phrase "man consciously or unconsciously" to restrict our attention to communication attempts by human beings; we thereby exclude such phenomena as the twinkling of a star and the dance of a bumblebee, which affect our cognitions, yet cannot be considered communication attempts. The communication process is *not* restricted to purely conscious attempts, however. Whether we realize it or not, we still communicate with others (such as by "body language" or involuntary gestures or facial expressions). Conscious communication attempts are important because of their purposefulness and goal orientation, and we will emphasize these more than those that are unconscious.

The word *affects* is an important part of our definition. A letter that is lost by the post office is not truly a communication because it does not affect the intended recipient. The lost letter represents a communication *attempt.* "In order to communicate, there must be an impact upon the receiver even if the effect is not the one intended or if the receiver is not the one intended. As long as the message affects a receiver, communication has taken place."[2]

The concept of another's cognitions stems directly from the use of the term *affects.* The difference here is that the recipient of the communication must have his stockpile of knowledge affected in some way. Certainly in conscious communication attempts, the receiver usually pays attention to the source, knowing that the source is attempting to communicate something. Affecting the cognitions of others, however, does not require the receiver to recognize consciously the effect of the communication on him nor even to relate the impact directly back to the message received. Nor does affecting the cognitions of another mean that the response from the receiver of the message will resemble in any way the one that the source *intended* to elicit. By investigating another's cognitions and the ways in which they are affected, we do not restrict our investigation to the receiver's responses and actions. Indeed, a change in the receiver's feelings may be a response to communications.

The final part of our definition, "materials or agents used in symbolic ways," forces us to recognize that interpersonal communication is largely symbolic. Some abstraction must usually be used in the message, by which the source's mind attempts to come into contact with the receiver's mind. Such contact between minds is physically impossible, of course, and thought transference has not yet been shown practicable. Therefore thoughts or desired actions must be *represented* through the use of some symbols to which are attached specified and commonly agreed-upon meanings. Examples of

[2]Ibid., p. 6.

these meanings or agents are telegrams (employing standardized words), gestures (such as the wave of a hand to show greeting), sounds (such as those you make in talking), or physical objects (such as the use of the flag of one's country to denote patriotism).

Having an initial understanding of what communication *is,* we can focus on *how* it happens. The process of communication may then be broken down into its component elements.

The Communication Model

We can classify and label the various parts of the communication process and incorporate them into a general model. The model can then help us to consider and analyze communication situations.

Figure 9-1 presents a model of the communication process, showing the sequence the elements of communication occur in. The *source* is the individual who is making the communication attempt. He has some idea, desired action, or meaning that is intended to be received by another. Remember that the communication attempt need not be a conscious effort on the part of the source; sometimes communication occurs despite the source's desire *not* to communicate. (Have you ever written a personal note to a loved one that fell into the hands of someone else?) A laborer may communicate a great deal about himself through his actions, symbols, or other agencies. Steel-toed boots, calloused hands, a union badge, even choice of words or phraseology may fairly shout with meaning.

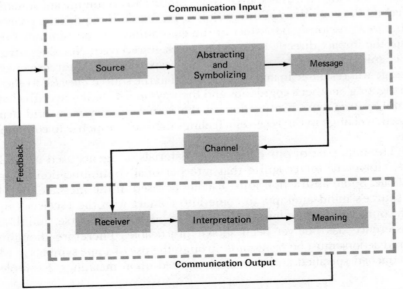

FIGURE 9-1   A model of the communication process.

A conscious communication attempt requires a rather formidable process of *abstracting* and *symbolizing* before communication can take place. The thought or desire, which exists only in the mind of the source, must be broken down and translated into symbols that have a high probability of conveying common meanings. Once the symbols are selected, either consciously or unconsciously, they are arranged into some sort of *message*. The content of the message and its structure may have to follow rather strict rules. In verbal communication, for example, the structure of the English language forces a certain basic format on messages in terms of sentence structure. For communication to take place in English, the words cannot be randomly generated but must follow a basic logic in the order in which they are presented.

Consistent with the content and choice of the message is the selection of the appropriate *channel* by which to transmit the communication. We have numerous choices open to us at any particular time for most of our communication attempts. Depending on the situation, we might variously choose to write a letter, make a telephone call, broadcast via television or radio, or make gestures. The channel and the message must be mutually consistent with each other. We could not meaningfully use gestures to convey meaning were we broadcasting over the radio. Similarly writing a note or letter to a person who is seated just across the table would be inappropriate. Television might be bypassed in favor of a high-speed printer when huge numbers of the communication must be sent from one place to another.

The recipient of the transmitted message is the *receiver*. This may be the intended receiver, one who intercepts the message, or whoever *chooses* to receive the message. National advertisers employ mass-broadcasting techniques (wide television coverage, for example) in the hope that of all the millions of people exposed to the message in the channel, receivers with particular characteristics and buying patterns will be reached. The role of the receiver is by no means passive; mass-mail advertisers have long recognized this fact. Should you receive an envelope, the contents of which you immediately classify as "junk mail," you may discard the letter unopened. The receiver, in this case, has actively rejected whatever the message was. No communication took place. "Personalized" envelopes or premiums are inducements widely used to make the *intended* receiver an *actual* receiver of the message placed in this channel.

Interpretation is the next necessary step in the communication process. The symbols that make up the received message must be "decoded" and the commonly agreed-upon definitions of these symbols must be applied. Then the next step of inferring *meaning* from the message can take place. The symbols and their interpretations can be used to attempt the reconstruction of the abstract thoughts or desires of the source of the message.

With the successful completion of each step in the communication process, the meaning that is abstracted from the message by the receiver is the same as the thought or desire that the source attempted to communicate.

Unfortunately the process is so complicated and so prone to error at each successive step that the meaning inferred by the receiver may be completely different from that intended by the source. *Feedback* is a process in which the receiver changes roles and becomes a source. He attempts to communicate to the person who originated the message the impact of the original message. Informal conversations provide many and immediate feedback opportunities for the source to observe the impact of his message on the receiver and for the receiver to indicate lack of understanding or to attempt clarification of the message.

Determinants of Effectiveness in Communication

The model of the communication process we have discussed looks deceptively simple. We have mentioned that many opportunities for failure exist in the communication process. Perhaps one of the major sources of failure in the communication process might be traced to the tradeoff that is made by a potential source between communication *efficiency* and communication *effectiveness*.

Efficiency Versus Effectiveness

The two terms *efficiency* and *effectiveness* do not mean the same thing. *Efficiency* in communication means making a communication attempt with the least possible cost. Cost may include such diverse elements as dollar expenditure, comfort foregone, or effort expanded. A machine is highly efficient if it works with very little loss of energy between power requirements and output. A communication attempt is relatively efficient if the message is transmitted through a channel at less cost to the source than that required by alternative channels.

A source almost always has several channels from which to choose in his attempt at communication. A manager might well wish to communicate a new policy to his subordinates. He might see several alternatives: he might call his subordinates altogether for a group meeting, call them individually into his office to talk about the new policy, distribute a memo to each employee, post a notice on the bulletin board, and so on. The *least efficient* communication attempt is probably that of calling each employee into his office for an individual conference. The next most inefficient method is probably that of calling a group meeting to discuss the policy. The *most efficient* communication attempt is that of posting a notice on the bulletin board, followed closely in efficiency by the distribution of memos to each individual employee. Mass mailing or mass advertising is usually quite efficient, particularly if one considers the cost per individual to whom the communication attempt is directed.

A communication attempt may well be highly efficient, yet the intended receiver may never receive the message, or the meaning inferred may be completely different from the meaning intended by the source. Should our manager attempt to communicate his new policy by posting its description on the bulletin board, possibly only a few of his employees might ever see, let alone read, the new policy. Those who do read it might dismiss it as irrelevant, or might simply misinterpret its meaning. Notice that this highly efficient communication attempt sacrifices effectiveness, primarily because of five missteps in the communication process.

Channel

The channel used, that of the written word and its inherent ability to reach the audience intended, is the first cause of the communication attempt to fail. What may be a highly complex and involved new policy may lose significance in the eyes of the intended receivers by its apparently being given little fanfare or notice. If all subordinates are to accept and implement the policy, a rather selective channel is not appropriate.

Receiver

Extending this thought somewhat, a policy statement must be uniformly applied and understood by those affected. The bulletin board notice might eventually be noticed by all employees and (assuming that the meaning of the policy statement is completely understood by each receiver) would probably be implemented at different times by different people. No assurances are given that any particular intended receiver has actually been communicated with.

Interpretation and Meaning

All receivers are individuals, with unique personality characteristics, backgrounds, experiences, and values. The interpretation of the symbols employed in the communication attempt might therefore differ widely. As a result, the meanings that individual receivers attribute to the same message could be quite different. It is important to recognize that meanings are not a part of the message but only "exist in the minds of people."[3] An identical message may have quite different meanings for different people, depending on their backgrounds and experiences, among other things. For example, the statement "I had a strike yesterday" seems unambiguous enough, yet consider how these various people would interpret that same phrase:

1. A bowler.
2. A major-league baseball pitcher.
3. A businessman with labor problems.

[3]Ibid., p. 10.

4. A fisherman.
5. A woman talking to her lawyer about a divorce from a brutal husband.

The extent of lack of communication *effectiveness,* traced to these four missteps in the process, may be attributed to a fifth element lacking in the overall communication mode—feedback. An impersonal notice allows no questions about content or meaning. Questions must be directed to the *author* of the notice. Lack of feedback allows poorly directed communications to continue unchecked. The intended receiver, without feedback opportunity, cannot compare his interpretation or the meaning he infers with that intended by the source.

Communication Efficiency and Effectiveness

Our example of the notice on the bulletin board as a communication attempt illustrates the differences between communication efficiency and communication effectiveness. The notice was quite efficient—that is, it minimized cost and effort—yet it also minimized effectiveness. Sometimes this tradeoff is acceptable. Our method of receiving up-to-date news information from television or the newspaper gives few feedback opportunities. News editors try to pay careful attention to eliminating ambiguity and interpretation difficulties from their messages. As a result, these media may carry an appropriate one-way message and still remain effective. The editor must ensure that the message is intelligible to the audience to whom the communication is directed. This also means that the content of the message must be appropriate. Polysyllabic or unfamiliar words might be appropriate for some scientific or professional audiences yet highly inappropriate for mass audiences. A lowest common denominator in communication content must be striven for, so that substantial portions of the audience need not be excluded from interpreting the message in much the same way as other segments of the audience.

Let us reanalyze one of the other communication channels not selected by the manager for communicating his new policy. We will look at the one we called the least efficient channel, that of calling each subordinate into the manager's office for an individual conference. We noted its lack of efficiency relative to the other channels, especially in time and effort expended. This communication attempt would probably be highly *effective,* however.

The message is individually attuned to each individual receiver, without distractions and in a setting that requires the receiver to devote his entire attention to the message. In an individual conference, the interpretation of the message content can be facilitated by the manager's using the terms and examples most highly relevant to the individual before him. This would also heighten the degree to which the meaning intended is the same as the meaning received by each subordinate. Face-to-face interaction builds in constant and significant opportunities for the manager to get feedback from the receiver regarding understanding and ability to implement the new policy.

Although highly inefficient, this communication attempt is highly effective. If the policy is important, then the tradeoff might well be heavily in favor of increased effectiveness. Should the policy be a minor matter of no great consequence, then efficiency might be more important.

Noise in the Communication Process

Another factor that affects the effectiveness of communication is "noise." Noise might be identified as "interference" or distracting stimuli that may occur anywhere—or everywhere—in the communication process and that lessens communication effectiveness. The term is analogous to the interference or static that interrupts and lessens the quality of radio or television reception. It interferes with our reception and interpretation of the message in its channel by distraction, lessening the strength with which the message is transmitted and overriding or blotting out portions of the message.

Similarly other messages may be received along with the intended message and provide the receiver with too much information or with contradictory information. A learned authority on finance and investment might disrupt his own message with unintended contradictory supplemental messages, should he address a seminar while attired in a rumpled and cheap suit with scuffed, untied shoes and with a dirty, wrinkled shirt. He would further add disruptive messages if he arrived at the seminar in a noisy, smoke-belching, dilapidated old automobile. Noise can also be added to the channel employed; a professor's drone as he lectures is one example. "Noise may totally destroy a message by making it incomprehensible or twisting its intended meaning. Bad telephone connections are an obvious example of noise. Loud conversation or frequent distractions can also be noise. Distracting stimuli, whether visual, tactile, or aural, and whether internal or external to the person, can be noise."[4]

The Role of the Receiver in Communication Effectiveness

The receiver of the communication attempt is by no means a passive element in the communication process. He does not merely respond to the stimuli that are presented by others:

He accepts or rejects, acts, refuses to act, or acts differently than the message suggests. Certainly determining his response to a message is a very important part of the receiver's role. But there are other important choices for a receiver. Usually he makes the decision of whether to enter into the communication transaction at all.

[4]Ibid., p. 11.

He may decide not to attend a concert or a meeting or not to talk with a certain individual. He decides whether to give his attention to the source or message, and, once he has given it, whether to continue. Further, the receiver often "creates" the source by asking a question or otherwise calling the source into being. His very presence may stimulate a need or desire to communicate.

The receiver does not merely respond to stimuli which others present. He controls his attention, comprehension, and acceptance. His motivations determine to whom and to what degree he will serve as a receiver. Because of the nature of the communication process, the source adjusts his communication to the receiver; thus the receiver affects and controls the source in many ways. Finally, in many situations, the receiver may take on the role of source and direct a response to the original communication or to the same or a different audience.[5]

Barriers to Communication Effectiveness

Interpretation is most influential in determining whether or not a communication breakdown will occur. Certainly noise can affect the ways in which we interpret the message. "Often the nonverbal external and internal stimuli play an important role in the interpretations we give to words. Sometimes, the stimuli are so strong that we interpret them instead of the words directed to us. When these factors sway our understanding to a degree which does not harmonize at all with the meaning intended by the communicator, they become *barriers* to the clear interpretation of ideas."[6] Another source of communication barriers stems from differences in experiences, which largely determine how we will react to specific stimuli. We tend to react according to our backgrounds and understanding of the stimulus. The communicator who fails to recognize that others can see the same objective statements or figures from different perspectives and impute different meanings to them is ripe for a breakdown in communication.

If a communication attempt is to be successful, some interest on the part of the receiver is ordinarily required. Although short-term interest can be raised by the mere process of communication itself, the end result of the attempt—influence—may or may not be realized. A manager may *order* interest to be aroused on the part of a subordinate, but this is hardly productive over the long run.

Common backgrounds are also important in determining the effectiveness of the communication attempt. An electrical engineer would probably have a bit of difficulty in explaining how and why he chose particular circuits to be included in the design of sophisticated aircraft, especially when his audience is a nontechnical cost accountant. "Associated with this might be those cases where the communicator's knowledge in a field is so thorough that he makes unconscious assumptions that the other person can't follow.

[5]Ibid., pp. 60, 61.
[6]Norman B. Sigband, *Communication for Management* (Glenview, Ill.: Scott, Foresman, 1969), p. 10.

The danger is to assume that the listener has adequate background or fundamental knowledge and then to try to communicate on the basis of this false premise."[7]

Breakdowns in communication can also occur when intrareceiver noise interferes with the process, such as the arousal of strong emotions. Hate or disgust can effectively blot out a message or might conceivably affect the interpretation of the message. This can be recognized on a smaller scale, in the effect of prejudice on communication effectiveness. Strong prejudice, for or against a concept or ideology, causes ideas to be rejected without consideration.

The major barrier to communication effectiveness, however, has been said to be "our very natural tendency to judge, to evaluate, to approve (or disapprove) the statement of the other person or the other group."[8] Rather than listening to the content of the communication, the *intent* or *credibility* of the source may be evaluated. In this way, the communication attempt itself may never get beyond the "channel" component of the communication process. The evaluation tendency may have effectively shut off the process before it ever had a chance to begin.

Evaluating Source Credibility

The tendency to evaluate the source or the message need not be a consistently negative factor in the communication process. Evaluating the credibility of the source gives us additional information about the intent of the source and the veracity of his persuasive arguments. Since we are constantly bombarded by persuasive appeals, we must realistically employ a defense, a filter for protection. As a result:

When the source is not well known or is not particularly important to another individual, when he must be judged without regard to topic, message, or any particular activity, research indicates that we tend to rely on two important bases for dimensions of judgment. The first and most important basis is labeled "evaluative." We use this as a basis by judging a person's character, knowledge, expertise, skills, and abilities. The second basis for judgment is "dynamism," that is, the activity, power, and energy of the person.

When a communication source is associated with an actual message, when he is interacting with us on a specific topic and in a specific situation, we base our judgments on a number of factors. Two of these seem to be independent elements arising from the evaluative dimension. The first is connected with the trustworthiness or safety of the source. This relates not only to his moral character but also to the degree to which we trust him to convey accurately to us what he knows. The second factor concerns his qualifications of authoritativeness. Does the source have

---

[7]Ibid., p. 12.

[8]Carl R. Rogers and F. J. Roethlisberger, "Barriers and Gateways to Communication," *Harvard Business Review* (July–August 1952), p. 46.

the necessary expertise? Does he have the information necessary to warrant his claims and conclusions? The third factor is again dynamism—a judgment about his power and activity.[9]

Communication as a Process of Influence

Expanding the model of the communication process allows us to observe the end result of communication effectiveness. In this expanded model the *result* of the communication attempt is instrumental in determining the overall effectiveness of communication, whereas the more limited view of effectiveness we discussed earlier merely addresses itself to the extent to which the *meaning* received coincides with the meaning intended by the source. If we consider that the overall *purpose* of communication is to influence another through the transmission of messages and meaning, then a simple measurement of effectiveness is simply that of the degree to which the receiver is affected by the message or does as is wished by the source.

This expanded model is rather realistic. Many advertisers are not satisfied simply with transmitting a message of product quality to potential customers; the intent of the persuasive appeal, rather, is to influence an audience to purchase a particular product rather than another. The manager, in his communication attempt, typically employs communication as a means to achieve a desired state—which may be any one of, or any combination of, the effects of changing opinion, perception, emotional relationships, or actions. Figure 9-2 illustrates how the communication process can result in specific, observable communication effects.

The source typically has in mind a particular purpose he wishes to accomplish. This creates the need for communication to take place. We have assumed all along that human behavior is purposeful, and there is no reason to exclude communication from this assumption. Even informal conversations take place to fill a social need among conversants. Communications within goal-oriented organizations must also display purposiveness, especially as they occur within the formal context of the task.

Given the rationale of goal-oriented communication attempts, we must regard the communication process as a major link in the attainment of some purpose. If the source's intent is to cause another to change his behavior, then measuring the effectiveness of the communication attempt by how well the meaning received compares with meaning intended seems incomplete. The receiver may understand the source's message fully, yet continue to behave as he always has. We will probably agree that the communication attempt has actually been a failure, from both the source's and the receiver's perspective.

Similar reasoning will show us that under unusual conditions a complete

[9]Andersen, p. 81.

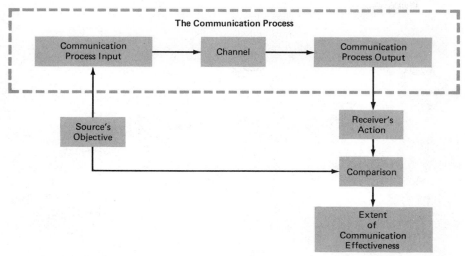

FIGURE 9-2   An expanded communication model: communication effectiveness as influence process.

communication "breakdown" may still yield a state of communication effectiveness! A foreman, attempting to get a worker to increase his productivity,
might take him aside for a personal chat about using new work methods.
The worker could interpret the total message received as meaning his work
has fallen off so far that the foreman has initiated the counseling step in the
dismissal procedure—and work harder! A purist would agree that a breakdown in communication had occurred. Pragmatically we observe that the
intent of the communication attempt has indeed been achieved, so that the
attempt has succeeded. We must hasten to note that a great similarity
between intended and received meaning will greatly increase the *probability*
that the intent of the communication attempt will result in the desired
behavior.

Figure 9-3 shows in a little more detail the types of objectives of the
source and how the communication process is central to the attempt to
achieve the purpose. The source might variously wish to change the opinion,
perception, interpersonal relationships, or actions of the receiver through
affecting his cognitions.[10]

Organizational Communication

Simply because an organization is composed of the intangible relationships and interactions among individuals, communication is a constant and

[10]The desired cognitive changes are adapted from Carl I. Hovland and Irving L. Janis
(eds.), *Personality and Persuasibility* (New Haven, Conn.: Yale University Press, 1959), p. 4.

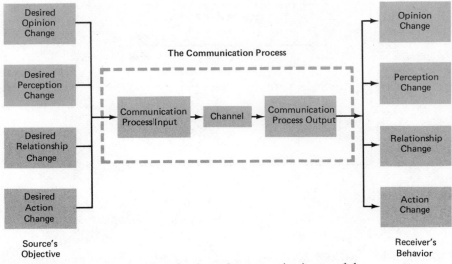

FIGURE 9-3   A general goal-oriented communication model.

critical factor. The typical pyramid-shaped organization, because of its dependence on specialization and hierarchy, requires at a minimum a downward flow of communication. Management employs many different formal communication channels. Typical channels include letters to employees, mass meetings, house organs (company newspapers or magazines), information racks, bulletin boards, plant tours, motion pictures, institutional advertising, community radio–TV–newspaper space, notes in pay envelopes, handbooks, and financial reports.[11] Yet one study indicated that employees' "principal sources of information are unofficial contacts."[12]

Formal devices are helpful in keeping employees informed. The mass communication techniques listed are generally efficient modes of communication but could hardly be considered very effective or influential. Notice the lack of feedback opportunities, for example. These one-way communication modes are typical of the formal communication techniques employed by management. There seems to be an intensity of downward communication that is optimum:

If there are too few of such formal communications, rumors will flourish in their absence, even on the executive level. On the other hand, the channels can get flooded with much irrelevant material so that the employe tends to "tune out" the whole system which is overloaded with messages. Even important messages may lose their saliency because they are imbedded in so much information of less consequence to the employe. Also there may be conditions under which a sense of frustration develops because the distribution of information results in everyone

[11]Bernard M. Bass, *Organizational Psychology* (Boston: Allyn & Bacon, 1965), p. 290.
[12]Ibid.

finding himself concerned with everyone else's problems, problems which he often cannot make any contribution to solving.[13]

Communication Technology

Communication is composed of processes, and these processes can be used to attain various purposes. Obviously the fast feedback associated with informal conversation is not a universal characteristic of all communication modes. The *technology* of communication must be selected and adapted to the situation. Several of these technological aspects of communication, discussed in the following sections, are direction of flow, information access, structure, and communication style.

Communication Flow

Two facets of communication flow are of direct relevance to organizational behavior. The first of these deals with *unilateral* (no feedback) and *bilateral* (feedback access built into the process) communication. The other, quite similar to the first, is comprised of *upward, downward,* and *lateral* organizational communication.

UNILATERAL AND BILATERAL COMMUNICATION   Unilateral communication entails the one-sided (one-way) transmission attempt. No feedback is provided for, and the source cannot receive information about the success of the attempt *during* the process—the degree to which communication actually occurred typically is not known until long after the attempt is concluded, when information is available from the *action* that resulted. Certainly, we might demur, no reasonable source would communicate unilaterally if he had a choice! Being pragmatic, we must recognize the efficiency of such a mode, even while questioning its effectiveness. Indeed, the sheer volume of unilateral communications is overwhelming when one considers the messages from television, radio, newspapers, lectures, letters, movies, and so on.

The efficiency of the unilateral mode is obvious; how *effective* is it? Are comparisons available between the effectiveness of unilateral and bilateral modes? Fortunately some evidence exists that supplements our hunches.

Leavitt and Mueller[14] experimented with the effect of various levels of feedback on task performance. The four feedback levels were

1. Zero feedback: the source was obscured from the receivers by a screen, and no questions or noises were allowed to be made by the receivers.
2. Visible audience: source and receivers were visible to each other, but receivers were not allowed to communicate with the source.

[13]Ibid., pp. 298, 299.
[14]Harold J. Leavitt and Ronald A. H. Mueller, "Some Effects of Feedback on Communication," *Human Relations,* **4**:401–410 (1951).

3. Yes–no feedback: source and receivers were visible to each other, and receivers could say only "yes" or "no" in response to questions from the source.
4. Free feedback: receivers were allowed to interrupt or ask questions of the source.

The task for the source was to describe orally a series of complex geometric patterns. The measure of effectiveness was the degree of accuracy with which the eighty receivers were able to reproduce the described (but unseen) patterns. The possible accuracy scores ranged from a minimum of zero to a maximum of 6.

As might be expected, average accuracy increased as feedback increased, from 4.7 (out of a possible 6, under zero feedback) to 5.3 (under visible audience) to 5.5 (under yes–no) to 5.6 (under free feedback). The confidence with which the receivers estimated their own accuracy was closely associated with actual accuracy, increasing with increased feedback opportunity. For efficiency, however, another pattern emerged. The average time required to describe the patterns increased as feedback opportunity increased. Zero feedback (229 seconds) required less than two thirds of the average time of the free feedback mode (363 seconds).

COMMUNICATION DIRECTIONALITY   One of the factors that distinguishes an organization is its hierarchy of positions and authority. The hierarchical arrangement and its consequent specialization create the need for direction to be provided from the superior position and for relevant information to be channeled up the hierarchy to the appropriate decision-making level. Downward direction and upward information flow are then necessary for the organization to be effective, as well as for its members to contribute meaningfully.

We noted earlier that authority gradations cement together the work relationships within the organization. We can add now that authority and formal communication flow through the same channels, supplementing each other. Authority can be considered relatively static and communication relatively dynamic. Authoritative communications are those influence attempts legitimized by the organization and are typically directed downward, from superior to subordinate. Through communication, authority and direction are exercised. Communication *effectiveness,* then, is important. Should any of the multitude of potential barriers or breakdowns occur within the authoritative communication attempt, serious results could stem from misunderstandings or failure to receive the message. Even the misplaced memo (perhaps giving permission for an emergency negotiation session with union leaders) can have impact.

At the same time, the upward flow of communication is important to the administrator. What with delegation of authority and decentralization of decision making, vital information can be lost simply because of the lack of channels set aside for information to flow *upward*. Many a chief executive has sat stunned in his office after being victimized by a wildcat strike. Others have been kept isolated from plant conditions or breakthroughs by the competitors because their communication channels were not engineered to yield these types of information from subordinates.

Even those executives who feel comfortable with an information system (which relies on their subordinates to transmit appropriate messages upward) may occasionally squirm with the realization that upward communications are frequently either distorted or absorbed by the links in the communication channel who mistake the intent or the content of the message. Some are distorted or absorbed for self-serving purposes, too.

Communication Engineering for Results

Built-in technological or structural factors affect the results of the communication process. The ways in which the communication processes are structured among more than two participants are major factors to consider in the engineering of the communication process to attain maximum effectiveness.

Communication Networks

The concepts of communication technology previously discussed can easily be applied to more complex communication situations. Complicating factors may include such diverse factors as numbers of participants, structure of communication flow, and hierarchy. When the communication process involves more than two people, communication *networks* emerge. Networks are simply diagrams of processes, and communication networks merely represent the direction and spatial arrangement of communication attempts.

The most common communication networks are those shown in Figure 9-4.

Each of these networks could be easily modified if the two-way communication (illustrated by the double-headed arrows) were reduced. The arrows depict the only channels open to each participant (shown as a circle) in the network. Thus in the wheel network each person can communicate *only* with the central person and not with the others. Obviously this central person is in a highly powerful position, because all must communicate through him.

Task Performance

We might well expect the task performance of each communication network to differ from that of the other networks. Many research efforts have investigated how, and why, performance varies with network configuration, when performance is measured by problem-solving efficiency.

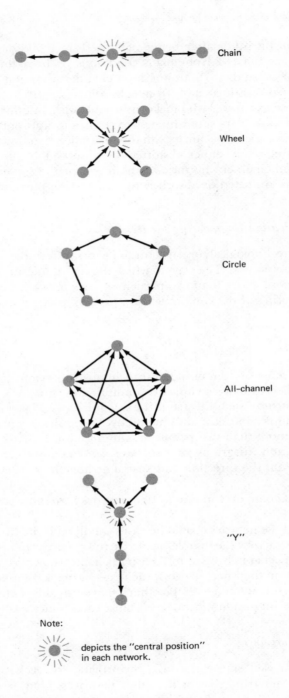

Chain

Wheel

Circle

All-channel

"Y"

Note:

depicts the "central position"
in each network.

FIGURE 9-4 Communication networks.

In general, the more highly centralized a network is (such as in the "wheel"), the greater the problem-solving efficiency—when the problems are *simple*. A simple problem requires only that information be gathered, "makes no demand upon problem-solving ability of group members ... [or] requires no manipulation of information."[15]

When the task is relatively complex, requiring analysis or manipulation of information, the more decentralized networks (such as the "circle") are more efficient. As an example, the leaderless "circle" allows two-way communication among adjacent members and a greater input to (and pooling of) knowledge.

The natures of the networks also have effects other than pure efficiency or accuracy. Speed, emergence of a leader, morale, and flexibility of job change are other features of communication networks.

A leader is more apt to emerge in those networks with central positions because of the structural requirement of passing information to or through the central position. Knowledge has been said to be power, and access to information seems related to being acknowledged as a leader. The group's ability to adapt to new task requirements is related in the opposite way to degree of centralization: the more decentralized networks adapt much faster than do the centralized networks.

When centralized and decentralized networks are compared with each other on simple problems, decentralized networks are *slower* in solving the problem and *less accurate,* yet *morale* is reported as being higher and *more messages* are transmitted among members than in centralized networks. For *complex* problem situations, however, the centralized networks are inferior; *centralized* networks are slower in problem solving as well as less accurate, with lower morale and fewer messages than in decentralized networks.

TABLE 9-1   **Effect of Problem Complexity on Selected Criteria for Types of Communication Networks**

	Decentralized (circle, all channel)		Centralized (wheel, chain, Y)	
	Simple Problem	*Complex Problem*	*Simple Problem*	*Complex Problem*
Speed of Performance	slow	fast	fast	slow
Accuracy	lower	higher	higher	lower
Morale	high	high	low	lower
Number of Messages	more	more	less	less

SOURCE: Adapted from Alex Bavelas and Dermot Barrett, "An Experimental Approach to Organizational Communication," *Personnel* (March 1951), pp. 370–71; and M. E. Shaw, "Communication Networks," in *Advances in Experimental Social Psychology,* Vol. 1, ed. by M. E. Shaw (New York: Academic Press, 1964), p. 123.

[15]Marvin E. Shaw, *Group Dynamics: The Psychology of Small Group Behavior* (New York: McGraw-Hill, 1971), p. 143.

Summary

Communication provides the vehicle for interaction and exchange among individuals. Isolating the common elements of communication attempts lets us identify source, abstracting and symbolizing, the message, the channel, the receiver, interpretation, and meaning as essentials. Feedback links the receiver's understanding to the source's original intended message.

Probably no communication attempt is perfectly successful, and specific factors decrease the probability or the degree of success. Often a conscious decision is made to lessen communication effectiveness in favor of increased efficiency, often through alternative media. Some media or channels have negative elements inherent in their makeup. Some of these are noise and barriers, which may lead to breakdowns in communication.

The communication process model may be expanded to include the source's intent or purpose and the receiver's consequent behavior. Communication effectiveness may then be described as a function of the match between the source's purpose and the receiver's behavior.

Finally, communication technology may be employed to maximize effectiveness in small groups, based on research studies of communication networks. Various network configurations (such as "circle," "wheel," "chain," "Y," and "all-channel") have different strengths and drawbacks that must be recognized in formal organizational communication.

The effectiveness of one-way and two-way communication attempts has many implications for the organization, especially because direction of communication (upward, downward, or lateral) makes built-in feedback difficult.

STUDY AND REVIEW QUESTIONS

1. What are some additional "barriers" to communication besides those mentioned in the text?

2. At what level in the organization—top management, supervisor, or worker—do you think communication effectiveness to be *most* important? *Least* important?

3. How realistic or useful is the expanded communication model (Figure 9-3)? Does it provide more or less practical insights into communication than Figure 9-1?

4. Can you think of some communication attempts that are both efficient *and* effective? (You may wish to consider the communication mode's alternatives in arriving at a conclusion.)

5. How can noise be eliminated from the communication process?

6. In which step of the communication process does noise have the most effect on communication effectiveness?

7. Compare and contrast the concepts of "noise" and "communication barriers."

8. How do organizational communications differ from informal conversations? In what ways are they similar?

9. Can you arrive at some generalizations on "decision rules" regarding how and when to trade off communication efficiency and effectiveness? List as many as you can think of.

10. Which network configuration would you choose as the most *effective* in the college classroom? The most *efficient*? (Hint: consider the purpose and nature of the task involved.) Why?

Chapter

10

The Matter of Perception

CHAPTER OBJECTIVES

1. To present perception as a process intervening between reality and the individual.

2. To analyze some common perceptual processes through which meaning is elicited and organized from one's environment.

3. To show the influence of perception on individual behavior, through considering perceived equity and dissonance.

4. To demonstrate the extent to which perceptual processes are employed in organizational behavior.

5. To introduce perceptual bases to managerial behavior through Theory X and Theory Y.

The importance of interpretation in the communication process has been heavily underscored. Any message must be *received and interpreted* before the communication attempt is complete. What complicates this seemingly straightforward process is the way in which we *organize* the information we receive, through perception.

Information comes to us in many forms besides communication attempts, becoming inputs. We can label all sensory inputs as *stimuli,* because they affect ("stimulate") our receptors and set the stage for a response. Communication attempts are only one type of stimulus to which we are constantly exposed. Other stimuli, different from communication attempts, also impinge on our hearing, sight, touch, smell, and taste. The five senses allow us to relate to the reality around us and to incorporate an understanding of our environment into our behavior.

The Purpose of Perception

We are constantly subjected to many diverse stimuli. Why are we not completely overwhelmed by their sheer volume? An internal process called *perception* serves both as a filter and as a method of organizing stimuli, thereby allowing us to cope with our environment. The perception process provides the mechanism through which stimuli are selected and grouped in a meaningful fashion. As a result, we are more nearly able to understand the total picture of the environment these stimuli represent.

One reason perception is central in interpreting the world around us is that we each perceive, yet may perceive *differently,* what is an *identical* situation. Perception is an almost automatic process and works in much the same way within each individual, yet typically yields *different* perceptions.

A logical question to ask at this point is, "Why do we perceive things differently? Isn't reality concrete and unchanging?" If *reality* is concrete and unchanging, then we would conclude that perceptions could not differ. Unfortunately, no matter how things actually are, we can only experience them through the stimuli associated with reality. Because information, people, and situations are always changing within our environment, stimuli also change and thus provide ambiguous clues to what is "really" there.[1]

We can extend the idea of perception as the mechanism through which meaning is derived from environmental stimuli (including communication attempts) to the conclusion that perception is extremely important to the understanding of organizational behavior. An individual does not react, or behave, in a certain way because of what the situation around him actually *is* but because of what he *sees* or *believes* it to be. The distinction is crucial. One's perception of a situation or message becomes the basis on which he behaves. We can see this with a few simple examples of how meaning is attached to

[1]Mason Haire, *Psychology in Management,* 2nd Ed. (New York: McGraw-Hill, 1964), pp. 55, 56.

actions or objects—which can be completely different from the meaning attached to the same action or object by another person. A construction helmet may be perceived merely as a protective device for the vulnerable cranium against falling objects on a construction site or as a symbol of extreme conservative philosophy in politics. The clenched fist can similarly be perceived either as an angry threat or as an expression of solidarity. An industrial engineer's stopwatch can be seen either as a device to measure the passage of time or as an instrument by which the worker is exploited by being forced to work harder for less money.

A hint on the nature of perception might be gathered the next time you discuss a controversial issue with another. You might find yourself saying, "I don't see it that way." The ways in which we each *see* things and the ways in which our beliefs affect what we do—these are the substance of perception. Actions or objects do not have meaning in and of themselves; meaning is *imputed* by the perceiver. The meaning so attached is uniquely derived from the desires, personality, and experiences of each individual. This does not, of course, rule out shared or widely held meanings for common objects; agreements as to meanings or similar backgrounds often furnish the means whereby symbols or actions are perceived in the same way by different people.

At this point we can capsulize the importance of perception in organizational behavior by drawing an analogy of perception to our concept of effective communications. No matter how "perfect" an attempt at communication may be, it must be considered ineffective if it does not accomplish what the source intends. Similarly, "A stimulus that is not perceived has no effect on behavior."[2] If one has never heard—nor heard of—classical music, he cannot perceive that classical music is "weird," only for snobbish intellectuals and consequently to be avoided. The stimulus (classical music) certainly exists, yet without perception there are no behavioral consequences.

Similarly a threatening message that is lost in the mails is not received and hence cannot be perceived. The supervisor's confidential appraisal of a subordinate's performance as "barely acceptable" cannot affect the latter's understanding of his own situation, unless the appraisal is communicated to *him*—and even then his ego defenses might make him perceive the appraisal differently than intended. Any attempt to affect organizational behavior must first run the perceptual gamut.

Components of Perception

What are the basic components of the perceptual process? We can easily identify information as a stimulus–input that must be perceived. For percep-

[2]Fremont E. Kast and James E. Rosenzweig, *Organization and Management: A Systems Approach,* 2nd Ed. (New York: McGraw-Hill, 1974), p. 252.

tion to occur, the stimulus must first be identified or recognized. This implies that some selection rule is used to differentiate between information that is to be perceived and information that is to be ignored. The information must then be organized in some meaningful way, that is, interpreted in the light of the situation and past experience. As a direct result of this process of perception formation, the individual is able to incorporate relevant information from his external environment into his behavior.

Selectivity

Myriads of stimuli seemingly clamor for our attention at any given time. We need to filter or screen out most of them so that we may deal with the important or relevant ones. A person being trained as a machinist normally finds the din of the shop floor deafening and distracting. He quickly becomes accustomed to the noise and ignores it, concentrating instead on the telltale hum of his machine for cues as to how it's working.

We have a "threshold" of perception. Stimuli below the threshold level in intensity or volume are ignored. When intensity or volume exceeds the threshold level, the stimuli begin to be sensed and we become aware of them, paying attention and reacting to them. This helps to explain how we can be so constantly immersed in stimulus bombardment at all times and yet cope with what must be an overwhelming sensory overload. Most of what we are familiar with we simply ignore, paying attention only to those things that are unfamiliar and thereby warrant attention or that become impossible to ignore—like a blaring radio in the next room while one attempts to concentrate on a difficult lesson.

Adaptation plays an important part in perceptual selectivity. We can become accustomed to stimuli (noises, for example), adapting our threshold of selectivity so that familiar stimuli do not arouse attention. We might think of the night watchman who routinely got a few hours of sleep between rounds in a noisy round-the-clock factory. When the power (and the noisy machines) went off one night, he jumped up out of a sound sleep and exclaimed, "What's that?!"

Perceptual Organization

When stimuli impinge on our consciousness, we attempt to make sense out of them, to organize them in such a way that we can derive meaning from their overall pattern. This is quite similar to the many data points on a graph. One data point by itself allows very little meaningful interpretation of trends or states of nature to be drawn; the more data points we assemble on the graph, however, the more able we are to infer a possible pattern. Eventually we may make a rather confident statement of a trend based on our interpretation and understanding of the graph. In a similar way, information is gathered and organized in the perceptual process. Over fifty years ago Wertheimer isolated eight principles of perceptual organization, factors involved in the gathering and patterning of information. The factors he derived were these:

1. *Proximity.* In a field of dots, like the starry sky, those that are near together are spontaneously seen as a group separate from others that are apart.
2. *Sameness and similarity.* A cluster of bright stars stands out as a unit from the background of dimmer ones. In a dot field of several colors, those of one color are likely to stand out together, the others retiring for the moment to the background.
3. *Common movement.* If some of the dots move together in the same direction and at the same speed, they stand out from the rest which remain stationary. An important example is the parallel retinal movement of objects at a certain distance resulting from any movement of the observer himself. . . . Thus the near objects are segregated from the distant ones.
4. *Continuity.* If several of the dots lie in a straight line or fairly simple curve, this unit stands out and catches the eye. A modern example, the lights of a road as seen from an airplane at night.
5. *Closure.* This factor operates in two ways. A closed figure has an advantage over a straight line or an open curve. And if a figure, otherwise continuous, has a small discontinuity, like a small gap in a circle, the gap tends to close itself automatically. "Closing the gap" is regarded as a dynamic factor also in problem solution.
6. *Pregnance.* A figure is "pregnant" if all parts of it conform to the general character of the whole. A perfect square is more pregnant than any sort of near-square.
7. *Familiarity.* Previous experience has conferred a perceptual advantage on letters of the alphabet and on the profile of the human face though these configurations have very little goodness in the sense of symmetry, regularity, or simplicity.
8. *Set.* . . . We find what we are looking for; at least what we are looking for has an advantage over other figures that are equally favored by all the other factors.[3]

In Figure 10-1 we see how the first five of these principles may be illustrated. The first figure (labeled *proximity*) shows how we tend to group similar items together on the basis of how close they are to each other. We might perceive the figure as being five groups of paired dots, rather than a simple line of dots. The second figure shows that proximity can be overcome by *sameness* or *similarity*. Each dot and X pair are physically closer than the dots are or the X's are. The dissimilar, yet close, figures are not the basis for grouping, but rather the X's are grouped together and perceived as a group, just as are the dots.

[3]Robert S. Woodworth, *Dynamics of Behavior* (New York: Henry Holt, 1958), pp. 193–195.

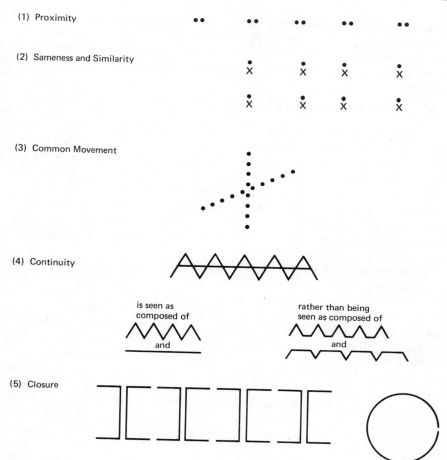

FIGURE 10-1   Illustrations of major principles of perceptual organization.

The third figure *(common movement)* shows dots arranged into two intersecting lines. The perceiver will probably assign the dots near the intersection to one or the other line with little trouble; they just "go with" the series of dots in a line. The influence of *continuity* is exhibited in the fourth figure. We see the compound figure as being composed of two continuous figures rather than the two discontinuous figures. Finally, the phenomenon of *closure* is displayed. In closure we are biased toward perceiving figures that are closed rather than open or incomplete.

When these principles are applied to the perceptual process undergone by all individuals, we can see that they are necessary if we are to make sense out of a very complicated and incomplete world. We rather readily group things together, whether they are people or data, according to how closely they are physically grouped or to how similar they appear in their external characteristics. Even incomplete data or information is not a deterrent to our being able to make sense out of the incompleteness. The perceptual processes involved in these everyday occurrences is a learned phenomenon, one that we learn to employ almost automatically and unconsciously.

Organizational Examples of Perceptual Processes

Within the formal organization the factor of proximity can be seen rather easily; for administrative purposes workers who are in close physical contact with each other may be grouped. If grievances emanate from the group, coupled with low production, management may perceive that the entire group is dissatisfied and exhibits this attitude in lower productivity and higher complaints. Naturally this perception may be erroneous; other factors may be causing the low productivity, with only a few of the group initiating grievances. In any event, the group may be perceived, because of proximity, as a single entity.

Common physical characteristics may also provide the basis for perceiving people as a group, such as classifying all black workers or all engineers or all blue-collar workers as belonging to a single homogeneous group, when in fact each member of that "group" is a unique individual. Continuity may be seen as being expressed by a supervisor's ability to identify readily the routine activities repetitiously performed by a subordinate, rather than random activities done sporadically. The repetitive activities may be much easier to pick out of the total job he does, to extrapolate a trend, and to perceive some measure of performance. Closure may be illustrated by the supervisor who thinks he has total agreement from his departmental subordinates on a problem when several of them are actually opposed. After discussion, the department head might perform closure and erroneously perceive unanimity.[4]

Luthans pointed out another demonstration of the perceptual process in an organizational setting. Hard-core unemployed workers are often trained by companies, the training sessions being conducted in quiet, classroom-type settings. One company found that the subsequent on-the-job performance of these trainees was inadequate and decided to find why.

The company discovered that the poor performance was due to the extremely loud noises that occurred on the assembly line. The workers were not accustomed to the noise because their training had taken place under nice, clean, and quiet conditions. When placed on the noisy factory floor, the contrasting din drew all their attention and adversely affected their performance. To solve this problem, the company concluded the training sessions right next to the noisy factory floor. By the end of the training sessions, the workers were used to the noise and they performed very well when subsequently placed on the job.[5]

[4]Fred Luthans, *Organizational Behavior: A Modern Behavioral Approach to Management* (New York: McGraw-Hill, 1973), pp. 351–352.

[5]Ibid., pp. 340, 341.

This example shows how the natural process of adapting to familiar stimuli—and opening wide the perceptual floodgates to unfamiliar or intense stimuli—may be incorporated into desired organizational behavior. Understanding perception and its element of adaptation allowed the company to *perceive correctly* the true state and then to respond effectively to that reality. (Notice how easy it would have been to *perceive* that the trainees were *untrainable* and then to curtail the hard-core training program).

Stereotypes and Halos

Closely related to these factors in the perceptual process are the phenomena of stereotyping and the halo effect. Walter Lippmann first pointed out the function of stereotypes over fifty years ago, because we define or categorize a situation *before* we see or perceive it, rather than the other way around: "In the great booming, buzzing confusion of the outer world, we pick out what our culture already has defined for us, and we tend to perceive that which we have picked out in the form stereotyped for us by our culture."[6]

Stereotyping

A person is classified by another as belonging to a group or category (sameness and similarity factor) because of certain characteristics. Often the attributes of the overall category may be rather widely agreed upon (which may not mean that they are correct), and these characteristics or traits are then attributed to the person assigned to that category. Many categories furnish the basis for stereotypes; one can attribute traits or behaviors to an individual if he knows, for example, that he is a Republican. Alternatively the traits or behaviors can be attributed to another, given that he is a black; still others flow from being categorized as a physician:

Stereotyping consists of classifying all new experiences, and especially persons, using symbols learned in the past. These symbols consist of significant cues for the classification. Important in this list of cues are race, ethnic background, socio-economic status, and others. Persons and situations are infinitely more complex than these simple cues will admit.[7]

While we emphasize that stereotyped behaviors and traits are often incorrect, stereotypes do furnish us with a most valuable mechanism. They allow us to short-circuit the process of independently evaluating a complex set of behaviors or traits for each individual before being able to have expectations or make predictions about behaviors or actions. Stereotypes furnish us with a shortcut route to predicting behavior. Naturally, when

[6]Walter Lippmann, *Public Opinion* (New York: Macmillan, 1922), p. 31.
[7]Abraham Zaleznik and David Moment, *The Dynamics of Interpersonal Behavior* (New York: Wiley, 1964), p. 35.

predicted and actual behavior do not coincide, then a more intensive investigation is necessary. Stereotypes quickly fall apart when an individual falls into a number of *different* categories that have stereotypes. Consider the Republican who is also a black physician. Each of the three roles or categories implied in this description might have stereotyped behaviors quite different from the others.

Halo Effect

The halo effect is similar in nature to the stereotype. The difference is that a *single trait* exhibited by the person forms the basis for an overall evaluation of the individual. Thus a highly articulate or very personable professor may receive higher overall student ratings for his teaching than one who stutters and stumbles or who is considered a "cold fish."

In a classic study Asch had two persons evaluated, each of whom exhibited identical personality traits—with the exception of one characteristic.[8] The list of character traits included *warm* for one and was replaced with *cold* in the other's trait list. The group that was informed that the person was skillful, practical, determined, industrious, intelligent, cautious, and *warm* judged him also to be wise, imaginative, popular, and humorous. A major difference appeared in the perceptions of those individuals who were informed that the person being evaluated was *cold*, yet also characterized by the same other traits; the perception of the "cold" individual was much less positive.

Kelley did a study similar to Asch's, but in a classroom setting at MIT. He also focused on different perceptions of the same individual as determined by the descriptive terms *warm* and *cold*.[9]

Various undergraduate classes were told that their regular instructor was out of town and that a substitute would take over. The experimenters indicated that as part of their own interest in the general problem of how various classes react to different instructors, the students would later be given some forms to fill out about him. (They were assured this wouldn't affect their own grades or the substitute's status.) A short biographical note about the newcomer was given out; the notes were identical, except that one form described him as being, among other things, "very warm" and the other form called him "rather cold." The material was given without people knowing that there were two kinds of information being distributed. The "stimulus person" then appeared and led the class in a twenty-minute discussion. A record was kept of how often each student participated in the discussion. Then subjects wrote free descriptions of the instructor, and rated him on a set of fifteen rating scales.

The results showed clearly that the instructor was consistently rated more

[8]S. E. Asch, "Forming Impressions of the Personality," *Journal of Abnormal and Social Psychology*, **41**: 258–290 (1946).

[9]H. H. Kelley, "The Warm–Cold Variable in First Impressions of Persons," *Journal of Personality*, **18**: 431–439 (1950).

favorably by those told that he was "warm" than by those who had been told that he was "cold." Although they all "saw" the situation, those set to see the person as "warm" rated him as being more considerate of others, more informal, more sociable, more popular, more humorous, and more humane. . . .

Did their set affect their own behavior or just the ratings? Apparently it affected the behavior also, for a larger proportion of those who had been told that the instructor was "warm" participated in discussions than of those that were told he was "cold." This is in line with the principle that perception serves to guide and steer a person's behavior in his social environment, and that an unfavorable perception set can lead to cutting down on our interactions with others.[10]

Perceptions of others are then apparently important in affecting the perceiver's behavior toward the person perceived. A *situation* can also be perceived, and this perception can be affected by the halo effect, as demonstrated by Grove and Kerr.[11] The morale of office workers was measured, together with salaries and working conditions. Salaries and working conditions were found to be better than those in similar firms in the area, even though the firm studied was then in receivership. The employees, when compared to employees in a financially sound company, were naturally less satisfied with job security. More importantly, "a form of halo effect operated with the employees expressing discontent with their actually superior pay and working conditions as well as with their work associates and immediate superiors."[12]

Perceptions, Behavior, and Attitudes

We have seen that perception is a process that is constantly between us and reality. Perception orders reality so that it fits our developing notions of the way that things are. The end result of perceiving then becomes an important input to the behavior of the individual. A situation or a single act may be seen in such a way (as a stimulus) as to bring forth rather complex behaviors in response.

In the next sections we will look into two constructs of perceptual organization, with emphasis on their implications for organizational behavior. In the first, the deep-seated value of social justice is shown to organize perceptions of effort and reward; equity theory furnishes a convenient framework. The second deals with man's penchant for consistency and abhorrence of incongruity; Festinger's theory of cognitive-dissonance gives us an opportunity to consider an interesting aspect of perception and behavior.

[10]Timothy W. Costello and Sheldon S. Zalkind, *Psychology in Administration: A Research Orientation* (Englewood Cliffs, N.J.: Prentice-Hall, 1963), p. 21.
[11]B. A. Grove and W. A. Kerr, "Specific Evidence on Origin of Halo Effect in Measurement of Morale," *Journal of Social Psychology*, **34:** 165–170 (1951).
[12]Costello and Zalkind, p. 35.

Equity Theory

An appreciation of "fair-play" and "fairness" seems characteristic of most people. Even though inequality does exist as a result of special training or skills, we think it only "fair" that men and women doing the same work should be paid on the same scale. Similarly we approve merit raises or bonuses to outstanding football players or industrial workers.

If a student puts in a certain number of hours studying for a quiz, he normally expects to get a grade similar to that received by another student with whom he studied and who studied the same number of hours. If the other student receives an A and the first student gets a C, offense may be taken. People compare the rewards they receive with the effort (costs) they expend—relative to the rewards received and the costs incurred by *other* people! We can express this as follows:[13]

$$\frac{\text{Rewards}_1}{\text{Costs}_1} = \frac{\text{Rewards}_2}{\text{Costs}_2} = \frac{\text{Rewards}_3}{\text{Costs}_3}$$

If these ratios are not roughly the same, then equity has not occurred. Interestingly, people will attempt to change the variables in the equity equation. In one case, proofreaders who perceived they were underpaid "adjusted" the equation by doing their jobs at a faster rate, carelessly making many errors.[14] Litterer summarized five ways in which the individual can reduce perceived inequity:

1. *Changing either the inducements or the contributions.* For example, if on hourly work and feeling underpaid, the worker can hold back his efforts costs . . . until it seems in proper proportion to his pay. . . . If the individual feels he is being unfairly overpaid, it seems a bit too much to expect him to request a reduction in salary, but he can and probably would work harder, raising his contribution and bringing the ratio into the "proper range."
2. *Perceptually distorting inducements or contributions.* Here the person would in some way, and there are many, convince himself that his contribution is actually much greater or less, than one might initially have thought it to be, or that the inducements received are much more important than initially perceived. This process ends in the "sour grapes" position.
3. *Leaving the field.* Escape . . . can take both physical and cognitive forms. A person can quit his job, can be absent, and so on. He can also become apathetic, daydream, or be there "in body only."

[13]Cf. John B. Miner, *The Management Process: Theory, Research, and Practice* (New York: Macmillan, 1973), p. 312; and David R. Hampton, Charles E. Summer, and Ross A. Webber, *Organizational Behavior and the Practice of Management,* Rev. Ed. (Glenview, Ill.: Scott, Foresman, 1973), p. 224.

[14]W. M. Evan and R. G. Simmons, "Organization Effects of Inequitable Rewards: Two Experiments in Status Inconsistency," *Administrative Science Quarterly,* **14:** 224–237 (1969); cited in Miner, p. 313.

4. *Getting comparison person to change.* People individually or in groups often put others under considerable pressure to bring their behavior into line with what is "proper." A piece work employee who has a loose rate will find himself under considerable pressure to hold production down, to not go over the informal group ceiling on earnings, and usually will comply. A member of a work group who holds back, does less than those around him, will find himself under great pressure to "do his share."

5. *Changing the basis of reference.* An individual who has had an increase in earnings that perhaps changes the ratio of inducements to contributions from what he has previously experienced may change his reference group to a higher status one.[15]

Perception, then, is an integral component of behavior because equity must be "seen" and subjectively evaluated. Equity theory can furnish clues to the manager as he attempts to isolate factors that contribute to the vagaries and inconsistencies in organizational behavior.

Cognitive Dissonance

Basic to the perceptual process is the grouping and interpretation of information so that we may gather meaning from the patterns observed and then base our behaviors on these patterns. This also hints at another characteristic of the process, that of *expectations* or predictions that we can reasonably make based on the perceptual process. If we perceive that a manager is a hard-driving authoritarian, then our expectation of his behavior would be based on the perception. Whenever new information comes into focus or crosses the threshold of selectivity, we attempt to incorporate it into the patterns we have already perceived. Thus we may observe the manager in a fit of rage over what he thinks is a subordinate's incompetence or lack of ability to perform a satisfactory job. This new information can fit readily into our previous perception of the manager. Our expectation of his behavior is not changed but confirmed.

We also have expectations about our *own* behavior. For most people rationality is central in their self-image; few would willingly recognize or characterize themselves as irrational. If you see yourself as friendly and extroverted, sitting sullenly in a corner at each party attended is *inconsistent* with your cognition of yourself. We try to appear consistent, at least to ourselves. If we perceive inconsistencies, we try to remove them.[16]

When information fits comfortably with the perceptual patterns and expectations we have, then we are in a state of *consonance.* When contradictory evidence is encountered or when our expectations about what things go together and what do not are encountered, a state of *dissonance* occurs; this is

[15]Joseph A. Litterer, *The Analysis of Organizations,* 2nd Ed. (New York: Wiley, 1973), pp. 490, 491.

[16]Robert B. Zajonc, "The Concepts of Balance, Congruity, and Dissonance," *Public Opinion Quarterly,* **24**: 280 (1960).

a psychological state of discomfort. Festinger used the example of a person caught out in the rain without benefit of raincoat or umbrella; he would obviously expect to get wet. If he observed a torrential downpour, yet saw that he was *not* getting wet, these two pieces of evidence and the expectations derived from them would not "go together." The person caught in the rain would naturally feel rather uncomfortable about the contradictions he is experiencing, and we can say that dissonance exists between the two pieces of information of interest here.[17]

Because our expectations do not conform to reality or because the evidence is mutually contradictory, this discomfort sets up a tension or drive to reduce the dissonance. Some explanation must be found for the discrepancies encountered. Only then can dissonance be reduced and the state of consonance be reattained.

Such dissonance does not constantly occur; perception must be first aroused. Perceptual arousal will more typically occur if the dissonance becomes important to the individual. If you observe two inconsistent pieces of evidence, such as the fact that it is raining and that meanwhile a water sprinkler is soaking another's lawn, some amount of dissonance is aroused.[18] The dissonance aroused could easily be reduced, with some rather trivial explanations. You might assume that the owner of the house set the sprinkler before going shopping and before the threat of rain was seen. Dissonance is generally aroused to the point of being important primarily in situations when perception of the person's own behavior is an element. "In perceptions of our own behavior . . . dissonance may be high and difficult to change, and perceptions also have a stubborn resistance to change."[19]

So a person's perceptions of *his* decisions and *his* behavior create conditions under which dissonance is most often aroused. When dissonance is aroused, it can become a motivating force, because the individual must strive toward consonance in some way. He can do this only by changing either his perceptions of the world or his actions.

Let us consider the case of a habitual cigarette smoker who has been exposed to the scientific evidence from the Surgeon General's Office that smoking is bad for his health. He continues to smoke, and the antismoking evidence is dissonant with his cognition or recognition of his continued smoking. A tension or drive is then set up by the individual's innate desire for consistency. How can he achieve consonance? We can see that there are two possible choices: he can change either his behavior or his knowledge. Dissonance is effectively reduced if he quits smoking; in this case his actions are consistent with his knowledge. Alternatively he can change the "information" to which he has been exposed, by rationalizing it away or by rejecting it outright. He can then continue smoking with dissonance reduced because of the lack of credibility assigned to the dissonant evidence.

[17]Leon Festinger, "Cognitive Dissonance," *Scientific American* (October 1962), p. 94.
[18]David F. Wrench and Chris Wrench, *Psychology: A Social Approach,* 2nd Ed. (New York: McGraw-Hill, 1973), p. 197.
[19]Ibid.

We might also consider the case of the ambitious young manager. He may have a high opinion of his abilities and capabilities and strongly desire a promotion. If he is bypassed for promotion in favor of another, then clearly his cognitions are inconsistent with reality because he perceives that outstanding performance is rewarded with promotion. Should our young manager see the promoted competitor as less qualified, then the dissonance becomes even more intense. His dissonance reduction choices seem to be these: (1) He can reevaluate and reappraise his perceptions of his performance and abilities. (2) He can reappraise his perception of the causal link between performance and promotion. (3) He can change his attitude toward the desirability of promotion. (4) He can maintain his cognitions *and* his perception of the reality, yet interject other explanatory elements into the promotion of his competitor (such as upper management's "playing favorites" or the other's greater seniority).

Festinger clarified these alternatives by identifying three ways to reduce dissonance. The individual can change a behavioral cognitive element, change an environmental cognitive element, or add new cognitive elements. The change of a behavioral cognitive element may be accomplished by the individual's changing his behavior, his attitude, or his opinion so that consonance is achieved with the outside reality. Under some conditions the environmental cognitive element may be changed so that the "reality" conforms to the individual's perceptions or beliefs. For example, if an individual is habitually hostile toward other people, he might make sure that he is surrounded with people who provoke and deserve hostility, in order to achieve consonance between his cognitions and the external situation. In the third way of reducing dissonance, adding new cognitive elements, the individual might actively seek new information that *increases* the present dissonance. He might also be able to generate rationalizations that suitably (to the person under dissonance, anyway) bring about consistency between perception and reality.[20]

Administrative Behavior and Perception

The place of perception in attitude formation and behavior is significant. All individuals must perceive, whether in organized settings or not. Perceiving events and people *as they really are* is even more critical because behaviors occur as the *result* of perception. The organization, as a goal-directed social entity, owes its existence to the effectiveness with which its functions are differentiated and the extent to which cooperation occurs in the integration of the functions into systematic and coordinated activities and outputs.

Should members perceive hostility and aggression, they will react with behaviors appropriate to such threats. If one subconsciously feels inferior to

[20]Leon Festinger, *A Theory of Cognitive Dissonance* (Evanston, Ill.: Row, Peterson, 1957).

another, he will act in a submissive, deferential manner as they interact. How the individual perceives his situation must *directly affect* how he behaves.

Managers are no different, except that they function in more complex and ambiguous situations than do subordinates or people in nonorganized settings. Even the research physicist, dealing with unknown laws and properties, is confronted with complex but definable relationships. The manager faces situations as dynamic and undefinable as life itself. His attention must continually shift from problem to problem, administering to the greatly differing needs of subordinates, peers, and superiors. He is exposed to a bewildering array of stimuli, from which he must perceive relevant patterns of activities so that he can fulfill his overall function.

Perception often is not a conscious process, and hence its effects are subtle. The manager cannot afford to be at the total mercy of an unconscious process because of his impact on others and his responsibilities. Most managers pride themselves, in fact, on their hard-headed and realistic approach to managing, dealing only with the facts.

Yet the manager's relationships with others are based on his *perceptions* of their basic natures and motivations. McGregor identified two major perceptual structures, which he labeled *Theory X* and *Theory Y*.[21] The manager who perceives people according to either structure, regardless of whether or not he recognizes or acknowledges such perceptions, will behave in predictable patterns because of his personal assumptions, beliefs, and attitudes.

Theory X Assumptions

To trace the effects of these perceptual structures, we will start with the assumptions that underlie Theory X. Although few in number, the Theory X assumptions are very powerful in influencing the perceiver's specific behaviors toward specific individuals.

1. The average human being has an inherent dislike of work and will avoid it if he can.
2. Because of this human characteristic of dislike of work, most people must be coerced, controlled, directed, threatened with punishment to get them to put forth adequate effort toward the achievement of organizational objectives.
3. The average human being prefers to be directed, wishes to avoid responsibility, has relatively little ambition, wants security above all.[22]

Given the nature of perceptual organization factors, closure, set, familiarity, and similarity all act to enhance the "validity" of the Theory X assumptions and the behaviors that are consistent with them. Hence we see

---

[21]Douglas McGregor, *The Human Side of Enterprise* (New York: McGraw-Hill, 1960).
[22]Ibid., pp. 33, 34.

detailed job instructions by which to perform tasks already rationalized to their lowest common denominators; extensive methods to check on workers and their performance, such as work sampling and quality control; close supervision, with supervisors hovering over subordinates and watching for slackers; and jobs with "surprises" (need for imagination or initiative) engineered out. The manager argues, logically enough, that these are necessary because (1) that's what the workers want, and (2) if these direction and control techniques weren't used, the workers would never work!

Is the argument valid? Are people really like the Theory X assumptions? If they are, did Theory X-based techniques make them *more* Theory X-like, which required *more* controls, coercion, and direction? Where does the cycle stop?

Theory Y Assumptions

The other perceptual structure is completely different in its assumptions. They stress the developing nature of the individual and possibilities for individual differences and growth.

1. . . . The average human being does not inherently dislike work. Depending upon controllable conditions, work may be a source of satisfaction (and will be voluntarily performed) or a source of punishment (and will be avoided if possible).
2. External control and the threat of punishment are not the only means for bringing about effort toward organizational objectives. Man will exercise self-direction and self-control in the service of objectives to which he is committed.
3. Commitment to objectives is a function of the rewards associated with their achievement. . . .
4. The average human being learns, under proper conditions, not only to accept but to seek responsibility.
5. The capacity to exercise a relatively high degree of imagination, ingenuity, and creativity in the solution of organizational problems is widely, not narrowly, distributed in the population.
6. Under the conditions of modern industrial life, the intellectual potentialities of the average human being are only partially utilized.[23]

Here again we can infer how such assumptions can influence behavior. If you *perceive* a person *as if* he were a responsible individual, you would probably have no second thoughts about entrusting him with tasks that required initiative and commitment. Such experience would, in turn, encourage him to *become* even more responsible and committed to organizational goals.

The initial key to managerial behaviors, however, is the primary percep-

[23]Ibid., pp. 47, 48.

tion of the nature of man. The perception is generalized to the specific individuals in the manager's situation. They become assumptions that underlie the manager's concept of *how* he should manage—*given the nature of the individuals in his situation.* His concepts are than translated into specific behaviors and activities. And, as we have seen, these behaviors can constitute a self-fulfilling prophecy—a prediction that an event will happen . . . and so it does, because the prediction *makes* it happen. A Theory Y-oriented manager, because of his assumptions about others, can—under certain circumstances—make these assumptions come true because he behaves as if they *were* true!

Theories X and Y represent only two extremes on a scale of managerial perceptions of the nature of organizational man. They serve to bring home once again that perception is a complex process whose results are often far broader than we give them credit for.

The assumptions of a given manager may be inferred if his actions are traced backward from how he *must* perceive people to cause him to act that way. If he is strongly authoritarian, insists on doing things "by the book," and gives orders and commands rather than suggestions and counseling, we might well predict a Theory X perceptual structure and be able to forecast other behaviors consistent with those assumptions.

The manager who is less aloof, spends time teaching and training his subordinates, emphasizes obtaining results rather than following procedures, and delegates authority shows the earmarks of embracing Theory Y assumptions. Perception can make a difference—where it counts, in behavior. Understanding this point can give the practicing (and potential) manager a basic insight by which he can evaluate the hidden causes—and all-too-apparent effects—of his behavior.

Perception in Perspective

Perception is then a process a great deal more complex than might be assumed at first glance. The perceptual process is an intensely personal one and cannot be lightly dismissed. In communication and in any organizational setting, the individual must perceive his environment. Whether his perception of reality corresponds to reality itself is rather immaterial. An Olympian judgment that a manager *should* see reality the way it is rather than the way he *wants* to begs the question. An individual "sees" a situation in ways unique to his own situation and in terms of his own personal frame of reference. He also brings to the perceptual process his mental "set" or propensity to see things in a particular way. Many junior executives have enthusiastically attempted to implement responsible management practices, so that workers would benefit through changed work methods while benefiting the company through decreased costs. They have usually encountered stiff opposition from the very people they most wanted to help—the workers. Skeptical of managerial motives, the workers *perceived* a dark ulterior motive, the exploitation of the worker. Even though this was not consistent with objective reality, the perception of the workers was their own perceived reality and formed the basis for their rejection of the recommended changes.

Similarly the secretary to the president has no formal authority, yet she is perceived to have considerable power by virtue of her access to the president and is treated accordingly. The way in which she is treated is the same as if she actually had formal authority, rather than merely being perceived as being powerful.

Finally, the question of perception must be reduced to *differences* in perception. Throughout this chapter we have recognized that different people perceive things differently. We must recognize, too, that different *groups* of people are similar to each other in their perceptions, which may be different from the perceptions of other groups. Table 10-1 illustrates how supervisors and their subordinates differ. Who is right? Chances are that supervisors and subordinates alike are convinced that the other is less than honest in answering the questions.

Webber also found perceptual discrepancies between superiors and subordinates—in communication between levels. Superiors reported that they started verbal interactions with their subordinates, to the tune of an average 2.8 hours per week. Subordinates reported *receiving* only 1.6 hours

TABLE 10-1   **Perceptual Differences Between Supervisors and Subordinates**

	Asked of Supervisors: "How do you give recognition for good work done by employees in your work group?" *Frequency with which supervisors say "very often":*	Asked of Employees: "How does your supervisor give recognition for good work done by employees in your work group?" *Frequency with which employees say "very often":*
"Gives privileges"	52%	14%
"Gives more responsibility"	48%	10%
"Gives a pat on the back"	82%	13%
"Gives sincere and thorough praise"	80%	14%
"Trains for better jobs"	64%	9%
"Gives more interesting work"	51%	5%

SOURCE: Adapted from Rensis Likert, *New Patterns of Management* (New York: McGraw-Hill, 1961), p. 91.

per week of these communications! "It would appear that the act of initiating a communication makes more of an impression on the initiator than does reception on the receiver. Because of the initiator's involvement, he tends to remember more or exaggerate what he has done."[24]

Stereotypes are useful because they allow us to generalize. They steer us into behaving in "standardized" ways toward the person so stereotyped. Such behavior may be either effective or counterproductive. The power of stereotypes to influence, through perception, individuals in organized settings is highlighted in a study by Haire.[25] Labor and management representatives were asked to describe the characteristics of two men for whom photographs and short biographical backgrounds were given. Unknown to the participants, a key description was systematically changed, just as was done in Asch's "warm–cold" experiment previously discussed. This time, however, half the time the person pictured was described as an industrial manager and the other half as a labor union official. A significantly greater percentage of the managers described one man presented as a manager as honest, conscientious, mature, practical, and dependable than did managers who were told he was a union official.[26] Union representatives, when told the other person was a union man, saw him to be more active, aggressive, and efficient than when he was presented as being a manager.

Haire's study of stereotypes shared by group gains in importance when we investigate the concept of *selective perception* studied by Dearborn and Simon,[27] in which a group of executives were presented with a standard case problem. Their identifications of the most important problems they recognized were analyzed. Five of the six managers in the sales department identified "sales" as the most important problem. Three out of four accounting supervisors also identified "sales" (these three held positions involving analysis of product profitability). Only two of the other thirteen executives mentioned sales as the most important problem.

Four of five production executives identified "clarifying the organization"; other executives (in public relations, industrial relations, and medical services) saw human relations as the most important problem! What perceptual processes were in action?

Each of these studies has been presented to reinforce the idea that perception is a common and powerful phenomenon that influences behavior. Perception may be internal to each individual, but perceptions are themselves affected by the situation and thus likely to be shared by group members. Shared perceptions abruptly stop, however, with organizational

---

[24]Ross A. Webber, "Perceptions of Interactions Between Superiors and Subordinates," *Human Relations* (1970), p. 238.

[25]Mason Haire, "Role-Perception in Labor–Management Relations: An Experimental Approach," *Industrial and Labor Relations Review*, **8**: 204–216 (1955).

[26]Ibid.

[27]De Witt C. Dearborn and Herbert A. Simon, "Selective Perception: A Note on the Departmental Identifications of Executives," *Sociometry*, **21**: 140–144 (1958).

barriers, such as departmental boundaries, leaving substantial gaps in perception and attitudes between members of different groups.

Summary

Perception is a filter for and organizer of information. Through the perceptual process, we select and shape environmental data into concepts of how reality is. We can then relate to the complexities and uncertainties of reality through our *understanding* of how it works. We "see" things according to our experiences, desires, and expectations. Perceptions may be completely unrealistic, but they constitute an individual's concept of a situation; for him, what he sees *is* real.

Stereotypes are perceptual devices through which involved observation of an individual's behavior is lessened. Categorizing one as belonging to a group to which certain characteristics are attributed allows those characteristics to be attributed to the member. In this way expectations and behaviors are based on perceptions. Stereotypes involve many problems, however, and often inappropriate stereotypes are derived and used.

The halo effect is a perceptual distortion in which a single trait is generalized to the overall evaluation of an individual. The halo effect then prevents all one's characteristics being considered.

Ways in which perceptual organization finds expression in behavior were discussed along with the concepts of equity and cognitive dissonance. Equity theory allows an individual to compare perceived relative fairness or justice among reference figures. If he sees that his reward per unit of effort is out of line with those of his reference figures, the individual can move to restore an equitable reward–effort ratio by increasing (or decreasing) his effort.

Cognitive dissonance is the state of psychological discomfort encountered when an inconsistency between one's beliefs and one's actions is perceived. The individual moves to restore consistency either by attitude change or by behavior change.

Managerial practices, too, result from perceptual processes. Theory X assumptions, that man is (among other things) inherently lazy and irresponsible, create the unconscious rationale for directing, controlling, authoritarian management. Theory Y assumptions, including the responsibility orientation of man and his potential for creativity and contribution, result in quite different practices. Both sets of assumptions incorporate many of the perceptual processes as they influence managerial behavior.

The perceptual process underlies behavior, especially in organizations in which both situations and environments are artificially established, yielding many ambiguities. Perception allows us to establish meaning and organize it in ambiguous situations, but it offers danger because differences in perceptions increase with ambiguity.

The next two chapters will look into the nature of motivation and how it influences behavior.

STUDY AND REVIEW QUESTIONS

1. Theories X and Y incorporate many factors of perception as they influence the manager's behavior. Carefully trace the influences of perception that finally culminate in Theory X or Y-based practices.

2. Show which of (and how) Wertheimer's eight factors of perceptual organization can explain the phenomena of (a) stereotypes, and (b) halo effect.

3. What is equity? Why is equity theory presented as perceptually based?

4. Compare and contrast cognitive dissonance and the personality defense technique of rationalizing.

5. What benefits can you see in using stereotypes? What dangers?

6. What are some ways in which differences in perceptions might be discovered? Reconciled?

7. What relevance has perception to an understanding of organizational behavior?

8. Selective perception was illustrated in the Dearborn–Simon study. What dangers and benefits do you see resulting from selective perception in specialized functional departments? In *training* for specialized positions?

9. Select any one of the research studies summarized in the section "Perception in Perspective." Show how you perceive that each of Wertheimer's eight factors of perceptual organization might be represented in the study.

10. How does perception directly influence an individual's behavior?

Chapter

11

Basics of Motivation

CHAPTER OBJECTIVES

1. To outline the broad nature of general motivation.

2. To compare and contrast several general motivational models.

3. To show the need for a deep understanding of motivation as a basic determinant of human behavior.

4. To prepare the student with the basics of motivation in order to apply motivational concepts to organizational settings and organizational behavior in Chapter 12.

CHAPTER OUTLINE

Static Models of Motivation
Instinct
Hedonism
Unconscious Motivation
Rational Man
Social Man
Static Models of Motivation in Perspective

Dynamic Models of Motivation
Maslow's Hierarchy of Needs
Vroom's Expectancy Theory
A General Motivational Model

People are different. Each person is a unique individual, different from—yet similar to—countless other individuals. We noted in Chapter 8 that our physical characteristics are all roughly the same, with standard numbers of arms and legs, placement of the head on our shoulders, and usage of our internal organs. Slight anatomical differences allow us to distinguish a friend from a stranger. By the same token, personality characteristics fall into patterns that may be quite similar, yet different enough to preclude accurate prediction of individuals' specific behaviors. The personality of each individual with whom you come into contact differs somewhat from that of every other person; social relationships would otherwise be quite dull.

Given our knowledge of the broad similarity in physical and personality characteristics of people, we are usually able to make predictions about them. If we know that Henry barely weighs 97 pounds in heavy work shoes, we might safely venture that his tenure as a defensive tackle on the university football team will be short-lived (as might Henry), or we might predict that domineering Bertha will be attracted to mild-mannered and docile George. But what do we know about *why* people behave the way they do? Personality characteristics can explain certain social behaviors but do not completely explain what happens in other, varying situations. Human actions are readily observable because a person changes his environment in some way through his behavior.

Some might argue that human activity is enough; why worry about what causes it? This would hardly suffice if when you were going to your next class, an old friend walked up to you and punched you in the mouth. The intent behind that action would be of great concern to you. Similarly, if you are attempting to persuade another to do a favor for you, you might be interested in learning why he behaves the way he does. You might learn his values from these patterns and use the incentive most likely to enlist his cooperation.

Your interest in learning what makes people behave the way they do—and learning how to influence their behavior—is not unique. From the beginning of time people have sought to influence others. Your professor probably tries to encourage certain patterns of behavior (learning) through the use of periodic quizzes. Production foremen also wish to encourage their workers to behave in more productive ways through the application of wage incentives.

What complicates the whole issue of explaining human behavior is that the *reason* behind an action usually cannot be directly observed. Why a person does something may well exist only within his own head, and he may have his own peculiar reasons. Any number of different and completely separate reasons can explain a single action. One person in your class may be persistently absent—why? Is it because he oversleeps? Does he have a job that does not allow him to make class consistently? Is he so bored by the class that he can't bring himself to come? Has he had the class before so that he doesn't need to attend the lectures to make a good grade in the class? Behavior can have many possible explanations.

If we reject the notion that people behave without any purpose or pattern, then we may be able to discover some broad patterns underlying why people behave in the ways they do. We are then concerned with discerning the internal forces that move ("motivate") a person to action. Just as we noted with physical and personality characteristics, we can think in generalizations about common properties of motivation and use them for predictive purposes. What are some of the explanations of behavior that have been developed? The next section will examine several that assumed the individual to be rather uncomplicated. These static models typically saw him as *responding to* outside forces, often blindly. Two dynamic models will then be explained, each of which sees man as a being questing for control over his life pattern.

Static Models of Motivation

Instinct

The simplest motivational model is that of behavior determined by instinct, inborn tendencies to respond in a particular way to particular conditions.[1] Instincts are not the result of learning and are identical patterns of behavior found in all people.[2] How one acts would then be determined primarily by heredity, having been transmitted from generation to generation through genes.

The individual's experiences and learning would have little or no effect on how he acted because behavior patterns are present; they await only the correct conditions to occur and then are automatically triggered. Using the instinct model, we might conclude that behavior is almost a reflex action, like jerking away one's hand from a hot surface. The nature of motivation—the process underlying the causes of behavior—would be that of predictable and predetermined reactions, with the individual able to exert little control over his "natural" impulses.

We might object that we are concerned with behavior that fulfills a purpose; are instincts or reflexes goal-oriented? If we assume that the ultimate purpose of all behavior is toward survival, then we might be able to make a case for this instinct-based model. We encounter some significant problems after that. Periods in which we are not responding to the environment should theoretically be periods of nonbehavior. Survival-oriented behavior also should logically be limited to the satisfying of biological and

[1]Bernard Berelson and Gary A. Steiner, *Human Behavior: An Inventory of Scientific Findings* (New York: Harcourt, Brace & World, 1964), p. 38.

[2]David T. Lawless, *Effective Management: Social Psychological Approach* (Englewood Cliffs, N.J.: Prentice-Hall, 1972), p. 81.

physiological needs. Probably the most complex behavior that we might expect would be that of laying up stores of food or money for the future.

Could we realistically explain complicated sequences of behavior through instincts alone? Some have attempted to. One typical list of basic instincts accounting for all behavior consisted of "flight, repulsion, curiosity, pugnacity, self-abasement, self-assertion, parental, reproductive, hunger, gregariousness, acquisitiveness, and constrictiveness."[3] A quickly lengthening list of instincts soon developed. Each author added a few more until by the 1920's the list totaled nearly 6,000 instincts, including an "instinct to avoid eating apples in one's own orchard"![4]

The instinctual basis of motivation is limited by its excluding previous learning and by its lack of a future orientation, in which behavior occurs *because* of an understanding of its *consequence*. Rather, instincts are "automatic, fixed responses released by certain fixed events; and the entire process goes blindly astray in a changed or unnatural environment. . . . In short, experience is both unnecessary and irrelevant for this instinct-controlled mode of adaption, and therein lies its chief advantage (no learning required) and its chief cost (lack of adaptability for the individual)."[5] In addition, the instinct models fail to account for the varying types and intensities of behavior by separate individuals—all of whom would share the same instincts.

Hedonism

As long ago as 500 B.C., Greek philosophers felt that they had developed a guide to living that would explain and direct human behavior. Their philosophy was simple: avoid pain and pursue pleasure. Few consciously seek misery and all strive to enjoy their lives, thus the hedonists reasoned that behavior must be dictated by the simple demands of minimizing pain and worry while seeking the most happiness and pleasure. Epicurus (341–270 B.C.) was a major proponent of this motivational model: "Pleasure is our first and kindred good. It is the starting point of every choice and every aversion, and to it we come back and make feeling the rule by which to judge of every good thing."[6]

As Epicurus interprets life, health of the body and tranquility of the spirit constitute lasting happiness. The happy life is a tranquil life, the life free from passion, from fear, and from pain. The great obstacle to happiness, he feels, is neither pain nor poverty, nor the absence of the good things in life; it is, rather, whatever tends to disturb our security and peace of mind, whatever causes fear, anxiety, worry. In the

[3]Edward J. Murray, *Motivation and Emotion* (Englewood Cliffs, N.J.: Prentice-Hall, 1964), p. 5.

[4]Ibid., pp. 5, 6.

[5]Berelson and Steiner, pp. 39, 40.

[6]Epicurus, cited in Robert F. Davidson, *Philosophies Men Live By* (New York: Holt, Rinehart, and Winston, 1952), p. 36.

pleasures of the mind of the moment, the surest way to real happiness is to be found.

.   .   .   .

These pleasures are singled out above others, it is important to note, not because pleasures of the mind are in themselves superior to the pleasures of the sense. All pleasure is equally good for Epicurus; it is simply the *amount of pleasure* that is important. The man of wisdom seeks to get the most pleasure in life and the least pain. An intelligent Hedonist will frequently choose to suffer more momentary pain if it enables him to gain lasting pleasure, and he will always avoid an indulgence of appetite or desire which brings unpleasant consequence. The temporary pain of a surgical operation, for example, is more than compensated for by the permanently improved health it can produce.[7]

While we may personally applaud the reasoning of Epicurus, we should note that the hedonistic model suffers from a painful deficiency: What is pleasure? What is pain? Certainly the pleasure of a masochist, who delights in being hurt, would be anything but attractive to almost all other people. How could you use the hedonistic model to *predict* what a person might do in a particular situation? Could we even draw meaningful conclusions about how pleasure compares when experienced by two different people?

Another major hurdle is encountered in the determination of short-term pain in order to reach long-term pleasure, as expressed by Epicurus. Because these questions all revolve around the measurement of such subjective factors as pleasure and pain, for our purposes the hedonistic model is not as useful as we might wish it to be.

Unconscious Motivation

Sigmund Freud, the famous father of psychiatry, used both the instinct and the hedonistic models in suggesting the existence and role of unconscious mental processes that influence behavior.[8] By recognizing both pleasure-seeking (and pain-avoiding) and unconscious motivations, he placed instinctive and hedonistic tendencies in positions as determiners of behavior—but outside the control of the individual. He even presented these influences as being unseen or unrecognized; they operated from within the unconscious, repressed, or buried portions of the human mind.

Behavior was then seen as stemming directly from the primitive and rather animallike segments of the human nature, obsessed with sexual and aggressive impulses. Man, by virtue of his cultural conditioning, constantly seeks to master these antisocial urges. Even then they may find expression in more socially acceptable actions. Aggressiveness may be turned from physical violence to vicarious release at boxing matches or on the football field.

[7]Davidson, p. 37.
[8]Floyd L. Ruch, *Psychology and Life*, Brief 6th Ed. (Chicago: Scott, Foresman, 1963), p. 10. See also Victor H. Vroom, *Work and Motivation* (New York: Wiley, 1964), pp. 9, 10; and Fred Luthans, *Organizational Behavior: A Modern Behavioral Approach to Management* (New York: McGraw-Hill, 1973), pp. 390, 391.

These processes, which find outcome in behavior, are neither noticeable nor noticed, even by the individual within whom they occur.

Freud's major contribution was his explanation of how man's behavior occurs. According to Freud, each person has less control over his day-to-day actions than he might wish to acknowledge because conscious activity is determined by unconscious, inborn, hedonistic processes. The dominating influence in man's life is not his rationality but his subjection to forces over which he has no control.

This unconscious motivational model has been found to be largely untestable; it does not lend itself well to making generalizations about behavior or predictions of what a person might tend to do in a particular situation. Each individual's unconscious motivational patterns are largely unique to his own experience and situation.

Besides, how could you explain the celibate life of priests and nuns? Or one's willingness to delay the gratification of his needs? What about the dangers and deprivations that explorers undergo? Freud's observations, based as they were on abnormal personalities, seem to be lacking in completeness for describing and predicting the behaviors of relatively normal individuals.

Rational Man

A model of motivation that places control over man's life back in his own hands is the rational man model. The major assumption of this model is that each individual is fully aware of the patterns of his personal needs and desires and will accordingly make intelligent and thoughtful decisions. Self-interest is what dictates what a person will do; no rational individual, it is felt, would do anything detrimental to himself. Whatever a person *chooses* to do (or however he chooses to behave) must then make a positive contribution to his well-being.

This sophisticated, hedonistically based model sidesteps the difficulties built into the simple hedonistic model; it divorces motivation from the technicalities of cataloging and measuring the contents of each human's pleasure–pain center. What matters is the behavior elicited, not the ultimate purpose of the behavior, nor how comparable are given levels of pleasure when experienced by various people.

The proponents of the rational man model can ignore the basic and unmeasurable differences between individuals and concentrate on the common ways in which they both strive to reach their own particular goals. It is then possible to infer motivational bases for a hardworking salesman as well as for the college professor; both might spend a great deal of energy and effort in their pursuit of their self-interests, to reap rewards for their endeavors. They might be said to be motivated by their desires for monetary rewards because money is instrumental in maximizing one's physical well-being. Investigation of how these monetary rewards were spent would be ignored because this would require unobtainable information of pleasure and pain measurements—the downfall of the simple hedonistic model. The rational or economic basis of behavior could logically be used to explain how the individual chooses what to do under widely varied circumstances.

This model of man's activities and motivation may still be seen in the basic assumptions on which modern economic theory is based. The model is not particularly new; Frederick Winslow Taylor, the father of scientific management, employed this model extensively in his management writings and practice at the beginning of the twentieth century, as did Adam Smith[9] in 1776. They felt that the common denominator for fulfilling most of man's desires was money; how the money was spent would be strictly up to the individual and his own peculiar complex of pleasure and pain activities. Of major importance in all of this is the complete reliance on man's economic well-being as the only effective reason for behavior. Economic well-being was a "true" measurement of pleasure achievement and pain avoidance, so any other motivations were inherently irrational, unmeasureable, and irrelevant.

A benefit of this model is that economic well-being lends itself quite well to rather objective measurement. It can be well represented by the number of dollars possessed by the individual. Although human pleasures are myriad and man is oriented only to his personal well-being (according to the hedonistic philosophy), then man must strive constantly toward greater and greater economic achievements. Another benefit of this model is its recognition of an effective way to motivate behavior in others—through the application of incentives. In order to influence the behavior of another, all one must do is allow him to achieve his own well-being at the same time that he does what you want him to do. Thus the concept of more pay for more work found expression in Taylor's writings.

The model overcame many of the limitations of previous models of motivation; behavior is observable, and the incentive for behavior can be readily measured in terms of dollars. Even the way in which the incentive affects behavior is consistent with intuitive reasons ascribed to actions, the maximizing of the individual's well-being.

As you might have guessed, this model—as descriptive and predictive as it appears—suffers from some major oversimplifications. Even Taylor recognized that this model did not take into account all of the forces that determine individual behavior; he warned about the role of social pressures in influencing actions that were not in the best interests of personal well-being. He noticed, for example, that even workers who were paid significantly more for producing more than quota would limit their productive efforts, consequently decreasing their own paychecks—a most irrational act according to the model!

Other real-world situations exist that are inconsistent with the rational

[9]Adam Smith, writing in *The Wealth of Nations*, put forward the idea of the "invisible hand," which, when individuals are free to pursue their own self-interests, directs these activities automatically in the best interests of society.

man model. We might notice that our neighbor trades in his perfectly good two-year-old automobile, which is just short of being paid for, for a brand-new and more expensive model. Is this decrease in spending power an example of a decision to increase one's economic well-being? Is an individual's decision to be a teacher consistent with a rational decision to maximize one's lifelong monetary income? Is the decision to retire from work at age fifty-five rational in view of one's ability to work for another ten years before retiring, thereby having an additional ten years of economic achievement? You may have even heard of business executives giving up $100,000-a-year jobs in order to take over university teaching positions that (it is rumored) pay substantially less.

Social Man

In order to find a model of motivation that took into account the many exceptions to the rational man model, the social man model was postulated. This model came about as a direct result of the Hawthorne studies discussed in Chapter 1. There, you may remember, researchers discovered that economic and rational factors were not sufficient to explain human behavior. They found that personal attention to a worker would influence his work activity positively. And they discovered that, far from each individual's being concerned only about his own individual well-being, the individual and his behavior were influenced by the expectations and social pressures of the people with whom he worked.

As a result, the critical factor in motivation was felt to be the satisfaction or happiness that the individual could gain. This you recognize as a further extension of the rational man model, but it is more general in its interpretation of individual well-being. Satisfaction was felt to be determined not by economic factors but by other, less tangible elements. Pressure to conform and compromise in order to gain social approval; striving to earn prestige; maintenance of friendly relationships; needs to belong to a compatible group—these are evidences of the social side of man. The social man model suggests that individual satisfactions arise from interpersonal relationships. They are then translated into personal contentment, pleasure, or happiness.

Becoming a more contented or happy person was therefore the end result most desired under this model. The results of the Hawthorne studies could be explained by the greater satisfactions derived from conforming to the group's standards (and thereby not being excluded from the social pleasures of the group) than from slightly higher economic rewards. Almost any social man might well make a trade-off between his ability to satisfy his economic needs and increasing his opportunities for social satisfactions.

The motivational emphasis would then shift from providing economic incentives to providing *social* incentives in order to bring about desired behaviors. This is one reason why such importance is attached to job satisfaction and morale today. This model could be carried too far, too; in its most extreme state, a work situation would turn into a "country club," in which no work was performed but in which individuals were having a good time. Further, this model was recognized as still not being inclusive enough. If social satisfactions are so important in determining behavior, why do individuals engage in antisocial behavior? Why do hermits separate themselves from human companionship? How does one explain the "loner" who violates the social expectations of people with whom he works?

Static Models of Motivation in Perspective

We can notice several things that these static models of motivation have in common. First of all, each seems to assume that there is a single factor toward which behavior is directed; behavior is caused or affected by the striving to attain some state of being or to achieve some goal. Each model's goal or motivating object is static in that it continues to motivate even after it is reached.

We might illustrate this by suggesting that money could be considered to be a motivator under a static model of motivation. Even a millionaire, then, would continue to be obsessed with amassing even more monetary holdings. Or put another way, under a static motivational model the last bite of steak would be just as satisfying as the first. The strength of the incentive and the intensity with which the incentive is striven for are static or unchanging in this model, even over time and at every stage of behavior.

Table 11-1 summarizes the static models, comparing the end purposes of behavior and the elements that determine how these end purposes will be achieved. The purposes of behavior presented would be constant or unchanging. This reinforces the prior idea that the static models assume each individual does not merely try to reach some state of existence through his actions. When the desired state is reached, he continues behaving to

TABLE 11-1   Summary of Static Models of Motivation

Model	Purpose of Behavior	Behavior Is Determined By
Instinct	Survival	Inborn automatic behavior
Hedonism	Happiness	Pursuit of pleasure and avoidance of pain
Unconscious motivation	Domination or aggression	Primitive buried impulses based on instincts and hedonistic tendencies
Rational man	Economic well-being	Self-interest
Social man	Happiness	Interpersonal satisfaction

increase the degree of attainment. This suggests that motivation is a constant, unvarying force.

In terms of the hedonism that underlies many of these models, the individual is primarily concerned with achieving more and still more pleasure or with successively lowering the amount of pain or unpleasantness to which he is subjected. In terms of economic theory these static models require that the satisfaction ("utility") one receives be constant with each successive addition to his store of satisfactions. The marginal utility from each unit of goal attainment is constant in static models.

How realistic are these conclusions? We might know an individual obsessed with achieving constant gustatory satisfactions—the proverbial glutton with an insatiable appetite, constantly eating for the sheer pleasure of eating. But how many other instances can you think of? How normal or widespread is that type of activity? Even a starving man will view his sixth or seventh jumbo hamburger with somewhat less than the same anticipation he had for his first. Would you be as ecstatic with a $100-a-month raise when you make $50,000 a year as when you make $5,000 a year? We've already remarked that one complicating factor these models do not take into account is that people's motivations are rarely constant or unchanging. Furthermore motivation is rarely simple; we can all think of times when we were faced with conflicting choices—we could, for example, either go to a great party tonight or study for the exam to be given tomorrow. If we felt that our studying tonight would make little or no difference in our score on the exam, then our behavior tonight would certainly be influenced. Our current grade in the course might also determine what we do. Of course, if we'd already been to parties for the last seven nights running, then we might not be nearly so eager to attend another tonight.

To sum up, the usefulness of static models of motivation is limited by their simple assumptions about the factors that determine or influence individual behavior. They fail to take into account different or conflicting motivations, as well as changes in motivation that occur over time.

Two models that do take into account these complicating factors are discussed as dynamic motivational models, those suggested by Maslow and Vroom.

Dynamic Models of Motivation

Maslow's Hierarchy of Needs

About twenty years ago Abraham Maslow of Brandeis University fashioned a more dynamic and realistic explanation of human behavior. He knew that man is a complex and changing being, and he felt that motivation must reflect man's nature. If one is moved to action and if man is rational and purposeful, then it stood to reason that the action was initiated by an attempt to achieve some desired end result. He drew on insights from actual behavior and presented a motivational model that reflects the progress and accomplishments of the individual.[10] What can be analyzed and used to predict behavior is the end results—satisfaction of needs—of the behaviors themselves.

He also pointed out that needs are ever-changing. People change their goals and redirect their activities in response to changing needs. Of major importance was his pointing out that unsatisfied needs serve as "magnets," which attract efforts to satisfy those needs. The thirsty person's activities would probably be directed toward obtaining a glass of water; the thirstier he gets, the more intense become his search and activities to secure thirst-quenching liquids. If he were stranded in the Sahara Desert, water might conceivably occupy his every thought and action. This particular need would serve to attract activities designed to satisfy that need, attracting more and more need-oriented activities as that need gained in strength.

After you've gone to the kitchen and drunk a glass of iced tea, would you remain there and gulp down gallon after gallon? Probably not. After a particular need is satisfied, it is "demagnetized." Satisfied needs are no longer effective motivators of behavior. The drive, which the unsatisfied need had originally set up in directing need-oriented activities, no longer exists. It can certainly recur, but for the moment it no longer drives us. We are free to focus our efforts on other matters. If our needs can attract our activity until each is satisfied, this hints that all of the needs that we face throughout our lives—or even at a particular moment in time—are not equally important. Some are more effective in driving us to action than others. And after a particular need has been demagnetized, it is no longer very important to us, at least insofar as its ability to influence what we do. Even though the basics of his ideas probably sound a little complicated and hard to handle, Maslow gave us an important framework for viewing human activity.

Physiological Needs

We all have basic and recurring needs to eat, drink, be protected from elements, sleep, and satisfy reproductive needs. These body and life-maintenance needs are essential to our very existence. They are powerful determiners of our behavior when they are not satisfied; physiological needs, such as thirst, can become all-powerful the longer they go without satisfaction. If they are unattended to for a sufficient length of time, of course, our very lives are threatened.

It has been estimated that the physiological needs of North Americans are relatively well, and relatively widely, met—about 85 percent satisfied. We

---

[10]His theory is set out in Abraham H. Maslow, *Motivation and Personality* (New York: Harper Bros.; 1954).

would not expect physiological needs to be powerful motivators of behavior for the vast majority of people in the United States. When the needs within this broad classification are satisfied, they more or less recede into the background and are no longer such important determinants of what we do; they no longer fill our thoughts and direct our activities toward their satisfaction. We are then free to do other things. This freedom is naturally linked to bodily rhythms, for hunger or thirst constantly reasserts its presence as a drive to satisfy a basic need. Physiological needs are easily satisfied but are short-cycle and recur regularly. The strength of these needs is obvious because of their capability to divert our attention from *whatever* we are doing until we relieve that need. Only then are we released.

Safety or Security Needs

Basic physiological needs are satisfied, for example, when thirst is quenched or when one's belly is full. One might then be concerned about making sure that these physiological needs will continue to be met tomorrow or next week or next month. The safety or security needs center around being free from the threat of being deprived of one's ability to satisfy physiological needs.

We might even look at this class of needs as representing man's desire to achieve some control over the uncertainties of life or over forces at whose mercy he may find himself. He may thus strive to achieve order out of chaos and ensure that he is more nearly able to be the master of his own destiny. We might then expect that, after having been stranded on a desert isle, one would first quench his thirst and soothe his hunger pangs. *Then* he would start to stockpile food and water and secure shelter from the elements. This safety classification of needs, too, is rather widely satisfied in our present society, with an estimated 70 percent of the safety or security needs of the average individual being satisfied.

Social or Belongingness Needs

The next rung in Maslow's hierarchy of needs is occupied by the social or belongingness needs. This need classification is relatively weaker than the more basic needs of the body and of security. This higher need can, however, become an effective and powerful motivator of behavior. Needs diminish in their abilities to affect what a person does as those needs become satisfied. With their satisfaction, a new class of needs comes into prominence, displacing the former needs. The patterns of behavior that were exhibited by the individual in his attempts to satisfy his lower needs would then become changed, because new goals or needs must be reached and satisfied. New activities would typically be necessary.

The social or belongingness needs are a reflection that man is a social being, needing the company and companionship of others. Feeling lonely or deprived of companionship, one might seek admission to a group with whom he can identify and feel comfortable. In his search for companionship and belongingness, the individual might behave in ways to be more socially acceptable to others.

Once man's needs for social relationships have been satisfied, then this need too decreases in its ability to motivate behavior. The average person in our society, in Maslow's estimation, has about 50 percent of his social or belongingness needs satisfied. This might indicate to us that the social needs are more widespread in their dominance in our society than the more directly physiological needs. Would this generalization help you to explain, for example, why conformity is so prevalent?

Esteem or Ego Needs

As the social needs become relatively satisfied, the new need of esteem emerges as a motivator of behavior. The social needs were concerned with belonging to a group or feeling accepted; the esteem or ego needs reflect man's wish (while being accepted by others) to set himself apart by being recognized as someone special. This might come about as a result of some achievement of which he is proud and for which he wishes to be recognized.

Or he may wish to enhance his self-image—the way he views himself. After all, the comparison between self-image and an ideal probably results directly in how well one likes himself. Self-confidence and self-respect stem from ego needs and their satisfactions.

This need can then be separated into two parts, internal and external recognition. Internal recognition is the self-respect one has and seeks. External recognition is public acclaim or esteem arising out of recognition and

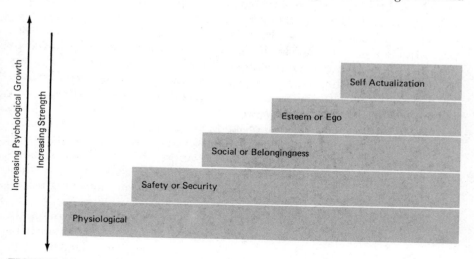

FIGURE 11-1   Maslow's hierarchy of needs.

appreciation of the individual or his deeds. Both have to do with one's personal feelings of importance or worth.

Esteem needs center around the individual, recognition of what he has done or who he is, and the deserved respect from others that these bring. These needs differ from social needs in that they reflect the worth of the person for what he has done, rather than mere acceptance of his existing or occupying a space in a group. The esteem needs are probably only about 40 percent fulfilled in the average person, again reflecting that they may be rather powerful in urging one to satisfy these needs. This esteem need is only slightly less satisfied than the belongingness needs.

Self-actualization

The highest and last class of needs on the hierarchy is that of self-actualization. It is also the weakest because all other needs on the hierarchy must be rather well satisfied in order for this class of needs to emerge. Figure 11-2 illustrates, by a flow chart, the process by which the individual ascends the needs hierarchy. Self-actualization needs go beyond the esteem needs in a significant fashion. Esteem needs reflect man's need to differentiate himself from his peers by virtue of his accomplishments and achievements. Self-actualization needs point to the individual's constant striving to realize his full potential—whatever it is.

Esteem may come from doing something better than others, but the self-actualized person may not be satisfied by that simply because he knows that he can do still better; he is not satisfied merely to be better than others. He must be as good as he is capable of being. We might notice this in certain athletes. Some exert only enough effort to win; with poor competition they loaf along. Others, however, constantly strive to break the national record. Once the record is broken, they try constantly to set a new one.

For self-actualization needs, a fundamental shift in orientation takes place. In belongingness needs, the individual measures himself with acceptance by others. In his esteem needs, he differentiates himself from his peers by higher accomplishment and consequent recognition. In self-actualization, he measures himself against his own internalized ideal of the greatest potential *of which he himself is capable.*

From this neat classification of man's needs and their sequential occurrence and motivational dominance, we must not assume that one particular needs class must be completely satisfied before the next level becomes operational. Rather, each successive level must be *relatively* satisfied, and then the next level of needs becomes *increasingly* important in motivating behavior.

With the aid of Figure 11-2 we can trace not only one's ascension up the hierarchy but one's *descent.* Assume you are currently at the level of satisfying your esteem or ego needs. Your actions would be determined by your situation and your motivation to fulfill ego needs. Until they are satisfied,

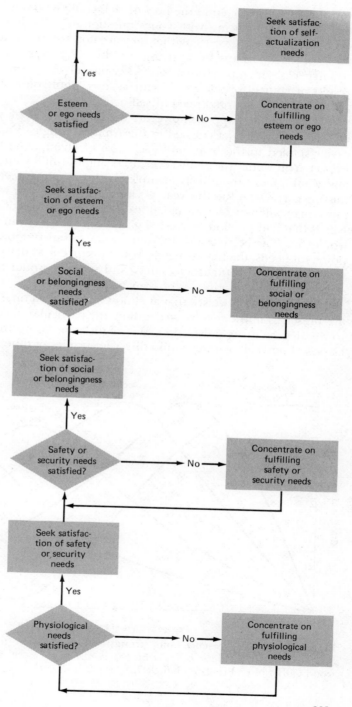

FIGURE 11-2
Flow diagram of needs satisfactions.

your behavior (depicted in the flow model) could be thought of as following the "loop" commencing with your "questioning" whether the esteem–ego needs are satisfied. Observing that they are not, you concentrate on fulfilling these needs—perhaps by studying for the CPA exam or increasing your country club membership efforts. Periodically you would compare the results of your efforts to needs satisfactions, until you could reorient your activities to the emerged need of self-actualization.

What would happen, however, if—in the midst of your esteem–ego efforts—your Lear jet crashed in the Amazon jungle? Your entire stock of caviar spoiled in the heat, and each case of champagne blew its corks on impact. You would suddenly revert to trying to fulfill your most basic needs and would, more than likely, completely dismiss the esteem implications of missing carnival in Rio this year. As a matter of fact, you would probably be more than willing to start a signal fire with the contents of your money belt. Needs that had previously exerted great force in determining your behavior would not now be relevant. In your trying to satisfy more basic and more powerful needs, the higher needs would disappear as drives. *Only* when you were found and returned to safety and security would these other needs serve as effective motivators of your behavior.

In Figure 11-3 we see that at almost any point in time all levels of needs are present, but the relative strength of any particular need varies according to the degree of its satisfaction. We might even notice that these different classes of need all operate within different frames of time. Thus our physio-

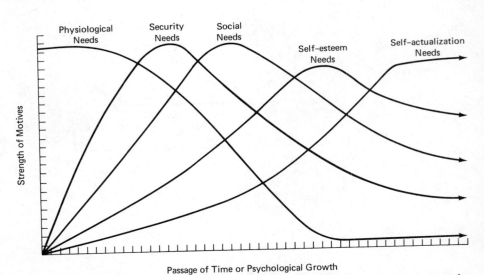

FIGURE 11-3 Presence and strength of needs with psychological growth. Source: David J. Lawless, *Effective Management, Social Psychological Approach* (Englewood Cliffs, N.J.: Prentice-Hall, 1972), p. 87.

logical needs recur relatively often, simply because of our own bodily rhythms. We typically eat three times a day and drink water more often, for example. At the other extreme, our attempts to achieve our full potential would probably be a lifelong endeavor.

The hierarchy-of-needs model is dynamic in that it presents motivation as a constantly changing force, expressing itself through the constant striving for fulfillment of new and higher levels of needs. Man is never satisfied. Instead of resting on his laurels when one goal is reached or a need is satisfied, the individual will typically redirect his efforts and capabilities toward the attainment of still higher goals.

Another dynamic motivational model, called *expectancy theory,* considers the process through which the individual decides which of his many choices of behavior will be put into effect.

Vroom's Expectancy Theory

Consider the following situation:

John Gordy has just reported to work; it's his first day at Bigtown Industrials. His new boss has chatted with him for a while and then introduced John around to his new co-workers. They seem like a likable bunch, having a pretty good time even while getting out the work. This is important to John because his last job was working on a noisy assembly line with no chance to socialize with the other workers. His old job, too, just required him to do mechanical and repetitive operations at the speed of a "flesh-and-blood machine."

Before leaving John at his new work station, his supervisor takes him aside and pointedly mentions to him that on his new job performance will depend completely on how well John himself wants to do; he will be paid for the amount of work that he does, and his performance will be taken into account when questions of raises and promotions are considered by management.

Shortly after his introduction to his new job, the co-workers let him know in no uncertain terms that if he wants to be considered one of the guys, John will fall in line with the informally determined work standard. No member of the group produces more than quota. The work group can deal quite harshly with a "rate-buster," with the ultimate threat being the "silent treatment" from the rest of the group members and being ostracized from social contact.

How will John behave? Will he ignore the demands of his peers and strive to meet management's goals? Or will he bow to pressure, restrict his output, and thereby be accepted by the group?

If we were analyzing this situation by Maslow's needs hierarchy, we would probably start by considering whether the belongingness (group acceptance) or the ego–esteem (achievement) needs were more basic. Belongingness needs are, but the *less* basic ego–esteem needs would motivate behavior if *belongingness* needs were satisfied. We might complicate the issue by recognizing that John might be motivated by a need still more powerful than that of belongingness, that of physiological or security needs, represented by striving to increase his paycheck by producing more.

Another way of looking at the situation is available in the expectancy model evolved by Vroom.[11] He presents a way of investigating the forces that underlie choices of behavior. According to expectancy theory, motivation occurs as a result of the individual's perception that a particular behavior will lead to a particular end result and of his degree of preference for that end result. We can examine this process more closely through the concepts of *instrumentality, valence,* and *expectancy.*

Instrumentality

People sometimes do one thing so that they may achieve something else. A football star may exert himself to score touchdowns (first-level outcome) *because* of the acclaim (second-level outcome) this brings him. In much the same way, the concept of instrumentality reflects how strongly one outcome is related to another, more distant outcome.

In John's case, he is faced with two alternatives and the behaviors each would require of him. In order to attain one of the two final outcomes (for instance, earning a promotion), John must appraise how *instrumental* more immediate outcomes are in helping him to attain the end result. He knows that in order to be considered for a promotion he will have to perform in a superior fashion, probably for above that of his co-workers. But how strongly associated is superior performance with being promoted? If John's fellow workers inform him that promotions do not come from the inside but are reserved for new college graduates hired from outside the firm, then John will see no direct association (instrumentality) between his preferred first-level outcome (high performance) and his second-level goal (promotion). Hence John would be given little incentive to perform in an outstanding fashion.

Valence

The decision he must make is whether to maximize his output (perform in a superior fashion) or restrict his output (adhere to group standards). For each situation, John will at least intuitively evaluate the value he places on the *outcome* of each alternative. If he doesn't particularly care for the members of the group, then he may be rather indifferent about the ostracism he would expect to receive from the group if he outperformed its members. A raise or promotion would then have a higher preference (or valence) than group acceptance. This would encourage him to increase his output at the expense of his social contacts with the group members. Vroom points out that "the

[11]Vroom, op. cit.

strength of a person's desire [positive valence] or aversion [negative valence] for [the outcomes] is based not on their intrinsic properties but on the anticipated satisfaction or dissatisfaction associated with other outcomes to which they are expected to lead."[12]

An interesting phenomenon occurs in the transference of valence. A first-level outcome instrumental to the attainment of a high-valence (strongly preferred) second-level outcome *acquires* a high valence from this relationship. This process occurs with negatively valenced (aversion) outcomes also. If John is strongly attracted to the second-level outcome of promotion, then he would transfer this preference to the first-level outcome instrumental to its attainments. He might then become strongly attracted to high job performance in its own right.

Expectancy

Another factor important to John's behavioral decision is "expectancy." This is merely his estimate of the likelihood that a choice will result in a particular outcome. For example, if John found both outcomes (promotion and acceptance) equally preferable, then his decision would more than likely be swayed by each choice's likelihood of resulting in its desired outcome. If he felt there were only a 50–50 chance that he would be able to meet the requirements for superior performance, but he knew without doubt that he could effectively restrict his output, then he would probably choose the latter. In this situation, more force would be applied to restrict his output, which could be equated with his motivation.

A more realistic refinement might be to point out that John actually encounters *two* expectancies in deciding between striving for promotion or for acceptance. Promotion requires (1) his ability to meet the requirements of superior performance, and (2) the rewarding of his efforts, provided he does in fact perform in a superior fashion. Both conditions have separate probabilities ascribed to them by the individual: John must evaluate his capabilities, job characteristics, and performance standards before he can estimate his chances for exceeding some quota (this is his first expectancy). Then he must consider the probability that his superior performance will actually result in a promotion (his second expectancy).[13]

Notice the slight, but significant, difference between expectancy and instrumentality. Expectancy is the probabilistic relationship between an *act* and an *outcome*. Instrumentality reflects the association between one *outcome* and another, more distant, *outcome*. We might clarify this still further by formalizing the relationships in Vroom's model.

---

[12]Ibid., pp. 15, 16.

[13]Cf. John P. Campbell, Marvin D. Dunnette, Edward E. Lawler III, and Karl E. Weick, Jr., *Managerial Behavior, Performance, and Effectiveness* (New York: McGraw-Hill, 1970), p. 346.

Motivational force = expectancy X valence (of first-level outcome) where valence = instrumentality between the first and second-level outcomes multiplied by the valence of the second-level outcome.[14]

Motivation

This complex series of behaviors and their anticipated outcomes are taken as a whole. We can see that, as in John's case, an intensely desired final outcome may not motivate behavior simply because his efforts may not be sufficient to allow him to reach it. On the other hand, a less preferred final outcome may be a strong motivator, simply because his efforts may be linked with certainty to the attainment of the final outcome.

Using John's situation, we might think of how he would be affected by the other situation he is faced with. In order to gain group acceptance, he must first limit his production to meet the group's standard. He knows that if he does not limit his production, he will definitely be kept out of the group. On the other hand, if John were completely certain that he met the personality interests expectations of the group members, then he might feel with certainty that limiting his production would result in full acceptance by the group. Even if he intensely desired the promotion and were only lukewarm about group acceptance, the relatively high expectancy associated with group acceptance (compared with that of promotion) could be enough to overcome the greater valence associated with the promotion-directed activities. John might then choose to forego performance on the job in favor of limiting his production.

Figure 11-4 shows one representation of the fashion in which Vroom's expectancy theory model works. The motivation of the individual could be measured by some "force" to behave in a certain way, through the individual's perception of the results of his efforts. On the job, for example, the worker might have work goals toward which he should strive. Given his job, the individual must consider for himself the chances that he will be able to meet those task goals—his expectancy with regard to his efforts. Further, he must consider the relationship between his achieving task goals and being awarded appropriately. A disproportionately high reward with little or no chance to attain it would, in most cases, fail to motivate. On the other hand, a lesser award with a higher probability of attainment might prove to be a very effective motivator. To summarize the model's relationships:

1. The valence of a first level outcome (incentive or reward) is a function of the instrumentality of that outcome for obtaining second level outcomes (need satisfactions) and the valences of the relevant second level outcomes.
2. The decision by an individual to work on a particular task and expend a

---

[14]Cf. Edward E. Lawler III, *Pay and Organizational Effectiveness: A Psychological View* (New York: McGraw-Hill, 1971), p. 88.

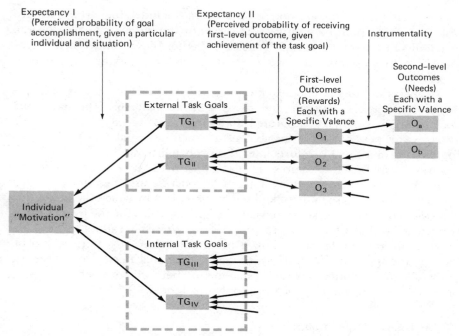

FIGURE 11-4   A schematic representation of an expectancy model of work motivation. Source: Campbell, *et al., Managerial Behavior, Performance, and Effectiveness,* p. 347.

certain amount of effort in that direction is a function of (a) his personal probability estimate that he can accomplish the task (expectancy I), (b) his personal probability estimate that his accomplishment of the task goal will be followed by certain first level outcomes or rewards (expectancy II), and (c) the valence of the first level outcomes.

3. The distinction between external and internal goals and rewards leads to a number of potential conflict situations for the individual. For example, an individual might estimate his chances for accomplishing a particular task as virtually certain (i.e., expectancy I = 1.0). However, the internal rewards which are virtually certain to follow (i.e., expectancy II = 1.0) may have a very low or even negative valence (e.g., feelings of extreme boredom or distaste). If external rewards, such as a lot of money, have a very high valence, a serious stress situation could result from outcomes which have conflicting valences. It would be to an organization's advantage to ensure positive valences for both internal and external rewards. Other conflict situations could be produced by high positive valences for outcomes and low estimates of type I expectancies (i.e., the individual does not think he can actually do the job).[15]

[15]Campbell et al., p. 348.

The first-level outcomes or rewards from the individual efforts toward task goals must then be appraised in terms of the individual's own overall goal and value system. He must consider whether these rewards are instrumental to his reaching his own personal goals or satisfying his personal needs.

Expectancy theory models shed a good bit of light on the activities involved in choices between alternative behavior patterns. The individual goes through a rather complicated and subjective procedure in which he evaluates his perceptions of his abilities to reach task goals, his preferences for the outcomes of his efforts, and the probability that his efforts will be rewarded. Finally, he measures all this against his own personal needs and wants. Expectancy theory does not give a concrete and descriptive model with which to work, for we are looking at the *process* by which the individual chooses to behave. We cannot develop insights or rules for the overall value framework within which this process goes on. We really cannot make statements from this model about how a particular behavior pattern would be seen by the individual and its satisfying his personal needs or desires. In point of fact, we cannot make good statements about what his personal needs or his desires *are,* when considering only this model.

A General Motivational Model

Maslow, in his needs hierarchy model, established a classification of end points toward which behavior is directed; he felt that people attempted to fulfill unsatisfied needs. Vroom, on the other hand, developed his model to explain how people choose between alternative courses of action and why a person might be more strongly motivated (exert greater effort) toward certain goals.

We might be able to put the two models together to develop a strategic model of motivation. Such a model would integrate broad classifications of drive-establishing needs with the process by which the individual chooses his behavior. Let's imagine the situation in which a college student may have fulfilled his physiological, security, and social needs. The need that would be operating to set up drives for its satisfaction would probably be the ego or esteem need. Satisfaction of this need would be the ultimate purpose of many of his behaviors. But what are the ways open to him so that he might fulfill this need? Because he is a college student, we know that he would typically be graded on his work in his courses. This might well prove to be a way in which he might be recognized for his achievements, thereby allowing him some self-esteem or recognition by others.

In terms of expectancy theory, we are suggesting that the student evaluates this particular path toward the satisfaction of his ego needs. He sees one alternative as being high marks in his courses. The preference (valence) that he has for this outcome of his efforts would be measured by his subjective appraisal of how instrumental high grades would be in satisfying his ego needs.[16] But how well is he able to influence his grades? If his professors all give true–false or multiple-choice quizzes—and this student is a notoriously poor performer on objective tests—then his expectancy that his efforts would result in the desired outcome (high grades) would be rather low. Therefore the motivating force, which would urge his actions in that direction, would be relatively low, mainly because of his perceived inability to influence the first-level outcome, which would be instrumental in his attaining his second-level outcome (satisfying his ego needs). Depending on what other choices are open to him, we might imagine that he would be more than willing to settle for a gentleman's C, putting his efforts somewhere else to get a reward for what he does. He might, for instance, devote his activities to student government functions, trying to work his way up to student body president if he were to evaluate this strategy as having a higher probability of success *and* being instrumental to his need satisfaction.

We might even be able to use this strategic model to explain what have been called the "blue-collar blues" and the "white-collar woes." If you worked on an assembly line, you would imagine that your physiological and security needs would be rather well satisfied. What about your social needs? Your ego or esteem needs? Are there opportunities available in the job situation by which you can satisfy these needs? On the typical assembly line your opportunity to socialize with your co-workers wouldn't be great, because your work station would probably be physically separated from those of the other workers. In those situations in which work stations are next to each other (such as in electronic assembly plants), you might have a chance to satisfy these needs. Let's examine these two situations.

Suppose that your social needs are not satisfied at work because your work station is physically separated from the stations of the other workers. Because this need is unsatisfied, a drive is set up on your part to satisfy it. What strategies or alternatives are available to you in the job situation to satisfy that need? Several possible ways exist: if you worked within speaking distance of a number of other workers, your social needs might be satisfied; if you were able to move around the plant and visit with other people, your social needs might tend to be met; and coffee breaks and lunch periods might provide you with some opportunity to socialize. How instrumental or relevant would one or all of these activities be in satisfying your social needs? Socializing only during coffee or lunch would probably satisfy these needs less than constant interaction on the job and so would probably have lower valence than socializing constantly at work.

But are you *able* to behave in these ways that would yield outcomes instrumental to your need satisfaction? If you work on a noisy assembly line or your work station is too far away from others, or your supervisor enforces a plant rule against talking on the job, then this path to your desired outcome would be effectively blocked. If your work speed is dictated by the speed of

---

[16]Ibid., p. 344.

the assembly line itself, or by the capacity of the machine on which you work, then your ability to be mobile or to move around the plant and converse with others would also effectively block your need satisfaction. And if, as is typically the case in mass-production plants, the assembly line cannot be shut down for lunch or coffee breaks, you may be relieved by your foreman or by an extra worker so that you can go to lunch or coffee—which wouldn't give you much opportunity to talk with your co-workers.

If your attempts to satisfy your social needs appear to be blocked at every turn by the technology of the work place, then your motivation to satisfy this need would be close to zero, no matter how strongly your desire to satisfy that need. This would probably result in apathy toward the work and increased drives to satisfy social needs *off* the job, perhaps through a bowling league or a fraternal lodge.

The same analysis could be done for an individual attempting to satisfy his ego needs, the next step in Maslow's hierarchy of needs. If his work allowed no chance for the individual to affect its performance, then recognition or achievement needs could not very well be satisfied through the job, no matter how strongly the need satisfaction is desired. So why should the worker be strongly motivated toward his job if he cannot influence his own performance, or if performance is not directly related to reward, or if the rewards for high performance are inappropriate (not instrumental) for satisfying the needs level at which he is operating—as in the case of putting a gold star in his personnel file?

Using this strategic model, we might be better able to explain and predict the actions—and nonactions—of your friends, colleagues, and associates. If we feel that human beings are somewhat rational in striving to satisfy their needs but are unwilling to butt their heads up against a stone wall, this combination of Maslow's needs hierarchy and Vroom's expectancy theory could be a powerful tool for us to use. We might be able to explain why some football players are motivated by performance on the field and not by performance in the classroom. Or we might consider why the revered grand master of our local lodge never seems to exert any initiative or show responsibility on the job and thereby is not considered supervisory material.

And what about you?

Summary

In this chapter, we have investigated the general nature of motivation and presented a series of models that attempt to explain why people behave the way they do. Static models, in which set and unchanging purposes of behavior are assumed, were examined and found to be rather unrealistic because of man's constantly changing and growing nature. Explaining behavior completely through instinct, hedonism (pleasure seeking and pain avoiding), the influence of the unconscious, the completely rational decision-maker, and social man models were too simple and failed to explain much.

Three dynamic models, which more nearly take into account the complexities of human behavior, were discussed. The first of these, Maslow's hierarchy of needs, presents man as a complex being whose activities are directed toward the satisfaction of his needs. These needs are felt to exist not on an equal priority basis but in a sequence of priority. Each classification of needs is effective in influencing behavior only when it is unsatisfied. These levels of needs are classified as physiological (the most basic of man's needs), safety or security, social, ego or esteem, and self-actualization (the highest and least powerful of the needs).

Whereas Maslow concentrated on the broad general objectives of man's behavior as being need satisfaction, Vroom presented his expectancy theory of motivation to explain why motivation may vary from person to person or from situation to situation. He felt that the individual subjectively assigns a preference (valence) to the outcome of his efforts. At the same time, he evaluates the extent to which his efforts will result in that outcome (expectancy, his subjective probability). The force of motivation is then the product of valence and expectancy.

A strategic model of motivation was developed in which the work of Vroom and Maslow was integrated. The strategic model points out that the process by which the individual evaluates his choices is oriented by the needs of the individual. The efforts that the individual expends will typically be in ways to satisfy the needs operating at the level of Maslow's hierarchy at which the individual currently exists.

These dynamic models more nearly represent explanations of why people behave the way they do. If we have this type of understanding and know something more about the motivating process, predictions of behavior can be more rationally and completely made.

STUDY AND REVIEW QUESTIONS

1. Explain why the five "static" motivational models are not "dynamic."
2. Compare and contrast the concepts of motivation and behavior.
3. Why is Freud's unconscious motivation model said to be based on a combination of the instinct and the hedonistic models?
4. *Evaluate* the effectiveness with which you could
  a. Explain an individual's observed behavior using each of the static models. Why?
  b. Predict an individual's behavior using each of the static models. Why?
5. *Evaluate* the effectiveness with which you could
  a. Explain an individual's observed behavior using each of the three dynamic models. Why?
  b. Predict an individual's behavior using each of the three dynamic models. Why?
6. Compare and contrast the static rational-man model and the dynamic expectancy-theory model.
7. Why is motivation of such great interest to managers?

8. Most people are interested in money. If an individual were observed to be "motivated by" money, analyze the situation using:
   a. Maslow's hierarchy of needs.
   b. Vroom's expectancy theory.
   c. the general motivational model.
9. Analyze your own motivation by using:
   a. Maslow's hierarchy of needs.
   b. Vroom's expectancy theory.
   c. the general motivational model.
10. Discuss how an understanding of basic motivational processes can be of use to you now and in the future.

Chapter

12

Motivation,
the Individual,
and Behavior

CHAPTER OBJECTIVES

1. To extend the discussion of basic motivation to implications for organizational behavior.

2. To introduce the role of incentives in motivation.

3. To add the concept of level of aspiration as a factor in the motivational process.

4. To give an indication of the difficulty involved in establishing a climate conducive to effective motivation.

CHAPTER OUTLINE

Organizational Motivation
Job Factors and Needs Satisfaction
Is the Needs Hierarchy Valid?
Intensity of Motivation

The Role of Incentives in Motivation
Positive and Negative Incentives
Incentives as Motivators
Implications for Motivating Organizational
  Behavior

Motivating with Money
The Many Facets of Money
Maintenance and Motivator Consideration
Perceptual Influences

Aspiration Level
Performance and Aspiration
Establishing the Aspiration Level
Aspiration Level and Motivation

Managerial Motivation

In the last chapter we explored some of the basics of human motivation, to provide background and a sense of what motivation processes imply for the individual's behavior. We saw that behavior is *motivated* and *goal-oriented*, intensely individualistic yet able to be generalized into broad statements.

In this chapter the general introduction to motivation will be built upon, so that we can examine the implications that individual motivation has for organizational behavior. Almost all managers and executives are highly involved in motivational programs; through motivation, the highest level of task performance and dedication of organizational members may be brought forth. Motivating its members means that the organization can attain its goals with less cost, greater productive efficiency, and greater human satisfaction. The motivated individual also gains through enhanced opportunities for development toward a more full realization of his potential and capabilities.

Organizational Motivation

Motives are forces, internal to the individual, that form the basis of behavior. Organizational motivation consists of the establishment of an environment—an entire complex of factors that surround the individual within the organization—that draws forth one's motives in appropriate ways. The individual motivates himself; all that the organization and its executives can do is to provide a setting and a task. Effective organizational motivation occurs when one's environment allows the simultaneous achievement of individual and organizational motives.

Job Factors and Needs Satisfaction

How may this be done? We first need to identify common environmental factors and their motivational implications. We can begin with Maslow's conceptualization of universal needs arranged in a hierarchy. These needs, starting with the most basic, are physiological, safety, social, ego, and self-actualization. We can investigate the extent to which these needs are satisfied within the context of the organization as conceived by Herzberg. A handy framework is provided if we note how well the needs hierarchy and Herzberg's dual-factor theory items appear to coincide.[1] Figure 12-1 shows how the two constructs may be related.

Job characteristics become part of a motivational program, especially when the individual's unsatisfied needs are taken into account. For instance, a worker whose safety and security needs (Maslow) are his driving forces would naturally be highly concerned with issues of job security (Herzberg). Questions of the "meaningfulness" of the work he does would probably be

---

[1]Herzberg's dual-factor theory was discussed in Chapter 6, "Technology, Structure, and Job Satisfaction."

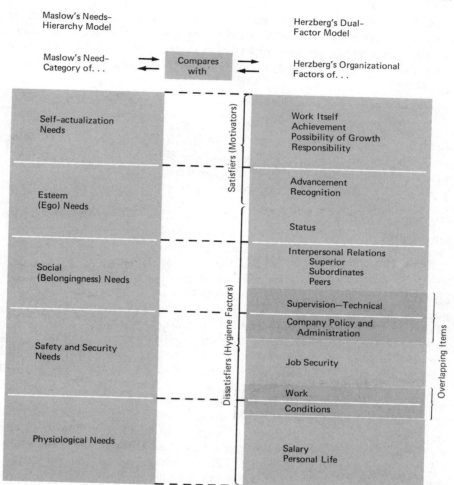

FIGURE 12-1   Comparison of Maslow's hierarchy-of-needs model with Herzberg's dual-factor model.

quite far from his mind at any particular moment, representing as this does the factors of the work itself, achievement, possibility of growth, responsibility, and advancement, as well as recognition. Of utmost importance to this worker is the satisfaction of his physiological needs and his needs at home that stem from his job. These needs are satisfied by salary and work conditions. The continued paycheck becomes more important than the higher-order but less tangible factors.

In a similar fashion, the person whose ego needs (Maslow) are in operation is interested in the opportunities that he has for advancement and recognition (Herzberg). These two factors are items that motivate his behavior. When he obtains advancement and recognition, they become positive sources of fulfilled motivation and hence job satisfaction. To satisfy these higher motivating needs, an individual might well leave job security behind to seek greater prestige and opportunity through starting his own company—which is ordinarily risky and offers little in the way of job security.

Is the Needs Hierarchy Valid?

What is the evidence on needs satisfaction? Unfortunately the studies that have been done specifically on the hierarchy of needs show some conflicting results. This may be because of the difficulty involved in measuring a need that has been gratified, or in expressing the relative strengths of needs that are in operation, not to mention the order in which they occur and are gratified.

Porter studied almost 2,000 managers, who represented the entire range of the managerial hierarchy, from first-line supervisors to presidents.[2] Omitted from the needs hierarchy categories was that of physiological needs; added between esteem and self-actualization was the category of autonomy or independence. He found that security needs were about equally satisfied on all of the managerial levels studied. The two highest-order need categories, autonomy and self-actualization, were the least thoroughly gratified of the need categories, even though self-actualization gratification tended to increase as the managerial hierarchy was ascended. Porter concluded that the three higher-order needs (esteem, autonomy, and self-actualization) and their gratification are linked to one's position in the organization. He also found that the two highest need categories are more important to higher-level managers in their jobs than they are to lower-level managers.[3]

Hall and Nougaim investigated the need hierarchy through data from the first five years of the careers of a group of managers. The study was longitudinal so that progression could be traced through the needs hierarchy. They confirmed that hierarchical position was related to need satisfactions. Instead of a hierarchy of needs that are successively gratified and give rise to emerging dominant new needs, they suggested that career stages explain better the changing needs found in the study. They conceptualized a career as "a series of salient personal issues, which emerge as the person passes through various status boundaries."[4] Passage through career stages occurs as a result of *occupational* changes and *maturity* and independently of satisfying successfully earlier stage concerns.[5] The career phases they suggested are these:

---

[2]Lyman W. Porter, "Job Attitudes in Management: I. Perceived Deficiencies in Need Fulfillment as a Function of Job Level," *Journal of Applied Psychology* (December 1962), pp. 375–384.

[3]Lyman W. Porter, "Job Attitudes in Management: II. Perceived Importance of Needs as a Function of Job Level," *Journal of Applied Psychology*, **47:** 141–148.

[4]Douglas T. Hall and Khalil E. Nougaim, "An Examination of Maslow's Need Hierarchy in an Organizational Setting," *Organizational Behavior and Human Performance*, **3:** 26 (1968).

[5]Ibid., p. 29.

1. Concern for security—gaining recognition and establishing oneself in a profession or organization. Concerned with defining the structure of his position and with feeling secure in it. Searching for means of integrating himself in the system. Struggling to define more clearly his environment and his relationship to it.
2. Concern for promotion and achievement—not so concerned with fitting into an organization (moving inside) as he is with moving upward and mastering it.
3. Concern for meaning and a sense of purpose in one's work—attempting to relate his efforts to some higher-order cause, such as commitment to the organization or service to youth; a means of self-actualization.[6]

In brief, the validity of the needs hierarchy theory is still in dispute. Researchers have approached the problem in many different ways and with varying degrees of scientific rigor, and we should expect diverse results to be obtained. The theory itself has been interpreted in different ways, which results in different ways of being operationalized. Methodologies have differed drastically, and measurement problems have been variously addressed and resolved. In the meantime, the needs hierarchy concept retains its usefulness if only for its controversy.[7] It also permits us a convenient framework within which to look at complex motivational matters.

To analyze individual behavior, we need to extend the broad organizational motivation framework of Herzberg and Maslow so that it includes elements of individual cognitive choices *and* the means by which needs are satisfied. We can do this by using the expectancy theory concepts discussed in the last chapter.

Intensity of Motivation

Motivation is a complex process that is expressed when an individual expends effort or energy in order to satisfy some need or attain some goal. The *strength* of the motivation is directly related to both the perceived expectancy that expending the effort will result in attaining the goal *and* the degree to which the goal is *desired* (valence).[8]

To extend our Maslow–Herzberg reconciliation to include strength and direction of motivation, think of a person motivated by his social needs. If he has only recently satisfied his safety and security needs, we would expect that his social needs would be ungratified and that his desire to fulfill them would be high. Developing satisfactory interpersonal relations and acceptance then would be the focus of his efforts. Assuming he saw a reasonable probability of his being accepted by his work group and thus becoming one of "in-

[6]Ibid., pp. 26–29.

[7]Mahmoud A. Wahba and Lawrence G. Briewell, "Maslow Reconsidered: A Review of Research on the Need Hierarchy Theory," paper presented to the annual meeting of the Academy of Management, Boston, Mass., August 1973, p. 18.

[8]Victor H. Vroom, *Work and Motivation* (New York: Wiley, 1964), p. 18.

group," the force of his motivation should be quite high. He might even flirt with lowering the extent of satisfaction of his lower needs, at least until he perceived a probability of their not being fulfilled. For instance, his work group might require that he adhere to an informally set production maximum that was below his own normal output. The dropoff in productivity could threaten his job security and therefore his salary. If he tries to satisfy his social needs by behaving as required by his work group, his lower, more basic needs may be threatened. The problem facing the manager is the lack of an alternative by which the member can satisfy his needs in *productive* ways.

The Role of Incentives in Motivation

A substantial challenge exists in designing motivational programs so that they encourage behaviors that contribute to the purpose of the organization. Employees usually know the lowest acceptable performance level. Why should they work harder than necessary? What may be needed is a conscious attempt to enlist enthusiastic contribution of effort and initiative above this bare minimum. Motivation is an *internal* state, beyond the ability of another person to manipulate directly. A situation *external* to the individual may be structured in such a way as to channel motivational forces and efforts into desired activities.[9] Obtaining the incentive for particular behaviors satisfies the need and thus removes it, just as drinking water removes thirst sensations.

Positive and Negative Incentives

Incentives may be either *positive* or *negative*. Those that satisfy needs and are pleasurable are positive incentives. Those that establish unpleasant consequences—outcomes to be avoided—are negative incentives.[10] Both types of incentives are common in organizations.

Security is often used to activate the individual whose performance falls below a certain standard. As a *negative* incentive the threat of being fired evokes a situation to be avoided so that his security may be maintained. Another incentive, money, is widely used in such positive incentive systems as piecework. Under piecework and similar systems, a worker is either paid a set rate for each satisfactory item he produces or is guaranteed a certain minimum wage level independent of performance, to which money is added based on his productivity.

[9]Norman R. F. Maier, *Psychology in Industrial Organizations,* 2nd Ed. (Boston: Houghton Mifflin, 1973), p. 330.
[10]Ibid., p. 339.

Incentives as Motivators

The use and effectiveness of such incentives are rarely questioned. We need to examine the rationale behind such incentives, however, to see their impact on motivation. Referring back to Figure 12-1, we can see that the threat of being fired corresponds to depriving an individual of his ability to satisfy his safety and security needs. Safety and security needs are quite basic and therefore quite strong. The appeal to fear and deprivation could prove to be a powerful motivating factor. The need that is activated and the goal to be attained are not necessarily contributions of effort and initiative in pursuit of organizational goals. Instead the individual becomes motivated to expend the amount of effort necessary to retain his job and thus his security. Certainly there is no enthusiasm involved in a fearful situation, merely dread and anxiety.

The threat of being fired can be called motivating. The object of the motivation is to *avoid* pain or discomfort, rather than the eager contribution of one's skills in the performance of his responsibilities. The threat of deprivation of security operates in a *negative* fashion. Interestingly enough, to the individual motivated by physiological needs, the threat of security deprivation holds few of the anxieties and motivating elements that it does for one at the security needs level. Satisfying one's physiological needs is dictated by an overwhelming priority associated with the immediacy of staying alive.

In a more positive vein, let us consider the person whose ego needs are in operation. He has satisfied rather completely his physiological, security, and social needs. His satisfaction with job security, salary, acceptance by peers, and status does not affect his job satisfaction. Should any of these fall below an acceptable level, they would increase his job *dis*satisfaction. Because these factors associated with his lower-level needs are hygiene factors, increased levels in any or all of them would not serve as stimuli for motivation to expend energy or effort to attain the greater state of status or whatever else.

His higher-order needs of esteem may be satisfied if recognition is given to him by peers and superiors, as well as with advancement based on merit. These factors of advancement and recognition are two of Herzberg's satisfiers or motivators. They are directly related to job satisfaction, indicating that they are directly related to positive attitudes toward the job held. The individual, by expending energy and effort in pursuit of advancement and recognition, can see a strong instrumentality between advancement or recognition and the satisfaction of his ego needs. The way in which advancement and recognition may be attained with the highest expectancy is through job performance. Therefore a high motivational force would be attached to job performance for the individual operating at the esteem needs level. This assumes that the job discussed is one in which individual contribution may be readily observed and measured, so that there is some identifiable level of performance to be recognized.

Implications for Motivating Organizational Behavior

At this stage, perhaps it is more readily apparent why some of the factors in Herzberg's dual-factor theory are called *motivators* and some are termed *hygiene factors*. The motivators are directly associated with needs satisfaction *through* the contribution of efforts and initiative to further the organization's purpose. They are directly related to the work itself. The hygiene factors, on the other hand, have very little to do with the work that one actually performs. They are job *context* factors, elements that surround the individual in his job yet, do not directly consist of factors involved in *doing* the job.

A major mistake made by many companies is confusing increased levels of hygiene factors with increasing motivation. Would another air-conditioned cafeteria on campus make you a better student? Would a newly painted office make a clerk a better clerk? Would a ten-year contract, replacing a three-year contract, make a star quarterback a better quarterback? The answer to all of these is "no." Inasmuch as they reflect neither recognition nor achievement, these factors cannot possibly motivate a person to doing a better job. Interestingly for several decades many companies across the country have spent millions of dollars training supervisors and executives in the niceties of human relations to establish better "interpersonal relations." The assumption behind this is that better relations between superior and subordinate will somehow increase the motivation ability of supervisors and the willingness to work of subordinates. We can see that such training *for that purpose* is probably wasted, because it is intended to increase a *hygiene* factor. Hygiene factors that are used to increase motivation are among the most expensive ways that a company can spend money on its employees, yet the return in increased motivational levels is probably minimal.

The true motivators—the work itself, achievement, possibility of growth, responsibility, advancement, and recognition—may "cost" no more than a pat on the back or a memo of congratulations. *But* the successful application of motivators to increase the contribution of organizational members requires that the members have satisfied their physiological, security, and social needs and that one of the higher-order needs be in operation. So motivation as a total program must recognize the specific needs that are motivating each individual organizational member. Workers whose desks are side by side may be motivated by entirely different needs and therefore will react differently to a single motivational stimulus.

Satiation of needs that are satisfied for most of the working population—physiological and security needs—makes very little sense. Instead, linking behavior to desired need gratification—and incentives—seems to offer more concrete possibilities for motivating organizational behavior.

Motivating with Money

If behavior is motivated by perceived probability of success, then the effective manager must have discretionary ability to administer rewards for task performance. The organizational reward system must similarly recognize the achievements of the individual. How then does money fit into the motivation of organizational members? Hardheaded businessmen may scoff at the notion that money isn't the all-powerful means through which increased effort is brought about. You may even feel much the same.

Many recent college graduates may privately admit that "It's not much of a job, but it pays well." Others may resolve a difficult choice between an interesting job and a well-paying one, perhaps in favor of more money. The question, though, is *motivation*. Will you work harder and accomplish more on a job that you detest, yet that is very high paying? To answer this question, we might do well to start by analyzing the concept of pay with Maslow's and Herzberg's models.

The Many Facets of Money

What does money represent? Certainly it is necessary to sustain life in a free enterprise system because it is a *medium of exchange*. Money may be exchanged for food, for example. Money is also a *store of value* because we may put the payment for last week's or last year's work in the bank for future use. The value associated with prior work may be stored and later redeemed for our choice of goods and services. Money can even represent *prestige*. Our higher-paid occupations, such as physicians or executives, are usually seen as having greater status or esteem than occupations that are rewarded substantially less, such as manual laborers. And finally, money can be the means through which an individual can do exactly as he *wishes*. The independently wealthy, for whom work is not necessary, may paint, travel, or do exactly as they wish without mundane worries.

Money represents many things to many different people. When we say that money motivates, we must look beneath the surface of this statement and see just what facet of money we are talking about. Money can be used to satisfy each need in Maslow's hierarchy. A five-thousand-dollar-a-year job would be barely sufficient to provide the means for satisfying the physiological needs of a starving person. At the same time, it should satisfy security needs, if the employment is relatively stable. What about social needs? A given level of income can sustain a social unit such as the family but may not allow significant opportunities for interaction with other compatible people.

Because of the large number of higher-paid family units, such a salary would probably not bring much status or esteem to the job holder. Nor would the level of income represented here go very far in allowing a person's self-actualization needs to be gratified.

So money for itself, we can conclude, is not really much of a motivator, according to Maslow's needs hierarchy; it can do relatively little to satisfy higher-order needs directly. Amount of money and position on the hierarchy are important considerations for determining whether or not a given monetary level can serve as a motivator.

Maintenance and Motivator Considerations

According to the dual-factor theory, money is not by itself a motivator. A given level of money income is necessary for *maintenance* (hygiene) needs. Money can be represented as a dissatisfier, a necessary condition *prior* to motivation, in such diverse elements as salary, personal life, work conditions, job security, company policy and administration, technical aspects of supervision, and status. We learned that these dissatisfiers cannot motivate, no matter what level of satisfaction is attained in any one or all of the hygiene factors. They merely contribute to a state of neutral satisfaction and set the stage for motivation to occur. The motivators (recognition, advancement, responsibility, possibility of growth, achievement, and the work itself) are set forth as the elements incorporated in a job that yields satisfaction. Their presence motivates the individual to job performance and their absence leads him toward a state of neutrality in attitude toward his job.

What does this have to do with money? Is money merely a hygiene factor that has no relevance to motivation? On the contrary, money can also be a motivator. Doesn't this contradict the earlier position taken, that money by itself is not a motivator? Money can be a motivator only insofar as it is *perceived* by the organizational member as representing factors that make up Herzberg's satisfiers. In other words, if a pay raise is seen as a reward or recognition for a job well done, then the money received will be a motivator. Such recognition should then bring forth increased efforts. A pay raise or given level of salary may be associated with advancement or change in position and then may take on characteristics that will motivate. Similarly money can be positively related to perceptions of responsibility and growth. The strongest correlation between money and motivation may be seen in the factor of achievement. If money is linked to the perceived successful performance of the individual, then money can be said to be motivating.

Perceptual Influences

The concept of money as a motivator is a little more complex than might be first indicated. Money itself does not motivate. What motivates is what the money stands for. This may help to explain conditions under which money is *not* a motivator. If you were given a raise of a thousand dollars a month, would you be motivated? Before you hasten to answer "yes," consider some additional hypothesized "facts" about your situation. Would you be as motivated to exert additional effort and initiative if you were making $500,000 a year as if you were making $5,000 a year? Probably not. The raise is rather insignificant, compared to the higher income level. As a matter of fact, at the higher income level, you may actually "see" this raise as being an insult, since it is so "little"!

Let's lower our sights a bit and more realistically suggest a raise of $100 a month. Let's imagine that you are a junior executive, making $15,000 a year. You would probably be quite happy with this raise of 8 percent, wouldn't you? How would you interpret this raise? Depending on your personal situation, we could say that such a raise might increase your ability to satisfy your physiological needs, although they are probably fairly well satisfied. Safety and security needs would also be more nearly gratified, and social needs would be more nearly satisfied through the additional money available. At the same time ego needs would be activated and relatively satisfied because of your interpretation of what the raise means. You could interpret such a raise as being recognition for the level and quality of work you have been doing, and further as marking your achievements. Such a raise would more than likely be seen as motivating.

But let's suggest that after a while the subject of pay raises comes up with your junior executive peers around the coffee pot. They tell you that the *smallest* raise that any of *them* received was a *12* percent increase, and the *average* raise they received was *15* percent! What about your motivation now? We can suggest that that raise is no longer perceived as representing recognition or achievement and so is no longer motivating. As a matter of fact, it may become a source of dissatisfaction! This phenomenon is called *relative deprivation,* because your needs have not been gratified to the extent those of your peers have been, and by comparison with them you see a deficiency. Looking at the situation through equity theory, if we assume that you see no difference in quality of work or contribution between you and your peers, then an inequitable situation is seen. Job-related motivation stemming from the pay raise would probably not be forthcoming. As a matter of fact, the pay raise will now be seen as rather insulting because of the inequity in pay raises.

Does money motivate? The answer is not simple. About the best we can do is to say that normally money itself does not motivate. What the money is perceived as representing, and the situation in which it occurs motivate.

We have talked rather loosely in the preceding sections about goal attainment and perceived achievement as being motivators. The concepts of degree of need satisfaction and goal attainment demand that we define the level of success that the individual establishes as necessary for satisfying his desire for competence or achievement.

Aspiration Level

At what level of effort and challenge does one direct his behaviors? What affects his perceived probabilities (expectancies) of a linkage between his efforts and reward? The concept of *level of aspiration* can help us. The concept also is useful in that it points out yet another way in which individual behavior can vary drastically. One way of looking at an aspiration level is to consider it as a "subjective goal toward performance . . . which . . . serves as a reference point for feelings of success or failure . . . performance which exceeds the level of aspiration is success, and performance which falls short of the level of aspiration is failure."[11] An aspiration level can then be considered the level of performance and its results that are set by the individual and against which he measures himself.

Performance and Aspiration

An obvious example of aspiration in action is the different criteria of performance we see in the classroom. We might think that performance is rather self-evident, but we must recognize that there is a range of rewards available to the student, each of which is supposedly geared to a different level of student performance. A C is a reward for an "average" level of performance and quality of output, whereas an A is intended to reward performance and output that is clearly superior and of the highest quality. This reward system is highly structured. Most industrial reward systems may range from being even more minutely spelled out (for production workers on piecework) or quite ambiguous (for top-level executives). Even with differences in certainty of rewards, what is important is that there is a reward structure established. For performance and given levels of quality, the student or the worker or the manager can expect a roughly commensurate reward.

Establishing the Aspiration Level

But what reward does one set his sights on? Is a D "good enough"? Is the student ecstatic with a B because it is far more than he dreamed of? If the student knows that a certain amount of work and performance on quizzes and papers is tied to a given grade, then he should have a range of expectations within which he establishes the amount of effort he is willing to expend. Similarly the production worker knows that the piecework system is directly geared to only one factor: the number of items he assembles that meet quality standards. A production worker can produce a bare minimum and expect the minimum wage, or he can work his shift at his greatest capacity in order to obtain the highest possible wage. Realistically we might

[11]H. Starbuck, "Level of Aspiration," *Psychological Review*, **70:** 51 (1963).

expect that he would pace himself at some rate between the two extremes. A student similarly might be expected to settle for something between an F and an A+. The level of aspiration chosen is something that depends on the individual, and a number of other factors. The process of *deriving* a given level of aspiration depends on a number of factors: the performance on the same or similar event, the setting of a level of aspiration for the next performance, the new performance itself, and the psychological reaction to the new performance.[12]

Figure 12-2 shows a typical sequence of events that occur in the establishing of a level of aspiration. This sequence can occur in almost any situation or series of situations that are similar or identical to each other. The classic example is that of a ring-toss in which the individual has scored 6 out of a possible 10. On the next try he may set his sights on scoring an 8 (a goal discrepancy of 2). He then executes the new performance and receives the new result. If he got a 5, then his "attainment discrepancy" was rather substantial and probably resulted in his reacting to the results of his new performance with disappointment. He might discontinue the activity altogether or start a new cycle with a new, adjusted level of aspiration—perhaps this time trying for a 6.

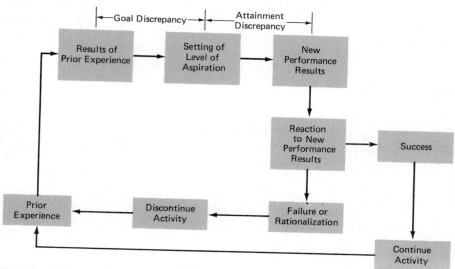

FIGURE 12-2   Typical sequence of events in a level of aspiration situation. Source: Adapted from Kurt Lewin, Tamara Dembo, Leon Festinger, and Pauline S. Sears, "Level of Aspiration," in J. McV. Hunt (Ed.), *Personality and the Behavior Disorders: A Handbook Based on Experimental and Clinical Research*, Vol. 1 (New York: Ronald Press, 1944), p. 334.

[12]Kurt Lewin, Tamara Dembo, Leon Festinger, and Pauline Snedden Sears, "Level of Aspiration," in *Personality and the Behavior Disorders: A Handbook Based on Experimental and Clinical Research*, Vol. 1, ed. by J. McV. Hunt (New York: Ronald Press, 1944), p. 334.

Aspiration Level and Motivation

Using the concept of level of aspiration, we can easily trace how success breeds higher self-imposed goals and how failure frustrates the individual. The concept also has implications for how the individual arrives at the expectancies in motivation regarding the linkage between his behavior and results obtained. With past successes his level of aspiration (and consequent subjectively derived probability of success) will be raised and so bring forth a higher level of motivation and willingness to apply initiative and expend more effort. On the other hand, frustration and failure creates a downward shift in aspirations because of lower perceived probabilities of linkage between behavior and success. Therefore motivation would be less and apathy would result if the activity cannot be discontinued.

There is a tendency in establishing levels of aspiration for the individual to evaluate the range of his ability when facing situations of varying difficulty. His level of aspiration is then anchored against this range. If a task is either too easy or too difficult, falling outside the range of his abilities, then no level of aspiration is established. You probably have no feeling of success or failure in connection with putting on your shoes and socks. You also probably have no level of aspiration of running a three-minute mile.[13] The range of capability of the individual must be seen as reasonable and allow for initiative to be demonstrated in establishing an appropriate level of performance in order to attain a related reward.

Managerial Motivation

The ideas regarding motivation we have expressed in this and the preceding chapter have dealt with organizational members in general. At this time we should point out some differences in motivating the two broad classes of organizational members, managers and nonmanagers. The importance of motivating nonmanagers or workers should be rather evident. Workers are those members whose direct contributions and performance explicitly affect the operations of the organization and the goods or services that are its output. Increasing their levels of performance can thus make a substantial difference in quality and quantity of output for given organizational budgets, and lower costs.

More humanistically, increased motivation implies that each worker has an opportunity to attain a higher level of psychological growth and more nearly achieve satisfaction of higher-order needs. Work conditions that do not allow for a motivated individual, unfortunately, simply force the organizational member to achieve whatever higher-order needs he has *off* the job, rather than on. This constitutes an important waste of the human resource,

[13]Ibid., pp. 339, 340.

both for the individual and for the organization within which he works. Socially responsible managements of today are beginning to recognize that their responsibilities extend to the development of the human resource as well as capital and managerial resources.

Motivating managers is also necessary. Most people do not recognize that managers are subject to the same pressures and frustrations as assembly-line workers. In terms of level of aspiration and expectancy theory, the manager is probably in a more difficult situation than many production workers. The production worker can usually see some sort of a result of his efforts, even if he cannot see the overall connection of his output with the goods or services produced by the organization as a whole. Rarely does the manager do any direct or substantive work that has a concrete output. He is measured by how well his subordinates do *their* work. The feedback on how well he does may be extremely subjective or even nonexistent in comparison with that of production workers. The connection between his efforts and the overall performance of his subordinates may take years to evaluate. His level of aspiration may then be established without any conception of what were appropriate behaviors in identical or similar situations, nor even what contribution they made to whatever success was obtained, not to mention the fact that success or failure in the previous experiences or situations may be impossible to evaluate!

Despite these drawbacks to both worker and manager motivation, the motivational concepts we have discussed do offer some starting points from which to initiate motivation. Especially for managers, the higher-order psychological needs are those in operation and thus are the motivating needs. Esteem and self-actualization can only be satisfied through Herzberg's elements of the work itself, achievement, recognition, advancement, and so on. How well the manager does is probably a direct result of his expectancy that his performance or behavior is linked in some way to some measure of performance and of the way in which his level of aspiration is set. This also provides for reinforcement of those activities that are beneficial to the organization and that contribute to performance in the individual's responsibilities. Through careful counseling, the superior can help his subordinate aspire to an appropriate level of performance, without too great a probability of failure nor too high a probability of success (so that success may actually be felt when it occurs, rather than not demanding any initiative).

Production workers and staff specialists alike need to be motivated. The most basic notion of motivation, however, is that a superior does not directly motivate his subordinate. He merely *establishes* the environment and the opportunities for the subordinate to motivate *himself*. The stimulus must be internally generated by the person to be motivated and by behavior initiated toward appropriate incentives. If the individual is given the opportunity and the essential tools to motivate himself, then the superior can be facilitated in his attempt to build a productive team.

If motivation is seen as an externally generated stimulus, then motivation can occur only when someone is motivating another. With this line of reasoning, when the boss is out of the office, we might assume that motivation would stop—hardly a desirable situation.

By inducing self-motivation, the work itself and the achievement and recognition obtained for performance are all the motivating elements necessary. It is up to the superior to initiate controls and feedback systems to measure and reward performance, as well as providing counseling, especially to give the subordinate advice on future behavior.

Summary

In this chapter we extended the notion of motivation to include more concrete implications for organizational behavior. The correlation between Maslow's needs categories and Herzberg's dual-factor items was developed to indicate how these theories influence individual motivation. The linkage between performance and need satisfaction, through job factors, was shown to affect motivational intensity, as predicted by expectancy theory.

Effective incentives, when appropriately applied, were seen to give direction and expression to behaviors of organizational members, as well as providing the first-level outcomes important to the individual. Incentives may not always motivate, since they may be directed at lower-level needs through maintenance factors. The correct meshing of needs level, motivational job factors, and incentives is essential for the individual to be motivated to contribute to the attainment of the organization's purpose.

The common conception of money's intrinsic motivating nature was shown to be misleading. Money by itself fulfills maintenance needs and *may* serve as a surrogate for *means* by which higher-order (motivational) needs may be satisfied. Perception and considerations of equity play important parts in money's motivational role.

Aspiration level—the level of performance set by the individual for achievement and success feelings—was shown to be an extension of expectancy theory. The aspiration cycle affects the establishment of subjective probabilities of reward through successful performance.

In the next chapter we will tie together the subsystems within the system of the individual, as they relate to—and affect—organizational behavior.

STUDY AND REVIEW QUESTIONS

1. Which need is satisfied by money? Why?
2. What is the difference between a *motive* and an *incentive*?
3. "A person cannot motivate another person. One can only motivate himself." Explain and discuss.
4. What are some incentives, positive and negative, you (as a supervisor) might

effectively employ to encourage the motivation of subordinates who are at the social–belongingness needs level?

5. Develop an argument, based on economic or cost–benefit factors, to show the value of developing motivational programs that are aimed at the higher-order needs rather than the lower-level needs. Would you favor scrapping existing incentive programs oriented toward lower-level needs when your program is implemented?

6. What motivates you?

7. What part does the perceptual process play in whether or not money is a motivator?

8. How does level of aspiration relate to the expectancy theory of motivation?

9. Discuss how the aspiration-setting sequence affects job satisfaction–dissatisfaction.

10. Discuss the types of incentives that are important in the motivation of:
a. College students.
b. College professors.
c. Executives.
d. Assembly-line workers.
e. Secretaries.
f. Engineers.

Chapter

13

Integrating Perspective: The Individual in the Formal Organization

---

CHAPTER OBJECTIVES

1. To show how the elements of the individual system separately and jointly affect each other.

2. To develop an integrated understanding of the individual system as an entity.

3. To display the interactions between individual and formal organizational systems, in order to better understand the major forces operating on the individual as an organizational member.

4. To trace major relationships between components of individual and formal organizational systems, allowing a deeper appreciation of the complexities and variables involved in organizational behavior.

CHAPTER OUTLINE

252

Individual and Formal
Organizational Systems:
Interface and Interaction
Personality and the Formal Organization

Communication and the Formal
   Organization
Perception and the Formal Organization
Motivation and the Formal Organization

In the last five chapters our focus has been on processes that are internal to the individual. We have looked at personality factors, which create the uniqueness of each person and of his patterns of behavior. We have seen that people relate and attempt to exert influence over their environments through basic communication processes. Perception plays an important part in organizing and interpreting external stimuli, directly affecting attitudes and responses. Motivation also is largely determined by forces within the individual, especially as they reflect his history, value structure, needs, and aspirations. The individual's response to managerially administered incentives becomes a function of motivation and many other elements within the individual.

We have examined each topic independently of its relationship with the other components of our organizational behavior model. We have done this not because the others can be ignored when we focus on one element in the human equation but simply to clarify the separate components before introducing additional complexities. The purpose of this chapter is to show some of the relationships and complications that do exist among the separate subsystems of the individual system and then to integrate the individual system into the formal organizational system. We will tackle this task systematically, examining in turn the effects of one component on another. Figure 13-1 shows the parts of the system whose interactions we will explore before looking to the effects of one system on another.

Personality and the Individual System

The organized and consistent patterns of an individual's behavior constitute his personality. We can predict an individual's behaviors to the extent that we have knowledge of his personality characteristics and thus his inclinations or propensities to behave in particular ways. There are no hard-and-fast rules nor a universal set of traits or types that we can use, yet the concept of internally generated propensities to behave in consistent patterns can help us to overcome the all too common tendency to ignore individual differences.

Personality's Effects on Communication

Even the *ways* in which we communicate are reflections of our personalities. As we communicate, we are faced with many decisions. We have a

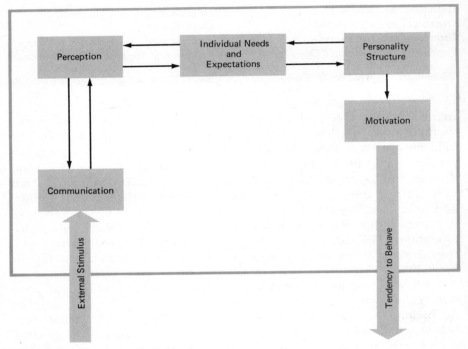

FIGURE 13-1   The individual system.

multitude of different words, intonations, and sentence structures available to us. The manner in which we choose to communicate reveals something of our intent, attitude, and personality. Shaw has developed four patterns of communication that are basic extensions of the personality of the communicator.[1] The communication patterns are termed *developmental, controlling, relinquishing,* and *withdrawing.* A person may use any one of these patterns consistently—yet unconsciously—because of personality considerations, most particularly those of tendencies toward influence and domination.

The Controlling Communicator

The person who has a high need for power might well find the controlling pattern of communication desirable because through this pattern he may best achieve his basic intent of getting the other person to do his will, staying in control, exerting his own influence, winning the argument. To accomplish his purpose, the controlling communicator has available two approaches: using persuasion or using force itself.

[1]Malcolm E. Shaw, *Developing Communication Skills* (Westport, Conn.: Educational Systems and Designs, Inc. 1968). The following discussion is based on his work.

Either method provides an avenue for attaining the objective of having the receiver submit, adopting the source's view or ideas. Persuasion is especially appropriate in trying to get another to "buy" one's ideas. The benefit or advantage to be gained may be pointed out in the persuasion attempt. Should the force of authority be on the communicator's side, he might choose to use that force in imposing his views or attitudes on another. He may use raw power, the authority of his position, or threats to accomplish his ends. A common characteristic of the controlling communicator is his use of negative incentives, or the undesirable results that may be expected if the other person doesn't do as the communicator suggests.

The Withdrawing Communicator

At the other end of the spectrum is the withdrawal pattern of communications. The communicator either retreats from a situation or attacks something other than what is frustrating him, indulging in an emotional outburst. Such nonproductive behavior might well be characteristic of the individual who has not matured emotionally. A problem situation can hardly be dealt with effectively when one refuses to come to grips with the problem or vents his frustrations on something outside the problem area rather than constructively using these energies in formulating a solution.

The Relinquishing Communicator

Closely allied with the withdrawal pattern is the pattern employed by the relinquishing communicator. The basic motive behind relinquishing is the source's need for social approval or affiliation. Just as with the person who has a high need of affiliation, the relinquishing communicator is more concerned with maintaining good interpersonal relationships than with task performance. To keep good relations, he accommodates or complies.

In accommodating, the source is influenced more by the opinions of others than by his own opinion. Riesman called this being "other directed."[2] The relinquisher will adapt or adjust to others, conforming even though unconvinced.

The other form of relinquishing, compliance, is observed when the source accedes to the wishes of another. He gives up all of his own influence, being completely willing to submit to the other. He goes along to keep other people happy or simply because he is afraid to take a chance. In any event, compliance is distinguished from accommodation by his being unconvinced of the value of the action but still being willing to give up his influence in favor of the other. Accommodation is marked by *acceptance* of the others' opinions. Adaptation, adjustment, and conformity to others are the hallmarks of the relinquishing communicator.

[2]David Riesman, *The Lonely Crowd* (New Haven, Conn.: Yale University Press, 1950).

The Developmental Communicator

The developmental communicator is not threatened by admitting that he needs help or that he does not have all of the answers. He also does not mind sharing his authority and influence with others but attempts to encourage the maximum contribution of all concerned. A stable and mature personality is typically needed to be as open and forthright, especially with subordinates, as is called for in the developmental pattern of communication.

A major point to be made on this interaction between personality and communication is that *both* elements must be considered together and also related to the situation at hand. There is no implied value judgment as to which of these is "best" or "worst"; each personality communication pattern has value—as well as disadvantages—under particular circumstances. The developmental pattern would hardly be appropriate on the front lines in a wartime situation, although it would probably be highly effective in performance appraisal or counseling sessions.

Personality's Effects on Perception

The way in which one tends to perceive a communication or a situation—his perceptual set—may also be determined to an extent by personality factors. Personality develops over time and as a result of past behaviors and their consequences. The extroverted person perceives a social situation as an opportunity to satisfy his needs and to develop pleasurable contacts. The introvert, on the other hand, perceives the same social situation as threatening and generally disagreeable.

Along the same line, consider how differently the chairmanship of a committee might be seen. The individual who scores high in need-Affiliation (n-Aff) brings his behavioral propensities with him to the task; the committee situation might very well be seen as an opportunity for developing and maintaining pleasurable social relationships, especially with attractive or compatible members. The position of chairman is easily used to further that end. Because of the characteristics of a high n-Aff chairman, we would expect the output of the committee—the accomplishment of the task for which it was formed—to be minimal, nonexistent, or the result of the hard work of an isolated member. The orientation of chairman would be toward social relationships and a friendly atmosphere. A task orientation usually means sacrificing social purposes.

The chairman who is oriented toward need-Achievement (n-Ach) would be rather frustrated by the necessity of group participation and contribution in attaining a particular objective. We remember that achievement-oriented individuals greatly prefer to work by themselves and maintain close control over their own ability to gain results. They also tend to hold many fewer meetings than others and prefer quick and substantive feedback on their performance. None of these can readily be obtained through committee efforts. Would it be any wonder that he would perceive the chairmanship as something less than an honor? As a matter of fact, he might perceive that the attempts of his members to contribute and to carve up the task into manageable individual portions are detrimental to his ability to maintain control over the process.

The power-oriented person would really be in his element as chairman. His appointment would be perceived as a major opportunity to influence others, backed by the authority of the formal organization. The relationship of member to chairman would probably be seen as confirmation of the latter's ability to control and direct the activities of others.

Personality's Effects on Motivation

Depending on stage of personality development, various needs emerge, and incentives are different in their effectiveness in inducing motivated behavior. A person may be characterized by a high level of submissiveness and need to be dominated by others. Because of his personality makeup, we would rather confidently predict that his motivation would not be activated through achievement, recognition, or the other factors associated with higher-order psychological needs. We would rather expect that an increased level of performance might be better attained through managerial practices such as close supervision, careful and detailed instruction, and carefully imposed standards for time and quality. Rosenfeld and Smith pointed out that organizational members may be able to be differentiated by basic clusters of personality factors, in order to provide incentives and motivational programs best suited for each group.[3] They defined four primary groups of organizational members according to behavioral stages, those termed *puritanical, power, group,* and *free.*

Those at the puritanical stage of behavior are operating at Maslow's safety needs level and constantly try to overcome perceived threats to their security. They also exhibit an overriding fear of the new and the unknown, because of the threats these can offer. They also exhibit "a general suppression of self, blind acceptance of rules, and predestination of work level,"[4] which is expressed in specific behaviors. Promotion desire is absent, changes are to be resisted, and money is not a sufficient incentive for increased performance. Rosenfeld and Smith suggested that the puritans should not be penalized for their lack of desire for promotion but that they should be employed in functions that are highly routine and demand exacting work. Piecework or incentive-based wage arrangements should not be used, nor should profit-sharing programs.

Power-stage individuals are self-centered and oriented to the use and

[3]J. M. Rosenfeld and M. J. Smith, "The Emergence of Management Theory Z: Part I," *Personnel Journal,* (October 1965), pp. 489–494.
[4]Ibid., p. 492.

growth of power. Fearless risk takers, they are dedicated to obtaining results, irrespective of the means. They respect force and authority as well as the trappings of status and are willing to work hard to achieve their purposes. Managerial incentives to elicit performance from power-stage members should be centered around incentive programs that offer the money, recognition, and resulting power desired. At the same time, their natural inclinations to beat the system for their own purposes should be carefully forestalled by the enforcement of organizational standards through the superior's authority.

Group behavior is the primary characteristic of those at the group stage. Each group-stage person identifies strongly with some particular group of people within his environment and wants group recognition and acceptance above everything else. He is status and social-needs conscious, accepting as his own the opinion of the majority of the group and the status conferred by group members. A major trait is conformity and consequent distress at being identified or recognized separately from the group. Managerial behaviors based on such characteristics are several. Groups should be encouraged that identify with the goals of the organization; incentive programs for work teams should be employed; status and recognition within the work groups should be provided and administered by the groups; and members should be regarded and treated as a group, rather than as separate individuals. Equity considerations will be uppermost in the mind of each group member, to see that there is little variance in fairness between the treatment of any individual and the other group members.

Those at the free stage are characterized by independence, autonomy, and individual and social freedom. Individualistic, they will not willingly take part in group efforts. By themselves they can contribute substantially to the purposes of the organization. Standard operating procedures and highly routine work conditions are abhorrent. Rather flexible and ambiguous conditions create an environment most conducive to their doing work that is of extremely high quality or that requires much effort or initiative. In the areas in which they are competent, they will exert leadership, yet they will not accept or follow irrational policies. Working in functions that are nonroutine allows them a great deal of autonomy in planning their work and in performing as individuals, best matching their characteristics and potential with work opportunities.

The importance of looking at the interaction between personality and motivation is underscored when we consider that managers continue to use inappropriate practices to organize and motivate their subordinates. Personality and behavior states and underlying value systems have changed while managerial practice has remained rather static.[5]

An interesting point about personality differences and motivation was

[5]M. Scott Myers and Susan S. Myers, "Toward Understanding the Changing Work Ethic," *California Management Review,* (Spring 1974), p. 15.

made by Eleanor Casebier, who compared characteristics of men and women in four companies: a bank, a utility company, a chemical company, and a paper company. Results were obtained from men and women in supervisory as well as nonsupervisory positions, from white-collar workers, hourly workers, and engineers. She found that Herzberg's motivators "are more important to men than to women":

It is more important to men to make the most of their talents, education, and training; feeling their views and opinions are taken seriously by those above them; having important responsibilities in the company; and helping to make important decisions affecting the work in the area. Men favor a supervisor who encourages their ideas and suggestions. Maintenance needs that are more important to men are economic and security needs.

Even though women are quite vocal about getting paid at the same rate as men for comparable work, the findings indicate that social factors are more important than economic and security factors are to women. They stress the importance of getting along well with fellow employees and working with people they like.

These data indicate a greater dependence upon and sensitivity to the supervisor on the part of women. That is, it is more important to women to be able to work for a supervisor whom they respect and admire. Women seem to look for more direction and guidance in doing their work.[6]

Communication and the Individual System

The process of transmitting information to attain some objective may be precipitated by either conscious or unconscious purposes of the communicator. The intent is generally to change a situation in some way so that it becomes more favorable to the communicator. Desired may be the changing of the behaviors of others or the changing of conditions that others control.[7]

Communication's Effects on Personality

The personality characteristics of the communicator have a significant effect on the content—as well as the intent—of the message. Bringing one's self-image and social self (the way that others see him) into congruity can only be done as a result of receiving and interpreting messages that reflect the perceptions of others. The young executive may see himself as a hard-driving, aggressive, and decisive person. If he receives information that his superiors see him merely as a brash, impulsive, and callow upstart, such

[6]Eleanor Casebier, "A Differentiation in Motivation of Men and Women Supervisory and Non-Supervisory Employees, Engineers and White Collar Workers," *The Southern Journal of Business* (November 1971), p. 64.

[7]Aubrey C. Sanford, *Human Relations: Theory and Practice* (Columbus, Ohio: Charles E. Merrill, 1973), p. 233.

communications may cause him to reevaluate of his behaviors, his projected personality traits, and his self-image.

In similar ways, the affiliation–needs–oriented supervisor might receive word that his subordinates are fighting among themselves and are discontented with his leadership. He may redouble his efforts to smooth over conflicts and create happy relationships. Should he fail in this, his social contacts may change in purpose, becoming more task-oriented, critical, and demanding—at the expense of cordial relations.[8] Those who have high n-Ach are also strongly affected by the availability of relevant feedback on performance. Without continual information on how well he is doing, the achievement-oriented person is frustrated in his ability to affect the outcome of a task or situation directly.

The initiation of communication, too, may be seen as reflecting control or superior status over the person receiving the communication. Communications may be so seen because of the intent of communication—to obtain the communicator's objective and influence another.[9] Certainly some communications are authoritative, being comprised of instructions or orders.

As influence attempts, communications can also directly influence one's perceptual set. Messages from the union that aver that management is exploiting its workers and only grudgingly grants decent working conditions and benefits—and only at the aggressive initiation of the union—will eventually condition members to see any unsolicited and humanistic moves by management as being motivated by cynical, self-serving purposes. The perceptual set will have been established by the barrage of communications. Perceptual processes will have been organized in such a way that the worker performs closure on information so that it conforms to patterns he *expects* to see.

Communication's Effects on Motivation

Communication is similarly important in the motivational process, for numerous reasons. Transferring information and meaning is necessary for the manager to establish what needs are operational for each of his employees. He also needs to remain informed of their attitudes and intentions, while receiving concrete and timely feedback on their perceptions of management actions and the consequences of the manager's practices.

Communication is a vital link in establishing expectancies between effort and results and between results and rewards. Communication need not be face to face nor even verbal; the receipt of a reward may be communication sufficient to establish such linkages. The way in which the reward is received may also communicate something quite different from what is intended. Receiving a raise would seem to be a clear-cut enough reward. Yet a junior

---

[8]Fred E. Fiedler, *A Theory of Leadership Effectiveness* (New York: McGraw-Hill, 1967), p. 195.

[9]William Foote Whyte, *Human Relations in the Restaurant Industry* (New York: McGraw-Hill, 1948), pp. 50–52.

clerk may receive the same dollar amount of raise as his more senior colleagues and therefore fail to recognize any differentiation and reward for superior performance. In fact, the more senior colleagues may have received a salary-percentage–based cost-of-living raise only, whereas the junior clerk's reward was for cost of living *plus* a merit increase.

Perception and the Individual System

As the gateway and organizing mechanism (filter) through which environmental data are organized into patterns that have meaning, perception has a profound effect on all elements within the individual system. An individual may have the basic tendency to act in certain ways, but his relationship with his environment and his behaviors are directly influenced by the perceived success or failure of prior actions. Learning theory tells us that unsuccessful behaviors tend to become extinct over time, whereas successful or rewarded behaviors are reinforced and generalized to similar situations.[10] In this way personalities develop and change.

Perception's Effects on Communication

In order for a communication attempt to be initiated, the source must first perceive a reason or purpose. Perception threads its way throughout the communication attempt. The personnel manager who concludes that workers are not informed of company benefits will have the necessary brochures distributed. His perception of the degree to which the problem is solved will depend on reports of how well the brochures have been read and understood.

The content or intent of the message may be variously perceived by the receiver. Identical communication attempts may be received from two different communicators and yet only one communicator might accomplish his intent. Outside sources of influence can affect the degree to which communication is successful, such as the perception of the credibility of the communicator or the receiver's past history of communications with the different sources. One example of this phenomenon may be observed rather commonly in the classroom situation. On a quiz paper a student might write what he considers a perfectly logical and reasonable statement of fact, yet his professor might refuse to accept that statement, even counting off points for failure to substantiate or trace the logic behind the statement. That same professor later may attend a learned seminar at which a noted authority speaks who uses the same phraseology and substance of the statement as the student. The authority's statement would probably be accepted without question, even though the student's conclusion was rejected or criticized.

[10]Learning theory and its behavioral implications will be treated in detail in Chapter 21, "Learning Theory and Positive Behavior Reinforcement."

The credibility of the source, in this case, is subject to the perception of the receiver, and the result of the communication varies accordingly.

Perception's Effects on Motivation

Motivation is also strongly affected by perception, as we noted in examining expectancy theory. The force of motivation is directly related to the perceived probability that effort and success are related, as well as the linkage between success and rewards.

Any external stimulus, no matter what its nature or source, is no stimulus at all unless it results in some cognitive change or change in overt behavior. This is one of the failings of money as an incentive or a motivator. Management perceives that money is effective in motivating a higher level of performance because of a rather simple model of man. The rational or economic man is perceived to be motivated by money, and hence management cannot understand why real people behave differently.

The difference lies in perception, among other things. The people who are assumed to be motivated by money do not perceive money in the same way that management does. And after a while, even if the money increase were large enough to motivate for a time, each individual adapts to the levels and intensities of stimuli to which he is exposed. In other words, a new and higher level of income soon becomes the standard or base line against which the individual evaluates his behaviors. Because the base-line income is no longer seen as representing a differential between the old salary and the new, it loses its motivating power. People adapt to the perceptions of stimuli. The dissatisfiers or hygiene factors, Herzberg noted, can affect behavior at best for only relatively short periods of time. Because of our understanding of the perceptual process, we may more nearly be able to understand why this occurs.

Motivation and the Individual System

Motivation is a process through which the individual organizes his resources and employs them in ways that will allow him to satisfy some need or attain some objective. The inputs to such a process, we have noted, are his contact with and understanding of his situation and environment, his characteristic patterns of behaviors, and the attempts he makes to influence his surroundings through communication. The result of this process of arousal and maintenance of activity (energy expenditure) is the attempted accomplishment of some purpose, which, in turn, satisfies a need.

Motivation's Effects on Communication

Katz and Kahn pointed out that motivation determines to a large extent the form, direction, and content of communication.[11] A person occupying a

[11]Daniel Katz and Robert L. Kahn, *The Social Psychology of Organizations* (New York: Wiley, 1966), pp. 239–247. The following discussion is largely influenced by this work.

superior position can satisfy many of his needs through task performance, which, to a manager, is typically composed of the individual and composite performances of his subordinates. Ego, status, peer group acceptance, recognition, and achievement all stem from his successfully administering the activities and accomplishments of subordinates. His communications, primarily directed downward to his subordinates, emphasize his motives. They basically consist of specific job instructions, general task information, organizational procedures and practices, performance feedback, and indoctrination with organizational goals.[12] Horizontal communications, which are communications between members who occupy the same hierarchical level, consist of two important elements: coordinating tasks as specified by policies and gaining social and emotional support from peers.[13] The greater the needs for belongingness and emotional support, the more numerous and intense we would expect horizontal communications to be.

Upward communication, from subordinate to superior, again tends to be task-related. Such flow is inherent in the nature of the hierarchical system, based as it is on successive breakdowns in the overall organizational task. Upward communication attempts may also be products of need deprivation, such as when the subordinate fails to receive support or encouragement from his superior. He may then initiate interaction attempts designed to elicit feedback or reassurance. The rate of upward communications intensifies as ambiguities of the situation or the need for approval and feedback increases.

Certainly we might expect those with high n-Ach to initiate a significant number of communication attempts directed to their superiors regarding their own performance. Affiliation-oriented subordinates' communication attempts would similarly be designed to enhance interpersonal relations between superior and subordinate. Peculiarly enough, upward communication attempts by the individual dominated by n-Pow would be attempts to influence his superior, to dominate him or, to change his behavior in favor of the subordinate. He can do this through greater technical knowledge than that possessed by his less-specialized superior or through selectively screening and passing upward information generated at a lower level.

Motivation's Effects on Perception

Perception of communication attempts, as well as one's sensitivity to or selectivity of environmental stimuli, depends a great deal on the extent to which the individual's needs are gratified. A person who is deprived views his environment through eyes that are sensitized to potential means of reducing the deprivation. The starving man sees food potential in his surroundings much more than his counterpart unthreatened by hunger pangs. Is it any wonder that subordinates who live under constant threat of being deprived

[12]Ibid., p. 239.
[13]Ibid., p. 243.

of security or esteem view the boss's scowl or offhand remark as something to be turned this way and that in a search for an interpretation that might reveal displeasure?

Individual and Formal Organizational Systems: Interface and Interaction

At this point we can more fully appreciate the extent to which the individual brings to his organization a unique set of behaviors, which may either mesh or conflict with the behaviors required by technology and structure. We saw in an earlier chapter how the elements of the formal organizational system affect each other, yielding productive efficiency and affecting job satisfaction. We can now make some more insightful observations about the individual–formal organizational relationship, using the framework provided by Figure 13-2.

Individuals have a unique set of needs and aspirations. The formal organization demands a given level of predictability and efficiency in the pursuit of its major purpose. Given the almost infinite variability possible among people, the need for standardized inputs and procedures would seem to offer some difficulties in organizational behavior. Argyris was one of the first to point out what he thought was a built-in and almost irreconcilable conflict between the organization and the individual, for these very reasons.

Personality and the Formal Organization

Personality–Technology Relationships

For effective task performance under any particular production technology, we would expect that personality factors would be important. Under mass production, for example, the individual who is highly creative and nonroutine, with a high tolerance for ambiguity, and has high n-Pow or n-Ach probably would not remain in a position long. There would be a basic mismatch between the formal expectations and requirements dictated by production technology and the needs and expectations of the individual.

Recognizing the importance of organizational–individual compatibility, some few innovative firms have specifically adapted their personnel screening to match individual qualifications and technological demands most effectively. One example is that of the electronic assembly plant in New York State that had been experiencing quality control problems, worker dissatisfaction, high turnover rates, and high labor costs. The assembly-line task consisted of the simple soldering of a few contacts before the part was transferred to another position in the line. Through careful consideration of the mismatch between worker characteristics and technology, plant officials were able to derive a new set of qualifications that effectively solved the

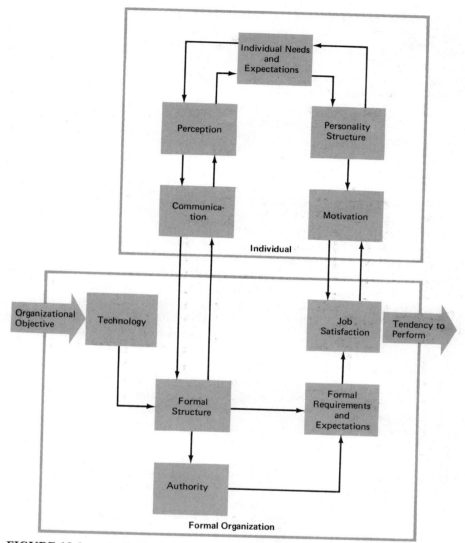

FIGURE 13-2   Individual–formal organization interactions and interfaces.

problem. Consideration was given to the hypothesis that the workers were overqualified and hence dissatisfied with the challenge in the work and the opportunities for promotion. Plant officials brought in mentally retarded people to work on the assembly line, doing exactly the same tasks as previous workers. The mentally retarded were able to do the repetitious yet simple tasks required with virtually no errors and without suffering boredom. Even further, these workers had a very low level of turnover and were extremely loyal to the company.

A firm in Texas was faced with a similar problem. The firm developed photographs for the geographic region. The color development laboratory, because of technological requirements, could not be lighted even with the usual red light. Workers were required to perform their duties in utter darkness. Turnover was astonishingly high and was compounded with significant levels of worker dissatisfaction. The use of blind workers, trained under a state job-training grant, enabled the company to continue first-rate photographic development, cut production time and costs, eliminate dissatisfaction and turnover, yet be a good corporate citizen.

Personality–Organizational Structure Relationships

Many formal organization structures seem to be predicated on a theory of human nature that assumes that people differ very little in personality factors rather than that differences are wide-ranging and variegated. Under this assumption of homogeneity, a single structure, authority system, and incentives may be employed uniformly, with uniform results to be expected. Actually, the single subsystem of perception can transform a uniform stimulus into perceptually different stimuli. If we agree with Argyris that the human personality has an inevitable tendency toward maturation, then bureaucratic organizational structure could well be construed as inhibiting the process. Grouping similar activities, rigid rules and policies, and increasing specialization as one descends the hierarchy tend to limit the scope and initiative assumed by the individual.

Before we overgeneralize that structure and technology affect personality development unilaterally, we must also acknowledge the reverse effect of personality on structure. Argyris pointed out the incompatibility between a rigid (bureaucratic) organizational structure and the tendency toward developing a fully mature personality. We must recognize that the fully mature personality and the rigid bureaucratic structure both represent extreme positions along their separate continua of personality development and of structural design of organization. A more realistic view is to recognize that the personality development potential is unique to each individual. Further, organizational structures may be similarly distributed along a scale by degree of authority, specialization, rigidity of controls, and tolerance of initiative and creativity.

The optimum situation is obviously that in which the personality characteristics of organizational members is exactly matched with the requirements of the organizational structure. In many organizations such a situation tends to exist. The structure and technology of research and development organizations allow a loose grouping of roughly compatible people, who may band together into interest groups or task teams as the situation dictates. Given a high level of creativity and need for independence, supervisors perform primarily administrative duties and delegate technical decisions. At the other extreme, Lawrence and Lorsch found that a rigidly structured firm that mass-produced containers, with a high degree of specialization, and with little authority at lower organizational levels, tended to match the personality needs and expectations of the vast majority of its members.[14] Managers in a high-technology plastics firm, on the other hand, "seemed to prefer more independence and had a greater tolerance for ambiguity, while those in the [bureaucratic, highly specialized] container company were perhaps better satisfied with greater dependence on authority and were more bothered by ambiguity."[15]

Personality–Authority Relationships

To be effective, the institutionalized right to influence the behaviors of others—authority—requires compliance. The legitimacy of the authority must be accepted by those who are to be influenced. The right to authority may also be interwoven with the concept of structure and technology. Even though a superior maintains overall authority and responsibility, he may choose to delegate the right to make decisions and the authority to implement them to subordinates in appropriate situations. Effective use of such delegated authority calls for a match between personality and the necessity of decision making. The overly dependent subordinate finds himself incapable of making a decision without first checking with his superior. Others may be confined by a deep distrust of trying anything new, preferring to fall back on old and proven solutions.

At the same time, personality and behavior patterns are subject to development, especially through adaptation and learning. The more an individual uses his behavioral capabilities, the more confidence he has in them and the more willing he is to experiment in his developed area of competence.

The reverse is true of situations in which learning is not encouraged and capability development is not allowed. Withholding authority creates a dependent relationship between subordinate and superior. The subordinate is unable to develop the particular skills required in making a decision and putting into effect the solution he sees. We must hasten to add that this is not necessarily a bad situation. In many situations delegation of authority should not be employed, even if it means curtailing the opportunity for skill and personality development of the subordinate. Obvious examples may be found in highly critical situations in which the repercussions of an error in judgment are irretrievable or in which the costs associated with an error are too large to risk. Diplomatic negotiations between countries, design of nuclear power plants, and floating a bond issue are examples. Others may be less dramatic, yet offer similar liabilities and risks, although at a lower level in the organization. A chief clerk may unilaterally establish a filing system for

[14]Paul R. Lawrence and Jay W. Lorsch, *Organization and Environment: Managing Differentiation and Integration* (Homewood, Ill.: Richard D. Irwin, 1969), p. 155.
[15]Ibid.

clerks to follow without exception, even though allowing them to design their own files would probably be more satisfying to the clerks.

Unbridled access to authority can affect the personality of the person with the influence. The authority holder can develop his ability to tolerate dissension or disagreement. His influence may also whet n-Pow. He may wish to extend the sphere of his domination over wider and wider areas and to attempt to deepen his influence by exacting more and more conformity and obedience.

Within an organized setting, functions and activities are divided and assigned to specific managers. "Clean breaks" between functions or responsibilities are rarely possible, even in the best-designed organization. Some overlaps almost always exist, which may be unacceptable to one or more of the managers involved. Conflicts may then occur over who is to control the area of overlap and just how far one peer should be influenced by the other and under what circumstances. Domination and control needs can create unpleasant interpersonal conflicts and dysfunctional organizational behavior.

Personality–Job Satisfaction Relationships

In Chapter 6 we saw that job satisfaction is no universal concept. Some people are happy with one particular job, whereas their work peers may be quite dissatisfied. Personality differences may offer significant leads and insights into differences in job satisfaction.

The design of a job creates behavior patterns that are necessary to fulfill the requirements of the job. These may or may not be compatible with one's natural behavioral inclinations as extensions of his personality structure. A traveling salesman who is expected to operate much as an independent businessman, obtaining customer leads and following through to product delivery and maintenance, should have strong independence and initiative characteristics. If he were conforming and dependent, the personality–job clash would most likely create severe job dissatisfaction.

Blood and Hulin pointed out some of the complexities involved in job satisfaction and personality correlates[16] in examining worker characteristics and job satisfaction. They suggest that a lack of job involvement, which creates job dissatisfaction, can be traced to the extent to which the worker's immediate environment encourages his acceptance of or alienation from middle-class norms. Those who are alienated from middle-class norms are characterized as being interested in their jobs only as a "provider of means for pursuing extraoccupational goals. The concern of these workers is not for increased responsibility, higher status, or more autonomy. They want

---

[16]Milton R. Blood and Charles L. Hulin, "Alienation, Environmental Characteristics, and Worker Responses," *Journal of Applied Psychology*, **51**: 284–285 (1967). See also Charles L. Hulin, "Effects of Characteristics on Measures of Job Satisfaction," *Journal of Applied Psychology*, **50**: 185–192 (1966).

money, and they want it in return for a minimal amount of personal involvement."[17] Those who are integrated with middle-class norms and who express more job satisfaction are those who are personally involved with the jobs they hold and who have goals of upward mobility.[18]

What causes such differences in characteristics and satisfactions? Blood and Hulin traced the cause to environmental conditions. Alienation has been associated with highly industrialized situations and lower social class, workers who are "separated from middle-class identification by low educational attainment or low occupational status and living in ghettos, slums, and highly industrialized communities. . . . Alienation from middle-class norms then is fostered by industrialized, socially heterogeneous, metropolitan conditions."[19]

The study tends to confirm an earlier one by Turner and Lawrence,[20] in which similar conclusions were reached. City workers were more satisfied with jobs that demanded less personal involvement. Workers with rural and small town backgrounds expressed more satisfaction when the jobs they held allowed more job-related freedom, "required more skill, were more varied, and contained more social interaction and responsibility."[21]

Communication and the Formal Organization

Because of the highly specialized and differentiated nature of the organization, communication is absolutely essential. Communication may be composed of information directly pertinent to the overall task of the organization or it may be of completely social content. In either case one fundamental reason for organization is to facilitate the interchange of job-related communication among people sharing activities or between individuals whose functions affect each other. The hierarchy provides prescribed channels through which authority and communication flow. Specialized communications flow upward, giving performance information and decision requests from subordinate to superior.

An effectively designed organization structure minimizes complexities in communication channels and provides opportunities for the decision maker to sit at the center of relevant channels in order to remain informed on all pertinent factors for which he is responsible. Computer-based management information systems supplement the more dynamic and personal interchange of ideas and information, reflecting changes in cash flow, sales figures, production discrepancies, and so on. An inappropriately designed structure can often cause communication attempts to be sidetracked through

---

[17]Blood and Hulin, p. 285.
[18]Blood and Hulin, pp. 284–285.
[19]Ibid., p. 285.
[20]A. M. Turner and P. R. Lawrence, *Industrial Jobs and the Worker: An Investigation of Response to Task Attributes* (Boston: Harvard University Press, 1965).
[21]Blood and Hulin, p. 284.

creating unnecessary "red tape" or by including individuals in the channel who have no responsibility for or interest in the matter.

Communication–Technology Relationships

Production technology similarly dictates the form and content of communication attempts. Craftsmanlike tasks or professional positions may be impossible to rationalize or fragment into component activities to be performed by specialists. A single craftsman or professional might be charged with the responsibility for everything involved in initiating and completing the task. Communication would be based largely on the *subordinate's* determining output requirements or design characteristics, and the *superior's* gathering of information about the worker's input needs and gaining information about progress, for planning and control purposes. Mass-production technology obviates many of these communication necessities, because the technology itself may be directly measured for progress data or input and output requirements, without direct communication with employees.

Informal communication develops among workers who develop new methods by which their jobs may be done more easily. These technological advances are often shared when physical layout permits easy communication and identification with each other.

Communication–Authority Relationships

Closely allied is the concept of authority and its relationship to communication. The centralization of authority—the formal withholding of authority from subordinates—is often precluded through communication difficulties. Decentralization of decision-making rights and authority over operations has typically increased as geographical dispersion of the firm's operations has spread. The president of a national company cannot keep close and personal contact with his far-flung plants because of the sheer inadequacies of communication with dispersed personnel. Of necessity he is forced to let go of the authority he holds, delegating it to his scattered subordinates as they need it.

A further requirement of such delegation and decentralization is the necessity to allow managers the ability to adapt their products or sales offerings to the characteristics of the local community or region. A central authority could not make enough decisions—and exceptions to decisions—to cover every possible contingency encountered in the operation of a nationwide firm. Far more typical is the setting up of a central policy-making body, whose responsibility is to set out in broad terms the general ways in which the firm is to be run. Operational authority—rights to run local plants or offices—is granted to subordinate managers who manage their concerns within the boundaries established by policies, making relevant decisions as necessary. With the increasing sophistication and availability of new communication technologies, however, some observers have noted that centralization of authority is on the resurgence.

Perception and the Formal Organization

Perception–Organizational Structure Relationships

Organizational structure allows the differentiation of activities and people into relatively specialized units. Through the hierarchical structure, these activities are integrated into a single contribution to the overall purpose. Such specialization, by its very nature, also creates a phenomenon called *tunnel vision*. Tunnel vision occurs when a person, typically a specialist or a member of a particular department, perceives either that the specialized activity in which he is involved is the organization's most important activity or that his unit's perspective on issues is the only correct one. The reinforcement of such a perception by a group that has the same values and duties is a natural occurrence.

Tunnel vision can create significant problems for organizational behavior, in addition to its obvious benefits for organizational effectiveness. A highly trained specialist in one particular discipline sees the world through eyes that have been trained to organize stimuli into the patterns familiar to his discipline. A production manager promoted to president might see the problems or opportunities of the firm as primarily those of production and scheduling. Marketing or financial difficulties might be relatively slighted because of his perceptual selectivity. To a personnel man, the firm's number one priority should be the establishment of effective performance appraisal and recruitment criteria. And to the student the professor not in his office from 8 A.M. until 8 P.M. for consultation is somewhat less than satisfactory.

Perception–Authority Relationships

If a person is perceived to have authority, then—realistically speaking—he does exert influence. For authority to be effective it must be accepted. Acceptance is not necessarily grounded in one's *right* to exert such influence. Perception of authority may stem from the perception of the other's competence in a particular field or from his control over positive and negative incentives, for example.

Perception–Job Satisfaction Relationships

Job satisfaction as an attitude is the result of perceptions of many factors, some job-related and some not. Some are more important than others in generating a given level of job satisfaction or dissatisfaction, but perceptions significantly alter understanding and conceptions of one's situation. If one perceives that his pay is inadequate, based on what others receive or what others in the community receive, such a perceived discrepancy can have negative effects on feelings of job satisfaction.

Whether or not the perception is based in reality or is true is immaterial. What is important is that an attitude is not an objective assessment of reality—it is a highly subjective and personal assessment of the reality as the individual understands it to be. As a result, he is concerned with what is deemed fair and right and also with what he understands the job conditions to be. If he perceives that he is not recognized for job performance, then his satisfaction suffers accordingly. He may have a "special recognition" sticker in his personnel file, and his file may be brought to the attention of top managers within the company as an example of a top-notch employee. If he does not *know* that, he cannot perceive that it is recognition for his achievements, and his dissatisfaction is not removed. A stimulus that does not affect cognitive knowledge or behavior is not a stimulus at all.

Perception is an individual's unique pattern of organizing stimuli in order to gain understanding of and meaning about his environment. This means that perception is not the same for all people. Different people perceive exactly the same situation in completely different ways. It is no wonder that such varying levels of job satisfaction have been reported in many studies. There is little agreement among people on the same job about the level of job benefits received. The halo effect operates in another way, allowing job satisfaction to influence perception. We remember that workers concerned about their job security generalized from this one negative aspect of their job to other positive job aspects. The resulting perceptions were that these other aspects were inferior to those enjoyed by employees in similar firms—even when they were in fact far superior!

Motivation and the Formal Organization

Motivation–Organizational Structure Relationships

Assumptions about states of motivation also affect the philosophy behind organization structure. If workers are assumed to be responsible individuals who are dedicated to management goals, then they need less close supervision and control. This means that a supervisor can supervise larger numbers of employees and much less attention can be given to the details of their work. He can also delegate more authority and decentralize his decision making to lower levels in the organization, while secure in the knowledge that responsibility will be utilized in the discharge of these privileges. On the other hand, workers who are seen as being lazy, apathetic, and uncommitted to management goals would seem to require closer control over their activities and duties. The supervisor would have to provide much closer attention to the ways in which they do their jobs and employ more severe punishments for unsatisfactory job performance.

The relationship is a two-way one, of course. If the individual is motivated to attain greater responsibility and achievement, then an organization structure that allows him to exert more initiative and independence is suitable to the level of aspiration displayed. Under conditions in which close supervision and close control of operation exist, he has very little opportunity to display the higher level of skills of which he is capable, resulting in frustration. The motivated individual under a "loose" structure has more opportunity to display his motivation and to achieve individual as well as organizational goals.

Motivation–Technology Relationships

Technology naturally affects how the relationship between motivation and structure may be implemented. There are very few alternatives in the short run to most mass-production technologies as we know them today. The fragmentation of the complex tasks involved in assembling electronic components or an automobile may require that the work be done in only one way, without variance. Such technological demands furnish the necessity for organizational structure to support the technological requirement, even at the expense of the motivation of the individual. Some few experiments have recently been performed on a plantwide basis in reorganizing production technology and redefining the structure to support the technology, with resultant increases in motivation of workers. Such solutions offer considerable hope that more effective meshing of individual motivation, organizational structure, and production technology may be attained. For now, we must recognize that such experiments constitute attempts at a more ideal production situation and are necessarily quite expensive.

The less highly specified technologies do allow for somewhat greater motivation to be expressed and used in organizational directions. Craftsman technology taps the individual's status, ego, esteem, social, and security needs when well managed. Such a technology allows the individual to satisfy these needs even while performing valuable tasks for the organization. High-technology enterprises similarly encourage the development of higher-level needs gratification in the pursuit of technological efficiencies.

Summary

The individual in the formal organization is subject to many opposing and contradictory forces. He may have needs for autonomy, initiative, and independence, yet the organization may demand varying degrees of compliance, conformity, predictability, and dependence on authority. The understanding of such a situation—and potential solutions—demands that we understand the processes behind the individual system, through which the individual adapts to his environment. At the same time, we must recognize the economic and rational aspects behind organizational requirements and the processes through which formal output must be attained. Certainly there is an area—largely unexplored—of compromise between the individual's needs and the organization's requirements. Explorations in defining the nature of such an area and the ways in which it affects both individual and organization are ongoing and offer promise for the future.

If we are to understand the individual in the formal organization more completely, we cannot ignore the fact that individuals in a group display different characteristics and processes than individuals as unique and separate entities. There are significant clashes between the individual and the social group, as well as between the individual and the formal organization. Similarly, formal organization and group have areas of overlap as well as conflict.

In Section IV we will explore the basics of the social system and integrate our findings so that we may have a better overall understanding of these three major systems of organizational behavior.

STUDY AND REVIEW QUESTIONS

1. What effect does a person's level of aspiration have upon his job satisfaction? Why?

2. What are some important technological and structural requirements that affect your "job" satisfaction as a student? Describe *how* they affect satisfaction. Is there a relationship between the student's "job" satisfaction and his motivation? Why or why not?

3. What are some important personality, technological, and structural considerations in the job satisfactions reported by members occupying different positions in communication networks (Figure 9-3)?

4. How would you go about including more of Herzberg's motivators in the jobs of your subordinates? What structural and technological factors would you have to consider?

5. Why is personality a determinant of job satisfaction?

6. Does a highly motivated subordinate need more or less influence exerted over him by his superior? Why?

7. Is there a built-in incompatability between formal organization and individual? Why or why not?

8. Why did Lawrence and Lorsch find that job satisfaction was high among managerial members of both a highly structured mass-production firm *and* a loosely structured advanced-technology firm?

9. What effect does cultural background have on job satisfaction?

10. What impact on personality development does a high degree of decentralization have? A high degree of centralization?

SECTION IV

THE SOCIAL SYSTEM

Chapter

14

The Group
and Its Dynamics

CHAPTER OBJECTIVES

1. To introduce the concept of the group as a basic social unit.

2. To identify characteristics common to groups.

3. To show some of the basic processes through which groups function.

4. To indicate the extent of group influence over individual behavior through norms, sanctions, and social pressure.

5. To introduce essential concepts on which to build the section on "The Social System."

CHAPTER OUTLINE

In the last sections we have seen how organizational behavior is affected by both the formal organization and the individual. We have gained some insights into the ways in which technology and structure provide the tools for accomplishing the organization's purposes. We have also seen that the individual consists of many complex processes and propensities that affect his functioning within the organization context.

Section IV, "The Social System," will be devoted to investigating the processes and characteristics of people in relationship with other people. Having an understanding of the basics of individual behavior will aid us in this endeavor because the basic building block of the social group is the person. Formal organizational requirements, as they give rise to and shape social behaviors, will provide valuable insights into the nature and processes of people in groups. The model we will employ in this section is provided again as Figure 14-1. In each chapter we will look into a major component of the overall system before considering the complexities of their relationships in Chapter 19.

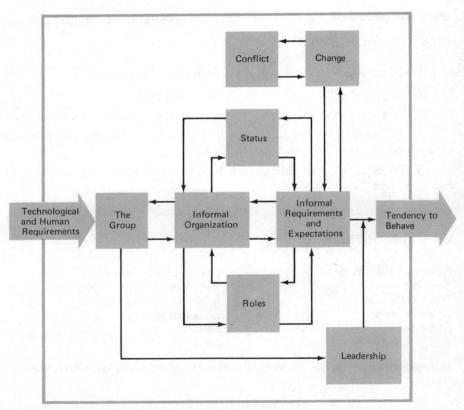

FIGURE 14-1   Framework for studying the social system.

The initial component will be that of the group itself and its workings, after which we will consider a special type of group, of unique implications for organizational behavior. The complementary concepts of roles and status are next to be considered, to be followed by the dynamic duo of change and conflict. The final component of the social system is that of leadership.

The concept of the group is fundamental to understanding the social system because individuals form social and task groupings to satisfy some basic and powerful needs, such as companionship, security, or task achievement. And there is a price exacted for the benefits provided by group membership. When one joins an organization or forms emotional attachments, his actual and desired behaviors are modified because of the interpersonal relationships established within a group setting. Group behavior is not the sum total of the behaviors of each of its members; it is something more, yet something less. The behavior of each member is modified, constrained, and directed into channels approved by the entity we call the group. In some ways, the group can be thought to behave almost as if it were a being independent of its separate members.

In order to understand what a group is and how it functions, we will look into what a group is, what the purposes of groups are, how groups are structured, what some basic structures of group processes are, and how group behavior is formed. Then we can more nearly understand group processes as they occur within the formal organization and the ways in which they influence organizational behavior.

Nature of the Group

Very few of us exist only for or by ourselves. Although we are each unique individuals, we also function in relationship with other people. A basic need is the social need, belonging and being accepted. This need can be satisfied only through social activity, which requires other people. If we are to "belong," then we must have something to which we can belong. This something is called a *group*.

In an extreme sense, we can consider that a formal organization is a group, as is your bridge club or fraternity. Each class you attend might also be considered a group. We can see that each of these things we call a group is composed of a number of people and a specific setting or situation. Is there more?

When you are riding on a crowded bus, do you and the other riders comprise a group? Certainly we have a number of people and a specific situation or setting, but there seems to be something essential that is missing. Even though you and the occupants of the bus have something in common, you are still merely a collection of individuals who happen to be gathered together in the same place at the same time. The same could be said of the audience in a movie theater. To make the distinction more concrete, a group and an aggregation of individuals differ in that group members relate both to each other and to the identifiable unit of which they are a part. Mere aggregations of people are simply individuals who happen to be collected together at any particular time, who do not really relate in a meaningful fashion to most of the other individuals in the collection, and who do not consider themselves members of an identifiable unit.

What Is a Group?

To be more specific still, we will define a *group* as

the largest set of two or more individuals who are jointly characterized by a network of relevant communications, a shared sense of collective identity, and one or more shared dispositions with associated normative strength.[1]

Implicit in this definition is the notion that even though a group is a real entity, it is at the same time *abstract*. We have no yardsticks against which we can measure groups, nor can we identity a group as a group merely by looking at the individuals who compose it. A group exists in the perceptions of its members *and* in the complex set of interrelationships that exist between and among the members of the group. This idea of the real but abstract nature of the group is vital to our understanding of the group in organizational behavior. We will see that group members define and modify both the existence and the purpose of the group. In addition, the group (because it is composed of relationships) exists merely from moment to moment and only because of the willingness of all group members to consider themselves as an entity.

Now let us look more carefully at our definition.[2] For a group to exist, it must have at least two members. Only with a minimum of two people can there be relationships, and the more group members there are, the more complex and numerous the relationships possible. The largest set of these individuals is considered so that group members are not excluded. Each group member affects what the group is and what it does. In turn, he is affected by the group's expectations and activities. Exluding group members from consideration would result in an incomplete conception of the group because a group consists of the relationships among all of its members. We can infer from the terminology of "the largest set" that a group may consist of smaller sets or subgroups that differ slightly in characteristics from the larger or parent group, in a fashion similar to the way in which we use subsystems as elements within an overall system.

Further, this set of members must have a *joint* set of characteristics, which are communication networks, shared identity, and shared goals. If any "member" is not included in any one or more of these required characteris-

[1] David Horton Smith, "A Parsimonious Definition of 'Group': Toward Conceptual Clarity and Scientific Unity," *Sociological Inquiry* (Spring 1967), p. 141.
[2] The following discussion is based on Smith, pp. 141–167.

tics, then he is not a member of the group about which we are talking. If one has never received communication attempts that relate to the purposes or existence of the group, his membership in the group is not possible.

By the same token, if any particular individual cannot communicate with every *other* member of the group, then he is not a member of the group. Some form of communication and ability to communicate is necessary for a group to exist. One of the purposes of communication is to share the nature and objectives of the group with its members as well as to provide the necessary means of gratifying social needs through the group itself. No particular form of communication is necessary. Face-to-face interaction is convenient and helps build a highly knit group, yet is not mandatory. Highly select groups of chess players, located all over the world, communicate with each other through the mails or by telegram. The form of communication is sufficient for them to communicate relevant messages to each other and to give each an identity as a member of a particular group. What constitutes a "relevant" communication differs according to the nature of the group, yet should convey information on the purposes, existence, standards of behavior, or whatever other characteristics are important to the group. For a group to exist, direct communications between a group member and every other group member is not necessary. There may be links in the communication process that intervene between group members. Even with indirect communications, communicator and communicatee would still fulfill this criterion as being members of the group.

Another important characteristic of the group is the shared sense of collective identity. Without this, major group processes cannot exist because of the inability of the group to enforce particular behaviors of its members or to elicit behavior consistent with that of the group as a whole. Each member of the group must believe that he is a member of, or a participant in, some specific group. He must also perceive or believe that there exists at least one other person who similarly identifies himself as a member of the group and who (in turn) perceives that other group members exist. This portion of the definition may be alternatively labeled *the concept of "we-ness."* That is, each group member identifies with each other group member through the nature of the group and sees that he is not an individual acting completely independently. He behaves in conjunction with group dictates and in unison with other group members. Then he can say that *"we* believe," *"we* feel," *"we* will," or *"we* have."

The fourth and final condition that must be met for a group to exist is that of shared goals. This means that each group member desires the attainment of some specific objective or the accomplishment of some goal. Furthermore each group member perceives that the other group members share this disposition and that they are aware that *other* group members share it. *"Associated normative strength"* is the obligation felt by each group member to contribute to the attainment of the shared goal. Such a compulsion or sense of social duty is normative (has implications of "should" or "ought to") and is strong enough to move the group member to behave accordingly.

Types of Groups

We find groups all around us, in every conceivable setting. Groups range in size from two to very large numbers and are formed to accomplish tasks varying from purely social functions to the most complex purposes of a research and development company. Depending on our perspective, we find groups within groups, each of which differ in important ways.

To clarify the nature of the group, we will point out that groups display common characteristics. A group has *formality of structure, permanence,* and *purpose.* Each characteristic may be considered as forming a continuum, with any particular group displaying a relative degree of formality, permanence, and purpose.

Formality of Structure

The completely formal group exhibits the characteristics of a formal organization. A hierarchy of authority is established, with specified member roles and functions. Rules, regulations, incentives, and sanctions guide the behavior of formal group members.

At the other end of the scale is the completely informal group. Individuals band together but without setting up a formal structure. Rather, member roles are loosely defined, based on member expectations and the needs of the group at any particular moment. A member's behavior is guided by his own internalized perception of what is appropriate and sanctioned by the bestowing or withholding of social approval.

Permanence

A group may be relatively permanent, such as the Roman Catholic Church, or quite temporary, as illustrated by a number of passers-by coming together to help a stranger by pushing his car to get it started. Immediately after the car starts, the group is disbanded.

Purpose

The purpose around which a group is formed may be either *task*-oriented or *socially* oriented. Accomplishing a particular task may tend to direct group members' activities in ways quite different from the activities of members of the purely social group. Naturally most groups will fall somewhere in the middle along this spectrum, with a mixture of task and social purposes.

Group Formation

Why does a group form? The definition of a group suggests that a number of isolated individuals may band together to increase the probability of accomplishing some purpose. Pooling resources or the concept of "strength in numbers" might be relevant considerations here. Technological requirements might also either dictate or give rise to the formation of a group. Multiples of four people are needed to play bridge; such a technological requirement, associated with a bridge club, may create such conditions that a group emerges from the club's membership. The shared purpose might then be to satisfy social needs and to acquire competence in a challenging game.

Technology can have another major influence on group formation, through structuring activities, interactions, and sentiments.[3] Activities are things that people do, actions and behaviors that occur both inside and outside formal organizations and groups. Technology specifies the activities required within the formal organization by specific individuals and within carefully defined environments.

As a result of activities and the ways in which work must be done for any specific technology, people are required to interact with each other. They must come in contact with each other, associate with each other, if only because each worker requires input for his task from another person and must provide his output for still another. A superior must interact—at least occasionally—with his subordinate. Students whose seats are next to each other generally interact. Waitresses and customers interact in a restaurant, as does the airplane pilot and his navigator. Interactions are thought of as being separate from the activities through which interaction takes place. Thus interaction is an element of social behavior by itself, and we do not bother to identify activities of which interaction is composed (such as moving the jaw up and down while exhaling, simultaneously shaping the mouth and tongue to form specified sounds in the process of talking).

Social contact can yield sentiments, which are emotions, feelings, or attitudes attached to the relationship or to the person with whom interaction occurs. The more we interact with a particular person, the better opportunity we have to know him, to form an impression of him, and to shape an attitude toward him.

We can trace the impact of technology on group formation by recognizing that technology dictates activities and the interactions necessary to the pursuit of these activities. As a result of interactions between people, sentiments arise—either positive or negative. Given these sentiments, individuals are given the opportunity to form into groups that have in common certain ideas or sentiments. Organization influences group formation, too. Establishing administrative units and putting together people who have activities in

[3]George C. Homans, *The Human Group* (New York: Harcourt, Brace, & World, 1950), pp. 34–40.

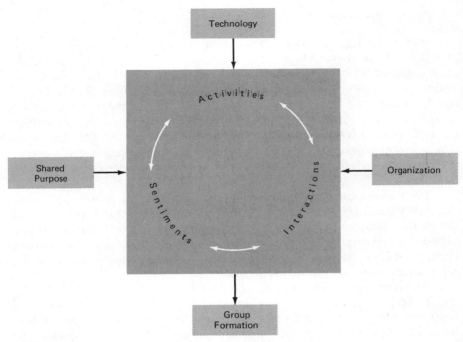

FIGURE 14-2   The group formation process.

common makes their interaction certain. Shared interests and activities help nurture positive interpersonal relations and attitudes. Can identification as a group be far behind?

The direction of cause is not necessarily from activities to interactions to sentiments. These three elements of social behavior affect each other, and any one may precipitate the others. For example, strong antiwar sentiment during the Vietnam war created strong sentiments and resulted in protestors' seeking each other out, interacting with each other, reinforcing their sentiments, and finally producing group activities such as demonstrations and picketing. Similarly, being forced into close contact with someone else can yield positive or negative sentiments. Rarely does one remain neutral toward a person with whom one interacts. Activities may occur based on the required interactions and the derived sentiments. The interaction involved and the accompanying sentiments provide the opportunity for individuals to communicate and develop a shared purpose and collective identity.

Group Structure and Process

A group, comprised as it is of a number of individuals, must yield satisfactions to its group members. After all, one of the major purposes behind the formation of a group is the gratification of the members' social needs. At the same time, the group must be making some headway toward the accomplishment of the formal purpose for which the group was formed. Should members fail to satisfy their social needs through the group *and* should they perceive that progress is not being made toward the attainment of the group's major purpose, then dissatisfactions will arise. Such negative sentiments may lead the member to part company with that group and seek another, more compatible or more successful group. If we restrict our scope for the moment to small (for instance, less than fifteen members) social groups, then exit from the group is rather easy. The smaller the group, the greater the ease of interaction with the other group members, and the freer communication attempts may be in assessing goal attainment. Smaller groups also readily allow group members' contribution to goal attainment to be seen and recognized. The efforts of a member of a three-person group are much more visible to himself and his group members than they would be in a 15,000-employee company.

Any social organization requires that someone do the leading and coordinating. In the formal organization this role is fulfilled by the manager. In the small social group a leader may not have a title or the ability to administer formal incentives. Yet a leader may exist just the same. The two extremes of groups, the formal organization and the small social group, require that we differentiate these roles.

The small social group is comprised of members and their interrelationships and is geared toward the shared goal attainment and needs satisfactions of its members. A leader is needed who must be quite different from the one necessary to the operation of the formal organization. A group leader may be appointed or may simply emerge. If he is appointed, then this is the result of a decision made by the group members he is to lead. If he emerges, then he assumes leadership naturally, and his right to influence is informally granted by the other group members. The small social group then offers a clear-cut demonstration of Barnard's "acceptance theory of authority."[4] The rights and abilities to influence group members are derived from the consent of those group members. Such a granted privilege may be withdrawn by its donors at any time. Because ability to influence stems from consent, we need to differentiate the influence held by a leader from that held by a manager.

We say that the leader has power—actual *ability* to influence group members—because the group members have agreed to follow him and accept his decisions. The authority of the formal organization's manager is only the organizationally granted *right* to influence subordinates. Because subordinates may choose to obey or disobey, the manager may or may not have the *ability* to influence them.

Group Functions

Because groups are goal-directed, the behaviors of group members must contribute to the accomplishment of those goals in some way. Member

[4]See Chapter 5, "Authority and the Human Effects of Formal Organization."

behaviors may be classified as either task-directed or group-maintenance–directed.[5] The purpose of task-related behavior is to make possible the mutual identification and solution of a common problem through group effort. Group-maintenance behaviors strengthen the group–member relationships and members' identification with the group as a whole. Such behaviors are important to the continued existence of the group, particularly as a vehicle through which members' social needs are met.

Specific activities typically found in group situations are listed in Table 14-1.

Group Characteristics

If a group is composed of members and their interrelationships, how can we define and delimit a particular group? A formal organization has an organization chart, job descriptions, authority limitations, and a formal hierarchy. The small social group is highly informal and exists in the perceptions of its members. Even the size of a small social group is a matter of group–member definition, and no independent means can assess an individual's membership in a particular social group. The most visible characteristic by which a group may be identified is the attraction between and

TABLE 14-1   Functional Activities of the Group

Task Functions (help the group accomplish its task)	*Group Maintenance Functions* (help build group feelings and attitudes)
1. Initiating: suggesting a new idea, new way of looking at a problem, or a new activity.	1. Harmonizing: compromising; reconciling disagreements; getting others to explore differences.
2. Seeking useful information or opinions: requesting facts; asking about feelings; asking for ideas or values.	2. Gate keeping: inviting others to talk; suggesting time limits or other procedures to permit wide participation; keeping talk flowing.
3. Giving useful information or opinions: offering facts; stating a belief; making suggestions.	3. Encouraging: being friendly, warm, responsive through words or facial expression; agreeing with others.
4. Clarifying: probing for meaning; defining terms; restating, enlarging, or stating issues.	4. Following: going along with the group; being a good listener; showing that words are heard.
5. Summarizing: reviewing; bringing related ideas together; restating suggestions of others.	5. Standard setting: testing group attitudes toward its procedures; suggesting procedures; stating values or ethics; supporting standards.
6. Consensus testing: checking to see if group is ready to decide; sending up trial balloon.	

[5]See, for example, Kenneth D. Benne and Paul Sheats, "Functional Roles of Group Members," *Journal of Social Issues* (Spring 1948), p. 42.

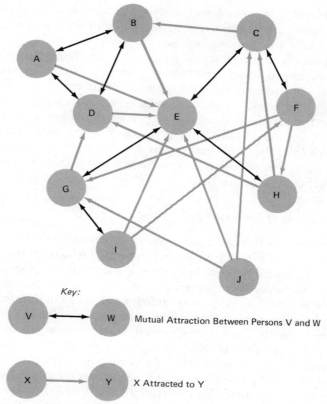

Key:

Mutual Attraction Between Persons V and W

X Attracted to Y

FIGURE 14-3   Sociogram of a ten-member group. Source: Adapted from Norman R. F. Maier, *Psychology in Industrial Organizations,* 4th ed. (Boston: Houghton Mifflin Co., 1973), p. 113.

among group members. If we could measure the attractions between the individuals in a department, fraternity house, or classroom, we could begin to have a good idea of which people constitute separate social groups.

Sociometry: Measuring the Group

As a matter of fact, that is exactly how one of the major tools of group research was developed. Recognizing the importance of interpersonal attraction in small social groups, Moreno was able to determine the structure of groups through the use of *sociometry.*[6] He simply asked group members to express their likes and dislikes of other group members. These preferences could then be charted, yielding a *sociogram.* Figure 14-3 illustrates how a sociogram represents the patterns of interpersonal attraction in a ten-person

[6]J. L. Moreno, *Who Shall Survive?* (Beacon, New York: Beacon House, 1953).

group. Each circle denotes a separate person, and the solid double-headed arrows indicate mutual attraction between two group members. The light single-headed arrows indicate one-way attraction.

Using sociometric techniques we can diagram rather well the relationships within any particular group, as reported by the group members themselves. For instance, the most popular members of a social fraternity could be easily spotted if members were asked to write down, in order of preference, the members whom they like. If we developed a chart like that in Figure 14-3, we could easily see that person E is the "star" because he was chosen by eight of the nine other group members. Person J could be termed an "isolate" because, although he was attracted to persons G and E, no one reported being attracted to him.

Applications of Sociometry

Sociometric techniques can be rather widely adapted to many uses. A manager might be able to check his perceptions of who his better workers are by asking his subordinates to relate the work-group members whom they contact on difficulties encountered at work. The applications of sociometric analysis are similarly diverse. Moreno first used the technique in reassigning delinquent girls to various communal cottages, in order to create happier home environments. Sociograms were developed from the questionnaires administered to the girls. He asked questions of interpersonal *rejection* as well as attraction, in order to avoid grouping incompatible people. The same type of analysis has been relatively rare in industry, yet it has yielded interesting results. We may remember from Chapter 6 that Van Zelst allowed construction workers to form their own work groups by selecting their own partners.[7] Job satisfaction increased for the sociometrically selected teams. At the same time, turnover, labor costs, and material costs declined.

Sociometric techniques help us to understand the ways in which subgroups occur within larger groups. If we refer again to Figure 14-3, we can see that persons A, B, and D compose a very definite subgroup. The manager might expect to encounter some resentments were he to try to reassign person B from his present shift to another. Who would be the better choice for promotion, E or J? The manager should expect difficulties should J be selected; he would hardly be a supervisor popular with his subordinates! E would probably prove to be a popular choice, yet he might find himself torn between loyalty to his erstwhile comrades and his new managerial role.

The wise manager could use an additional sociogram derived from answers to the question, "Who in your work group would be the best supervisor?" A combination of popularity, work-group acceptance, and demonstrated competence could be used as inputs by which a highly effective supervisor could be selected.

[7] R. H. Van Zelst, "Sociometrically Selected Work Teams Increase Production," *Personnel Psychology* (Autumn 1952), pp. 175–185.

Cohesiveness

Another dimension along which we may classify a group is *cohesiveness*. As the term implies, cohesiveness relates to the strength of the interpersonal attractions among group members. A highly cohesive group is composed of members who value their association with the group as a whole as well as with the other group members. A group marked by a low degree of cohesiveness, on the other hand, is one in which the members are not especially dedicated to the group and its purposes. Members may not find the other group members particularly attractive either.

What makes a group cohesive? Factors that influence degree of cohesiveness include homogeneity, communication, isolation, size, outside pressure, status of the group, and success.[8]

Homogeneity

The more alike the group members are, the more likely they are to see each other as similar to themselves, and the easier it is to identify with the others. Such perceived similarity can create a strong basis for mutual attraction. By contrast, a collection of individuals who have nothing in common would experience a great deal of difficulty in establishing a social group, let alone a cohesive social group. Stability of membership, too, affords group members opportunities to get to know each other, learn and identify with the operation and purposes of the group, and so internalize group values and behaviors.

Communication

We pointed out earlier that a requirement for a group to exist is opportunity to communicate. Obviously the more group members are able to communicate (interact), the stronger the sentiments and the greater the interpersonal attractions among members. Difficulty in communication, perhaps because of noisy surroundings or rules against talking, imposes a great deal of difficulty in formulating, absorbing, and passing on information on the purposes and operations of the group. Such difficulties further discourage members from forming attachments to each other, as well as resulting in the decrease of identification with the overall group.

Isolation

If a group is isolated from the distractions and competition of other groups, then group members can more readily devote their time, energies,

---

[8]David R. Hampton, Charles E. Summer, and Ross A. Webber, *Organizational Behavior and the Practice of Management,* Rev. Ed. (Glenview, Ill.: Scott, Foresman, 1973), pp. 221–223. The following section is based on their discussion.

and attention to the group. Alumni of small, isolated colleges may have developed such cohesive and long-lasting relationships during their college days that the sense of "we-ness" persists long after graduation, to be periodically renewed by reunions to which members go to a great deal of effort to attend.

Physical boundaries may also effectively isolate a group by making more obvious the limits and membership of the group. The physical boundaries may clarify the group membership, thus encouraging stability. Clearly identifiable groups, and certainly cohesive groups, emerge only with great difficulty on assembly lines or in huge auditoria. Large classes in college may display some of the difficulties of developing cohesive groups even among a group of relatively homogeneous individuals who share a relatively limited space and whose membership is quite clear.

Size

The size of the group has an obvious effect on the ability of the individual member to identify with the group as a whole, as well as his ability to communicate readily with other group members. In a small group of, say, five members, face-to-face interaction among members is quite easy and uncomplicated. If we consider a group of thirty or forty members, each group member needs to formalize his interactions with others and coordinate dealing with a large number of diverse personalities. In larger groups, because of the greater opportunities for differences between and among individuals, smaller groups composed of members who find each other relatively more compatible than others tend to emerge within the context of the larger group. Referring back to Figure 14-2, for example, we can see that persons A, B, and D form a subgroup of mutual attraction within the larger ten-person group. As the size of the group increases, such subgroups tend to emerge more clearly.

Outside Pressure

When the members of a group perceive that the group is in danger or threatened by an outside force, internal differences are minimized. Cohesiveness increases as the group and its members strive to combat the collective threat. This ability to band together in the face of a common enemy is one of the great strengths of the group. Disruptive or threatening forces external to the group, especially as they are perceived as detrimental to the fundamental purpose of the group, create tighter bonds among group members and increased commitment to the group, coupled with shared resistance to the threat. Just as with individuals, the threatened deprivation of the physiological (existence) needs of the group is a powerful motivator and occurs in conjunction with the powerful security motives of individuals, as well as the threatened social needs of its members.

Status of the Group.

Probably in an attempt to satisfy ego and esteem needs, individuals in high-status groups display greater cohesiveness. Certainly membership in such a group is more highly valued than membership in a group that is widely held in contempt. Given the perceived value of membership in such a group, the individual tends to resist losing his association and therefore submits to a greater extent to the dictates and activities of the group as a whole. Cognitive dissonance might also play a part. Some civic and social organizations allow membership only by approval of existing group members and then require extensive and arduous initiation rites. Dissonance might be rejected because the individual could not willingly see himself as going to a lot of trouble for a group that had no value, or he might impute great status or value to the group, creating a great attraction to the group.

Success

We would ordinarily expect a group that experiences continual failure to attain its major goal to disintegrate eventually. A group that enjoys success is more attractive to its members and hence more cohesive. The impact of group success on cohesiveness may be related to the degree to which membership is voluntary and informal. Lack of success encourages members to forgo further frustration and to seek satisfactions elsewhere.

Social Control

Implicit in our previous discussions has been the concept of a group as an entity, which almost has existence, processes, and functions independent of its component members. In a way this may be a handy way of looking at a group. Depending on the cohesiveness of the group and the value associated with membership, members give up a certain amount of self-determination and initiative, giving precedence to the "will of the group." In a sense, this is submission of the individual to the group and willingness to be influenced by the leader and the values or standards of the group. The small social group shows many of these functions in clearest form because of its informal nature, based only on the willingness of the individual to belong and submit. We will base our discussion of the power and importance of group standards and norms on the small social group.

Norms

A norm is a rule of conduct that has been established by group members to maintain consistency in behavior.[9] Many different individuals share a

---

[9]Marvin E. Shaw, *Group Dynamics: The Psychology of Small Group Behavior* (New York: McGraw-Hill, 1971), p. 247.

common purpose and compose the group. Individual behaviors must be standardized and not allowed to detract from the efforts of the group to attain its goals. Norms are "standardized generalizations concerning expected behavior in matters that are of some importance to the group."[10]

The difference between an imposed rule and a norm is that a rule dictates what must be done by another, whereas a norm refers to what *should* be done and therefore what should guide his own behavior. A norm that is not accepted by group members is not a norm at all. A norm might arise in a group that drinks coffee together each morning at the office. Each day a different member of the group is expected to buy coffee for the other members. Another may be that the newly accepted addition to the group buys coffee for the old-timers. Still another typical norm might be observed at the weekly bridge club sessions; winners should not boast about their superior skills, and the losing teams should replay the hands that proved to be crucial in their downfall, so that they may learn from it.

A norm, as a standard of behavior, must allow for noncompliance. Obviously not all group members can or will follow group norms at all times. What course of action is taken against group members who fail to comply ("deviate") with group standards? Nonconformity to group norms requires that some *sanction* be leveled at the deviant by the other group members. He may accordingly be influenced to behave in a way acceptable to the group and thereby contribute to the purposes of the group.

Sanctions may range all the way from expressions of mild disapproval to the ultimate sanction in the social group, ostracism, in which the deviant is rejected and ignored by the group members and is not allowed to participate in group activities. For other groups, sanctions may be even more extreme, including the death penalty. The severity of the sanction depends on the impact of the nonconformist behavior on the group and its purposes, as well as the circumstances under which it occurs. Further, some norms require that they be strictly adhered to, whereas others exhibit an entire range of behavior that is acceptable.

Social Pressure

Through the influence of norms and group members, social pressure can be either a deterrent or a stimulus to individual behavior. Approval is the result when the norms and behaviors of the individual are in accordance with those of the group. Should the individual find that his behavior is different from that indicated by group norms, he has four choices: to conform, to remain a deviant, to leave the group, or to change the norms. Another choice, a function of the other group members, is that he be removed from the group without his consent.[11]

[10]Ibid.
[11]A. Paul Hare, *Handbook of Small Group Research* (New York: Free Press, 1962), p. 24.

Asch showed the extent of influence of the group on the behavior of the individual.[12] He set up an experiment in which subjects were to choose which of three comparison lines were the same as another, standard line. Each subject orally reported his decision, in sequence, and in the presence of other subjects. The total number of subjects in any particular session ranged between seven and nine, with one "naïve" subject providing the basis of the experiment. All of the other group members in a session had been coached to give unanimous—but incorrect—responses. In the face of an incorrect majority opinion, naïve subjects also gave incorrect responses that agreed with the majority. Over a third of the naïve subjects gave these erroneous responses, compared to almost no errors in control groups (in which all members responded normally). "Thus, influence of group opinion on the individual was in many cases sufficient to dissuade him from responding in terms of his immediate sense impressions, which were clearly in contradiction to the group."[13]

Enforcing Norms

The group employs several specific functions in order to ensure that individuals within the group comply with its norms. Enforcement is accomplished through the processes of education, surveillance, warning, and sanctions.

Education

Education is accomplished early in the initiation phase of acceptance to group membership. The "right" way of behaving is presented to the initiate, and any deviations are admonished. Through this process the new group member can become exposed to approved behavior patterns and modify behaviors that are not in accordance with group norms.

Surveillance

Surveillance, especially of new members, is performed in order that deviance from group norms may be detected. This is largely a function of each of the group members because adherence to group norms is essential for group survival.

Warning

A warning is issued when a deviation from group norms is detected. Group members increase the intensity of their interaction with the deviant,

[12]Solomon E. Asch, "Effects of Group Pressure on the Modification and Distortion of Judgments," in *Groups, Leadership and Men,* ed. by H. G. Guetzkow (Pittsburgh: Carnegie Press, 1951), pp. 174–183.
[13]Hare, p. 28.

with the interaction progressing from quite friendly and supportive contact. Should the deviate refuse to bring his behavior back into compliance with group norms after the educational process and explaining has been done, the interaction becomes threatening and may consist of razzing, argument, or threats of discipline.

Sanctions

Sanctions or actual discipline is imposed only when it becomes clear that the deviant is not going to change his behavior into that approved by the group. Ostracism is a common and severe form of discipline, although actual physical violence or tampering with personal possessions may also be imposed.[14]

Rituals

In order to maintain the integrity of the group, rituals are quite common. Rituals take many forms, ranging from nicknames all the way to formal and elaborate rites. The intent of the ritual is to isolate the group, to set it apart, and to give forms and methods of identification to each individual group member. A widespread form of ritual is the use of technical language or "jargon." The language is shared by individuals, particularly those in a specialized or exotic job, who may then more easily discuss work-related occurrences or objects. Not only does jargon allow them to communicate in a more concise and exact manner, but it sets the group members apart from those not belonging by the simple exclusion of others from the basic communication process.[15] Passwords, handclasps, chants, and so on are also forms of rituals.

Summary

To accomplish complex tasks and to fulfill social needs, individuals band together into a social unit called a *group*. A group is composed of, yet separate from, members and their interrelationships. It may be defined as "the largest set of two or more individuals who are jointly characterized by a network of relevant communications, a shared sense of collective identity, and one or more shared goal dispositions with associated normative strength."

Shared purposes, technology, and organization influence the formation of groups. They may operate individually or in combination, by establishing the conditions through which activities, interactions, and sentiments allow groups to coalesce and emerge as entities.

[14]Joseph A. Litterer, *The Analysis of Organizations,* 2nd Ed. (New York: Wiley, 1973), pp. 245–247.

[15]Delbert C. Miller and William H. Form, *Industrial Sociology: The Sociology of Work Organizations,* 2nd Ed. (New York: Harper & Row, 1964), p. 263.

Sociometry furnishes a means by which a group may be diagramed, by schematically representing reported attractions among group members and the value placed on group membership. Factors affecting group cohesiveness are homogeneity, communications, isolation, size, outside pressure, group status, and success.

To maintain existence and integrity, the group exerts social control over its members. Norms are internalized standards of conduct by which group members guide their own behavior in ways important to the group. Social pressure is brought upon the deviant who violates group norms or fails to conform. Norms are enforced through education, surveillance, warning, and sanctions.

To further group cohesiveness and identification, rituals are common to groups. They vary in form and elaborateness but allow members to employ symbols of belonging and acceptance, as well as separation from and rejection of nonmembers.

The group forms the basic social unit of the organization. Basic familiarity with the nature and process of the group provides a framework for investigating the social system in organizational behavior. In the next chapter we will extend our understanding of the group to its unintended occurrence as the informal organization.

STUDY AND REVIEW QUESTIONS

1. List five units, with which you are familiar, that meet the definition of a group. Discuss how each meets all of the criteria of a group.

2. What are the benefits an individual member gains from group membership? What are the benefits the group gains from his membership? What "costs" (disadvantages) are simultaneously incurred?

3. Which of the three criteria of a group is the most important? least important? Defend your answers.

4. What is "collective identity"?

5. Discuss how Homans' activities-interactions-sentiments model may be used to explain group cohesiveness.

6. List and discuss three applications each you would make with sociometry if you were

a. a manager

b. your college professor

7. Compare and contrast power and authority. Which would you rather have?

8. Discuss the cohesiveness of this class. (You should include considerations of the six factors that affect cohesiveness; you might wish to do a sociogram based on questionnaire responses of class members.) How would you increase its cohesiveness? *de*crease its cohesiveness?

9. What part do norms play in the group? What norms operate in a classroom setting? What sanctions are imposed to ensure conformity by class members?

10. Discuss how rituals affect group cohesiveness.

Chapter

15

Informal Organization

CHAPTER OBJECTIVES

1. To relate group dynamics concepts to the social system at work.

2. To introduce the student to the nature of the informal organization and its implications for organizational behavior.

3. To show some major social processes through which individual behavior is modified.

4. To give guidelines for integrating informal and formal organizations.

CHAPTER OUTLINE

Emergence of the Informal Organization

Human Needs and the Purposes of the Informal Organization
Security
Social Purposes
Identification
Competence

Informal Organizational Processes
Norms and Standards

Informal Communication
Cohesiveness
Cohesiveness and Productivity

Managing the Informal Organization
Organizational Members and the Informal Organization
Managers and the Informal Organization
Identifying the Informal Organization
Influencing the Informal Organization

In the last chapter we developed an appreciation of the basic processes and characteristics of groups, although from a rather theoretical viewpoint. Groups are natural parts of our lives, both at work and throughout everyday life.

Technology and organization establish task-oriented groups, units that have as their major purposes the attainment of organizationally established objectives. Their formal functions may include such diverse work-related activities as assembling television sets, drawing up a set of construction plans, or selling foodstuffs to the consuming public. In terms of the classification scheme set up in the last chapter, these types of groups have a formal structure, are task-oriented, and are rather permanent. Their activities contribute directly to the formal organization's purpose, having been consciously organized for this reason. We may rather easily discern such groups by plotting workflow and by examining the organization chart.

Other groups, although not intended or anticipated by the formal organization, also exist. They emerge from the informal interactions and attractions among members of the formal organization. Such unanticipated groups, which display many of the characteristics of the small social group, function alongside and in parallel with the work-related activities of the formal organization. As a result, they are termed *informal* organizations.

Informal organizations, because they are real and powerful influences on behavior, are the subject of an extended discussion in this chapter. Functioning in many ways, at many levels, and for many purposes, informal organizations are a fascinating phenomenon that alternately baffles and amuses the practicing manager.

Emergence of the Informal Organization

The enterprise is a rather rational and efficient device through which objectives are reached. The primary purpose of many enterprises is often seen as being something quite different from the satisfaction of members' needs. Such needs exist nonetheless. Man, being the goal-oriented organism he is, actively strives to arrange his surroundings or manipulate his situation in ways that will allow the satisfaction of his motivating needs.

One such powerful need is that of social behavior or belongingness; most people are by nature gregarious, enjoying the company of others. The task-oriented formal organization rarely considers social needs as anything other than dispensable and counterproductive luxuries, so no formal allowances or opportunities for purely social interaction are established. Even such social situations as lunch or coffee breaks are intended to relieve fatigue, refuel the body, or obey union contracts and governmental requirements!

People interact nevertheless. Technology and organization may stipulate who must contact whom in the conduct of the job, but such interactions have consequences other than those intended. The project engineer and the cost accountant may discover a common passion for building and flying model airplanes, leading to friendship. Turret-lathe operators may find identity and status in a tightly knit group that bowls together off the job and forges a bond of mutual interest on the job. Even the car pool group, made up of members from six different departments, may find that pooling news and information is as rewarding as—and more stimulating than—sharing driving chores.

From the structure and technology of the formal organization emerges a uniquely human organization dedicated to serving *its* members' needs. It is called the *informal* organization to distinguish it from the task-related formal organization, as well as because of its casual nature and composition of informal interactions among its members. We can see indications of its existence in the gathering around the office water cooler, the clique that systematically excludes all but a chosen few, and the work group that sets its own productivity goals—regardless of goals set by management.

The informal organization emerges on its own, without conscious intent, as a natural and human consequence of formal organization. If we look carefully, we can observe the informal organization functioning in every conceivable circumstance, within each task-directed organization. It emerges more clearly—and becomes more powerful—as its host formal organization increasingly ignores the human needs of its members, workers and executives alike.

The informal organization takes on many forms, has a range of purposes, and can be either benign or malignant in its relationship with the formal organization. In a well-managed firm, with members' needs well attended to by company policy and administration, a healthy symbiotic relationship develops; formal and informal organizations complement and gain advantages from the other. As a result, the firm's objectives and the members' needs are simultaneously satisfied. When the informal organization must battle for human satisfactions, however, internal conflicts can tear the company apart.

Human Needs and the Purposes of the Informal Organization

What are the human needs capable of satisfaction through the informal organization? Security, social and belongingness, competence, and identification needs are common bases.

Security

Protection is afforded the individual through the informal organization, especially against injurious competition from fellow workers and against the work requirements of the formal organization. Both individual and collective security are available through recognition of mutual benefits to be attained. The pressure of management demands for increases in productivity or for procedural changes is cushioned—and sometimes absorbed—through the concerted efforts of group members guided by shared attitudes, values, and standards. Job insecurity can threaten workers, who act to assure continued employment by restricting output. The rate buster who continually exceeds his production quota is punished by group members for making the rest of the workers look bad in comparison.

Social Purposes

Just as man cannot live by bread alone, so also is unremitting work insufficient. Even on the job, companionship and social relationships form an element important to each person. Through the informal organization one can relate to other people as a person and not as just another pair of hands. One's social contacts have the further advantage of being pleasing (otherwise he would not be part of the social group) and familiar with frustrations and tensions undergone by other members. They can furnish a sympathetic understanding and empathy that soothes the distress of the member's problems.

Perhaps even more important is the sense of belonging imparted by the informal organization, of having a specific place with a specific status in a social group comprised of members chosen solely for their compatibility and attraction. A lack of belonging becomes a matter of some proportion in working conditions that preclude it in one way or another. If a worker is isolated from other work-group members, he may feel he shares a job title with them but little else. Or a clerk who performs his duties in an office filled with other clerks—doing the same thing—may feel faceless, a mere number, deprived of some aspect of his humanness. The informal organization allows human relationships and satisfactions to be superimposed over the spartan structure created by technology and organization, adding a human dimension to the formal organization.

Identification

A purpose that follows directly from social and belongingness needs is that of identification with a definable and specific set of individuals, a sense of shared expectations and experiences, of mutual interests and sentiments. Such identification has a by-product, the desire to influence factors that affect the group. The sense of shared destiny—the belief that group members are subject to having the same things happen to them individually and collectively—encourages the members to pool their resources and efforts to achieve mutually desirable outcomes.

Competence[1]

Task competence is also developed through the informal organization, although this purpose is not often recognized. A person new to his job, in particular, cannot have all aspects explained satisfactorily by his supervisor. Eventually he encounters a problem that requires a new solution or experienced handling, or he needs to know how nearly company policies are enforced—what the limits and kinds of acceptable behavior are.

Learning and Tasks

The informal organization provides the vehicle through which technical assistance may be granted, without showing the novice's ignorance to the boss. Additional information on expected or approved behaviors similarly is provided:

Most employees don't want to violate the generally accepted "rules of the game"; at the same time they don't want to conform to restrictive rules that everyone else ignores. They want to know the "right" thing to do. The group fills an important need by providing all its members with a kind of "guide to correct behavior"— correct not in terms of any written policies, but in terms of what is actually acceptable.[2]

The group may also ease task burdens by transmitting new, more efficient work methods to its members. Usually such innovations are *not* the result of management but are shortcuts or new tools that may violate standard operating procedures and consequently are to be hidden from superiors and other representatives of the formal organization. Such developments might be welcomed by management but, members fear, would cause the reanalysis and increase of production goals. Work-group members would then have to work harder than before, with no real benefit reaped from the innovation. Instead new techniques or tools are kept careful secrets to lighten the work burden of members, leaving more time available for joking and relaxation when the supervisor leaves the area.

Monotony is alleviated through the informal organization. When feasible, specialized workers may swap jobs with each other, even if such practices are not formally allowed: "extra work breaks can be obtained because employees spell each other; unpleasant tasks assigned to one man can be rotated or shared by group agreement."[3]

In attending to and satisfying the needs of its members, the informal organization is essentially a shadow organization. It springs up as an unin-

---

[1]This section is based in part on George Strauss and Leonard R. Sayles, *Personnel: The Human Problems of Management* 3rd Ed. (Englewood Cliffs, N.J.: Prentice-Hall, 1972), pp. 72, 73.

[2]Strauss and Sayles, p. 72.

[3]Ibid.

tended (and unrecognized?) complement to the formal organization. The informal organization publishes no organization chart, yet its members know their functions and status, leaders and rejects, enemies and aspirations. It has no corporate charter, yet behavior standards, duties, and obligations guide its activities. No identifiable product is produced, yet its objectives are striven for zealously.

The complex relationship and mutual dependence between formal and informal organizations may be clarified if we briefly examine behavioral results. We can identify and label three classes of types of behaviors, formal, nonformal, and informal behaviors or activities.

Formal Behavior

Those activities performed as a direct result of one's job may be called *formal behaviors*. They may be stipulated in the position description or may be the movements through which the worker produces output. Formal behaviors are those required by the formal organizational system of the individual or the work group. These formal activities are the reason for which the individual was hired in the first place. The typist's formal behaviors include operating a typewriter, perhaps proofreading for errors, performing these duties for eight hours a day, arriving for work at 8:30, and leaving at 5:15.

Formal behaviors are the activities necessary to actuate the formal organization's technology and structure in pursuit of the firm's objectives. They are strictly task-related and task-determined.

Informal Behavior

Behavior that is socially and emotionally based is informal behavior. It is not undertaken in order to achieve a company-decreed goal or to perform a formal duty, but it occurs in the pursuit of satisfying purely human needs. The formal organizational system and its resultant formal behaviors may provide the opportunity and the setting for informal behaviors, by grouping together people who discover they like each other or share some values. Informal behaviors emerge as individuals relate to each other. Various forms may be taken. Horseplay and joking are types of informal behaviors, as are expressions of group identity such as work restriction.

Nonformal Behavior

Job expectations and requirements are established by the formal organization so that predictable amounts and types of work activity will occur. Often the technology or organization, created to support the individual, is insufficient or inadequate. He must then resort to nonformal (that is, outside that stipulated by the formal organization) behavior to see to it that his job is done.

Workers on an assembly line may swap jobs to relieve monotony, even though forbidden by official policy. A machinist may devise a tool that lets him cut down on measurement errors in grinding smooth faces onto parts. Assistant professors may review and critique each other's journal articles. Students may set up study groups before final exams. These are activities that are not prescribed by the formal organization, yet that emerge because of some inadequacy in technology or organizational structure. Nonformal behaviors *complement* the formal organization's prescribed activities and behaviors and are thus work-related.[4]

Comparing Formal, Informal, and Nonformal Behaviors

The three behavior classifications may be related by their purposes. Figure 15-1 illustrates that formal, informal, and nonformal behaviors differ in orientation. Formal behaviors are much more directed toward task accomplishment than are informal behaviors, which are dedicated to satisfying

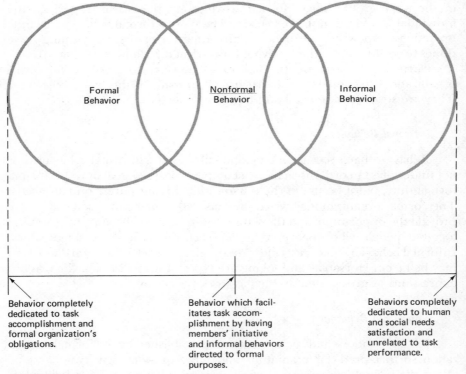

FIGURE 15-1   Formal, nonformal, and informal behavior.

[4]Cf. Edwin B. Flippo, *Management: A Behavioral Approach*, 2nd Ed. (Boston: Allyn & Bacon, 1970), p. 195.

individual and group needs. Nonformal behaviors are pictured as occupying a middle ground between formal and informal behaviors, *linking* them together. Overlapping areas similarly indicate that no sharp dividing lines exist between these behavior types.

Individual and group behaviors and interactions provide the dynamics of the informal organization. To better relate its impact on organizational behavior, we must next go to the basic processes of the informal organization.

Informal Organizational Processes

Although we have covered some processes in our previous discussion of group dynamics, the special case of the informal organization should offer many insights. Major processes are those of norms and standards, informal communication, and cohesiveness.

Norms and Standards

The group is the mechanism through which individuals reinforce their own sentiments and the sentiments of group members, as well as attitudes and other values important to them and to the group. Design engineers may decry management attempts to trade off product quality in favor of manufacturing efficiency or cost savings; the common sentiment easily leads them to talk together during lunch hour about management's latest cost drives. An informal organization centered around the value of professional pride in quality emerges, perpetuating the performance standard of the *profession* as the relevant measure of status rather than the standard established by cost-conscious management. Informally approved activities, predicated on this value and subscribed to by group members, emerge. Engineers swap tales and techniques of keeping the minimum high-quality level of design while seeming to lower quality or cost. Heightened perceptions and many ears pick up the telltale signs of new management cost-cutting drives.

Because of the engineers' group norms and the consequent circulation of design innovations that lower costs while increasing quality, several results are obtained. Costs are reduced, quality is increased, engineers are upgraded in technical expertise, trade of job information is encouraged, engineers have a stronger group and professional identification, conflict with management has been heightened and resolved, professional standards have been upheld, and management is ultimately satisfied.

Group norms reflect the values important to group members and the purposes for which the informal organization exists. Norms are guides to members' behaviors, which members believe should be followed. Machine-shop work-group members place great emphasis on equitable treatment, every member being treated alike; the new member, falling short of quota while learning his job, may well return from his coffee break to find the top operator busily working at the novice's machine to produce enough to meet the quota, then returning to his *own* machine. Such generosity is simply the way they "should" look after other members, and it naturally flows from commonly held group values.

Informal Communication

Communication opportunities and channels are also provided through the informal organization, satisfying a need for information. Often the formal organization's communication network—which either follows the hierarchical structure or is composed of plant newspapers or other in-house organs—does not provide information that is directly relevant, up-to-date, or specific enough for members. The communication process provided by the informal organization is called the *grapevine* and consists of the human contacts through which information is passed. The grapevine complements or replaces the formal communication system.

The grapevine plays an important part in the effectiveness of the informal organization. The interpersonal contacts that make up the overlapping informal organizations within the formal organization provide a highly effective technique through which information can be quickly passed from member to member, until all interested personnel are informed. The grapevine is not formally established, even by the informal organization. It is a natural outgrowth of the fact that people spontaneously form social groups and have a normal desire to know.

In choosing classes to attend, the student may have access to a number of alternative sources of information regarding his prospective professors. He can go to the university bulletin to determine their degrees and where they studied; a local service fraternity or the academic departments may provide short biographical sketches; the bookstore may list the information that one professor requires $22.50 worth of texts whereas another hands out free notes on the course; and old copies of syllabi that spell out the professor's expectations and work load may be available from other sources. Many of these sources of information are either established or derived from the formal organization.

The source of information that is probably most widely used, however, is none of these. The student grapevine, which may be formalized to varying degrees, is seemingly the source of information that is perceived as having the highest credibility and relevance. In its most formalized sense, the student government may publish ratings and evaluations of professors, based on questionnaire returns from students. At the other end of the spectrum, the individual prospective student may rather unsystematically and haphazardly inquire of people he happens to know what they have heard about a particular professor. In the latter case, the grapevine can be seen as operating.

How reliable is the grapevine? Surprisingly enough, one noted authority estimates that grapevine accuracy in business organizations of between 80 and 99 percent is typical for company information that is noncontroversial. For personal or highly emotional information, such accuracy is probably not duplicated.[5] We typically tend to underestimate the grapevine's accuracy primarily because we are swamped with communications that we absorb and never consciously ascribe to the grapevine. Yet when the grapevine errs, it is highly visible and may then be attributed to the "rumor mill."

Information can be transmitted through direct, face-to-face contacts, by telephone, or by any combination of communication devices—all that is necessary is a sharing of information not provided by the formal organization. Even formal organizational *channels* may be used by the grapevine. Keith Davis relates how a teletype link between company warehouses in separate cities was used by two clerks to swap information on local conditions and to compare notes.[6]

Three common grapevine networks are diagramed in Figure 15-2, the chain, gossip, and the cluster chain. In the chain, the source (S) relates the bit of information to one other person, who relays it in turn to another, and so on, until the chain is broken by failure to repeat. The chain may end because the information has become old or common knowledge or is considered irrelevant. The chain differs from the other networks diagramed in the high

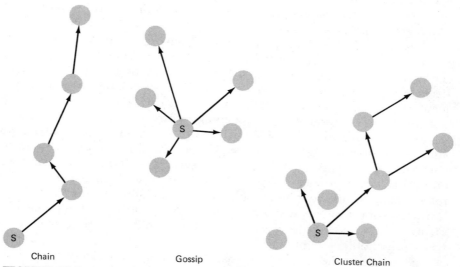

Chain   Gossip   Cluster Chain

FIGURE 15-2   Networks of informal communication. Source: Adapted from Keith Davis, "Management Communication and the Grapevine," *Harvard Business Review* (September–October 1953), p. 45.

[5]Keith Davis, *Human Behavior at Work: Human Relations and Organizational Behavior,* 4th Ed. (New York: McGraw-Hill, 1972), p. 263.
[6]Ibid., p. 262.

degree of selectivity exhibited by each succeeding source; only one receiver is chosen for communication.

The gossip, by contrast, rather indiscriminately broadcasts the information to almost everyone who will listen. The middle ground between the chain and the gossip is occupied by the cluster chain. Selectivity—but not exclusive selectivity—is used by the source and also by some other link in the network. In Figure 15-2 we note that S selects three receivers (and thereby excludes three others). Two of these receivers elect not to pass on the information, and the third communicates with two others.

Cohesiveness

Having such a wide-ranging and fast-reacting communication network, which is also responsive to member needs, allows a high degree of cohesiveness to develop among group members. We saw in the last chapter that cohesiveness is primarily a measure of the attraction among group members and their commitment to the group itself. By its very nature the informal organization is quite valuable to the individual member. It has the potential to satisfy some very basic needs that may not be otherwise gratified—security, social, ego, and status. Highly cohesive groups expect and demand a high degree of compliance with group norms. Compliance can be enforced because of the perceived value of membership, and threatened deprivation of membership is usually sufficient to ensure conformity to the values and standards of the group.

The cohesiveness of any particular informal organization—and, for that matter, the *existence* of any particular informal organization—is a function of the ever-changing situation. A loose group of acquaintances may be suddenly transformed into a tightly knit informal organization with antimanagement and militant attitudes. What may set it off? The stimulus may be something as innocuous as an impending visit from central headquarters' director of organization planning—which breeds fears of a far-reaching job analysis, possibly in order to eliminate inefficient jobs or departments, or to pare unnecessary personnel. Even the appearance of an industrial engineer on a shop floor is usually sufficient to set off hosts of plausible explanations for and conjectures about his activities. Even at that, his impending presence is usually known well in advance of his actual visit, through the grapevine. Plenty of time is usually available in which those affected can become efficient and otherwise prepared for a "surprise" visit.

The highly cohesive group is characterized by deep loyalty on the part of its members to the norms, values, and standards of the informal organization. What this means to management is that intended changes will be vigorously resisted by a group which is organized to protect members' self-interests. Perceptions of threats are just as real in the formation and solidification of an informal organization as an actual threat. If computer programmers anticipate that a layoff is coming, then formal communications will be interpreted through that perceptual set and will give fuel to the formation of the informal organization.

A very common norm exists in most production-related work groups and is based on perceptions of equity. Management has its idea of a "fair day's work for a fair day's wage," which may be based on engineering studies of jobs and human capacities. The workers, on the other hand, may have a quite different conception of what is fair, both in wages and in output. One of the widespread myths in many industrial firms is that demand for the company's good or service is limited. Increased production therefore means fulfilling demand, which may mean the lessened desirability of a full work force or of prevailing wage rates. For a given wage rate, too, there may be a given level of output that is deemed as just. Naturally if there were no informal organization, the great variances possible between individuals doing the same task would be easy to spot and sanction. The informal organization allows the standard to be established for an entire group of people at a given level of effort.

The effect that the informal organization has on worker and group productivity is an indirect result of the cohesiveness of the social group, combined with the values and norms of the group and the amount of perceived external pressure. Behaviors and sentiments of informal organization members may *result* from work-related activities and interactions and may *affect* work performance. Yet the purpose behind informal behaviors is the satisfaction of human—not necessarily organization—needs.

Cohesiveness and Productivity

One confusing aspect of the relationship between the informal organization and productivity occurs in the process of creating social and emotional satisfactions. When a highly cohesive informal group coincides with the work unit, task performance may be either increased or lowered. The direction depends on the ways open for the informal group to satisfy the emotional and social needs of its members, through existing values and norms.

Seashore examined the role played by group cohesiveness in group attitudes and productivity.[7] The company in which the study took place was a midwestern manufacturer of heavy machinery, located in a medium-sized city and employing between ten and twenty thousand people. About 90 percent worked in the factory, manufacturing and assembling. The great majority of the factory jobs were classified as skilled or semiskilled. He found that

Members of highly-cohesive groups were less anxious about job-related matters than were members of low-cohesive groups; this may be related to higher degrees of satisfaction of security needs through the group.

[7]Stanley E. Seashore, *Group Cohesiveness in the Industrial Work Group* (Ann Arbor, Mich.: Institute for Social Research, University of Michigan, 1954).

Productivity varied significantly less among highly-cohesive group members than among low cohesive group members.

The productivity of highly-cohesive groups differed (above *and* below) from plant standards more often and to greater extents than did productivity of low cohesive groups.

Attitude toward management affected whether group productivity would be higher or lower than plant standards.

Group cohesiveness increased with the prestige attributed to group members' jobs.

Group cohesiveness increased with opportunities for interactions among group members.[8]

Major implications may be drawn from the study because high cohesiveness may increase positive attitudes among group members yet affect productivity negatively—*or* positively. The ability to influence group members' work behaviors toward an informally established productivity standard is significant power indeed. When one considers the attractiveness of the informal group to the member (as measured by its cohesiveness) and the social control devices available to the group to enforce conformity, the extent of such influence becomes understandable.

Managing the Informal Organization

The informal organization is a form of group and exhibits characteristics of groups even though it is not a readily identifiable entity. The informal organization emerges within work groups, springs up in management conferences, creeps into every corner of the organization. With rare exception every organization member belongs to at least one informal organization. And with rare exception the power of the informal organization can make itself felt.

Organizational Members and the Informal Organization

What gives the informal organization its strength are its inevitability, its attraction, and its ubiquity. People inevitably seek social interaction and satisfactions. The informal organization exists because of such desires and feeds on dissatisfactions and fears. Members of the formal organization are attracted to the socially based relationships offered through the informal organization and come to value the commonly held beliefs or attitudes that distinguish group members from "outsiders." The more valued informal group membership is, the more open to influence the member must be. Conformity to group norms is a prerequisite to acceptance and membership, so the norms acquire a central position in the informal structure. Finally,

[8]Ibid., pp. 98, 99.

such informal groups are not isolated occurrences; they can—and do—appear almost everywhere people come into contact with each other. Informal organizations do not differ in frequency or location of occurrence, merely in strength and visibility.

When we say that the informal organization exists within and in parallel with the formal organization, we must stop to put this element into perspective. People are naturally gregarious and tend to band together under numerous circumstances. Especially when people are thrown into interaction, as by the requirements of technology or organization, activities and sentiments emerge and are strengthened through the interactions. In addition, social needs may be better satisfied through interactions that are initiated by work-related circumstances, yet blossom into relationships that have a more or less social base. An informal organization cannot be readily picked out from the organization chart, or even from the observation of people performing their duties. Just as with the social group, the pattern of *interactions* under various circumstances and the nature of social interchanges may be the only clues available to the interested observer who wishes to identify an informal organization. The observer may be frustrated in his attempts simply because of the difficulty involved in separating "legitimate" work-related interactions from emergent interactions that make up the binding element in the informal organization. The simple act of his observation attempts affects those observed and lessens informal interchanges.

Managers and the Informal Organization

Why is the concept of an informal organization of importance to organizational behavior? We have seen in previous chapters that the individual plays an important part in determining how well technology and formal organizational factors are implemented. Individuals have their own peculiar levels of aspirations, which set the range for performance and effort. The expectations and sanctions of the group to which he belongs is a further input to how the individual responds in a work situation. At the same time, group standards and norms affect attitudes, satisfactions, and behaviors common to the group.

Managing groups of people has become the only realistic and economically feasible way of administering the formal organization. Yet the groups of people may be managed as they are set out in the organization chart and not as they actually and informally evolve. Such informal groups may also have standards and values divergent from those of their superiors.

To summarize to this point, a common thread that underlies the derivation of the informal organization is in its being a human adaptation of the formal organization and its requirements. If the job does not of itself satisfy social needs, then the job and its required reactions can be modified to provide social satisfactions. If the technology established for doing a job proves to be more difficult than necessary, then the individual may modify the technology without permission of the formal organization. Such modifications are shared and passed on through the informal organization. At the same time, a social entity has been set up to provide the individual member with a peer group, with which he can identity and find solace and also pool his knowledge and resources in the event the formal organization becomes oppressive of the individual. Such an informal pooling provides the basis for a form of countervailing power through which the relatively powerless individual can more equally relate to the powerful formal organization. As an individual he may consider himself at the mercy of the formal organization, yet as a member of a group he finds confidence, identity, and support.

Any manager must understand that the informal organization exists and cannot be wished away, banished, or outlawed: "As long as there are people, there will be informal groups."[9] Attempting to abolish it without understanding its causes and processes can yield disastrous results because antagonistic management actions can quickly coalesce a loose social organization into a militant and powerful foe.

Even if the informal organization could be done away with, its benefits and advantages would also disappear. The informal organization encourages and supports *non*formal behavior as well as the purely social interactions. Nonformal activities are task-related and supplement deficiencies of technology and organization. Few managers could achieve their goals if the policy manual were strictly followed by their subordinates. To illustrate this point, we need only remember that a most effective technique used by railroad union members in work slowdowns has been their following all formal procedures and policies to the letter!

Some informal organizations are detrimental to formal goal-attainment, but the effective manager does not consider this anything but a symptom of a more deep-seated problem. Often the problem actually stems from inadequate company policies or poorly thought out formal communications that merely raise threats or questions. People need some source of security and social satisfactions. If the formal organization cannot or will not provide them, the informal organization will, and it will become more powerful as a result.

Identifying the Informal Organization

The informal organization does not advertise its presence, purpose, or membership; its nature and characteristics must be inferred by the manager through his sensitivity to processes and patterns of behaviors. He can chart informal membership through sociometric techniques or by diagraming observed interactions. A complete program for studying the informal organization is succinctly put by Miller and Form:

1. Keep your eye *primarily* on people, and secondarily on what they are producing or servicing.

[9]Davis, p. 252.

2. Observe how they *react to each other.*
3. Listen to what they say and don't say; observe what they do and don't do in reference to each other.
4. Note the degree to which saying and doing jibe with each other.
5. Find the ideas, beliefs, and attitudes on which they generally agree or disagree.
6. Appraise how stable or unstable your findings are as situations change.
7. Do not become a factor in the situation you are observing. If this is impossible, try to analyze your relations to the group as you would analyze any other person's.[10]

Influencing the Informal Organization

Knowing the membership and values of the informal organization, the manager is in a much better position to influence it. This is not a suggestion that he suppress or manipulate it but that he integrate formal and informal organizations for the benefit of both.

The informal organization provides a strong impetus to raise the quality of managerial practices. Arbitrary or counterproductive actions will generally tend to be informally resisted. The manager is then encouraged to ensure that conflict is minimized or negated *before* making changes rather than trying to resolve destructive conflicts that occur as the result of poorly thought out plans and policies. With such an incentive the formal and informal organizations provide checks and balances in favor of a better overall situation.

Overdefining the content and processes of jobs, that is, establishing job procedures in minute and exacting detail, may similarly prove detrimental to overall goal attainment. Activities that are somewhat less well defined (or less thoroughly policed and sanctioned) allow nonformal behaviors to fill the gaps in the formal specification of procedures. The nonformal behaviors will often consist of shortcuts or new, better ways to do the job, developed and initiated by those members who know the jobs best.

Understanding the nature of the social system, the manager then knows that he cannot relate to subordinates, peers, or superiors as separate and unrelated individuals. Whenever he idly mentions conjectures, data, or projections to another individual—and especially a subordinate—he speaks into the ear of the informal organization. Social relationships wire the subordinate into a network with purposes of its own. The individual cannot be considered as merely an independent person; he should be treated as a representative of an entire group, a channel to the entire informal organization. Through sociometry, the "star" of the social system may be identified. He is usually the person looked to for guidance and given credibility by the informal system members. The thoughtful manager can utilize the star's

[10]Delbert C. Miller and William H. Form, *Industrial Sociology: The Sociology of Work Organizations,* 2nd Ed. (New York: Harper & Row, 1964), pp. 228, 229. Emphases in the original.

informal position and influence to keep members informed of management intentions and activities. Naturally, manipulating the star or planting misleading information will quickly rebound. Credibility will be lost and gone will be the manager's ability to influence the informal organization.

To integrate formal and informal activities most effectively, management must:

1. Let employees know that management accepts and understands informal organization.
2. Consider possible influence on informal systems when taking any action.
3. Integrate the interests of informal groups with those of the formal organization.
4. Keep formal activities from unnecessarily threatening informal organization in general.[11]

By considering the implications and reactions of the informal organization, the manager can see the power of social influence at work. Everyday occurrences and interactions assume a new dimension of meaning. Individual behaviors are modified by group values and processes, making an influential but invisible partner—or foe.

Summary

The informal organization exists in parallel with the formal organization, emerging as an unintended consequence of technology and organization. It consists of the informal relationships and interactions among people who share values and sentiments.

Three types of behaviors may be classified in the consideration of the effects of informal organization: formal, nonformal, and informal. Nonformal behaviors link formal activities and informal actions, being work-related while addressing human and social needs. The informal organization's major purpose is to facilitate the satisfaction of its members' security, social, competence, and identification needs.

The major processes underlying the informal group are norms and standards, communication, and cohesiveness. These processes provide guides to member behavior, access to relevant information not available through formal channels, and attraction to the group.

Cohesiveness is a powerful determinant of group and individual productivity, reducing the variances in output between members to a range centered in the group's informally established standard. Depending on many factors, the major one of which is extent of acceptance of management goals, such productivity standards can be either above or below management's standards.

[11]Slightly modified from Davis, p. 271.

The informal organization will never just go away. The manager must learn to accept it, deal with it, and integrate it with the formal organization.

STUDY AND REVIEW QUESTIONS

1. How can the informal organization be a "shadow organization," existing "in parallel with the formal organization"?

2. What are some steps the manager can take to eliminate the informal organization?

3. Identify three informal organizations to which you belong, and draw sociograms of the relationships within each. What are the norms and standards of the three groups? How cohesive—and "productive"—are they?

4. Carefully distinguish between nonformal and formal behaviors. What are some examples of nonformal activities with which you are familiar?

5. How can the manager influence an informal organization that is highly cohesive and antagonistic to management?

6. What are some factors that would affect the rate at which information is transmitted via the grapevine?

7. What are some ways in which the manager can avail himself of the grapevine, to receive and to transmit?

8. How can a sociogram of the informal organization aid the manager who must institute a major work-related change?

9. What are the steps you would take as manager to *lessen* the cohesiveness of an antagonistic informal organization?

10. How would you as a manager build a cohesive and productive work group dedicated to management goals?

Chapter

16

Role and Status

CHAPTER OBJECTIVES

1. To identify the organization as a complex system of interrelated roles.

2. To present the process by which role behaviors are established and modified by requirements and expectations.

3. To show the far-reaching implications for organizational behavior of role behaviors and role conflicts.

4. To trace the relationship between role and status attributed by others.

5. To illustrate the uses of status in the organization.

CHAPTER OUTLINE

Concept of the Role
Activities and Roles
Expectations of Behavior
Establishing Role Behavior
Role Conflict
Roles and Attitudes
Role Ambiguity
Resolving Role Conflict

Status
Status as Ascribed Value
Status and Organizational Role
Status Determinants
The Status Implications of Role
Symbols of Status
Status Congruence
Status Discrepancy

The formal organization is composed of people performing assigned duties. Any member's job contains functions and tasks for which he is responsible. Until the functions are performed and tasks accomplished, the job or position contributes in no way to the organization's purposes. After all, even the most routinized assembly line needs workers to perform the assembly operations. The job—being an abstract set of duties—cannot produce anything by itself.

What is lacking? Formally prescribed *behaviors* by the person holding the position are needed to transform the static group of duties into dynamic productivity. The complex of job behaviors—and the ways in which they are established and modified—are subject to many ambiguities and conflicts, misunderstandings and misapprehensions, expectations and influences.

The concept of *role* offers insights into the problems of establishing and modifying goal-directed behaviors, in informal as well as formal organizations. We will examine roles as they reflect expectations and behaviors associated with formal and informal positions. Types of conflicts inherent in the nature of formal roles, and how they may be managed, will be examined.

The second major part of the chapter is devoted to the *status* or prestige implications of roles. Status is a perceived attribute and may actually be inconsistent with role, to the discomfort of the position holder and to the detriment of his effectiveness. The place of status symbols as attempts to differentiate individuals and positions will be considered.

Concept of the Role

Within an organization—formal or informal—a variety of functions must be performed, and behaviors must be enacted by the members. These functions are divided up into jobs, which consist of duties, obligations, and formal expectations of the behaviors of the job holders. To accomplish the purpose for which the job was created, the job holder must do something— behave in such a way that his duties are successfully done and his obligations discharged.

Specialization allows each organizational member to know the intricacies of his job and accumulate experience and competence. Becoming proficient in a job means that alternative behaviors can be tested and either discarded or retained, depending on how effective they prove to be. The marketing manager can develop over time a sense of timing for special product promotions, and the machinist can learn how to meet quality standards most efficiently.

Activities and Roles

A major point to be made is that a position or a function encourages the development of specific behaviors (activities) that are directly associated with achieving a specific objective. Such behaviors recur or are consistently performed over time in the pursuit of formal objectives. The set of these recurrent behaviors, associated with a particular function, is called a *role*.

Usually behaviors are prescribed and formalized as job descriptions, so that the job holder knows what general activities make up his role. At other times role behaviors emerge or are the result of less formalized duties. We can see this most easily by recognizing that any given person occupies many different roles, either simultaneously or according to the situation. Common roles are those of student, daughter, subordinate, father, deacon, wife, or executive. Each of these roles is associated with a given set of behaviors.

Expectations of Behavior

Such roles are so widely recognized that their role behaviors are almost stereotyped. A given role is filled by individuals who behave quite similarly, which gives rise to expectations of how another will behave in that role.

Role expectations derive from two major sources: the duties and obligations of the position or function and past experience in dealing with the individual who fulfills the role. In some cases a certain amount of stereotyping occurs, through which we expect specific behavior patterns from an individual, even though we have never before observed that particular individual in the performance of his duties. A new acquaintance, a salesman, might be expected to be outgoing, jovial, glib, and probably insincere, but not necessarily because we have experienced those traits in our acquaintance. Rather, we have a conception of his duties, as well as generalizations of behaviors of other salesmen with whom we have come into contact.

Similarly a minister is expected to be concerned, temperate, calm, and dedicated. He should get along well with many diverse types of people, be a good organizer, and be continually available for consultation or emergencies. Our expectations would be violated—or at least shaken—should we see him frequenting the local bar, leaving an R-rated movie, or gossiping about his parishioners.

The duties and obligations of an office or position, coupled with our experiences with role incumbents, generate expectations of behaviors. One often-overlooked aspect of the roles we play is that role behaviors are not determined solely by the role incumbent. The people with whom he comes into contact have their *own* conceptions of appropriate behaviors as he *should* enact them. When a person's behavior is observed and evaluated as not being "right," the next step is typically an attempt to communicate the disparity in hopes that a behavior change will occur—which is in line with the communicator's idea of appropriate behavior. Attempts to influence how the role incumbent (the "focal person") plays his role are quite common. After receiving and evaluating influence attempts, the focal person may or may not adopt them or integrate them into his behaviors.

Establishing Role Behavior

Although the concept of the role is not particularly difficult to grasp, we recognize that the process whereby role *behaviors* are established is quite complex. With the help of Figure 16-1 the ways in which role behaviors are established and modified can be traced.

The diagram illustrates that any particular role behavior is affected by many variables external to the role incumbent or focal person. To place the role process in perspective, we must point out that role behavior is composed of "the recurring actions of an individual, appropriately interrelated with the repetitive activities of others so as to yield a predictable outcome."[1] The entire set of organizational behaviors is then mutually dependent on the behaviors of other appropriate individuals, composing a collective pattern that is stable and in which members play their assigned parts.[2]

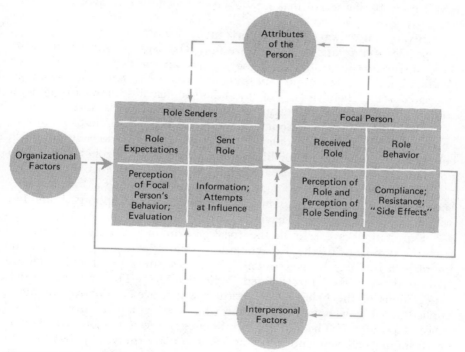

FIGURE 16-1   Role behavior and its influences. SOURCE: Adapted from Daniel Katz and Robert Kahn, *The Social Psychology of Organizations* (New York: Wiley, 1966), p. 187.

[1] Daniel Katz and Robert L. Kahn, *The Social Psychology of Organizations* (New York: Wiley, 1966), p. 174. The discussion of roles and role conflict is largely based upon their work, especially pp. 171–198.

[2] Ibid.

We can start by concentrating on the two central boxes in the figure, headed "Role Senders" and "Focal Person." The focal person is the role incumbent, and the role senders are individuals with whom he relates in performing his role. Because role senders comprise a major audience for the ways in which he fulfills his role, they are also important in evaluating and influencing the focal person's role behavior. They are called role *senders* because they send (transmit) their expectations, evaluations, and influence attempts to the focal person, to reinforce or modify his behaviors.

Role behavior is made up of specific acts and activities performed by the focal person. Just as with determining basic personality features, we can sift a number of basic and stable characteristics from the focal person's behaviors, identifying them as roles. The manager's role is quite well defined. We can consider his functions and activities in general terms, even though we recognize that we could not predict with any certainty how he will go about performing specific acts or making the day-to-day decisions involved with his overall role.

In very similar ways we each perform a variety of roles, depending on the specific circumstances in which we find ourselves. Such roles might be those of student, husband, churchgoer, sports fan, mother, or job holder, to mention but a few. The important thing to recognize is that each role has an associated set of behaviors. The focal person usually knows the general outlines of the types of behaviors he should perform in his role.

Those other persons who interact with the focal person in the course of performing his duties and obligations also have expectations about which behaviors are appropriate for him to enact. When actual role behaviors do not coincide with expectations, an attempt is made to influence the behavior of the focal person. In so doing, the other person becomes a "role sender," because he is attempting to implement his own conception of another person's appropriate role behavior.

Expectations are sent to the focal person in the hope that he will respond positively to the expectations of those persons with whom he interacts in fulfilling his role duties. We can see this represented in Figure 16-1 in the left-hand box headed "Role Senders." The role sender has expectations of the behavior of another, which are "evaluative standards applied to the behavior of any person who occupies a given organizational office or position."[3] The attempt to influence the focal person's role behavior, bringing behavior and expectations into conformity, is called the *sent role*.

The focal person, the recipient of the sent role, is the target of a communication attempt. We have seen that a message sent is not necessarily the message received, nor is a role sent necessarily the role received by the focal person. He must perceive the sent role and interpret it, along with many other messages from diverse sources (including policy manuals, job

[3]Ibid., p. 182.

descriptions, and other role senders) and compare its content with his expectations of his own appropriate behaviors.

You may have seen an example of this process. A professor may make assignments in readings, homework, and term papers that his students feel are not consistent with the requirements of other professors. They might see that his behaviors (requirements) are inappropriate and initiate attempts to influence the professor toward behaviors or expectations more appropriate, as seen by his students. The students may complain about the disparity in requirements, even going so far as to present copies of others' syllabi. The students' evaluation of the professor's role behavior then generates role-sending activities in an attempt to influence a change in the focal person's role behavior.

The behaviors actually elicited by the process constitute still another step in the process. The focal person has his own expectations about what his appropriate behaviors are and, in a sense, "sends" roles to himself. Role behavior is the focal person's response to the role situation and influence attempts of role senders. His role behavior directly affects his role senders (represented by the feedback arrow from the focal person to the role senders). If no change in the focal person's role behavior is observed, then the role senders may give up the influence attempt, continue the role sending, or bring other forms of influence to bear. If the focal person responds in a hostile fashion to the sent role, further influence attempts are likely to be quite different from those caused by submissive compliance. Compliance may be expected to reduce influence attempts.[4]

The diagram shows further that there are still more factors that affect the process through which roles are established and modified. These are organizational factors, interpersonal factors, and the attributes of the person. Organizational factors include such things as the design of the task, job description, formal sanctions, and organizational structure. After all, these are the basic technological and structural characteristics of the organization that determine formal expectations and requirements, making up the duties and obligations for which the role incumbent is responsible. Procedures and policies are also important because they may require specific formal interactions or communications between various role incumbents. Interpersonal factors include such items as the quality and extent of interpersonal relationships enjoyed among members of the relevant focal person–role senders set. Certainly the member of the informal organization will respond differently to roles sent by his group members than to roles sent by isolates, group deviates, or superiors.

The attributes of both role sender and focal person can also have important effects on role setting. Personality factors can also strongly influence role behavior, especially in terms of the focal person's perception of the sent role. His understanding of appropriate role behaviors, too, may be a

[4]Ibid., p. 183.

function of basic personality patterns. Reaction to influence attempts by others (such as submission versus resistance) may also be due to engrained personality attributes.

Role Conflict

The establishing and modifying of role behaviors, although simplified conceptually in our diagram, is by no means a simple or straightforward process. The focal person is constantly bombarded with influence attempts from role senders, each of whom evaluate the focal person's behaviors in terms of their own requirements and criteria. Further complicating the process is the realization that *every* person in an organization is a focal person. The web of role behaviors becomes tangled quickly when we see the mutual role sendings and receivings, all done simultaneously by all organizational members, and all attempting to influence different combinations of other persons.

What with the complexities, differences in formal requirements, perceptual biases, and consequent divergencies in role expectations, any particular focal person may be placed under conflicts that are quite stressful and frustrating. Perhaps role conflict is as uncomfortable as it is because it entails a basic incompatibility between expected patterns of behavior. Katz and Kahn defined role conflict as:

The simultaneous occurrence of two (or more) role sendings such that compliance with one would make more difficult compliance with the other. In the extreme case, compliance with one expectation as sent would exclude completely the possibility of compliance with the other; the two expectations are mutually contradictory. For example, a person's superior may make it clear to him that he is expected to hold his subordinates strictly to company rules. At the same time, his subordinates may indicate in various ways that they would like loose, relaxed supervision, and that they will make things difficult if they are pushed too hard. Here the pressures from above and below are incompatible, since a style of supervision which satisfies one set of expectations violates the other set.[5]

We can identify four distinct types of role conflict: intrasender, intersender, interrole, and person–role. Each creates unique pressures on the focal person.

Intrasender Conflict

Intrasender conflict occurs as the result of the role sendings of a single sender. In transmitting his role expectations, the role sender may be demanding two separate sets of behaviors that are contradictory or incompatible. A purchasing agent may be ordered by the materials manager to buy certain raw materials at whatever cost necessary and from whatever source

[5]Ibid., p. 184.

necessary, yet not to go outside previously approved suppliers—none of whom have the needed materials because of a shortage.

Intersender Conflict

Role conflict occurs when the role behaviors demanded by one role sender are inconsistent with the expectations of one or more other role senders. Production workers often experience intersender conflict when their supervisor demands increased production and group members set an informal work restriction on the number of units to be turned in. Students may experience such a conflict when separate professors assign time-consuming projects due the same morning.

Interrole Conflict

Conflict between the behaviors associated with separate roles held by the same individual also creates stress. The expectations for one role may conflict with the expectations for the focal person's other role. Many managers (and professors) find themselves in this uncomfortable position when they must periodically evaluate the performance of subordinates (students); the role of judge—and potential role of punisher—interferes with the ability to fulfill the important role of trainer, developer, or teacher. Working wives find difficulty in reconciling completely the demands of the roles of careerwoman and housewife.

Person–Role Conflict

The fourth type of role conflict differs somewhat from the other three. Intrasender, intersender, and interrole conflicts stem from inconsistencies in the expectations of *others*. Person–role conflict is the result of role requirements that are incompatible with the focal person. A sales manager may find himself caught between pressures to meet competitors' actions by adopting shady practices, even as his own ethical code forbids them. Another form of person–role conflict exists when the focal person's behavior is not accepted by others as consistent with his role. The rate buster violates the role expectations of his work group by his production activity.

Role Overload

These four fundamental role conflicts can create other and more complex forms of conflict. *Role overload* is an example of one. A form of intersender conflict, overload occurs when the roles sent by the members of the focal person's role set are legitimate and compatible, yet physically impossible to fulfill. The sent roles may each consist of a number of tasks, the sum total of which cannot be completed by the focal person within the time available nor at given standards of quality. He then experiences overload as a result of a conflict between priorities or as conflict between maximizing quality or quantity. Under such conflicting pressures, the focal person must attempt to balance the demands on his time and efforts, setting priorities of his own. As a result, he may slight the sent roles of some members of his role set. If the conflict cannot be resolved, then he has the impossible task of attempting to satisfy everybody without adequate resources or capacity.[6]

Roles and Attitudes

The requirements and behaviors associated with different roles may be quite obvious and formalized, as in a job description, or subtle and "natural," like the culturally imposed role of women. Role influences are pervasive and powerful, shaping our expectations of ourselves and others, and thus creating behaviors and attitudes. Roles create perceptual selectivity, as was pointed out in Chapter 10. We have seen how departmental affiliation was strongly related to the types of problems that executives identified in a written case situation. Roles also influence attitudes. Because attitudes are central in formulating behaviors, we can see the causal link between role perceptions, attitudes, and behaviors.

To underscore the impact of roles, Lieberman studied the relationships among perceptions, attitudes, and roles.[7] He obtained attitude questionnaires from almost the entire set of factory personnel at a medium-sized midwestern home appliance producer—over 2,000 workers, 145 union stewards, and 151 foremen. Within six months, 23 workers were promoted to foremen and 35 workers became union stewards. The same questionnaire forms were readministered to these workers who had experienced a change in role, as well as to several control groups.

The experimental (new foremen and stewards) groups were found to have developed attitude changes on experiencing their role changes, whereas the control groups did not undergo such attitude changes. The new foremen saw the company as a better place to work than other companies, had more positive perceptions of company executives, and became more in favor of the company's incentive system. New stewards, however, were more positive toward labor unions in general, had more positive perceptions of the local top union officials, and came to prefer seniority over ability in determining which workers should get better jobs.

Yet another phase of the study was made possible by an economic downturn shortly after the resurvey. The company's work force was cut, and 8 of the initial 23 workers who had become foremen were returned to the worker role; 12 remained foremen, and 3 had left the company. The 35 new stewards had also experienced major changes: 14 had left the steward role,

[6]Ibid., p. 185.
[7]Seymour Lieberman, "The Effects of Changes in Roles on the Attitudes of Role Occupants," *Human Relations,* **9** (1956).

either because of not seeking reelection or because they had not been reelected; 15 others had either left the company or been laid off; and only 6 of the original 35 remained stewards. The same questionnaire was then administered a third time, to these original group members who remained with the company.

Those who remained foremen either retained their favorable attitudes toward management or increased the favor with which they saw management. The foremen who had been demoted showed attitude changes to the *previous* level of attitudes they had held when they had been merely workers. Ex-stewards showed no marked tendency to revert to the attitudes they had held before they became stewards, probably because the initial attitude changes they had experienced in entering the steward role had not been as great as those experienced by the new foremen. New stewards, after all, still retained work-group membership while performing their essentially part-time union duties. Their roles had been added to, whereas the new foremen experienced a complete new set of roles.

Role Ambiguity

If we refer once again to Figure 16-1, another underlying factor in the role behavior process can be identified. Expectations are important, and hence the way in which expectations are formed can influence behavior. The less information available about role content, duties, authority, or criteria of performance evaluation, the higher the level of anxiety and dissatisfaction.[8]

Ambiguous or ill-defined roles are naturally more prone to role conflict because of the lack of a formal specification of expected duties, functions, or behaviors. The role incumbent is placed in the unenviable position of determining what he is supposed to do—and how to do it—by trial and error.

Role senders are quite active in trying to influence the establishing of role behaviors because of the tentative nature of the ambiguous role. In a company with a newly established research and development department, the R & D director can expect many visits and not-too-subtle role sendings from the heads of the other departments. They will be influencing his conception of what R & D will do in the future—and for whom—according to their own expectations and needs.

The less ambiguous—the more structured and specified—a role is, the more nearly its incumbent can get feedback on performance. On the assembly line a worker can directly observe whether or not he is falling behind. Top-level executives, on the other hand, may find that their roles change rather drastically as the firm's external environment changes randomly. They must structure new roles and restructure old ones as external expecta-

[8]W. Clay Hamner and Henry L. Tosi, "Relationships Among Various Role Involvement Measures," a paper presented before the Academy of Management, August 1973, in Boston, Mass. p. 1.

tions and demands ebb and flow. The executive's role behavior may be evaluated in terms of boycotts, antitrust suits, multi-million-dollar fines for discriminations in promotion or pay, too-late entry into an emerging market, and so on. Ambiguous roles must still be performed effectively, yet the pressures and frustrations are unrelenting. Role sendings must be evaluated and often incorporated into the conception of what the ambiguous role entails. A major question always occurs, however, of how legitimate others' demands are.

Role ambiguity complicates the establishing of role behaviors. The manager must be aware of the frustrations, pressures, and conflicts he builds into a subordinate's job when he fails to define his expectations and criteria clearly. If he goes too far in detailing them, on the other hand, he eliminates initiative, judgment, and flexibility. The role of the manager is then rather ambiguous itself as he influences subordinates' role behaviors.

Resolving Role Conflict

Conflicts in the expectations by others of how one should act creates severe frustration. The role player is frustrated in his attempts to do his job successfully, especially as he is bombarded with role sendings, each of which try to influence him into different behaviors. Role senders are frustrated because their abilities to fulfill *their* roles may depend on how another does his job, and their role sendings may be ineffective. All of these frustrations and perceived behavior inadequacies must eventually mean that the organization as designed becomes less effective.

Clarifying role ambiguities and resolving role conflicts then become a key to the successful implementation of formal expectations. Also made possible is the avoiding of the anxieties associated with both initiating and receiving attempts to influence behavior. Depending on the nature and source of the conflict, the focal person is placed under considerable pressure and stress to accommodate at least some of his senders.

Generally speaking, the manager experiencing role conflict has available a number of ways of responding. Some are less effective than others, but they have in common the easing of some of the strain imposed on the focal person.[9]

1. The manager can adopt the position that hierarchical level outweighs any other consideration. Under this clear-cut rule of thumb, the expectations of subordinates or peers are rejected in favor of the expectations of the focal person's superior. Ranking role sendings, dismissing those from one group, and enacting the expectations of another lessen the strain of weighing the relative legitimacy or authority of the senders. Such an

[9]Most of these resolution mechanisms are based on those in Jackson Toby, "Some Variables in Role Conflict Analysis," *Social Forces* (1952), pp. 324–327.

option may also be taken by nonmanagers; assembly-line workers may reject the role sendings of the foreman and the time-study engineer, instead accommodating the expectations of fellow workers.

2. He can screen himself from others' expectations by subordinating himself to impersonal (and rigid) rules or policies. In this way he disavows any capability to behave differently by pointing to his powerlessness to violate organizational dictates. Such a response can effectively remove stress because role senders can be informed that the focal person's actions are beyond his control. It is not *he* that behaves in such a way, he is just doing what the rules require. Another form of this basic response may be noticed when the focal person seeks relief from superiors' rulings by removing himself from responsibility. The negative consequences of a new policy may be forecast not because of his performance but because his work group (or sales territory or research project) will not accommodate it. "Thus, he has an excuse for not living up to the expectations of his superiors because of the unfortunate conditions with which he is faced."[10]

3. Another manner of removing his perceived personal involvement in his role behavior is the desocialization of his role through impersonal rituals. He may become rather formal in his interactions with others, identifying himself—and calling others by—"Mister" or other suitable titles. Such a process is evident in classroom settings, with titles ("Professor," "Mister") diminishing the possibility of a socially based role interfering with the focal person's ability to perform his task-related role. If the roles are allowed to coexist, then friendship or social obligations may bias the objectivity with which the professor (or purchasing agent or personnel administrator) performs his duties.

4. Tact or deceptive practices may be employed, especially in social situations. A tactful excuse for not fulfilling a social obligation may be beneficial to both parties. Deception usually involves a less humane motivation; a role sender may be given false or manipulated data that indicate compliance with his expectations, whereas the actual role behavior is completely different. Dalton related[11] the experience of one corporate headquarters in trying to reduce unnecessary inventory. A corporate representative was ordered to conduct surprise plant inspections to determine compliance with prescribed inventory levels and thereby reduce overall inventory stocks. The inspecting executive found the expectations of headquarters incompatible with those of the production managers, yet realized that not conducting the checks would be spotted by his superiors at headquarters. His role conflict was resolved through deception; inspections were held, yet they came as no surprise. He carefully informed each

---

[10]Joseph A. Litterer, *The Analysis of Organizations,* 2nd Ed. (New York: Wiley, 1973), p. 712.

[11]Melville Dalton, *Men Who Manage: Fusions of Feeling and Theory in Administration* (New York: Wiley, 1959), pp. 47–49.

production manager well in advance of his audits. Reports to his superiors documented his fulfilling formal expectations and his finding inventory levels to be within acceptable ranges.

5. Stalling until the pressures subside can reduce role conflict, but only if the pressures are temporary and only if the focal person possesses the deft touch necessary to placate the senders. If the stalling tactic works, the focal person can avoid a commitment until at least one of the competing senders relaxes or abandons his demands. Then the remaining sender's expectations may be met.

6. Rather than changing his behaviors, one may resolve role conflict by redefining the situation or expectations. The production executive may try to educate the new marketing-oriented president about the necessity for cost consciousness and standardization. In other cases, seemingly irreconcilable demands can be met by actions that meet both sets of expectations. A student with heavy report-writing assignments may find his girl friend's demands for companionship at odds with his professor's expectations—until he starts a series of library dates with the girl friend.

7. The focal person may try to negotiate with his role senders, pointing out conflicting demands in order to reduce their expectations to a level where they are no longer mutually exclusive. Negotiations may be rather formal or may be implicit, such as when a person partially meets each of conflicting sets of demands in hopes of effecting a compromise.

8. Avoidance of the conflict may result from several actions. The focal person may ignore *all* role senders. In a way, this option is similar to the first discussed above, in which one set of expectations was complied with and the rest ignored. Complete avoidance requires that the focal person reject all influence attempts, with only his own role sendings to guide his actions. In the long run, complete avoidance of sendings would probably result in dismissal. Other avoidance patterns involve escape, too, such as resigning the position or seeking a transfer. These latter actions effectively remove one from the range of the role senders, their expectations, and their sanctions.

9. Finally, illness may result from unbearable pressures, if the devices mentioned above do not seem appropriate to the person in role conflict. Either mental or physical illness can be caused by severe psychological strain and may effectively resolve the role conflict by forcing the focal person to remove himself without the implications of failure found in the avoidance patterns in number 8.

Status

A phenomenon closely linked to the concept of role is that of status. One of the characteristics of any form of social organization is that members tend to adopt behaviors appropriate to the task to be completed and also to place a value on other people and the functions they perform. A medical doctor generally has more prestige in a community than does the owner of a small neighborhood laundry. The physician's services have, after all, required much more extensive and specialized training, and his skill is important to the well-being of the local residents.

Status as Ascribed Value

We must not confuse the prestige attached to the role held by particular individuals with moral judgments about one person's being "better" than another. The question of status and prestige is simply a result of a natural desire to rank-order positions according to some criterion of importance.

Status cues furnish valuable information about the individual in social behavior, too. In conversing with a new acquaintance, you will probably find yourself searching for cues to his status, as he will about you. Information will be exchanged about the occupation of one's father, schools attended, the type (and year) of car driven, the type of job held, and so on. Such information eases the difficulties experienced in establishing a relationship. Persons identify more readily and relate more freely to those of approximately the same social status because values and interests tend to be roughly similar. Even in a society founded on egalitarian principles, as are the United States and Canada, a shared ranking of common characteristics is widely used. Status cannot—and must not—be ignored because it exists and is important to most people. Maslow's esteem needs and Herzberg's factors of advancement, recognition, and achievement are closely related to the concept of status.

Status and Organizational Role

The formal organization is made up of a number of defined positions arranged in order of their increasing authority. The president occupies a position that is superior to the position occupied by a clerk-typist, primarily because his role is composed of rights and duties pertaining to the direction of the entire organization.[12] The role of the clerk-typist is similarly composed of concrete rights and duties, which differ in content and scope from those of the president.

We intuitively realize that the two roles—president and clerk-typist—differ in another way too, in prestige. Unfortunately, one's position in the formal organizational hierarchy may not be sufficient to describe the amount of value his position has in the eyes of his peers. We must differentiate between the value ascribed to a position by the formal organization and that ascribed by members of the social system. Value in the formal organizational system may be termed *rank* and reflects the holder's place on the organiza-

[12]R. Linton, *The Study of Man* (New York: Appleton-Century-Crofts, 1935), p. 113.

tional ladder. Social status, on the other hand, is the measure of informally established value and its comparison with other positions, as perceived through the informal organization or the social system.

Even though "all men are created equal," we still ascribe more prestige to some people than we do to others. Even within an office composed of holders of the same title, an informal ranking invariably occurs. The best machinist or the most creative advertising specialist occupies a special place in the eyes of his fellows.

Status Determinants

What determines status? Status is a result of prestige or value attached to the holder of a position. Status need not be conferred only by organizational members. Supreme Court justices have status outside the courtroom, prestige attached to the position they hold by the general public. Within the ranks of the justices, however, there may also be another—informal—status system in which the individual justices are ranked by their fellow justices. Such complications in status suggest that we might benefit from examining several different types or scales of status. Four scales by which we can describe these types of status are those of ascribed–achieved, functional–scalar, positional–personal, and active–latent.[13]

Ascribed–Achieved

The ascribed–achieved dimension of status measures the extent to which prestige or value is earned or is a matter of birthright. A certain amount of prestige derives merely from being born into a prominent family. On the other hand, a person may earn through his own hard work the admiration of others. Within the work environment, especially, the means for achieving a specific position in the social system are education or skill.[14]

Scalar–Functional

The scalar–functional dimension relates status to position held in the formal organization. Scalar status is what we have previously called organizational status or rank, the prestige attached to a position in the vertical hierarchy. Functional status derives from the particular type of task, function, or job performed by a person. An accountant and a statistician may have the same scalar status, yet the position of accountant may have more or less functional status than that possessed by the statistician because of the relative perceived value of their jobs. The corporate controller has greater scalar status than either.

[13]Fremont E. Kast and James E. Rosenzweig, *Organization and Management: A Systems Approach*, 2nd Ed. (New York: McGraw-Hill, 1974), p. 277. The following is based on their discussion.
[14]Ibid.

Personal–Positional

Quite similar to the scalar–functional continuum is that of personal–positional. This scale relates status to the extent to which prestige or value is based on characteristics of the individual himself or based on the position he holds without regard to the person who occupies it. Positional status may be illustrated if we compare the prestige attached to the position of Supreme Court justice and that of county dogcatcher. No matter who occupies these two positions, there are certain inherent status differences between them. Personal status may be illustrated if we compare the extent to which different amounts of prestige are conferred on individual Supreme Court justices because of the estimation of competence of each justice relative to the others. Other determinants of personal status may be sociability, "connections," or attractiveness.

Active–Latent

Active and latent status considerations are important because of the varieties of functions and behaviors possessed by any particular individual. Different status degrees are conferred to each of his roles, and there may be varying degrees of spill-over from one status to another. The status conferred by a local congregation because of his role of deacon will probably have very little to do with the status one enjoys at work as a design engineer. At work his status as deacon would be latent, yet in a conference with the minister, such status would be very active.

The Status Implications of Role

From our discussion of status, we can see how different roles are evaluated by others along some continuum of prestige or value. In the evaluation phase of role sending, the role sender compares his perceptions of the role behaviors of the focal person with his own perceptions of what those behaviors should be. Such a comparison may be in terms of how well the focal person is performing his duties or whether the duties he is pursuing are the appropriate ones. Such a process can yield positional or functional status, through which several role incumbents may be differentiated by status, even though they perform the same duties. One clerk might then have higher status in the eyes of his supervisor than another. Or a physician who practices on Park Avenue might be held in higher esteem than one who practices in the slums. Professors are also subject to evaluation and status differentials, even though they might teach exactly the same subjects. Their activity in professional associations, consulting activities, and publication in learned journals are several possible sources of comparison, as is relative teaching effectiveness.

A major complication in status considerations is that so many different status systems are in operation at any particular time. The supervisor of a work group may see the members as being different in job performance and work-related functions and thus different in status. The workers themselves may have several status systems in operation, one of which may regard seniority or job knowledge. Others may be dictated by seemingly extraneous factors, such as a worker who has a son in graduate school or a brother who is a vice-president at another company, thus deriving status from another. Another set of status inputs can stem from personality factors. The person who is relatively sociable tends to be held in higher status than the recluse, and people with generally pleasing traits are accorded greater personal preference and prestige.

In much the same way, informal organizations—and other group forms—have their own status hierarchy. The leader tends to be the one who typifies the values and norms of the group most nearly and thereby serves as an "ego ideal." As the central person in the group and the person to whom deference and informal position are accorded, he anchors the status ladder in the group. Depending on how well they contribute to the purpose, values, and norms of the group, others are ranked below the leader.

Symbols of Status

The maze of roles and positions in any organization creates a certain difficulty in their integration. Cooperation, teamwork, and coordinated specialization require sound communication about the duties and obligations of one's role and about one's organizational rank. Symbols effectively relate information about each role incumbent, furnishing cues of "correct" ways of treating each other. Symbols tell the amount of authority possessed, without a job description or a statement of responsibility posted on the office door. Status symbols are necessary, in short, because ordinary communication is inadequate to describe a position, an amount of prestige, and cues for how to interact with the focal person. Besides, status symbols continually—and silently—broadcast their message to all, yet with subtlety. We can see, with the help of the tongue-in-cheek Table 16-1, how hierarchical or formal status is differentiated through the display of various accouterments.

A less obvious set of status symbols is used to differentiate role occupants who perform the same function, as might be the case with design engineers whose desks are side by side. One might prominently display a membership certificate in a selective professional engineering organization, whereas the other keeps a sophisticated minicomputer at his desk. While in the office, both engineers might well be expected to work in their shirt-sleeves, yet when they are called on to investigate conditions in the plant, they will invariably don their jackets and will probably carry a slide rule. They are simply—and relatively unconsciously—making sure that they are not mistaken for members of a lower-status occupational group while on the factory floor.

For these engineers we can see another aspect of status, the separate ways in which rank and performance are symbolized and communicated to others. Goffman clarified this point:

Status symbols designate the position which an occupant has, not the way in which he fulfills it. They must therefore be distinguished from *esteem symbols* which designate the degree to which a person performs the duties of his position in accordance with ideal standards, regardless of the particular rank of his position. For example, the Victoria Cross is awarded in the British Army for heroic performance of a task, regardless of what particular task it is and regardless of the rank of the person who performs it. This is an esteem symbol. It rates above a similar one called the George Cross. On the other hand, there is an insignia which designates Lieutenant-Colonel. It is a status symbol. It tells us about the rank of the person who wears it but tells us nothing about the standard he has achieved in performing the duties of his rank. It *ranks* him above a man who wears the insignia of a Captain, although, in fact, the Captain may be *rated* higher than the Lieutenant-Colonel in terms of the esteem that is accorded to good soldiers.[15]

In organizations, symbols of status may be rather formally assigned. Occupying an office differentiates one from the large numbers of members who share a huge room. But with how many people does one share his office? A private office indicates high status, as does its relative size. Other status determinants are the office's furnishings (desk: steel or wood? dictating unit? how big is the desk? what kind of chair?), location (corner office? which floor is the office located on? is there a view from the window?), number of windows, secretary (if *she* has a secretary, you're big-time!).

Such considerations are often seen as rather silly by nonmembers. We must remember, though, that status symbols concretely differentiate the esteem in which individuals and their functions are held. Status *is* important:

In a large manufacturing company, for example, an executive promoted to a new job was transferred to an office at company headquarters. The office to which he was moving had formerly housed a vice-president—although our executive's promotion was to a position lower than that of vice-president.

The new office was well furnished, including wall-to-wall carpeting, paintings, and the other amenities of a high-status business office. Before top management would let the executive occupy his new office, however, they told maintenance to cut a 12-inch strip from the entire perimeter of the carpet. Why? Because wall-to-wall carpets convey a message of position and power in this company and belong exclusively to executives of vice-presidential rank or above. With a single action, the company had put the executive "in his place" and conveyed the message to all his future visitors.[16]

Status Congruence

We have pointed out the central position of roles in encouraging stability and predictability in the organization. Given well-communicated

[15]Erving Goffman, "Symbols of Class Status," *British Journal of Sociology* (December 1951), p. 295.

[16]Paul Preston and Anthony Quesada, "What Does Your Office 'Say' About You?" *Supervisory Management* (August 1974), p. 29.

TABLE 16–1   Status Differentiation in Organizations

Visible Appurtenances	Top Dogs	V.I.P.s	Brass	No. 2s	Eager Beavers	Hoi Polloi
Brief cases	None—they ask the questions	Use of backs of envelopes	Someone goes along to carry theirs	Carry their own—empty	Daily—carry their own—filled with work	Too poor to own one
Desks, office	Custom made (to order)	Executive style (to order)	Type A "Director"	Type B "Manager"	Cast-offs from No. 2s	Yellow oak—or cast-offs from Eager Beavers
Tables, office	Coffee tables	End tables or decorative wall tables	Matching tables Type A	Matching tables Type B	Plain work table	None—lucky to have own desk
Carpeting	Nylon—1 inch pile	Nylon—1 inch pile	Wool-Twist (with pad)	Wool-Twist (without pad)	Used wool pieces—sewed	Asphalt tile
Plant stands	Several—kept filled with strange exotic plants		Two—repotted whenever they take a trip	One medium-sized, Repotted annually during vacation	Small—Repotted when plant dies	May have one in the department or bring their own from home

Vacuum water bottles	Silver	Silver	Chromium	Plain painted	Coke machine	Water fountains
Library	Private collection	Autographed or complimentary books and reports	Selected references	Impressive titles on covers	Books everywhere	Dictionary
Shoe shine service	Every morning at 10:00	Every morning at 10:15	Every day at 9:00 or 11:00	Every other day	once a week	Shine their own
Parking space	Private in front of office	In plant garage	In company garage—if enough seniority	In company properties—somewhere	On the parking lot	Anywhere they can find a space—if they can afford a car
Luncheon menu	Cream Cheese on Whole Wheat, Buttermilk, and Indigestion Tablets	Cream of Celery Soup, Chicken Sandwich (White Meat), Milk	Fruit Cup—Spinach, Lamb Chop—Peas, Ice Cream—Tea	Orange Juice, Minute Steak, French Fries—salad, Fruit Cup—Coffee	Tomato Juice, Chicken Croquettes, Mashed Potatoes, Peas—Bread, Chocolate Cream Pie, Coffee	Clam Chowder, Frankfurter and Beans, Rolls and butter, Raisin Pie á la Mode, Two Cups of Coffee

SOURCE: Adapted from Meyer Weinberg and Oscar E. Shabat, *Society and Man* (Englewood Cliffs, N.J.: Prentice-Hall, 1956), p. 150.

role expectations and behaviors, the ways in which members relate are smoothed by role considerations and mutual understanding. Another factor that complicates organizational relationships even further is multiplication of statuses. We have noted the fact that we all play many roles, behaving differently according to the specific situation in which we find ourselves and the expectations of that particular role set. As long as each role and role set are kept separate, few conflicts in status-based expectations should occur.

Unfortunately roles and role behaviors often overlap. Consequently, status incongruencies can occur. Status incongruency stems from the different valuations of various roles held by the same person. For the focal person—and the members of his role set(s)—to avoid status discrepancies and discomforts, the status of each of his relevant roles should be roughly similar.[17] The confusion that is created by status incongruence might be illustrated by the student who also happens to be the founder of his own successful business, yet who carries a D average. How does another student relate to him? The status of the student role is shared by another student, who may see students as being somewhat low in status. A successful business-man is generally ascribed a rather *high* status. However, *low* status is usually attributed to students with severely deficient academic records.

Status incongruence creates confusion in interpersonal relationships. A high-status person is generally treated with some respect and deference, whereas low status may elicit contempt and impatience. "Prestige or status are (sic) frequently defined as a set of unwritten rules about the kind of conduct that people are expected to show in one's presence: what degree of respect or disrespect, familiarity or unfamiliarty, reserve or frankness."[18]

Status Discrepancy

Another consideration important to organizational behavior is per-ceived discrepancy in status. Interaction with others perceived as lower in status can be threatening because of potential identification with that group or individual. Because status is abstract and is ascribed through the percep-tions of others, one's status can be quite tenuous. It may be withdrawn or downgraded through misperceptions as readily as through active participa-tion by the individual. Status can become so important that it is jealously guarded lest a careless word, acquisition, or acquaintance diminish one's prestige.

The reference group—the set of individuals or social class with which one identifies and whose values and behaviors are adopted—can be instru-mental in establishing or maintaining status. To preserve status one cannot long leave the reference group for a lower-status group, for a *new* reference

---

[17]George C. Homans, *Social Behavior: Its Elementary Forms* (New York: Harcourt, Brace & World, 1961), p. 264.
[18]David R. Hampton, Charles E. Summer, and Ross A. Webber, *Organizational Behavior and the Practice of Management,* Rev. Ed. (Glenview, Ill.: Scott, Foresman, 1973), p. 219.

group will be used to ascribe status. Implications exist for formally required interactions between groups dissimilar in status or prestige. The high-status staff officer (without formal authority) may find himself in conflict with the aspects of his job. One of his functions may be to solicit problems from line executives, analyze them, and then present the proposed solutions to line officers. In a sense his work is *initiated* by perceived lower-status individuals, and his function is to *serve* or *support* them with his specialized abilities. Such discrepancies in status and formal role can create hostility between line and staff.

Summary

In this chapter we have seen that consistent behaviors become associated with specified organizational roles. The manner in which any incumbent performs the duties and discharges the obligations of his role depends on the expectations of what the role behavior should be. Role senders evaluate role behaviors and initiate influence attempts at the suitable modification of how the role is performed. The sent roles are received by the focal person and accepted, rejected, or modified.

Conflicts between the expectations that others have of one's role behavior are common, especially in ambiguous roles. Conflicts may stem from inconsistencies in the role expectations sent by separate individuals (intersender conflict) or by the same individual (intrasender conflict). Separate roles occupied by the same individual may cause conflicts between their respective expected behaviors (interrole conflict). Role requirements may conflict with the values or abilities of the incumbent (person–role conflict). These fundamental role conflicts can combine to create role overload.

Selective perceptual processes cause attitudes to change so that they become consistent with the functions and values appropriate to the role. Resolving role conflicts then becomes more difficult. Specific conflict resolution mechanisms include weighting expectations by the hierarchical level of the sender, strict rule-adherence, desocializing the role, deceiving role senders, stalling, redefining the situation or expectations, negotiating and compromising, avoiding the conflict, and becoming ill from the stress.

Status (prestige) is attributed to role and role behavior. Organizational status is termed *rank,* and social status is informally established. Status may be classified as being ascribed or achieved, functional or scalar, positional or personal, and active or latent. Symbols of status serve as silent communications and indicators of acceptable patterns of interaction, as well as serving ego needs.

Status congruence—the compatability of statuses attributed to one's diverse roles—eases confusions that can interfere with effective interactions. Status discrepancy occurs when interactions occur between occupants of different status levels.

We have seen the place of roles and status in organizational behavior, especially as they provide an interface between formal and informal expectations, modifying the individual's propensity to behave. In the next chapter we will continue with discussions of broader organizational conflicts and the problems of implementing changes.

STUDY AND REVIEW QUESTIONS

1. Identify three major roles you play. What behaviors do they each call for? What role sendings do you receive for each and from whom? Do these roles conflict with each other? If they do, how do you resolve the conflicts?

2. How and why does role affect the attitudes of the incumbent?

3. How is role ambiguity related to job satisfaction and job performance?

4. Why do others act as role senders to the focal person?

5. Which of the four forms of role conflict is the most frustrating for the role incumbent? Why?

6. Which of the four forms of role conflict is the most detrimental to organizational effectiveness? Why?

7. Distinguish between symbols of status and esteem.

8. How does the concept of status interfere with organizational effectiveness?

9. How does the concept of status facilitate organizational effectiveness?

10. If you were a manager, how would you treat the problems of status symbols, status congruence, and status discrepancy?

Chapter

17

Change and Conflict

CHAPTER OBJECTIVES

1. To identify change as an organizational process and a managerial responsibility.

2. To present insights into the effective management of change.

3. To show the close relationship between change and conflict.

4. To discuss ways in which various forms of conflict may be resolved.

5. To develop an appreciation for an analytical approach to change and conflict in order to remove perceived goal incompatibilities among formal organizational, individual, and social subsystems.

CHAPTER OUTLINE

Change
The Importance of Change
Change as a Process
Analyzing the Change
  Situation

Conflict
Internal Conflict Forms
Organizational Conflict
Managing Conflict
Managing Change

One of the most important duties of the manager is decision making. The very nature of a decision implies a *change* from the current situation toward a desired *future* state of being. Decisions are not the sole property of top executives; day-to-day decisions are routinely made by supervisors, as well as by nonsupervisory or operative workers. What does differ is that the scope and impact of executive decisions are much more far-reaching and commit organizational resources much more and for longer periods of time than do the decisions of members with less authority.

Any change must necessarily conflict in some way with the way things are done now. In the extreme case, present activities are completely abolished in favor of a completely new set of activities. The more general situation in which change is encountered is that of modifying previously established behaviors to fit a new situation.

Whatever the change situation, a certain amount of conflict is bound to be encountered. Separate individuals or groups have their ability to attain their own objectives blocked or hampered by the other. When this happens, conflict results, generally as a result of competition for some scarce resources. The resource may be prestige, budget allotment, market share, security, and so on.

Change

Change is one of the facts of life in organizational behavior. The manager, in creating change, creates conflicts. The repercussions and implications of change and conflict must be well understood so that they may be managed and controlled. In extreme cases, poorly managed conflict and change can completely wipe out the ability of team members or departments to work effectively together. Improperly introduced changes can also nurture resentment and sabotage.

The Importance of Change

Life itself is almost synonymous with the concept of change. All organisms must adapt to the demands of their environments and their own stages of growth. Throughout history, animals and plants that have not been able to adapt or change when necessary have become extinct. Similarly humans "grow up," leaving behind the characteristics of earlier stages of development and adopting new behaviors more appropriate to age, environment, and expectations.

An organization is not much different. Even firms in rather stable and static environments find that some change eventually becomes necessary, if only to accommodate changes in the work force. New technologies are constantly being developed, and competition must be met in new marketing offerings and pricing policies. Population centers shift and new communications techniques are found to be necessary. New managerial tools and techniques may be implemented.

If these variables can change in static environments, just think about those firms which encounter drastic change routinely, as do aerospace industries! Simply reacting to or coping with change is insufficient. Change must be anticipated because of the conflicts it can bring. Minimizing the negative impact of an imposed change and clearing the way for its implementation is an essential part of the managerial role.

The effects of change upon the formal organization are great. Technology and organization are two major causal factors in the operation of the firm. Reorganizing and modifying technological bases is a huge undertaking, of course. But the effect of change upon individual and social systems may be even greater.

Change as a Process

Change can (and does) occur haphazardly. For our purposes change can be considered a process, a series of related activites. We can identify the activities and their effects on human responses, acquiring basic knowledge by which effective and ineffective changes may be differentiated.

Change cannot take place unless it occurs through people. People must *decide* that the change should be made, plan on how the change will be done, modify the organization of the firm to incorporate the change most effectively, hire or replace members with newly appropriate skills and retrain those with obsolete abilities, and finally make the change *work*. Ultimately the concept of change boils down to how to make sure that the change is effectively implemented. A "perfect" change that is not accepted by workers will not work to the extent that it should. A "poor" change, if wholeheartedly embraced by those most affected, can work better than it should.

The central focus in the concept of organizational change is the reduction of forces that lower the probability of the change's successful implementation, while increasing the effects of the forces that favor the change.

Forces Favoring Change

Probably the most immediate and apparent factor influencing change is recognition that a problem exists. A manager realizes that his factory production is seriously out of line with that needed to meet sales projections. During static tests, a new booster rocket flames out. Turnover and absenteeism dramatically increase at a plant. Consumers bring a class action suit against the company, charging safety hazards from product failure. Workers vote to be represented by a union. Two executives refuse to speak to each other. A competitor introduces a new product that immediately captures a substantial share of the market. A safer turret lathe is invented. Manual assembly becomes too costly to allow a product to compete with those made by automated means. All of these instances have in common something that favors the introduction of a change. Some problem is recognized as existing, some factor is seen as detracting from goal attainment, and some modification in technology or organization must be made.

These forces for change can be conveniently classified as belonging to one of two groups, either external or internal forces.[1] The external forces may be identified as being composed of changes in the marketplace, in technology, and in social environment. Forces internal to the organization consist of process- and people-related causes; organizational processes are the activities by which work is performed and managed, and behavioral factors are those associated with attitudes, satisfactions, motivation, and so on.

Miner points out that sweeping changes are often initiated "under conditions of some degree of crisis or at least where there are strong pressures for improvement,"[2] such as falling profits. Change is usually accompanied by high tension as well as some powerful advocate pressing for the change to be implemented. In most cases, the advocate of change is a higher-ranking manager or staff group, having determined that the change is necessary and beneficial.

Factors Counteracting Tendencies Toward Change

Resistance to change is a natural phenomenon. Even so, we can identify built-in restraints to unnecessary or thoughtless change both in the formal organizational system and in the human system of individual and group.

ORGANIZATIONAL RESTRAINTS   The very technological and organizational processes of the firm tend to counteract tendencies toward change. The requirement for stability and predictability ensure that carefully specified formal expectations are met in ways sanctioned by the formal organization. Changing these expectation means changing to some extent the basic nature of the organization, a difficult undertaking and justifiably so. Major technological or organizational changes may be initiated *only* after considerable study has been given the proposition and after the benefits to be derived are shown to be significantly more than the not inconsiderable costs and more inconveniences necessary to implement the change. Such natural restraints can also be overly restrictive, when a sound or needed change is dismissed solely because of the trouble required to implement it.

HUMAN RESTRAINTS   Whether change is actually beneficial or not, resistance is almost always encountered in one form or another. Only in very rare instances, in which the manager thoughtfully and carefully paves

---

[1]James H. Donelly, Jr., James L. Gibson, and John M. Ivancevich, *Fundamentals of Management: Functions, Behavior, Models* (Austin, Texas: Business Publications, Inc., 1971) p. 234.

[2]John B. Miner, *The Management Process: Theory, Research, and Practice* (New York: Macmillan, 1973) p. 270.

the way, does change occur without difficulty or hard feelings. In the extreme case, human resistance is so great that the attempt to initiate the change is met by extreme negative reactions such as wildcat strikes, increased turnover, low morale, and plummeting production.

Why should this occur? We can trace resistance to change through the three major subsystems in organizational behavior. We know, because of the systems nature of the organization, that a change in one unit or subsystem will eventually be felt throughout the entire organization or will manifest itself in interactions with other subsystems. The impact cannot be limited only to the unit or subsystem most directly related to the change.

The change and its consequences are perceived by the individual in his social context. Through the closure phenomenon, he will probably embellish the raw change with all manner of meaning and value. The change will then take on the meaning read into it, and those affected by the change will react to it in ways determined by their attitudes or sentiments toward the meaning they ascribe to it.

Change and Human Response

The response may take any form, depending on the meaning with which the change is imbued and the associated sentiments. Figure 17-1 illustrates the process. The change is announced, and sentiments are immediately aroused. Whether they are positive or negative is influenced by psychological factors and the social situation, coupled with a sense of history that the individual understands is relevant to the present situation. He may remember that the last time a major work-methods change was initiated, production quotas were raised shortly thereafter. His sense of history would certainly affect his perception of a similar change.

One psychological factor that affects response to change is reaction to stress. Some individuals are rather comfortable under conditions of anxiety and stress and seem to welcome the excitement of change. To others, change is extremely threatening to the status quo as they have finally been able to understand it. The norms and values of the informal group cannot be dismissed either. Technological changes can disrupt the current social situation, especially when teamwork is replaced by assembly-line production technology.

EVALUATING THE CHANGE   Given these additional factors that affect the change process, the individual must eventually evaluate the net impact of the proposed change on his personal situation and his ability to attain his own goals. The change may be seen in any of a range of possible ways. It may be seen as totally destructive, as anxiety-producing or threatening, as neutral (as having no net impact one way or the other), as relatively acceptable, or as having very positive and satisfying consequences.

RESPONSE TO THE CHANGE   With evaluation is associated a tendency to respond to the proposed change in an appropriate way. The appropri-

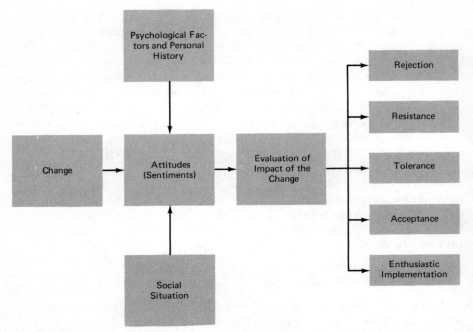

FIGURE 17-1   Response to change. Source: The left-hand side of the figure is adapted from Fritz J. Roethlisberger's "X" chart, *Management and Morale* (Cambridge, Mass.: Harvard University Press, 1941), p. 21.

ateness of the response is dictated by human and nonrational criteria, not necessarily by logic and argument. Response is an emotional matter, colored by sentiment and perhaps not understood even by the individual reacting to the change.

REJECTION   If the change is perceived as potentially destructive, outright rejection is called for. If the change is not withdrawn, walkouts and strikes will probably occur. Certainly increased turnover, alienation, drastic reductions in productivity, and severe job dissatisfactions will follow.

RESISTANCE   Threatening or anxiety-producing changes elicit either overt or covert resistance. Sabotage and other counterproductive behaviors can be expected, along with the more common work slowdowns and informal quotas associated with the work-restrictive informal organization. Most work-related or pay-related changes will probably be classified as threatening or anxiety-producing.

TOLERANCE   If the change is evaluated as being neutral in impact, perhaps having positive and negative factors that offset each other, the result will probably be tolerance of the change. No effective rationale can be seen for resisting the change, nor will there be positive benefits sufficiently strong to encourage acceptance. Workers and managers alike, in tolerating a change, will probably make no strenuous effort to ensure the success or the failure of the change.

ACCEPTANCE   The positive evaluations of a change proposal can bring forth—if properly implemented—support and active participation in seeking the success of the change. They differ primarily in degree and not in kind. The worker who sees positive benefits for himself in a change will, unless prevented by social or formal expectations, accept the change—at least on a trial basis. If the trial supports his evaluation, the change will be carried out. Only rarely, unfortunately, is a change seen as so over-whelmingly positive and beneficial that those affected by the change enthu-siastically embrace it.

MANAGERIAL ACTION   A single change may elicit a different response from different members. Attitudes and sentiments are intensely personal. The manager must focus his attention on the subjective and nonrational aspects of perception and interpretation if he is to implement the change effectively. In addition, by virtue of what he does—or fails to do—the manager can affect the response to a given change. If he actively seeks to reduce resistance to change and intelligently analyzes the forces for and against change, he can increase the probability that a positive response will be forthcoming. On the other hand, if he chooses to ignore personal, social, and attitudinal factors and blindly seeks to enforce the change, he will be increasing the probability of a negative response. The critical factor in the success of organizational change is then the manager and how he goes about managing change.

Resistance to Change

Some specific reasons for resistance to change may help show the extent to which resistance occurs, its diversity, and the importance of thorough analysis for effective change. Three major categories are used—work-related, individual, and social reasons—to link resistance to factors in each subsystem in organizational behavior.

1. Work-related factors.
    a. Fear of technological unemployment.
    b. Fear of changes in work conditions.
    c. Fear of demotion and reduced based wage.
    d. Fear of speedup and reduced incentive wages.
2. Individual factors.
    a. Resentment of the implied criticism that the present method employed is inadequate.
    b. Resentment of the implied criticism that present performance is inad-equate.
    c. Fear that the need for level or type of skill and ability will be reduced or eliminated.

  d. Fear that greater specialization will occur, resulting in boredom, monotony, and a decreased sense of personal worth.
  e. Inconvenience of having to unlearn present methods.
  f. Inconvenience of having to learn a new method.
  g. Fear that harder work will be required.
  h. Fear of uncertainty and the unknown.
3. Social factors.
  a. Dislike of having to make new social adjustments.
  b. Dislike of the necessity of breaking present social ties.
  c. Fear that the new social situation will bring reduction in satisfaction.
  d. Dislike of outside interference and control.
  e. Dislike of those initiating the change.
  f. Resentment of lack of participation in setting up the change.
  g. Perception that the change will benefit the formal organization more than the individual, the work group, or society.[3]

Analyzing the Change Situation

A constructive technique of analysing the change situation is Kurt Lewin's force field analysis, in which the forces operating for and against the change are identified and specified. If the forces operating for change are met with resisting forces of equal magnitude, equilibrium—no change in the status quo—occurs.

We can think of the present situation, which we wish to change, as being represented by a line on which are acting factors for and factors against the change. In a situation in equilibrium, the forces for ("driving") and those against ("resisting") change must be just equal to each other in strength, and the line will remain stationary. If the driving forces were more powerful than the resisting forces, then the situation cannot be in equilibrium or be stable.

With the help of Figure 17-2(a) we can see how such a situation might be represented. The length of each arrow is proportional to its force or magnitude. In equilibrium the total strength of the driving (D arrows) forces is just equal to the sum of the resisting (R) forces. The scale at the bottom of the figure, from −5 to +5, may be used to represent the comparative benefits of different situations.

The situation is now anchored at a neutral position, and the desired situation (represented by the dotted line) is seen as being relatively more beneficial. The problem then becomes finding a way of moving from the present situation to the desired situation. We can adopt the approach of adding more driving forces to move the situation, or the strategy of *removing* resisting forces and thus allowing current driving forces to move the situation to that desired. These two alternatives are illustrated in the other portions of the figure.

---

[3]Adapted from Keith Davis, *Human Behavior at Work: Human Relations and Organizational Behavior*, 4th Ed. (New York: McGraw-Hill, 1972), pp. 163–64.

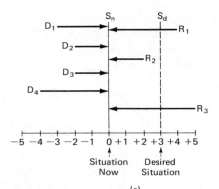

(a)
Current and Desired Situations,
with Present Forces in Equilibrium

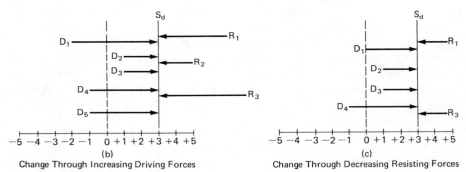

(b)
Change Through Increasing Driving Forces

(c)
Change Through Decreasing Resisting Forces

FIGURE 17-2   Force-field change analysis.

In Figure 17-2(b), change occurs through the adding of other driving factors to the situation, as well as by an increase in the force of present factors. Figure 17-2(c) shows that decreasing the resisting forces can also result in achieving the desired situation, if we completely remove some resisting forces and decrease the magnitude of others.[4]

A danger exists if the factors for change are simply increased, because resisting forces are not diminished. Under increased pressure, resistance can acquire additional force, eventually erupting with explosive results. This is the so-called *coiled-spring effect,* representing as it does the parallel of adding more and more pressure to squeeze a coiled spring. The spring pushes back with greater force as more force is added. Increased levels of force are required to *maintain* the spring in its new configuration.

[4]Note that the (b) and (c) figures are intended to represent the situation immediately *after* the forces have been modified. As they are shown, the situations are unstable and not in equilibrium. The magnitudes of the driving and resisting forces are not equal. Should this imbalance continue, the situations would continue to change. What generally happens is that the effectiveness of increasing the driving forces (or of removing the resisting forces) is gradually diminished until the force field once again attains equilibrium.

One example of force field analysis in action is a situation that occurred during World War II. Female factory workers objected to wearing the required safety glasses. Despite the company's extensive efforts and potential punishment for noncompliance, the women would not wear the safety glasses with any consistency. Force field analysis was employed to determine how to get from the present situation (female factory workers' refusal to wear safety glasses) to the desired situation (female factory workers' wearing safety glasses). Driving forces for the change were summarized as being the necessity to protect one's eyes, desire to cooperate with the company, and willingness to follow the rules. A little leg work revealed that resisting forces were composed of the women's feeling that the glasses were too heavy, that the glasses were unattractive, and that the rule hindered the women's ability to determine their own activities.

The immediate respone of many managers facing such a situation would be to add more driving forces, such as sending home without pay workers who failed to wear the safety glasses, firing them, imposing fines for noncompliance, putting up safety posters, or holding safety training programs. Rather than adding forces to the driving side of the situation, it was decided to try to remove or reduce the *resisting* forces. The company agreed to substitute lighter and more comfortable frames for the glasses, at the cost of about five cents more per frame. Next, each woman was encouraged to decorate her glasses as she wished, and a contest was held for the most attractive glasses. Each woman was then able to express herself in a unique way and resistance was effectively removed.[5]

Force field analysis can be applied to almost any change situation, although it does require some ingenuity and thought. The usefulness of the analytical technique derives from the fact that it encourages the manager to examine the entire situation and to take constructive actions to solve problems, the true nature of which may not be readily apparent. To illustrate the wide range of situations in which force field analysis may be used, consider the production level of work teams in factory settings. Production levels, as we have seen, generally tend to remain relatively constant. Using the insights developed from force field analysis, we may infer that production remains at a given level because forces acting to increase production are just balanced by forces tending to decrease production. Driving forces might consist of pressures from supervisors for higher production, higher salary because of an individual incentive system, or interteam competition. On the other hand, restraining forces might be unwillingness to work harder, displeasure with poor supervision, or inadequate maintenance of machinery.[6]

Another situation might occur in a group to which you belong. Perhaps a member does not contribute, remaining silent and uncommunicative. Forces to increase his contribution might consist of pressures from the other

[5]Kurt Lewin, "Frontiers in Group Dynamics," *Human Relations,* **1:**5–42 (1947).

[6]David A. Kolb, Irwin M. Rubin, and James M. McIntyre, *Organizational Psychology: An Experiential Approach* (Englewood Cliffs, N.J.: Prentice-Hall, 1971) pp. 306, 307.

group members, rewards or recognition given for amount of participation, and projects in which he is interested or topics in which he is knowledgeable. Factors tending to reduce his participation might be the wish to avoid hurting the feelings of other members, concern about retaliation for intruding on another's area, or fear of exposing himself to criticism or ridicule.[7] Constructively changing either of these situations is aided by the insights developed through force field analysis.

Conflict

One of the factors that may lead to resistance to change is a lack of similarity between the needs and goals of the formal organization and those of its members. The formal organization may, by inducing changes in work methods or organization, be more nearly able to be productive and efficient. Individual and social groups may resist such changes because their abilities to satisfy their human and social needs may be lessened as a result. We have seen that the economic benefits and productive efficiency theoretically possible have not attained because of other, unintended results of specialization of labor: the demands of specialization for routine and predictability conflict with human needs for exercising judgment and fulfilling recognition and esteem needs. Argyris contended that there is a basic incompatibility or built-in conflict between the goals of the formal organization and the psychological development of the individual member.

The notion of conflict covers a wide variety of forms, from warfare to industrial strikes to competition to simple dislike. In a broad sense, conflict occurs whenever the attainment of a goal is hindered. Most forms of observable conflict occur when two or more parties are each trying to attain mutually exclusive goals. The attainment of a goal by the first party precludes the second party's reaching its goal. Simpler forms are those that occur within a single individual.

Internal Conflict Forms

Two conflict forms, frustration and goal conflict, are common even though their occurrence is typically less than dramatic. They do affect the individual in his relationship with his social and organizational environments and so are considered here for the additional light they shed on the varieties and intensities of conflict.

Frustration

The simplest form of conflict, frustration, occurs when one's ability to attain a goal is hampered by the imposition of a barrier. An employee may

[7]Ibid, p. 307.

strongly desire to perform in a superior fashion yet (perhaps because his abilities are not sufficient) his performance evaluations are consistently in the "average" range. The motivated individual then "normally tries to circumvent, remove, or otherwise master"[8] the inadequacy. He may take night courses at the local university, insist on seniority-based privileges, take his work home or come to work on weekends, and so on. If any of these behaviors are not sufficient, then frustration results and less productive behaviors may consequently be adopted:

1. "The barrier itself may be attacked, physically or symbolically."[9] Frustration is transformed into aggression and these impulses may be taken out either on the appraisal system or on the appraising supervisor. The form of the aggression may range from tearing up the appraisal sheet to belittling the supervisor behind his back. One extreme example of this reaction to frustration was the shooting of assembly-line supervisors by a laid-off auto assembler in Detroit.

2. "When the actual barrier is physically, psychologically, or socially invulnerable to attack, aggression may be displaced to an innocent but more vulnerable bystander ('displaced aggression')."[10] This behavior is even less realistically adaptive and certainly does nothing to allow adjustment or resolution to the conflict. One may get some relief temporarily by kicking the cat or losing his temper at the wife or children, yet such behavior can hardly be considered effective.

3. "Under conditions of frustration, behavior may revert to earlier, less adaptive modes; and it may show general deterioration, even in areas unrelated to the frustrating event."[11] The frustrated employee may resort to sulking and sabotage or to lowering the quality of his work in retaliation. Naturally these reactions would tend to be counterproductive because they would hardly result in higher performance appraisals.

4. "Frustration, especially when produced by or coupled with punishment, may produce extremely rigid and nonadaptive behavior, which may endure even when the barrier is removed to make the goal directly accessible."[12] The person may fixate, that is, continue his unproductive behaviors while ignoring their lack of effectiveness.

5. "Sometimes prolonged or intense frustration produces flight rather than further fight for the goal. When survival is not at stake—and sometimes even then—people may give up and leave the situation, physically or psychologically."[13] Apathy and alienation may occur in situations of prolonged or intense frustration. The individual striving for superior perfor-

[8]Bernard Berelson and Gary A. Steiner, *Human Behavior: An Inventory of Scientific Findings* (New York: Harcourt, Brace & World, 1964), p. 267.
[9]Ibid.
[10]Ibid.
[11]Ibid, p. 270.
[12]Ibid.
[13]Ibid, p. 271.

mance may simply give up his goal, being content merely to perform at a satisfactory level. Alternatively, he may refuse to acknowledge his inadequacy, quitting to find a job in which he can be successful.

Goal Conflict

Another form of conflict, more complex than frustration, is goal conflict, in which the attainment of one goal excludes the possibility of attaining another. Three major forms of goal conflict may be distinguished:

1. *Approach–approach conflict.* The individual is caught between trying to decide upon one or another of two attractive goals, which are mutually exclusive.
2. *Approach–avoidance conflict.* The individual has both positive and negative feelings about trying to attain a goal, because the goal possesses both attractive and repulsive characteristics.
3. *Avoidance–avoidance conflict.* The individual must choose between two mutually exclusive goals, each of which possesses unattractive qualities.

APPROACH–APPROACH   Approach-approach conflicts hardly seem like conflicts are all, because whichever choice the individual makes he will attain a positively valued outcome. The problem comes in when the valences or desirabilities of the choices are roughly equal. Who has not experienced such a conflict in a restaurant in trying to choose between lobster and steak? Such a decision is rather difficult to make, and takes much longer to make than in the other types of conflicts. Certainly after the decision has been made, cognitive dissonance will ensure that (whichever choice was made) the choice was the *right* one!

APPROACH–AVOIDANCE   Approach-avoidance conflicts embody different types of delays in arriving at a decision. The goal has both positive and negative qualities. Organizational goals often exhibit this set of characteristics. Superior performance most likely will result in a great deal of organizational rewards (desirable) yet the time and effort required to achieve that goal mean that time must be taken away from the family and other outside pursuits (undesirable). Some research studies have shown that:

When goals are at once satisfying and threatening, pleasant and painful, attractive and anxiety-arousing, people's behavior vacillates at a point near but not too near the goal: at a distance the tendency to approach predominates, near the goal the tendency to avoid is greater. The result is a stable or self-maintaining conflict that tends to keep the organism at the point where the two tendencies cross.[14]

Luthans pointed out the very real implications of approach–avoidance conflict within the organizational setting:

[14]Ibid., p. 272.

In general . . . it is safe to assume that the positive aspects of a given organizational goal are stronger and more salient at a distance (in time and/or space) than are the negative aspects. On the other hand, as a person gets nearer to the goal, the negative aspects become more pronounced and at some point he may hesitate or cease to progress further. For example, managers engaged in long-range planning typically are very confident of a goal (plan) they have developed for the future. Yet, as the time gets nearer to commit resources and implement the plan, the negative consequences seem to appear much greater than they did in the developing stage. The manager or managers involved may reach the point where approach equals avoidance. The result is a great deal of internal conflict which may cause indecision, ulcers, or even neurosis.[15]

AVOIDANCE–AVOIDANCE   Unless other choices are available, avoidance–avoidance conflicts have a tendency to stay unresolved. We pointed out just above that the closer one gets to a decision, the more the negative aspects of the choice create a tendency to *avoid* that choice. If the individual does make a decision toward one of the avoidance–avoidance choices, the closer he gets to implementing that decision the more likely he is to be repelled by the negative characteristics of the choice, retreating toward the other decision. Ultimately he can be seen to bounce back and forth, from dilemma to dilemma.

Such a situation is stressful and anxiety-arousing because of the perceived inability to escape either of two painful options. Realistically most organizational members do have a third alternative, that of leaving the organization should they find themselves in avoidance–avoidance conflict. Yet even this may lead to *another* avoidance–avoidance situation. The choice then shifts to starting the anxiety-producing search for another job (with no guarantee that it will prove better than the present one) versus the other painful decision to remain in the current unpleasant situation.

The use of negative incentives also has conflict implications for management. Berelson and Steiner concluded that using punishment as an incentive to get another to perform something disagreeable or threatening is effective only to the extent that the individual cannot leave the situation. "When intense fear attaches to all alternatives and physical or psychological distance is small, such conflicts produce acute anxiety; ultimately, even when the physical barriers are impenetrable, people may escape psychologically. In the extreme case there may be complete loss of contact with reality, as in some forms of psychosis."[16]

These general reactions to internal conflicts by the individual may be generalized to many other situation, of course. We can see that they represent conflict situations for the individual and the ways in which he can react. More dramatic and perhaps more traumatic conflicts are readily observed in situations in which two or more parties are competing for scarce resources.

[15]Fred Luthans, *Organizational Behavior, A Modern Behavioral Approach to Management* (New York: McGraw-Hill, 1973), pp. 468, 469.
[16]Berelson and Steiner, p. 276.

Organizational Conflict

Individual conflicts are quite common. The organizational context within which they occur and that create special types of conflict should also be considered. These we may term *organizational conflicts* because they are either institutionalized (a direct result of formal organization and technological processes) or emergent (emerging informally within the formal organizational context as a result of individual and social goals). Because the organization is a goal-directed system composed of interdependent goal-seeking subsystems, it is probably inevitable that subsystems or individuals within the organization will experience conflict. Competition for scarce resources or goals is the substance of organizational conflict.

Institutionalized Conflict

Division of labor and organizational form often go hand in hand with productive efficiency. Such divisions and separations of individuals, work responsibility, and goal structure can create some severe conflict situations. The existence of several different departments or divisions implies that their goals are distinct and separate from each other and that the contributions of each unit may be separately measured, established, and rewarded. To the extent that the work of each unit is truly independent—is affected in no way by the work of the other units—this concept is a valid one. Yet because of the systemic nature of the organization such independence is relatively rare. Litterer told of one such conflict situation:

Not long ago a major airline was faced with considerable conflict between two of its managers at a western city. Upon investigation it was found that the Sales Manager, in order to increase his sales volume, wanted to provide certain services for the customers. These, however, would be provided by the employees and from the budgets of the Ramp and Services Manager. There was considerable effort to decentralize and promote as much autonomy for individual managers as possible and handsome bonus systems were set up on certain standards of individual managerial performance. If the Sales Manager could increase his sales, he would have many advantages. Conversely, if the Ramp Services Manager could keep his costs down he too would have many rewards coming to him. Hence the problem, and the conflict; the Sales Manager could not get his bonus unless the Ramp Services Manager were to forego some of his own. This condition, although not always clearly recognized, exists in many organizations where reward systems are based upon individual performances which are not independent but are very much interdependent.[17]

ORGANIZATIONAL SANCTIONS   Competition for organizational rewards can also create conflict between members of the same department, just as competition for budget allocations can create conflict between the

---

[17]Joseph A. Litterer, "Conflict in Organization: A Re-examination," *Academy of Management Journal* (September 1966), p. 181.

heads of two units as they compete for scarce resources. Competition can be fostered through the reward of individual performance. Once again, such competition requires that the work of the members be independent in all ways. For instance, one large auto dealership systematically fires the bottom two or three salesmen every month. In this situation, in which one's job depends on maximizing individual performance, very little in the way of personal relationships with one's competitors is allowed, and very few training tips and learning experiences (from older and more experienced salesmen to novices) will occur, nor will assistance in closing a sale. These are termed *win–lose* situations: for one to "win" or reach his goal, another must necessarily "lose" or fail to meet *his* goal.

HIERARCHY-BASED INCOMPATABILITIES   Other conflicts may occur as a direct result of the creation of a hierarchy. We have pointed out that specialization occurs as the hierarchy is descended, and broader and more long-range responsibilities are found near the top of the hierarchy. This implies that a foreman will have rather different perspectives and goals than the president of the company. The president may be deeply committed to long-term development and consideration of organizational members, perhaps to the extent of sacrificing some profit in order to create a humane and satisfying work environment. A supervisor, on the other hand, is evaluated by his superior in terms of work schedules and production quotas and will probably use whatever means are at hand to reach his goals, even if the president's goals are short-changed.

FUNCTIONAL CONFLICTS   Interdepartmental conflict similarly arises from the organizational framework. When business functions are divided up into departments, many benefits accrue. At the same time, there are many differences that are institutionalized and formalized between these groups. The manufacturing division will tend to have a short time perspective and will seek to maximize its own goals of long production runs and standardized products in order to meet unit cost goals. Marketing personnel will have their own goals to strive for, which are diametrically opposed to those of manufacturing. Marketing will tend to have a relatively longer time perspective, will usually evaluate product and service from the viewpoint of the customer, and will endeavor to customize and provide many options to suit each individual customer. Conflicts between the two departments are ready-made whenever they must meet to resolve problems or to conduct yearly planning sessions.

In similar fashion research groups and product development groups differ quite drastically in their own goals and perspectives. Research may insist that another three to five years are needed to establish the characteristics of a new polymer, whereas product development insists that it merely meet certain minimum standards in order to get the product on the market as soon as possible.

LINE AND STAFF   Line and staff personnel conflict as a result of organizational form. Staff and other advisory or support groups are responsible for measuring, monitoring, analyzing, and projecting the work and results of the organization. Line management often cannot take the time to analyze problem situations, being concerned with reaching a "workable" solution as quickly as possible in order to avoid interruptions in producing the output of the organization. Line perceives that staff personnel are abstract, impractical, overeducated, inexperienced, and too young. Staff sees line personnel as being unimaginative, dull, narrow in mind and scope, and inflexible. When a staff adviser attempts to sell his solution to a line manager, these mutual perspectives can get in the way of reaching a common solution.

The criteria for goal attainment similarly contrast in the line and the staff groups. Staff personnel tend to view themselves as members of a profession and look to their professional peers for approval and evaluation. Line managers are evaluated for their efforts by line superiors and consequently are results-oriented. Should the line manager adopt a staff solution that proves to be unworkable, *his* is likely to be the head to fall.

Emergent Conflict

Conflicts may also be derived from uniquely personal and social causes, even though they occur within the context of the organized setting. They may encompass informal as well as nonformal behaviors that result in conflict.

FORMAL AND INFORMAL ORGANIZATIONAL CONFLICT   One such major conflict is the conflict between the formal and the informal organization. Once again, the matter of goal incompatibility rears its head. The informal organization, as a group, has specified goals around which the group forms and that are protected by its norms and values. Informal expectations which support group goals may differ quite drastically from formal expectations, which are important to attaining formal economic objectives.

The illustration of work behavior may be used briefly to show goal incompatibility and the conflict that arises. Productive effort is expected from organizational members in return for salary and other benefits. The sum total of the work contributes to producing the firm's output. The informal organization, to which the individual may belong, has other goals. A common value or standard for behavior is determining an acceptable and rather standardized level of output or effort of group members. A range of acceptable behaviors may be available, with unacceptable behavior being defined as producing too much more (or too much less) than is produced by group members. Work restriction can satisfy the group goals of demonstrating belongingness or solidarity, conserving energy for leisure activities, extending the total amount of work available over longer periods of time, and so on. Such goals interfere with the attainment of the firm's economic objectives. Yet they do coexist.

STATUS   Status conflicts, as we pointed out in the last chapter, can also create difficulties, especially when incongruency and discrepancy exist. The threatened deprivation of one's status can be a powerful motivator to action. Because numerous status scales are in action at any particular time, most people are quick to defend and announce their status position relative to another. Litterer points out that status problems in industry have arisen because of the impact of changes in technology.[18] Before the recent onslaught of accelerated technological and social change, men had entered companies and slowly risen as they proved themselves. To them, status may be determined by seniority and age, the symbols of the respect due them. Highly qualified and trained young specialists may supersede these senior members, moving into higher-level positions because of their more current expertise. Working for another who both is younger and has less seniority results in status conflicts for the older subordinates.

Another status incongruency occurs as a result of giving orders. He who gives orders to another—initiates action for another—is attributed higher status than those who are obligated to receive and carry out the orders or to do the work that has been initiated for them. A ready example of such a status incongruency may be observed in the line–staff relationship, wherein staff advisers suggest or initiate plans that the line managers are encouraged to implement. Line management may see this as threatened status deprivation, even though the suggested change or plan may have considerable merit.

POLITICS   Another conflict factor, and one that is relatively little understood or studied, is the political process within the organization. Striving to get ahead, even at the expense of others, by whatever means necessary is a characteristic ascribed to company politics. The political maneuverings of the aspirants are predicated by the fact that scarce resources or rewards are available, and many are attempting to reach them. For many, the striving is mutually exclusive—if another gets the promotion that means that he cannot. A win–lose situation is defined by the organizational reward system. The behaviors that occur are most definitely not those prescribed in the company manual, yet they may be widely observed. Competition and conflict are derived from the organizational reward system, yet the means to goal attainment may be largely devoted to informal or nonformal activities.

Managing Conflict

Conflict is a troublesome phenomenon and can have disruptive and counterproductive results. But not *all* conflicts are harmful and thus to be avoided. The very structure of the organization itself creates conflicts. The process by which conflicts are resolved can often result in new and unique

[18]Ibid., pp. 182, 183.

solutions being adopted that meet the criteria of both parties in question, yet create higher levels of performance—a positive attribute as far as the organization is concerned. From our previous discussion of the nature of change, we must observe that any change brings with it inherent conflicts. Yet if we were to adopt the short-sighted view that conflict is wholly negative and to be avoided, then no change would ever be presented or implemented.

A more realistic way of viewing conflict is that conflict cannot be avoided. It is inevitable and may be the result of many different factors. A performance evaluation system, the shape and design of the organization structure, even the shape of the building or furnishings in an office can create conflict. Change is also inevitable, and without conflict change cannot occur. The problem for the manager of organizational behavior is to see that conflict is constructively used as a tool in reaching new, creative, and better organizational processes and outputs. He must ensure that conflicts do not become ends in themselves. Conflict cannot be abolished—nor should the attempt be made—because a certain amount of conflict simply means that organizational members at all levels must be responsive to change and attempt to resolve creatively whatever barriers exist in individual and group goal attainment.[19]

Resolving Conflicts

Robbins presented a number of frequently used methods by which conflicts are resolved. They include problem solving, superordinate goals, expansion of resources, avoidance, smoothing, compromise, authoritative command, altering the human variable, and altering the structural variable.[20]

PROBLEM SOLVING   The first two conflict-resolution techniques, problem solving and superordinate goals, are considered to be the most generally positive techniques available, because they emphasize the attaining of the common interests of both conflicting parties. In mutual problem-solving the parties in conflict must come together with the responsibility of solving the mutual problem that faces them rather than merely finding a way to accommodate their different perspectives. Questions of who is right and who is wrong, who wins and who loses are not allowed, but sharing and communicating are required in order to find areas of common interest. This process causes the doubts and misunderstandings that underlie the conflict to become more obvious to the parties, so that they may more effectively deal with them.

Problem-solving approaches to resolving conflict are most effectively

[19]Cf. Joe Kelly, "Make Conflict Work for You," *Harvard Business Review* (July–August 1970), p. 104.

[20]Stephen P. Robbins, *Managing Organizational Conflict: A Nontraditional Approach* (Englewood Cliffs, N.J.: Prentice-Hall, 1974), pp. 59–77. The following discussion is based on his work.

applied when there are merely misunderstandings or conflicts developed from misunderstandings. Problem solving then lends itself well to a thorough analysis of the problem, finding suitable definitions of terms, and mutual understanding of the other's ideas. The technique requires great patience in order to reduce or resolve conflicts that have existed for a long time.

A major weakness in the problem-solving approach is that it may not be effectively used in conflicts that stem from value systems that differ and that are one of the major sources of conflict. If value systems are incompatible (as they often are), forced problem-solving merely increases the level of conflict by letting each party more clearly understand the depth to which they *disagree*.

SUPERORDINATE GOALS   Although a superordinate goal is similar in nature to a goal common to several parties, it differs in that it is highly appealing and compelling, yet beyond the reach of the resources of any single group by itself. Mutual dependence of two or more groups is required in order to reach the superordinate goal. It is also a goal that is desired by each of the conflicting parties and that has a high degree of value. Superordinate goals also are those that take precedence over other goals that may separate the conflicting parties. Churchill used the threat of invasion by Germany as a superordinate goal to heal the rifts between conflicting groups in the British government. The existence and well-being of the Commonwealth took precedence over the relatively minor differences between the groups, and they were able to reduce their conflicts by the necessity of working together in achieving the mutually desirable overall goal.

EXPANSION OF RESOURCES   Conflict is often the result of scarcity of resources. When this situation exists, one party may be able to attain its goals only by securing relatively larger amounts of resources, which must be taken away from another group. The usefulness of this technique may be illustrated in a notion attributed to Napoleon. He suggested that giving a promotion is a harrowing experience because in promoting one of a hundred, no matter whom you choose, there will be ninety-nine unhappy soldiers and one ungrateful one. In the same vein, a set pool of money for raises to be distributed among departmental members simply means that one member's raise must come at the expense of another's, creating conflict between departmental members.

The technique of expansion of resources, although limited to appropriate situations, may be illustrated by the experience of the Ford Motor Company in 1969. After Semon Knudsen left the presidency of Ford, three vice-presidents vied for the position. Henry Ford II was required to decide the next president, but he recognized that giving but one of the candidates the position would create one winner and two losers. Conflict existed because of the three aspirants' seeking to secure a scarce resource—the presidency. The conflict was resolved by the creation of an office of the president, which resulted in the position's being expanded, and each of three vice-presidents was "promoted" to the presidency over separate but equal areas of the entire company. Three winners (rather than only one) resulted. Ford expanded the resource and then allowed each of the competing parties to "win."[21]

AVOIDANCE   If a possibility of conflict exists, certainly one way to eliminate conflict is through avoiding the conflict entirely. The conflict is not effectively resolved, nor is the conflict permanently eliminated, but under some conditions avoidance is still a viable alternative.

The party or parties to conflict may either withdraw from the conflict or conceal the incompatibility. The first of these, withdrawal, may be observed when the field of conflict is left by one or more parties. As a result, another party may "win" by being in sole possession of the goal in dispute. Alternatively, the goal may be redefined through *mutual* withdrawal from the field and the redefinition of other and nonoverlapping goal priorities. People who cannot get along together generally find this to be an acceptable way of eliminating conflict, merely avoiding the presence of each other.

Concealing the incompatibility is another form of avoidance and may be necessary when withdrawal or mutual evasion is not possible. Conflict may be eliminated by the withholding of the information that the parties are in conflict because of goal incompatibilities. Many a husband has learned to suppress certain information or beliefs, knowing full well that should they be aired his wife's ire will be aroused. No conflict has been effectively resolved, yet it has been avoided.

SMOOTHING   The process of playing down the differences between individuals or groups and highlighting their common interests is called *smoothing*. Just as in the avoidance technique of concealing or suppression, differences between conflicting parties are withheld, but accenting similarities if added to the process. Finding and emphasizing similarities between conflicting parties, while suppressing differences, can eventually lead the parties to realize that the two are not as far apart as was first believed. With shared viewpoints on some issue, the ability to work together toward a commonly held goal must be facilitated. We must hasten to recognize, however, that smoothing does not completely resolve conflicts. Differences between conflicting parties are not specifically confronted and remain under the surface. The chances are that they will surface sooner or later. It is at best a temporary solution, for the short run.

COMPROMISE   Compromising is a well-accepted method of resolving conflict, yielding neither a definitive loser nor a distinct winner. A decision does result, even though it may not be the "perfect" one for either of the parties. Compromise may be effectively used when the goal object may be divided up in some way among the competing groups. In cases in which this is not possible, one group may yield to the other something of value in exchange for a concession of value. Both parties then give some-

[21]Cited in Robbins, p. 68.

thing up. Such a technique is often found in situations in which overt or physical conflict is not acceptable and in which the conflict must be resolved in some way. Offers and counteroffers are made in the compromise process between the parties. Each may successively give up more of its demands (as in labor–management negotiations) in the attempt to get the other party to modify its position toward an agreement relatively agreeable to both sides.

In a compromise situation the outcome will primarily depend on the relative strength of the parties. In situations in which one of the bargainers is much stronger than the other, little actual compromising may occur, and one side dictates to the other. In all but this one-sided "compromise," we must recognize that *neither* compromiser may be happy with the final position taken. After all, each has had to give up a portion of his ability to attain his own goals in favor of reaching a mutually agreeable decision. Because of this, the compromise technique of conflict resolution is usually only temporary, and the conflict that initiated the compromise situation will probably recur.

AUTHORITATIVE COMMAND   Conflicts may effectively be resolved through the hierarchy. If resolution cannot be attained by two organizational members, they may take the issue to a common superior who resolves the conflict by making a decision. Such judgment is usually accepted by organizational members because of the recognized superior authority of the higher-ranking individual. The decision may not necessarily bring *agreement*, but it will usually be accepted. Authoritative command does not and cannot solve the source of the conflict. It only resolves the conflict that results.

ALTERING THE HUMAN VARIABLE   Another way of resolving conflict is to focus on the behavior of the individuals involved. Conflict is usually the result of individual perception, and consequently changing the human portion of the conflict equation may yield substantial results in alleviating the source of the conflict, in addition to resolving the apparent conflict itself. Attitudes and beliefs may be changed through educational efforts, such as in the training program used by many industrial firms to teach management personnel new insights into human relations. More recently, T-group or sensitivity training has allowed the exploration and changing of ideas, beliefs, and attitudes. Interpersonal and intergroup conflict may be reduced through the shared knowledge of how another feels and why he behaves in the way he does.[22]

ALTERING STRUCTURAL VARIABLES   The formal organization structure itself may be altered in order to reduce conflict. Members of conflicting groups may be transferred or exchanged, positions may be created to serve as "go-betweens" between conflicting groups, an appeal system may be developed to eliminate arbitrary use of power, and the organization's

---

[22]David R. Hampton, Charles E. Summer, and Ross A. Webber, *Organizational Behavior and the Practice of Management*, Rev. Ed. (Glenview, Ill.: Scott, Foresman, 1973), p. 768.

boundaries may be redefined to encompass the source of an external conflict.

If a relatively few organizational members are seen as sources of conflict, one ready alternative is to remove them from the situation, thus reducing existing tensions. In other situations, conflict results because members of different units have insufficient contact with each other and cannot understand the others' perspectives. When this occurs, individuals may be transferred from one unit to the other on a temporary basis, to broaden their perspectives and to encourage interunit cooperation and understanding. If manufacturing finds that the research and development department, because of goal incompatibility, is furnishing product development designs unsuitable to the firm's technology or cost structure, a ready way to reduce the conflict between the two groups is by having R & D incorporated within the manufacturing unit. The unit would then be exposed to the criteria and evaluations of manufacturing, and attitudes and beliefs would necessarily be forced to change, given the new perspectives and reward structures. Without this organizational restructuring, research and development may well continue to create conflict because manufacturing cannot influence their activities.

Interactions required by the formal work structure or organizational structure may result in conflicts, and the formal work requirements may be adapted to eliminate the conflict. An executive need not advertise for, interview, test, and select a new assistant, all of which activities require substantial time investment away from his normal duties. Rather, the personnel department takes on these duties as part of their normal routine. Goal incompatibility is resolved by alteration of structure and the definition of the total process involved which creates a specialized unit to handle the problem.

Management's Role in Conflict Resolution

One might form the impression, after examining the major conflict resolution techniques discussed above, that conflicts are largely determined by—and must be resolved by—the people or parties involved in the conflict. Further, one might assume that only in rare instances ("authoritative command") may the manager intervene in the conflict situation. Such is not the case at all. Conflict resolution is not the same thing as conflict *solution*. One may avoid conflict and still meet the terms of resolving the conflict for himself. Even further, often conflicting parties may not formally nor consciously recognize that they are actually in conflict, nor even *why* they experience so much difficulty in working together or coming to a mutual understanding. Perhaps even more damaging is the tendency to have attempts at domination take precedence over the true conflict issues.

One of the difficulties experienced by the manager in performing his role is the effective management of conflict. Conflict that gets out of hand and then produces negative or counterproductive results diminishes the manager's ability to facilitate both organizational and human goal attainment. His is the difficult task of diagnosing a conflict situation as having occurred or as currently occurring, finding the root or source of the conflict, structuring alternative techniques by which the conflict may be resolved (preferably by the parties experiencing the conflict), and following up to ensure that the conflict has truly been resolved and its source abolished through the resolution.

Once again, the role of the manager may be quite similar to that of the tightrope walker; he cannot go too far either way, completely eliminating or incompletely resolving the conflict. An organization without some level of conflict stagnates and furnishes no challenge to its members. On the other hand, a chaotic, ambiguous, and frustrating environment creates too many anxieties for the individual to handle and simultaneously to perform his duties. The manager must see that whatever conflicts do exist are *productive* conflicts and that nonproductive conflicts are eliminated through remedial actions.

Yet another pitfall ready to entrap the unwary manager is the tendency to use the expeditious resolution technique rather than the long-term but more effective technique. An authoritarian manager may be disposed to use the "authoritative command" technique when he recognizes conflict, imposing his decision on the conflicting parties. He may never recognize that the conflict has not been resolved and that just the immediate result of the conflict has been decided—by him. The management of conflict demands a steady hand at the helm and a watchful eye, as well as a quick hand on the rudder. Conflict cannot—and should not be—completely prevented from happening, and it is the manager's job to see that the results of conflict contribute positively to the goal attainment of organization and organizational members alike.

Managing Change

Just as the manager cannot allow conflict to run rampant through the organization, so change and its implementation must be managed. We have pointed out several times that change encompasses conflicts for the individual, the group, and the organization. The conflicts that tend to encourage resistance to change must be resolved through appropriate techniques. Without this attention to reducing the forces that will restrain the effectiveness of the change, the manager is relying on random and unreliable fates to see that the desired change comes about. The effective manager intervenes in the process and plans ahead to presolve potential problems and constructively eliminate those elements that will tend to reduce the effectiveness of the planned change.

Understanding the nature of conflict situations and the forces that tend to encourage resistance to change, the effective manager can introduce a change situation in a manner calculated to reach his design objectives and satisfy the needs of those most directly affected by the change.

Implementing a change requires that the manager follow five basic steps to secure maximum possible effectiveness. These are as follows:

1. Is the change necessary? The manager must evaluate the benefits as well as the costs involved in making the change. He cannot afford to make changes in areas where the returns are minimal, while ignoring other problem areas of greater consequence.

2. Is the proposed change the correct one? In almost all situations there are alternative changes, any one of which will accomplish the desired result. Choosing one of these requires that the manager know the full and true underlying nature of the problem that the change is intended to correct. Solving symptoms does not remove the problem and will probably create other problems.

3. The impact of the change must be evaluated. Preferably this impact—on the problem itself, the people affected, the social system, and the formal organization—must be predicted and evaluated *before* the change is implemented. Only in this way will resisting forces be forecast, so that they may be reduced or eliminated. A further benefit is that the manager can conceptually trace through the effectiveness with which the proposed change actually solves the problem at hand.

4. How may acceptance of the change be secured? Those most directly affected by the change hold the key to the success of the change. Unless their anxieties are eliminated and their cooperation obtained, even a sound change has very little chance of reaching its full degree of effectiveness.

5. What follow-up is necessary? After the change has been implemented, the manager must obtain information about how well the change actually has solved the problem and the degree to which it is effective. Problems that occur as a result of the change will come to his attention in this stage, too, to be reduced.

How may these steps be most effectively taken? There are four major touchstones that must be built into any effective change program. They are participation, communication, empathy, and reduction of anxiety.

Participation

Often the manager is tempted to decide unilaterally that a problem exists, that he knows what the problem is, and that he has the solution. Once he has gone through these steps, his next logical step is to inform his subordinates of the changes that will take place in their activities and behaviors. Such an approach has a number of inherent weaknesses, because the manager may not have all the necessary information. The nature, extent, and complexity of the change will typically be known by those people who deal with the problem situation on a day-to-day basis, his subordinates. Especially in technical matters, their analysis and proposals for solution may be substantially more effective than those of the manager. After all, they may know what will work and what won't. Subordinates, at whatever level, constitute an important source of information for the manager in identifying and implementing a change.

Participation also has another major benefit, that of reducing resistance to change. Discussing the problem and its effects can help the people affected to understand why a change is necessary and may secure their willingness to try something new. Especially when leaders of the informal organization see the necessity for change, the social system can be used to encourage support for the change and reduce resistance. Full participation means that the manager must allow his subordinates to participate in the decision-making process itself and not merely in the discussion phases. Almost all people will more enthusiastically embrace their own ideas (or ideas that they had a major part in formulating) than decisions made by someone else and in isolation.

Communication

Full participation similarly requires open communication channels and two-way communication between all parties affected by the problem area and the proposed change. The wise manager keeps all parties informed of every stage in the change process. Open communication allows him to verify that the change is necessary and that the proposed change is the change that will correct the situation. He can also read between the lines, observing the forms of complaint and anxiety, and thereby deducing what major forms of resistance to change will be brought to bear. He may then take steps to eliminate them by communicating openly and fully about the nature of the change and the impact it will have upon those affected. His subordinates will also be able to secure additional information important to themselves through the open channels.

Empathy

Empathy may be defined as the ability to put oneself in another person's shoes, understanding his feelings and attitudes. Without empathy, the manager cannot truly understand the nonrational fears common to people affected by a proposed change. Any time one is forced to unlearn patterns of behavior developed over time in response to formal expectations and to learn new patterns, he experiences anxiety, discomfort, and reluctance. Empathy means that the manager can evaluate what the *behavioral* impact of the proposed change will be on individuals and groups and what forms of resistance may be expected. Understanding that anxiety and resistance are a natural phenomenon and not the product of sabotage, laziness, or animosity, the manager can then see his way clear to ease his subordinates over the traumatic transition period, eliminating the fears and discomforts that attend change.

Removing Anxieties

Participation, communication, and empathy furnish tools by which the manager can reduce the anxieties so natural to the change process. Any time one leaves familiar and comfortable patterns of behavior and embarks on new ones, anxiety is aroused about how effectively the new patterns will work and how he will be evaluated. These fears and anxieties stem from exposure to the unknown, as well as knowledge that formal organizational rewards will still be administered. But what new criteria will be used? How long will it take the individual to learn the new skills and techniques, in order to reach acceptable performance levels—if ever? The manager must pay close attention to these fears, because they are the most basic factors in inducing resistance to change, because of the threatened security needs of his subordinates.

Fears and anxieties may be removed through removing penalties for failure in an experimental period. The change may be tried without measurement of individual failure or performance, so that those affected by the change may become familiar with what is involved in it and how they may adapt to it. Linking the goals of the change to the goals of the individuals and groups involved can also help to eliminate built-in conflict. Using some of the conflict resolution techniques we talked about earlier may help to bring individual, group, and change goals into line with each other, thus reinforcing the positive benefits of the change.

Acceptance of the change is critically important in the overall process. Eliminating anxieties goes a long way toward reducing resistance to change and allowing the change to be implemented in an effective fashion. Enthusiastic acceptance of a change can mean that despite the difficulties involved in the change, the change can be effectively put into action.

A specific follow-up program is also important, and communication and participation should also be employed in the process of determining the impact of the change and what further problems remain to be resolved. Once again, the subordinates are allowed to have a hand in appraising performance and to participate in the decision-making process. They also serve as a direct link with the informal organization and other social systems, keeping all interested members fully informed of matters that are critical to their well-being.

The effective manager who employs these major elements in his change program can realistically say that the change has resulted in a change for the better. His subordinates are also more likely to agree with such a statement. We have seen that change consists of many elements that create conflict and that the unwary manager fails to notice how these conflicts will detract from the potential effectiveness of any change. But managing the change process through conflict management allows mutual goal attainment to take place and makes subordinates partners in identifying and implementing change.

Summary

An inescapable part of the managerial role is initiating and managing change. Both organizational and human forces act to restrict the effectiveness of a change attempt, and the manager must understand the factors behind resistance as well as those that favor change.

Adaptation to changing environmental, technological, and organizational opportunities creates major forces to use new methods or systems. Recognition of a problem situation also encourages the imposing of a change in order to attain formal goals more nearly. The formal organization's need for predictability and stability serves to restrain arbitrary or minor changes, as does the basic technological process.

Human and social resistance offers significant challenge in the implementing of change. Force field analysis is a tool with which driving and resisting forces may be identified and analyzed. Knowing the specific factors acting in the change situation, the manager can formulate a strategy through which resistance may be overcome and driving forces adapted as appropriate.

Change brings conflict, and often conflict creates the need to change existing situations or relationships. Conflict may be internal to the individual, such as frustration and goal conflict, or external and within the organizational context. Frustration occurs when goal attainment is blocked by some barrier, and goal conflict results from the desirable and undesirable attributes of choices between which the individual must decide. Approach–approach, approach–avoidance, and avoidance–avoidance dilemmas are examples of goal conflict situations.

Organizational conflict stems from a basic goal incompatibility between two or more parties. Both cannot attain their goals because of competition for scarce resources. These conflicts may be institutionalized (the result of formal organization) or emergent (resulting from individual or social processes, yet within the formal organization).

Conflicts may be resolved through problem solving, superordinate goals, expansion of resources, avoidance, smoothing, compromise, authoritative command, altering the human variable, and altering structural variables. The situation determines the effectiveness of any particular resolution technique.

Conflict management is integral to the managing of change. Conflict resolution techniques must be incorporated within the elements of an effective change program. Specific parts of such a program include participation, communication, empathy, and reduction of anxiety.

In the next chapter the role and function of leadership will be explored. Basic processes, especially as they relate to the social system, will be the focus. Organizational leadership will be considered as part of the manager's intervention and modification system in Section V.

STUDY AND REVIEW QUESTIONS

1. Why is conflict discussed as being part of the change process?
2. How might conflict create change?
3. Carefully compare and contrast internal and organizational conflict.
4. Identify a situation with which you are familiar and that you would like to change in some way. Analyze the situation through force field analysis and formulate a change strategy based on your analysis.
5. Is conflict good or bad? Defend your answer.
6. Identify an organizational conflict situation with which you are familiar. Evaluate and discuss each conflict resolution technique's effectiveness in solving the conflict.
7. Why is participation a key to effective change?
8. Why is labor–management conflict so disruptive? What conflict resolution techniques would you try as a manager if you encountered labor–management conflict? Formal–informal organization conflict? Line–staff conflict?
9. Why must the manager take an analytical and active part in organizational change? Discuss the relative merits of managed change and change presented to (imposed on) members.
10. Discuss the nonrational or emotional elements in response to change. How do the elements of participation, communication, empathy, and reducing anxiety affect response to change?

Chapter

18

Leadership: Groups, Goals, and Functions

CHAPTER OBJECTIVES

1. To introduce the leadership process as a role differentiation to facilitate the attainment of group goals.

2. To show the importance of the leadership function in the group-goal process.

3. To differentiate between contemporary and person-centered analyses of leadership.

4. To discuss the nature and results of common leadership styles.

5. To explore briefly the facets of the contingency theory of leadership effectiveness.

CHAPTER OUTLINE

Concept of the Leader
The Leader as "Great Man"
Leadership Traits
Leader Behavior
The Situational Approach

Leader Versus Manager
Sources of Difference

Role of the Leader

Leadership Functions

Leadership: A Function of Individual and Group?

Factors in Leader Determination

Contemporary Approaches to Leadership
Leadership Styles
Contingency Theory of Leadership

In examining the social system in organizational behavior, we have concentrated on groups, their functions, and their processes. Because informal groups pervade all organizations, we must know how and why they operate as they do.

A key element has been omitted so far. We have seen some of the dynamics of group formation, operation, and perpetuation. We have *not* dealt in a systematic fashion with what distinguishes a successful group from an unsuccessful group—its leadership.

In this chapter we will look into the intriguing subject of leadership, focusing on what it is, what it *isn't,* the role of the leader, the nature of his functions, criteria of effective leadership, and different perspectives on—and theories of—leadership. To see more clearly what a leader is and what he does, we must examine leadership in a rather "pure" form, in the social group or informal organization. The primary reason for limiting our conception of leadership is so that we can examine what leadership is without complicating the discussion by mixing in elements of organizational requirements, sources of authority, extent of decentralization, acceptance by the followers, morale levels, and so on.

Concept of the Leader

Leadership has fascinated mankind for thousands of years. The one-in-a-million person who overcomes great odds, battles seemingly insurmountable obstacles, rallies his followers, and achieves great victories is a favorite fantasy—and a widely held image of the leader. Naturally enough, great interest has been shown in finding out who leaders are, what makes them leaders, and how they differ from mere mortals.

The Leader as "Great Man"

One way of investigating leadership is by the study of great leaders. The "great man" theory of leadership presumes that great events are set in motion by equally great men. The theory is that those individuals who display leadership would be leaders under almost any other circumstances besides those in which they emerged. They are leaders because of inherent and unique sets of qualities that are recognized and accepted by the followers. We must hasten to point out that Churchill, the great British leader in World War II, was rejected by his countrymen before the war and then made a remarkable comeback to unite his country. His was an example of a leader's being appropriate for one specific situation and not for another.

Leadership Traits

The "great man" theory implies that leaders are born and that leadership qualities are inherent and immutable—and, by implication, that if one is not destined to be a leader, then he must be resigned to a lifetime of being a follower. A more realistic view is that leaders differ from followers in specific ways. By isolating and identifying these distinguishing characteristics we can recognize emergent leaders and even train them to be more effective as leaders.

The "trait" theory of leadership states that there are identifiable and common characteristics that are unique to leaders. Leaders are tall, intelligent, aggressive, dominating, fluent, and persuasive. They also wear white hats and ride white horses. Whether we are talking about physical or psychological traits, much research has been done to identify the traits that distinguish leader and follower. No consistent patterns have been found. We may admire the tall, attribute leadership qualities to them, and point to Charles de Gaulle and Abraham Lincoln as prime examples. (At the same time, we hope that someone doesn't ask about Napoleon Bonaparte!)

Studying the traits that are common to leaders has resulted in a lengthy list of physical, intellectual, and personality factors. In his review of leadership studies, Stogdill reported that height, weight, physique, and health were each slightly related to leadership, but not consistently.[1] Intelligence is similarly related to leadership, yet intellectual *level* complicates the relationship; a leader may be brighter than his followers but cannot be too much brighter because he loses the ability to communicate and identify with them.[2]

Personality traits display inconsistencies and weak relationships with leadership. Stogdill reported that dominance, introversion–extroversion, sociability, and aggressiveness (among others) cannot be concretely linked to leaders as identifiable or predictable traits.[3] In other words, personality traits cannot be reliably used to distinguish leaders from followers or good leaders from bad leaders.[4] A major reason for the overall lack of fruitfulness of the trait approach is that the *behavior* of the leader is what distinguishes him from the follower, rather than what he looks or acts like.

Leader Behavior

Another major school of thought emphasizes what the leader *does* to fulfill his role. If there are consistently displayed activities, poor leaders may train to be good leaders by building the skills necessary. The behavior emphasis constitutes an important step formed in the study of leadership because leader attributes as critical factors are played down, for "leadership is not a matter of passive status, or of the mere possession of some combination of traits."[5]

[1]Ralph M. Stogdill, "Personal Factors Associated with Leadership: A Survey of the Literature," *Journal of Psychology* (1948), pp. 35–71.

[2]L. S. Hollingworth, *Gifted Children* (New York: Macmillan, 1926).

[3]Ralph M. Stogdill, *Handbook of Leadership: A Survey of Theory and Research* (New York: Free Press, 1974), pp. 49–63.

[4]William G. Scott and Terence R. Mitchell, *Organization Theory: A Structural and Behavioral Analysis*, Rev. Ed. (Homewood, Ill.: Richard D. Irwin, 1972), p. 228.

[5]Stogdill, *Handbook of Leadership*, p. 65.

The concept of leadership suggests a process of goal attainment, follower satisfaction, and group support—actions and activities performed by and for the leader. Few leaders can remain leaders or inspire their followers with a policy of status quo or doing nothing. Rather, leadership requires a dynamic and innovative approach to problems commonly perceived by an identifiable group of people.

Two broad classes of leader behavior are those of *consideration* and *initiation of structure*.[6] Consideration is the showing of understanding, concern, and sympathy for the feelings and opinions of followers, being considerate of their needs and well-being, and showing willingness to explain what he does. Initiation of structure covers task-related behaviors, such as assigning roles and duties to group members, scheduling work assignments, defining goals and establishing task procedures, setting standards, and evaluating followers' performance.[7]

Identifying leader behaviors is an important method of finding out about the leadership process. Unfortunately even this pragmatic approach has built-in problems. Mitchell pointed out that data on leader behaviors are derived from three different sources: leaders, followers, and independent observers. Agreement among the three about the behavior of one specific individual is difficult to obtain, leading to questions of data validity.

Another difficulty with the behavior approach lies in results. Korman found that a specific set of leader behaviors differed in effectiveness *in different situations*.[8] Many diverse variables may affect how well the leader leads.

The Situational Approach

The multiribboned, combat-hardened top sergeant may be readily conceded to be a first-rate battlefield leader. Would he do as well in civilian life as chairman of the community United Way campaign? Probably not, we agree. The situations are too different. Pinning the matter down, *what* is different? Why should such differences affect the ability of the leader to lead effectively?

The sergeant has combat *experience* appropriate to the task at hand. His followers recognize, accept, and accede to his superior *experience* and *judgment*. He leads his platoon in a *crisis* situation, in which a mistake has serious consequences. He is backed by, and has been granted, appropriate decision-making and punitive *rights from the organization;* few realistic *alternatives* are open to his followers other than to obey immediately and to the letter whatever he orders. These are just a few of the characteristics that make a hard-driving, no-nonsense leader effective.

---

[6]Ralph M. Stogdill and A. E. Coons, "Leader Behavior: Its Description and Measurement," Research Monograph No. 88, Ohio State University, 1957.

[7]Fred E. Fiedler and Martin M. Chemers, *Leadership and Effective Management* (Glenview, Ill.: Scott, Foresman, 1974), p. 48.

[8]A. K. Korman, "Consideration, Initiating Structure and Organizational Criteria: A Review," *Personnel Psychology,* **19**:349–363 (1966). See also Fiedler and Chemers, p. 49.

In a volunteer organization few members would follow the leader who behaved as if under combat conditions. Members are participating because they *want* to, not because they must. If they fail to do their duties, money will not be raised for charity—serious, but not a matter of the members' life or death. The individual usually works independently, rather than as part of a unit. Alternatives to obedience are simply seized: leave the campaign, refuse to listen to or to obey the leader, and so on. Punishment of a serious nature cannot be meted out by the leader because of lack of authority and because of the ability of the member to refuse to accept the punishment.

The matter of leader behaviors and the situation in which they are enacted are extremely important. By thinking just for a moment of the different leadership situations possible, one can appreciate that the situational approach cannot be boiled down to a simple set of universal rules. Classifying types of situational variables and relating behaviors and situational variables to performance measures can yield realistic explanations and predictions of leadership effectiveness. One such major situational theory, Fiedler's contingency theory of leadership effectiveness, will be discussed later.

We must make it clear that *organizational* leadership is just *one* leadership situation. Leadership qualities are important to the effective manager but are hardly limited to managers or to industrial situations. In fact, how many managers are also leaders is a hotly contested issue.

Leader Versus Manager

In any activity we accept—almost take it for granted—that someone has to take charge, rally a group of disorganized individuals into a cohesive unit, establish clear-cut purposes and standards, and urge members on to feats they never dreamed possible, all the while setting an example for them by his own behavior. We accept, almost without question, the hierarchical notion that someone must perform managerial types of duties, coordinating the separate activities of group members in the direction of organization (group) goals.

Perhaps we can relate to the consequences of a group *without* a leader by thinking about a number of people who decide to get together to play football for fun. Without a clear consensus of who is to do what, disorganization and confusion can quickly result. ("Me bring the football!? I thought *you* were going to bring it!") Someone needs to make the hard decisions that, even in a social group, result from conflicts between either cliques or individuals. (Who is to decide how to allocate the three high school All-American running backs between two teams?) If the group tries to raise a little money to provide jerseys and cleats, who is going to discipline and counsel a member who flags in his efforts? Who is to mediate and soothe hostile feelings that may erupt on the field?

Sources of Difference

The leader we are talking about is not a manager, although the leader *may* be a manager. Certainly all managers are not leaders. For our purposes, we must make a distinction between the concept of the leader and the concept of the manager. They also have many similarities, but the differences will serve to point out some important factors in the managerial *situation* and the leader *situation*.

Influence Bases

The major differences between leader and manager lie in their respective sources of influence. The manager obtains his authority from the organization and employs it to obtain results from his subordinates and to achieve organizationally prescribed task objectives. The leader, on the other hand, exists in relationship with his followers and receives his power directly from his followers. This is the difference between the formal theory of authority and the acceptance theory of authority in rather pure terms.

THE LEADER'S INFLUENCE   The leader holds his position on the sufferance of his followers. They can rescind the leader's influence rights at any time they feel that he is no longer worthy of their respect and following. Because of this relationship, and because of the unique structure of groups, the leader wields real power in terms of his ability to influence the behaviors of the group members. Group members have *given* him the right to influence them, and an individual who goes against this group norm or value finds that the leader is not the only source of sanction—the other group members must necessarily sanction a deviant in some way.

The leader without the acceptance, wish, and willingness of his followers cannot be a leader. A major characteristic of a leader is that he must have *followers*. Should they refuse to follow him, then the leader is no longer a leader.

THE MANAGER'S INFLUENCE   If the manager's subordinates feel that his commands are inappropriate or that he makes poor decisions, their choices are two: obey or leave the organization. A third alternative is that of disobeying, hardly viable in anything but the short run. The manager is manager irrespective of the acceptance of his group members. After all, they have not granted him influence rights; the organization has. Whether or not they obey him, he is still the manager as prescribed by the formal organization.

Sanctions

The manager has at his command the allocation and distribution of organizational sanctions. These include pay and promotion and are awarded for task performance and contribution to formal organizational objectives.

Negative sanctions, such as *withholding* raises or promotions, are also controlled by the manager. The leader in the social group is able to apply sanctions that are probably more powerful. He can grant—or withhold—access to satisfying the very purposes for joining the group, social satisfactions and related task rewards. In winning the monthly tournament, a highly regarded member of a bridge club may be given purpose-related rewards through warm praise, increased social interaction, prestige and status, and so on. A little-preferred group member who accomplishes the same honor by winning the tournament may have the self-satisfaction that goes with winning, but gratification from group members and leader may be withheld if he is not deemed worthy of his accomplishment.

Both manager and informal leader control rewards and punishments appropriate to the purposes of their own organizations. The relative strengths of these sanctions are functions of their valence and instrumentality to the individual's goal attainment. Organizational sanctions are strongly geared to physiological and security needs, whereas informal sanctions may be more relevant to the individual with belongingness or ego needs operating. Certainly the *probability* of receiving a sanction may be higher in informal groups than in formal organizations, and punishments or rewards are more immediate. Informal sanctions are distributed informally, as behaviors occur, rather than semiannually, when formal performance appraisals are *scheduled*.

Role Continuance

Continuance is yet another difference between the leader and the manager. The harsh taskmaster manager may continue in his office as long as his performance is accepted by the formal organization. By contrast, the leader maintains his position only through the day-to-day wish of his *followers*. Their criterion for continuing to accept him as leader is how well he is facilitating the group's accomplishment of their objectives. The highly personable leader, who is a flop at arranging facilities and refreshments for the football game and who cannot handle the interpersonal problems that arise between members will soon be seen as a detriment to the group's goal attainment rather than as a contributing factor. After a while acceptance of his decisions and influence will be withdrawn, and another leader will take his place.

Leadership and managership are different roles requiring different behaviors. They differ in their overall situations, and especially in influence bases, sanctions, and role continuance criteria. The distinction is very important to bear in mind as we consider leadership. The overlap between leadership and managerial functions will be taken up in Chapter 20, "The Manager as Leader." First we must learn more of the basic functions and processes of leadership.

Role of the Leader

The primary function of the leader in any group situation is to facilitate the accomplishment of group goals. Without fulfilling this function, a leader cannot remain a leader. Whatever the primary purpose of the group, the group cannot remain a group for long unless it has some perceived success in attaining its purposes for being a group. The football team that fails to win a single game eventually loses its cohesiveness, its sense of togetherness, and its satisfactions. Bickering and alienation from the group will soon occur, and the group will dissolve.

Within any group, successful or not, interpersonal difficulties are bound to arise. Frictions and conflicts are bound to develop whenever individuals come together in a cooperative setting for a specified reason, whether this be for informal and social purposes or for formal and organizational purposes. We have seen in our discussion of group dynamics that group members must consider themselves a group and must subordinate some conflicting personal preferences to processes and values that are important to group goal accomplishment. Often the leader must help this process along, by arbitrating conflicts between group members or between a group member and the behaviors expected of him.

There then seem to be two separate dimensions of what the leader must do in performing his leadership function. First, he must maintain the group as a group, resolving internal difficulties and relating to group members. Maintaining the group is essential because being a leader requires having followers; to perform his duties the leader must have a group consensus of major purposes toward which he directs their activities. So group membership maintenance is critical for leadership effectiveness.

Second, the leader must facilitate the attainment of group objectives. In this role he must act as an executive, an administrator, a planner, and a motivator. These are all task-related functions, necessary and important to reach group goals. Without internal harmony the group is not consistently a group, and without some perceived movement toward reaching group goals, the group will lose its cohesiveness. So the leader must make a concerted and conspicuous effort toward goal attainment. Even if internal social relations are good, lack of perceived success in moving toward group goals will diminish group cohesiveness and member acceptance of the leader. The two functions go hand in hand; the leader cannot slight one function in favor of the other.

Some other subsidiary functions of the leader relate to group maintenance. The leader is usually the ego ideal for group members. No matter what the values and norms of the group, the leader is expected to exemplify behaviors that support group ideals. He serves as a pattern by which other group members may shape their own behaviors. In addition, he is the source of sanctions for deviation from group norms and is responsible for influencing deviates to adopt behaviors more nearly consistent with group norms. His lead is followed, too, when a deviate can no longer be tolerated within the group. He must make the decision, and implement it, by which the deviate is expelled from the group.

Leadership Functions

This conception of the leadership role implies that the role must be a weak one because the leader is a group member whose function is to aid the group in achieving a common goal. This being the case, the leader must arise from the group according to the nature of the situation at hand. This function of leadership determination suggests that the group is most likely to follow, in a particular situation, the member of the group who possesses the greatest technical knowledge related to the situation, who presents what is perceived to be the most practical idea or solution for the problem, or who provides the greatest potential direction and momentum for achieving the group goals.

The leadership role is still based on group consensus and acceptance. An individual may retain the leadership role for as long as the group perceives that the individual is fulfilling the requirements of the leadership-task accomplishment. Working under this concept of leadership, it is proba-ble that the leadership role will change as the situation changes, from one member to another. Carter supported this phenomenon in noting that "leaders and followers fulfill their sterotyped roles only in the statistical sense" because specific activities may be performed by individual members according to their individual areas of expertise.[9]

Group task roles are considered to be those behaviors related to the task that the group has decided to undertake. The purpose of these behaviors is to facilitate and coordinate group effort in the selection, definition, and solution of a common problem. Group building and maintenance roles are those behaviors related to the functioning of the group as an entity. The primary consideration of these behaviors is the alteration or maintenance of the group way of working, in order to strengthen, regulate, and perpetuate the group as an entity. Finally, individual roles are expressed in group interaction. These are actions that do not fulfill a group need (either group task or group maintenance) but that are directed toward the satisfaction of the needs of the specific individual.

Additionally, Hemphill distinguished five functions common to the leader irrespective of the specific group or specific situation.[10] These func-tions are (1) to advance the purpose of the group, (2) to administrate, (3) to

[9]Launor Carter, "Leadership and Small Group Behavior," in *Group Relations at the Crossroads,* ed. by M. Sherif and M. O. Wilson (New York: Harper, 1953), p. 261.
[10]John K. Hemphill, *Situational Factors in Leadership* (Columbus, Ohio: OSU Personnel Research Monographs, 1949).

inspire greater activity or set the pace for the group, (4) to make the individual member feel secure of his place in the group, and (5) to act without regard to his own self-interests.

Successful leadership behaviors tend to fall into four general categories, according to Bowers and Seashore:

1. Support: that behavior which enhances the feeling of personal worth and importance of someone else.
2. Interaction Facilitation: behavior which encourages members of the group to develop close, mutually satisfying relationships.
3. Goal Emphasis: behavior which stimulates an enthusiasm for meeting the group's goal or achieving excellent performance.
4. Work Facilitation: behavior which helps achieve the group goal by such activities as scheduling, coordinating, planning, and providing resources such as information, technical knowledge, tools, and materials.[11]

The importance of the leadership role may be observed in the very nature of these functions. They are highly related to the conceptions of task performance (goal attainment) and membership maintenance. The tight-rope on which the leader must walk is the necessity of balancing goal orientation with member social satisfactions. Should the leader err by over-emphasizing one or the other, group cohesiveness and group acceptance must suffer. If too much emphasis is put on goal attainment, a leader becomes a taskmaster; social satisfactions would then be sacrificed by the leader in order to reach group objectives. Especially in the informal group, one of the major purposes of group coalition is the derivation of belonging-ness or social needs satisfaction. On the other hand, if group goals are ignored in favor of maximizing quality of interpersonal relationships and social satisfactions, then the group can make little headway toward reaching its major purposes for being a group. A stagnating but happy group may result. Over time, the members will leave for another group that offers more achievement and goal progress. A mix in orientation is necessary, because the leader must maintain acceptance by the group members.

Leadership: A Function of Individual or Group?

We have assumed that leadership is embodied in the activities of a single individual. The single-leader idea is widely accepted; its validity is open to question, however. The leadership role consists of many specific activities and behaviors. That they must all be performed by only one person seems rather far-fetched. One-person leadership in informal situations or organizations is even less likely. Member satisfactions of a very basic nature would

[11]David G. Bowers and Stanley E. Seashore, "Predicting Organizational Effectiveness with a Four-Factor Theory of Leadership," *Administrative Science Quarterly* (1966), pp. 238–263.

be slighted; the sense of involvement and participation in group processes—so important to the informal group—would not be available to full degree if one person performed all leadership activities.[12] Besides, some observers have noted the multiplicity of separate roles involved in leadership. One such classification includes eight primary and six subsidiary behavior patterns in leadership:

Primary: Executive, Planner, Policymaker, Expert, External group representative, Controller of internal relations, Purveyor of rewards and punishments, Arbitrator and mediator.
Subsidiary: Exemplar, Symbol of the group, Substitute for individual responsibility, Ideologist, Father figure, Scapegoat.[13]

The physical impossibility of fulfilling all role behaviors results in some role differentiation; the leadership roles are distributed among group members according to their interests and abilities.[14] The individual who fills the roles most important or most directly related to group goal attainment will be generally acknowledged as "leader," even though the term is misleading.

Factors in Leader Determination

Under what conditions does a group member assume the leadership role? What factors encourage other members to accept him as leader? Probably the most important single factor in gaining acceptance is the perceived extent to which he possesses the skills, qualities, and knowledge necessary to achieve the purposes and accomplish the tasks of the group. Members of a mountain-climbing expedition will automatically look to the most experienced individual for leadership, accepting his authority of expertise. Another may be the recognized socioemotional leader, but his leadership would be rejected because of the inappropriateness of his skills to the task.

Another factor is the potential leader's active support of—and allegiance to—group norms and values. Few groups would recognize as leader the individual who ridiculed and flagrantly violated those ideals most dear to all members.

"Knowledge is power" and information provides a form of leadership. Access to information can be a powerful determinant in leader emergence, if the information is seen as relevant to the purposes of the group. Members must come to the individual who has the information they need, and such

[12]David J. Lawless, *Effective Management: Social Psychological Approach* (Englewood Cliffs, N.J.: Prentice-Hall, 1972), p. 306.
[13]D. Krech, R. Crutchfield, and E. Ballachey, *Individual in Society* (New York: McGraw-Hill, 1962), pp. 428–432.
[14]Bernard Berelson and Gary A. Steiner, *Human Behavior: An Inventory of Scientific Findings* (New York: Harcourt, Brace & World, 1964), pp. 344, 346.

dependence forms the basis for the leader to emerge and gain acceptance. In similar fashion the individual who fills the central position in a communication net—so that information and messages must pass through his position—can also be accepted as leader. By virtue of location he knows the sum total of all transmitted information pertinent to group process and goal achievement. Such centralization of pertinent knowledge gives him a significant opportunity to wield power and influence group members. Another side of the knowledge–information–leadership factor is the central person's ability to *withhold* or *refuse to transmit* messages and information, a powerful threat because of the essential nature of intermember communication in group dynamics.

Stogdill summarized the results of dozens of research studies on leadership emergence:

The member who talks and participates most actively in the group activities is the one most likely to emerge as a leader. Leaders differ from followers in ability to initiate and sustain interaction with a wide range of personalities.

.   .   .   .

A group member tends to make more attempts to influence the group when his status is high, his control is high, he is highly motivated, he is highly esteemed, he is promised high rewards, he has a reasonable expectation of task success, his influence attempts are accepted by members, and he is perceived by members as competent in the group task.

The group member who possesses information enabling him to contribute more than other members to solution of the group task tends to emerge as leader. However, an excess of information that strains the credulity of group members may operate as a handicap.

Observational studies have identified several patterns of leader behavior not anticipated by the trait theorists. The emergent leader is experimental and in natural groups tends to be valued because his spontaneity is contagious and stimulates spontaneity in others. He widens the field of participation for others and expands the area of group freedom for decision and action. He protects the weak and underchosen, encourages participation of less capable members, is tolerant of the deviate, and accepts rather than rejects a wide range of member personalities.[15]

Leadership is then a process rather than a person. We might summarize to this point by saying that leadership exists in the relationship among three critical components: leader, group, and situation. The situation includes such things as the characteristics of the task, types of skills needed to accomplish the task, the nature of group goals, perceived probability of goal attainment, and urgency. Group factors include communication networks, norms and values, cohesiveness, commitment to group goals (valences), and the satisfactions, personalities, and expectations of members. Factors relating to the leader include his behaviors, skills, pertinent knowledge, acceptance by the group, balance between initiating structure and consideration, personality, and perceived effectiveness.

[15]Stogdill, *Handbook of Leadership*, pp. 230, 231.

Leadership is the process through which the group is maintained while goal attainment is facilitated through behaviors appropriate to the situation, the leader, and the group. The overall leadership process may be centralized in one person or may be differentiated into component roles that are distributed throughout the group. Leadership is a dynamic process because the leader must constantly evaluate, direct, and motivate member behavior toward overall goals. Goals change, members change, and the situation changes—the leader and his behaviors must change accordingly. Leadership is also a constrained process. The leader cannot arbitrarily impose his will on the group, nor can he flagrantly violate group norms. He is as much a prisoner of the group and their attitudes as members are influenced and directed by him.

Leadership is an essential part of the effective group, the group that makes meaningful progress toward its goals while offering significant satisfactions to its members. Not everyone can be—nor should wish to be—a leader. True leadership is demanding, arduous, frustrating, and hazardous—failure means the revoking of status, privilege, esteem, respect, power, and sometimes even membership in the very group led. Success brings many satisfactions, however. Recognition, achievement, and dominance are just three that attend the effective leader.

Contemporary Approaches to Leadership

Two contemporary leadership approaches—one of patterns of leader behaviors and one of leader effectiveness—are discussed in the following sections. The first, leadership styles, considers distinctive behavior patterns associated with the leader. The second is Fiedler's contingency theory, which relates the match between leader behavior and the situation.

Leadership Styles

What the leader does, rather than who he is, is the determinant of how well he leads. From previous discussions we know that *patterns* of behaviors or activities become associated with specific roles. The leadership role is no different. Leaders behave in characteristic ways. Three such patterns of leader behavior have been distinguished: democratic, autocratic, and laissez-faire. They are usually termed leadership "styles." A style of leadership is "a relatively enduring set of behaviors which is characteristic of the individual regardless of the situation."[16]

Lewin and Lippitt pioneered the study of leadership styles with their investigations of the effects of different styles on group member behavior.[17]

[16]Fiedler and Chemers, p. 40.
[17]Kurt Lewin and Ronald Lippitt, "An Experimental Approach to the Study of Autocracy and Democracy: A Preliminary Note," *Sociometry*, 1:292–300 (1938).

Although many of the leadership style studies have been rather artificial (e.g., children's groups, created or laboratory situations), their general conclusions have been embraced by many.

The Autocratic Style

The autocratic leader makes all decisions that relate to the group and is the major source of influence in the group's activities. Because of his control over the group and its resources, group members are dependent on him. He controls the future (giving one-step-at-a-time instruction), information (giving only orders, not sharing his knowledge), work (making all task and team assignments), member satisfactions (allowing no initiative or judgment to be used and using personal terms in criticism or praise), and relationships (each member is dependent on the leader for instructions and training, must get the leader's decision each time anything new comes up—quite ego-building for the leader!). "His most effective technique in maintaining this leadership position is by withholding knowledge of goals, not sharing information required for the task, and not providing feedback to members on their progress. As he is the only group member with complete knowledge of all functions and accomplishments, the members are dependent upon him for goal achievement."[18] The group figuratively revolves around the autocratic leader and is dominated by him.

The Democratic Style

In sharp contrast to the autocrat is the democratic leader, who shares his influence with the group. Decisions are made by the leader only after full discussion and participation by members, whose feelings and reactions are given full weight. The participative process, although time-consuming, effectively encourages each member's input and familiarity with the problem. The leader gains additional information from group members, as well as a greater commitment to the decision than would occur under autocratic conditions. "He tries to keep as many members as possible personally involved in problem solution and in awareness of goal progress."[19]

The Laissez-Faire Style

The laissez-faire (literally, "let them alone") leader is not really a leader at all. As the term implies, he is a figurehead who exerts no influence and makes no contribution to group goal attainment (except possibly by *not* detracting from the group's activity through becoming involved in it). No direction is given. Individual members or the group as a whole must incor-

[18]Lawless, p. 314.
[19]Ibid., p. 315.

porate the leadership function into their activities, which can yield role overload, role ambiguity, and other conflicts. Under normal task conditions such a leadership style would appear most frustrating. Table 18-1 summarizes the major behavior differences among the autocratic, democratic, and laissez-faire styles.

Response to Leadership Styles

We may notice a bias toward—or away from—one of these leadership styles. Such a reaction should be avoided, because we still must apply the pragmatic test: if it works, it's "good." No one of the styles has been found universally effective (or ineffective), even though our democratic heritage and values may lead us into a philosophical—but unscientific—acceptance of the democratic style. At the same time we may have an unconscious aversion to the other styles. We must restrain such tendencies and evaluate the results of the three styles.[20]

Work Quality and Quantity. Autocratic leadership resulted in higher levels of work activity and greater quantities of work than under either of the two other styles; work quality differed considerably, with quality under laissez-faire being much lower than under democracy.

Motivation. Work continued, under democratic leadership, even after the leader left the room; when the autocratic leader was not present the members stopped their task activities. Interest in the task was slightly higher under democracy than under autocracy.

Efficiency. Laissez-faire conditions resulted in disorganized activities, in failure and setbacks, and loss of interest. Little difference in efficiency was observed between autocratically and democratically-led groups.

Satisfactions. Hostility was expressed much more often under autocracy than under democracy, as were aggressive demands for attention. Displaced aggression—venting frustrations on an object or person other than the source of frustration—was conspicuous in the autocratic group, but occurred scarcely at all under democratic leadership. Nineteen of twenty members who experienced both autocratic *and* democratic leadership reported preferring their democratic leader. Democratic-group members were more friendly and "group-minded" than were autocratic-group members. Submissive or dependent behavior was more common in the autocratic group than in democratic groups. Originality was also higher under democracy.

These results show—under the conditions studied—that different leadership styles can affect groups in different ways. Before making too-quick generalizations, we must remember that these classic experiments were composed of groups of ten-year-old boys, and the tasks were *hobby* activities. The groups were primarily *socially* oriented groups, with *adult* leaders.

[20]The following results are drawn from Ralph White and Ronald Lippitt, "Leader Behavior and Member Reaction in Three 'Social Climates,'" in *Group Dynamics: Research and Theory,* 3rd Ed., ed. by Dorwin Cartwright and Alvin Zander (New York: Harper & Row, 1968), pp. 326–334.

TABLE 18-1   Comparison of Leadership Styles

Function	Autocratic	Democratic	Laissez-faire
Policy Decisions	Determined by leader.	Determined by group discussion and decision, encouraged and assisted by leader.	Complete freedom for group *or* individual decision; minimum of leader participation.
Planning	Leader dictates techniques and activity steps one at a time; future steps always largely uncertain.	Discussion period provides perspective on activity. Leader sketches general steps to group goal; when technical advice is needed, leader suggests two or more alternatives from which choice can be made.	Leader supplies various necessary materials; provides information only when asked. Takes no other part in work discussion.
Task Assignments	Leader dictates each member's work task and work companion.	Members choose their own work companions; group determines division and assignment of tasks.	Leader takes no part in assignments.
Direction by Leader	Leader praises and criticizes each member's work in "personal" terms; remains aloof from active group participation except when demonstrating.	Leader is "objective" or "fact-minded" in his praise or criticism; tries to be a regular group member in spirit without doing too much of the work.	No attempt to intervene in (appraise or regulate) task processes; unless questioned, only gives infrequent spontaneous comments on member activities.

SOURCE: Adapted from Ralph White and Ronald Lippitt, "Leader Behavior and Member Reaction in Three 'Social Climates,'" in *Group Dynamics: Research and Theory*, 3rd Ed., ed. by Dorwin Cartwright and Alvin Zander (New York: Harper & Row, 1968), p. 319.

Contingency Theory of Leadership

Although the autocratic–democratic–*laissez-faire* studies may have been overgeneralized by businessmen and academicians to many situations, we must realize that there are few universal or simple "rules." Often a technique—highly appropriate for one narrow application—is carelessly used under conditions for which it was never intended, with disastrous results.

Common sense tells us that democratic leadership under battlefield conditions is neither satisfying nor effective. Nor is it likely that inmates in penal institutions will be consulted on matters of security. One researcher who has carefully extended this common-sense approach is Fred Fiedler. A result of his two decades of investigation is a typology or classification of the leadership approaches most likely to be effective under carefully defined conditions.

Leader, Style, and Behavior

Fiedler focused on the leader as the individual who directs and coordinates task-related group activities. His effectiveness may then be evaluated through the group's task performance.[21] Fiedler distinguished between two major leadership styles: task-oriented and relationship-oriented. The task-oriented leader's basic goal is task accomplishment, from which he derives self-esteem. A relationship orientation by the leader implies that he has

as his basic goal the desire to be "related." That is, he seeks to have strong emotional and affective ties with others. If this basic goal is achieved, if he feels that he has achieved such an affective relationship, he will also seek, as his secondary goals, status and esteem. He will want to be admired and to be recognized.[22]

The relationship-oriented leader thus differs in his purposes and motivations from the task-oriented leader. The latter, when he perceives no task-related problems, has *secondary* interests in friendly and pleasant relations with the group members. His interests in good interpersonal relations occur *only* when task accomplishment is assured and takes a definite back seat to the task itself.[23]

Situational Characteristics

Which is the "better" leadership style? The characteristics of the leader's specific situation determine how effective either style will be. Three specific dimensions—leader–member relations, task structure, and position power—form the basis for a classification of leadership situations. The

[21]Fred F. Fiedler, *A Theory of Leadership Effectiveness* (New York: McGraw-Hill, 1967), pp. 8, 9.

[22]Fiedler and Chemers, p. 76.

[23]Ibid., p. 77.

groups on which the contingency theory is based are called "interacting" groups, those in which member cooperation is required in accomplishing the task as compared to "groups" made up of members whose work is independent of each other. The distinction is akin to the difference between a basketball team and a bowling team.

LEADER–MEMBER RELATIONS   In a small group, especially, the interpersonal relationship between the leader and the group members is the most important single factor in determining the influence of the leader. The wholeheartedly endorsed leader has a favorable situation because of the willingness of his followers to follow *him*. If relationships are strained or poor, the leader finds himself in a rather unfavorable situation. Group members must be urged and influenced in the performance of task activities, hardly satisfactory for promoting enthusiasm and involvement.

TASK STRUCTURE   The second most important determinant of leadership effectiveness is the extent to which the nature and requirements of the task are specified. The highly structured task influences member behavior through the impersonal requirements of job instructions, policy statements, and workplace arrangement. The leader need not rely on interpersonal (and hence tenuous) relationships, for the situation itself influences behavior in task-related directions. The leader can rather quickly ascertain performance, and sanctions may be applied as necessary. The leader in a highly structured task situation faces a rather favorable (for him) situation.

A task with low structure is an ambiguous, poorly defined task. Little direct support is given the leader through technological requirements, and he enjoys no such favorable situation as in a highly structured task. No formal specifications are available, nor are readily observable performance measures. The leader has no more appropriate knowledge than his members, and he operates under rather difficult conditions. His influence and ability to specify behaviors are inappropriate, and motivation is more important than authority. A committee chairman might find himself in such a position, as would a research and development supervisor.

Task structure depends on:

1. Goal clarity: the extent to which task requirements are specified or known by members.
2. Goal-path multiplicity: the extent to which there are alternative ways to accomplish the task.
3. Decision verifiability: the extent to which task accomplishment can be evaluated by objective, logical, or feedback means.
4. Decision specificity: the extent to which the task has but one correct outcome (an arithmetic problem) or several equally good results (establishing several alternative budgets from which the president will choose).[24]

[24]Fiedler, p. 28; Fiedler and Chemers, pp. 67, 68.

POSITION POWER   The right of the leader to "direct, evaluate, and reward and punish"[25] group members is related to the power he has by virtue of being the leader. High position power, characteristic of most management positions in industry, goes with the positive and negative incentives and sanctions available to the leader. Low position power, associated with committee chairmen, implies that the leader has very few means at his disposal to influence members into compliance.

Situational Favorableness

All three dimensions occur in any given leadership situation. To complicate the matter, each can vary independently of the others. The leader can find himself with low position power, high task structure, and good leader–member relations. What style is more effective, task- or relationship-oriented? What about under the same situation but with *poor* relations? We can see that each of the dimensions are favorable or unfavorable to the leader's exercise of influence. High position power is favorable, whereas low power is unfavorable to his ability to affect task accomplishment. Good relations are a favorable quality, whereas poor relations detract from his ability to influence. High task structure supports and supplements his influence, whereas low structure detracts from his ability to affect task accomplishment.

We can classify any situation through these dimensions. We can also classify the situation in the rough terms of its overall favorableness for the leader by remembering that the most important element is relations, followed by task structure, and then by position power. Figure 18-1 shows such a scheme.

The chart shows the characteristics of eight different situations, representing all possible combinations of their three characteristic dimensions and the rough extent to which each quality exists. Situation I, for example, displays good leader–member relations, high task structure, and strong leader position power. Such a situation is highly favorable for the leader.

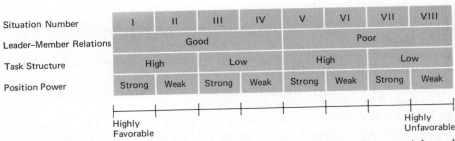

FIGURE 18-1   Situational characteristics and favorableness. Source: Adapted from Fiedler and Chemers, p. 70.

[25]Fiedler and Chemers, p. 68.

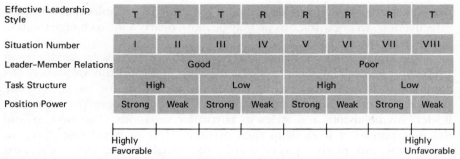

FIGURE 18-2 Contingency model of leadership effectiveness. Source: Adapted from Fiedler, p. 146.

Situation VIII, on the other hand, reflects poor relations, low task structure, and weak position power—a most unfavorable and frustrating combination of circumstances for the leader. Other situations range between these two extremes according to their characteristics and relative net favorableness.

Contingency Model

So far we have seen that two general leadership styles, task- and relationship-oriented, are available to the leader. At the same time the leader must operate within a specified situation. His problem is this: which style is better in a given situation? The results of Fiedler's research are summarized in Figure 18-2, in which the effective leadership style is shown for each of the eight situations. In general, we can say that, under relatively *favorable* conditions (situations I–III), the effective leader is task(T)-oriented. The combination of good relationships, task structure, and position power enables him to concentrate on task matters. Under relatively *unfavorable* conditions (situations IV–VII), the effective leader must show diplomacy or concern for developing trust and support. Under situation VIII, the worst of all possible situations, the leader has no choice but to revert to being task-oriented. With an unstructured (perhaps creative) task, low position power, and poor relations, the leader must keep his group somehow goal-oriented.

Contingency Implications

Inherent in the contingency model is the implication that simple prescriptions, such as those espoused by the "human relation" or "participative management" schools, are neither valid nor effective. The considerate leader who consults his followers on all decisions may be unconsciously adopting the "easy" leadership style, not a more effective one.

Further, one assumes that the leader in an organized setting will continue to be effective in another role—through promotion or other change—which may have just enough differences to render his "natural" style ineffective. The leader should remain aware of the external variables that affect his effectiveness. In organizations he may be more nearly able to change them to enhance his effectiveness.

The contingency model of leadership effectiveness is by far the most useful and well validated concept of leadership. It is especially valuable for its adaptability to wide varieties of situations, as well as for its prescriptive powers. The contingency model enables us to develop a perspective on the leader, his behaviors and styles in particular situations. The process and dynamic nature of leadership then becomes clear as it provides the goal orientation and motive power within the social system. After the next chapter, which will integrate the concepts of the social system, we will apply our leadership findings to the *managerial* setting, as a technique for modification and integration of the organizational behavior systems.

Summary

In this chapter we have examined leadership as a process, a series of activities that facilitate group goal attainment. Such an approach requires emphasis on the dynamics of the activities, rather than on universal qualities of either leader or group.

The leader and the manager roles were differentiated. The manager *may* exhibit leadership qualities in *addition* to his formal role, but such need not be the case. Differences between the roles stem from influence bases, sanctions available, and role continuance.

Task and interpersonal-relationships–maintenance (group-building) functions were explored, as were the expanded functions of support, inter-action facilitation, goal emphasis, and work facilitation. Group-member role differentiation can occur for supplying the leadership function when the single leader cannot provide all the necessary skills. Factors that encourage the emergence of a specific individual leader include skills, qualities, knowl-edge, support of group norms, information access, participation, and so on.

Two contemporary approaches to leadership, that of leadership styles and a situational approach, were presented. Leadership styles include auto-cratic, democratic, and laissez-faire. The situational (contingency) approach suggests an optimum style under separate carefully defined conditions. The situation may be classified along the dimensions of leader–member relations, task structure, and position power. Although complex, the contingency approach offers significant insights and valuable prescriptions.

STUDY AND REVIEW QUESTIONS

1. Why are the "great man" and trait theories of leadership of little practical use?

2. When is a leader a manager? A manager a leader?

3. Two distinct sets of leadership styles were presented: task and interpersonal-relations orientations, and democratic–autocratic–*laissez-faire* styles. Are these style sets consistent with each other? Do they conflict? Can they be reconciled?

4. Consider this course as a "situation." Analyze the situation by using the contingency model. According to your analysis, should your leader (professor) be task- or relationships-oriented to be an effective leader? Specify a program or series of activities through which he can implement his new style (or if he is already "effective," what activities enable you to *identify* his style?).

5. What qualities do you look for in a leader? What qualities *detract* from a leader?

6. Compare and contrast the "leader behavior" and "situational" approaches to the study of leadership.

7. Can leadership be taught? If yes, defend your answer and outline a program for doing so. If no, defend your answer.

8. "A leader is only a leader for as long as his group accepts him as its leader." Discuss.

9. Using Fiedler's contingency model as a base, identify two specific situations (and their dimensions) under which the democratic style is highly effective. Repeat for both the autocratic and laissez-faire styles. (Hint: do not limit yourself to Fiedler's dimensions; you may wish to develop others.)

10. Why are leader–member relations more important to leadership effectiveness than task structure or position power?

Chapter

19

Integrating Perspective: Individuals, Groups and Formal Organizations

---

CHAPTER OBJECTIVES

1. To trace some basic relationships among major components of the social system.

2. To show briefly the place of the individual in the social system.

3. To identify major interfaces between social and formal organizational systems.

4. To illustrate some ways in which system interactions occur in actual situations.

CHAPTER OUTLINE

In the last five chapters we have looked at the separate components of the social system. All organized settings are comprised of people, and people naturally form associations besides those dictated by organizational structure. In this chapter we will look at the relationships among the various components of the social system in order to establish a better understanding of the ways in which organizational behavior is influenced. Then we will briefly investigate the interactions among individual, social, and formal organizational systems.

The Social System and Its Components

While looking into the social system, we must bear in mind that we are looking at a network of interrelated groups of individuals that displays a stable and persistent structure,[1] such groups being related by common processes. Figure 19-1 repeats an earlier representation of the social system. We see that the basic unit of analysis in this system is the group. Processes such as conflict, change, status, and roles create the structure and process within the system, and informal organization and expectations arise from the formal organizational context. Leadership is the dynamic process by which the group adapts and coordinates its activities toward goal attainment. This overview shows some basic relationships and how closely entwined the entire system is.

The only way to understand each of the major systems is to understand the complexities of relationships among their components. We will review below how the components of the social system interact, creating behavioral tendencies and changes in behaviors.

Human Requirements for Social Activity

Social and affiliative needs provide the motivation for individuals to identify with others and band together in social relationships. The benefits of pooling interests and resources further support such tendencies. A tribe is more powerful than an individual hunter, and a group member has more opportunities for relaxation, contentment, and task accomplishment than he does when isolated, by himself.

Within an organized setting, social or group activity is usually a requirement of task structure. Shared tasks, close proximity, or organizational grouping force people into contact with others. The technological and organizational processes in the formal organization encourage and require interactions and shared activities among individuals. Common activities and shared task goals give common ground for interactions at first; eventually, shared sentiments about nonformal activities emerge from these formally-dictated interactions and activities. These pave the way for sentiments and

[1]W. H. Scott, "The Factory as a Social System," in *Human Relations and Modern Management,* ed. by E. J. Hugh-Jones (Amsterdam: North-Holland Publishing Co., 1958), p. 20.

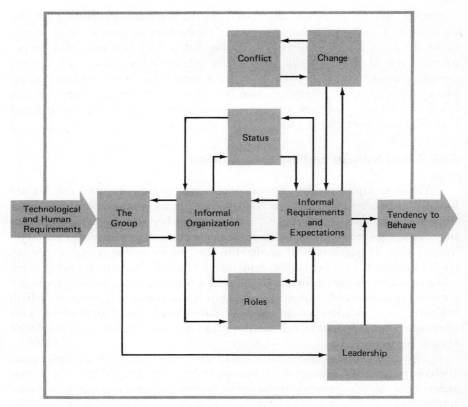

FIGURE 19-1   The social system.

shared interests in hobbies or sports. Informal interactions and shared sentiments create the structure within which values and expectations emerge, to be eventually codified in roles and status of an ongoing *group,* perhaps an informal organization.

Informal Organization and Expectations

All groups have goals, purposes for being; the informal organization is no exception. Its major purpose is to give identity and social satisfaction to its individual member while contributing to the security and special interests of the group as a whole. As in all groups, organized or not, members must conform to group expectations. The informal organization, after all, really exists only in the perceptions and interactions of individual group members. It exists only so long as the group contributes to the individual member's well-being while effectively pursuing overall purposes.

One may be tempted to reify the informal organization, to consider an abstract relationship as if it had existence as a concrete being. On the contrary, the informal organization is made up of the separate behaviors and perceptions of its members. These behaviors must conform to the broad outline of behaviors necessary to the informal organization's purposes and must create a suitable social environment for its members. Individual members are integral components of the organization, and their behaviors substantially affect the character and intensity of the group process. Informal policies—informal requirements and expectations—are essential to the continued existence of the informal organization. An antisocial member in a socially based group may create conflicts and detract from the other members' enjoyment. He may be excluded from social interactions because of his having violated the expectations of behavior suitable to the purpose of the group.

Expectations and Roles

Informal expectations and norms stem directly from the major purpose of each specific group. They also create specific roles to be played by group members and so facilitate social control and establish behavior patterns that are consistent with group purpose and process. Group members, because of their identification with the group and its purpose, act as role senders. They influence every other group member into behaving in ways that are consistent with perceptions of behavior appropriate for a group member. Even though there may not be absolute consistency between the role sendings of each member, a broad consensus may be reached for any individual role receiver. He, in turn, sends—both to himself and to other group members—his own conception of appropriate role behaviors, as well as behaviors he expects from other members. Each group member then attempts to influence the behavior of every other member according to his own perception of the organization's expectations and behavior that will contribute to the purposes of the group.

The Leadership Role

More specifically, broad behavior expectations are an important part of role sendings, and they orient each member to behaving in ways that are constructive to the group. Even more finely detailed *functional* roles are also sent and received. These are sets of activities "assigned" to specific individuals, much as overall component tasks are divided up and assigned in the formal organization. Two such roles are those of leader and follower. The leader in the social system, and especially within the informal organization, tends to be he who best exemplifies behaviors valued by group members. The most successful young executive is generally looked up to as leader by a clique of aspiring junior executives. The most widely popular girl on campus is listened to carefully when she offers social advice to her acquaintances. The leader of a street gang may be the one who most successfully and audaciously defies the authorities.

Other roles are important to the group's ability to attain its objectives, such as being able and willing to mediate disagreements and conflicts between group members. Another member may relieve tension and provide sanctions through playing the role of humorist, making jokes and ridiculing those who fail to conform to the group's standards. Group cohesiveness is enhanced by identification and ideological separation from groups that hold other values. Such "us–them" feelings increase the sense of belongingness and identity, as well as strengthening internal ties among members. One of the major roles of the leader is to minimize internal conflict and to maintain satisfactory member relationships. A disharmonious informal organization quickly loses cohesiveness and identity, dissolving into factions and cliques.

The content of these roles stems directly from the nature of the informal organization. Task-related and social roles are dictated by the overall purpose for which the group is formed. The roles are the formalization of the requirements and expectations of the informal organizations, comprising consistent patterns of behavior that are constantly modified and adjusted in accordance with other members' expectations and group norms. The type of role that the individual plays—or the extent to which he plays it—is a function of his personality, commitment to group goals, acceptance by group members, and the extent to which he subscribes to the standards of the group.

Expectations and Status

Consistent with the nature of the role process is the status attributed to the role players within the group. The highest status is usually granted to the person who enacts the role of leader, with the other group members being attributed less status according to several different criteria. Probably the most important factor is the extent to which the individual contributes to the success of the group, followed closely by how well he fulfills his role expectations. Completely individual characteristics, such as personality traits, will contribute relatively little to status within the group. A "hanger-on," who contributes nothing to the group nor to its ability to attain its goals, may be tolerated because of unique personal qualifications and characteristics. Yet in group meetings or discussions, his credibility and inability to affect the group will be quickly noticed.

Formal status, on the other hand, is attributed on the basis of one's hierarchical position and task ability. This is again quite similar to the concept of status in the informal or social group because formal status reflects potential ability to contribute to overall organizational goals. The process of differentiating the amount of respect that is "deserved" results in a ranking of individuals along a status scale. Such status may be functional, in which people doing the same task are accorded different status, or scalar, in which the position held is the determinant.

Status can be a powerful motivator, as we saw in Maslow's hierarchy of needs. Those operating at the ego needs level find that achievement and recognition by peers and superiors greatly magnify motivational force. Many managers find outlets for their ego–status needs through organizational success and promotion. Many other organizational members find this path inappropriate, because of either their inability to perform or their unwillingness to pay the price, and so seek other ways to fulfill status needs. The informal organization furnishes several opportunities for fulfilling status needs, as do some off-the-job activities. Status is granted by the people with whom one identifies, group members, and such status is granted for perceived contribution to a small group rather than to a large, impersonal organization. The large organization typically cannot feed back performance reports and recognition to each individual nearly so quickly as the immediate feedback given by individuals interacting face to face.

The rewards that accompany this recognition and esteem are those of immediate importance to the individual, those that further reinforce his identification with—and dependence on—his social group. The informal organization then controls some very powerful needs satisfactions and grants rewards and punishments as they are merited, rather than quarterly or semiannually. Not being able to belong is a powerful deterrent to the potential deviate.

Formal Organization and Social System

For these reasons the very natures of the social and formal organizational systems come into conflict through the substance and direction of behaviors of individuals. The formal organization demands formal task behaviors, for which it reimburses the member, whereas the informal organization requires the individual to conform to its own expectations in exchange for social and esteem needs satisfaction. The economic institution demands profit maximization and productive efficiency, whereas the informal organization has no such formal output requirements. It is, rather, concerned with maximizing member satisfaction and social purposes. Formal organization structure and technological requirements cause people to be grouped together and to interact with each other in task-related ways, yet from this maze of required behaviors emerges the web of interpersonal and informal contacts and shared nonformal interests.

Increasing production rates and decreasing production costs are two common goals associated with fulfilling the economic mission. The formal organization may completely disrupt its social system in its search for more efficient ways of organizing production and minimizing costly waste time. Entirely new production technologies are often imposed on a social system that has emerged and become well established over the years. Severe dislocations follow of group members and their comfortable sets of relationships with people they value. Even in relatively minor technological changes severe individual and social consequences occur that were not anticipated. Technological changes, especially, require major changes in social relationships and create anxieties about the net impact of the change on the individual and his valued group membership. Resistance is encountered because of great conflict between those things of value to the individual and those things felt to be necessary to the formal organization.

Manager and Social System

Why is the social system considered one of the three major organizational behavioral systems? Unless we consider the psychology and sociology of *people in groups,* we limit our understanding of the things that affect organizational behavior. People as individuals are assumed to behave in ways that maximize their own self-interests, irrespective of how this affects others. People are viewed as separate, compartmentalized resources, with the minimal and strictly task-oriented communications made necessary by their formal activities. The authoritarian leader relates to his followers on a one-to-one basis, attempting direct personal contact and influence. He rarely considers his followers as a social group with a shared fate and identification. Is the social system supportive of—or antagonistic to—the manager? We cannot say; it depends on the situation. There is nothing in the nature of the social system that makes it hostile, but there is much in its nature that can conflict with the arbitrary demands made by the unwary manager who does not know of its existence nor understand its characteristics.

Such information and understanding are very important, because the understanding of individual psychology and motivation cannot completely allow the manager to predict individual behaviors. Each individual has constraints on his range of acceptable behaviors, imposed by his social group or informal organization. Individual and social behavior can conflict in as many ways—and just as seriously—as the formal organization can conflict with the social system. The individual may seem to be motivated by recognition and achievement yet be unwilling to sacrifice friendships and group acceptance by outproducing his peers. He must operate within the norms and standards of his reference group or be excluded from it. Few indeed are those who can chart their own courses without taking into consideration what their friends and associates regard as acceptable aspirations and activities! No reasonable manager can or should place a subordinate in the conflict-filled position of choosing between mutually exclusive formal and informal expectations. Doing so will only create a substantial probability that the choice will be in favor of the more powerful and immediate rewards offered by peers. Choosing the informal organization's norms causes rejection of the formal organization and alienation. Even should formal expectations be chosen, ignoring informal norms, the subordinate will not be supported by his associates within the social system. Withdrawal of peer group support weakens the network of formalized cooperation so essential to the functioning of the firm. In either choice the manager would have opted for ineffective performance.

Instead whatever conflicts do exist must be minimized and, hopefully, resolved. This requires an analytical and knowledgeable manager—knowing more than the technical aspects of his job, knowing the problems and possible solutions and processes involved in each of the three major organizational behavioral systems. We have seen time and time again that the manager must take an active role in establishing the overall environment for goal attainment and must mesh the conflicting objectives and processes of individual, group, and formal organization to the best of his ability.

The meshing and interactions of the separate components of the social system make rather good sense from a theoretical point of view. How do they function in actual organized settings? What are some examples of the social system in action? To consider the organizational realities of social processes, in the next section we will make a detailed analysis of the social system in real situations.

Social Structure: The Case of the Restaurant

We often take very much for granted the purpose and functioning of the familiar restaurant. The customer is waited on, is served, and leaves after paying. The ways in which these processes happen are rarely examined closely, and one may overlook the fact that the restaurant is an organized setting and consequently possesses a social system. Fortunately one researcher was curious—and patient—enough to study the social workings in a number of restaurants.[2]

Technological Requirements and Organization

The fundamental purpose of the typical restaurant is service—satisfying customers' basic hunger drives through the timely and tasty serving of prepared foodstuffs in an appropriate environment and for a suitable fee. How well this objective is attained may be measured in several ways, including repeat business, extent to which restaurant capacity is filled, and gratuities left for waiters. The customer is the focal point in the restaurant. His satisfaction and his evaluation (of food quality, portion size, service, and so on) immediately affect the employees with whom he comes into direct contact (unlike many other types of businesses). Unless he receives what he selects, as he wishes it prepared, in a reasonable period of time, at an appropriate temperature, and with the proper attitude, he is unhappy.

[2]William Foote Whyte, *Human Relations in the Restaurant Industry* (New York: McGraw-Hill, 1948); and, by the same author, "The Social Structure of the Restaurant," *American Journal of Sociology* **54**:302–310. (January 1949). Unless otherwise noted, this section is based on these two works.

Customer service	Production	Transportation
Waiters	Chef and cooks	Runners
Bartenders	Kitchen workers	Busboys
Cashier	Pantry workers	
	Dishwashers	
	Checker	

The ways and means that support the restaurant's purpose require that three major functions be provided: customer service, transportation, and production.

Indirect and supervisory contribution is made by the manager, the supervisors of food production and of the dining room, and the cost-control supervisor. Checker and cashier are two roles of less direct contribution than the others because the checker inspects the portion sizes and the correctness of the food order and verifies and totals the bill for the order. The cashier is responsible for receiving payment from the customer.

The pantry is a holding area in which food prepared in the kitchen is "served" to waiters for delivery. Runners carry the food from kitchen to pantry and bring food orders from the pantry (where the waiters leave them) to the kitchen.

Finally, the kitchen is the hub of all production in the restaurant. It is the "manufacturing" division, where the basic product is prepared. Preparation entails many different types of operations, such as processing (cooking or frying), assembly (making sandwiches or salads), preparation (boning fish, slicing meat, peeling potatoes), and so on. Dishwashing is a support activity, not directly related to food preparation, yet a necessary function in the total delivery to the customer.

The kitchen operation is headed by the food production manager, and preparation activities are under the immediate supervision of the chef. Reporting to the chef are a number of cooks, who specialize in cooking particular materials, and supervisors of work stations, each station specializing in the preparation of specific materials.

Status Structure in the Kitchen

The status system in the restaurant kitchen is complex because of the many roles and functions involved in food preparation. Generally, though, preparation of the finished food product is held in higher esteem than the earlier stages. Those who actually cook are at the top of the status ladder, whereas those who prepare foods to be cooked hold lower status. Complicating this general role is the varying prestige of the food materials themselves, a factor powerful enough to reverse expected status.

Without considering the food material, cooks would be expected to occupy top status below the chef, followed by salad makers, then chicken and meat preparers, and anchored by vegetable preparers. Overall this pattern is valid, yet the characteristics of the materials and duties *within* each rough category create exceptions. For example, chicken cooking and fish-related activities are low status; in fact, the fish station is actually the very lowest in status.

Even vegetables have status! Vegetable-related activities display the usual cooking–noncooking status differences, and the noncooking activities have their own complex and rigid status structure that arises from the great specialization of labor:

At the top were the luxury or decorative items such as parsley, chives, and celery. At the top of the regular vegetables were green beans. Next came spinach and carrots. Next to the bottom were sweet and white potatoes, and onions were considered the most undesirable of all vegetables.

.   .   .   .

Comments of the workers showed that they valued lack of odor, crispness, and cleanness of handling mostly highly in vegetables, whereas the vegetable that had an odor and that stained the hands or was sloppy to handle was held in low esteem. . . . Perhaps spinach might have ranked with potatoes or below except that it did not reach the preparation table until it had been thoroughly cleaned of soil and sand at another station.[3]

A kitchen worker tends to perform activities that are roughly congruent with other status factors, such as social background, skill, wages, and seniority. The system is well developed and accepted by all workers. That function and status are related, and not just by coincidence, is indicated by the shifts that occur when a rather high-status function is unattended because of its occupant's absence. Workers on lower-status materials each move up one notch, with the person immediately below the status of the absent worker taking over his duties and being replaced in turn by the worker just below him in status, and so on.

Often, because of customer demands or low stock, both high- and low-status workers have to prepare the same vegetable. When this happens, status differentiations still occur, and those workers with higher status "[handle] later stages in the preparation process. This [places] them in direct contact with the range—the social pinnacle of the kitchen—and they [are] also in a position to criticize the workmanship of those handling preceding stages."[4]

Initiating Activity and Status Discrepancy

Another status element arises from the work activity itself. We might well expect workflow to create status differences because of the activities–interactions–sentiments cycle. Work is often accomplished through a

[3]Whyte, *Human Relations in the Restaurant Industry,* p. 36.
[4]Ibid., p. 38.

sequence of separate activities, and the restaurant is no exception. The customer instigates a complex series of functions and behaviors when he places his order. The waiter creates work for the kitchen by transferring the order to the cooks. The cooks, in turn, cause runners and stockmen to perform functions because of inventory levels or foods being ready to transport. Cooks and runners complete the cycle by furnishing the prepared orders to the waiter for delivery to the customer.

Restaurant organization and technology dictate who will perform which function and who will cause other organizational elements to initiate their technological specialities. Workflow seems highly rational and efficient as the customer's order is received, prepared, and delivered. Conflict can and does arise, however. Role behaviors and status incongruity are two major sources of conflict between formal and informal expectations.

Such conflict is best seen in the results of the process of *initiating activity* for others. The person who orders another to action occupies a higher-status position, as does the manager in relation to his subordinate. When the social systems derived from different formal organizational functions come into contact, socially based conflicts may flare. The kitchen has its own system of social relationships, as do waiters and the other restaurant functionaries. Sequential work activities, such as in the conduct of the restaurant's business, create formally required interfaces among these social systems.

The activities transmitted across system interfaces may be identified as stimuli intended to evoke particular responses. When the stimulus (order) is administered by a higher-status person, the chance that the proper response will be forthcoming is quite large. Resentment of being told what to do rarely occurs because of the higher-status person's right to influence the other. Proper role behaviors of initiator and responder are mutually agreed upon.

What about actions being initiated by a *lower*-status person? Whyte documented a number of cases in which the restaurant's technology and structure *require* a lower-status person to initiate a higher-status person's activity and the resentments, conflicts, and informal adjustments made.

Runners and Cooks

Runners are responsible mainly for the transportation of food orders to cooks and prepared foods to waiters. In trying to perform their duties they initiate activities for the cooks with orders and often try to influence the speed with which foods are prepared. High-status cooks typically resent such behavior from low-status (barely higher than potwashers and sweepers), inexperienced, low-paid, low-seniority, young runners.

Cooks usually react in ways calculated to quash runners' affrontery, by responding aggressively or by initiating action for the *runner*. Aggressive responses remind the runner abruptly that he has no authority over the cook. An example of responding by initiating action might be the salad maker's refusal to bring the runner eggs from the refrigerator, telling him to get them himself.

Ignoring the status discrepancies in women's initiating activity for men, runners and cooks' relative status differences can create conflicts. One adjustment was the use of a "buffer" between the two. Whyte related how a revolving spindle was set up so that the runner's order was placed on the spindle, and the cook merely handled each order in turn. No direct contact, and no direct conflict, then occurred between runner and cook. The impersonal spindle absorbed status differences and discrepancies and initiated action. The same spindle buffer, often reinforced by a high counter, is usually interposed between service pantry worker and waiter. The service pantry worker receives foods from the kitchen and prepares each order for the appropriate waiter. The spindle removes the need for personal confrontation and automatically removes favoritism by holding each order for attention in its turn. Role sendings and influence attempts are largely useless because of the impersonal technology interposed between social systems and role behaviors.

Bartenders and Waitresses

Another common conflict from status discrepancy stems from the required interactions between bartenders and waitresses. Waitresses often double as takers of drink orders and hence initiate activity for bartenders. In Whyte's study, the male bartenders found several ways to reduce the status discrepancy they experienced, all of which were primarily centered on turning aside waitress-initiated activity.

One bartender reorganized the process of taking orders. He refused to accept drink orders from waitresses unless they stood in line and gave their orders in turn. Another responded in quite another way when tensions and pressures built up: "when too many girls tried to originate action for him at the same time, or when one girl seemed unduly aggressive—he just slowed down or stopped working until the waitresses responded to him in the desired manner."[5] Such behaviors put the bartenders on the initiating end of the work transaction, for the waitresses were forced to respond in "appropriate" ways to get their orders filled.

How serious is conflict from status and role discrepancy? Tensions build under the pressures for task performance in each functional area in the restaurant, and close coordination among them is essential to satisfying the customer. Yet each area—order taking and delivery, food preparation, and transportation—directly affects the ability to attain the overall goal. Such joint responsibility and required dependence on others over whom one has no influence can create serious frustration. As a matter of fact, tempers do

[5]Ibid., p. 78.

flare quite routinely, heated words are exchanged, and tears flow from conflicts across system interfaces. Production can slow down or stop because of perceived inappropriate behaviors from lower-status individuals. Orders are deliberately delayed for specific waiters in the attempt to influence them to behave in accordance with informal expectations.

System Interactions

Throughout the book, and especially this chapter, we have recognized that no single behavior system component produces organizational behavior. Each system interacts with the other systems, sometimes in seemingly unpredictable ways. Because we now have a better idea of the separate natures of these systems—formal organization, individual, and group—and some rudimentary knowledge of how they interface with each other, we can now trace *interactions.*

Our original systems model developed in Chapter 3 assumes a great deal of importance because it shows in concrete form the important relationships *across,* as well as *within,* systemic boundaries. Figure 19-2 provides a handy reference to the earlier model but is modified to exclude the modification and integration processes for analytical ease. Although we obviously cannot trace every possible series of relationships—there are a stupendous number of these—we can see how the model can be employed to analyze almost any conceivable situation and predict behavioral effects.

An Intersystem Example

"I just don't understand it," Harry shook his head slowly, bewildered. "My micromotion studies and work analyses were all conclusive that production would increase by better than 20 per cent. . . . Instead it went *down* by 12 per cent. . . . Most of all, though, I'm sorry that I let you down, Charlie. After all, you gave me the opportunity to try my hand on a project. It's not often that a brand-new industrial engineer can do that and I blew it."

Charlie patted Harry on the shoulder soothingly. "Don't sweat it, kid. Look, the only real way to learn practical stuff is by trying it out and seeing if it works. Theory's fine, but a lot of the time what the textbooks tell you just doesn't work." Harry looked up in surprise, and Charlie continued, "Don't get me wrong, now . . . the big thing is just that things are never as simple in real life as they are in books. Take your production project, for example. Tell me how you went about it."

"Well, you know about my analysis; it's all in the report I turned in to you before you gave the go-ahead." Charlie nodded. "Then I took my stop watch and data sheets and went into the production area. All five of the three-man teams were at work—if you call it work, laughing and talking and carrying on. I asked the foreman to pull one of the teams off duty to test out my ideas; I took them over into the empty shed and told them that they were to learn a new production setup that would be easier and less fatiguing and that would increase production and, therefore, their pay. (As you know, they're paid on the basis of the team's production.)

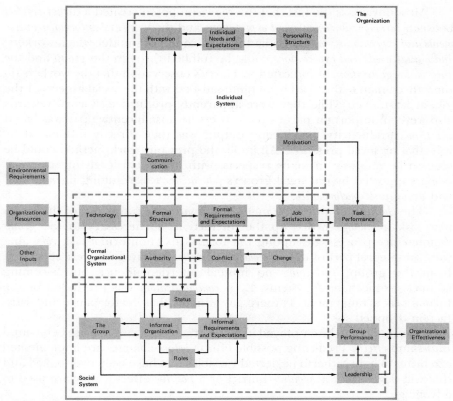

FIGURE 19-2   A systems model of organizational behavior.

"I showed them the new procedures and workplace layouts, then let them get used to it before timing them. You know, they should have been happy as larks— here they worked less hard then before but were able to make more money. I timed them in their new procedures for two weeks. Do you know that the *best* they did was a production rate 12 per cent lower than the old way? I couldn't believe it. My figures all checked, though.

"Paying each worker for his own production should have encouraged each one to put out more. And getting them out of each other's way by spacing their work stations five feet apart and connecting them with a conveyor belt should have increased efficiency, too. So why didn't it?"

"Hmmmm," said Charlie.[6]

Could Harry have predicted that production would drop and that his carefully calculated change would fail? To what can we attribute the results he experienced? The systems model helps trace what happened.

[6]Robert M. Fulmer and Theodore T. Herbert, *Exploring the New Management* (New York: Macmillan, 1974), p. 256.

Most obvious is the fact that the *change* imposed created a direct *conflict* between *formal requirements and expectations* and the workers' *informal requirements and expectations; technology* had created conditions under which workers' *individual needs and expectations* could be fulfilled through the *group* and the *informal organization,* as indicated by Harry's observation that the workers (in their three-man teams) had been quite satisfied with the social aspects of the job, at least, even while they were apparently productive. Formal rewards also were an important part of the process because incentive pay was based on *team* productivity; production output was then directly influenced by informal or social pressures. All in all, the previous work method could be seen to be *satisfying* in many respects, with individual levels of *motivation* being supported by the small group's *job satisfaction,* resulting in *individual* and *group* task *performance.*

The *change* did away with many of the *satisfying* conditions of the job. A new task *technology* broke up the interactions so necessary to the *group* maintenance process, disrupting the formal and nonformal task *roles* that were an integral part of the *informal organization.* Individuals were separated from the group, *perceiving* no mutual interdependence but becoming adjuncts to mechanical systems. Even *communication* was precluded by the formal task arrangement. Is there any wonder that performance and satisfaction dropped so?

The model can be employed in many other situations to trace behavioral *causes* and *effects.* Predicting possible effects *before* changes are implemented can bring to light hitherto neglected variables that have been overlooked and that will have either a *negative* impact or a *positive* effect if they are used to advantage.

Social System: Hostile or Benign?

We musn't consider the social system a deterrent to efficient operations, however. Well-communicated role expectations and status perceptions contribute to well-organized efforts. When such emergent behaviors support and reinforce task technology, overall goal attainment is made easier, as was the case in the kitchen's status structure. When formal and informal expectations clash, then counterproductive results are inevitable, as we saw at the restaurant activities' interfaces.

The manager, to be effective, should understand the effects of task technology and organization on individual and social structure alike. Knowing what the potential conflicts are, he can move confidently to remove frictions and inconsistencies in expectations. Organizational behavior that meets the *compatible* requirements of individual, group, and firm is encouraged. Behaviors are enacted that allow the mutual needs satisfaction and goal attainments of the three major systems in organizational behavior. A total environment capable of evoking the highest aspirations and growth possibilities is created.

But understanding is not truly enough. The manager must *intervene* in the fashioning of organizational behavior, changing and molding the organizational climate in ways that ensure mutuality of purpose among the three systems. He cannot accomplish this by exhorting members to try harder or by being friendlier to his subordinates. He must identify and reformulate the critical organizational behavior components—no small task. The tools available to him are the subject matter of the next series of chapters.

Summary

The social system is composed of interacting components that include groups, the informal organization, status, roles, conflict, change, and leadership. They have in common the association with social interrelationships and purposes shared by individuals. Some of the ways in which the social system operates were discussed, such as the impact of group norms on individual behaviors and the conflict between formal and informal expectations. Informal leadership is the dynamic process that gathers and directs social energies in concert toward accomplishment of group goals and that encourages appropriate behaviors by the use of example and sanction.

The individual finds himself a member of what are usually two competing systems, social and formal organization. Each makes demands of him, seeking to secure behaviors consistent with its own systemic goals. At the same time, the social system can act as a buffer between the weakness of the individual and the vast authority of technology and organization, giving safety and belonging in the group. Finally, the formal organization seeks to deal with its members through the administrative device of departmentation and task teams, securing task efficiency and predictability.

The social system's characteristics in a familiar setting, the restaurant, were offered. Especially evident were the dictates of technology and organization as they create the framework within which the social system flourishes. Status, roles, and conflict are the three social system components of greatest interest.

The next section of chapters offers insights and applications of managerial tools for the effective modification and integration of organizational behavior. With these techniques, the manager can intervene in the organizational behavior system, identify and change major components, and create a more effective and satisfying environment. If we trace the interactions and components of the organizational behavior system, a design can be set up so that mutually supportive systems are created, each successfully accomplishing its own goals while contributing to broader goal attainment.

STUDY AND REVIEW QUESTIONS

1. How are informal expectations capable of influencing individual behavior?

2. Leadership is represented (Figure 19-1) as a role emerging from the group that acts in conjunction with informal expectations to yield behavior tendencies. Given this perspective, under what conditions can a manager be a leader?

3. Why is higher status usually attributed to the leadership role?

4. How does a group differ from an informal organization? How important is this distinction?

5. What part does the informal leader play in the effective implementation of change?

6. Identify a social system with which you are familiar. Briefly relate the interactions among its constituent elements. (Hint: you might wish to review the restaurant study for pointers.) What conflicts and interfaces does this system have with the formal organizational system?

7. How do roles cause group members to conform to informal expectations?

8. Why do the norms and values of the informal organization create conflict with the requirements of the formal organization? How may these conflicts be resolved?

SECTION

V

MODIFICATION AND INTEGRATION PROCESSES

Chapter

20

The Manager as Leader: Managerial Styles

CHAPTER OBJECTIVES

1. To explore the leadership dimension of the manager's role through the concept of managerial style.

2. To present three major styles or consistent patterns of behavior of interest to the manager.

3. To evaluate the managerial styles' effectiveness under varying conditions and to point out their strengths and pitfalls.

CHAPTER OUTLINE

Through this point in the text we have examined in some detail the separate systems in organizational behavior. We have traced the impacts of the formal organizational system, the social system, and the individual. These three coexisting systemic elements interact to produce organizational behavior.

The Manager's Role in Modifying and Integrating Organizational Behavior

Conflicts will always occur: between formal organization and individual, between formal organization and social system, and between individual and social system. The manager must fulfill his responsibility for attaining results. His task is to find a strategy and a set of tools with which effective organizational behavior is maximized and destructive conflicts minimized. Such a responsibility is enormous in scope and complexity. The effective manager must first understand the nature of the systems with which he is dealing before he can effectively modify organizational behavior or integrate the major systems.

Without a basic understanding, he stands the very great risk of simply aggravating an already harmful situation. He could, by undertaking inappropriate actions through ignorance, completely disrupt whatever constructive behaviors currently result from the interactions and interchanges among the organizational behavior systems. The current status of effective behaviors must be evaluated, the major systemic inputs to the creation of the behaviors estimated, counterproductive conflicts within the systems determined, and the desired configurations of behaviors forecast. Only then can he undertake appropriate actions to modify the components of the organizational behavior system in order to integrate these systems more effectively. If he is successful, an overall climate or environment will be created that is conducive to organizational behavior and that mutually satisfies the purposes and needs of the three *separate* systems.

The essence of these modification and integration techniques is the manager's *intervention* in organizational behavior. He must actively take a part in, and restructure, the factors that make up the separate components producing organizational behavior. He cannot, by force of personality, make people behave differently or react more constructively to formal requirements. Only by acting directly on the people, groups, and organization involved can he modify organizational behavior into more desirable paths.

In this section we will look at four major ways available to the manager in modifying organizational behavior and integrating the three systems. The first of these, the subject of this chapter, is managerial styles. The overall manner in which the manager performs his activities and sets the environment for his subordinates is related to the results he might expect to obtain. The second is the application of learning theory and positive behavior reinforcement. The third is job enrichment, in which the individual task is redesigned to give more satisfying elements to its holder. Finally, we will investigate the broad outlines of organizational development; this is an overall approach to changing organizational structure that uses planned intervention and change in order to make the organization more responsive to human and social needs.

The Case for Managerial Style

All managers are not leaders, nor are all leaders managers. Yet a manager must inspire confidence and facilitate the accomplishment of his work group's objectives. He cannot be a true leader in the full sense of the word, of course. We saw in Chapter 18 the essential differences between leadership and managership. Few managers are directly appraised by their subordinates, and few are deposed simply because their subordinates no longer wish to obey them. Other major differences exist, too, between the two roles. Probably the most obvious difference is the nature of the goals of the respective groups. The leader's group has internally generated goals— goals that the members have set for themselves and tasks that they have agreed to undertake in order to reach these goals. The manager's work group, on the other hand, rarely has very much to say about the nature of the goals nor the ways in which they are to be attained. These goals are imposed on the manager and his work group by the formal organization. Such a series of critical differences makes the task of the manager as leader all the more difficult.

The manager recognizes that he is attempting to manage more than just a work group; he is also attempting to manage both informal groups and highly diverse individuals. Individuals possess great potential for initiative and creativity, which the manager seeks to tap in appropriate situations. He needs to draw forth their productive efforts through the means at his disposal. Yet the informal group serves as a buffer between the formal requirements of the manager and the powerlessness of the individual. It allows a coalition of individuals who share common interests and thereby increases their total power to resist arbitrary or detrimental requirements and to influence the manager in turn. There are powerful forces at work all around the manager, which can either complicate or facilitate his role performance.

Styles of Managerial Behavior

The findings and implications of the Lewin and White studies on leadership styles (cited in Chapter 18) have been held out to practicing managers for application in organizational settings. The concepts of managerial style that have been most widely accepted and used center around

Theory X–Theory Y assumptions and the autocratic–democratic–laissez-faire styles. We will investigate the results of using these styles after we introduce the notion of characteristic managerial patterns of behavior and activity.

The Managerial Grid: Production and People

The managerial grid was developed to give a pictorial representation to the practicing manager of his basic orientation. Essentially the grid is composed of two axes, one labeled "Concern for Production" and the other "Concern for People." Through a test, the manager can determine his own particular style, "pure production," "pure people," or (as is usually the case) a mixture of focus on production and on people.[1] The practicing manager can establish where on the grid his own behavior pattern lies.

We see in Figure 20-1 that there are five squares shaded, which represent rather clear-cut style mixes. The square at the bottom left-hand corner of the grid—1,1 or the "impoverished" square—identifies a style with low concern for production coupled with low concern for people. The bottom right-hand square, indicating maximum concern for production—9,1 or the "task-oriented" style—is highly related to the characteristics of a leader who shows initiating structure behavior and no consideration. The task-oriented manager would give the work objectives of his group much higher priority then the needs to maintain friendly relationships or to minimize conflicts between group members.

The opposite of this extreme task orientation is that of square 1,9, the "country club" manager. This style is represented by the square at the top left-hand corner of the grid. Here "Concern for People" is maximum and "Concern for Production" is minimum. This manager would give top priority to the satisfactions and relationships of the work group. If work or formal requirements conflicted with their satisfactions, the formal requirements would be relaxed or waived. Such a style would probably make for a very comfortable social environment on the job yet would be ineffective in terms of a high or prolonged level of task performance.

Midway between these two extreme styles is that of square 5,5, the "middle-of-the-road" manager. Under this style concern for production is balanced with concern for people, to attain a satisfactory level of morale *and* of task performance. The position of the grid that Blake and Mouton represented as the "best" managerial style is square 9,9, the "team" style. Such a style is characterized by the integration of interpersonal relationships and task performance, through the molding of a task-oriented group with the manager as leader.

[1]The managerial grid was developed by Robert Blake and Jane S. Mouton, *The Managerial Grid* (Houston, Texas: Gulf Publishing Company, 1964).

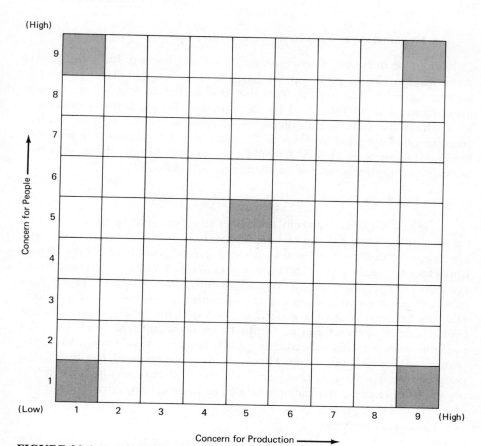

Concern for Production ➝

FIGURE 20-1   The managerial grid.

(1,1) or "Impoverished" Manager: Exertion of minimum effort to get required work done is appropriate to sustain organization membership.

(9,1) or "Task-oriented" Manager: Efficiency in operations results from arranging conditions of work in such a way that human elements interfere to a minimum degree.

(1,9) or "Country-Club" Manager: Thoughtful attention to needs of people for satisfying relationships leads to a comfortable friendly organization atmosphere and work tempo.

(5,5) or "Middle-of-the-road" Manager: Adequate organization performance is possible through balancing the necessity to get out work while maintaining morale of people at a satisfactory level.

(9,9) or "Team" Manager: Work accomplishment is through committed people, interdependence through a "common stake" in organization purpose leads to relationships of trust and respect.

SOURCE: From Blake and Mouton, *The Managerial Grid;* and Robert R. Blake, *et al.,* "Breakthrough in Organization Development," *Harvard Business Review* (November–December 1964), p. 136.

An Introduction to Free-Rein, Democratic, and Authoritarian Styles

When we discussed Theories X and Y we emphasized that assumptions about human nature make up the basis for handling people in consistent patterns of ways. The assumptions that lead to behavior styles are largely unconscious and unrecognized by the manager. So too is the overall style with which the manager implements his philosophy of human nature, conveniently expressed in terms of Theories X and Y. Obviously a manager holding the tenets of Theory X would not—and could not—be an effective manager using democratic or laissez-faire methodologies.

The Free-Rein Style

The laissez-faire ("free-rein") manager supervises indirectly if at all. The conduct of the work and the making of decisions directly relevant to the task are delegated to the subordinates who have greater knowledge of the factors important to the decision. The free-rein manager recognizes his limitations regarding the technical aspects of the job and, with confidence, gives to his subordinates decision-making rights and authority over day-to-day affairs. His role becomes that of a general supervisor who establishes merely the broad policies and outlines of things to be done and then delegates the implementation to his subordinates. Such behavior would seem to fit the pattern of beliefs underlying Theory Y, which expressed the belief that people can enjoy work and seek responsibility and can exert initiative in the accomplishment of organizational as well as personal objectives.

The Democratic Style

The democratic style is characterized by the soliciting of subordinates' input, desires, and information, and relatively little psychological distance between manager and subordinate. The democratic manager cannot be aloof, cold, or unconcerned with his subordinates. He must instead have a great deal of respect for and confidence in them. The manager still maintains control and does not relinquish his responsibilities. *He* makes the ultimate decisions, but only after consulting his subordinates to determine their feelings and to utilize their knowledge. In these ways he seeks to make the decision that is best for all concerned.

The democratic manager expresses basic consideration for his subordinates and recognizes his own limitations. He would appear to have a mixture of Theory X and Theory Y assumptions, if we were forced to make a categorization.

The Authoritarian Style

The autocratic or authoritarian manager differs quite drastically from the democratic and the free-rein managers. As was noted with the autocratic leadership style, the authoritarian manager retains for himself the decision-making rights, keeps himself aloof from the group, is extremely task-oriented, and relates to his subordinates through the commands and orders he gives them. He initiates all activity, and communication is typically one-way, being downward only. His behaviors may be directly traced to Theory X assumptions.

A Continuum of Managerial Styles

A rough idea of the relationships among these three leadership styles is given in Figure 20-2; we can see that the authoritarian style is not an "all-or-nothing" style. Rather, there are *degrees* of authoritarianism, ranging from "pure" authoritarianism to authoritarianism mixed with substantial amounts of democracy. The "pure" authoritarian behaves in the fashion indicated by the "pure" Theory X assumptions and makes all decisions by himself, without input from subordinates. He is highly task-oriented and tends to perceive his subordinates as mere commodities, without capacity or willingness to perform of their own volition. It is his perceived role to coerce and force them to live up to formal organizational requirements. He must then closely supervise their activities lest they take advantage of the freedom and indulge in nonproductive behaviors. He is the source of all authority regarding his work group and jealously guards his influence rights. Should his authority be questioned, the authoritarian leader would perceive an attack on his right to manage and would probably react in a forceful and direct manner.

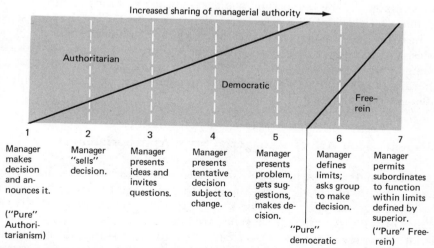

FIGURE 20-2 A continuum of managerial behavior and managerial styles. Source: Adapted from Robert Tannenbaum and Warren H. Schmidt, "How to Choose a Leadership Pattern," *Harvard Business Review* (March–April 1958), p. 96.

The extent of authoritarianism diminishes as the manager increases the sharing of his authority with subordinates. In the other extreme case, that in which the manager completely shares authority with his subordinates, we have the "pure" free-rein style. The free-rein manager, as previously pointed out, establishes the broad policy limits and overall task objectives but allows his subordinates to make relevant decisions and to achieve the objectives in any manner they see fit.

Subordinates under successful free-rein managers are those who, by virtue of technology or personality, are ego-involved, oriented to organizational as well as personal objectives, highly responsible, and possessing great initiative—Theory Y assumptions. Given this type of subordinate, a complete centralization of authority in the person of the manager would be clearly counterproductive. Also the nature of the task to be done and other technological requirements may make inappropriate the centralization of decision making in the person of the manager; he may be not qualified to make decisions of a highly technical nature and of grave consequences. Research and development groups are generally administered under free-rein management, as are other knowledge-based and creativity-intensive organizations. Even under the free-rein style we can see that this is just one end in a continuum of possible styles and that the "pure" free-rein managerial style is not the only form of free-rein style. Instead, it can be readily mixed with varying degrees of democracy.

Falling in between the two extremes in managerial styles is that in which a rather substantial amount of the manager's authority is consistently shared with subordinates, the *democratic managerial style*. Here manager and subordinate are seen to be relatively equal in their abilities to contribute toward the unit's task goal. The democratic manager—probably rating around 9,9 on the managerial grid if he is effective—is more of a "leader" in the pure sense of the word than the managers who employ either authoritarian or free-rein styles. The extremely democratic manager is represented in Figure 20-2 as falling between points 5 and 6 on the "sharing of managerial authority" axis, where manager and subordinates have the same approximate amount of influence on activities and decisions.

Elements That Affect Managerial Style Appropriateness

Each of these "pure" styles of management has very definite advantages—and disadvantages—associated with it. In objectively appraising the three managerial styles, we must keep four major points in mind: (1) the names of the three managerial styles are "value-laden," conjuring up emotional responses to the ideas associated with the terms and not necessarily with what the styles themselves represent; (2) we will be talking in terms of "pure" styles but must remember constantly that the pure or ideal forms are relatively rare; rather, the multitude of "mixed" styles predominate in practice; (3) there is no universal managerial style that is "best" in all situations;

the characteristics of the situation dictate which style is most effective; and (4) the manager's style is the pattern of ways in which he seeks to attain organizational objectives, his first and primary responsibility.

How can the manager realistically appraise which managerial style is most appropriate for his situation? Four elements offer insights: need for participation, the result of commitment, closeness of supervision required, and the supportiveness of the manager.

How Important Is Participation?

One of the implicit questions that underlies the subject of managerial styles is the importance of participation by subordinates in the optimizing of managerial effectiveness and organizational goal attainment. The question is highly pragmatic because information relevant to managerial decisions may be possessed by subordinates as a result of their more direct involvement in work activities.

Ego Involvement

Participation in the decisions that affect subordinates can encourage ego involvement in the activities and functions of the work group. Ego involvement can be important for heightening levels of commitment, involvement, and motivation. The worker has a clearer understanding of his place in the work group and the constraints and difficulties involved in coordinating and managing the unit.

Decreasing Status Differentials

There is also gratification from being asked one's opinion, rather than merely being informed of what one is going to do without having any say in the matter. Another way of looking at this is to remember some of the factors important in the status differential. An individual who initiates activity for another is ascribed higher status, and hence the person whose work is initiated by another is of relatively lower status. The organizational hierarchy does differentiate in status and authority because of its very nature. Participation and consultation among workers and managers can diminish the status differential somewhat. Decreasing status differences can also mean that the psychological distance between managerial levels is decreased. This, in turn, tends to ensure that communication channels and relevant communications and information are more effectively transmitted—both upward and downward.

How Far Should Participation Go?

Participation does not—and should not—extend to every managerial decision. Participation techniques are probably most appropriate to matters of work activity, work methods changes, work assignments, vacation schedule preference, and other decisions that directly relate to subordinates and their satisfactions. There still remain a number of areas in which workers cannot participate formally.

Some of these are in policy determination in which the overall direction of purpose of a company or work group is established. Another is in the formal allocation of promotions and raises. Major reasons for excluding participation in the broad and basic decision areas reflect the fact that the manager is ultimately responsible for his contribution to attaining organizational objectives. His task is to direct and coordinate the activities of others in the pursuit of those objectives. Should he lose control over what objectives are given priority—organizational, social, or individual—he places himself in serious role conflict.

The organization is an economically based institution, the major purpose of which is to produce goods and services for the elements of society it serves. The marketplace and that society must eventually determine how well it does that job, and its management must attempt to satisfy its clientele by operating as effectively as possible. Participation by major groups in the determination of the basic nature of the firm and its purpose can place serious constraints on the firm's economic viability, especially in highly competitive situations. Those formally in charge must have the capability to influence that for which they are responsible, with as little confusion as possible.

Participation that is limited to the areas in which subordinates are competent and directly affected are the areas in which participation can most effectively be used. These comments do not rule out the idea of subordinate *representation* in major policy decisions, which can give needed balance to the decision process. But for workers to be allowed to participate fully, with equal influence in making decisions, can result in authority's being effectively withdrawn from those held responsible and to short-term accommodations being favored over longer-term considerations.

The Importance of Commitment

Together with the ego involvement brought on by participation and consultation, commitment to organizational goals is an important element that can more nearly integrate the behavior of the individual with the activities required by the formal organization for goal attainment. The rationale is that if the individual identifies with an end product or end purpose and is committed to attaining it, he will be more motivated to exert additional energy and initiative toward that end. The uncommitted individual merely performs the bare essentials required of his employment, at the rate and the quality level expected of him. These expectation levels are largely determined by the concept of "the average," hardly an incentive to superior levels of performance and high aspiration levels. The committed individual is not content to perform at *expected* levels, however. His purpose is to attain the end result with which he strongly identifies, even if it means some sacrifice on his own part.

Commitment to organizational objectives is especially important in organizations in which work is not extremely routine or programmed and in which initiative and creativity are important. In some few organizations commitment to organizational goals is identical with commitment to the individual's goals. Research scientists, for example, find that by striving to meet their own professional purposes, they are also directly contributing to the formal expectations and requirements of the organization. In other organizations such congruency between individual and organizational goals is rarely found. In most situations there is an implicit assumption that individual and organization must necessarily conflict in their objectives. The securing of commitment, through participation, motivation, and redefinition of goals, makes possible the integration of individual and organization, and also the modification of individual and group work behaviors to higher levels and qualities.

Closeness of Supervision

The third element that influences managerial style appropriateness is the closeness of supervision required by the nature of the task and the organizational purpose. In many cases the term *closeness of supervision* is synonymous with *control*. Closeness of supervision is also closely allied with the extent of delegation and decentralization permitted within the formal organization and implemented by the manager. A "close" supervisor is a supervisor who is constantly checking and evaluating the procedures and activities of his subordinates. The phrase "always looking over your shoulder" is typically applied to such a superior. The "general" supervisor, on the other hand, focuses on results and allows the individual to accomplish those results as he wishes, as long as he does not exceed his authority or organizational guidelines. The close supervisor has many of the same characteristics as the Theory X manager, whereas the general supervisor is highly correlated with the manager who uses the assumptions of Theory Y.

One of the advantages of general supervision, in those jobs in which some initiative and originality are important, is the stress on the final purpose of what the subordinate is doing, rather than the *way* in which he is doing it. This reinforces the concept of identification with the purposes of his task and encourages him to see how that task interrelates with organizational purpose. The close supervisor, on the other hand, forces his subordinates to be more concerned with doing their activity the "right" way, rather than reaching the end point in a manner consistent with organizational purpose.

A bureaucratic phenomenon called *goal displacement* is typical of what can happen under close supervision. Under goal displacement, the *way* in which something is done, the procedure, is more important than *what* is to be accomplished. Thus rules and regulations cannot be bent, and people jealously guard their authority territorial rights even to the point of detriment to the overall organization.

The close supervisor should not be arbitrarily dismissed, however. In many cases the way in which the work is done is extremely important. Allowing individuals to assemble an atomic bomb as they wish, under general supervision, and being concerned only if the final product works is a little short-sighted. The general supervisor in such a situation may never get the chance to inspect the final product because of an experimenting and creative technician!

The Supportive Manager

In his important study of effective managers Likert found that managers of highly productive units differed in major ways from ineffective managers. High-producing managers developed and maintained supportive relationships. Under these high-producing managers, "The leadership and other processes of the organization must be such as to ensure a maximum probability that in all interactions and all relationships with the organization, each member will, in light of his background, values, and expectations, view the experience as supportive and one which builds and maintains his sense of personal worth and importance."[2] Low-producing managers were more oriented toward Theory X and attempted to control through their authority. In contrast, the high-producing managers used extensive participation and group-leadership techniques in building an integrated team that was committed to organizational goals.

Evaluating the Managerial Styles

The three managerial styles display varying amounts of closeness of supervision, commitment to organizational goals, participation, and supportiveness. To evaluate the three styles objectively we must know the advantages and disadvantages of each. We will consider both positive and negative sides, in order to establish more objectively the limitations associated even with these "pure" styles and to point out that no one of them is universally effective or without flaws.

The Positive Side of Authoritarianism

Here we will look into the positive and negative aspects of the authoritarian manager, beginning with what is easily overlooked, its positive side. We will try to keep a balanced view, so that we may be objective.

[2]Rensis Likert, *New Patterns of Management* (New York: McGraw-Hill, 1961), p. 103.

High Productivity over Short Periods of Time

In cases of temporary work groups or a new manager, an authoritarian style can result in increased productivity by subordinates. Such measures may quite effectively stimulate physiological or security needs, increasing motivational force to do just as the authoritarian says. Fear of losing one's job can, over the short run, be powerful. The subordinates will more than likely have low morale and few satisfactions from happiness, but the increased production may, under appropriate circumstances, be maintained for a year or so.[3]

High Consistency and Uniformity

The authoritarian manager may find his style extremely appropriate in those situations in which uniformity and consistency are essential. Union contracts, for example, may dictate that certain matters be handled in exactly the agreed-upon manner and without a great deal of leeway. Similarly antitrust laws and legal contracts may also make essential the performance of duties according to clearly stipulated and imposed criteria. Finally, accounting practices furnish a major illustration of the critical needs for uniformity in reporting and interpreting data.[4]

Expediency Organization

Certain types of organizations (the military, the police, and fire departments) require a great extent of control over work processes and absolute adherence to policy and procedure. Under the emergency conditions of war, riot, or fire, one person may direct the activities of all organizational members; organizational effectiveness may hinge on the unquestioning acceptance and performance of assigned duties by those members.[5]

Highly structured organizations, and especially those with mass-production or process technologies, require rigid adherence to carefully formulated organizational policies and procedures that stem directly from the nature of the production technology. Extreme specialization of task, many hierarchical levels, small spans of management, and limited delegation similarly encourage authoritarian management.

Personality Characteristics

Subordinates may be much more receptive to authoritarian and firm management than they are to more open and permissive managers, whom

---

[3]William Fox, *The Management Process* (Englewood, N.J.: Prentice-Hall, 1963), p. 209.
[4]Harold Koontz and Cyril O'Donnell, *Principles of Management,* 4th Ed. (New York: McGraw-Hill, 1968), p. 417.
[5]William T. Greenwood, *Management and Organizational Behavior Theory* (Cincinnati: South Western Publishing Co., 1966), p. 442.

they perceive as being weak and indecisive. Whether this is because they have become accustomed to authoritarianism or whether they merely prefer it is beside the question. Personality traits are extremely difficult to change, certainly over a short period of time, and authoritarianism may be forced on the manager because of the expectations and demands of his subordinates.[6]

Forces in the supervisor himself may lead him to authoritarianism for effective performance; because of a highly structured personality, intolerance of ambiguity, or high achievement needs, the manager may exercise direct authority over all relevant activities of his subordinates. Once again, adapting a style that conflicts with his underlying personality will hardly be appropriate over the long run. Instead of so doing, he should make sure that his "natural" managerial style is appropriate for the situation in which he finds himself.

Negative Aspects of Authoritarianism

Authoritarianism has a number of negative considerations, based on the extent of dependence on a single person.

The Authoritarian Personality

In a study of the authoritarian personality Adorno and his colleagues were able to determine significant attitude patterns very consistent with the assumptions of Theory X.[7] They found that individuals with authoritarian characteristics were generally conventional and conforming and less apt to be open to change, resulting in rather rigid beliefs. Authoritarians' standards for evaluating others were based on such matters as power and toughness and were little attuned to motivational matters or the individual needs of others.

Alford suggested that the authoritarian manager is also insecure, compensating for this feeling through a show of strength. He fears losing his power and hence cannot delegate authority with ease.[8] Some continual need to emphasize superiority—and hence the inferiority of others—may also be part of the authoritarian personality, which explains his behavior. This may result in the creation of "a relationship of personal dependency . . . that is highly destructive of the personality and self-respect of his subordinates."[9]

Competence of the Authoritarian

Centralized decision-making in the person of the manager requires that the manager have all appropriate information regarding the nature of the

[6]Erwin S. Stanton, "Which Approach to Manage . . . Democratic, Authoritarian, or (What)?" *Personnel Administration* (March 1962), p. 46.

[7]T. Adorno, E. Frenkel-Brunswik, D. Levinson, and R. Sanford, *The Authoritarian Personality* (New York: Harper, 1950).

[8]L. P. Alford, *Principles of Industrial Management* (New York: McGraw-Hill, 1968), p. 112.

[9]Mason Haire, *Organizational Theory in Industrial Practice* (Homewood, Ill.: Richard D. Irwin, 1961), p. 137.

problem, the full range of alternatives, their relative effectiveness in solving the problem, full knowledge of the results of each alternative solution, and the manner in which the solution can be implemented most effectively. As long as the authoritarian manager does, in fact, possess all the information and technical competence, then the authoritarian managerial style may be highly appropriate.

Under many mass-production technologies, information naturally flows to a higher centralized position, that of the manager. The nature of decisions tends to be relatively routine, and the information necessary to solve them naturally occurs in the manager's position. In these types of production technologies, the role of the manager is strongly geared to the function of coordination of closely related specialized activities, and no one of these units has all the information. He may then effectively make the decisions. His problem then becomes that of securing the confidence of subordinates and overcoming resistance to the changes and decisions he imposes.

Should the manager be operating in an area that is more dynamic or knowledge-intensive at his subordinates' level, then his competence to make decisions (especially technical decisions) diminishes rapidly. Yet the authoritarian manager, perhaps because of his basic nature, is hardly likely to relinquish his absolute authority even under these conditions. The authoritarian who is remiss in technical knowledge loses the respect of his subordinates and strains leader–member relationships even further.[10]

Reaction from Subordinates

The dependent relationship of subordinate on superior can create severe anxieties and frustrations, especially when the subordinate wishes to participate in decisions important to his activities. Dependence on the superior also creates anxieties because this is a *personal* relationship, and the authoritarian manager usually rewards his subordinates not on the basis of their performance but according to how well they submit and are loyal to him personally. The authoritarian motivation to dominate others can be received rather submissively or with hostility. The informal organization may well gain strength as subordinates seek to equalize a unilateral influence.

The authoritarian manager can also be the source of a job dissatisfier of significant dimensions. The authoritarian will not share task-related information or plans and maintains step-by-step control over each succeeding sequence of his subordinates' activities. Hence subordinates are kept in a perpetual state of confusion and lack of awareness regarding the total nature of their function and its purpose. Frustration can easily occur in an environment so filled with uncertainties and ambiguities. A lack of job satisfiers— and a preponderance of dissatisfiers—coupled with threats to security and esteem needs can strongly affect motivation and job satisfaction. The satis-

[10]Cf. Ernest Dale and L. C. Michelow, *Modern Management Methods* (New York: McGraw-Hill, 1964), p. 26.

faction of the authoritarian manager, however, would probably be quite high because of the satisfaction of *his* ego, status, security, and power needs.

Task Effectiveness

Bradford and Lippitt pointed out that the overall work-group effectiveness can be seriously hampered under the authoritarian manager, assuming that this style is inappropriate for the situation:

The lack of team work, intense competition among employees, buck-passing, knifing of others, lack of acceptance of responsibility, letdown of production when the supervisor was absent, resulted from the employees being frustrated in achieving basic personal needs from their work efforts. First, every employee needs to belong to and participate in a work group. Under the hardboiled autocrat there was no group to which to belong, but merely a collection of individuals dominated by one person. Second, every person needs a feeling of individual importance and satisfaction from personal effort. The only status possible to the employee was to be recognized and possibly favored by his supervisor. The supervisor, by assuming the central role of total responsibility and credit, frustrated any efforts of the employees to gain a sense of personal achievement and worth.[11]

In summary, the authoritarian managerial style possesses some very dramatic characteristics. It can be highly effective—when the situation calls for it. Some writers have suggested that authoritarian management is a thing of the past, primarily because of changing values and characteristics of the work force and new concepts of industrial democracy. Is authoritarianism dead? Authoritarianism may go against some widely held values, yet in certain situations there does not really seem to be an effective alternative. Perhaps a common characteristic of authoritarianism is not its demise but its shift along the "sharing of managerial authority" scale, with more clear demarcation between decisions that *must* be made only by the manager and those decisions that the manager need *not* decree, which really are more appropriate for subordinates to decide.

Across-the-board authoritarianism may indeed be gone, even from the bastion of bureaucratic centralization, the military. Decisions of length of hair, increased freedom in decorating one's dwelling quarters as he pleases, and lessened amounts of "make-work" tasks such as KP and litter removal are indications of increased personal freedom. Yet we would still expect to see rigid adherence to battlefield orders.

The democratic managerial style contrasts in several important ways with the authoritarian. The democratic manager shares his authority with his subordinates, uses several different types of techniques to encourage meaningful participation by subordinates in the decision-making function, employs two-way communication channels for full and thorough informa-

---

[11]L. P. Bradford and R. Lippitt, "Building a Democratic Work Group," *Personnel Journal,* **22**:145 (1945).

tion exchange, and is much more concerned with creating and maintaining sound interpersonal relationships between manager and group member, as well as among group members. The democratic manager is apt to be effective in a majority of industrial situations because of their characteristics and demands, which coincide with democratic characteristics.

Positive Aspects of the Democratic Style

The democratic manager employs techniques consistent with the assumptions of Theory Y, to a great extent. He believes that he does not have all of the information and that his subordinates are ready, willing, and able to accept the responsibility of participating in decisions that affect them. As a result he relinquishes an amount of his authority because he solicits input and gives it significant weight in his decision-making process. We must point out that the democratic manager still makes the decision. What is different is that he opens communication channels and information sources, allowing subordinates to influence the decision. He is still responsible for the decision's effectiveness, and because of limitations we will go into later he seeks to maximize the quality of the decision through participation and commitment.

Sutermeister summarized some characteristics of the democratic managerial style:

A democratic leader is likely to encourage his followers to take part in setting goals and methods and to contribute ideas and suggestions . . . the leader tries primarily to maintain good human relations and a smoothly running organization. He does not give detailed instructions or check frequently on his followers; he relies on their initiative and judgment; they have much freedom in planning their work.

. . . .

A democratic leader will carry out all aspects of his job in such a way as to indicate that he considers his subordinates important individual human beings, like himself, with ideas of their own and an eagerness to put their brains as well as their brawn to work when given a chance.[12]

Nature of the Task

The effective democratic manager employs his style best under conditions in which the activity he supervises is relatively routine yet still requires subordinate initiative and judgment. Mass-production work would not typically fall under this heading. The work must also be under the control of the subordinate, and not machine-paced, for example, so that the motivation and attitude of the subordinate affects productivity. At the same time, the nature of the tasks must be relatively flexible and changing so that worker perceptions and information may be a continuing process rather than a one-time-only input to be secured.

[12]Robert A. Sutermeister, *People and Productivity* (New York: McGraw-Hill, 1963), pp. 40, 41.

   This also suggests that major decisions that affect the nature of tasks and such things as work assignments or reorganization must be relatively common. None of these factors could typically occur frequently in process or mass-production technologies. Instead we will probably find democratic managerial styles especially apt for batch production and craftsman technologies. The purpose of using the democratic managerial style in these technologies is to secure the motivation, participation, and commitment to organizational objectives of the subordinates. Because they have relevant information regarding the state of affairs and technical factors of which the manager may not be aware, he is only wise to secure their participation. Further, we remember, under such technologies the individual himself affects his productivity, which is especially influenced by his satisfactions and motivations.

   The manger, then, cannot assume that the intrinsic satisfactions of work are sufficient to encourage the subordinate to maximize his efforts toward organizational goals. If precautions are not taken and if significant dissatisfactions arise, the informal organization can be quite powerful as well as extremely detrimental to high productivity. Work restriction can be especially damaging, as it decreases the potential production of the entire work group and also makes the work group more resistant to managerial efforts to integrate their purposes with that of the overall organization. Modification attempts on the manager's part are also met with extreme hostility and resistance.

   Because the democratic managerial style employs an entire program dedicated to securing participation in and commitment to overall goals, we can see that such a style can effectively mold a work group that displays more of the characteristics of a team, with the manager as leader, than could be obtained under authoritarian management. The integration of informal organization and work group, as well as formal organizational goals, is critical to the effective contribution to overall purposes.

Integrating Individual and Formal Motives

   The nature of the task we have just discussed indicates that subordinates under these technological conditions require more opportunity for growth and expression. The democratic manager, with his participation and commitment program, provides significant opportunities for such development. Security is enhanced through open and two-way communication, and also with full sharing of relevant information and plans that will affect the work group. Ambiguity and uncertainty about what the future holds are then diminished, creating a more secure work environment.

   Status differentials are also lessened because of the democratic manager's attention to creating sound interpersonal relations and the less aloof attitude that he must take toward his subordinates. Lessening the psychological distance between manager and subordinate, and at the same time creating less status differential, can be interpreted in one of two ways: either the manager is lessening his own status, or he is increasing the relative status of his subordinates. In either case such conditions would make for freer and more open communication and exchange of ideas between superior and subordinate.

Resistance to Change

A major detriment to the authoritarian style's effectiveness lies in securing acceptance and implementation of the decisions and changes made unilaterally. The democratic manager, through the very process of his management style, minimizes the chance of such negative consequences' occurring. After he has secured participation, commitment, and relevant information from his subordinates, he still must make the decision. Yet the manner in which he has gone about the decision-making process encourages subordinates to identify with the overall nature of the problem, the full range of possibilities open, and their relative consequences.

The Situation for Democratic Management

An obvious point to remember is that democratic management cannot succeed where workers are alienated, apathetic, or hostile to organizational goals. Democratic management allows the successful linking of individual and informal organizational needs to those of the formal organization. Relatively greater autonomy or freedom is granted the individual by the democratic manager. The overt hostility that creates a powerful informal organization is dissipated through open communication and heightened sensitivity to the manager's relationship with the work group.

The characteristics of the subordinates, too, are important to an effective democratic managerial style. If they are not willing to assume the responsibility that goes with participation, the manager cannot manage democratically. Effective participation additionally requires some identification by subordinates with the goals and objectives of the formal organization. They also need to have sufficient background and perspective, not to mention experience and knowledge, to make realistic suggestions on common problems and inform the manager of factors that he should know.[13]

The Negative Side of the Democratic Style

Democratic management, for all the positive results and values associated with it, is still not a universally effective style. Under some conditions it is much less effective than the other two managerial styles, and in still other cases it is completely inappropriate.

[13]Stanton, p. 47.

Time

Although a major benefit of democratic management is the full participation of those affected in the decision-making process, a negative factor
that goes hand in hand with the soliciting of all available inputs is the amount
of time that is demanded. The democratic managerial style imposes a huge
time commitment on the manager, and he must spend large blocks of it as he
solicits participation.

Subordinate Personality and Responses to Democratic Management

We pointed out earlier that some subordinates are not willing to participate in decision making and see the democratic manager as weak and hence
unworthy of leadership. Still others see democracy as an opportunity to
manipulate the manager to their own ends, rather than being objective in
their inputs. Certainly organizational members who more nearly fit the
assumptions of Theory X than Theory Y will not be comfortable under
democratic management and will not be *able* to participate effectively.

Lack of Commitment to Organizational Goals

Similarly members who cannot identify with, or are not committed to,
organizational goals cannot meaningfully participate in democratic management. Such a situation can become quite dangerous when they see democratic management as a way to satisfy their own personal or work objectives,
without attempting to integrate them with the broader purposes of the entire
work group and its manager. The situation is dangerous because of the
hostility evoked when the manager fulfills his responsibility by making a
decision that does not incorporate suggestions made by alienated members
or members who did not put in suggestions of high enough quality. Such
employees can well feel that they have been let down because an implication
of democratic management is the use of subordinate input. The manager is
still the ultimate decision-maker, and hence he must under many conditions
reject or modify certain of the suggestions made.

Lack of Equifinality

The term *equifinality* suggests that there are many different paths, all of
them terminating at the same level of goal attainment, and with the same
purpose. Many different salesmen employ entirely different techniques, yet
the end result may be sales ratios of roughly the same percentage. Under
many production technologies, however, such freedom may not be possible.
The workers in the industrial relations section may not be able to go on a
flexitime system (under which they each come in at their choice of time, for a
required number of hours, and then go home), simply because of the

random occurrence of labor grievances, which requires a full staff to be on hand all during plant working hours. And the design of an accounting information system may need to meet very specific criteria, imposed by the accounting practices management needs, and information-handling capability. Very few options may then be open for participation, and unsound design innovations may create serious problems later. In much the same way, many programmers may try to stick to relatively common routines as they program computers, because of the need for an independent check on the program in a process of debugging. An innovative "loop" may not work right or may require an inordinate amount of time for another programmer to understand its logic.

Physical Dispersion

A major prerequisite for participation and democratic management is access to and by subordinates. Many industrial firms are widely decentralized geographically, and thus getting people together for consultation may be time-consuming, expensive, and infrequent. A vice-president at central headquarters with a number of subordinate managers scattered throughout the country cannot call them in every week for consultation, and even long-distance telephone calls lose effectiveness in the gathering of information and in participation. Quarterly meetings also are too infrequent, and usually numerical data and performance review data take up the bulk of the time available. Under such conditions a relatively authoritarian establishment of general policies, subject to review and modification, may be initiated, with free rein being given to the managers to operate within the policy constraints. Full democratic management may simply be inappropriate.

At the end of the continuum at which the manager completely shares his authority with subordinates is the laissez-faire or free-rein managerial style. The free-rein manager may establish broad parameters of performance and of objectives and then completely withdraw from operational decisions. He delegates tasks almost completely and decentralizes decision making to the level where it is most appropriate. He still remains active in planning and performance review and is readily available whenever an exceptional circumstance arises or a decision needs to be made. Yet in almost all normal decisions and activities, the subordinates are responsible for handling their own affairs.

The Positive Side of the Free-Rein Style

The free-rein managerial style is rather controversial. Depending on its interpreter, it is regarded either as abdication of managerial responsibility or as the epitome of industrial humanization. Such wide divergence is probably the result of the free-rein style's being clearly appropriate in a limited and highly specific number of situations and clearly inappropriate in others.

Autonomy and Freedom

The broad areas of job freedom and decision capability granted by the free-rein manager are substantial grants of authority. In essence the manager is delegating major portions of his managerial job to his subordinates. Self-control and responsibility are enhanced and demanded under such a managerial form. The subordinate who is ready to assume such responsibility is rewarded only for the results he obtains and not for the ways in which he reaches them. Experimentation is encouraged, as are learning and self-growth.

Free-rein management requires that the subordinates' tasks be rather ambiguous in the nature of the activities and functions that compose them. It also requires that the subordinates be the critical elements in the success of the function. Research scientists and university professors typically function best under such management because it is impossible to coerce creativity or teaching effectiveness. The scientist or professor must *wish* to accomplish these purposes, and there is no one "right" way to accomplish such a purpose—performance is entirely a result of the individual and his personal approach. The manager simply evaluates the end results of the performance, within the stipulated policy guidelines. What this does is to allow the individual a great deal of freedom to meet organizational objectives in ways that also fulfill his own personal needs satisfactions. Such a situation can then lead to a highly meaningful and satisfying job.

Motivational Intensity

Because performance and activities are entirely dependent on the individual, he must be committed to performance objectives. Such commitment, in conjunction with professional pride and satisfaction, can increase the valence of work behaviors and also the instrumentality of its linkage to broader objectives, as well as subjective probabilities of success and reward. All these factors combine to increase significantly the motivational force exerted by the individual in the conduct of his duties. This may be one major reason why dedicated scientists and professors are usually found hard at work, often seven days a week, and well into the night.

Another amount of freedom, not usually recognized, is the freedom of the manager from the close supervisory controls usually necessary when subordinates' activities are carefully monitored for conformity with organizationally prescribed procedures. The free-rein manager need not do that but merely maintains a rather loose control, receiving periodic reports on goal attainment and finally "debriefing" his employees as they attain their organizational goals. Consequently the manager is able to spend much more time on the longer-range managerial functions, such as planning and organizing, rather than the shorter-range and more time-consuming functions of directing and controlling. His function is also made much easier because organizational rewards can be geared strictly to performance and not to other measures of process or activity.

Psychological Development

The freedom that is granted under free-rein management also requires that psychological development and personality development possibilities be well provided. Personal maturity and responsibility are encouraged, of course, as are managerial capabilities and the needs for achievement and independence. The manager's ability to trust and delegate is similarly developed, and a need to maintain close supervision over everything going on under his supervision is discouraged.

Negative Aspects of the Free-Rein Style

Although free-rein management offers many interesting possibilities, its thoughtless use in inappropriate situations can bring disastrous results. Such a style requires *much more sophisticated* managerial skills—not less.

Coordination Difficulties

The free-rein managerial style differs from the other two styles in that it is individual-centered rather than being boss-centered or group-centered. In essence, the manager delegates authority *to the individual* on tasks that are individual in nature and not dependent on the performance and input of other individuals. What this can mean is that the inexperienced or ineffective free-rein manager can ignore his coordination functions, to the detriment of his own ability to attain results. He can easily wind up with a number of separate individuals, each going in entirely uncoordinated different ways, and each arriving at quite different end points. The free-rein manager must use considerable patience and skill in the planning and communication of guidelines and end objectives to be striven for by subordinates.[14]

Personality Characteristics

We have previously noted that free-rein management demands mature and responsible subordinates. If subordinates do not meet these characteristics, then the lack of close supervision can quickly yield frustration, anxiety, and a sense of helplessness on the part of subordinates. An environment under free-rein management is either open and free or chaotic and uncomfortable, depending on one's perception and personality characteristics. Worker expectation similarly has a great deal to do with the effectiveness with which the style is put into effect.

[14]Cf. Sutermeister, p. 39.

Managerial Style and Motivation

Each of the three managerial styles has both positive and negative aspects. One of the major generalities we can make from looking at them is that each of the styles is an effective motivator—under specific conditions. Each can allow subordinates to satisfy their own personal needs, given the *right kind* of needs. Authoritarian management satisfies security and dependence needs. Democratic management satisfies ego, esteem, and social needs. Free-rein management satisfies independence and achievement needs.

The task for the manager is to examine the characteristics of his situation carefully, examine the needs and expectancy linkages appropriate for his task orientations, select an appropriate managerial style, and concentrate on raising the expectancies of both individuals and groups for attaining individual, group, and organizational goals. By so doing he can more nearly modify organizational behavior from its current state into that more nearly consistent with organizational requirements, and at the same time he can satisfy the expectations and needs of *each* of the three major systems in organizational behavior. As a result, inherent conflict can be minimized between system and human, and integration of purpose can more nearly be attained.

Managerial Style and Productivity

Each managerial style is unique in its characteristics, assumptions, and benefits. But what effect does managerial style have on attaining formal goals and performing duties? The end result of major interest to the manager of modification of organizational behavior must be the net impact on *his ability to obtain results.* Adopting a pattern of behaviors that make subordinates happy—but under which productivity drops—is hardly an effective managerial style.

Relatively little is known about the actual productivity differences between the various styles, holding constant the task type, workers, and so on. One study, which allows us to draw conclusions about appropriate managerial styles under one specific set of conditions, was performed some years ago at the Harwood Manufacturing Company in Marion, Virginia.[15] The company's main plant employed mostly women who produced pajamas under an individual piecework incentive system. Pay was directly related to the worker's average production for the week, and the production records of each worker were published every day.

Four different groups of workers—three experimental groups and one

[15]Lester Koch and John R. P. French, Jr., "Overcoming Resistance to Change," *Human Relations,* **1**:512–532 (1948).

control group—were selected and used to test the different effects of several managerial styles of introducing change. Table 20-1 summarizes the characteristics of each group and their respective tasks, the changes in work methods, the ways in which the changes were introduced, and the results after forty days.

The control group was exposed to the routine or traditional way of changing work methods. The job was modified by the production department and a new piece rate was established. The control group was then informed, in a group meeting, of the change and questions were answered. An authoritarian style was apparently used. No participation in designing the change or making any decisions was employed. Very little production improvement resulted, and much hostility and aggression were noted. Deliberate restriction of output occurred, cooperation with the supervisor failed to develop, grievances were filed about the rate established, and 17 percent of the control group quit within forty days.

Experimental group 1, on the other hand, was subjected to quite different conditions. A group meeting was held, as with the control group, but with a critical difference: the meeting was held *before* any changes were made or suggested. The critical need for reducing costs was dramatically presented to the group, and a general approach was approved by the experimental group:

1. Make a check study of the job as it was being done.
2. Eliminate all unnecessary work.
3. Train several operators in the correct methods.
4. Set the piece rate by time studies on these specially trained operators.
5. Explain the new job and rate to all the operators.
6. Train all operators in the new method so they can reach a high rate of production within a short time.[16]

The group chose the operators to be trained in the new methods. The special operators helped work out the details of the new methods. A second group meeting was held to present the changes to the entire group, and the special operators trained the group members in the new techniques. At the end of forty days production had increased about 10 percent. Worker attitudes were notably cooperative and permissive. The experimental group experienced no quits in the forty days, and there was only one act of aggression directed against the supervisor.

The second and third experimental groups went through the same general steps as did the first experimental group—group meeting, dramatic presentation of the need for change, general plan. The only difference was that *all* members were designated special operators; each member participated directly in the design of the change and the setting of the new piece rate. Results were quite impressive. Production quickly returned to normal

[16]Ibid., p. 521.

TABLE 20-1   Summary of Harwood Study

Group	Number in Group	Former Job	Changed to	Change Method	Result
I (Control)	18 hand pressers	Stack pressed garments in lots of 6 on a cardboard form.	Stack pressed garments in lots of 6 in a box.	Announcement of change to be made.	Little production improvement; resistance; grievances and hostility; 17% quit in first 40 days.
I (Experimental)	13 pajama folders	Fold coats with prefolded pants.	Fold coats with unfolded pants.	Participation through representation in designing change to be made.	10% production improvement; cooperation; no quits in first 40 days.
II (Experimental)	7 pajama examiners	Clip threads from entire garment; examine every seam.	Clip only certain threads; examine every seam.	Total participation of all group members in designing change to be made.	14% production improvement; no quits in first 40 days.
III (Experimental)	8 pajama examiners	Clip threads from entire garment; examine every seam.	Clip only certain threads; examine every seam.	Total participation of all group members in designing change to be made.	14% production improvement; no quits in first 40 days.

SOURCE: Adapted from Koch and French, "Overcoming Resistance to Change," pp. 520–522.

after the change and maintained constant improvement. After forty days production was about 14 percent higher than before the change. No aggressive incidents were observed, cooperation was outstanding, and no quits occurred.

These changes were, we must remember, relatively minor job changes and occurred in rather simple jobs. Yet the implications of increasing production with more democratic styles—together with less grievances, hostility, and turnover—are of concern to us. Alleviating anxieties and encouraging participation in decisions affecting employees' jobs are natural results of a democratic style of introducing change.

Summary

The manager's characteristic style of behaving influences his ability to obtain results through the efforts of others. A completely production-oriented style ignores the human and social needs of subordinates and can diminish motivation and job satisfaction. Too much concern for people and not enough for task accomplishment, on the other hand, may make happy and sociable subordinates but no contribution to organizational goals.

The democratic, free-rein, and authoritarian managerial styles were presented as pure types of behavior patterns employed in the managerial role. Each is characterized by different levels of employee participation in decision-making, commitment to organizational goals, closeness of supervision, and supportiveness.

Although our culture may encourage us to value the democratic and free-rein styles more than the authoritarian, the only pragmatic approach to be taken is to evaluate each style for optimum effectiveness in the given situation. No single style is universally effective, and each has positive as well as negative aspects.

The free-rein style offers considerable freedom to subordinates through the complete sharing of managerial authority. The manager assigns substantial responsibility for the directing and controlling functions to subordinates, allowing more time for the longer-run considerations of planning and organizing. Yet such a style requires close coordination and communication lest subordinates lose sight of overall objectives. Mature, responsible, and committed employees are essential to the effective use of free-rein management. Its success has typically been in isolated and uncommon conditions such as research and development laboratories or academic settings.

The democratic manager maintains decision responsibility yet solicits inputs from the subordinates directly affected by the decision. By so doing the manager recognizes that he has only limited information and that his subordinates may be closer to the problem, that they can contribute effectively, and that they should be given every consideration in voicing their feelings and opinions. The democratic manager is probably most effective when participation is used in the design of work methods changes, when the work is relatively routine, and when task performance is a function of motivated behavior.

Authoritarianism has its place, too. The reservation of all decision-making rights to the manager may be necessary under emerging conditions when more time-consuming participatory methods are not appropriate. The effective authoritarian is the one who does, in fact, possess all relevant information and who is in the position of being the sole person able to integrate conflicting demands. The authoritarian may have to make a difficult decision that is best for the entire unit or organization, even though it is bad for some subordinates. If he is to be effective under these conditions, the tasks supervised should be very routine and highly structured, probably of the mass-production type. He must still rely heavily on effective downward communications to remove anxieties and must ensure that resistance is minimized.

STUDY AND REVIEW QUESTIONS

1. Discuss the concept of "the *effectiveness* of managerial styles." What are the purposes to which managerial styles contribute, in the estimating of their effectiveness?

2. List and discuss the negative consequences to be expected when the free-rein style is used in an inappropriate situation.

3. List and discuss the negative consequences to be expected when the democratic style is used in an inappropriate situation.

4. List and discuss the negative consequences to be expected when the authoritarian style is used in an inappropriate situation.

5. Which managerial style do you think would be most effective for each of the five production technologies discussed in Chapter 4?

6. Which managerial style do you think would be *least* effective for *each* of the five production technologies discussed in Chapter 4? Why?

7. Discuss the "usual" managerial style employed by professors in your degree program. How effective is this style (be careful how you define *effective*)? How would the other styles rate in effectiveness in the classroom? Why?

8. Which style (or combinations of styles) would be most natural to the manager with high achievement needs? High power needs? High affiliation needs? Given the manager's role, evaluate the deficiencies or weaknesses of each manager and his natural style. What would be his unique strengths?

9. Does managerial style serve as a motivator to subordinates? Why or why not?

10. Which managerial style results in greater subordinate productivity? Explain.

Chapter
21

Learning Theory and Positive Behavior Reinforcement

CHAPTER OBJECTIVES

1. To furnish an overview of relevant concepts and theories of learning.

2. To provide insight into the applications of learning theory in organizational behavior.

3. To specify successful approaches to modifying organizational behavior through the positive reinforcement of desirable activity.

4. To alert the aspiring manager to the dangers of the inappropriate use of punishment and extrinsic rewards alone.

CHAPTER OUTLINE

Toward More Effective Behavior Alternatives

Concepts and Theories of Learning
Classical Conditioning
Operant Conditioning
Contingencies of Reinforcement
Reinforcement Schedules and Extinction
Acquisition of Complex Behaviors: The Learning Curve

Transfer of Training
Conditions Affecting Transfer

Stimulus Discrimination and Generalization

Organizational Applications of Learning Theory
The Need for Systematic Management of Feedback and Rewards
Positive Behavior Reinforcement
Organizational Examples of Positive Behavior Reinforcement
What About Punishment?
Implementing Positive Reinforcement

The ways in which the manager relates to subordinates—managerial style—have a direct influence on the behaviors of his subordinates. We can make a generalization about the process through which this impact occurs; the appropriate use of managerial style affects organizational behavior because it affects *attitudes*. Subordinates may have needs and expectations that are met through the manager's characteristic style of behavior as he discharges his task responsibility.

An assumption implicit in the concept of managerial styles is that attitudes intervene in the process by which behavior occurs; that is, attitudes are central in determining behaviors. If the manager operates on a subordinate's attitudes in appropriate ways, behaviors beneficial to the organization can be elicited. Subordinates' interests are integrated with those of the formal organizational system as more democratic techniques are employed. Resistance is reduced, commitment to organizational goals built, clear and two-way communication channels created, and more positive and involved attitudes developed that increase motivation and performance.

Toward More Effective Behavior Alternatives

Yet attitudes cannot be empirically defined, and the various cause–effect relationships that ultimately yield configurations of attitudes are difficult to influence.[1] Being able to predict the probable effects of various managerial styles is useful, yet it may be extremely difficult to change one style for another, should the manager decide that his present style is ineffective. At the same time, knowing of alternative ways in which to deal with common problems makes a broader range of effective behaviors available to the manager.

Attitude-based processes—such as motivation, communication, and recognition—usually create the most significant problems of the supervisor. Because they are subjective and individualized, the manager can act maladaptively when confronted with such problems. An example of maladaptive behavior is "the manager who, in an attempt to motivate an employee to improve poor performance, actually threatens him to the point where the employee becomes even less effective and [more] hostile toward the manager."[2]

A repertoire of adaptive, effective behaviors should aid the manager to fulfill his role better. An approach through which the manager can directly affect organizational behavior is available through the application of learning theories. For direct contrast with the use of managerial styles, we can say that the application of learning theories results in direct changes of *behavior*,

[1]Cf. Craig Eric Schneier, "Behavior Modification in Management: A Review and Critique," *Academy of Management Journal* (September 1974), p. 529.
[2]Melvin Sorcher, "A Behavior Modification Approach to Supervisor Training," *Professional Psychology* (Fall 1971), p. 401.

which creates changes in *attitudes* through cognitive dissonance processes. The managerial styles approach, in contrast, focuses on changing attitudes in order to change behavior. How can this be? How can behavior be directly changed?

We intuitively know that most of the knowledge and skills we possess were not inherited. They have been acquired in some fashion throughout our lives; they have been *learned*. Thus learning amounts to a process through which our behaviors and cognitive processes are modified, over time. Many of the things that we have learned seem "natural," such as the ways in which we use a knife and fork in eating. Yet these too are learned and are acquired skills. Many Orientals have never had contact with Western eating utensils and cannot use them with the facility they have learned in using chopsticks, for example. The highly complex behaviors by which a computer is programmed are also a set of acquired behaviors based on knowledge that is learned. A course in organizational behavior similarly provides a learning situation through which your cognitive processes and behaviors may be affected and modified.

The manager may be likened to a teacher, that is, one responsible for administering a learning situation. The major difference between the "real" teacher and the manager–teacher is that the professional teacher is able to employ the learning process in a carefully constrained, artificial, and specific environment with concrete and mutually understood goals and performance criteria. The manager–teacher must administer the learning process in a setting that has been formally established not for teaching but for perform-ing a task and for contributing toward organizational objectives. How that is done is the focus of organization learning and usually occurs unsystemati-cally, haphazardly, and individually. The manager can employ tools from learning theory, however, to reduce the haphazardness of organizational learning while increasing the extent to which effective learning occurs. Systematic management of organizational learning provides an important opportunity for individual and formal organization to be integrated in the pursuit of effective organizational behavior.

The nature of these tools will be implied as we investigate the underly-ing concepts and basic theories of learning. Then we will consider their application in organizational settings and in modifying organizational behav-ior.

Concepts and Theories of Learning

In very general terms, we can consider as learning any change in behavior that occurs as the result of experience. The experience may be either direct (previously encountered behaviors that are quite similar to the present situation) or symbolic (acquired conceptually, as through knowledge or nondirect behavior). Learning has occurred whenever a particular response is associated with a given stimulus. Simple learning can be termed *conditioning,* in which the association between stimulus and response is made explicit. There are two different types of conditioning, classical and operant.

Classical Conditioning

The father of classical conditioning was Ivan Pavlov, a Russian physiologist who worked at the beginning of the twentieth century. He observed a direct and simple association between a stimulus (food) and a response (salivation) in dogs with which he was studying gland secretion. Pavlov found that the response (salivation) could be elicited by a stimulus to which a dog did not normally salivate. He could *condition* the dog to respond in a "natural" way to an "unnatural" stimulus. He did this by pairing the neutral (non-saliva-eliciting) stimulus with the unconditioned (saliva-producing) stimulus. When food was presented (unconditioned stimulus), a bell was simultaneously rung. After a series of repetitions of the stimulus pairing, the dog would salivate at the sound of the bell alone, the food being withheld.

What caused this artificial association between a previously neutral stimulus and a response so automatic and uncontrollable as to be termed a *reflex?* The dog had associated the bell with the presentation of food. When the bell rang, the reflex salivation began because the bell aroused the expectation of food. Pavlov then observed another interesting phenomenon, which we could probably predict. In successive ringings of the bell during which food was still withheld, the dog's salivation rate diminished. Eventually the ringing of the bell produced no saliva. The response had been *extinguished* because of the weakening association between the conditioned stimulus (the bell) and the unconditioned or natural stimulus (food).

To introduce another term, the conditioned behavior was extinguished because it was not *reinforced* (rewarded). Lack of reinforcement allowed the association between the unconditioned and the conditioned stimulus to diminish and the conditioned *response* to become extinct. What would have happened if every time the bell was rung, food was presented? We would predict that such reinforcement would stop or reverse the extinguishing of the conditioned response.

Classical conditioning, then, represents the simplest and most direct method through which learning occurs. Behavior is modified through the process by which a given natural response becomes associated with a previously neutral stimulus. The applications of classical conditioning may be exemplified by several very simple situations. The administrator of a paratroop-training school is responsible for teaching people to jump from an airplane when given a signal. Further, the signal is given at the exact time that the men are to jump, and they must jump *then.* Under normal conditions, all one needs to do is give the command "Go." In actual jump conditions, however, the aircraft's doors have been removed and so a voice command cannot be heard over the roar of the wind and the engines. Still the command to jump must be given, communicated, in some other way. A vigorous slap on the buttocks is one way in which the command may be communicated. When the men are being trained to jump, a full-scale model of an aircraft door may be used, through which men are to jump at the command "Go." The command is the unconditioned or natural stimulus, and the response (jumping) may be considered the unconditioned response. If the voice command is given simultaneously with a slap across the buttocks, the slap becomes paired or associated with the command, becoming the conditioned stimulus that can elicit the desired response. After the voice command and the slap are successfully associated, the voice command can be omitted and the slap will still produce the desired response.[3]

In similar fashion:

let us look at a supervisor, Mr. Knox, and his relation to an employee, Joe. Mr. Knox operates with the philosophy that an employee gets paid for doing a job. Thus, he believes that doing a good job is what he pays Joe for. So Mr. Knox never praises Joe because, after all Joe is expected to do a good job. But when Joe fails to do something or makes a mistake, Mr. Knox is quick to rebuke the unfortunate Joe.

How does all this fit together? When Joe first went to work for him, he did not dislike Mr. Knox. In fact, Joe, like most employees, wanted to please his supervisor by doing a good job.[4]

Joe feels bad, however, every time he is rebuked by Mr. Knox. Because Mr. Knox never praises Joe, Mr. Knox comes to be directly associated with rebukes, which yield the response of bad feelings. Through this process, the presence of Joe's supervisor becomes associated with these bad feelings. "Eventually, every time Mr. Knox comes around Joe experiences negative feelings toward him. Now, he no longer likes Mr. Knox. More importantly, he no longer attempts to engage in job behavior designed to please Knox."[5]

Operant Conditioning

A somewhat more complex learning form is that of operant (instrumental) conditioning. In classical conditioning, given behaviors change as the stimuli that elicit responses are modified. Under operant conditioning, the *response* creates the modification of behavior, rather than the behavior's creating the response. This learning form is termed *operant* because the individual *operates* on his environment as he modifies *his own* behavior. The reward is administered for desired behaviors and not for other behaviors. A fundamental relationship in operant conditioning is expressed in Thorndike's law of effect, which states that:

[3]Roger N. Blakeney, Michael T. Matteson, and Donald R. Domm, "Classical and Instrumental Learning," in *The Individual and the Organization,* ed. by Donald R. Domm, Roger N. Blakeney, Michael T. Matteson, and Robert S. Scofield (New York: Harper & Row, 1973), p. 22.

[4]Ibid., p. 23.
[5]Ibid.

Of several responses made to the same situation, those which are accompanied or closely followed by satisfaction . . . will be more likely to recur; those which are accompanied or closely followed by discomfort . . . will be less likely to occur.[6]

Behaviors that we find rewarding are apt to be repeated in similar circumstances. Behaviors that result in punishment, or a decrease in comfort, will be *less* apt to be repeated in similar circumstances. The law of effect summarizes quite concisely a basic learning process that occurs over time, in which one changes his behavior based on his past experience in similar circumstances. Notice the requirement of having learned the valence (desirability) of the results of the behavior.

Piegons which are fed only after they have pecked at a certain-colored key will eventually learn, when hungry, to peck only that key. Children who burn their hands on a hot stove eventually learn not to touch this stove. Subordinates who are chastised for pointing out problems to their bosses soon learn to present only pleasant information and to absorb or modify unpleasant news. "The difference between this type of conditioning and the Pavlovian or classical conditioning lies in the fact that the organism is reinforced as a result of something it does. Out of an infinite number of acts, some bit of behavior is reinforced; other behavior is not. The reinforcement of that bit of behavior makes it more likely that the organism will engage in that act in the future."[7]

Operant conditioning and its applications are generally traced to the pioneering work of B. F. Skinner, who in the 1930's developed the famous "Skinner box' in which animals or birds could be placed and in which they could press a bar or peck a key to receive food pellets or water for reward.[8] Skinner also noticed that frequency and variability of reinforcement had a significant effect on the rate with which the conditioned behavior was extinguished. Different reinforcement schedules had different and dramatic effects. Not only did they influence *extinction* rates, but they also affected the manner in which conditioned responses were able to be *obtained*.

A critical distinction between classical and operant conditioning is in the manner in which the conditioned response is elicited. Classical conditioning simply requires a natural response and its natural association with a given stimulus, which is then associated with a neutral stimulus until the neutral (conditioned) stimulus elicits the natural response. In operant conditioning, however, the behavior classified as the *desired* response is just one of an infinite number of possible responses. The problem for the experimenter is to bring forth that response. Think of how long it would take a pigeon in a Skinner box to peck a key of a specific color randomly, especially when pecking a key is not a natural behavior pattern and when there are a number

---

[6]Edward L. Thorndike, *Animal Intelligence* (New York: Macmillan 1911), p. 244.

[7]Blair J. Kolasa, *Introduction to Behavioral Science for Business* (New York: Wiley, 1969), p. 178.

[8]See, for example, B. F. Skinner, *The Behavior of Organisms* (New York: Appleton-Century-Crofts, 1938).

of keys present, each of various hues. The experimenter must have a behavior to reinforce in order to condition the pigeon to peck the key. How does the pigeon ever learn what he is supposed to do?

In operant conditioning, the specific desired behavior or response may occur as a result of random movement, and thus the behavior may be reinforced. A more systematic approach is through the reinforcement of *successive approximations* to the desired response, a process called *shaping the response*. Shaping behaviors simply means that the organism under study is rewarded for behaving in a way that approximates the final desired response. After this first approximation has been learned, then the reward is withheld until a *closer* approximation occurs, which is then reinforced until *it* in turn is learned. After this second approximation is mastered, then reinforcement is withheld again until still closer approximations are mastered, and so on. Through this series of successively closer approximations to the final desired response pattern, the organism is "led" to learn the desired response through reinforcement. The desirability of such a step-at-a-time approach is intuitively recognized in the statement that "One must walk before he can run, and crawl before he can walk."

The power of the shaping approach is indicated in the following summary, which reports a study:

designed to increase interpersonal responsiveness in *severely withdrawn schizophrenics*. Working on the assumption that motor responses could be more easily elicited from those patients than verbal or social behavior, the therapists first set them the task of performing a simple motor response which brought social and material rewards. In successive phases, the complexity of the task was increased, and verbal and interpersonal responses were elicited and rewarded. Also, in later phases, rewards were presented only when the patients communicated verbally and cooperated with the therapist and other patients in order to solve problems of some complexity. Three other groups of patients, matched with the reinforcement group for severity of disorder and length of hospitalization, concurrently participated in either traditional interview therapy, recreational therapy, or received no treatment. The reinforcement approach proved more efficacious than all other three techniques in producing favorable changes in social behavior.[9]

Contingencies of Reinforcement

In shaping behavior or in classical conditioning, how often should reinforcement be provided for the desired behavior to be learned? The reward may be applied after *every* correct response, or after *every other* correct response, every *n* times, or even completely randomly. How is one to know how often and in what pattern the reward should be administered?

[9]G. F. King, S. G. Armitage, and J. R. Tilton, "A Therapeutic Approach to Schizophrenics of Extreme Pathology," *Journal of Abnormal and Social Psychology*, **61**:276–286 (1960); summarized in Albert Bandura, *Principles of Behavior Modification* (New York: Holt, Rinehart and Winston, 1969), pp. 232, 233.

What effect does the schedule of reinforcement chosen have on the organism under consideration and his behavior? Many of the findings have been based on experiments with lower-order animals, such as flatworms and rats, and so we must be wary of their generalizability to human beings. Nonetheless, we will review briefly the patterns that have been found in order to establish that schedules of reinforcement can affect behavior and should be considered when we are dealing with individuals in organized settings, too. We will investigate the effects of reinforcement on a fixed-ratio, variable-ratio, fixed-interval, and variable-interval schedules.

Fixed-Ratio Schedules

Reinforcement on a fixed ratio simply means rewarding the desired behaviors when the operant response has been performed a fixed number of times. This can range anywhere from reinforcing every operant response (a condition termed *continuous reinforcement*) to reinforcing the operant response every ten thousand times it occurs, or any other ratio of reward to numbers of operant responses. A fixed ratio schedule is the most effective of the four types in eliciting an immediate, high rate of desired responses, simply because the fixed ratio schedule "places a premium on rapid responding,"[10] no matter what the ratio. Responses under higher ratios of reinforcement occur faster than under a lower ratio of reward, because it will take a larger number of responses to receive the reward then under the lower ratio. Piecework incentive systems are fixed-ratio schedules because each item completed by the worker is rewarded by the accumulation of given amounts of money.

Variable-Ratio Schedules

The variable-ratio schedule of reinforcement is similar to the fixed-ratio schedule in that the operant response is rewarded according to some ratio of reinforcement for every number of desired responses. The difference occurs in that the ratio varies randomly, or from time to time. In a variable ratio situation, operant responses may be rewarded every five times they occur—*on the average*. Thus the first operant response may be reinforced, and then the operant response may not be rewarded until the tenth or twentieth time it occurs, and the next time reinforcement may not occur until the third response, and so on. The ratio of reward to operant response varies randomly, yet over the entire number of operant responses, the number of times they are reinforced averages a given ratio.

The variable-ratio schedule is an elicitor of a rapid rate of response, as is the fixed ratio. At the same time, the variable-ratio reinforcement system is

[10]Jon L. Williams, *Operant Learning: Procedures for Changing Behavior* (Monterey, Calif.: Brooks/Cole Publishing Company, 1973), p. 44.

extremely. resistant to extinction, because the organism can never know whether his next three desired responses will each be rewarded, or whether a reinforcement will not occur for another hundred responses. The value of the reward and its unpredictability keep the organism responding. In a direct comparison between continuous and variable-ratio reinforcement, the variable-ratio schedule was found to be significantly more effective in increasing work productivity.[11]

Compulsive gamblers cannot quit because of the random possibility of winning; the slot machine is the source of a variable ratio reinforcement powerful enough to cause extensive (and expensive) commitments of time and money. A still further example is that of the cigarette smoker who cannot quit because of the possibility that the *next* cigarette will be the one that tastes so good. Variable-ratio schedules are common—and powerful—modifiers of behavior.

Fixed-Interval Reinforcement

A schedule in which rewards are administered according to a fixed passage of time is termed a *fixed-interval schedule*. Here the organism receives a reward not according to the rate of response or even for a given number of desired responses but simply for giving the operant response within a specified interval of time. Accordingly the organism usually maintains a rather constant number of responses between rewards, and Skinner maintained that "with interval schedules of reinforcement the rate of responding usually is inversely proportional to the interval between reinforcements."[12]

Under fixed-interval reinforcement schedules, the *pattern* of responses is quite interesting. Immediately after a reinforcement, at the beginning of the next interval of time, few responses are made. As the interval progresses, but before the reward is due to be administered, responses become more and more frequent, gradually accelerating until the reinforcement, after which responses fall off again. The office worker whose paycheck is scheduled every two weeks may notice that his productivity slackens quite dramatically immediately after his paycheck comes and slowly builds back up until he receives the next. Similarly during a classroom lecture the glances made by a student at his watch may show the same pattern!

Variable-Interval Reinforcement

The variable-interval schedule of reinforcement is similar to the variable-ratio schedules. In both the reward is administered on a random basis.

---

[11]Gary Yukl, Kenneth N. Wexley, and James D. Seymore, "Effectiveness of Pay Incentives Under Variable Ratio and Continuous Reinforcement Schedules," *Journal of Applied Psychology*, **55**:19–23 (1972). The study reported was a laboratory study with temporary, part-time employees.

[12]Skinner, cited in Williams, p. 47.

The variable-ratio schedule is characterized by the reward's being administered for a variable number of responses. In variable-interval reinforcement the reward is administered at the end of randomly determined intervals of time. Thus the period of time changes from one reinforcement to the next, perhaps three minutes before the first reward, then thirty seconds for the next, then five minutes, and so on. Reward is not obtained for responding at a fast rate but for responding in a randomly changing interval. The response rate, then, tends to be relatively low, compared to the ratio schedules, but steady.

Reinforcement Schedules and Extinction

That behavior is *acquired* through reinforcement provides a potentially powerful tool to the practicing manager, but what can be learned can be unlearned, and the various schedules also differ from each other in the rates at which learning is extinguished. In the simple learning process, rewards are administered for desired responses, according to some particular scheme. What happens when rewards *cease* to be given? Generally speaking, the behavior that has been acquired is exhibited less and less often when reinforcement ceases, until eventually the behavior is completely extinguished.

The continuous-reinforcement form of the fixed-ratio schedule, we noted, is most effective in instilling a particular behavior response because every correct response is rewarded. This schedule is effective, however, only when the rewards are continued. When the reinforcement is withheld, the organism immediately knows that reinforcement has stopped, and consequently the extinction of the acquired behavior begins almost immediately. Figure 21-1 illustrates typical differences in the extinction patterns of the reinforcement schedules we have discussed. Notice that with continuous reinforcement, desired responses quickly cease, whereas responses in the other schedules decay relatively gradually.

Responses rewarded on a fixed-interval schedule continue to display the characteristic heightened response rates prior to the expected reward. When reinforcement fails to be obtained, these periods of heightened activity diminish until the behavior ceases. Once again, the organism receives relatively immediate feedback that the accustomed reinforcement schedule has been altered, and consequently the lack of expected reward becomes quickly learned.

The schedule that ranks in the middle of the five in terms of resistance to extinction is that of the variable-interval schedule. Response rate continues unaffected, primarily because the randomness of the previous reinforcement does not allow the organism to "learn" that reinforcement has ceased. He must infer that this has happened because of the successively lengthening period without reward. Then response is extinguished rather quickly.

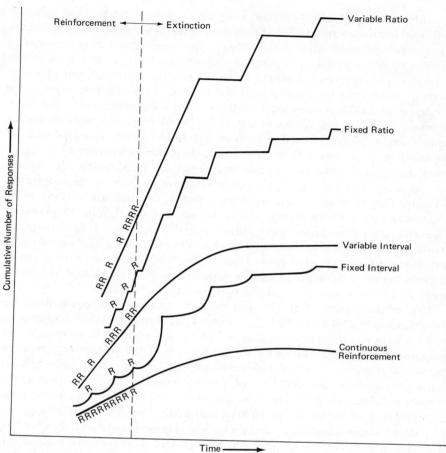

R: A Single Reinforcement

FIGURE 21-1   Typical extinction patterns of five reinforcement schedules. Source: Adapted from Williams, *Operant Learning: Procedures for Changing Behavior*, (Monterey, Calif.: Brooks/Cole Publishing Co., 1973), p. 51.

The fixed-ratio schedule is characterized by a rapid rate of response, because the organism knows that a reward is to be obtained for a given and fixed number of desired responses. When reinforcement ceases, the organism continues his rather rapid rate of response, followed by successively lengthening periods of rest, until extinction occurs. The schedule most resistant to extinction is that of the variable ratio. Responses are emitted at the same rate when reinforcement is withheld as they were under reinforcement, for a considerable length of time. A period of no activity follows, after which the previous response rate is again exhibited, but for a shorter period of time, until the behavior is eventually extinguished.

Thus we may observe that learning is not a permanent process. Acquired behaviors are exhibited only so long as they are rewarded, however infrequently or randomly. In real life, extinguishing human behaviors can require an entire lifetime, in some cases, perhaps because of the subjective estimation that the reinforcement is "due" even though it will not be forthcoming. What may be important is the manner in which one expects the reinforcement to be administered. If the reward is expected after equal fixed intervals, and it is not forthcoming, the desired behaviors may be rather quickly extinguished. But if one does not know which random ratio of appropriate responses will be rewarded, then the estimation from unrewarded response to the next unrewarded response must be that the reward may soon be administered. Motivation to continue responding at a high rate, until this subjective estimation declines, is then a result. Managing response acquisition—and maintenance—then, seems to be a significant problem. The contingency (continuous reinforcement) that optimizes rate of response acquisition also shows the fastest extinction. Yet reinforcing every response is time-consuming and may prove expensive. *Shifting* contingencies offers obvious benefits. A response can be acquired under continuous reinforcement and then *maintained* under a variable ratio schedule.

Another important insight that must be underscored, particularly for future reference, is the effect that *delay* of reinforcement has on learning and extinction. Obviously the shorter the period of time between operant response and reward, the faster the acquisition of the response. When the period of time lengthens between response and reward, incorrect responses cannot be immediately pointed out and corrected in favor of appropriate responses. Thus the individual is deprived of immediate feedback. He must experiment and approximate, by trial and error, the desired behavior.

Perhaps this is one major reason for the acquisition of bad habits and the learning of incorrect techniques on the job. Unless immediate feedback is given regarding the incorrect method used and the correct method is demonstrated, the bad habit itself becomes acquired and must become extinguished *after* feedback is eventually given. And then the learning process of the *correct* method must begin, the sum total of which time is considerably greater than would have been the case under immediate feedback and reinforcement. Periodic performance evaluations suffer from this handicap, unless they are supplemented by informal and immediate on-the-job training procedures, provided by the administrator of the reward.

Acquisition of Complex Behaviors: The Learning Curve

When the behaviors to be learned are relatively complex, as in the case of skills or sequences of behaviors, we cannot expect that the individual will be able to master the skill the first time he attempts it. Instead we know that novice typists find the positioning of the fingers on the appropriate keys awkward, and each stroke of each finger must be consciously commanded.

As a result, the number of correctly typed words per minute is rather low at first. With increasing confidence and practice, the rate of speed with which one types increases, until a maximum rate for the individual is reached. The limiting factor may depend on motivation, coordination, or some other physical or psychological constraint.

Figure 21-2(a) illustrates the typical learning curve as we have described it. The curve has been smoothed out and actually consists of a series of ups and downs, which still conform to the general pattern displayed. It is called a *diminishing-returns curve* because of the decreasing increment of performance that is attained over time. As the individual repeats the skilled behaviors, he gets better and better, and consequently his increase in performance goes

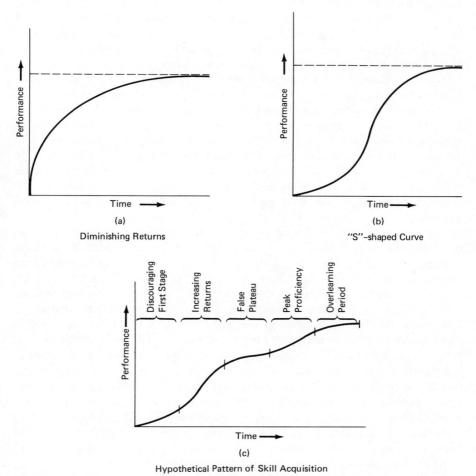

(a)

Diminishing Returns

(b)

"S"–shaped Curve

(c)

Hypothetical Pattern of Skill Acquisition

FIGURE 21-2   Learning curves. SOURCE: Figure (c) adapted from George Strauss and Leonard Sayles, *Personnel: The Human Problems of Management,* 3rd ed. (Englewood Cliffs, N.J.: Prentice-Hall, 1972), p. 451.

up, but at a decreasing rate. The diminishing-returns curve is a very commonly observed one. The horizontal line above the curve is intended to suggest that there is some limit beyond which performance may not go, an absolute ceiling on performance. Given the proper motivation and learning, the individual may, over time, approach this absolute limit rather closely.

Another form of learning curve is shown in Figure 21-2(b), the S-shaped curve that many psychologists claim is *the* learning curve. The lower portion of the S-shaped curve represents the very beginning forms of acquiring a particular skill, with very slow learning initially, followed by successively greater returns. Eventually the pattern displayed in the diminishing-returns curve becomes paramount, with performance capability leveling out at some absolute limit.

Hence the diminishing-returns curve is said to be merely the S-shaped curve in situations in which the elementary skills (the bottom part of the S-shaped curve) are transferred from other situations and therefore need not be acquired. Because they are not part of the behaviors to be learned, they do not show up on the learning curve. It is then argued that the diminishing-returns curve is just a special case of the S-shaped learning curve.

A rather complex pattern of skill acquisition is diagramed in Figure 21-2(c). The initial stage is one of very slow learning of the basics of the techniques and skills to be acquired, a rather discouraging portion of the learning process because of its newness and the learner's relatively slow rate of learning. How long this initial stage lasts is a function of how complex the skills are and how adept the learner is. This stage may last from a few minutes (perhaps for one learning to operate a dictating machine) to several weeks (for a student aircraft pilot).

The second stage is that of increasing returns. The learner gains confidence and has established the rudimentary knowledge of what he is to do and the basics of how he is to go about it. With practice he can become more proficient, gaining skill over time.

Following this period of increasing returns is a plateau, on which little or no increase in performance is observed. Such a plateau can occur when the learner is shifting his mental gears from one way of doing the task to another, more efficient method. Thus the budding typist may exhibit several plateaus. The first may be experienced when he has developed proficiency in typing each individual letter. The plateau occurs because of the physical constraint on how fast he can order each finger to do its individual task. Great improvements in performance come about after this initial plateau, when the typist learns to type entire words without thinking of them as being composed of individual letters. This may, in turn, be followed by yet another plateau because of the limitation of looking at each individual word and sending a given signal for each word to the fingers.

The top typist may then increase his performance still further by scanning entire phrases and transmitting complex commands automatically, without the intervention of stopping to transmit a separate signal for each letter or word. This can be demonstrated as being the period of peak proficiency, as seen in the diagram. The final phase, that of overlearning, truly constitutes the ultimate in performance. It is termed *overlearning* because at this stage the skill becomes second nature, habitual, automatic, unforgettable. Most people who have driven stick-shift automobiles for substantial periods of their lives and then go to automatic transmissions never really forget how to shift gears. Were they to be placed in a straight-shift auto, even after many years of driving autos with automatic transmissions, the effective performance of the required behavior would be exhibited with very little relearning necessary—as a result of the overlearning period.

Transfer of Training

We noted that the S-shaped curve has been considered by some to be the general learning curve, with the diminishing-returns curve being a special case in which the rudimentary portions of the learning have been acquired elsewhere. This assumes that in certain circumstances previous learning can be *transferred* to other situations. If this is true, then such positive transfer has important implications for job training, as well as other types of skill acquisition and learning.

Conditions Affecting Transfer

Under what conditions can learning be transferred from one situation to another? Berelson and Steiner suggested that the extent to which learning transfers from one situation to another is a function of the extent of similarity in the stimulus and/or response.[13] The situation that is extremely similar to the previous learning situation has an obvious advantage; the learner is familiar with the things to look for and the manner in which he is to be presented with conditions to which he must respond. When his responses are similar to the responses he previously learned, then he is helped by his previous experiences. His learning time is significantly decreased because of this positive transfer of learning.

If the situation is the same (or similar) but the response that he must make is quite different, then the previous response can interfere with his ability to respond in this newly acquired way. Such a phenomenon is called a *negative* transfer of learning because the old response must be unlearned and the new response acquired in its place. The old response interferes with the individual's ability to learn to respond in a highly efficient manner.

When the situations are significantly different from each other, and the responses are also very different, then there is no transfer effect. The two

[13]Bernard Berelson and Gary A. Steiner, *Human Behavior: An Inventory of Scientific Findings* (New York: Harcourt, Brace & World, 1964), pp. 160–162.

situations and their respective responses are independent of each other. But when the responses are the same or quite similar, even in different situations, some increase in the rate of learning is experienced, although not a great deal. After all, the individual "already knows what to do and how to do it—all he has to learn is where and when."[14]

A summary of the effects of learning-situation and learned-response similarity is provided in Table 21-1. An obvious conclusion to be drawn is that learning and training situations should be rather highly related to the situations for which skills are to be acquired and applied. The less similar the situation in which the learned skill is to be transferred, the less the skill will be transferred. And the specific response or skill to be acquired should be as similar as possible to that to be applied in the new situation.

One condition to be avoided is negative transfer, wherein the applied response is dissimilar to the training response. This is to be avoided because of the interference with the acquiring of a new skill, coupled with the necessity for extinguishing the previous response *and* learning a new one. Berelson and Steiner also warned that under crisis or emergency situations, the older or previous behavior patterns tend to emerge and replace the newly acquired skill. "For example, seasoned pilots have crashed when, in an emergency, they reverted to responses learned earlier and appropriate in former airplanes but disastrous with the present control system."[15]

Stimulus Discrimination and Generalization

Two concepts that can help to explain transfer of learning are *discrimination* and *generalization*. Most individuals are able to respond to stimuli or situations that are not identical to previous stimuli or situations. The new stimuli are, however, similar enough so that the previously conditioned response is *generalized* to the new and similar stimulus.

TABLE 21-1   Learning Transfer Summary

| | | Previous and New Learning Situations Are | | |
		Identical	Similar	Dissimilar
Response Is	Identical	100% positive transfer	High amount of positive transfer	Slight amount of positive transfer
	Similar	Slight amount of positive transfer	High amount of positive transfer	Slight amount of positive transfer
	Dissimilar	High amount of negative transfer	High amount of negative transfer	No transfer

SOURCE: Adapted from Berelson and Steiner, *Human Behavior: An Inventory of Scientific Findings*, pp. 160–162.

[14]Ibid., p. 161.
[15]Ibid.

Generalization

The less similar the new stimulus is to the conditioned stimulus, the less will be the tendency to respond with the frequency or intensity one did to the conditioned stimulus. Training and learning situations, to be effective, should be designed in such a way that the acquired knowledge or skill may be readily generalized to other, different situations. It is usually difficult and expensive to provide training and learning in the *actual* situation in which the learner will ultimately find himself. Thus the college of business administration typically cannot set up an ongoing business in which its students may be coached by their professors in situations identical to those to which they are aspiring. Educational experiences may include analyzing written case descriptions of actual businesses, in hopes that the insights developed will be *generalized* to career experiences.

Discrimination

Discrimination, on the other hand, refers to the ability to tell the *difference* between relatively similar stimuli, under conditions in which generalization can yield negative consequences. Almost all automobile drivers have learned to discriminate between a red and a green traffic light, even though both represent light and color stimuli. The red traffic light will elicit a completely different response (it is hoped) than the green. A supervisor may, over time, learn to discriminate between two equally productive workers. One may produce at a high rate, at the expense of quality, whereas the other has very few rejects. The supervisor may respond more positively to the high-quality producer and negatively to the low-quality producer, hoping to reinforce the productive behavior and extinguish the low-quality performance.[16]

Now that we have considered the nature and concepts of learning, what applications have they in the manager's role and for organizational behavior? There are obvious applications to industrial training and management development, but can the manager use learning theory to integrate individual, group, and organizational patterns of behavior? Applications of learning theory in organized settings, and as a tool of the manager, will be taken up in our next section.

Organizational Applications of Learning Theory

One of the roles of the effective manager is that of a teacher. He manages a learning process whereby his subordinates acquire the skills

---

[16]Fred Luthans, *Organizational Behavior: A Modern Behavioral Approach to Management* (New York: McGraw-Hill, 1973), p. 373.

necessary for effective job performance and unlearn counterproductive behaviors. He performs this role because it stems directly from his major responsibility for achieving results, primarily through the efforts of his subordinates. The authoritarian may conceive of his role as the taskmaster. He may feel that his subordinates are hired to do a good job and that it is his responsibility to punish those who fall short. A more constructive perception is that the organization is composed of a complex series of interrelated activities, some of which are very sophisticated and require extensive periods for the development of capability. The manager always retains the responsibility of evaluating individual performance, but the effective manager sees that by helping his subordinates to do a better job, he fulfills his major responsibility more effectively.

The Need for Systematic Management of Feedback and Rewards

The manager can be a coach or a teacher, providing feedback to his subordinates regarding their performances and the relationships between what they are doing and the rewards available. The manager is the source of some powerful reinforcements: social, status, monetary, and ego. If he restricts his rewards to the fixed-interval application of financial rewards, then he is not actively shaping effective subordinate behaviors and is not furnishing the feedback and reinforcement necessary for optimum sustained contribution.

Few frustrations are greater than those encountered in doing one's job for a period of time, only to find out that he has been doing it wrong and also that the superior knew it all the time and failed to let him know. Equally frustrating is the trial-and-error process of acquiring skills thought to be important, yet without benefit of feedback from one's superior—who *evaluates* skills and performance. Any ineffective acquired behaviors, which detract from personal task competence, may negatively affect the willingness of the individual to identify with the goals of the formal organization and to see his interests as coinciding with the organization's. When such a disparity occurs, the manager has placed himself at a distinct disadvantage. By his inaction he has decreased his ability to perform effectively his role and to achieve formal organizational purposes.

The learning process is continual and involves both subordinate and manager. The simple process of applying reinforcement for appropriate behaviors and shaping successive approximations to desired behaviors constitutes the core of the manager's applications of learning theory. The process may be called *positive behavior reinforcement* and has been used with a great deal of success in several companies. The process has also been called *behavior modification*, a term that has some distinctly negative connotations and implications of Machiavellian thought-and-behavior control and that will not be used here.

Positive Behavior Reinforcement

Most supervisors find that they do not have enough time to scrutinize closely the work and consequences of each of their subordinates. Instead they rely on managing "by exception." Managing by exception simply means that a range of "acceptable" behavior is established, such as producing at least one hundred items per eight-hour day to meet minimum quota. Anything over the minimum is acceptable, and the supervisor's attention is directed to such unacceptable behaviors as failing to meet the quota.

What is the matter with this? Note that focusing on undesirable behaviors is not in itself bad, but it does put the supervisor–subordinate relationship into terms of a punishment situation. The worker is "caught" doing something his supervisor doesn't want him to do, and a reprimand is issued. An assumption of many managers is that subordinates perform unsatisfactorily as a matter of *choice;* and the subordinate must be punished for making that choice so that next time he will choose to perform satisfactorily and so avoid punishment. Because of this assumption, notification about poor performance is rarely accompanied by constructive information—*what* was being done wrong and *how* to correct it and therefore perform satisfactorily. The manager feels that the employee knows this but just doesn't do it.

Just as seriously, those behaviors that constitute *effective* performance may be noticed and approved by the supervisor, but he will rarely make a point of applauding the employee—after all, the worker was *hired* to perform, he will receive a pay raise and a "superior" performance evaluation on the semiannual performance review—isn't that enough? We know it's not, because of the phenomena of extinction, reinforcement schedules, and delay of reward.

In terms of learning theory the supervisor is ultimately responsible for shaping the behaviors of his subordinates into patterns that are both highly effective and highly productive. This requires that he reward successive approximations to the final desired patterns, until the subordinate has mastered each successive step along the way to acquiring superior skill in all facets of his job. Effective behaviors must be systematically reinforced, and undesirable behaviors must be quickly extinguished. These are activities for which the manager must be responsible and that must constitute a specific portion of his overall role. No subordinate can provide such reinforcement for himself nor appraise and extinguish inappropriate actions. Formal contribution to organizational goals must be evaluated and shaped by the manager.

Failure to provide positive reinforcement is equivalent to withholding a reward, which is a specific strategy effective in extinguishing the behavior. If the employee feels that the correct things he does are ignored, then extinction can occur. This amounts to the supervisor's accomplishing exactly what he *doesn't* want to accomplish: good behaviors can be extinguished and negative behaviors *not* be decreased. After all, when the supervisor reprimands a subordinate for not wearing his safety goggles or for miscalculating a cost estimate, the behavior by which this result was accomplished has not been effected—merely the subordinate's being *caught* at it. You can be sure that the subordinate will exert every effort—to avoid being caught the next time he decides not to wear his safety goggles or the next time he is careless in his calculations.

How may the supervisor employ the concepts of learning theory to shape his subordinates' behaviors into desired and productive channels? The answer seems intuitively simple. The manager must know specifically what the end objective of each subordinate's task is and exactly what constitutes average, unacceptable, and superior performance in quantitative, verifiable terms. He must interact with the subordinate on the job, and when the employee behaves in a way that constitutes a step toward ultimate effective performance it must be immediately rewarded in a positive fashion, perhaps by an encouraging comment or praise. Behaviors that detract from the subordinate's ability to perform effectively must be immediately extinguished through the withholding of reinforcement or by immediate feedback that the behavior is counterproductive, coupled with suggestions of behaviors to replace the ineffective behaviors. In any event, the positive reinforcement of desirable behavior will ultimately, if conscientiously applied, lead the subordinate into successively learning and mastering the phases of his job so that he may perform all of them effectively.

Positive behavior reinforcement in organizational settings demands that two different types of reinforcers be used:

Extrinsic reinforcements are those that bear no inherent relationship to the behavior itself, but are selected artifically, and in some cases, arbitrarily, to reinforce the behavior in which change is sought. A suggestion system that awards money for acceptable suggestions is an example. The money unquestionably serves to reinforce the behavior of providing suggestions, but the award is not a natural consequence of the behavior. *Intrinsic reinforcements* are those that are a natural consequence of the behavior; from the individual's point of view they bear a psychologically expected relationship to the behavior itself. Knowledge of a job well done, the experience of knowing that you have worked up to capacity, or becoming qualified to do a different kind of work are illustrations.[17]

Extrinsic rewards are the only rewards that many supervisors feel are effective and available for use, notably salary increments, bonuses, and so on. Intrinsic rewards are more nearly related to Maslow's higher psychological needs and Herzberg's motivator factors and are less visible, tangible, and controllable than extrinsic, formal rewards. Achievement, praise, recognition, esteem, feedback, growth, challenge, and responsibility are just a few intrinsic rewards that can be controlled by the supervisor. We noted in

[17]Timothy W. Costello and Sheldon S. Zalkind, *Psychology in Administration: A Research Orientation* (Englewood Cliffs, N.J.: Prentice-Hall, 1963), p. 214.

discussing group dynamics that they are typically more powerful than extrinsic reinforcements; for this reason the social control powers of the informal group may override the ability of management to affect how an individual will behave. Should management employ intrinsic rewards in a systematic and job-related fashion, intrinsic rewards could *support* the extrinsic rewards system, furnishing a powerful means of influencing behavior.

The manager's control devices include statistical quality control, performance evaluation checklists, production quotas, customer surveys, and so on. Such controls provide the manager feedback on how well his subordinates and productive operations are performing, compared with organizationally determined criteria of performance. Rarely do they establish more than the fact that formal goals and expectations have *not* been met. It is up to the manager to determine what happened and who was responsible. In using extrinsic rewards and control procedures, the rational manager places his faith in the assumption that the rational employee will conduct himself in an acceptable fashion when his performance is monitored by his supervisor and therefore that highlighting and punishing unsatisfactory performance will yield acceptable levels of performance. We have seen how erroneous this assumption is. After all, even this assumption implies that a subordinate knows what acceptable behavior is and how to attain it. It further fails to recognize that each subordinate must learn and acquire skills appropriate to his task and the levels of performance required. The assumption of rational control also implies that he is *motivated* to perform at formally prescribed levels. Each of these assumptions and implications is shaky at best. For these reasons the manager must actively intervene and modify behavior and skill acquisition successively toward those optimum behaviors most effective for organizational purposes, productivity, satisfaction, and achievement.[18] Ways in which positive behavior reinforcement concepts have been successfully used are illustrated below.

Organizational Examples of Positive Behavior Reinforcement

One of the requirements of all organizations is having a predictable and stable workforce on hand through whom formal goals will be attained. (Sometimes one wonders whether fringe benefits such as sick pay and extensive holidays do not reward the worker for staying *away* from work!)

Improving Work Attendance

Nord tells of two different organizations that attempted to modify the attendance behaviors of their employees. Both sought to reduce absentee-

[18]Everett E. Adam, Jr., and William E. Scott, Jr., "The Application of Behavioral Conditioning Procedures to the Problems of Quality Control," *Academy of Management Journal* (June 1971), p. 176.

ism, and both developed similar systems for rewarding the desired behavior, rather than punishing undesirable behavior.[19]

LOTTERY IN HARDWARE STORES   The first is a large retail hardware chain composed of six stores located in a large metropolitan area. In 1966 the management of the hardware chain considered that tardiness and absenteeism were serious enough to embark on a new and innovative program. The program consisted of a lottery, with monthly prizes being awarded and a separate major lottery being held at the end of six months.

What was unique about the lottery was its eligibility requirements. Only company employees who had recorded perfect attendance and no tardiness during the entire preceding month were eligible for each monthly lottery. Only those employees who had perfect attendance and punctuality for the entire six months were eligible for the major six-month lottery.

The grand prize was a color television set. Each monthly prize was an appliance worth around $25. One monthly prize was provided for every twenty-five employees, and each store had its own monthly lottery.

The program was a rousing success. Sick leave payments were reduced 62 percent, and absenteeism and tardiness were reduced to about one quarter of the previous level in the first year of the program. The program was so popular that even a snow storm was not able to deter employees from leaving home early enough to ensure that they were at work on time!

FIXED-INTERVAL REWARD IN SCHOOLS   A slightly different technique was used in a major city's public school system: rewards were distributed for perfect attendance to *all* teachers who met the standard. Only teachers were included in the program. The program was instituted because of rising costs and difficulties in obtaining qualified substitute teachers for those teachers who reported in sick, using their annual ten-day sick leave allowance. Also, an additional reward for regular attendance was felt to be important.

Fifty dollars was awarded every teacher who had reported to work every day the previous semester. Over the five-year life of the program, the percentage of eligible teachers who had perfect attendance ranged from 41 to 60 percent, with an average of almost 50 percent. The result was reduction in the cost of substitute teachers and the stemming of an upward trend in absenteeism.

ALTERING ATTENDANCE MEASUREMENT   Still another positive reinforcement program was set up in a unit of the telephone company. The thirty-eight operators had an overall 11 percent rate of absenteeism, which was to be reduced. Attendance records had been kept, on a monthly basis. Attendance recognition plans that had been previously used had not affected the absenteeism rate at all. Investigation revealed that the reason for the previous plan's failure was that "the operators felt that if they had

[19]Walter Nord, "Improving Attendance Through Rewards," *Personnel Administration* (November–December 1970), pp. 37–41.

missed a day early in the month, they had already messed up their own monthly attendance record as well as their group's chance for positive recognition. Thus, it made little difference if they took a day off later in the month."[20] The attendance records were quickly put on a weekly basis, and absenteeism declined because the operators could still be rewarded even if they had missed a day early in the month. Supervisors were encouraged to comment positively on operators' attendance records. Within six weeks the pilot group's absenteeism rate dropped from 11 percent to 6.5 percent. The positive reinforcement program was broadened to over one thousand operators in Detroit, and absenteeism there decreased from 7.5 percent to 4.5 percent in the first quarter of the year.

Reinforcing Task Performance

In another company, Emery Air Freight, positive behavior reinforcement has been adopted as a far-ranging program, with significant results.[21] Emery uses positive reinforcement in three areas at present: sales and sales training, operations, and containerized shipments. Significant benefits in all three areas have been realized and (perhaps more impressive) sustained for between three and four years. Additionally, Emery does not use financial incentives at all; the results of their positive reinforcement program are strictly through the use of feedback of individual performance, establishing reasonable performance goals, and giving consistent praise and recognition for reaching the standard. Several examples may help to show the results that such an approach can yield.

SHIPMENTS   In the containerized-shipment operation, the purpose of the packers is to package small shipments that are going to the same destination in large containers, rather than sending them separately. Containerized shipments are subject to lower rates than their equivalent weight in small shipments. Emery management had felt that employees were making use of these containers on about 90 percent of the possible occasions. On investigating the situation, however, they found that the containers were used for only 45 percent of all possible shipments. A checklist was set up for each dock worker to mark each time he used a container. The worker then totaled his own results at the end of his shift to see whether he had hit the 90 percent goal. Supervisors and regional managers were also encouraged by top management to praise performance improvement. "The results were impressive. In 80% of the offices where the technique was tried, the use of containers went from 45% to 95% in a single day."[22] Emery has reported an annual saving of $650,000 using this system.

SERVICE   Customer service operations were also substantially

[20]"Where Skinner's Theories Work," *Business Week* (December 2, 1972), p. 54.
[21]"At Emery Air Freight: Positive Reinforcement Boosts Performance," *Organizational Dynamics* (Winter 1973), pp. 41–50.
[22]"Where Skinner's Theories Work," pp. 64, 65.

improved. Before the positive reinforcement program was implemented, standards for the customer service area were being met only 30–40 percent of the time. The standards included answering all of each customer's telephone inquiries within ninety minutes. After the positive reinforcement program was established, standards were met between 90 and 95 percent of the time, and in the first office in which it was tested, performance leaped from 30 percent to 95 percent of standard—in a single day!

As a direct result of the positive reinforcement program in only three areas, Emery estimated that they had saved over $3 million in the past three years. Certainly this is an impressive record that indicates that operant conditioning and positive reinforcement offer significant opportunities for improving organizational effectiveness.

What About Punishment?

Rewarding or reinforcing desired behavior certainly seems an effective approach. But what about punishing *undesirable* behaviors, causing them to be extinguished? We had previously noted that punishment, if inappropriately applied, simply causes displacement. The person being punished can perceive the punishment as a result of being caught rather than as an incentive to replace those undersirable behaviors with another set of behaviors:

The two soundest arguments against punishment are: (1) punishment causes anxiety and suppresses the response which reappears when the punishing stimulus is absent and (2) the effectiveness of the punishing agent diminishes over time and the punisher may never be perceived in a favorable light again—even in non-punishing situations. In other words, there are some undesirable side effects accompanying the use of punishment. The punished organizational participant may become anxious and only temporarily suppress the undesirable behavior and the punishing manager may become less effective as the employee learns to avoid, distrust, and not allow the manager to administer positive reinforcement.[23]

Punishment causes learning to occur—learning to *avoid*—but fails to remove the undesirable tendency to respond. The tendency is simply overcome at the moment by the acquired knowledge that behaving in a particular way will result in punishment, a consequence to be avoided.[24] When the threat of punishment is removed, the undesired behavior tendency may then reemerge. If an office worker tells off-color jokes to his co-workers, the supervisor may stop the activity by disapproval or ridicule. As soon as the supervisor leaves the work area, the behavior will probably reappear quickly.[25]

[23]Fred Luthans and Robert Kreitner, "The Role of Punishment in Organizational Behavior Modification (OB Mod)," *Public Personnel Management* (May–June 1973), pp. 158, 159.
[24]Berelson and Steiner, p. 142.
[25]Stephen F. Jablonsky and David L. DeVries, "Operant Conditioning Principles Extrapolated to the Theory of Management," *Organizational Behavior and Human Performance,* **7:**345 (1972).

Punishment or negative reinforcement can be soundly integrated into an overall program of positive reinforcement but only under certain carefully controlled conditions. Punishment that is far removed in time from the undesirable behavior or that provides no cue to the subordinate for changing his behavior to more appropriate activities will be ineffective. But by the same token instituting immediate feedback to the employee regarding the specific inappropriate behavior coupled with suggestions for how to rectify the situation can offer considerable assistance in modifying behaviors into desirable channels.[26]

Implementing Positive Reinforcement

Positive reinforcement seems to offer some sound considerations for management in the intervention and modification of the organizational behavior process. Positive reinforcement focuses on organizationally required task goals and objectives and specifically identifies the individual's contribution to the attainment of those goals. Using learning theory, the manager can modify the subordinate's behaviors as appropriate. He can change them from counterproductive or unproductive behavior into more desirable activities through the use of specified and communicated verifiable task objectives, immediate feedback of individual performance as measured against the standard, integration of intrinsic rewards with extrinsic rewards, and accentuating the positive.

Jablonsky and DeVries summarized the ways in which organizational behaviors may be systematically influenced:

Avoid using punishment as a primary means of obtaining desired behavior.

Positively reinforce desired behavior and, where possible, ignore undesirable behavior.

Minimize the time lag between desired response and reinforcement, or bridge the gap via verbal mediation.

Apply positive reinforcement relatively frequently, preferably on a variable ratio schedule.

Ascertain the response level of each individual and use a shaping procedure to obtain a final complex response.

Ascertain contingencies which are experienced as positive and/or negative by the individual.

Specify the desired behavior in explicitly operational terms.[27]

Using these methods, the manager is allowed a higher probability of modifying organizational behavior in a more consistent and productive fashion. Ignoring them simply means that he cannot use the newer techniques of behavior modification, coupled with techniques that have been demonstrated to be effective in many different types of situations. Although

[26]Luthans and Kreitner, ibid.
[27]Jablonsky and DeVries, p. 356.

positive behavior reinforcement calls for an in-depth look at the specific behaviors and performances of individuals toward organizationally determined objectives, the effective manager cannot afford to bypass the incremental amount of control the techniques put at his command. Through the utilization of intrinsic rewards, notably those of praise, recognition, challenge, and so on, the manager is able to motivate the individual through applying incentives directed at his higher-order psychological needs on a systematic and goal-oriented schedule.

Summary

Another behavioral tool available to the manager is positive behavior reinforcement, based on the concepts and theories of learning. Learning theories explicitly recognize that behavior is modified (learned) as a result of experience.

Simple learning forms are classical and operant conditioning. In classical conditioning a neutral stimulus is paired with a stimulus that already elicits a response. With successive presentations of the paired stimuli, the neutral stimulus acquires the effective (unconditioned) stimulus's ability to elicit the response, even when the unconditioned stimulus is withdrawn. Operant conditioning derives its basis from the law of effect, which states that rewarded behavior will tend to be repeated and that unrewarded behavior will tend to be extinguished. In other words, behavior is determined by its consequences!

Because of the law of effect, behaviors are acquired at different rates, depending on how they are rewarded. They are also extinguished at different rates, according to how they have been acquired. Schedules of reinforcement discussed were continuous reinforcement, fixed ratio, variable ratio, fixed interval, and variable interval.

The learning curve traces the acquisition of ability to perform rather more complex behaviors. The S-shaped curve is characterized by several distinct stages and rises slowly at first, then rapidly, decaying into a plateau wherein little or no improvement in performance is noticed. Consistent with the notion of learning curves is the ability of learning to be transferred from one situation to another. Transfer may be either positive or negative, depending on whether the previous learning facilitates or hinders the acquisition of the new response behavior. Stimulus generalization and discrimination also play important roles in transfer.

Learning theory may be applied to organizational situations. Successful use depends on carefully determining criteria of performance, giving timely performance feedback to subordinates, supporting feedback with intrinsic rewards, and shaping behavior through reinforcing successively closer approximations to the final desired behavior. Such reinforcement is most effective when positive reinforcement is used. Negative reinforcement should be used carefully if at all.

Through a program of positive behavior reinforcement the manager is able to modify the behavior of subordinates directly. Unproductive behavior may be extinguished and behavior desirable to individual *and* organization may be specifically encouraged.

STUDY AND REVIEW QUESTIONS

1. Carefully distinguish between classical and operant conditioning. Give two examples of each.

2. Why is positive reinforcement "better" than negative reinforcement?

3. In learning and skill acquisition, when are rewards (reinforcements) necessary? Unnecessary?

4. If you were the training director for skilled employees in a large corporation, how would you use learning theories and transfer of training concepts effectively?

5. If you were the director of management development in a large corporation, how would you use learning theories and transfer of training concepts effectively?

6. When is punishment "good"?

7. Evaluate the extent to which the ideas presented in this chapter are embodied in a "typical" college classroom. How would *you* implement them, if you were a college professor?

8. To what extent is a manager a teacher?

9. Over what specific *intrinsic* reinforcements does the manager have control? How could these be used in a program of positive behavior reinforcement?

10. Evaluate the "costs" and "benefits" you feel would be associated with a positive reinforcement program in a specific situation with which you are familiar.

Chapter

22

Job Enrichment

CHAPTER OBJECTIVES

1. To describe the major intervention technique of job enrichment.

2. To compare job enrichment results with the results of its rival job design approaches.

3. To illustrate current applications of job enrichment.

4. To point out inhibiting factors in the effective implementation of a job enrichment program.

CHAPTER OUTLINE

The manager intervenes in the organizational behavior process in many ways as he pursues his objectives. He relates to his subordinates via consistent patterns of behavior (managerial styles), shapes their acquisition of effective job behaviors (positive behavior reinforcement), and structures the very nature of formal task expectations and activities. In this chapter we will consider job design as another method through which the manager is able to influence organizational behavior and integrate the individual and the formal organization.

Job satisfaction stems from the nature of the formally prescribed work activities of the individual. His expectations, aspirations, personality characteristics, motivations, and rewards—subjective, individual, and attitudinal factors—all tend to affect his performance. Positive behavior reinforcement is attuned to operating directly on the behavior of the individual, ignoring the attitudes that intervene between formal task requirements and individual behavior. The assumption is that attitudes are less open to change than end behaviors and that changed behaviors can modify attitudes through cognitive dissonance.

Both integrative techniques—managerial styles and positive behavior reinforcement—are devices by which to modify behavior, yet neither is explicitly capable of doing more than affecting behavior and attitudes *within* a task structure regarded as fixed, constant, unchanging. In one way, a cynic might argue that managerial styles and positive reinforcement are unable to accomplish more than adapting the individual to his job. The same criticism was also leveled at the scientific management movement for failing to modify jobs to meet the characteristics of the workers who held the jobs.

Although such criticism may be regarded as reflecting a limited perspective, we should nonetheless consider the nature of the job—the work itself—as an important variable in influencing organizational behavior. It stands to reason that changing the job can change the organizational behavior process. The manager's ability to define and establish task characteristics is then another method by which he can modify and intervene in the behavior associated with individuals and groups in organizations.

Job, Motivation, and Performance

We saw in Chapter 6 that job characteristics directly affect attitudes. Herzberg pointed out[1] that the nature of the work itself is a powerful motivator and that achievement, recognition, growth, and responsibility are elements that encourage motivated behavior as well as job satisfaction. A conflict seems to exist between these motivating elements and organizational dictates for predictability, stability, and specialization of labor, especially in large mass-production–based companies.

[1]Frederick Herzberg, *Work and the Nature of Man* (Cleveland: World, 1966).

Economic and Human Results of Job Design

Significant economic benefits derive from the systematic division of work activities into their smallest constituent tasks. Lower wage rates, short training time, short work cycles, ready replaceability of an individual worker, and low skill requirements are some results of value to the goal-directed organization. The search for efficiency in operations leads to minute specialization, extensive coordination, and large-scale production.

Such arrangements can have *human* results, too. Monotony, boredom, and dissatisfaction can be created, with a motivation-based gap opening between actual and potential productivity. In other words, the structural elements of the work activity itself affect the attitudes of the job holder and then find expression in dissatisfaction, lowered motivation, and unsatisfactory performance.

Redesigning the Job for People

If the job-related requirements and activities are changed, attitudes may be directly influenced. This approach amounts to a considerable revolution in job and organizational design. The manager may be concerned with developing satisfied employees, but if the job itself does not *allow* satisfaction, then there is very little that can be done except to recruit specific employees who can tolerate the job condition and to pay them premium wages for such tolerance. Yet the early 1970's saw considerable revulsion by young workers to working in mass-production, highly rationalized jobs—even at premium wages.

Such negative attitudes toward the nature of the job suggest a need to reevaluate work design principles in light of human experience, with an eye to restructuring job content to achieve a better match with man's nature. Redesigning the job itself offers an attractive alternative. After all, if the job is boring and creates high turnover, the job may be reconstituted to include variety, challenge, and achievement. Turnover would be expected to drop; motivation, performance, and resulting job satisfaction would be expected to increase.

Alternatives in Job Design

The concept of restructuring and redesigning the activities and elements that make up a job is called *job enrichment*. It differs very substantially from the engineering-based approaches of dividing work up for optimal efficiency and lowest possible skill use. Instead job enrichment takes as a starting point those elements that motivate and satisfy individuals. The way in which the total work is divided into jobs is evaluated against motivational characteristics.

To what extent does job enrichment sacrifice economic efficiency for intangible job satisfaction and motivation? As we will see later, job enrich-ment does call for higher wage rates and some duplication of facilities, yet these costs may be recouped in higher levels of productivity and quality, not to mention the savings from lower turnover and hence training and skill acquisition costs. Additionally there are the subjective and intangible factors involved in providing opportunities for psychological growth and meaning-ful work for organizational members.

Specialization/Division of Labor

The successful rationalization and specialization of individual jobs cre-ate an overwhelming necessity for extensive coordination and supervisory control over productive activities. Coordination and control needs stem from task specialization and individual workers losing sight of their contribution to the final output of the firm. Comprehensive rules and regulations are necessary to ensure that the task will be done as dictated, which results in *more* alienation and dissatisfaction of workers. Dissatisfaction similarly increases for the holder of a craftsman's job that, over time, has its tasks narrowed down and nonrepetitive activities (such as planning) trimmed off and assigned to other specialists.[2]

In order to evaluate the problem—and compare alternative solutions—we will represent a department composed of four activities in Figure 22-1. At the top of the diagram is a box that represents the traditional managerial functions of planning, organizing, directing, and controlling. The depart-mental supervisor does all these things because his major responsibility is summarized as "managing."

The lower, large box represents the operational technology of the department, the total transformation process through which input becomes output. In our model the input undergoes four separate and sequential operations, each of which is performed by separate, specialized workers. The input could be a steel plate, to be milled, deburred, polished, and inspected. It could be a customer in a cafeteria, with workers dispensing meats, vegeta-bles, desserts, and operating the cash register. It could be a sales order form that is posted to a sales ledger, broken down into inventory classes, entered on a manufacturing schedule sheet, and used to initiate a customer's bill. Whatever the specific process is, four separate workers perform specialized activities on the input. Worker A does Task 1, Worker B does Task 2, and so on.

Under this work design concept, each worker's responsibility consists of "doing" something. The supervisor retains the managerial activities of plan-ning, organizing, directing, and controlling. His responsibility, in short, is to "manage," performing those responsible and nonroutine elements of the total process. Such a division of activities into *doing* and *managing* is based on

[2]John B. Miner, *The Management Process: Theory, Research, and Practice* (New York: Macmillan, 1973), pp. 236, 237.

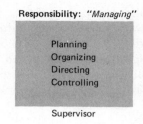

Responsibility: *"Managing"*

Supervisor

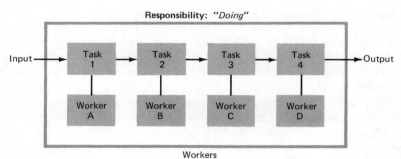

Responsibility: *"Doing"*

Workers

FIGURE 22-1   Hypothetical work flow and task responsibilities. Source: Adapted from M. Scott Myers, "Every Employee a Manager," *California Management Review* (Spring 1968), p. 11.

economic efficiency. The skill levels demanded of workers are low compared with the skills needed for managing, and each worker is freed of distractions such as making decisions, thinking ahead, and evaluating quality of output.

Division of labor also enables each worker to attain peak proficiency quickly because of short cycle time and carefully specified work methods and procedures. Yet such job characteristics, we have seen, are precisely those associated with job dissatisfaction, high turnover rates, alienation, low motivation, and diminished productivity and task performance.

Are there any job design alternatives to this approach? Expanding the scope of narrowed and routinized jobs has been presented as a way of redesigning jobs for increased motivation and satisfaction. Reversing this scope-narrowing specialization process calls for the addition of nonroutine activities and the including of motivating elements in the design of the job. Several different approaches exist by which job requirements are changed in order to increase job satisfaction and productivity. We will consider job rotation and job enlargement as stops along the way to the enriched, motivating job.

Job Rotation

Under job rotation, the job held by the individual is considered to be unchangeable, even though it is recognized by the management as being without challenge and opportunity for growth and is both boring and monotonous. Given a number of related tasks, the individual is "rotated" through the other tasks, successively holding each of them for a period of time. In this way, he is taken off his boring job for a while. He is allowed to develop other skills and also a perspective of where his own activity fits into the overall flow of work, hopefully increasing his identification with the final output. In a cafeteria a server might swap jobs for a week, ladling out potatoes and peas instead of slicing and serving roast beef. An inventory clerk, in an enlarged job, might get to make out customer bills for a change.

The problem with job rotation is that neither the job nor the individual has been changed, either in formal expectations or in attitudes. Monotony may be relieved for a while, but the individual still returns to the same old boring job. While he has been rotating, some critics charge, he has merely been exposed to *other* boring and monotonous jobs.

Job Enlargement

A more sophisticated approach to the problem of increasing motivation, satisfaction, and productivity is that of job enlargement. In a sense, job

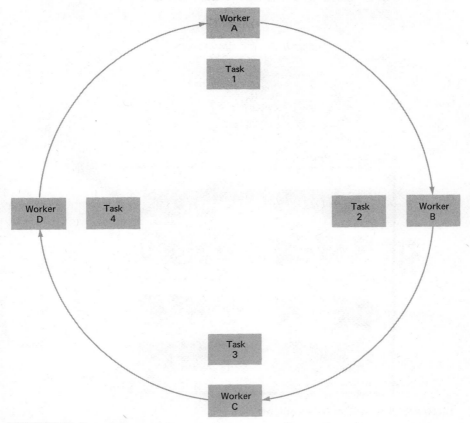

FIGURE 22-2   Job rotation.

enlargement recognizes that dissatisfaction and monotony may be traced to extremely short cycle times built into the nature of the job because of overspecialization. As a solution to the problem, the job is made larger, with requirements for broader skill development and longer cycle time. The job is enlarged to include activities that were formerly the domain of other specialized workers, thus increasing the number and variety of skills and activities required of the individual.

Figure 22-3 shows how the activities in Figure 22-1 might appear under job enlargement. Monotony is expected to be reduced, with a resulting positive effect on satisfaction. Notice that attempting to build in some variety is central to both job rotation and job enlargement. Job enlargement is intended to expand the total amount of capability or potential of the individual demanded by the task.

Under the job specialization concept, separate bookkeepers in a large utility were assigned to separate activities. One saw that all new accounts were opened properly; another took care of closing all accounts; a third posted all payments. When the utility's total of over a million customers is considered, the volume of each activity seemed to justify such specialization. Yet satisfac-

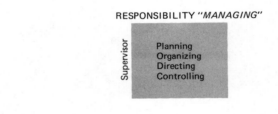

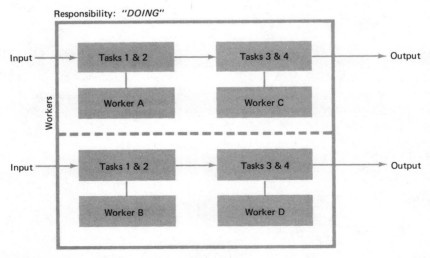

FIGURE 22-3   Job enlargement.

tion and productivity were low. The jobs were enlarged so that a bookkeeper is now responsible for handling *all* routine transactions that occur within the accounts for a given group of fifteen thousand customers.[3] Each bookkeeper now has more variety and a longer cycle time in performing a complete task and can better identify with the overall bookkeeping and customer service functions.

The ultimate objectives of job rotation and enlargement are the same— increasing satisfaction, motivation, and productivity—and are intended to create positive attitudes by changes in job activity. We can employ Herzberg's dual-factor theory to see how task changes affect job satisfaction. In looking for motivating factors in the design of an enlarged job, we observe no essential inclusion of achievement, recognition, advancement, or responsibility. Possibility of growth and the duties of the work itself are the only two motivators that might be considered as being designed into an enlarged job. The possibility of growth is implicit in the requirement for increased skill development. The duties of the work itself as a source of good or bad feelings are *assumed* because of the greater variety and hence decreased feelings of boredom and monotony.

In short, job enlargement seems to suffer from a lack of motivators. Variety, the requirement of more skills, and increased capability are part of job enlargement, but the job has been made larger and less boring rather than intrinsically more satisfying. Herzberg called job enlargement the result of a horizontal loading of job factors. The job is not made more meaningful and capable of securing initiative, sense of accomplishment, individual responsibility, and identification with the final product. Instead a new approach is needed to build in motivators in a concrete and systematic fashion. The job has to be *enriched,* rather than made larger.

Job Enrichment

A dramatic comparison to these approaches of job enlargement and job rotation, as well as to the other integrative techniques, is that of job enrichment. The design of the job itself is changed as in job enlargement, but it is changed in such a way as to require the job holder to exercise initiative and achievement, accept responsibility, develop new skills, prepare for advancement, accept evaluation and recognition for the quality of work he does, and otherwise become involved in the nature of the job itself. This, in turn, creates the necessity for variety, autonomy (relative independence), identify with the task, and continual feedback of task-related performance.[4]

Jobs are referred to as "enriched" when the employee participates in planning his or her work, organizing the sequence and schedule of it, and controlling the

[3]"The Renewed Interest in 'Job Enlargement,'" *Administrative Management* (April 1964), p. 22.

[4]Edward E. Lawler, III, *Motivation in Work Organizations* (Monterey, Calif.: Brooks/Cole Publishing Co., 1973), p. 160.

quantity and quality of the work by measuring effort expended against the objectives set in the planning phase, in addition to making the product or performing the service implicit in the job. The basic "doing" aspects of the job may or may not be changed; the enrichment is the addition of the planning and control responsibilities—functions traditionally thought of as managerial.[5]

What does the worker receive from the enriched job? He exercises initiative and judgment, accomplishes a task objective, assumes responsibility for his performance of an increased scope of duties, and manages a complete and meaningful module of work. Motivation and satisfaction are resultants of these attitude-based factors, and increases in measures of productivity are then assumed to follow.

Figure 22-4 allows a comparison between a specialized task and an enriched one. The enriched task incorporates duties that were once centralized in the position of the manager, notably those of planning, scheduling, organizing, evaluating, and controlling. Under task specialization what had been left to the worker was the routine "doing" activity. The nonroutine activities that affected what, when, how, and why the worker did his task were performed by his supervisor.

We have seen that participation in the managerial function elicits commitment and satisfaction. Separation of the managerial from the implementation phases of work activity precludes major participation. In addition, the repetitive and routine functions are left for the worker for what appear to be sound and economic reasons. He can specialize in a particular activity full time, developing that skill to its utmost, without bothering about broader concerns. Reducing the task to its lowest dimension also allows a lower wage rate to be assigned and much less nonproductive time while learning the task and being trained for full productivity.

The Enriched Job

Decisions ultimately affecting each operative worker under such a system are structured to be made at a managerial—not a subordinate—level. Hence information and communication flow must be a personal result of relationships between superior and subordinate, not a natural and necessary part of participating in managerial decisions or the workers' making decisions by themselves that affect their own work.

Decision-Making Locus

Job enrichment calls for an essential decentralization of decision-making rights to each individual, over areas that directly affect his own task func-

[5]Harold M. F. Rush, "Motivation Through Job Design," *The Conference Board Record* (January 1971), p. 54.

Manager

Worker A: Responsibility—Managing Job Module

Input ———→ TASKS 1, 2, 3, & 4 ———→ Output

Job planning:
problem-solving, organizing
work, scheduling, methods
improvement

Job control:
inspect, test, evaluate, record,
adjust, repair

Input ———→ TASKS 1, 2, 3, & 4 ———→ Output

Job planning

Job control

Worker D: Responsibility—Managing Job Module

FIGURE 22-4   Job enrichment.

tions. The job is enriched with the inclusion of these managerial activities and also by the emphasis on the *result* of the worker's efforts rather than the procedure by which he does his job. The manager delegates authority over task-related concerns to the operative level, together with decision-making rights commensurate with the responsibility assigned each worker for obtaining the results and meeting the standards established. So long as they are met or exceeded, the manager need not interfere or intervene in the operative activity, instead focusing his attention on long-range planning matters and other areas of managerial concern that are time-consuming yet vitally important. Workers control themselves, internalizing standards of quality and quantity because of the necessity of policing their own performance and being held accountable for it. A group of workers meeting in a goal-setting conference dramatized the extent of the change from a job enrichment program:

During the discussion of the merging role of the supervisor, the group concluded that an effective supervisor is one who *provides a climate in which people have a sense of working for themselves.* In terms of their day-to-day relationships, they further defined the supervisor's role as:

Giving visibility to company (customer) goals.
Providing budgets and facilities.
Mediating conflict.
But primarily, staying out of the way to let people manage their own work.[6]

Example: Stockholder Correspondents

A report of an actual situation may help to clarify the essence of job enrichment.[7] A large corporation employed about 120 women as stockholder correspondents. They were divided into five departments. They were extensively trained before they began the task of answering stockholder queries. In replying to letters, the correspondents used stock paragraphs and standard answers that were on file. Supervisors handled any unusual or especially difficult letters. All of the correspondents were relatively young and all held college degrees.

After the correspondent put together the stock phrases and paragraphs into an answer, the letter was turned over to the supervisor for checking and for the supervisor's signature. This job was chosen for job enrichment because of extremely high and costly turnover, a problem additional to relatively low performance and very low job satisfaction. Those choosing to leave the job reported that the job was boring. One of the departments was chosen for study, with the others being control groups, without changes being introduced into them.

Significant changes were made in the experimental group's jobs and responsibilities. No longer were the difficult and unusual inquiries referred to supervisors; the correspondents handled them themselves, with fellow workers being assigned specific areas of expertise. In this way the correspondent could consult an expert peer about a difficult letter before answering it. Another change occurred in which supervisors no longer signed and checked each correspondent's letters. Correspondents checked, verified, signed, and mailed their own letters without consulting or passing through the supervisor. Each correspondent was held responsible for the quality of the answer because any further requests from stockholders for additional information or clarification were referred back to the original correspondent for handling. Finally, each correspondent was urged to answer each letter individually, in her own words, and without using stock phrases or paragraphs.

What were the results of enriching this task? The enriched group's performance index rose from 50 percent to over 90, whereas the control group's performance remained rather steady at around 70 percent. Job satisfaction rose significantly in the enriched group and fell slightly in the

[6]M. Scott Myers, "Every Employee a Manager," *California Management Review* (Spring 1968), p. 17.
[7]Frederick Herzberg, "One More Time: How Do You Motivate Employees?" *Harvard Business Review* (January–February 1968).

control group. Absenteeism and turnover decreased substantially in the enriched group.

Enrichment, Theory X, and Theory Y

What are the critical differences that account for the increased job satisfaction, motivation, and productivity? Why did turnover decrease? In this example we can see that the job of the stockholder correspondents was enriched, redesigned, and restructured to include several formerly managerial functions. In addition, the correspondents were given responsibility for their own work, were allowed to exercise initiative and creativity in the pursuit of their duties, and were freed from controls that had formerly been exercised by their supervisors. One way of looking at the difference between the old and the new jobs is to view them from Theory X and Theory Y perspectives. Under the old system, the supervisor had sought productivity above all else. To ensure that requisite quality attended the productivity, the supervisor checked and evaluated each letter that went out before signing it. Further, to make sure that the individual correspondent did not write a "poor" letter, preselected phrases and paragraphs were supplied for selection and inclusion in the letter. In other words, the job was designed to be as predictable and routine as possible, with the supervisor exercising the evaluating and controlling function and the correspondents performing the "doing" phase of the work.

This pattern seems to fit a Theory X philosophy quite nicely. An essential part of such a job system is an assumption that the workers are not responsible enough to do a good-quality job and hence must be constantly checked to ensure that the job they do meets minimum standards. As a result, the job is made as foolproof as possible, with extensive guides and rules. Low motivation and satisfaction are almost assumed in the design of the job, and the question then becomes how the job can be controlled so that output meets or exceeds minimum standards.

In direct contrast are the assumptions of the enriched job approach. First of all, the correspondents are assumed to be responsible and competent. Second, the job itself—securing the final output—is assumed to be able to be changed. Further, poor job attitudes are felt to be a product of the *job* rather than deficiencies in the character or motivation of the *job holders*. Third, the correspondents are felt to be capable of becoming involved and interested in their jobs. Finally, the job holders are considered to be capable of responding productively to a challenge and to meet it through task accomplishment when such an opportunity is provided and rewarded.

Sanctions

Another critical distinction between the specialization and the enriched approaches is in the nature and source of sanctions. Under the previous technology, sanctions were typically negative in fashion, with the control system implemented by the manager and dedicated to ferreting out *inferior* work and intended to force people to do a minimum of satisfactory work. Inferior performance was punished, but we saw no ready-made device by which the superior performer was individually recognized. (How does one distinguish a "superior" combination of stock phrases and paragraphs?) The source of these negative sanctions is the manager. He controls organizationally provided rewards, all of which are extrinsic rewards—salary, promotion, perhaps a bonus, and so on. We might, as an aside, refer to the concepts in learning theory to question how effective these extrinsic rewards are in securing effective behavior, especially when they are aimed at providing negative reinforcement for ineffective behaviors. What reinforcement factors do we notice for effective performance?

The enriched approach does take a more positive orientation. Controls are loosened and the manager delegates the day-to-day control function to its lowest possible level, the correspondents themselves. Such responsibility is supported with equal authority, however, so that the amount and type of work done constitute a complete and natural "module" of work.

The Work Module and Intrinsic Rewards

The job is redefined and reconstituted into a "natural" cluster of closely related functions and activities rather than being artificially separated and assigned to various levels in the organization. In this way the individual correspondent can identify with a given complete product over which she has had complete control from beginning to end, and she receives recognition and responsibility for the quality of the job she has done.

An enriched job continues to have extrinsic rewards for performance, but these are directly supported with the intrinsic rewards that are much more immediate and powerful to the individual himself. The motivator factors in Herzberg's dual-factor theory are, as we see, consciously made a part of the redesigned job. The job is loaded *vertically,* rather than merely horizontally, because the job becomes "deeper," more complex, and more demanding of responsibility, achievement, and initiative.

The Autonomous Work Group

In cases in which the nature of the product or technology precludes designing a self-contained natural work module for the individual worker, establishing an *autonomous work group* has proved effective. The autonomous work group is most obvious in Saab's and Volvo's automobile assembly plants in Sweden. The Volvo facility was the first auto assembly plant built around the group assembly concept, and the Saab plant was the pioneer in auto subassembly with autonomous work groups.[8]

The Swedish Experience

Saab found itself, in 1969, in the unenviable position of being forced to be innovative. Total employee turnover was 45 percent annually. In the auto assembly plant alone, turnover ran 70 percent. Absenteeism was incredibly high—almost 20 percent.[9] Humanizing the auto assembly process was the only economically viable alternative.

The assembling of auto engines by small groups was instituted, replacing the traditional assembly line. Production groups range in size from five to twelve. They all have related duties and decide among themselves what their work assignments and methods will be. Job rotation is used by the groups, because assembly tasks vary in desirability and can be shared by rotation. Further responsibilities were added to the tasks of the production groups, making each group responsible for inspection and quality control, housekeeping, and simple service and maintenance activities.

Each group also assembles cylinder block, cylinder heads, connecting rods, and crankshaft in putting together the entire engine, a thirty-minute job. Work pace is group-determined, as are the number and length of work breaks taken—just as long as 470 engines are assembled in each ten-day period.

The results? Lower capital investment, improvement in quality, lower turnover, higher productivity, and better worker attitudes.

Volvo faced many of the same problems experienced by Saab: turnover was 40 percent annually; absenteeism was 20–25 percent; 45 percent of the employees were non-Swedes because Swedes refused to work in a factory job. Volvo too found enrichment to be helpful, both to employees and to the firm. The extent of Volvo's commitment may be measured by its investment in its new auto assembly factory at Kalmar, Sweden. The factory's environment was designed for group work and enriched jobs.

The assembly line, so representative of monotonous labor, has been completely done away with. In the assembling of the autos, responsibility for different installations (electrical systems, brakes, wheels, and so on) falls to teams composed of fifteen to twenty-five members. Each team is autonomous, has its own work area, and decides all work-related matters.

Self-propelled electric trolleys furnish transportation of autos to each "bay" (work area) from storage areas. Even this retrieval is done by team

---

[8]See, for example, "Job Redesign on the Assembly Line: Farewell to Blue-Collar Blues?" *Organizational Dynamics* (Autumn 1973), pp. 55–60; and Noel M. Tichy, "Organizational Innovations in Sweden," *Columbia Journal of World Business* (Summer 1974), pp. 18–22.

[9]"Job Redesign on the Assembly Line," p. 55.

members. Each team is also responsible for managing its own parts inventory.

Finally, the architecture of the plant directly supports the new technology. Work areas are physically separated from each other by walls. Each team has its own entrance, changing room, and rest rooms. Extensive use of windows was made to make the work environment as pleasant as possible. Whether such a total commitment to a new humanistic enrichment technology is supported by economic results, time will tell.

Meanwhile, in Topeka . . .

In 1971 a new pet-food plant was opened in Topeka by the General Foods Corporation. The plant and job characteristics were designed to "incorporate features that would provide a high quality of work life, enlist unusual human involvement, and result in high productivity."[10]

An important part of the program was the design of autonomous work groups:

Self-managed work teams are given collective responsibility for large segments of the production process. The total work force of approximately 70 employees is organized into six teams. A processing team and a packaging team operate during each shift. A team is comprised of from 7 to 14 members (called "operators") and a team leader. Its size is large enough to include a natural set of highly interdependent tasks, yet small enough to allow effective face-to-face meetings for decision making and coordination. Assignments of individuals to sets of tasks are subject to team consensus. Although at any given time one operator has primary responsibility for a set of tasks within the team's jurisdiction, some tasks can be shared by several operators. Moreover, tasks can be redefined by the team in light of individual capabilities and interests. In contrast, individuals in the old plant were permanently assigned to specific jobs.[11]

The range of the managerial functions included in the work group's duties may be seen in the following: coordinating and handling production problems, task reassignments, screening and selecting new team members, counseling team members who fail to meet group production–attendance standards.[12]

The results of the autonomous work-group concept are impressive: 70 workers man the plant rather than the 110 estimated necessary; quality rejects are 92 percent below the industry norm; absenteeism rate is 9 percent below the industry norm; annual savings of $600,000 result from reductions in variable manufacturing costs; turnover is far below average for the company; attitudes are positive.[13]

[10]Richard E. Walton, "How to Counter Alienation in the Plant," *Harvard Business Review* (November–December 1972), pp. 70, 71.
[11]Ibid., pp. 74, 75.
[12]Ibid., p. 75.
[13]Ibid., p. 77.

Implementing Job Enrichment

The nature of the enriched job should be fairly clear by now. But how does a job *get* enriched? Enriching a job constitutes a significant change for a relatively large number of people within the organization. Such a change can create significant conflicts and resistance. Even further, there conceivably could be individuals who simply do not *want* an enriched job—they are perfectly happy and content with a job that makes little demand of them.

Establishing the Change Need

At one end of a scale of securing participation in enrichment efforts is the relatively authoritarian method of simply decreeing that a change will be made. In many cases management may feel that the situation is serious enough to redesign a job without securing participation and involvement by job occupants. Through consultants or other engineering studies and guided by the principles of including motivator factors in a newly designed job, management investigates the extent to which a problem is perceived to exist. Attitude surveys, productivity measures, turnover rates, and job-exit interviews alert the manager that the job is dissatisfying and incapable of motivating the individual. The manager then investigates the nature of the workflow and considers his role in the system. Each job that he supervises is analyzed for hygiene as well as motivator factors to provide a base line or status quo and to provide direction for the nature of the design effort.

Principles of Enrichment Design

Herzberg suggested the following principles to be followed in designing motivators into a job to be enriched:

1. Remove some controls while retaining accountability—building in the motivators of responsibility and personal achievement.
2. Increase the accountability of individuals for their own work—building in the motivators of responsibility and recognition.
3. Give a person a complete natural unit of work (module, division, area, and so on)—building in the motivators of responsibility, achievement, and recognition.
4. Grant additional authority to an employee in his activity; job freedom—building in the motivators of responsibility, achievement and recognition.
5. Make periodic reports directly available to the worker himself rather than to the supervisor—building in the motivator of internal recognition.
6. Introduce new and more difficult tasks not previously handled—building in the motivators of growth and learning.
7. Assign individuals specific or specialized tasks, enabling them to become

experts—building in the motivators of responsibility, growth, and advancement.[14]

Even more specific are the steps found by Ford to make a job more meaningful and satisfying for competent people with demonstrated ability:

1. Give the employee a good module of work.
   Pull responsibilities back down to this job level if they have been assigned higher up only for safety's sake.
   Gather together the responsibilities that are now handled by people whose work precedes or follows, including verifying and checking.
   Push certain routine matters down to lower-rated jobs.
   Automate the routine matter completely if possible.
   Rearrange the parts and divide the total volume of work so that an employee has a feeling of "my customers," "my responsibility."
2. Once an employee has earned the right, let him really run his job.
3. Develop ways for giving employees direct, individual feedback on their own performance (not group indexes).
4. Invent ways of letting the job expand so that an employee can grow psychologically. ("There's always something new coming up on this job!")[15]

In this approach to job restructuring, Herzberg specifically suggested that employees be *excluded* from directly participating in the enrichment process, for:

their direct involvement contaminates the process with human relations *hygiene* and, more specifically, gives them only a *sense* of making a contribution. The job is to be changed, and it is the content that will produce the motivation, not attitudes about being involved or the challenge inherent in setting up a job. That process will be over shortly, and it is what the employees will be doing from then on that will determine their motivation. A sense of participation will result only in short-term movement.[16]

Instead the criterion to be observed is the extent of improvement in important measures such as turnover, satisfaction measures, and productivity. These must be measured before any change is made, and a control group must be established to guard against other extraneous factors that actually create improvement rather than the structural changes in the job. After the changes are implemented, there typically occurs a drop in productivity in the newly enriched job—but the drop is only temporary. Performance quickly improves to the old level and finally stabilizes at a level significantly higher than before.

[14]Herzberg, "One More Time," p. 59.
[15]Robert N. Ford, *Motivation Through the Work Itself* (New York: American Management Association, 1969), p. 188.
[16]Herzberg, "One More Time," pp. 61, 62.

Advantages of Job Enrichment

Throughout our discussion of job enrichment we have seen that job enrichment can play a powerful role in creating significantly greater opportunities for job satisfaction and motivation while raising employee productivity. Thus its greatest advantage may be relatively philosophical: redesigning and restructuring a job with the intent of providing more meaningful work is an important philosophical difference, one that stipulates that individual and formal organizational objectives may be—under appropriate conditions—mutually consistent rather than antagonistic and irreconcilable. If the job is, in fact, demeaning, degrading, and incapable of providing any satisfactions, then the total workflow should be reanalyzed and restructured in the process of creating a more human work environment. If a job cannot be enriched and if it fails to provide satisfaction and motivation, then it should be automated—taken over by a machine. Tasks that cannot be enriched are so short cycle, routine, and repetitive that they could be done better by a machine, which is unaffected by attitude and motivational considerations.

In addition to structuring formal expectations to be consistent with psychological growth considerations, job enrichment provides significant opportunities for individuals to display and develop native initiative and judgment. Managerial functions, such as scheduling, planning, organizing, evaluating, and controlling, become the domain of the operative worker. Superior task performance in an enriched job provides a significant opportunity for the formal organization's never-ending search for managerial talent. In the typical unenriched and repetitive job, all the employee does is "do"; *doing* skills are much different from conceptual and analytical managerial skills, and even the conscientious manager cannot evaluate his subordinates on their managerial aptitudes. This is one reason why the best punch-press operator may become foreman—for lack of relevant information, management is forced to assume a connection between operative performance (motivation) and managerial aptitude. But the enriched job requires the development and display of *managerial* as well as operative skills. The supervising manager can evaluate each employee on his ability to plan and schedule, organize and set priorities, coordinate and evaluate, follow up and control his natural module of work.

As the manager has been relieved of the onerous and time-consuming duties of checking and evaluating performance and quality, he can devote much more of his time to the longer-range considerations of planning and forestalling potential problems. He can also devote much more of his time to training his employees because of the amount of time that he has had freed. Two-way communication can more nearly be facilitated because of an increased congruence between managerial and operative objectives and the necessity of the subordinate to learn from his manager. Communications between subordinate and superior can become goal-oriented, and hence the manager may become apprised of emerging problem situations much more quickly.

Finally, because of increased satisfaction and motivation, overall productivity per employee rises, sometimes dramatically. Although this may not be a prime objective of job enrichment, productivity may increase so much that quite a number of jobs may be eliminated, offering direct payroll savings. The assumption of responsibility and the evaluation of the worker's own work further support the raising of quality and the lowering of defect rates in output.

Disadvantages in Job Enrichment

Each individual is different in personality makeup and hence in motivation. Even though there are no relevant statistics on the matter, job enrichment may be met with differing amounts of enthusiasm by various employees. Job enrichment is a task-oriented device, albeit one that is humanistic and devoted to meaningful work. One might well expect that workers relatively high in n-Ach would welcome such an opportunity. But what about workers low in n-Ach? We might argue that few workers who are achievement-oriented would willingly seek a job in a routine, repetitive, unchallenging task. Rather the task might have been sought and maintained by those *low* in achievement needs. A major inconsistency may be encountered in the requirements of job enrichment and the personality characteristics of those holding the jobs most open for job enrichment.

The supervisor of the workers whose jobs are to be enriched can also be a source of conflict. Again we must start with personality considerations, for the supervisor of a routine and repetitive task is likely to be a rather authoritarian individual who thoroughly enjoys the power and dominance over others that his position and the task technology demand. Changing his responsibilities from dominance of others to the more abstract areas of long-range planning, and also requiring a lesser amount of psychological distance (more equality) between him and his workers may create a great deal of dissonance and dissatisfaction on *his* part. After all, job enrichment forces rather free and open communication channels between the two levels and also requires the manager to work relatively closely—almost as a team member—with his employees as he attempts to assist them and develop them in acquiring managerial skills.

In addition, the supervisor can create enormous amounts of resistance because of his being forced out of his comfortable pattern of behavior into new and unfamiliar ones for which he will be held accountable. Even managers can be sources of resistance to change! If the routine task technology that is being enriched has required that substantial portions of his time be devoted to controlling, checking, and directing his subordinates, he has probably had very little time to do more than pay scant attention to his other managerial functions of planning and organizing. Hence those skills that the manager had developed to a rather high degree are threatened to be shorn away from his responsibility, and he will be forced to develop skills and ability in areas that he has not had time to develop over his career.

Job enrichment requires a development effort—not only for the employees whose jobs are to be enriched—but for their supervisor in *managerial* skills that will come to occupy almost all of their time and that will become critical. This can amount to a rather substantial investment by the top management of the organization in training and development, as well as periods of relative decline in productivity as the managers learn, experiment, and attempt to implement real managerial skills.

Personnel costs will also increase because of the need for higher levels of skills and initiative to be sought among new job holders. Job incumbents may also perceive a lack of equity if they are not granted substantial increases in pay commensurate with their increased responsibilities.[17] Less control over individual workers and their job performance will also require a substantial effort to determine how the individuals should be evaluated and how they should be rewarded for differential levels of job performance.

On Balance, However . . .

On balance, however, the concept of job enrichment offers many significant improvements in the basic nature of the task of the organizational member. Through a restructured and redesigned job the motivational and personality needs of the individual may be effectively integrated with the objectives of the formal organizational system. By taking such an approach, the organizational member has an alternative path open to him for satisfying his needs and realizing his potential. We must point out, too, that this path toward attainment of his goals becomes a viable alternative to the other path, the informal organization and work restriction. There are even some managerial positions that could conceivably benefit from a reanalysis of function and contribution, in the pursuit of productivity through heightened satisfaction and motivation.

How widespread is job enrichment? No one really knows at this point, but we can safely assume that it offers the practicing manager a realistic approach to integrating the individual into the formal organizational system, making his objectives consistent with those of the larger system while making possible a work environment more attuned to more qualified, more motivated, and more aspiring workers.

[17]Judson Gooding, "It Pays to Wake Up the Blue-Collar Worker," *Fortune* (September 1970), p. 168.

Summary

Structural redesign of job characteristics is a tool available to the manager in influencing organizational behavior. Redesign offers significant opportunities to eliminate dissatisfying task components while the manager includes motivator elements. By building motivating factors into the structure of the formal expectations entailed in the job, individual and organizational goals may be more nearly aligned.

Achievement, recognition, variety, interesting work, advancement, professional growth, challenge, and responsibility are examples of factors that are associated with satisfaction and motivation. The job can be redesigned to provide these elements as formal task objectives are attained.

The traditional specialization–division of labor approach to job design was compared to newer alternatives. Job rotation takes task characteristics as unalterable and attempts to furnish variety for the worker by rotating him through related jobs. Job enlargement is an alternative that conceives the task as artificially established and hence changeable. To relieve the pressures of monotony and boredom incurred by repetitive, short-cycle tasks, the job is restructured to include other specialized tasks. The worker is then exposed to a variety of job requirements and develops new skills.

Job enrichment is the most thorough and effective approach to redesigning the job for human needs and motivation. Job enrichment may call for horizontal loading of job factors (as in job enlargement) and does require vertical loading with managerial functions. Decision-making rights are decentralized to the operative worker, who is granted responsibility and control over his job activity. The job is designed to include all activities "natural" to its objective, so as to constitute a module and to further responsibility for and identification with a specified end product. Meaningful work, challenge, and personal growth are the purposes of job enrichment.

When job enrichment is not feasible, autonomous work groups with managerial control over total task activity may be established. Such work groups have been found effective in several studies in increasing productivity and satisfaction and decreasing turnover and absenteeism.

Finally, job enrichment is not for everyone. Not all employees are achievement-oriented, and some enjoy working in a task that demands little. Managers can furnish resistance to enrichment programs because of the fundamental change enrichment requires in the managerial role. Yet, on balance, job enrichment provides a major and innovative way in which to humanize work and provide a meaningful opportunity for growth.

STUDY AND REVIEW QUESTIONS

1. Compare and contrast job enlargement and job enrichment.
2. Describe the personality characteristics of the worker for whom an enriched job becomes motivating and satisfying.

3. Describe the general characteristics of the job that *should* be enriched.

4. Can a manager's job be enriched? If yes, under what conditions? If no, why not?

5. Carefully evaluate the opportunities for effective implementation of job enrichment under each of the production technologies.

6. Using force field analysis, analyze the forces for and against implementing job enrichment. How would you, as a manager, overcome resistance to enrichment?

7. What are some advantages to the autonomous work-group concept? Some disadvantages?

8. Describe a job with which you are familiar. Using Herzberg's principles of enrichment, redesign the job into an enriched job. Then evaluate the characteristics of the enriched job with the dual-factor theory.

9. What arguments *against* job enrichment can you think of?

10. How likely is job enrichment to catch on and be widely implemented in organized settings? Discuss your arguments and reasons.

Chapter

23

Organizational Development

CHAPTER OBJECTIVES

1. To provide a broad perspective on organizational development (OD) as a major integrating device.

2. To review the natures and applications of OD interventions.

3. To evaluate the current status of OD as an organizational improvement program.

4. To give an understanding of, and a familiarity with, the philosophies and values that underlie OD.

5. To develop an appreciation for the potential of OD as a total program for integrating individual, group, and organization.

CHAPTER OUTLINE

The organization is successful to the extent that it mobilizes its resources effectively in the pursuit of organizational *and* human goals. Its resources are defined far more broadly than comprising merely financial, machinery, or raw materials inputs—they include the organization's reservoir of human and managerial talent. Applying these human resources offers substantial challenge because of the difficulties involved in measuring, inventorying, and allocating them. They are also highly volatile and subject to many intangible pressures and conflicts.

Within the organizational behavior system, frictions and conflicts are created by the differing natures of the three component subsystems. Each has its own characteristics and needs, and each relies on its interactions with the other two subsystems, yet some trade-offs and compromises are necessary. The formal organizational subsystem's needs for predictability and stability must be modified by the human desires for autonomy, challenge, and competence. The individual's desires to be independent and answerable only to himself are inconsistent with the social subsystem's requirements of adhering to group norms and standards. Individual autonomy and self-actualization conflicts also with the formal organizational subsystem's requirements of coordination and accountability in task performance. The social subsystem's conflicts with the formal organization find expression in the compromising of task performance to a level that allows the group to meet performance criteria while satisfying belongingness needs.

Improving the Organization's Effectiveness

Conflicts and inconsistencies among the requirements of the three subsystems cannot be wished away by the manager. Under appropriate conditions innovative solutions can be found by which conflicts may be reduced *and* each subsystem allowed to seek its own goal attainments, even while supporting and contributing to the overall effectiveness of the organization in human, social, and economic terms. Yet the technology and the knowledge employed in establishing and maintaining an organization changes over time. The "truths" of yesterday can become outmoded and unworkable as conditions change. Today, in the last twenty-five years of the twentieth century, no other society has experienced the drastic and continual buffeting of major social and technological change that we have. These are translated into dynamic organizational environments, unstable at best, that require sophisticated management merely to keep up with—let alone predict—the amount and nature of change that will affect internal operations and external relationships.

The tendency in our society is toward rather large organizations, which evolve through various growth stages. Each growth stage is accompanied by problems and crises, which must be overcome before the next stage may be successfully entered.[1] Table 23-1 shows the stages of growth.

[1]Larry E. Greiner, "Evolution and Revolution as Organizations Grow," *Harvard Business Review* (July–August 1972). The following discussion draws heavily on his work.

TABLE 23-1   Organizational Growth Stages

Organizational Characteristics	Phase	Growth Through	Leading to Crisis of
Small, young	1	Creativity	Leadership
	2	Direction	Autonomy
	3	Delegation	Control
	4	Coordination	Red Tape
Large, mature	5	Collaboration	-?-

SOURCE: Adapted from Larry E. Greiner, "Evolution and Revolution as Organizations Grow," *Harvard Business Review* (July–August 1972), pp. 41–44.

In the *creative* stage, the firm is usually established to fill a need. Its originators are usually creative and nonmanagerial in orientation; individualism is encouraged. *Leadership* quickly becomes important and a strong manager must take up the reins of the larger, more complicated firm. The growth is sustained through *direction* by the manager, who installs techniques to channel creative energy more efficiently. An organizational structure is set up, as are accounting systems, decision making by managers, incentives, budgets, and so on. The *crisis of autonomy,* the need for less controls and more initiative, is encountered as the firm continues to grow.

Autonomy needs are successfully met through *delegation* and establishing responsibility and decentralized decision-making. Motivation at lower levels increases, yet the crisis of *control* evolves. Too much freedom can result in field managers' failing to coordinate plans, money, technology, and manpower with other organizational units.

The *coordination stage* is entered to solve the crisis of control. Formal systems are implemented and administered by top officers. Examples are the merging of units into product groups, formal planning and review procedures, and capital budgeting techniques. Such centralized control and coordination create the *red-tape* crisis, leading to resentment and lack of confidence between line and staff.

The final stage, *collaboration,* is entered to overcome the red-tape crisis by strong interpersonal cooperation. Confrontation of interpersonal differences and team management lead to social control and self-discipline instead of formal control. The fashion in which collaboration is engendered is the substance of organizational development (OD). The characteristics of firms needing collaboration-building assistance, large and rather mature organizations, suggest that OD may most profitably be initiated in response to overspecialization and overcontrol in large firms, victims of their own growth stage.

Changing Managerial Philosophies and Organizational Realities

The organization must be just as dynamic as its relevant environments. As the needs of its members and the characteristics of customers and workers change, managerial philosophies must change. What once was a "good" job on the assembly line may today be seen as demeaning and overly restrictive. Philosophies and methods of effective management change—and have changed—with time and circumstances. Table 23-2 summarizes the major trends that are even now occurring in managerial values. Traditional managerial values are represented (probably simplistically) as being rather Theory X- and controlling-oriented, appropriate to bureaucratic organizations, stable environments, highly centralized decision-making, and authoritarianism.

Emerging values are more akin to those of Maslow, McGregor, and Likert—"humanistic" values—which emphasize the individual's innate worth, dignity, and potential for contribution to formal objectives. These emerging values explicitly recognize the importance of interpersonal trust, openness, collaboration, and the confrontation of unproductive conflicts. "Process work" is the facilitation of productive accomplishment through "such activities as team maintenance and development, diagnosis and working through of interpersonal and intergroup communication barriers, con-

TABLE 23-2   Changing Managerial Values

Away from . . .	Toward . . .
A view of man as essentially bad.	A view of man as basically good.
Avoidance or negative evaluation of individuals.	Confirming individuals as human beings.
A view of individuals as fixed.	Seeing individuals as being in process.
Resisting and fearing individual differences.	Accepting and utilizing individual differences.
Utilizing an individual primarily with reference to his job description.	Viewing an individual as a whole person.
Walling-off the expression of feelings.	Making possible both appropriate expression and effective us of feelings.
Maskmanship and game playing.	Authentic behavior.
Use of status for maintaining power and personal prestige.	Use of status for organizationally relevant purposes.
Distrusting people.	Trusting people.
Avoiding facing others with relevant data.	Making appropriate confrontation.
Avoidance of risk taking.	Willingness to risk.
A view of process work as being unproductive effort.	Seeing process work as essential to effective task accomplishment.
A primary emphasis on competition.	A much greater emphasis on collaboration.

SOURCE: Adapted from Robert Tannenbaum and Sheldon A. Davis, "Values, Man, and Organizations," *Industrial Management Review*, **19**:69–79 (Winter 1969).

frontation efforts for resolution of organizationally dysfunctional personal and interpersonal hangups, and assessment and improvement of existing modes of decision-making."[2] Process skills' place in task accomplishment is seen as vital and hence important additional behaviors to be acquired. In other words, the components of one or more of the organizational behavior subsystems can—and do—change, creating imbalances in the overall organizational behavior process. The formal organizational subsystem, as we have seen, tends to resist change and adaptation, whereas the social and individual subsystems continually change, although at varying speeds.

Managerial technologies are available to attempt to rectify the imbalances created by the changing interactions among the subsystems. We have discussed, in the last two chapters, two of these methods as being job enrichment and positive behavior reinforcement. They are managerially initiated techniques for more effectively integrating human and organizational requirements and goals. Job enrichment is relatively far-reaching because it recognizes that the nature and characteristics of the job must be reevaluated and modified when necessary in order to integrate the expectations of individuals for meaningful and challenging work with the needs of the formal organization for effective output. Positive behavior reinforcement similarly specifies that the individual must be integrated into the formal organizational network by the channeling of his effective behaviors into paths that will result in rewards and achievements for him—and the organization.

From our knowledge of the entire organizational behavior process and the systems-based model we have investigated, we know that such integration technologies are only two major tools, with specific and necessarily limited purposes.

Overcoming Barriers to Effectiveness: Organizational Development

If we consider that the organization is the artificially created vehicle by which behaviors, tasks, and technologies are integrated, then we may notice that task behaviors may be relatively modified by the manager, yet other barriers to organizational effectiveness may still detract from his efforts. Perhaps this concept of barriers should be explored a little more.

In our model of organizational behavior we adopted, for simplicity's sake, a positive conception. The components of the model were seen as processes important to creating given levels of qualities of organizational behavior. Specified leadership styles can increase—or decrease—the probability that effective and satisfying behaviors will be elicited. Certain personality orientations result in various perspectives and inclinations toward satisfaction with tasks of various natures, and so on. One assumption that we were making was that if all of the "right" components were put together, then

[2]Robert Tannenbaum and Sheldon A. Davis, "Values, Man, and Organizations," *Industrial Management Review,* **10:**78 (Winter 1969).

organizational effectiveness and optimized organizational behavior would result.

The OD Climate

Adherents of a technology called *organizational development* (OD) have pointed out that the implementation of organizational behavior requires that the members of an organization operate in a climate conducive to effective behavior. That is, a manager and his subordinates must perceive each other as being receptive, without mistrust, and working together as a team. Conflicts that may be institutionalized—or may spontaneously erupt—between departments cannot be allowed to disrupt the necessary cooperation in their mutual attempts to contribute to overall organizational goals. And organizational members must be able to relate to each other in open and realistic ways, without counterproductive stereotypes. Communication—up and downward—may be enhanced through the appropriate managerial style and available channels, yet open and free communication requires mutual trust and respect—something that cannot be commanded.

Barriers to effective interpersonal behavior are built in and require a different method of handling. Through organizational development methods, effective behavior patterns and interpersonal relationships are created, built, and reinforced. The ways in which this is done are usually based on learning through doing, experience-based learning, rather than cognitive (intellectual) learning. How this is done will be taken up shortly.

Margulies and Raia put it succintly:

Unlike other techniques, which tend to focus on solving current and specific problems, OD technology is aimed at developing new organizational learning and new ways of coping and dealing with problems. The focus is on improving the ways in which the technical, administrative, and personal-cultural systems interact with each other, as well as the way in which the organization relates to the external environment.[3]

Organizational development may be defined as "a planned, systematic process in which applied behavioral science principles and practices are introduced into an ongoing organization toward the goals of effecting organizational improvement, greater organizational competence, and greater organizational effectiveness."[4]

Objectives and Characteristics

Two major objectives of OD are to enhance organizational effectiveness and to develop methods for coping with and adapting to change. To

[3]Newton Margulies and Anthony P. Raia, *Organizational Development: Values, Process, and Technology* (New York: McGraw-Hill, 1972), p. 5.

[4]Wendell L. French and Cecil H. Bell, Jr., *Organization Development: Behavioral Science Interventions for Organization Improvement* (Englewood Cliffs, N.J.: Prentice-Hall, 1973), p. 3.

accomplish these purposes, OD is characterized by a professional behavioral scientist's "intervention" in the processes of the organization. OD is still very much an art, but there are some similarities in OD approaches that have been recognized. First of all, the OD specialist, the professional behavioral scientist, is usually (but certainly not always) an external consultant unaffiliated with his client except by his consultant contract. Second, the OD specialist comes into the organization without preconceived notions of existing problems and without attempting to sell packaged wares or programs. Third, he participates in "action research," through which he gathers data and develops tentative hypotheses about the nature of the problems in the firm. Fourth, these data and hypotheses are fed back to appropriate organizational members for testing and reactions. Fifth, after the problems have been identified, groups of organizational members are gathered for sharing experiences designed to cope with the problems identified and to encourage the practical use of new behaviors back on the job. Sixth, a program of measurement of improvement and further data analysis is undertaken to identify results and further problems for solution. Finally, the entire process is a continuous one, not a "one-shot deal," yet it may be eventually turned over to an "internal consultant," an organizational member with formal responsibility for continuing the OD process.

A major distinction, too, is that the OD consultant does not merely identify the problems in the firm, develop solutions and recommendations, present them for implementation by the firm, and then leave. Instead he is a part of the solution implementation process, acting as a resource person through whom problems are solved. His is a continuing relationship with his client, until the client has developed sufficiently to stand on his own.

Action Research

The term *action research* summarizes the basic methodology of organizational development. Research—gathering data, identifying problems, formulating possible solutions—is the focus of OD. Action coexists with the research, for organizational members and consultants jointly generate data and evaluate the problems pointed out. Then action plans are jointly established by which members may implement their solutions. A model of the action research process is shown in Figure 23-1.

More specifically, action research "is the process of systematically collecting research data about an ongoing system relative to some objective, goal, or need of that system; feeding these data back into the system; taking actions by altering selected variables within the system based both on the data and on hypotheses; and evaluating the results of actions by collecting more data."[5]

What might precipitate the calling in of an OD specialist? Beckhard identified a number of specific situations that might call for an OD specialist.

[5]Ibid., pp. 84, 85.

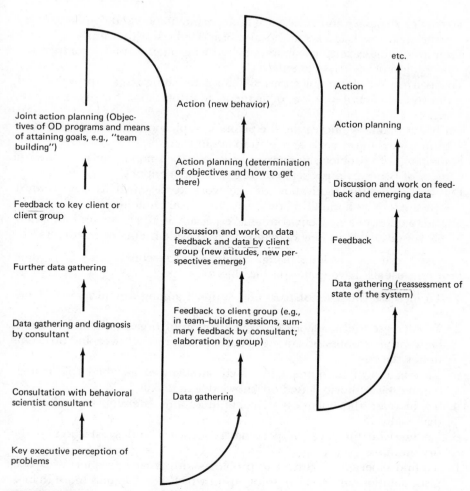

FIGURE 23-1   An action research model for organizational development. Source: Wendell L. French and Cecil Bell, Jr., *Organization Development: Behavioral Science Interventions for Organization Improvement,* 1973, p. 86. By permission of Prentice-Hall, Inc., Englewood Cliffs, New Jersey.

These goals may occur either singly or in some combination:

To change a managerial strategy, the basic objectives and processes by which the firm operates.

To make the task-related characteristics of the organization more consistent with both individual needs and changing characteristics of the firm's environment.

To change the firm's internal "culture," such as values, ground rules, norms, and power structure.

To change structure and roles, such as departmentation and responsibilities, or behavior expectations and duties of individuals within units.

To improve intergroup collaboration, reducing inappropriate competition between units or departments.

To open up the communications system, eliminating gaps in upward and downward communication, or inadequate information for decision-making.

For better planning, increasing the planning sophistication and effectiveness of members to set goals and plan to attain them.

For coping with problems of merger, especially the smooth transition toward unity of two previously separate organizational entities.

For change in the motivation of the work force, such as new reward structures or task modification through job enrichment.

For adaptation to a new environment, especially if a firm moves into a new market or adapts to new demands from outside clients or customers.[6]

As a result of problems' being recognized, OD techniques are brought to bear and usually have quite specific objectives:

1. To increase the level of trust and support among organizational members.
2. To increase the incidence of confrontation of organizational problems, both within groups and among groups, in contrast to "sweeping problems under the rug."
3. To create an environment in which authority of assigned role is augmented by authority based on knowledge and skill.
4. To increase the openness of communications laterally, vertically, and diagonally.
5. To increase the level of personal enthusiasm and satisfaction in the organization.
6. To find synergistic solutions to problems with greater frequency. (Synergistic solutions are creative solutions in which 2 + 2 equals more than 4, and through which all parties gain more through cooperation than through conflict.)
7. To increase the level of self and group responsibility in planning and implementation.[7]

OD as Education

The methods by which these types of problems are solved are, as was pointed out, various and dependent on the needs and resources of the firm, its members, and the values and perspectives of the OD specialist. They all

---

[6]Richard Beckhard, *Organization Development: Strategies and Models* (Reading, Mass.: Addison-Wesley, 1969), pp. 16–19.

[7]Wendell French, "Organization Development Objectives, Assumptions and Strategies," *California Management Review,* **12:**23 (Winter 1969).

have in common the fact that they are all *educational* strategies because the focus of OD is on permanent change in behaviors and abilities to cope with change. The OD methodologies may be differentiated from more traditional efforts:

In many traditional educational and training activities, learning and action taking are separated in that the knowledge and skills are "learned" in one setting, say, in a classroom, and are then taken back to the organization with the learner being admonished to practice what he has learned, that is, to take actions. This artificial separation is minimized in most OD interventions in several ways. First, in many intervention activities there are two goals: a learning and an educational goal and an accomplishing-a-task goal. Second, OD problem-solving interventions tend to focus on real organizational problems that are central to the needs of the organization rather than on hypothetical, abstract problems that may or may not fit the members' needs. Third, OD interventions utilize several learning models, not just one.[8]

OD as Planned Change

OD purposes and methodologies might be summed up as "planned change." All change is not planned; unplanned change may be unconscious, evolutionary, or revolutionary, either a natural adaptation to new conditions or imposed by authority.[9] Planned change "involves the conscious and deliberate establishment of shared goals and means for their attainment," and thus connotes an ongoing process built into the organizational technology.[10]

OD Interventions

Some of the tools in the OD specialist's kit include the following interventions: job enrichment, management by objectives, process observation, conflict resolution experiences, sensitivity training, and team development. We will briefly describe the applications of each of these methods to the types of problems that they may help to eliminate.

Job Enrichment

Job enrichment is a relatively marginal tool in OD use, and yet when appropriate it can be one of the more powerful tools. We saw in the last chapter that job enrichment calls for the including of greater challenge, achievement, opportunities for accomplishment, and increased responsibility for planning and control of a complete module of work. Under an OD

[8]French and Bell, p. 41.
[9]Margulies and Raia, p. 57.
[10]Ibid.

methodology, job enrichment is one of the methods by which problems identified may be solved in an ongoing fashion. It then is of importance as a *result* of organizational development. The characteristics of organizational members and their interactions with the formalized task-related expectations of the firm can be more nearly brought into line if the task is enriched to include elements that were formerly assigned to another member, either horizontally or vertically. Thus the role activities and responsibilities of an individual may be more responsive to the needs of the individual. As a result of such restructuring, the nature of the task becomes more consistent with the nature of its holder.

Management by Objectives

Another end result of the organizational development methodology is management by objectives (MBO). In its purest form, MBO is a managerial device that formalizes and institutionalizes joint goal-setting between superior and subordinate. It also allows the focusing of performance appraisals on *results* of behavior rather than on the manner or *procedures* by which the results are attained. MBO further creates the formal expectation and vehicle for task-related upward as well as downward communication.

Under MBO a superior and his subordinate separately establish in writing what the duties of the subordinate are and the outcomes that are associated with these duties. Given this role specification, the manager and his subordinate separately establish what they consider to be reasonable and attainable yet challenging levels of results for which the subordinate should strive over the next identified period. In a problem-solving and goal-setting session, the superior and his subordinate sit down in an open and free atmosphere. Comparing perceptions of the duties for which the subordinate is responsible allows continued dialogue about a set of behaviors and duties agreed upon mutually.

In a give-and-take session, superior and subordinate discuss the performance of the subordinate over the past period. They discuss reasons for failure to meet agreed-upon objectives or share congratulations for objectives exceeded and recycle the planning and organizing sequence for the next period. They establish reasonable goals, yet goals that challenge the subordinate. They cannot be too attainable or easy because then there is no sense of accomplishment, given the level of aspiration of the subordinate. At the same time they allow the subordinate to develop professionally and technically, yet to maintain control over his own rewards. He knows for sure what the criteria are for his performance, exactly what is expected of him, and at what level. His attention is not diffused through lack of comprehension about what the boss wants, and he can focus on attaining the objective agreed upon. Further, because the objectives and final end behaviors are mutually agreed upon, the subordinate is committed to attain them to the best of his ability. They are not *imposed* on him by an uncommunicative superior.

Such a device allows role ambiguity and role conflict to be diminished through open communication channels between superior and subordinate. The subordinate has more of a psychological attachment to both his job and the purposes of his job and can more nearly identify with its place in the total hierarchy as a result of his discussions with his manager. Problems and difficulties that he is having can also be brought up in these sessions for action and further resources as they relate specifically to the task.

The MBO vehicle allows specification of formal objectives and the individual's identification with them so that he may prove more nearly effective in his goal orientation. Once again, MBO is a formalization or institutionalization of a device that is intended to solve organizational problems that have been encountered in the past. It is an ongoing device or process and hence needs continued support at all levels to function effectively. In its worst condition, MBO can become another authoritarian device by which the autocrat imposes his perception of what the subordinate *should* be able to accomplish without the true participation of the subordinate. The mutually agreed-upon objectives can then become sources of negative incentive and punishment rather than constructive and positive reinforcement and reward.

Process Observation

One of the major methods of acquiring data on or insights into organizational problems is process observation. While focusing on improving the output in goal attainment of the unit under study, the consultant pays attention to the *ways* in which problems are solved. The inputs into the decision-making process could be considered to be the skills, backgrounds, technical expertises, personality structures, and so on of each of the individuals who contribute. Identifying the relevant inputs allows the observation of the specific ways and techniques by which the participants transform the inputs into their decision output. The assumption is that results can be improved if the process (by which results are attained) is improved. Improving interpersonal and decision-making processes demands that *present* processes be diagnosed so that specific recommendations may be made upon which to base new patterns of behavior.

The OD consultant then sits in on meetings, or structures situations for organizational members to experience, observes the processes that occur, feeds back his observations on data to participants, and assists participants in learning how to diagnose and restructure those processes that hinder effective interactions in decision making. Roles and functions of group members, group problem-solving and decision-making, group norms and growth, communication, leadership, authority, and cooperation in competition between groups are some of the major types of processes to be observed and diagnosed.[11]

---

[11]Edgar H. Schein, *Process Consultation: Its Role in Organization Development* (Reading, Mass.: Addison-Wesley, 1969), p. 13.

Schein described one such process observation situation:

In the Apex Company, I sat in for several months on the weekly executive-committee meeting, which included the president and his key subordinates. I quickly became aware that the group was very loose in its manner of operation: people spoke when they felt like it, issues were explored fully, conflict was fairly openly confronted, and members felt free to contribute. This kind of climate seemed constructive, but it created a major difficulty for the group. No matter how few items were put on the agenda, the group was never able to finish its work. The list of backlog items grew longer and the frustration of the group members intensified in proportion to this backlog. The group responded by trying to work harder. They scheduled more meetings and attempted to get more done at each meeting, but with little success. Remarks about the ineffectiveness of groups, too many meetings, and so on, became more and more frequent.

My diagnosis was that the group was overloaded. Their agenda was too large, they tried to process too many items at any given meeting, and the agenda was a mixture of operational and policy issues without recognition by the group that such items required different allocations of time. I suggested to the group that they seemed overloaded and should discuss how to develop their agenda for their meetings. The suggestion was adopted after a half-hour or so of sharing feelings. It was then decided, with my help, to sort the agenda items into several categories and to devote some meetings entirely to operational issues while others would be exclusively policy meetings. The operations meetings would be run more tightly in order to process these items efficiently. The policy questions would be dealt with in depth. Once the group had made this separation and realized that it could function differently at different meetings, it then decided to meet once a month for an entire day. During this day they would take up one or two large questions and explore them in depth. The group accepted my suggestion to hold such discussions away from the office in a pleasant, less hectic environment.

The full-day meetings changed the climate of the group dramatically. For one thing, it was easier to establish close informal relationsips with other members during breaks and meals. Because there was enough time, people felt that they could really work through their conflicts instead of having to leave them hanging. It was my impression that as acquaintance level rose, so did the level of trust in the group. Members began to feel free to share more personal reactions with each other. This sense of freedom made everyone more relaxed and readier to let down personal barriers and report accurate information. There was less need for defensive distortion or withholding.[12]

Process observation is a fundamental skill common to many OD techniques. It requires substantial experience and expertise to focus on patterns of behaviors as *processes* and relate deficient processes to ineffective performance, diagnosing and correcting such hinderances. Sensitivity training, too, demands becoming attuned to interpersonal processes.

Inside a T-Group

At the fifth meeting the group's feelings about its own progress became the initial focus of discussion. The "talkers" participated as usual, conversation shifting rap-

---

[12]Ibid., pp. 106–107.

idly from one point to another. Dissatisfaction was mounting, expressed through loud, snide remarks by some and through apathy by others.

George Franklin appeared particularly disturbed. Finally pounding the table, he exclaimed, "I don't know what is going on here! I should be paid for listening to this drivel! I'm getting just a bit sick of wasting my time here. If the profs don't put out—I quit!" George was pleased; he was angry, and he had said so. As he sat back in his chair, he felt he had the group behind him. He felt he had the guts to say what most of the others were thinking! Some members of the group applauded loudly, but others showed disapproval. They wondered why George was excited over so insignificant an issue, why he hadn't done something constructive rather than just sounding off as usual. Why, they wondered, did he say their comments were "drivel"?

George Franklin became the focus of discussion. "What do you mean, George, by saying this nonsense?" "What do you expect, a neat set of rules to meet all your problems?" George was getting uncomfortable. These were questions difficult for him to answer. Gradually he began to realize that a large part of the group disagreed with him; then he began to wonder why. He was learning something about people he hadn't known before. " . . . How does it feel, George, to have people disagree with you when you thought you had them behind you? . . ."

Bob White was first annoyed with George and now with the discussion. He was getting tense, a bit shaky perhaps. Bob didn't like anybody to get a raw deal, and he felt that George was getting it. At first Bob tried to minimize George's outburst, and then he suggested that the group get on to the real issue; but the group continued to focus on George. Finally Bob said, "Why don't you leave George alone and stop picking on him. We're not getting anywhere this way." With the help of the leaders the group focused on Bob. "What do you mean 'picking' on him?" "Why, Bob, have you tried to change the discussion?" "Why are you so protective of George?" Bob began to realize that the group wanted to focus on George; he also saw that George didn't think he was being picked on, but felt he was learning something about himself and how others reacted to him.

"Why do I always get upset," Bob began to wonder, "when people start to look at each other? Why do I feel sort of sick when people get angry at each other?" . . . Now Bob was learning something about how people saw him, while gaining some insight into his own behavior.[13]

One of the most controversial methodologies in organizational development is sensitivity training. In fact, some observers feel that OD is really nothing *but* sensitivity training. The types of problems sensitivity training is intended to remedy stem primarily from the interpersonal and group relationships between organizational members. Sensitivity training (sometimes called *T-group training*) is focused on allowing members to become more *sensitive* to the ways in which they relate to others. It is an experience-based educational methodology, typically conducted away from the plant and extending from several hours (a "microlab") to several weeks. It is characterized by a facilitator or resource person, a trained behavioral scientist, who introduces a brief overview of the purposes of sensitivity training and then

[13]R. Tannenbaum, I. R. Weschler, and F. Massarik, *Leadership and Organization: A Behavioral Science Approach* (New York: McGraw-Hill, 1961), p. 123.

lapses into silence. He has then initiated a leaderless and agendum-free group situation. All members of the group are required to relate to each other in the here and now, without bringing up factors or items from their companies or other outside activities. The ways in which they act and relate to each other are the raw material from which the training sessions draw, as individuals are allowed to focus on behaviors rather than duties and other perceptions. Individuals typically become extremely frustrated by the ambiguous circumstances of the group, without being told what or how to do something specific. As a result they are shorn of handy defense mechanisms and social devices, expressing their feelings in more open ways. Eventually, with the skillful help of the facilitator, individuals can gain trust and confidence in each other as they learn to express their feelings and attitudes openly and to *receive* the perceptions of others:

One of the goals . . . in sensitivity training programs is to break through the barrier of intellectualization and verbalization to facilitate the participant *experiencing* his own behavior and effect. Thus, one of the major goals of the intensive group experience is to provide the participant with a suggestive environment in which he may experiment with new ways of behaving, and to facilitate his development of new, more effective ways of perceiving his reality.[14]

The group may be a "stranger," "cousin," or "family" group. A stranger group consists of individuals, probably from different companies, who do not know each other. A cousin group consists of members of the same organization or firm, yet whose work is unrelated, typically being in different departments. A family group consists of unit members who work with each other, often including the supervisor. As individuals learn to express trust and confidence in each other, they can relate more openly and are not nearly so afraid to show their feelings, thus expressing hostilities effectively— without regard to personalities and focusing on exactly what it is that bothers them—and becoming more nearly able to be constructive and honest in dealing with others. They also gain constructive and open *feedback* from others about themselves and their own activities and relationships with others. Such a procedure can be quite a shock and should not be conducted by amateurs.

As a result of sensitivity training, the individual takes away a more nearly realistic view of the processes by which he characteristically deals with others and the ways in which he affects others by his own behavior. He develops these insights in the unstructured group, and with the help of group-member feedback he learns more about himself and also about others. Especially in family groups, unit members get to know each other better and can communicate and relate more freely and openly, without hostility and without fear of being rejected. Interpersonal barriers to working together as an effective team may be substantially reduced.

[14]Daniel L. Kegan, "Organizational Development: Description, Issues, and Some Research Results," *Academy of Management Journal* (December 1971), p. 455.

Conflict Resolution Through Intergroup Team-Building

Conflicts can erect major barriers to effective cooperation and task accomplishment. We saw in Chapter 17, "Change and Conflict," that various methods exist through which conflicts may be resolved. OD specialists prefer confrontation as the method most able to resolve conflicts *and* attain OD objectives.

If conflicts are to be confronted, they must be recognized and identified. Merely telling the conflicting parties that they *are* conflicting, for specific reasons, handles only one aspect of resolving the conflict, cognitive knowledge. The roots of the conflict usually go much deeper than cognitions, often to the emotional or affective level. Resolving deep-seated conflicts requires reeducation and an emotional adjustment based on experience. Allowing conflicts to be "resolved" through the hierarchy or through edict results in one party's winning while the other loses—aggravating the still unsolved conflict. Smoothing over conflicts also fails to attack the problem.

Open confrontation between the conflicting parties is the method espoused by OD advocates. The meeting is generally scheduled for a half day and is designed to facilitate bringing into the open and:

addressing differences in beliefs, feelings, attitudes, values, or norms to remove obstacles to effective interaction. Confrontation is a process that actively seeks to discern real differences that are "getting in the way," surface those issues, and work on the issues in a constructive way. Many obstacles to growth and learning exist; they continue to exist when they are not actively looked at and examined.[15]

When the organizational reward system tends to reward one party at the expense of another, for example, negative stereotypes quickly develop and effectively aid in decreasing the communication between the conflicting parties. Collaboration ceases and relationships come to be based on "winning" the conflict or making the other "lose," a competitive situation through which the *overall* organization may itself "lose." Confronting the conflict in a productive way can result in reduced misunderstandings and the setting up of joint collaboration. The specific steps through which these objectives are to be attained are given below:

1. Agreement is obtained between the two groups to work directly on improving mutual relationships.
2. Each group writes down its perceptions of both their own and the other group.
3. The two groups are then formally brought together, and a representative from each group presents the written perceptions obtained in the previous step. Only the two representatives may speak, since the primary objective is to make certain that the perceptions and attitudes are presented as accurately as possible and to avoid the defensiveness and

[15]French and Bell, p. 108.

hostility that might arise if the two groups were permitted to speak directly to each other.

4. The two groups separate, each armed with four sets of documents—two representing their own group's perceptions of itself and the other group, and two representing the other group's perceptions of itself and the other. At this point, a great number of discrepancies, misperceptions, and misunderstandings between the two show up.

5. The task of the group (almost always with the help of a process observer) is to analyze and review the reasons for the discrepancies. In other words, the process observer works hard at getting the group to work at understanding *how* the other group could possibly have arrived at the perception they have, e.g., "what actions on your part may have contributed to that set of perceptions? How did they get that way?" The emphasis is on problem-solving rather than on defensiveness.

6. The two groups are again brought together to share both the discrepancies they have identified and their problem-solving analysis of the reasons for the discrepancies. Again the focus is primarily on the behavior underlying the perceptions. At this point, either the formal representatives may be used or the groups can talk directly to each other.

7. If formal representatives are used, the next step is to allow more open discussion between the two groups, with the goal of reducing misperceptions and increasing intergroup harmony.[16]

Such an activity allows misunderstandings, stereotypes, defensive or aggressive behavior, and general misperceptions to be brought out in the open. A new action plan, which illustrates the need for collaboration and reduced competition, is set up by the participants and tends to solidify major changes in the two parties' relationships. Where could such an activity be used? Production and sales departments could be called together when sales jeopardizes production's budget because of excessive overtime to meet sales commitments, for example. Or representatives of a field organization and of central headquarters could minimize the conflicts that occur, say, between an auto producer and its dealerships. Labor–management groups could also benefit.

Team Development

The concept of the work unit as a team comes close to connoting the ever-increasing dependence of task effectiveness on how well the team members function interdependently. The temporary team is encountered more and more as task forces, project groups, and committees become

[16]Edgar F. Huse and James L. Bowditch, *Behavior in Organization: A Systems Approach to Managing* (Reading, Mass.: Addison-Wesley, 1973), pp. 296, 297. For more information on this approach, see R. R. Blake, H. A. Shepard, and J. S. Mouton, *Managing Intergroup Conflict in Industry* (Houston, Texas: Gulf Publishing Company, 1964); or Beckhard, pp. 34, 35.

accepted. An ongoing unit, too, must work well together, and so team development (or team building) interventions have many practical uses, all of which have as objectives "the improvement and increased effectiveness of various teams within the organization."[17]

The team is brought intact to a session, usually conducted away from the plant. During the session some or all of four distinct areas of interest may be addressed: diagnosis, task accomplishment, team relationships, and team and organization processes.[18]

Diagnosis

The diagnostic phase is concerned with team members' evaluating group performance and *identifying* (not solving) problems. Information regarding these problems is drawn out and shared through discussion among all team members, discussion in smaller groups and subsequent reporting back to the total group, or discussion–interviews between two individuals who report back their ideas to the entire team.

Once ideas ("data") are generated on the nature and extent of group problems, the problems may be grouped (role ambiguity problems, planning problems, and interpersonal acceptance problems, for example) so that they can be discussed. The discussion of these issues occurs not to take action steps to solve them but to decide *how* to take the necessary action steps.

Diagnosis enables a team to step back from its task involvement and criticize itself, identifying areas of strength and weakness. Every team member participates and thus influences the planning of future actions to be taken to improve group functioning. These important activities are done with only minimal investment of time, either a halfday or one full day.

Relationships

Group members perform both task and relationship functions, contributing both to goal attainment and to building and solidifying positive interpersonal attitudes. Both are important to the well-functioning team and are interrelated. Margulies and Raia stated that group development is affected by the extent to which members identify with their team as a primary group rather than as a secondary group. The primary group is one's major referent, characterized by identification with the group, sense of belonging, "we-ness," personal ties among members, informality, and commitment to shared goals. Secondary groups, in comparison, are impersonal, guided by formal or contractual obligation, and composed of members pursuing their own self-interests.[19]

---

[17]French and Bell, p. 112.
[18]Ibid., p. 113. The following discussion on these items draws heavily on their work, especially pp. 114–120.
[19]Margulies and Raia, p. 353.

Developing trust and openness is a result of team development experiences. In free exchanges, role ambiguities may be alleviated by specific role sendings and comparisons, opening the way to agreement on behavior expectations. Clarifying and defining roles, especially task roles, can go far to relieve frustrations and conflicts. Equalizing power distribution and exploring the nature of the superior's authority and task expectations are often a result of team development because of the emphasis on positive affective (emotional) relationships among team members regardless of formal position.

Task

A natural variant on the relationship-oriented group development method is the focus on task procedures and attainment. The session may be rather more aimed at solving specific difficulties uncovered in the diagnostic phase. Methods of solving problems, techniques of planning, and procedures for setting goals are examples of items on the task agendum. Conflicts with other groups as a result of task characteristics may also be taken up but not without all conflicting parties' involvement in the session.

Process

The final team-development area is that of team and organization processes. Team members meet to discuss means of improving their processes, such as reducing communication breakdowns, increasing the quality of decisions, or making task allocations more equitable. The same general format holds for process-oriented sessions as for the other team-development sessions. Individuals meet and share their feelings and ideas about the specific topic assigned, coming to an open expression of the nature of perceived problems and taking action steps to eliminate these problems or to bring about the changes deemed to be desirable in light of the discussions.

When the session is lengthy and many complex issues must be addressed, the problems may be tackled in rank order of priority. Especially when a complicated master strategy or several action plans are to be undertaken, a follow-up meeting is desirable. The follow-up meeting is held to evaluate how effectively the action plan was implemented, what subsidiary related problems still exist, and what the effects of the implemented action plans are.

Evaluating OD

Organizational development offers some very attractive methodologies and philosophies to practicing manager and academician alike. OD's humanistic philosophy and focus on human development are consistent with the very latest advances in behavioral science. OD has its devotees, its fanatical adherents, and also its detractors.

The values of OD are implicit in its methodologies, embodying the advanced humanism of Maslow, McGregor, and Likert. But what about its results? How well does OD do what it attempts to do?

Difficulties in OD

As a rather new approach, OD suffers the same types of difficulties of other emerging disciplines—lack of research, lack of documentation, far more heat than light. It operates under another substantial handicap, the difficulty of defining in verifiable, measurable terms its processes and results. How does one define the organization's "climate"? How does one measure the extent of interpersonal "openness and trust"? In what ways may traditional management development methods be compared with OD—comparative task effectiveness or dollar savings? These are some of the many difficulties inherent in evaluations of OD. Another perspective on these difficulties may be found in a perusal of the OD literature: few OD authors agree on what OD is, let alone what composes its inventory of intervention methodologies.

We have taken a rather broad approach to the subject because of the lack of clear definition or delineation in its lore. OD may be frustrating to some who desire a clear-cut conceptualization of its processes and structure. OD may be a source of inspiration and hope to others who feel the need for human-based approaches to organizational problems.

Effects of Sensitivity Training

Most of the work in OD has been in sensitivity training, perhaps a measure of the popularity of the T-group. Yet in a comprehensive review of research on sensitivity training, Campbell and his colleagues concluded rather glumly that:

The evidence, though still limited, is reasonably convincing that T-group training and the laboratory method do induce behavioral changes in the "back-home" setting. . . . there remains the vexing problem of specifying the nature of these changes. . . . Several researchers . . . strongly resist discussing the nature of any "typical" training effect; they imply that each trainee's pattern of change on various behavioral dimensions is unique . . .[and therefore] no basis exists for judging the potential worth of T-group training from an institutional or organizational point of view. Instead, its success or failure must be judged by each individual trainee in terms of his own personal goals.

Still another problem in evaluating the back-home changes is that the perceived change measures have not usually related observed changes to actual job effectiveness. Observers have been asked to report changes in behavior, not changes in performance. . . . [One study's] results lead to the suggestion that while laboratory training seems to produce more actual changes than the simple passage of time, the relative proportion of changes detrimental to performance is also higher for the laboratory method.[20]

MBO Results

Management by objectives is the subject of a substantial volume of writing and research. It is well documented in all its processes and procedures. Surprisingly enough, however, "only one study has attempted to relate changes in the economic performance of the organization to the installation of an MBO program"—productivity increased.[21] Studies of managers' attitudes and perceptions are more numerous and are generally positive, even though the increased paperwork and time demands are felt to be excessive.[22]

Integrated OD Programs

What about the effects of integrated OD programs? Once again, concrete evidence is skimpy. Huse and Beer offered one of the few studies that purport to measure—in cost and productivity figures—the results of having implemented an OD program.[23] The program was started in 1966 in a small plant, one of fifty in the corporation. The factory employed thirty-five hourly employees (mostly women), fifteen technical and clerical personnel, and eight salaried professional and managerial personnel. It produced a variety of medical and laboratory instruments and was basically an assembly operation.

Through the use of job enrichment, autonomous work teams, and "integrating" work groups with differing objectives and goals, substantial productivity increases were obtained: hot-plate department, 84 percent increase in productivity; glass shop, 20 percent; and instrument department, 17 percent. The parts shortage list in the materials control department was reduced from fourteen computer printout pages to one. The manufacturing manager's job—and the jobs of one third of the first-line supervisors—was eliminated. And the plant's profit was noted to be one of the highest among the corporation's fifty plants.

Not-so-measurable improvements that accompanied the quantitative

---

[20]John P. Campbell, Marvin D. Dunnette, Edward E. Lawler, III, Karl E. Weick, Jr., *Managerial Behavior, Performance, and Effectiveness* (New York: McGraw-Hill, 1970), p. 323.

[21]Stephen J. Carroll, Jr. and Henry L. Tosi, Jr., *Management by Objectives: Applications and Research* (New York: Macmillan, 1973), pp. 121, 122. The study to which they refer is A. P. Raia, "Goal Setting and Self Control," *Journal of Management Studies,* **2:** (1965); see also Raia, "A Second Look at Goals and Controls," *California Management Review,* **8:** (1966).

[22]Ibid., pp. 122, 123.

[23]Edgar F. Huse and Michael Beer, "Eclectic Approach to Organizational Development," *Harvard Business Review* (September–October 1971), pp. 103–112.

changes were the development of trust, the opening of communications channels, departmental monthly meetings, weekly plant manager–employee coffees, increased participation and delegation by supervisors, mutual goal-setting, interdepartmental conflict-reducing sessions, and the development of cohesive work teams. How many of these positive changes can be attributed to which OD tool is impossible to tell. Yet the results do indicate that there may be empirical evidence favorable to OD.

Contrary results were observed in an evaluation of the impact of a major OD program on the total climate of a governmental agency. The only results were small changes in individual behavior, with no changes in the agency's work climate.[24]

Argyris suggested[25] that OD efforts may be incompatible with the operational philosophies of chief executives—internalized values and traits that guide daily behavior—and hence end up unsupported by the top officer in the organization. Argyris cited characteristics he has found to be common to chief executives. They are articulate, competitive, and persuasive. They are dominating in their relationships with subordinates, stimulate win–lose competition, encourage conformity among subordinates, and discourage innovation and risk-taking behavior. Feedback to the effect that the chief executive officer (CEO) has negative impacts on others is disturbing and hence suppressed. MBO, confrontation meetings, T-group sessions, and comprehensive OD programs seem inconsistent with the CEO's behavior patterns. His behavior invariably undermines the OD program's goals and eventually causes it to fail.[26]

Greiner summarized six trends that may explain OD's questionable results:

Beginning with the individual before the total organization, ignoring broader (perhaps causal) problems in favor of individual attitude change.

Stressing informal values over formal organization, explicitly ignoring alternative formal organizational forms in favor of creating new social norms and behaviors.

Prescribing behavioral actions without diagnostic skills, emphasizing behavioral and emotional processes to the exclusion of cognitive, intellectual decision making.

Focusing more on behavioral relationships than task accomplishment, without understanding that task demands influence the behavioral process, not just *vice versa*.

Adhering to standardized programs over situational needs, creating specific

[24]Larry Greiner, D. Paul Leitch, and Louis B. Barnes, "The Simple Complexity of Organizational Climate in a Government Agency," in *Organizational Change: Explorations of a Concept*, ed. by R. Tagiuri and George Litwin (Boston: Division of Research, Harvard Business School, 1968).

[25]Chris Argyris, "The CEO's Behavior: Key to Organizational Development," *Harvard Business Review* (March–April 1973), p. 56. The following discussion is based on his findings.

[26]Ibid., p. 58.

and tangible "products" which the consultant develops, bringing in *his* set of programs and values rather than tailoring programs to the firm's problems.

Placing the expert ahead of the manager, creating overdependency on the skills and efforts of the OD consultant, deferring to the judgments of an outside person who may recommend solutions irrelevant to the time problems, and failing to develop OD skills in organizational members for continuing the programs after the consultant leaves.[27]

Finally, even those few studies of the effects of OD programs may be open to question. Golembiewski and Munzenrider investigated the common technique of using self-report data gathered from OD participants. They found that before–after research designs, intended to measure the impact of the OD program, are affected by the phenomenon of "social desirability" (the tendency to describe something in terms that will gain the approval of others).[28]

An Optimistic Recap

A major shortcoming in the state of the art of OD is the apparent dichotomy between the "attitude only" and the "task–technique" adherents. The former are concerned primarily with developing positive and open interpersonal attitudes—difficult to measure—and the latter *may* (through MBO and job enrichment) be just more sophisticated cost cutters of the scientific management school. One author decried the limited perspectives of OD specialists, and hopefully predicted that OD in the future will include consideration of organizational technology and structure and eventually "include *any* method for modifying the behavior of organization, thereby encompassing the entire spectrum of applied behavioral science."[29]

Integrating organizational and technological variables in OD is often dismissed because of participants' inability to contribute meaningfully in questions of organizational structure. A fascinating breakthrough in structural design has recently been announced by Kilmann and McKelvey.[30] They use multivariate analysis, high-speed computers, and participation by all relevant organizational members to generate information by which to handle the complex issues of organizational design *and* to help managers periodically evaluate how well the present design is adapted to the organization's environment.

[27]Larry E. Greiner, "Red Flags in Organization Development: Six Trends Obstructing Change," *Business Horizons* (June 1972), pp. 19–24.

[28]Robert T. Golembiewski and Robert Munzenrider, "Social Desirability as an Intervening Variable in Interpreting OD Effects," paper presented before the annual meeting of the Academy of Management, Boston, Mass., August 1973.

[29]William E. Halal, "Organizational Development in the Future," *California Management Review*, **16**:37 (Spring 1974).

[30]Ralph H. Kilmann and Bill McKelvey, "Organization Design: A Participative Multivariate Approach," *Administrative Science Quarterly* (March 1975), pp. 24–36.

In short, evaluating OD is difficult at best, given the state of the art and its research. Soundly designed studies of concrete effects are few, and even they may be compromised by the heavily value-laden and subjective results that are the targets of OD. Conceptually and intuitively the humanistic philosophy and values of OD may appeal to us. Yet the shamanlike qualities of the OD consultant and the aura of mystique that surrounds OD[31] should provide warning about its uncritical acceptance. The developing nature and tendency toward more rigor and scientific methodology are encouraging, however, and may yet substantiate the claims of OD devotees.

OD is of particular interest because it is an attempt to integrate the organizational behavior subsytems, diagnosing and changing systemic barriers to overall effectiveness. The separate components of behavior are, almost without exception, represented in some way in a broad, total OD program. Therefore OD represents a substantial step forward in the integration of human and organization and is a significant addition to the total set of tools of the practicing manager.

Summary

An overview of organizational development purposes and methods was presented. OD is a systematic research and action-based effort designed to enable the organization to cope with change and to make it more effective. Effectiveness stems from making the formal organization responsive to human needs.

The underlying values of OD are primarily humanistic, assuming individuals to be responsive and willing to participate. The OD specialist, a professional behavioral scientist, functions as a "change agent," a resource person for diagnosing problems and assisting the organization. He uses action research techniques to gather data and hypotheses from organizational members regarding existing and potential problems. Members and consultant evaluate the data and initiate action plans by which to remedy the problems pointed up. Problems found are typically attitudinal in nature. OD is a continuing process, a cycle of data gathering, evaluating, and action planning.

Major interventions, component parts in the OD approach, are job enrichment, management by objectives, process observation, sensitivity training, conflict resolution, and team development. Each have specific purposes and applications. Each may be the action agreed to in the action planning phase, in which organization members see the need to develop new behaviors through these interventions.

Evaluating OD is difficult indeed, primarily because it is still very much

---

[31]Newton Margulies, "The Myth and Magic in OD: Powerful and Neglected Forces," *Business Horizons* (August 1972), pp. 78–80.

an art, with few research studies based on quantifiable and verifiable processes. Some authors point out that the types of skills and behaviors developed as a result of OD may have nothing to do with job performance *or* with
organizational effectiveness. Others argue just as vehemently that the skills
and behaviors improve the organization's climate, and hence motivation,
while removing interpersonal barriers to productive efforts.

A clear-cut evaluation is not possible, yet OD offers considerable potential—and promise—as the major unifying program by which the subsystems
of the organizational behavior system may be effectively integrated, through
the scientific application of behavioral science.

In the next, and last, chapter we will summarize briefly where we have
gotten to at this point and try to extrapolate the exciting challenges of
organizational behavior in the future and in current application.

STUDY AND REVIEW QUESTIONS

1. Why do you think that OD methodologies are called "interventions"?
2. Six OD interventions are discussed. At which organizational growth stage
would each intervention be most appropriate? Why?
3. Why is open expression of feelings important to conflict resolution and
team development?
4. Would an integrated OD effort be helpful in your college setting? What
types of results might you expect? Why?
5. Why is OD termed an *educational strategy?*
6. What is the difference between experiential (experience-based, emotional)
learning and traditional (intellectual, cognitive) learning? Which is most effective?
Why?
7. Why is planned change preferred to unplanned change?
8. Evaluate the reasoning that better interpersonal relationships will make the
organization more effective.
9. Compare and contrast positive behavior reinforcement with organizational
development. Which is "better"? Why?
10. How would you go about evaluating the effects of an OD program, if you
were the company's president?

SECTION VI

ORGANIZATIONAL BEHAVIOR: PERSPECTIVE FOR TOMORROW

Chapter
24

Challenge in Organizational
Behavior

Throughout this book we have emphasized the fact that behavior in organizations is a complicated subject. Because it is so complex, behavior can best be investigated through the process of breaking the total subject down into its constituent elements and studying the relatively simple pieces one at a time and then in combination. Behavior consists of—and is influenced by—many specific factors that can yield complex results, patterns, and tendencies. Through the framework provided by the organizational behavior systems model we have seen some of the major influences on the total behavior process and the ways in which organizational behavior is affected.

Now the next step must be in the *systematic application* of the knowledge of systemic elements and their relationships. Such an orientation has been fostered by the attempt to summarize and integrate each major subsystem and to show some of the ways in which the three major subsystems affect each other. If nothing else, the approach taken should make you wary of attributing behavior to a single cause. Instead you should now have a rather sophisticated grasp of the fact that almost nothing happens by itself in a direct cause–effect relationship. Multiple influences, determined by the situation, *intervene* in the behavior process, sometimes even changing the nature of relevant factors or the total behavioral process itself. Understanding and recognizing the variable nature of behavior elements—and the conditions and relationships under which they change—yields a flexible yet action-oriented conception of organizational behavior.

Throughout this book we have looked at these processes—and modifiers of behavioral processes—from two distinct perpectives, one being that of the participant or member of the organization and the other the viewpoint of the manager responsible for managing organizational behavior. The organizational member should have some understanding of the forces that mold his work-related activities and the influences that affect his formal, informal, and nonformal behaviors. By understanding the influences and their relationships, the organizational member frees himself from the prison of ignorance about those things that cause him to behave. Knowing them, he acquires power over them—at least to the extent that their ability to exact blind obedience is diminished. He acquires power over his immediate environment and becomes able to identify more nearly with organizational processes and to participate in productive and satisfying behaviors.

By the same token, the manager soon recognizes that his ability to fulfill his responsibility rests on the ever-shifting sands of individual and social behavior, a tenuous basis at best, yet one with considerable unanticipated as well as formalized powers. His every word, facial expression, decision, or *lack* of decision is an input into the organizational behavior process—whether or not he intends (or wishes) it to be. By understanding the elements and processes of organizational behavior, he becomes more able to anticipate or predict the final results of any given action. Expecially when the manager must fulfill his responsibilities by making decisions about work activities or personnel, he can anticipate and negate resistance to change or other untoward results. The systems model also provides the manager with a road map with which he can trace changes in productivity, job satisfaction, or other effects back to their sources or root causes, an aid just as valuable as prediction.

The net result of familiarity with the applications of the systems model of organizational behavior could well be the identification and internalization of the set of decision rules most nearly applicable to the individual manager's specific situation. The relevant characteristics of his situation and the components under study can be isolated, identified, and considered. The individual is not then bound by a set of simplistic, abstract, and untested "rules" intended to cover every *possible* situation, but he is able to generate relevant guidelines that will help *him*.

After all, we have seen that different production technologies create (for example) entirely different organizational processes and procedures by which formal tasks are most effectively performed. Each distinctive production technology generates different requirements for individual and group behavior and hence affects individual and social system elements and relationships uniquely. The extent of decision making, for example, at any given level depends for its appropriateness on member capability, decision importance, and the level in the hierarchy at which the requisite and relevant information exists. These factors vary from situation to situation, as well as from organization to organization, and differ quite dramatically with each production technology.

The blanket assertion that decisions should be pushed down to as near the operative (worker) level as possible is true *only* in situations and organizations in which this is appropriate, as in advanced technology firms regarding design or engineering questions. Granting assembly-line workers the right to decide for themselves at which hour they will come in to work—or when during the week they may take two days off—or whether to build a new plant would hardly be appropriate. Instead routine mass-production technology, with its high degree of specialization and interelatedness of tasks, seems to require that major decisions be made at a relatively high level in the hierarchy.

Is it important to be able to distinguish among situations, their characteristics, the relevant factors, and their relationships? The world and its phenomena are rarely as simple and clear-cut as we perceive (or wish) them to be. Complications exist in that any factor we choose to use to categorize or classify a situation is not a "yes–no" factor. That is, no factor—especially no factor involving humans—either exists or does not exist; it will almost always exist to *some extent* in any situation we choose to investigate. Even the most hard-bitten authoritarian, for example, will *occasionally* seek suggestions. Our ability to differentiate levels of existence, or the extent to which a factor exists, in some situation is critical in establishing where on a scale any given factor lies.

One might label as "great" the extent to which subordinate participation in the superior's decision-making process exists in a mass-production firm because the manager solicits input regarding procedural changes or preferences in desk arrangement or vacation schedule. *For that specific situation* this may be a rather substantial amount of participation. Yet were this exact situation transferred to an *advanced technology* firm, we would be forced to classify it as rather minimal because we would be comparing it to what the *optimum* level of participation should be, given the demands of advanced technology for continuing and deep involvement by subordinates in decision making.

Thus we can state that organizational behavior is situationally determined. What is right for one situation can be completely wrong for another. It is critical in today's society and complex times that the manager be able to determine what is most effective for *his* organization and *his* subordinates, as he attempts to accomplish formal goals through the efforts of subordinates. He must manage organizational *behavior* as well as production processes or marketing programs. Very rarely is the opportunity presented to rectify a mishandled or critical behavioral problem—it can fester unrecognized, yet show damaging symptoms in turnover, productivity, and dissatisfaction.

Although the state of the art in organizational behavior has not yet reached a final, sophisticated form, we are embarked on a road that will (hopefully) lead us to the development and application of a complete typology of situations, with their relevant characteristics and their effects on organizational behavior. The systems model is a step in that direction, for it outlines relevant factors and relationships. The model could be initially applied in, for example, different production technologies. Then, within each production technology, different organizational forms could provide another breakdown, followed by levels of decentralization and types of authority, and so on.

Given such an approach, and a complete study, a true contingency theory of organizational behavior could be formulated. The individual would then be able to choose proven approaches as *strategies* for maximizing overall organizational effectiveness through the derivation of organizational behavior that simultaneously satisfies the requirements of *each* of the three organizational behavior subsystems. Until we reach that stage, we must look to the application of the conceptual model that we have derived and attempted to apply in a consistent fashion. Conscientious and insightful application of the model should then allow the individual to develop the most relevant portions of the model.

Yet such limited applications of our conceptual model are really not enough. A complete understanding of the entire model is now—and will become even more—important to practitioners and researchers in organizational behavior. The world and its organizations are now changing at a rate almost breathtaking in scope and magnitude. Bennis has warned of the impending death of the bureaucratic form of organization and its replacement by temporary organizations composed of short-term teams and assignments. Such a revolutionary change would then mean an end to traditional concepts of formal authority and stable organizational forms with their dependence on thorough role prescriptions.[1]

Product life cycles—the time and stages through which products develop from inception to decline—also seem to be shortening, and even traditionally stable markets like the automobile market are exhibiting fluctuations that require less organizational stability and production predictability in order to handle and anticipate changes. The changing nature of the work force, as we have pointed out earlier, is having a profound and continuing impact on managerial applications and strategies. We have seen how management techniques are predicated on a model of the nature of the individual. As individuals in our postindustrial society continue to evolve and manifest new characteristics, needs, and motivations, new managerial applications will continually evolve in response. Tried-and-true management tools will accordingly become obsolete and ineffective. Only a systematic and flexible approach to organizational behavior, which builds in a continuing analysis of relevant elements, will allow the manager to adapt to—or anticipate—such major changes.

Using our systems model we can attempt to get beneath the surface of behavioral activities and identify the changing characteristics of people and their ultimate impact on organizational behavior. We are not content merely to react to changes but must intervene in behavior as effectively as possible in

---

[1]Warren G. Bennis, *Changing Organizations: Essays on the Development and Evolution of Human Organization* (New York: McGraw-Hill, 1966), pp. 3–15.

order to make the organization the specific vehicle for economic attainment, individual satisfactions, and group achievement.

The role of the formal organization and of formal activity, whether it be business, government, or education, has changed from the utilization of internal human resources in pursuit of external objectives. Outside clientele must still be served, yet an emerging and important function of the organization is also to serve the needs of its *internal* clientele, its members.

All of these considerations constitute the challenge in organizational behavior—a challenge at once awesome and exciting. Organizational behavior, after all, is based on the scientific and systematic analysis of that most dynamic phenomenon, human behavior, yet such a study is for very pragmatic and important purposes. We do not investigate human behavior in organizations to lock up the results in an ivory tower but to translate the findings into applications in the real organizational world. The results are of great social—as well as economic—significance, for they speak to the continued evolution of an economic postindustrial society *and* the increased adaptation of organizational vehicles to the *needs and aspirations of man.*

Such a quest—idealistic, to be sure, yet eminently practical—inspires researchers and practicing managers alike. The simultaneous satisfaction of three dynamic, independent equations—formal organization, individual, and social system—offers potential immense enough to enlist many contributors. Economic maximization will result as organizational effectiveness and productivity soar, with the resultant delivery of socially desired goods and services at rock-bottom prices. Individual achievement and development are enhanced as the workplace and the job become sources of positive accomplishment and satisfaction, encouraging the development of each member's own personal potentialities. And social satisfactions will stem from the integration of informal and formal expectations, the consolidation of the strength and involvement of the social system with the task orientation of the formal organizational structure.

Indeed, organizational behavior furnishes a challenge. Much has been learned, and much more remains. Even as rapidly as behavioral science applications are made to the field, the elements and processes themselves change in their dynamic relationships, requiring even more and newer knowledge. The future portends even more change, even more challenge, even more complexity. All these considerations should point up the fact that a sound yet flexible framework is necessary—and becoming critical—in the management of organizational behavior. The conscientious application of the systems model, we feel, provides such an aid. With it you can face the challenge in organizational behavior.

Subject Index

Author Index

DATE DUE